KV-194-830

HISTORICAL DICTIONARIES OF CITIES OF THE WORLD
Series Editor: Jon Woronoff

1. *Tokyo*, by Roman Cybriwsky, 1997.
2. *Stockholm*, by Dennis E. Gould, 1997.
3. *Warsaw*, by Adriana Gozdecka-Sanford, 1997.
4. *Paris*, by Alfred Fierro, 1998.
5. *Honolulu and Hawai'i*, by Robert D. Craig, 1998.
6. *Guangzhou (Canton) and Guangdong*, by Graham E. Johnson and Glen D. Peterson, 1998.
7. *Greater Johannesburg*, by Naomi Musiker and Reuben Musiker, 1999.
8. *Vienna*, by Peter Csendes, 1999.
9. *Osaka and Kyoto*, by Ian Martin Röpke, 1999.
10. *Sydney*, by Arthur Emerson, 2001.
11. *London*, by Kenneth J. Panton, 2001.

For Carol,
with all my love

Historical Dictionary of London

Kenneth J. Panton

Historical Dictionaries of Cities of the World, No. 11

The Scarecrow Press, Inc.
Lanham, Maryland, and London
2001

SCARECROW PRESS, INC.

Published in the United States of America
by Scarecrow Press, Inc.
4720 Boston Way, Lanham, Maryland 20706
www.scarecrowpress.com

4 Pleydell Gardens, Folkestone
Kent CT20 2DN, England

British Library Cataloguing-in-Publication Information Available

Library of Congress Cataloging-in-Publication Data

Panton, Kenneth J. (Kenneth John), 1945–
Historical dictionary of London / Kenneth J. Panton.
p. cm.—(Historical dictionaries of cities of the world ; no. 11)
Includes bibliographical references.
ISBN 0-8108-4015-4 (alk. paper)
1. London (England)—History—Dictionaries. 2. London (England)—History—Chronology. 3. London (England)—Encyclopedias. I. Title. II. Series.

DA677 .P33 2001
942.1'003—dc21

2001020180

∞™ The paper used in this publication meets the minimum requirements of American National Standard for Information Sciences—Permanence of Paper for Printed Library Materials, ANSI/NISO Z39.48-1992.
Manufactured in the United States of America.

Contents

Illustrations

Editor's Foreword

Few world cities have as much to offer as London. Historically, there are remains and reflections of the Roman era (and before), centuries of rule by English kings and queens, the policies and programs of Whig, Tory, Liberal, and Labour, the glory of being the capital of an empire on which the sun never set, and the ignominy of the Blitz. Economically, the muscle of manufacturing has largely dwindled, but the financial might is more prominent than ever, as are flourishing commerce and services. Socially, there seem always to have been (and to be) social and religious experiments, including those of Henry VIII, Cromwell, the Wesleys, the Chartists and Fabians, and Lady Thatcher. Culturally, London often comes up with the best, be it in literature and theater, music and dance, art and architecture. This has consistently kept London at the top of the charts with a title of "great" city for most and "cool" for the rest.

This series on the world's leading cities would not be complete without an edition for London, and this *Historical Dictionary of London* is certainly one of the best books in the series and also a particularly useful guide for those interested in London. Its broad introduction presents this fascinating city, from the time of Londinium on, showing how it grew into today's metropolis. The *Dictionary* includes entries on persons, places, events, and institutions connected with the above facets of history, economy, society, religion, and many more. Other entries describe numerous neighborhoods and districts in a city that is often regarded as a collection of villages, each with its own personality, each worth knowing. The chronology makes it easier to scan a long and lively history, and the bibliography points toward some of the countless books on London's varied and complex makeup.

This volume was written by an admirer who, while not born in London, got to know the city exceedingly well and, moreover, has a talent for describing it to others. Part of this gift may be natural, the rest came through sheer practice. Although born in Edinburgh, Kenneth J. Panton visited London often enough and received his Ph.D. at King's College, University of London. As a professor of geography at London Guildhall University, as a matter of routine, he taught British students about London's shape and structure, not once but many times. As organizer of the United States' largest summer program in London for the University of Southern Mississippi, where he now teaches, he is expected to present London to over 300 Americans, not once but every year. As coauthor of the two-volume *Historical Dictionary of the United Kingdom*, he has written on the broader context. This professional activity, overlaid with a delight in exploring the city, has produced an informative and also readable account that many visiting or living in London will doubtlessly consult with some pleasure.

Jon Woronoff
Series Editor

Acknowledgments

Along with those readers who slide this book from a library shelf (or, bless them, buy it), I owe a considerable debt of gratitude to three groups of people.

First, there are those who, over a period of more than 30 years, have taken time to talk about London, show me its warts and its dimples, and thus shape my understanding of a great city. Some of them (like countless taxi drivers) are individuals whose names I never knew. Some, regrettably, have gone and I never thanked them properly because it is only with hindsight that I know how much I learned. They include many friends and neighbors, including Czech refugees Henry and Marianne Kay, master carpenter Jim Slogrove and his family, and the regulars on the 8:24 from Earlswood to London Bridge, notably Mike Segre. Knowledgeable British scholars (including Dr. Peter Allen, Dr. Martin Bridge, Mr. James Bromwich, Dr. Keith Cowlard, Dr. Andrew Haggart, Dr. Barrie Morgan, and Dr. Peter Shoebridge) have peered behind the physical and social facade, providing insights into the city's economy, society, and structure. Many American companions have looked at London from a different cultural perspective, asking questions I would never have thought of asking. In particular, I am grateful to Dr. Lawrence Clinton, Dr. Clifton Dixon, Dr. Tim Hudson, Dr. Amy McCandless, Dr. Mark Miller, Dr. Jim Schnur, Frances and Phil Sudduth, and Dr. Jerry Waltman. In addition, there are aspects of the city I would probably never have known intimately without the guidance of specialists such as politicians Donald Anderson, MP, and Tony Banks, MP, barrister Ros Mandil-Wade, and educators Dr. Alan Little and Christine Mabey. Most of all, perhaps, interest in the city has been continually stimulated by generations of students who have argued in tutorials, analyzed census data in practical classes, trudged the streets doing field work, and continued the debates long after graduation.

Second, there are many people who have made a direct—and invaluable—contribution to the production of the book. Jon Woronoff, editor of the Historical Dictionaries of Cities of the World series, has given unstintingly of his time and advice, providing, through his own work, a standard of scholarship that I cannot claim to match. Don Shewan of City Cartographic has rendered the handsome maps that enhance this book. The effervescent Eva Yocum and Andrew Batt, curators of the picture library at the Museum of London, guided me through their institution's enormous collection of photographs, and staff at the London Metropolitan Archives, Redhill Public Library, and the University of Southern Mississippi Library were never once stumped by requests for assistance. Tim Hudson, dean of the College of International and Continuing Education at the University of Southern Mississippi, very generously approved a grant to cover the cost of the illustrations, and Jennifer Foil, with other colleagues, donated much time to assist with translations from British to American English.

Perhaps the greatest personal debt is to my family. My mother, Elspeth Panton, fostered an interest in books and learning long before I knew what she was up to, and it has lasted a lifetime, bringing enormous pleasure in its train. Carol, my wife, could not possibly have known what she was letting herself in for when we married back in 1969; she has spent much of the past three decades driving a geographer in the never ending search for geography and I cannot thank her enough. My daughter, Mhorbhaine, has been a consistent source of support, asking questions, querying accepted philosophies, and sharing the inevitable ups and downs of authorship. This work is principally dedicated to those three, but that does not diminish in any way my gratitude to all those who helped, knowingly or not. The faults in this work are not of their making.

Notes to the Reader

It is impossible to separate the history of a capital city from the history of the state within which it functions. However, in order to keep the size of a volume such as this within reasonable bounds, some, essentially subjective, editorial decisions must be made. As with other books in the Historical Dictionaries of Cities of the World series, the emphasis is on the people, institutions, political forces, economic trends, and social values that gave the metropolitan area its shape and character. Thus, individuals and events that had a clear impact on London are included, but those that were essentially national are excluded unless there are specific implications for London itself. For example, all English monarchs for the past thousand years have lived in London, but most had limited effect on London's structure and evolution, so they are not considered here. Those readers who wish to put London's development into an explicitly British context are advised to consult the two-volume *Historical Dictionary of the United Kingdom,* written by myself with Dr. Keith A. Cowlard and published by Scarecrow Press in 1997 (volume 1) and 1998 (volume 2).

Similarly, many learned societies, international companies, and large businesses (such as banks) maintain headquarters in London but have a national, rather than a metropolitan, focus. These too are excluded in order to devote adequate attention to organizations that affect the character of the city as a financial and cultural center. Also, for reasons of space, greater emphasis has been placed on more recent social and economic history, although the earliest stages of London's settlement and growth are certainly not ignored.

ABBREVIATIONS

This section of the book lists all abbreviations used in the text with the exception of those likely to be familiar to readers in the United States (such as the abbreviations for state names used in the bibliography).

CHRONOLOGIES

The chronologies provide simple checklists, in date order, of historical events, lord mayors of London, chairmen of London County Council, chairmen of the Greater London Council, and population growth from 1801 until 1996.

THE DICTIONARY SECTION

The conventions employed in the text are noted below.

Entry Conventions

Entries in this section are listed alphabetically in **UPPER CASE BOLD PRINT**. When several entries begin with the same word, they are ordered according to the alphabetical sequence of the second word (thus, **ROYAL MEWS** appears before **ROYAL MINT**).

In some cases, the first word in the entry may be different from that used first in spoken English. For example, all London boroughs are listed in the form **BRENT, LONDON BOROUGH OF**, rather than **LONDON BOROUGH OF BRENT**. Also, individuals are listed by family name (as in **BARNARDO, THOMAS JOHN**) with the exception of members of the royal family, who appear under their given (or first) name followed by their title (for example, **ALBERT, PRINCE**).

Cross References

Cross references to related entries elsewhere in the Dictionary are shown within the body of individual entries in **bold print** and should be consulted by readers seeking further information.

Names, Foreign Words, Publications, and Quotations

The names of ships, planes, and trains are given in italic print. The same convention is used for noting the words from which place names are derived, for foreign words, for publications, and for lengthy quotations.

The City of London and the city of London

The term City of London (often abbreviated to the City) is used to refer to the square mile of the urban area that is administered by the Corporation of London. The term city of London is used to refer to the metropolitan area as a whole.

BIBLIOGRAPHY

The bibliography is divided into thematic sections in order to facilitate the search for citations. Further details are provided in the introduction to the bibliography.

Acronyms and Abbreviations

A.D.	In the year of Our Lord (anno domini)
ALA	Association of London Authorities
ALG	Association of London Government
BBC	British Broadcasting Corporation
B.C.	Before Christ
c.	about (circa)
d	old pence
FA	Football Association
GLA	Greater London Assembly
GLC	Greater London Council
GMT	Greenwich Mean Time
GPO	General Post Office
HMS	Her (or His) Majesty's Ship
ILEA	Inner London Education Authority
IPE	International Petroleum Exchange
LB	London Borough
LBA	London Boroughs Association
LCC	London County Council
LCH	London Clearing House
LDDC	London Docklands Development Corporation
LDMA	London Discount Market Association
LHE	London Health Emergency
LIFFE	London International Financial Futures and Options Exchange
LIRMA	London International Insurance and Reinsurance Market Association
LME	London Metal Exchange
LPAC	London Planning Advisory Committee
LPO	London Philharmonic Orchestra
LPTB	London Passenger Transport Board
LRB	London Residuary Body

LRPC	London Regional Passengers' Committee
LRT	London Regional Transport
LSE	London School of Economics and Political Science
LSE	London Stock Exchange
LSO	London Symphony Orchestra
LT	London Transport
Ltd.	Limited Liability Company
LTE	London Transport Executive
MCC	Marylebone Cricket Club
MP	Member of Parliament
NFT	National Film Theatre
NHS	National Health Service
PLA	Port of London Authority
plc	Public Limited Company
PRO	Public Record Office
RADA	Royal Academy of Dramatic Art
RAF	Royal Air Force
RPO	Royal Philharmonic Orchestra
RSA	Royal Society of Arts
Rt. Hon.	Right Honourable
SEAQ	Stock Exchange Automated Quotations
TWA	Thames Water Authority
UK	United Kingdom
US	United States of America
V&A	Victoria and Albert Museum

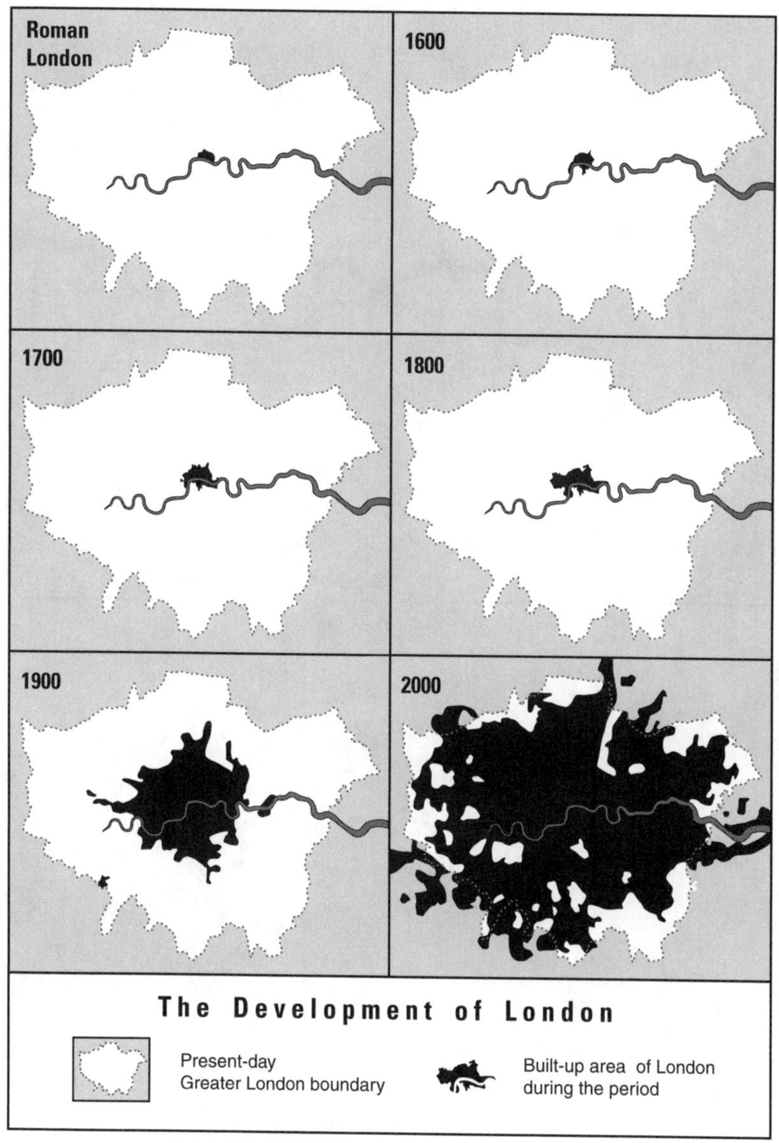

Courtesy of Don Shewan

Courtesy of Don Shewan

Courtesy of Don Shewan

Chronologies

HISTORICAL EVENTS

In the following list, entries for each year are listed in alphabetical order.

c. 55 B.C. According to legend, Julius Caesar leads his Roman army across the River Thames at Brentford.

54 B.C. An invading Roman army battles with native Celtic Catuvellauni people at the site of modern Stanmore.

43 The Romans invade the British Isles.

60 London (with a population of about 30,000 people) becomes the capital of Roman Britain.

61 Boadicea attacks the Roman settlement at Londinium.

c. 100–c. 400 The first London Bridge is built.

179 The Romans erect a basilica in Londinium.

190–220 The Romans encircle Londinium with a defensive wall.

410 The Romans abandon Londinium and the city's population falls.

457 Invading Jutes defeat native Britons in battle at Crayford.

604 Ethelbert, the first Christian King of Kent, founds St. Paul's Cathedral.

605 The Bishopric of London is established.

c. 666 St. Erkenwald founds Barking Abbey.

685 The first stone church is erected on the site of St. Paul's Cathedral.

c. 750 Sebert, King of the Saxons, builds a church on the site now occupied by Westminster Abbey.

787 Offa, King of Mercia, holds a synod on the site of present-day Chelsea.

800–900 Danish invaders pillage London.

1030 Waltham Abbey is founded as a collegiate church of secular canons.

1060 Edward the Confessor, King of England, builds a palace on the site of modern Westminster and orders the construction of an abbey dedicated to St. Peter.

Waltham Abbey is rebuilt by Harold, son of Earl Godwin of Wessex and future King of England.

1066 The Normans invade England and make London their administrative center.

1078 Work begins on the construction of the Tower of London.

1091 London Bridge is destroyed by a storm but rebuilt.

1097 William Rufus (son of William the Conqueror) orders the building of Westminster Hall.

1099 According to the *Anglo-Saxon Chronicle*, the River Thames floods, causing much damage.

c. 1100 London's population reaches 14,000–18,000.

1101 Matilda (wife of King Henry I) builds a leper hospital in the fields beyond the western wall of the City of London.

1106 St. Thomas's Hospital is founded.

1114 Gilbert the Knight acquires land at Merton and endows an Augustinian priory.

1120 St. Margaret's Church is built at Westminster.

1123 Rahere, a courtier of King Henry I, founds an Augustinian priory named in honor of St. Bartholomew at Smithfield.

1132 King Henry I grants the City of London a charter empowering it to appoint a sheriff.

1133 King Henry I gives St. Bartholomew's Priory the right to hold an annual fair for three days from St. Bartholomew's Eve (24 August). The event survived until 1855.

1135 William de Montfichet founds Stratford Langthorne Abbey for the Cistercian order.

1136 London Bridge is burned down but rebuilt in elmwood.

1160–1185 Temple Church is built.

1170 Ranulf de Glanville, chief justiciary of England, founds a priory at Stanmore.

Waltham Abbey is refounded as a community of Augustinian monks.

1176 Work begins on replacing the wooden London Bridge with a stone structure.

1178 Lesnes Abbey is founded for Augustinian monks by Richard de Luci as a penance for supporting King Henry II in a dispute that led to the murder of Thomas Becket.

1185 The Knights Templar build a church on the north bank of the River Thames close to present-day Charing Cross.

1189 Henry FitzAilwyn is appointed first Lord Mayor of London.

1197 The Corporation of London pays King Richard I the sum of 1,500 marks for rights of control over the River Thames.

c. 1197 Walter and Rose Bruno found an Augustinian priory, known as St. Mary Spital, to the east of the City of London.

1200 A Court of Aldermen is formed to provide local government for the City of London.

c. 1200 London's population reaches 20,000–25,000.

1221 Dominican monks found a monastery at Shoe Lane, in the area now known as Blackfriars.

1224 Franciscan friars establish a monastery on land gifted by John Travers, sheriff of London.

1236 The Statute of Merton, signed at the Augustinian priory and sometimes said to be the first Act of Parliament, gives lords of the manor power to enclose common lands.

1237 The City of London appoints its first city chamberlains.

1243 A community of French Protestants, known as the Hospital of St. Anthony, is established north of Threadneedle Street.

1245–1532 Westminster Abbey is built.

1253 Carmelite monks build a priory in the City of London.

1273 London's first customs house is erected at Old Wool Quay.

1290 The Bishops of Ely establish a London residence at Ely Place.

1291 The heart of Queen Eleanor, wife of King Edward I, is buried by the altar at Greyfriars Monastery.

1297 The Stone of Scone, coronation stone of Scotland's monarchs, is seized by King Edward I of England and placed in Westminster Abbey.

c. 1297 Work begins on the construction of Lambeth Palace.

1300 St. Etheldreda's Church is built in Holborn.

Work begins on the construction of Eltham Palace.

1348 King Edward III establishes the Order of the Garter (the oldest knighthood in Europe) at Eltham Palace.

1348–49 The Black Death (a form of bubonic plague) ravages London, killing about half of the city's population.

c. 1350 London's population reaches 40,000–50,000.

1370 The Legal Society of Lincoln's Inn is formed.

Sir Walter Manny founds a Carthusian Monastery at what is now Charterhouse Square.

1381 During the Peasants' Revolt, Wat Tyler leads a group of protestors into London, where it sets fire to the Tower and beheads the Archbishop of Canterbury at Lambeth Palace.

1388 Tyburn becomes a site for public executions.

1390 Construction of the nave in Westminster Abbey is completed.

1397 Richard Whittington is appointed Lord Mayor of London.

1400 Geoffrey Chaucer is buried in the south transept of Westminster Abbey, an area later known as Poet's Corner.

c. 1400 Lincoln's Inn is built.

1410–20 The Bishop's Palace is built at Fulham.

1411–39 A Guildhall is built for the Corporation of London. After the Great Fire of 1666, it was the only pre-17th-century stone structure left standing in the City of London.

1415 King Henry V founds a Bridgettine monastery on the land later occupied by Syon House.

1426 Humphrey, Duke of Gloucester and brother of King Henry V, builds Bella Donna, a residence later known as Greenwich Palace.

1433 Greenwich Park is created as walls are built around the Bella Donna estate.

1480 King Edward IV establishes a Franciscan monastery at Greenwich.

1484 King Richard III founds the College of Arms.

1485 King Henry VII creates the Yeomen of the Guard.

1497 King Henry VII builds Richmond Palace.

1500–6 King Henry VII rebuilds Greenwich Palace.

1503–12 King Henry VII's chapel is built at Westminster Abbey.

1509 King Henry VIII founds the Honourable Corps of Gentlemen at Arms.

1512 King Henry VIII creates England's second Royal Naval Dockyard at Woolwich (the first was at Portsmouth, on the south coast).

1513 A third Royal Naval Dockyard is built at Deptford.

1514 The City of London's Court of Aldermen establishes an order of precedence for livery companies.

The Deptford Guild of Mariners is granted a royal charter authorizing it to provide pilotage on the River Thames.

Thomas Wolsey begins building Hampton Court Palace, intending that it will be the finest residence in England.

1515–20 King Henry VIII builds Bridewell Palace.

1518 The Royal College of Physicians of London is founded.

1520–32 The Church of St. Andrew Undershaft is erected.

1529 King Henry VIII orders the building of Whitehall Palace.

Thomas Wolsey gifts Hampton Court Palace to King Henry VIII.

1531 King Henry VIII buys a leper hospital outside the western walls of the City of London, gives each inmate a pension, and builds St. James's Palace in its place.

1536–41 English monasteries, including those in London, are dissolved and their assets transferred to the Crown.

1537 The Fraternity or Guild of Artillery of Longbows, Crossbows, and Handguns (now the Honourable Artillery Company) is formed.

1538 The area now occupied by Bushy Park and Hampton Court Park is enclosed as a hunting forest by King Henry VIII.

King Henry VIII builds Nonsuch Palace.

1539 A court of law is built beside Newgate Prison in a street named Old Bailey.

1547 The Corporation of London buys the buildings of St. Mary Bethlehem Priory (known as Bedlam) and converts them into an asylum for the mentally ill.

The Deptford Guild of Mariners is renamed The Corporation of Trinity House on Deptford Strand.

1551 King Edward VI confiscates the property of the Hanseatic League.

1552 King Edward VI gifts estates at Covent Garden to John, Earl of Bedford.

1553 The City of London Corporation accepts Bridewell Palace as a gift from King Edward VI and converts it into a prison.

King Edward VI establishes a school on the site of Greyfriars Monastery. (Now known as Christ's Hospital, the institution moved out of London in 1897.)

1557 The inmates at Bedlam asylum are moved to Moorfields and become a popular attraction for city residents.

1564–65 The River Thames freezes over. Archery contests are held on the ice.

1567 The Old Curiosity Shop is built on Portsmouth Street. Still functioning, it is claimed to be the oldest store in London.

1568 The Royal Exchange opens as a meeting place for merchants.

1572 Farmer John Lyon founds Harrow School.

1576 Sir Thomas Gresham buys Osterley Park House.

The Theatre, London's first playhouse, opens at Shoreditch.

1577 Francis Drake sets off from Deptford on his circumnavigation of the world.

A theater opens in Blackfriars, attracting the city's literati and making the area a fashionable place in which to live.

1579 Thomas Gresham endows Gresham College, creating seven lectureships in arts and sciences.

1587 Philip Henslowe builds the Rose Theatre, the first playhouse at Bankside.

1595 A Marshall is appointed to maintain order in the City of London.

1596 The Swan Theatre opens at Bankside.

1598 Playwright Ben Jonson kills actor Gabriel Spencer in a duel.

Queen Elizabeth expels merchants of the Hanseatic League from London.

1598–99 Cuthbert and Richard Burbage build the Globe Theatre at Bankside.

1600 The East India Company is founded.

Philip Henslowe builds the Fortune Theatre, the largest of its day, at Bankside.

c. 1600 London's population reaches 200,000–250,000.

1603 King James VI of Scotland enters London, by way of Aldersgate, to claim the throne of England as James I.

A plague epidemic kills 30,000 people.

1605 Actor and theater manager Edward Alleyn endows a college at Dulwich for 12 poor scholars.

A group of Roman Catholic conspirators attempts to blow up the Houses of Parliament. Guy Fawkes (the explosives expert) is found in a

cellar packed with gunpowder and, under torture, reveals the names of his colleagues, all of whom are executed.

The River Thames freezes over.

1606 Settlers leave the port of Blackwall to found the first permanent English colony in North America at Virginia.

Walter Cope, Chancellor of the Exchequer, builds Cope Castle (now known as Holland House) in Kensington.

1608 England's first golf club is formed on Blackheath.

1610 Sir Thomas Vavasour builds Ham House.

1611 Thomas Sutton buys the former Carthusian monastery at Charterhouse and converts it into a school (for boys) and hospital (for gentlemen).

1613 The Globe Theatre is destroyed by fire but rebuilt.

Philip Henslowe opens the Hope Theatre at Bankside.

1616 Inigo Jones is commissioned to build the Queen's House at Greenwich for Anne of Denmark, wife of King James VI and I.

1620 The *Mayflower* leaves Rotherhithe for the Americas.

1621 Poet John Donne is appointed dean of St. Paul's Cathedral.

1622 The Banqueting House, designed by Inigo Jones, opens with a performance of Ben Jonson's *Masque of Angers*.

1630 Frances Russell, Earl of Bedford, commissions Inigo Jones to plan a development at Covent Garden.

1631–35 The Earl of Leicester erects a mansion on the north side of what is now Leicester Square, initiating urban development on agricultural land.

1633 St. Paul's Church, Covent Garden (the first Anglican place of worship to be built in London after the Reformation), is completed.

1635 The first postal deliveries to private citizens in London are made as part of the Royal Mail service.

Hyde Park is opened to the public.

1637 King Charles I encloses Richmond Park as hunting forest.

1638 A cattle market is formally established at Smithfield by the Corporation of London (but the site had been a focus for trade in animals since the early 12th century).

William Newton develops Lincoln's Inn Fields for housing, despite the objections of the Inn.

1642 Puritan authorities close the Globe Theatre.

Royalist troops defeat a parliamentarian force at Brentford and advance (temporarily) on London.

1644 The Globe Theatre is demolished.

1649 King Charles I is executed at the Banqueting House, and England becomes a republic.

1652 The Fleet River is clogged with rubbish and impassable to boats.

1657 Jews are allowed into England and settle in Mile End.

1660 The Earl of Southampton lays out Southampton (now Bloomsbury) Square.

The East India Company is formed, with monopoly rights to trade with East Asia, India, and Southeast Asia.

The English monarchy is restored, and Charles II's court returns to London.

The Society of London for the Promotion of Natural Knowledge is founded.

1660–69 Samuel Pepys records the minutiae of London life in his *Diary*.

1661 At Blackwall, the East India Company builds a wet dock, the first with gated access to the River Thames.

1662 King Charles II grants a royal charter to the Society of London for the Promotion of Natural Knowledge, founded in 1660. The organization is now known as the Royal Society.

1663 Diarist Samuel Pepys records that the River Thames flooded Whitehall.

1664–66 London suffers an epidemic of plague.

1665 Henry Jermyn begins to develop St. James's Square.

1666 The Great Fire kills nine people and destroys over 13,000 buildings (including 89 churches) in the City of London.

The *London Gazette* is published.

1669 Christopher Wren is appointed surveyor general for London.

The Royal Exchange reopens in new premises (its previous building was destroyed by the Great Fire of 1666).

1670 The Earl of Bedford obtains a royal charter entitling him to hold a daily fruit and vegetable market on his estate at Covent Garden.

Leicester Square is laid out.

1670–83 St. Mary-le-Bow Church is built to Christopher Wren's designs.

1671 A 202-foot-high monument is built to commemorate the Great Fire of 1666.

Diarist John Evelyn introduces woodcarver Grinling Gibbons to the royal court.

1671–1703 St. Bride's Church is built to designs prepared by Christopher Wren.

1672 John, Earl of Lauderdale, converts Ham House into one of the most sumptuous mansions in England.

1672–1717 St. Stephen Walbrook Church is built to Christopher Wren's designs.

1675 An astronomical observatory, established by royal warrant, is built at Greenwich.

1675–1710 St. Paul's Cathedral is rebuilt.

1676 The Apothecaries' Company establishes Chelsea Physic Garden so that its members can conduct research into the properties of medicinal plants.

Fire destroys much of Southwark.

1676–84 St. James's Church, Piccadilly, designed by Christopher Wren, is erected.

1677–83 St. Benet Church, Paul's Wharf, is built to Christopher Wren's designs.

1679–82 Christopher Wren rebuilds St. Clement Danes Church.

c. 1680 Edward Lloyd's coffeehouse, a popular meeting place for ship masters and merchants, becomes the best place in London at which to arrange insurance deals. From these beginnings, Lloyd's of London evolves into one of the world's principal insurers.

1681 Soho Square is laid out.

1681–86 Christopher Wren rebuilds St. Mary Abchurch Church.

1682 King Charles II founds Chelsea Hospital as a home for soldiers who are no longer able to undertake military duties.

Nonsuch Palace is bought, and demolished, by Lord Berkeley, who uses the stone to build a mansion at Epsom (Surrey).

1683 Abraham Boydell Cuper (gardener to the Earl of Arundel) opens Cuper's Gardens as a place of recreation for Londoners.

A spa, with entertainment for visitors, opens at Sadler's Wells.

1683–84 When the River Thames freezes over, stall holders set up booths on the ice.

1684 Nicholas Barbon lays out Red Lion Square.

1684–90 Christopher Wren designs the Church of St. Andrew, Holborn.

1685 Islington Spa attracts Londoners to its supposedly health-giving waters.

King Louis XIV of France revokes legislation giving French Protestants freedom of worship. As a result, Huguenot refugees flee to London.

1685–95 St. Andrew by the Wardrobe, Christopher Wren's last church in the City of London, is erected.

1689 King William III moves the royal court from Whitehall Palace to Kensington Palace because air pollution in central London is affecting his asthma. Christopher Wren is commissioned to refurbish and extend the building, which was previously known as Nottingham House.

1691 Nicholas Hawksmoor is appointed clerk of works at Kensington Palace.

1692 John Campbell founds the bank, now known as Coutts and owned by the Royal Bank of Scotland, which holds the account of Queen Elizabeth II.

1694 Scotsman William Paterson founds the Bank of England at Mercers' Hall.

1696 Howland Great Dock is built at Rotherhithe to accommodate 120 merchant ships. In the 19th century, when it is known as the Greenland Dock, it becomes part of the Surrey Commercial Docks development.

1696–1702 Christopher Wren, Nicholas Hawksmoor, John Vanbrugh, and other architects build Greenwich Hospital (which became the Royal Naval College in 1873) on the site of Greenwich Palace.

1697 The first tea auctions are held in London.

1698 Fire destroys much of the interior of Whitehall Palace and the Banqueting House. As a result, the royal family makes St. James's Palace its principal residence.

Parliamentary legislation abolishes the cartel controlling sales at Billingsgate Fish Market.

1699–1700 The Ranger's House is erected at Greenwich.

c. 1700 London's population reaches 575,000–670,000.

1701 Development of a spa attracts fashionable Londoners to Hampstead.

1702 The *Morning Chronicle*, London's first newspaper, is published.

1704 The first houses are built in Queen Anne's Gate.

1705 The Queen's Theatre (now known as Her Majesty's Theatre) opens in Haymarket under the management of architect John Vanbrugh (who designed the building) and dramatist William Congreve.

1707 William Fortnum and Hugh Mason found the grocery store that still bears their names.

1709–11 Marlborough House, designed by Christopher Wren, is built next to St. James's Palace for Sarah, Duchess of Marlborough.

1711–18 St. Alfege's Church, Greenwich, is rebuilt to Nicholas Hawksmoor's designs.

1713 Thomas Doggett leaves a will requiring that a portion of his estate be used to provide a coat and badge for the winner of a sculling race on the River Thames. The race is now the oldest fixture in Britain's sporting calendar.

1714 Architect James Gibbs sets up practice in London and wins a commission to design St. Mary-le-Strand Church.

1715 Following an explosion which kills 17 people, the Royal Arsenal (then known as The Warren) moves from the City of London to Woolwich.

1715–16 The River Thames freezes over. Booths are set up by retailers and entertainments held on the ice.

1717 The Bank of England is made responsible for the management of government securities.

Cavendish Square, the first urban development north of Oxford Street, is laid out by John Prince.

1719 A school for prospective army officers is established at Woolwich.

Westminster Hospital is founded.

1720 Haymarket Theatre opens.

1722 Drainage works initiate a process of land improvement on Clapham Common.

1722–26 James Gibbs builds St. Martin-in-the-Fields Church.

1724–29 Marble Hill House is built for Henrietta Howard, Countess of Suffolk and mistress of the Princess of Wales.

1725 Guy's Hospital is founded.

1725–29 Richard Boyle, Earl of Burlington, builds Chiswick House, fuelling a resurgence of interest in classical architecture.

1725–31 Grosvenor Square (the second-largest square in London) is built as the focus of the Grosvenor Estate's Mayfair development.

1729 Christ Church, Spitalfields, regarded by many critics as architect Nicholas Hawksmoor's masterpiece, is consecrated.

A wooden bridge built across the River Thames links Putney (on the south bank) to Fulham (on the north).

1730–31 The Serpentine is built in Hyde Park at the suggestion of Caroline of Ansbach, wife of King George II.

1731–33 St. Giles-in-the-Fields Church is rebuilt to the designs of Henry Flitcroft.

1732 Entrepreneur John Rich builds a lavish new theater in Drury Lane, opening with a performance of William Congreve's *Way of the World*.

No. 10 Downing Street becomes the prime minister's official residence.

1733 St. George's Hospital is founded.

1734 The Bank of England moves to Threadneedle Street.

1735 John Rich (founder of Covent Garden Theatre) and George Lambert (a scene painter) form the Beefsteak Club, a society for 24 gentlemen of noble birth.

1738 George Dance the Elder is appointed architect and surveyor to the Corporation of London.

1738–50 Westminster Bridge is built.

1739 Work begins on the development of Berkeley Square.

1739–40 The River Thames freezes. As in 1715–16, stall holders set up booths on the ice.

1739–52 The Mansion House, official residence of the Lord Mayor of London, is built to the designs of George Dance the Elder.

1740 The London Hospital is founded.

1741 Actor David Garrick makes his first appearance (as Harlequin) on the London stage.

The army officer training school at Woolwich is given the status of Royal Military Academy.

1741–44 St. Botolph's Church is built to plans prepared by George Dance the Elder.

1742 Thomas Coram founds a children's hospital at Lamb's Conduit Fields.

1744 Samuel Baker, a London bookseller, opens the auction house that becomes Sotheby's.

1745 The Middlesex Hospital is founded.

1747 Actor David Garrick leases Drury Lane Theatre in partnership with James Lacy.

London's first Corn Exchange is built at Mark Lane.

1747–76 Author Horace Walpole buys a small property at Strawberry Hill and appoints a Committee of Taste to advise on its conversion into a Gothic castle.

1748 Novelist Henry Fielding is appointed magistrate at Bow Street and forms the Bow Street Runners.

1750–60 Horse Guards Parade is laid out by John Vardy to William Kent's designs.

1751 The Bank of England assumes responsibility for administering the national debt.

1753–56 John Brooks perfects the art of printing transfers on porcelain, selling the products as Battersea China.

1754 William Shipley, a Nottingham teacher, founds the Society for the Encouragement of Arts, Manufactures, and Commerce. The organization was renamed the Royal Society of Arts in 1908.

1755 The first Trooping the Colour ceremony is held.

1757 Horace Walpole installs a printing press at his home in Strawberry Hill and publishes many of his own works, as well as those of other writers (such as poet Thomas Gray).

1758 Architect Robert Adam establishes a practice in London.

1758–59 A wooden bridge is erected across the River Thames between Kew and Gunnerbury.

1758–62 Houses are removed from London Bridge and the structure's arches strengthened.

1759 The British Museum opens to the public (but visitors are admitted only if they request permission in writing).

The Royal Botanic Gardens are laid out by Augusta, widow of Frederick, Prince of Wales.

1760 Bishop's Gate, the point at which the Romans' Ermine Street entered London, is demolished, along with Cripplegate (one of the Romans' northern entrances to the city), so that the road system can be improved.

Cuper's Gardens closes and a vinegar distillery is built on the site.

Ludgate, originally an entry to the western areas of Roman London, is demolished.

The Society for the Encouragement of Arts, Manufactures, and Commerce holds Britain's first art exhibition.

1760–69 A new bridge is built across the River Thames between Blackfriars and Southwark to provide the only crossing between Westminster Bridge and London Bridge.

1761 Aldgate (the site of the eastern entry to Roman London) and Aldersgate (one of the northern entries) are demolished.

Portman Square is laid out.

Rivals Robert Adam and William Chambers are appointed architects to King George III.

1761–62 William Chambers builds the Great Pagoda at Kew Gardens.

1761–68 Robert Adam redesigns Syon House for Hugh, Duke of Northumberland.

1762 Edward Boodle founds Boodle's as an apolitical gentlemen's social club based in Pall Mall.

John and Francis Baring establish a merchant bank in the City of London.

1763 James Boswell and Samuel Johnson meet for the first time.

1763–67 Robert Adam is commissioned to remodel Osterley Park House.

1764 Robert Adam is commissioned to remodel Kenwood House.

1765 Thomas Roseman builds a theater at Sadler's Wells.

1766 Midshipman James Christie establishes an auction house in Pall Mall.

1767 Newgate, originally one of the western entry points to Roman London, is demolished.

1767–73 The gardens at Syon House are laid out by Capability Brown.

1768 Captain James Cook leaves from Deptford to search for Terra Australis.

George Dance the Younger succeeds his father as architect and surveyor to the Corporation of London.

Robert, James, and John Adam begin work on the Adelphi development.

The Royal Academy is founded.

1770 The discovery of a spring with allegedly health-giving properties leads to the establishment of a spa at Bermondsey.

1770–78 Newgate Prison is rebuilt to the designs of George Dance the Younger.

Robert Adam finalizes plans for Apsley House (now the Wellington Museum).

1771–72 A wooden bridge is built across the River Thames between Chelsea and Battersea.

1771–81 The cutting of wood for fuel reduces the area of Epping Forest from 9,000 to 3,000 acres.

1773 A group of brokers forms a stock exchange in Threadneedle Street.

1774 The first cricket match in England is held between Kent and an All-England team at a site in City Road.

The River Thames is bridged at Richmond.

1775 Dr. Samuel Johnson publishes his two volume *Dictionary of the English Language*.

1775–80 Builders Thomas Crewer and William Scott lay out Bedford Square, now considered one of London's finest Georgian developments.

1776 Manchester Square is developed.

1776–86 Somerset House is built to William Chambers's designs.

1777 Charles and John Wesley, founders of Methodism, visit Bethnal Green, in the East End, and declare that the area is scarred by "such poverty as few can conceive without seeing it."

George Dance the Younger lays out Finsbury Square.

1780 Lord George Gordon leads a series of protests designed to prevent the Tory government from repealing anti-Catholic legislation. During the disturbances, the Bank of England is stormed and several prisons (including Newgate) ransacked.

Public executions at Tower Hill are abolished.

1783 Public hangings are transferred from Tyburn to a gallows outside Newgate Prison.

1784 The City Day Police is formed to maintain law and order in the City of London during daylight hours.

General William Roy establishes, at Hounslow, a baseline for the mapping of the British Isles.

1785 John Walter publishes the *Daily Universal Register*.

1787 Marylebone Cricket Club is formed.

1788 The *Daily Universal Register* is renamed *The Times*.

1788–89 The River Thames freezes and a fair is held on the ice.

1790 Violinist and impresario Johan Peter Salomon commissions the music now known as the London Symphonies from Joseph Haydn.

1791 Flogging of women prisoners at Bridewell is abolished.

James Boswell's *Life of Samuel Johnson, LL.D.* is published.

The Veterinary College of London (now the Royal Veterinary College) is founded.

1792 Henry Walton Smith opens a newsagent's store in Little Grosvenor Street. (The firm's name changed to W. H. Smith in 1828 and by 2000 the company had become the largest retailer of books and stationery in the United Kingdom.)

1798 Patrick Colquhoun and John Harriott form a force of river police.

1799 The Royal Institution is founded by Benjamin Thompson as a means of "diffusing the knowledge and facilitating the general introduction of useful mechanical inventions and improvements."

1800 Bedlam asylum for the mentally ill moves from Moorfields to Lambeth.

Russell Square is laid out by architect James Burton.

1801 The first British census indicates that London has 959,310 citizens.

Paddington Canal opens.

1802 The West India Company builds London's first large enclosed wet dock on the Isle of Dogs.

1803 The Surrey Iron Railway (the world's first public railroad service) links Wandsworth to Croydon.

1805 London Docks open at Wapping.

No. 11 Downing Street becomes the official residence of the Chancellor of the Exchequer.

1806 The East India Docks at Blackwall are expanded.

John Smith builds the Sans Pareil Theatre (now known as the Adelphi Theatre) in the Strand so that he can further his daughter's acting career.

1807 Frederick Winsor presents a display of gas lighting in Pall Mall to celebrate the birthday of George, Prince of Wales.

Surrey Docks (the only enclosed docks on the south bank of the River Thames in London) open at Rotherhithe.

1808 Addington Palace, Croydon, becomes the official London residence of the Archbishops of Canterbury.

1811 George, Prince Regent, commissions architect John Nash to convert Marylebone Park into a place for public recreation. The result is the Regent's Park development.

1813 The East India Company loses its monopoly rights to trade with India and with east and southeast Asia.

1813–14 The River Thames freezes over and a great fair is held on the ice.

1814 Dulwich Picture Gallery (now Britain's oldest public art collection) opens.

The first Grand Union Canal is opened, linking London to the East Midlands of England.

The Gas Light and Coke Company provides London's first permanent street lighting by placing lamps on Westminster Bridge.

Much of St. James's Palace is destroyed by fire but immediately rebuilt.

1814–19 The River Thames is bridged between Southwark and the City of London.

1815 Doulton and Watts begin porcelain production in Lambeth.

1815–17 William Montague lays out Finsbury Circus to the designs of George Dance the Younger.

1818 Charing Cross Hospital is founded.

The passage of the Church Building Act (a thanksgiving for Britain's victory over the armies of Napoleon Bonaparte at the Battle of Waterloo) leads to the construction of 38 places of worship in London.

Rudolph Cabanel builds the Royal Coburg Theatre (now known as the Old Vic).

1819 Piccadilly Circus takes shape as Regent Street links with Piccadilly.

1820 Conspirators meet in Cato Street to plot the assassination of the whole British cabinet but are betrayed and arrested.

King George III commissions architect John Nash to prepare plans for Buckingham Palace.

Regent's Canal opens, allowing barges to move between Paddington Basin and the River Thames at Limehouse.

1820–40 Trafalgar Square is laid out.

1823 The Baltic Club is founded to regulate trade between London and the Baltic states.

Marc Brunel begins work on the first tunnel underneath the River Thames, linking Rotherhithe to Wapping.

The Royal Academy of Music is founded by a group of aristocratic arts patrons.

1823–31 The construction of a replacement for London Bridge improves the flow of the River Thames and prevents the channel from freezing over.

1823–47 A new home is built in Great Russell Street for an expanding British Museum.

1824 John Wilson Croker forms The Society (later known as the Athenaeum gentlemen's club) for scientists, writers, and artists at Somerset House.

The National Gallery opens, with 38 old masters (purchased by the government from the estate of John Julius Angerstein) forming the nucleus of the collection.

1825 Builder Thomas Cubitt starts work on Belgrave Square, the focus of now fashionable Belgravia.

The foundations of Lancaster House are laid.

1825–28 Clarence House is built.

1826 Poet Thomas Campbell and other religious dissenters found University College as a center of learning for nonconformists excluded from Oxford and Cambridge.

1827 A new bridge across the River Thames links Hammersmith (on the north bank) to Barnes (on the south).

1828 London Zoo opens in Regent's Park.

Marble Arch is erected as a gateway to Buckingham Palace.

St. Katharine's Dock, designed by Thomas Telford, opens.

Supporters of the Church of England establish King's College as a rival to the nonconformist University College, created in 1826.

The Wellington Arch is erected outside Apsley House.

1829 The first boat race between Cambridge University and Oxford University is held on the River Thames. Oxford wins.

George Shillibeer introduces a service of horse-drawn carriages that transport passengers between the City of London and Paddington.

The Mansion House is refaced with Portland stone.

Robert Peel creates a Metropolitan Police Force.

1829–32 The Travellers' Club, designed by Charles Barry, is built in Pall Mall.

1830 The hay market at Haymarket closes, and the land is colonized by the entertainment industry.

The Royal Geographical Society is founded.

The Society moves from Somerset House to Pall Mall and renames itself the Athenaeum.

1831 The Duke of Sussex founds the Garrick Club.

John Nash designs the Theatre Royal, Haymarket.

The Royal Horticultural Society holds its first exhibition.

1832 The Carlton Club is founded (and later evolves into the social headquarters of the Conservative Party).

The Society for the Encouragement of Arts, Manufactures, and Commerce holds Britain's first exhibition of photography.

1833 Bank of England notes become legal tender.

Individual fire brigades merge to form the Fire Engine Establishment.

London's first commercial cemetery is laid out at Kensal Green by the General Cemetery Company.

The Royal Coburg Theatre is renamed the Royal Vic in honor of the 14-year-old Princess (later Queen) Victoria.

Sir John Soane arranges for his eclectic collection of curiosities, acquired over a lifetime, to be preserved in a museum.

Using Boz as a pen name, Charles Dickens begins to publish stories that draw on his experiences of London.

1834 Much of the Palace of Westminster is destroyed by fire.

1835 Madame Tussaud opens a gallery of waxworks in Baker Street.

1835–60 The Palace of Westminster is rebuilt to designs prepared by Charles Barry and Augustus Welby Northmore Pugin.

1836 London's first steam-driven rail service connects Bermondsey to Deptford.

The Reform Club is founded as a meeting place for gentlemen with radical political views.

The Whig government creates a University of London, based at Somerset House.

1837 The Geological Museum is founded.

The London and Birmingham Railway builds Euston Station.

Queen Victoria moves the Royal Household from St. James's Palace to Buckingham Palace.

A school of design, predecessor of the Royal College of Art, is established at Somerset House.

1838 The Great Western Railway opens a London terminus at Paddington.

The London and Southampton Railway opens a terminus at Nine Elms.

The Public Record Office is created by an Act of Parliament.

The Royal Exchange is destroyed by fire.

The University of London holds its first examinations (for 23 students).

1839 The Bow Street Runners are disbanded.

The London Cemetery Company opens a burial ground at Highgate.

1839–42 Nelson's Column is built in Trafalgar Square.

1841 The City of London's first railroad station is opened in Fenchurch Street by the London and Blackwall Railway.

Following its destruction in the fire of 1838, the Royal Exchange is rebuilt to plans prepared by William Tate. The work involves the demolition of St. Benet Fink Church, designed by Christopher Wren.

The Royal Botanic Gardens are gifted to the nation by Queen Victoria.

1841–45 Hungerford Bridge is built, providing access to Hungerford Market from the south bank of the River Thames.

1842 Fleet Prison closes.

Pentonville Prison accepts its first inmates.

Robert Peel's Conservative government buys land on which to lay out Victoria Park, in the East End.

1845 Surrey Cricket Club is formed, with headquarters at the new Oval ground.

The Treasury Buildings are erected in Whitehall to Charles Barry's designs.

Waterloo Bridge, designed by John Rennie, links Lambeth to the Strand.

1846 The character of Sweeney Todd makes his first appearance in a story published in the *People's Periodical and Family Library*.

Parliament passes legislation authorizing construction of a public park on Battersea Common.

1846–49 Barnes Bridge is erected for the London and South Western Railway.

1848 The London and South Western Railway builds a station at Waterloo.

A medical officer of health is appointed for the City of London.

The Windsor, Staines, and South Western Railway builds a bridge to carry its services over the River Thames at Richmond.

1849 Bedford College (now part of the University of London) is founded specifically to provide a liberal education for women.

Harrods store opens in Knightsbridge.

1850 Sir Robert Peel (founder of the police force) dies following a fall from his horse on Constitution Hill.

Thomas Cubitt lays out Gordon Square, the last of the Bloomsbury Squares.

1851 Artist G. F. Watt moves into Holland House as a guest of Sara Prinseps and establishes the Holland House Circle.

Dr. Charles West founds the Great Ormond Street Hospital for Sick Children.

The Great Exhibition attracts six million visitors to Hyde Park in 14 weeks.

Henry Mayhew's writings on *London Labour and the London Poor*, originally published in the *Morning Chronicle*, appear in a three-volume collection.

Marble Arch is moved from Buckingham Palace to its present position at the junction of Oxford Street, Edgware Road, Hyde Park, and Bayswater Road.

1851–58 A suspension bridge links Chelsea (on the north bank of the River Thames) to Battersea (on the south).

1852 At the instigation of Prince Albert, profits from the Great Exhibition are used to purchase a site for the construction of museums and educational institutions in south Kensington.

Crystal Palace, centerpiece of the Great Exhibition, is dismantled and moved to Sydenham.

The Great Northern Railway opens Britain's largest railroad station at King's Cross.

Holloway Prison is built.

The Palace of Westminster, much rebuilt after the fire of 1834, is opened by Queen Victoria.

1853 Battersea Park opens for public use.

The University of London moves from Somerset House to Burlington Gardens.

1854 During an outbreak of cholera in Soho, Dr. John Snow persuades the authorities to remove the handle from a water pump in Broad Street. The epidemic ends within days, confirming Snow's belief that the disease is carried by water.

The premises of the small arms factory opened at Enfield in 1804 are expanded to facilitate production of the Enfield rifle.

1855 Bartholomew Fair, first held in 1133, is closed because of drunkenness and disorder.

Bridewell Prison is closed and inmates are transferred to Holloway.

Claridge's Hotel opens.

A college for Jews is founded in Golders Green.

The Metropolitan Board of Works, London's first citywide local authority, is appointed to replace a plethora of bodies, each dealing with a specific function.

The Metropolitan Cattle Market moves from Smithfield to Holloway.

The Royal Victoria, first of the Royal group of docks, is opened by Prince Albert.

1856 Joseph William Bazalgette is appointed surveyor to the Metropolitan Board of Works and initiates a program of improvements to roads and sewage disposal systems.

The Society for the Encouragement of Arts, Manufactures, and Commerce introduces examinations designed to help young people from working-class families learn vocational skills. By 1989, when the Examinations Board became an independent body with charitable status, nearly one million students were being presented annually.

1857 The Science Museum is founded.

The Victoria and Albert Museum is created through the merger of collections of fine and applied arts held by the School of Design and the Museum of Manufactures.

1858 Blackheath Football Club, the oldest public rugby union club in London, is formed.

Covent Garden Theatre (renamed the Royal Opera House in 1892) opens on the site of the theater built in Drury Lane by John Rich in 1732.

During an exceptionally hot summer, sewage carried by the River Thames emits a stench that becomes known as the Great Stink.

The opening of the Alhambra Theatre proves to be the first step in the growth of an entertainment complex at Leicester Square.

Westminster Bridge is lit by electricity.

1859 The chimes of Big Ben ring out over London for the first time.

HMS *Warrior*, Britain's first iron-hulled battleship, is launched at the Thames Ironworks in Canning Town.

A National Portrait Gallery opens, partly because of Prince Albert's enthusiastic support for the venture.

Samuel Gurney founds the Metropolitan Drinking Fountain and Cattle Trough Association in an attempt to reduce levels of cholera and drunkenness.

1860 The Grosvenor (or Victoria) Bridge is built across the River Thames by the London, Chatham, and Dover Railway to provide access to Victoria Station.

Hungerford Market closes.

The London, Brighton, and South Coast Railway, and the London, Chatham, and Dover Railway open stations at Victoria.

The Royal Victoria Dock, at Plaistow Marshes, is extended by construction of the Royal Albert Dock.

1861 Tramcars appear on London streets.

A wrought iron bridge is built across the River Thames between Battersea and Chelsea to give the West London Railway access to the station at Clapham Junction.

1862 The London Cooperative Society is founded by railway workers in West Ham.

Westminster Bridge is replaced.

1863 Alexandra Palace is opened as an exhibition center in north London. It is destroyed by fire after only two weeks but rebuilt.

London's first underground railroad company (the Metropolitan) offers services between Paddington and the City of London.

A railroad station, now Britain's busiest, opens at Clapham Junction.

The Royal College of Art is founded.

1864 Completion of a wrought iron bridge allows the London, Dover, and Chatham Railway to carry passengers across the River Thames from Southwark to the Metropolitan Railway at Blackfriars.

The first Peabody Buildings open at Spitalfields.

The former Bridewell Prison is demolished.

The Hungerford Railway Bridge links Charing Cross to the south bank of the River Thames.

John Lewis, a buyer of dress fabrics, opens a shop in Oxford Street that evolves into a major national department store business.

The South Eastern Railway builds a station at Waterloo.

1864–65 The Langham, the first of London's luxury hotels, is built in Portland Place.

1865 Daniel Nicholas Thévenon, a Parisian wine merchant, opens the Café Royal in Glasshouse Street.

Parliament approves legislation creating the Metropolitan Fire Brigade.

William Booth establishes his first mission in Whitechapel.

1866 Bishops of the Church of England convene for the first Lambeth Conference.

The gates at Mile End, London's last major turnpike, are removed.

London's first blue plaque (honoring Lord Byron) is erected.

1867 The Hurlingham Club is formed.

The Metropolitan Asylums Board is created and introduces a limited ambulance service.

1868 The construction of Parliament Square involves demolition of some of London's worst slums.

A covered hall for meat trading is built at Smithfield Market.

Millwall Dock opens.

Parliamentary legislation ends the spectacle of public hangings in London.

St. Pancras Station opens as the terminus of the Midland Railway.

1869 The All England Croquet Club is formed at Wimbledon.

The bridge over the River Thames between Blackfriars and Southwark is replaced.

The Royal Naval Dockyards at Deptford and Woolwich are closed.

1870 Charles Dickens is buried at Westminster Abbey.

Dr. Thomas John Barnardo opens his first children's home in Mile End.

The Gas Light and Coke Company builds a plant, designed to serve the whole of London, on the north bank of the River Thames at Beckton.

A London School Board is appointed to provide education for children aged five to 13.

The Vaudeville Theatre is built in the Strand, opening with performances of James Albery's *Two Roses*, a comedy that helped launch the acting career of Henry Irving.

1870–73 Wandsworth Bridge is built across the River Thames between Wandsworth and Fulham.

1871 Mary Tealby moves her home for unwanted cats and dogs from Holloway to Battersea.

The Royal Albert Hall is opened by Queen Victoria.

1871–73 The Albert Bridge is built to carry traffic across the River Thames between Chelsea (on the north bank) and Battersea (on the south).

1872 Charterhouse School moves out of London to Surrey.

The first London School Board institution opens in Berners Street.

1873 The East India Company is terminated.

The Royal Naval College transfers from Plymouth to Greenwich.

1874 The Criterion Theatre (one of the first to be constructed underground) opens.

Liverpool Street Station opens as the London terminus of the Great Eastern Railway.

Wormwood Scrubs Prison is built by convict labor.

1875 Liberty's Store opens in Regent Street.

The rules of polo are formalized at the Hurlingham Club.

1876 The Albert Memorial, erected in Kensington Gardens as a tribute to Queen Victoria's late husband, is completed.

St. Etheldreda's Church, Holborn, becomes the first place of worship to revert to Roman Catholic use since the reformation.

1877 The All England Croquet Club, founded in 1869, admits tennis players as members.

The Corporation of London provides a trading hall for Billingsgate Fish Market.

Peter Jones's department store opens for business at Sloane Square.

1878 Cleopatra's Needle is erected on the Victoria Embankment.

The Corporation of London and the livery companies found the City and Guilds of London Institute to provide technical and scientific education.

The Corporation of London takes control of Epping Forest in order to preserve it as a recreational amenity.

A Criminal Investigation Department is formed to coordinate detective work within the Metropolitan Police Force.

Parliamentary legislation creates a Senate to act as governing body for the University of London.

The University of London allows women to receive degrees.

William Booth coins the phrase "Salvation Army" to describe his growing band of missionaries in east London.

1879 Dan Harries Evans opens the D. H. Evans drapery store in Oxford Street, specializing in lace work.

Fulham Football Club, the oldest still playing in the top flights of English soccer, is formed.

The passage of the Thames Flood Act leads to construction of embankments alongside the river.

1880 The Corporation of London founds the Guildhall School of Music.

1881 The Comedy Theatre opens in Panton Street, presenting comic operas.

The Natural History Museum opens.

The Royal Albert Dock opens.

The Savoy Theatre (the first public building in London to be lit by electricity) opens in the Strand.

1882 Electricity begins to challenge gas as a source of lighting in London after Parliament authorizes the use of overhead and underground cables as a means of providing power.

The Playhouse Theatre is built in Northumberland Avenue by speculator Sefton Parry, who believed that the South Eastern Railway would eventually purchase the site.

The Royal College of Music is founded.

The Royal Courts of Justice open in the Strand.

1882–86 The wooden bridge across the River Thames between Putney and Fulham is replaced by a granite structure, designed by Joseph Bazalgette.

1883 The Wellington Arch is moved to its present location at the west end of Constitution Hill.

The world's first electricity generating station opens at Holborn Viaduct.

1883–87 The central span of Hammersmith Bridge is replaced.

1884 Construction of the underground railroad system's Circle Line is completed.

Delegates at an international conference in Washington, D.C., agree that the prime meridian (0° longitude) will pass through Greenwich.

The footbridge across the River Thames at Teddington is completed.

The National Agricultural Hall opens as an exhibition center.

The Prince of Wales becomes patron of Battersea Dogs' Home, setting a precedent for royal support for the institution.

The Prince's Theatre (later known as the Prince of Wales Theatre) opens in Coventry Street.

Samuel Barnett founds Toynbee Hall as an educational center in London's East End.

The Savoy Hotel opens.

1886 A bridge is built across the River Thames from Southwark to St. Paul's railroad station for the Holborn Viaduct Station Company.

The South Eastern Railway opens a terminal at Cannon Street Station.

Tilbury Docks open.

Tower Bridge is built, linking the Tower of London to Bermondsey docks.

1886–90 New Scotland Yard, designed by R. Norman Shaw, is built as a headquarters for the Metropolitan Police.

1887 Arthur Conan Doyle creates the fictional detective Sherlock Holmes.

The Imperial Institute (now the Commonwealth Institute) is founded to commemorate the golden jubilee of Queen Victoria's reign.

1888 Female employees at the Bryant and May match factory in Bow go on strike in the first British attempt to involve women in labor union activity.

Jack the Ripper cuts the throats of six women in Whitechapel.

The London Clearing House is formed.

The London County Council replaces the Metropolitan Board of Works.

The Lyric Theatre opens in Shaftesbury Avenue.

The Royal Court Theatre is built in Sloane Square.

1889 The Garrick Theatre is built for lyricist W. S. Gilbert.

London dockers strike and win concessions from managements, encouraging labor in other British industries to form trade unions in an effort to improve working conditions.

Queen Victoria allows public access to the state apartments at Kensington Palace.

Wyndham's Theatre is built in Charing Cross Road for Charles Wyndham (the only person whom the Marquis of Salisbury would allow to erect a playhouse on his estate).

1889–1903 Charles Booth, in his 17-volume *Life and Labour of the People of London*, draws attention to the extent of poverty in the city.

1890 A cast iron bridge across the River Thames replaces the wooden structure linking Battersea to Chelsea.

Electricity is used by the Underground railroad, for the first time, on the line linking Stockwell to King William Street.

Frederick Horniman provides the basis for the modern Horniman Museum by allowing the public to view the objects he has amassed during his travels.

Louis Rothman opens a tobacconist's shop in Fleet Street. In 1999, the firm that developed from that inauspicious birth was acquired by British American Tobacco for US $7.55 billion.

1891 Arsenal is the first London football club to turn professional.

The London Shipping Company is formed to serve the growing ocean liner industry.

The Royal English Opera House (renamed the Palace Theatre in 1892) opens with performances of Arthur Sullivan's *Ivanhoe*.

1891–97 A 4,000-foot-long tunnel is built to link Blackwall (on the north side of the River Thames) with Greenwich (on the south).

1892 John Burns and James Keir Hardie win seats in Parliament, becoming the first members of working-class organizations to represent London constituencies in the House of Commons.

Covent Garden Theatre is renamed the Royal Opera House.

The Royal English Opera House is renamed the Palace Theatre.

The Trafalgar Square Theatre (now known as the Duke of York's Theatre) is the first playhouse to open in St. Martin's Lane.

1892–95 The Brewer Car—the first British automobile to use an internal combustion engine—is built at Walthamstow.

1893 A statue of Eros is erected in Piccadilly Circus as a memorial to the seventh Earl of Shaftesbury.

1894 Lincoln's Inn Fields becomes a public park.

1895 A Jewish Cemetery is laid out at Golders Green.

The London School of Economics is founded with funds from the estate of Henry Hunt Hutchison, a left-wing sympathizer.

1895–1903 The Roman Catholic Church builds Westminster Cathedral.

1897 The Anglican Church of St. Saviour and St. Mary Overie is raised in status, becoming Southwark Cathedral.

Christ's Hospital School moves out of London to Horsham (Sussex).

The Coburg Hotel (now the Connaught) is erected in Carlos Place.

Frederick Temple, Archbishop of Canterbury, sells Addington Palace, London residence of the Primates of the Church of England since 1807.

Horse-drawn carriages face their first competition from electric-powered taxis.

Motorized omnibuses appear on London streets.

The Tate Gallery, gift of sugar refiner Henry Tate, opens at Millbank.

1897–1906 University College Hospital is built.

1898 The Drain—the underground rail link between Waterloo Station and the City of London—is opened.

The first London boroughs are created.

1899 The Hospital for Tropical Diseases is founded.

The London County Council assumes responsibility for running the Metropolitan Fire Brigade.

1899–1909 Aston Webb designs a new facade for the Victoria and Albert Museum's Cromwell Road frontage.

1900 The Church of England donates nine acres of land at Lambeth Palace to the London County Council for use as a public park in an inner city area with limited green space.

The Wallace Collection of European art, bequeathed to the nation in 1897, is placed on permanent display in Manchester Square.

Westminster is given city status.

1901 The Apollo Theatre opens in Shaftesbury Avenue as a venue for musicals.

The Baltic Club and the London Shipping Company merge as the Baltic and Mercantile Shipping Exchange Limited.

The Bechstein Concert Hall (later known as the Wigmore Hall) opens with a performance by Evelyn Stuart.

The census shows that the County of London has a population of 4,536,267.

Electric trams are introduced in London.

Frederick Horniman's museum (established in 1890) is acquired by the London County Council.

The Metropolitan Police create a Fingerprint Bureau.

Whitechapel Art Gallery opens.

1902 The British Academy is founded.

A foot tunnel is built under the River Thames between Greenwich and the Isle of Dogs.

The London County Council buys Marble Hill House (Twickenham) and the Ranger's House (Greenwich).

A Metropolitan Water Board is created to manage London's water supplies.

Newgate Prison is demolished to provide space for the erection of the Central Criminal Court.

1902–7 Buildings for the Central Criminal Court, designed by Edward Mountford, are erected at Old Bailey.

1903 The Abbey Theatre opens.

The first Wolseley cars are manufactured at Crayford.

The New Theatre (later known as the Albery Theatre) is built in St. Martin's Lane for Charles Wyndham.

1904 Actor and producer Herbert Beerbohm Tree founds the Royal Academy of Dramatic Art.

The Coliseum Theatre (also known as the London Coliseum) opens with a repertoire of variety shows.

George Barker makes his first films at the Barker Motion Photography studios in Ealing.

The London Symphony Orchestra is formed.

Responsibility for children's education passes from the London School Board to the London County Council.

Simpson's restaurant opens in the Strand.

The Stephen family move into 46 Gordon Square, establishing the Bloomsbury Group.

1905 The Aldwych Theatre opens, featuring musical comedies.

The Waldorf Theatre (now known as the Strand Theatre) opens with a repertoire of operas and dramatic productions.

1906 Admiralty Arch, designed by Aston Webb, is built across the eastern entrance to The Mall as part of the nation's memorial to Queen Victoria.

The Baker Street and Waterloo Railway and the Great Northern, Piccadilly, and Brompton Railway introduce underground services.

1907 The Charing Cross, Euston, and Hampstead Railway introduces underground services.

The Queen's Theatre opens in Shaftesbury Avenue.

The Rugby Football Union makes Twickenham its headquarters.

Wyldes Farm, in north London, is put on the market. Much of the land is purchased by a trust fund that develops it as Hampstead Garden Suburb.

1908 The cast iron railroad bridge across the River Thames at Richmond is replaced by a stronger steel structure.

London's first escalator is installed at Harrods store.

The Society for the Encouragement of Arts, Manufactures, and Commerce is renamed the Royal Society of Arts.

White City Stadium is erected.

1909 The Port of London Authority is created to manage the city's docks.

Selfridge's store opens in Oxford Street.

1910 The London Palladium Theatre opens, featuring variety shows.

1911 Claude Graeme-White establishes Hendon as a center of innovation in the infant aircraft industry.

The Prince's (known from 1962 as the Shaftesbury) Theatre opens with a performance of *The Three Musketeers*.

The Queen Victoria Statue, at the western end of The Mall, is unveiled.

The University of London moves to a site in Bloomsbury.

The Victoria Palace Theatre opens, providing music hall entertainment.

1911–22 County Hall is built, on the opposite side of the River Thames from the Houses of Parliament, as the headquarters of the London County Council.

1912 The Baltic Exchange moves into new premises at St. Mary Axe.

George Frampton's statue of Peter Pan, the little boy who never grew up, is placed in Kensington Gardens.

The University of London appoints its first female professor.

1912–21 The cast iron bridge between Southwark and the City of London is replaced by a five-span steel structure designed by Ernest George.

1913 Aircraft manufacturer Handley Page builds a plant at Cricklewood.

The Ambassadors Theatre opens in West Street, off Shaftesbury Avenue.

Big Ben's winding gear is automated.

The Royal Horticultural Society holds its first Chelsea Flower Show.

1914 The London County Council opens the Geffrye Museum.

1916 The last of the horse-drawn carriages, which provided a public transport service in London, disappear from the streets.

St. Martin's Theatre opens in West Street.

1919 Great Britain's first civil airport is opened on Hounslow Heath, providing service to Paris and Australia.

The Palais de Danse (usually known as the Hammersmith Palais) opens on the site of a former tramcar garage in Shepherd's Bush Road.

Parliamentary legislation (known as the Addison Act) provides government subsidies that allow London's local authorities to erect 27,000 low-rent homes.

1919–20 The Cenotaph, designed by Edward Lutyens, is erected in Whitehall as a memorial to service men and women of the British Empire and Commonwealth who were killed during the First World War.

1920 The Imperial War Museum is established by an Act of Parliament.

London Airport is opened at Croydon.

1921 Construction of the George V Dock is completed.

Hammersmith Palais is the first British dance hall to have a jazz band on stage.

High construction costs result in the abandonment of the housing subsidies introduced by the Addison Act (1919).

1922 The British Broadcasting Corporation (BBC) makes its first radio transmissions from Savoy Hill.

1923 Horace Walpole's Gothic revival castle at Strawberry Hill is bought by the Catholic Education Council and turned into a teacher training college.

Wembley Stadium opens in time to host the Football Association Cup Final, attended by over 200,000 people.

1924 Legislation introduced by the Labour government reestablishes subsidies for local authority house building and results in the construction of 64,000 low-rent homes over the next decade.

1924–25 The British Empire Exhibition, held at Wembley, attracts over 27 million visitors.

1927 Lord Iveagh bequeaths Kenwood House to the London County Council.

1928 The airstrip at Croydon is officially named London Airport.

Lloyd's of London moves from the Royal Exchange to Leadenhall Street.

The River Thames floods.

1929 The Duchess Theatre opens in Catherine Street.

Managers of London's tram, underground railway, and bus companies agree to coordinate their services.

A second Grand Union Canal is completed, linking London to Birmingham.

1930 The London County Council assumes responsibility for the city's ambulance service.

The Phoenix Theatre opens with a performance of Noel Coward's *Private Lives*, featuring Coward himself in the cast.

The Prince Edward Theatre opens.

The Royal Bethlehem Hospital for the mentally ill (Bedlam) moves out of London to premises in Addington, Surrey.

The Whitehall Theatre opens, featuring Walter Hackett in his own play, *The Way to Treat a Woman*.

1930–35 Embankments alongside the River Thames are raised in order to prevent further flooding.

1931 Chessington Zoo opens.

The Dorchester Hotel opens in Park Lane.

Ford Motor Company starts car production at Dagenham.

Industrialist Samuel Courtauld founds the Courtauld Institute of Art.

Ninette de Valois creates a ballet company (later known as the Royal Ballet) at the Old Vic theater.

The Saville Theatre opens.

1932 The Jewish Museum is founded.

Lambeth Bridge is replaced.

Thomas Beecham creates the London Philharmonic Orchestra.

1933 Battersea Power Station opens.

The city's transport service is nationalized and placed under the control of a London Passenger Transport Board.

1935–50 Dr. Scott Williamson supervises the Peckham Experiment, conducting research into human biology in the south London community.

1936 The British Broadcasting Corporation builds the world's first television transmitter at Alexandra Palace and begins regular broadcasts.

The Crystal Palace is burned to the ground.

A pro-fascist rally led by Sir Oswald Mosley breaks up following violence between marchers and their opponents in Cable Street.

1936–40 The lattice girder bridge across the River Thames between Fulham and Wandsworth is replaced by a cantilever structure designed by T. Pierson Frank.

1937 Earl's Court Exhibition Hall (the largest reinforced concrete structure in Europe at the time) opens.

Lupino Lane popularizes the dance known as the Lambeth Walk.

The National Maritime Museum opens at Greenwich.

St. Paul's railroad station is renamed Blackfriars Station.

1938 A Green Belt of land protected from development is designated around London by Parliament.

Michael Balcon acquires the former Barker Motion Photography site, renames it Ealing Studios, and, for more than a decade, produces a highly successful string of movies now known as the Ealing comedies.

1939 Building work is completed at the Bank of England in Threadneedle Street.

Evacuation of schoolchildren begins after the United Kingdom declares war on Germany at the beginning of the Second World War.

Irish terrorists make an unsuccessful attempt to blow up Hammersmith Bridge.

The Royal Exchange ceases to function as a place for general merchant trading due to the development of specialist markets.

1939–45 John Rennie's Waterloo Bridge is replaced by a new structure designed by Giles Gilbert Scott.

1940–41 During the Blitz, an estimated 18,800 tons of explosive are dropped on London by German aircraft, killing 15,000 people and damaging 3.5 million homes.

1941 The Dorchester Hotel becomes General Dwight D. Eisenhower's British headquarters after the United States enters the Second World War.

German bombs destroy the Queen's Hall, forcing the Henry Wood Promenade Concerts to move to the Albert Hall, where they have remained ever since.

1945 Walter Legge forms the Philharmonia Orchestra.

1945–50 The House of Commons is rebuilt following bomb damage suffered during the Second World War.

1946 The Bank of England is nationalized.

The City of London (Various Powers) Act gives local councils the authority to create smokeless zones in an effort to reduce the incidence of smog.

Covent Garden Opera Company and Sadler's Wells Ballet make the Royal Opera House their base.

The General Assembly of the United Nations holds its first meeting in Methodist Central Hall.

Heathrow is recognized as London Airport and provides direct services to the United States.

Thomas Beecham founds the Royal Philharmonic Orchestra.

1947 Hansom cabs disappear from London streets.

The Royal Military Academy at Woolwich is merged with its counterpart at Sandhurst and part of its barracks converted into a museum for the Royal Regiment of Artillery.

1948 The Labour government nationalizes electricity supply and appoints a London Electricity Board to manage power distribution in the city.

The London Passenger Transport Board is replaced by the London Transport Executive.

The National Trust acquires Ham House.

The Royal Observatory moves from Greenwich to the clearer skies of Herstmonceux (Sussex).

1949 The Earl of Jersey gifts Osterley Park to the nation.

1950 Four Scottish nationalist students steal the Stone of Scone (the coronation stone of Scotland's first kings) from Westminster Abbey. It is recovered after four months (though rumors persist that the authorities were deceived into returning a replica to London).

Timothy Evans is hanged at Pentonville Prison for the murder of his wife and daughter despite widespread doubts about his guilt. The event fuels the (ultimately successful) campaign to have capital punishment abolished in the United Kingdom.

1951 The Labour government promotes a Festival of Britain in an effort to raise public morale at a time of food rationing and economic reconstruction following the Second World War. The focus of the celebrations is on the dockside between Waterloo Bridge and Hungerford Bridge, where the Royal Festival Hall is built. Battersea Park is redesigned as part of the celebrations.

1952 The last tramcars are withdrawn from service.

The London County Council buys Holland House and converts it for use as a youth hostel.

The Mousetrap, the world's longest running play (still being performed at the end of the millennium), opens at the Ambassador's Theatre.

One hundred and twelve people are killed, and 340 injured, when two express trains collide at Harrow and Wealdstone and a third runs into the wreckage.

A smog lasting from 5 to 9 December leads to the deaths of 4,700 Londoners with respiratory diseases.

The Wellington Museum opens.

1953 The British Film Institute builds a National Film Theatre on the South Bank.

1954 *Cutty Sark*, built in 1869 and one of the fastest of the tea clippers, is placed in dry dock at Greenwich as a tourist attraction.

Excavations under Queen Victoria Street, in the City of London, uncover the remains of the Roman Temple of Mithras, built during the second century A.D.

The London Commodity Exchange is established.

1956 Big Ben's operating mechanism is overhauled.

The British Broadcasting Corporation moves its television studios from Alexandra Palace to Shepherd's Bush.

The Clean Air Act introduces tighter controls on sources of air pollution in London.

The Royal Ballet is created through the award of a royal charter to the Sadler's Wells Company.

1957 Boutiques begin to appear in Carnaby Street, which becomes a symbol of "swinging London" during the 1960s.

A Royal Commission, chaired by Sir Edwin Herbert, is appointed to consider the reorganization of local government in London.

1958 The City of London Corporation buys the Barbican site by compulsory purchase order and commissions a new housing estate, with provision for public buildings such as premises for the Museum of London.

Gatwick Airport is opened on farmland 25 miles south of central London to accommodate growing air traffic to the capital.

A planetarium is built adjacent to Madame Tussaud's waxworks.

1958–61 The United States's embassy is built at the western end of Grosvenor Square.

1959 Croydon Airport, increasingly hemmed in by urban development, is closed.

The Mermaid Theatre, the first playhouse to open in the City of London for over three centuries, offers its first productions at Puddle Dock.

1960 The Royal Commission established to consider the reorganization of local government in London recommends formation of a Greater London Council and the creation of new boroughs with enhanced powers.

1960–67 A second tunnel is built under the River Thames between Blackwall and Greenwich in order to relieve traffic congestion.

1961 The Royal Navy's victualling yard at Deptford closes.

Steam engines are withdrawn from the London Underground railway.

1962 An Act of Parliament establishes the Covent Garden Market Authority to manage London's principal food and vegetable wholesalers.

Brunel College of Advanced Technology is renamed Brunel University and given authority to award its own degrees.

The Prince's Theatre is acquired by Charles Clore and EMI, who rename it the Shaftesbury Theatre.

St. Mary-le-Bow Church, originally designed by Christopher Wren, holds its first services after being largely rebuilt and refurbished following damage by German bombers during the Blitz.

1962–72 London Underground's Victoria Line is built between Stockwell and Walthamstow.

1963 Bankside power station is commissioned.

The London Government Act creates the Greater London Council.

The Mayfair Theatre is built as an extension to the Mayfair Hotel in Stratton Street.

A Museum of the Theatre opens in Kensington.

1963–66 The British Telecom Tower is built. Over 600 feet high, it dominates central London's skyline and allows radio and television waves to travel above buildings.

1964 The London Boroughs Association is formed.

1965 London's local government is reshaped as the Greater London Council and 32 London boroughs replace the London County Council.

1966 The British Airports Authority assumes responsibility for the management of Gatwick and Heathrow Airports, initiating a series of improvements to runway and terminal facilities.

City University is founded.

Marble Hill House is converted for use as a museum of 18th-century art and furniture.

Trinidadian immigrants hold the first Notting Hill carnival.

1967 Construction work begins at Thamesmead, which will house a community on land reclaimed from River Thames marshes.

East India Docks close.

The Hayward Art Gallery opens on the South Bank.

A major rehabilitation scheme, designed to reduce pollution of the River Lea and convert the area into a regional park, is unveiled by local authorities.

The Queen Elizabeth Hall (named after Queen Elizabeth II) opens on the South Bank.

The Royal Arsenal at Greenwich closes.

Thames Television is founded to provide programming for the London region.

1968 Covent Garden Opera Company is renamed the Royal Opera.

St. Katharine's Dock closes.

1968–72 London Bridge is replaced.

1969 The Beckton Gas Production Plant, opened in 1870, closes as natural gas from the North Sea replaces town gas as a source of fuel and power.

The London Docks close.

Regent's Canal is closed to industrial traffic.

The Transport Act denationalizes the city's public transport system, transferring management responsibilities to the Greater London Council.

Twins Ronald and Reginald Kray, leaders of London's major criminal organization, are convicted of murder at the Old Bailey.

1970 The British Museum, lacking space to exhibit ethnographic material at its Great Russell Street site, opens a Museum of Mankind in Burlington Gardens.

Central London Polytechnic, City of London Polytechnic, Kingston Polytechnic, North East London Polytechnic, South Bank Polytechnic, and Thames Polytechnic are created in order to enhance opportunities for higher education in London.

John Rennie's London Bridge is sold to American interests, transferred to the United States, and reerected at Lake Havasu City, Arizona.

Surrey Commercial Docks close.

The Young Vic is founded as part of the National Theatre.

1971 HMS *Belfast*, the largest cruiser ever built for the Royal Navy, is berthed at Symon's Wharf as a tourist attraction.

The National Army Museum moves from the Royal Military Academy Sandhurst to a site beside Chelsea Hospital.

North London Polytechnic is founded.

Plans to convert London's declining docklands into office and commercial space are shelved in the face of a public outcry.

1971–72 Embankments along the River Thames are raised in an attempt to prevent flooding.

1971–81 The 600-foot-high National Westminster Tower is built. At the time, it was the tallest building in London.

1972 The Conservative government authorizes construction of a flood barrier across the River Thames at Woolwich.

Hangars at the former airstrip in Hendon are converted for use as a Royal Air Force Museum.

Soho residents initiate a campaign to change the area's image as the center of London's sex industry.

1973 The British Museum Library, the National Central Library, and the National Lending Library merge to form the British Library.

The London Stock Exchange unites with the Dublin exchange and those operating in provincial cities of the United Kingdom. It also admits women as members.

Middlesex Polytechnic is founded.

The Water Act creates a Thames Water Authority with responsibility for water supply, pollution control, sewage disposal, and provision of recreational facilities in the Thames river basin.

1974 Covent Garden fruit and vegetable market transfers to Nine Elms. The old site is redeveloped as a tourist focus, with boutiques, stalls, and outdoor cafés.

The Ranger's House at Greenwich is converted into an art gallery and museum of musical instruments.

1976 Guildhall Museum and the London Museum merge to form the Museum of London.

The London Docklands Strategic Plan proposes community-based development, including housing, in the city's former dock area.

The Notting Hill carnival is marred by rioting.

Work on the National Theatre is completed, 25 years after the foundation stone was laid.

1977 The Astoria Cinema, in Charing Cross Road, is converted for use as a theater.

The Bryant and May match factory at Bow is closed and redesigned as flats.

Heathrow Airport is linked to the Underground railway system by an extension of the Piccadilly Line.

The Public Record Office opens a new base at Kew.

1978–79 Disputes between management and labor at *The Times* lead to frequent disruption of printing schedules but end with the introduction of new working practices.

1978–86 Richard Rogers and Partners design the controversial steel and glass Lloyd's Building.

1979 The Bank of England is made responsible for the supervision of all banks based in the United Kingdom.

London Underground's new Jubilee Line (named to commemorate Queen Elizabeth II's 25 years on the British throne) improves access between Bond Street and Charing Cross.

The New Victoria Cinema is renamed the Apollo Victoria, refurbished, and opened as a theater presenting musicals and pop concerts.

1980 Alexandra Palace is destroyed by fire for the second time.

The last of Blackwall's docks closes.

The London Transport Museum opens in a converted flower market building at Covent Garden.

Millwall Docks and West India Docks close.

1981 Bankside power station is decommissioned.

The London Docklands Development Corporation is established, with a brief to regenerate the former dock area of the city.

The London Symphony Orchestra takes up residence at the Barbican Centre.

Riots in Brixton lead to an official government inquiry into relationships between the Metropolitan Police and London's black community.

The Royal group of docks (the Victoria, Albert, and King George V) close, becoming the last of the 19th-century harbor developments to cease operations.

Rupert Murdoch's publishing empire absorbs *The Times*.

1982 The Barbican Arts Centre opens.

Billingsgate Fish Market moves to the Isle of Dogs.

Construction of a flood barrier across the River Thames at Woolwich is completed.

The London International Financial Futures and Options Exchange (LIFFE) opens as a trading base for companies whose transactions involve a considerable element of financial risk.

1983 Battersea power station is decommissioned.

The Duchess Theatre is the first London playhouse to perform musicals regularly on Sundays (*Snoopy* was the initial production).

London Health Emergency is formed to campaign against the Conservative government's plans to close hospitals in the city.

Thirteen local authorities, all dominated by the Labour Party, withdraw from the London Boroughs Association and form the Association of London Authorities.

1984 London's public transport system is renationalized and a management body, known as London Regional Transport, created to oversee provision.

Parliamentary legislation creates a London Regional Passengers' Committee to consider complaints about bus and rail services in the city.

1985 The Geology Museum and the Natural History Museum merge.

Stansted is designated London's third airport.

1986 The Big Bang revolutionizes financial practices in the City of London.

The London Planning Advisory Committee is created to advise the government and London boroughs on strategic planning issues and major development proposals.

London Transport replaces some of the advertising on its underground services with poems, a policy that meets with widespread approval from travellers and leads to the publication of a successful book series.

London's last gas street lamps are extinguished at Temple.

A major development of Liverpool Street railroad station includes construction of offices, restaurants, and shopping facilities.

Part of Hampton Court Palace's south wing is destroyed by fire.

Prime Minister Margaret Thatcher's government abolishes the Greater London Council.

The Stock Exchange converts from an association of members into a nonprofit-making limited company and replaces face-to-face dealing with a computerized system of trading.

1987 The Docklands Light Railway links the City of London to the Isle of Dogs.

A fire at King's Cross Underground railway station kills 31 people.

London City Airport opens in the Docklands.

The London Commodity Exchange renames itself London Fox, the Futures and Options Exchange.

London's Corn Exchange business transfers to the Baltic Exchange.

Plans are prepared for an 850-foot-high tower, incorporating offices, a concert hall, and a railroad station, at Canary Wharf.

A special Act of Parliament allows the Great Ormond Street Hospital for Sick Children to continue receiving financial benefits from the copyright of J. M. Barrie's play, *Peter Pan*, after the normal period for receipt of royalties expires.

The Tower of London and the area that includes Westminster Abbey, the Palace of Westminster, and St. Margaret's Church, are declared World Heritage Sites by the United Nations Educational, Scientific and Cultural Organization (UNESCO).

1987–88 Excavations reveal the foundations of a Roman amphitheater underneath Guildhall Yard.

1988 Alexandra Palace, rebuilt after a fire in 1980, is opened as a sports, leisure, and exhibition center.

A Museum of the Moving Image opens on the South Bank.

1989 A Design Museum, showing the best of British manufacturing, opens in a former warehouse at London's Docklands.

1990 The Courtauld Institute of Art moves from Portman Square to Somerset House.

The Inner London Education Authority is abolished by the Conservative government, with which it had frequently crossed swords.

The London Philharmonic Orchestra is made the resident orchestra at the Royal Festival Hall.

Thames Water Authority is privatized by the Conservative government.

1991 Electricity supply is denationalized, returning the industry to private companies.

The London International Insurance and Reinsurance Market Association (LIRMA) is formed.

The Queen Elizabeth II Bridge carries southbound traffic across the River Thames at Dartford (at the eastern edge of the metropolitan area) and relieves congestion at the Dartford Tunnel.

The Roche Consortium, a development company that had received planning permission to convert the former Battersea power station into a theme park, runs out of money.

West London Polytechnic is founded.

1992 A bomb planted by the Irish Republican Army damages the premises of the Baltic Exchange but has little effect on trading.

Commercial organizations create London First to coordinate public and private attempts to improve investment in the city, increase the quality of transport provision, encourage tourism, and reduce air pollution.

The London International Financial Futures and Options Exchange (LIFFE) absorbs the London Traded Options Market.

Parliamentary legislation allows the London polytechnics to call themselves universities.

1993 Buckingham Palace is opened to the public. Admission fees are used to pay for rebuilding work at Windsor Castle.

County Hall, former headquarters of the Greater London Council, is bought by a development company and converted into a hotel, restaurant, and entertainment complex.

1994 The Baltic Exchange moves to new premises in St. Mary Axe.

The Conservative government announces its decision to close the Royal Naval College at Greenwich.

London Transport assumes responsibility for The Drain (the underground rail link between Waterloo Station and the City of London).

Prime Minister John Major vetoes a proposal by his defence secretary, Michael Portillo, to sell Admiralty Arch to a private developer who would develop its office potential.

1995 The Association of London Authorities and the London Boroughs Association merge as the Association of London Government.

Barings, the oldest merchant bank in the City of London, collapses financially after one of its employees takes excessive risks with the firm's funds on the Singapore futures market.

The Conservative government decides against construction of additional runways at Gatwick and Heathrow Airports.

London bus services are denationalized, returning to private sector control.

In response to a European Union directive, Dublin business on the London Stock Exchange is redirected to a new exchange in the Republic of Ireland.

1996 The Irish Republican Army bombs Canary Wharf Tower, killing two people and injuring 100.

Lloyd's of London reaches a £3.1 billion settlement with most of the names who alleged that losses experienced between 1987 and 1992 were, in part, due to bad management.

London International Financial Futures and Options Exchange (LIFFE) absorbs London Fox.

The Royal Philharmonia takes up residence at the Royal Festival Hall.

The Stone of Scone, coronation stone of the early Scottish monarchs, is removed from Westminster Abbey and returned to Scotland.

1997 The Bank of England is given responsibility for altering interest rates, a task previously reserved for government.

The British Library moves to a purpose-built site at St. Pancras.

Cars are banned from Hammersmith Bridge but buses, cyclists, and pedestrians retain rights of access.

Greenwich is designated a World Heritage Site by UNESCO.

The new Globe Theatre opens its first season of plays.

The newly elected Labour government announces plans to privatize part of the Underground railway system but later shelves them following internal disputes over funding.

The Swansea to Paddington express train passes a red signal and crashes into a goods locomotive at Southall. Seven people are killed, 150 injured, and Great Western Trains (operators of the express service) are fined a record £1.5 million for breaching safety legislation.

1997–99 The British Film Institute builds a seven-story IMAX cinema (the largest in Europe) on a site near Waterloo Station.

1998 The Londons Dockland Development Corporation is dismantled and its powers transferred to the London boroughs.

Tea auctions are held in London for the last time.

1999 The Millennium Dome opens at Greenwich amid complaints about its cost, design, and management.

2000 Andrew Lloyd Webber buys the Stoll Moss theater empire in the West End.

Australian Ross Stretton is the first foreigner to be appointed director of the Royal Ballet.

The Athenaeum, one of London's principal gentlemen's clubs, votes to admit ladies as members.

London citizens elect Ken Livingstone, a left-wing member of parliament, as their first mayor.

The London Eye, a giant wheel, is erected outside County Hall, allowing visitors a view of the city from 450 feet above the River Thames.

The London International Financial Futures and Options Exchange (LIFFE) announces a joint venture with NASDAQ (the North American exchange for high technology stocks) to form a market for stock futures.

The Real Irish Republican Army bombs the British Broadcasting Corporation Television Centre, but damage is limited and only one person is injured.

The Tate Gallery opens new exhibition rooms for its modern art collection in the former Bankside power station.

The Underground's Jubilee Line is extended through the Docklands to Stratford.

2001 The Royal Shakespeare Company decides to move out of Barbican Centre, leaving it wihtout a permanent base in London.

The Stock Exchange announces plans to list itself on its own market.

LORD MAYORS OF THE CITY OF LONDON

Office holders are listed by year of appointment.

1189	Henry FitzAilwyn
1212	Roger FitzAlan
1215	Serlo le Mercer
	William Hardel
1216	James Alderman
1217	Salomon de Basing
1218	Serlo le Mercer
1222	Richard Renger
1227	Roger le Duke
1231	Andrew Buckerel
1238	Richard Renger
1239	William Joynier
1240	Reginald de Bungheye
1241	Ralph Ashwy
1244	Michael Tovy
1246	John Gisors
	Peter FitzAlan
1247	Michael Tovy
1249	Roger FitzRoger
1250	John Norman
1251	Adam de Basing
1252	John Tulesan
1253	Nicholas Bat
1254	Ralph Hardel
1258	William FitzRichard
1259	John Gisors
	William FitzRichard
1261	Thomas FitzThomas
1265	Hugh FitzOtho
	John Walerand
	John de la Linde
1266	William FitzRichard
1267	Alan la Zuche
1268	Thomas de Ippegrave
	Stephen de Eddeworth
1269	Hugh FitzOtho
1270	John Adrien
1271	Walter Hervey
1273	Henry le Waleys
1274	Gregory de Rokesley
1281	Henry le Waleys
1284	Gregory de Rokesley
1285	Ralph de Sandwich
1289	John le Breton
	Ralph de Sandwich
1293	John le Breton
1298	Henry le Waleys
1299	Elias Russell
1301	John le Blund
1308	Nicholas de Farndone
1309	Thomas Romeyn
1310	Richer de Refham
1311	John de Gisors
1313	Nicholas de Farndone
1314	John de Gisors
1315	Stephen de Abyndon
1316	John de Wengrave
1319	Hamo de Chigwell
1320	Nicholas de Farndone
1321	Robert de Kendale
	Hamo de Chigwell
1323	Nicholas de Farndone
	Hamo de Chigwell
1326	Richard de Betoyne
1327	Hamo de Chigwell
1328	John de Grantham
1329	Simon Swanlond
1330	John de Pulteney
1332	John de Prestone
1333	John de Pulteney

1334	Reginald de Conduit
1336	John de Pulteney
1337	Henry Darci
1339	Andrew Aubrey
1341	John de Oxenford
1342	Simon Frauncis
1343	John Hamond
1345	Richard le Lacer
1346	Geoffrey de Witchingham
1347	Thomas Leggy
1348	John Lovekyn
1349	Walter Turke
1350	Richard de Kislingbury
1351	Andrew Aubrey
1352	Adam Fraunceys
1354	Thomas Leggy
1355	Simon Frauncis
1356	Henry Picard
1357	John de Stodeye
1358	John Lovekyn
1359	Simon Dolseley
1360	John Wroth
1361	John Pecche
1362	Stephen Cavendisshe
1363	John Nott
1364	Adam de Bury
1366	John Lovekyn
1367	James Andreu
1368	Simon de Mordone
1369	John de Chichester
1370	John Bernes
1372	John Pyel
1373	Adam de Bury
1374	William Walworth
1375	John Warde
1376	Adam Stable
1377	Nicholas Brembre
1378	John Philipot
1379	John Hadle
1380	William Walworth
1381	John de Northampton
1383	Sir Nicholas Brembre
1386	Nicholas Exton
1388	Sir Nicholas Twyford
1389	William Venour
1390	Adam Bamme
1391	John Heende
1392	Sir Edward Dalyngrigge
	Sir Baldwyn Radyngton
	William Staundon
1393	John Hadle
1394	John Fresshe
1395	William More
1396	Adam Bamme
1397	Richard Whittington
1398	Drew Barentyn
1399	Thomas Knolles
1400	John Fraunceys
1401	John Shadworth
1402	John Walcote
1403	William Askham
1404	John Heende
1405	John Wodecok
1406	Richard Whittington
1407	William Staundon
1408	Drugo Barentyn
1409	Richard Merlawe
1410	Thomas Knolles
1411	Robert Chichele
1412	William Walderne
1413	William Crowmere
1414	Thomas Fauconer
1415	Nicholas Wotton
1416	Henry Barton
1417	Richard Merlawe
1418	William Sevenoke
1419	Richard Whittington
1420	William Cauntbrigge
1421	Robert Chichele
1422	William Walderne

1423 William Crowmere
1424 John Michell
1425 John Coventre
1426 John Reynwell
1427 John Gedney
1428 Henry Barton
1429 William Estfeld
1430 Nicholas Wotton
1431 John Welles
1432 John Perneys
1433 John Brokle
1434 Robert Otele
1435 Henry Frowyk
1436 John Michell
1437 William Estfeld
1438 Stephen Broun
1439 Robert Large
1440 John Paddesle
1441 Robert Clopton
1442 John Hatherle
1443 Thomas Catworth
1444 Henry Frowyk
1445 Simon Eyre
1446 John Olney
1447 John Gedney
1448 Stephen Broun
1449 Thomas Chalton
1450 Nicholas Wyfold
1451 William Gregory
1452 Geoffrey Feldynge
1453 John Norman
1454 Stephen Forster
1455 William Marowe
1456 Thomas Canynges
1457 Geoffrey Boleyn
1458 Thomas Scott
1459 William Hulyn
1460 Richard Lee
1461 Hugh Wiche
1462 Thomas Cooke
1463 Matthew Philip
1464 Ralph Jossleyn
1465 Ralph Verney
1466 John Yonge
1467 Thomas Oulegrave
1468 William Taillour
1469 Richard Lee
1470 John Stockton
1471 William Edward
1472 Sir William Hampton
1473 John Tate
1474 Robert Drope
1475 Robert Bassett
1476 Sir Ralph Josselyn
1477 Humphrey Hayford
1478 Richard Gardyner
1479 Sir Bartholomew James
1480 John Browne
1481 William Haryot
1482 Edmund Shaa
1483 Robert Billesdon
1484 Thomas Hill
1485 Sir William Stokker
John Warde
Sir Hugh Bryce
1486 Henry Colet
1487 William Horne
1488 Robert Tate
1489 William White
1490 John Mathewe
1491 Hugh Clopton
1492 William Martin
1493 Ralp Astry
1494 Richard Chawry
1495 Sir Henry Colet
1496 John Tate
1497 William Purchase
1498 Sir John Percyvale
1499 Nicholas Ailwyn
1500 William Remyngton

1501	Sir John Shaa
1502	Bartholomew Rede
1503	Sir William Capel
1504	John Wynger
1505	Thomas Kneseworth
1506	Sir Richard Haddon
1507	William Browne
1508	Sir Lawrence Aylmer
	Stephen Jenyns
1509	Thomas Bradbury
1510	Sir William Capel
	Henry Kebyll
1511	Roger Achleley
1512	William Copynger
1513	Sir Richard Haddon
	William Browne
1514	Sir John Tate
	George Monoux
1515	William Boteler
1516	John Rest
1517	Thomas Exmewe
1518	Thomas Mirfyn
1519	James Yarford
1520	John Brugge
1521	John Milborne
1522	John Mundy
1523	Thomas Baldry
1524	William Bayley
1525	John Aleyn
1526	Sir Thomas Semer
1527	James Spencer
1528	John Rudstone
1529	Ralph Dodmer
1530	Thomas Pargeter
1531	Nicholas Lambarde
1532	Stephen Pecocke
1533	Christopher Ascue
1534	Sir John Champneys
1535	Sir John Aleyn
1536	Ralph Warren
1537	Sir Richard Gresham
1538	William Forman
1539	Sir William Hollyes
1540	William Roche
1541	Michael Dormer
1542	John Cotes
1543	William Bowyer
1544	Sir Ralph Warren
	William Laxton
1545	Sir Martin Bowes
1546	Henry Huberthorn
1547	Sir John Gresham
1548	Henry Amcotts
1549	Sir Rowland Hill
1550	Andrew Judde
1551	Richard Dobbis
1552	George Barne
1553	Thomas Whyte
1554	John Lyon
1555	William Garrarde
1556	Thomas Offley
1557	Thomas Curtes
1558	Thomas Leigh
1559	William Hewet
1560	Sir William Chester
1561	William Harper
1562	Thomas Lodge
1563	John Whyte
1564	Richard Malorye
1565	Richard Champyon
1566	Christopher Draper
1567	Roger Martyn
1568	Thomas Rowe
1569	Alexander Avenon
1570	Rowland Heyward
1571	William Allen
1572	Lionel Duckett
1573	John Ryvers
1574	James Hawes
1575	Ambrose Nicholas

1576	John Langley
1577	Thomas Ramsay
1578	Richard Pype
1579	Nicholas Woodroofe
1580	John Branche
1581	James Harvye
1582	Thomas Blanke
1583	Edward Osborne
1584	Thomas Pullyson
1585	Wolstan Dixie
1586	George Barne
1587	George Bonde
1588	Martin Calthorp
1589	Richard Martin
	John Harte
1590	John Allot
1591	Sir Rowland Heyward
	William Webbe
1592	William Rowe
1593	Cuthbert Buckell
1594	Sir Richard Martin
	John Spencer
1595	Stephen Slanye
1596	Thomas Skinner
	Henry Billingsley
1597	Richard Saltonstall
1598	Stephen Soame
1599	Nicholas Mosley
1600	William Ryder
1601	John Garrarde
1602	Robert Lee
1603	Sir Thomas Bennett
1604	Sir Thomas Lowe
1605	Sir Leonard Halliday
1606	Sir John Watts
1607	Sir Henry Rowe
1608	Sir Humphrey Weld
1609	Sir Thomas Cambell
1610	Sir William Craven
1611	Sir James Pemberton
1612	Sir John Swynnerton
1613	Sir Thomas Middleton
1614	Sir Thomas Hayes
1615	Sir John Jolles
1616	John Leman
1617	George Bolles
1618	Sir Sebastian Harvey
1619	Sir William Cokayne
1620	Sir Frances Jones
1621	Edward Barkham
1622	Peter Probie
1623	Martin Lumley
1624	John Gore
1625	Allan Cotton
1626	Cuthbert Hacket
1627	Hugh Hammersley
1628	Richard Deane
1629	James Cambell
1630	Sir Robert Ducye
1631	George Whitmore
1632	Nicholas Rainton
1633	Ralph Freeman
1634	Thomas Moulson
	Robert Parkhurst
1635	Christopher Clitherow
1636	Edward Bromfield
1637	Richard Ven
1638	Sir Morris Abbot
1639	Henry Garraway
1640	Edmund Wright
1641	Richard Gurney
1642	Isaac Penington
1643	Sir John Wollaston
1644	Thomas Atkyn
1645	Thomas Adams
1646	Sir John Gayer
1647	John Warner
1648	Abraham Reynardson
1649	Thomas Andrewes
	Thomas Foot

1650	Thomas Andrewes
1651	John Kendricke
1652	John Fowke
1653	Thomas Vyner
1654	Christopher Pack
1655	John Dethick
1656	Robert Tichborne
1657	Richard Chiverton
1658	Sir John Ireton
1659	Thomas Alleyn
1660	Sir Richard Browne
1661	Sir John Frederick
1662	Sir John Robinson
1663	Sir Anthony Bateman
1664	Sir John Lawrence
1665	Sir Thomas Bludworth
1666	Sir William Bolton
1667	Sir William Peake
1668	Sir William Turner
1669	Sir Samuel Starling
1670	Sir Richard Ford
1671	Sir George Waterman
1672	Sir Robert Hanson
1673	Sir William Hooker
1674	Sir Robert Vyner
1675	Sir Joseph Sheldon
1676	Sir Thomas Davies
1677	Sir Francis Chaplin
1678	Sir James Edwards
1679	Sir Robert Clayton
1680	Sir Patience Ward
1681	Sir John Moore
1682	Sir William Prichard
1683	Sir Henry Tulse
1684	Sir James Smyth
1685	Sir Robert Geffery
1686	Sir John Peake
1687	Sir John Shorter
1688	Sir John Eyles
	Sir John Chapman
1689	Thomas Pilkington
1691	Sir Thomas Stampe
1692	Sir John Fleet
1693	Sir William Ashurst
1694	Sir Thomas Lane
1695	Sir John Houblon
1696	Sir Edward Clarke
1697	Sir Humphrey Edwin
1698	Sir Francis Child
1699	Sir Richard Levett
1700	Sir Thomas Abney
1701	Sir William Gore
1702	Sir Samuel Dashwood
1703	Sir John Parsons
1704	Sir Owen Buckingham
1705	Sir Thomas Rawlinson
1706	Sir Robert Bedingfield
1707	Sir William Withers
1708	Sir Charles Duncombe
1709	Sir Samuel Garrard
1710	Sir Gilbert Heathcote
1711	Sir Robert Beachcroft
1712	Sir Richard Hoare
1713	Sir Samuel Stanier
1714	Sir William Humfreys
1715	Sir Charles Peers
1716	Sir James Bateman
1717	Sir William Lewen
1718	Sir John Ward
1719	Sir George Thorold
1720	Sir John Fryer
1721	Sir William Stewart
1722	Sir Gerard Conyers
1723	Sir Peter Delmé
1724	Sir George Merttins
1725	Sir Francis Forbes
1726	Sir John Eyles
1727	Sir Edward Becher
1728	Sir Robert Baylis
1729	Sir Robert Brocas

1730	Humphrey Parsons
1731	Francis Child
1732	John Barber
1733	Sir William Billers
1734	Sir Edward Bellamy
1735	Sir John Williams
1736	Sir John Thompson
1737	Sir John Barnard
1738	Micajah Perry
1739	Sir John Salter
1740	Humphrey Parsons
1741	Daniel Lambert
	Sir Robert Godschall
1742	George Heathcote
1743	Robert Westley
1744	Henry Marshall
1745	Richard Hoare
1746	William Benn
1747	Sir Robert Ladbroke
1748	Sir William Calvert
1749	Sir Samuel Pennant
1750	John Blachford
	Francis Cockayne
1751	Thomas Winterbottom
1752	Robert Alsop
	Crisp Gascoyne
1753	Edward Ironside
	Thomas Rawlinson
1754	Stephen T. Janssen
1755	Slingsby Bethell
1756	Marshe Dickinson
1757	Sir Charles Asgill
1758	Sir Richard Glyn
1759	Sir Thomas Chitty
1760	Sir Mathew Blakiston
1761	Sir Samuel Fludyer
1762	William Beckford
1763	William Bridgen
1764	Sir William Stephenson
1765	George Nelson
1766	Sir Robert Kite
1767	Thomas Harley
1768	Samuel Turner
1769	William Beckford
1770	Barlow Trecothick
	Brass Crosby
1771	William Nash
1772	James Townsend
1773	Frederick Bull
1774	John Wilkes
1775	John Sawbridge
1776	Sir Thomas Hallifax
1777	Sir James Esdaile
1778	Samuel Plumbe
1779	Brackley Kennett
1780	Sir Watkin Lewes
1781	William Plomer
1782	Nathaniel Newnham
1783	Robert Peckham
1784	Richard Clark
1785	Thomas Wright
1786	Thomas Sainsbury
1787	John Burnell
1788	William Gill
1789	William Pickett
1790	John Boydell
1791	John Hopkins
1792	Sir James Sanderson
1793	Paul le Mesurier
1794	Thomas Skinner
1795	William Curtis
1796	Brook Watson
1797	John Anderson
1798	Sir Richard Glyn
1799	Harvey Christian Combe
1800	Sir William Staines
1801	Sir John Eamer
1802	Charles Price
1803	John Perring
1804	Peter Perchard

1805 James Shaw
1806 Sir William Leighton
1807 John Ansley
1808 Charles Flower
1809 Thomas Smith
1810 Joshua Smith
1811 Claudius Stephen Hunter
1812 George Scholey
1813 William Domville
1814 Samuel Birch
1815 Matthew Wood
1817 Christopher Smith
1818 John Atkins
1819 George Bridges
1820 John Thomas Thorp
1821 Christopher Magnay
1822 William Heygate
1823 Robert Waithman
1824 John Garratt
1825 William Venables
1826 Anthony Brown
1827 Matthias Prime Lucas
1828 William Thompson
1829 John Crowder
1830 John Key
1832 Sir Peter Laurie
1833 Charles Farebrother
1834 Henry Winchester
1835 William Taylor Copeland
1836 Thomas Kelly
1837 John Cowan
1838 Samuel Wilson
1839 Sir Chapman Marshall
1840 Thomas Johnson
1841 John Pirie
1842 John Humphrey
1843 William Magnay
1844 Michael Gibbs
1845 John Johnson
1846 Sir George Carroll
1847 John Kinnersley Hooper
1848 Sir James Duke
1849 Thomas Farncomb
1850 John Musgrove
1851 William Hunter
1852 Thomas Challis
1853 Thomas Sidney
1854 Francis G. Moon
1855 David Salomons
1856 Thomas Finnis
1857 Sir Robert Carden
1858 David Wire
1859 John Carter
1860 William Cubitt
1862 William Rose
1863 William Lawrence
1864 Warren Hale
1865 Benjamin Phillips
1866 Thomas Gabriel
1867 William Allen
1868 James Lawrence
1869 Robert Besley
1870 Thomas Dakin
1871 Sills Gibbons
1872 Sir Sydney Waterlow
1873 Andrew Lusk
1874 David Stone
1875 William Cotton
1876 Sir Thomas White
1877 Thomas Owden
1878 Sir Charles Whetham
1879 Sir Francis W. Truscott
1880 William McArthur
1881 John Ellis
1882 Henry Knight
1883 Robert Fowler
1884 George Nottage
1885 Robert Fowler
John Staples
1886 Sir Reginald Hanson

1887 Polydore de Keyser
1888 James Whitehead
1889 Sir Henry Isaacs
1890 Joseph Savory
1891 David Evans
1892 Stuart Knill
1893 George Tyler
1894 Sir Joseph Renals
1895 Sir Walter Wilkin
1896 George Faudel-Phillips
1897 Lieutenant Colonel Horatio Davies
1898 Sir John Moore
1899 Alfred Newton
1900 Frank Green
1901 Sir Joseph Dimsdale
1902 Sir Marcus Samuel
1903 Sir James Ritchie
1904 John Pound
1905 Walter Morgan
1906 Sir William Treloar
1907 Sir John Bell
1908 Sir George Truscott
1909 Sir John Knill
1910 Sir Thomas V. Strong
1911 Sir Thomas B. Crosby
1912 Colonel Sir David Burnett
1913 Sir Thomas V. Bowater
1914 Colonel Sir Charles Johnston
1915 Colonel Sir Charles Wakefield
1916 Sir William Dunn
1917 Charles Hanson
1918 Sir Horace Marshall
1919 Sir Edward Cooper
1920 James Roll
1921 Sir John Baddeley
1922 Edward C. Moore
1923 Colonel Sir Louis Newton
1924 Sir Alfred Bower
1925 Sir William Pryke
1926 Sir George R. Blades
1927 Sir Charles Batho
1928 Sir John E. K. Studd
1929 Sir William Waterlow
1930 Sir William P. Neal
1931 Sir Maurice Jenks
1932 Sir Percy Greenaway
1933 Sir Charles Collett
1934 Sir Stephen Killik
1935 Sir Percy Vincent
1936 Sir George Broadbridge
1937 Sir Harry Twyford
1938 Major Sir Frank Bowater
1939 Sir William Coxen
1940 Sir George Wilkinson
1941 Lieutenant Colonel Sir John Laurie
1942 Sir Samuel Joseph
1943 Sir Frank Newson-Smith
1944 Sir Frank Alexander
1945 Sir Charles Davis
1946 Sir Bracewell Smith
1947 Sir Frederick Wells
1948 Sir George Aylwen
1949 Sir Frederick Rowland
1950 Denys Lowson
1951 Sir Leslie Boyce
1952 Sir Rupert De La Bère
1953 Sir Noel V. Bowater
1954 H. W. Seymour Howard
1955 Cuthbert L. Ackroyd
1956 Sir Cullum Welch
1957 Sir Denis Truscott
1958 Sir Harold Gillett
1959 Sir Edmund Stockdale
1960 Sir Bernard Waley-Cohen
1961 Sir Frederick Hoare
1962 Sir Ralph Perring

1963 Sir James Harman
1964 Sir James Miller
1965 Sir Lionel Denny
1966 Sir Robert Bellinger
1967 Sir Gilbert Inglefield
1968 Sir Charles Trinder
1969 Lieutenant Colonel Sir Ian F. Bowater
1970 Sir Peter Studd
1971 Sir Edward Howard
1972 Rt. Hon. The Lord Mais
1973 Sir Hugh Wontner
1974 Sir Murray Fox
1975 Sir Lindsay Ring
1976 Sir Robin Gillett
1977 Sir Peter Vanneck
1978 Sir Kenneth Cork
1979 Sir Peter Gadsden
1980 Sir Ronald Gardner-Thorpe
1981 Sir Christopher Leaver
1982 Sir Anthony Jolliffe
1983 Dame Mary Donaldson
1984 Sir Alan Traill
1985 Sir Allan Davis
1986 Sir David Rowe-Ham
1987 Sir Greville Spratt
1988 Sir Christopher Collett
1989 Sir Hugh Bidwell
1990 Sir Alexander Graham
1991 Sir Brian Jenkins
1992 Sir Francis McWilliams
1993 Paul Newall
1994 Christopher Walford
1995 John Chalstrey
1996 Roger Cork
1997 Richard Nichols
1998 Lord Levene of Portsoken
1999 Clive Martin
2000 David Howard

CHAIRMEN OF THE LONDON COUNTY COUNCIL

1889–1890	Earl of Rosebery
1890–1892	Sir John Lubbock
1892	Earl of Rosebery
1892–1895	Sir John Hutton
1895–1897	Sir Arthur Arnold
1897–1898	W. J. Collins
1898–1899	T. McKinnon Wood
1899–1900	Lord Welby
1900–1901	W. H. Dickinson
1901–1902	A. M. Torrance
1902–1903	Sir John McDougall
1903–1904	Lord Monkswell
1904–1905	J. W. Benn
1905–1906	Sir Edwin Cornwall
1906–1907	Evan Spicer
1907–1908	H. Percy Harris
1908–1909	R. A. Robinson
1909–1910	Sir R. Melvill Beachcroft
1910–1911	W. Whitaker Thompson
1911–1912	Sir Edward White
1912	Captain G. S. C. Swinton
1912–1913	Major-General Lord Cheylesmore
1913–1914	Cyril S. Cobb
1914–1915	Viscount Peel
1915–1916	Cyril Jackson
1916–1917	Alfred F. Buxton
1917–1918	Marquess of Crewe
1918–1919	R. C. Norman
1919–1920	Lord Downham
1920–1921	John W. Gilbert
1921–1922	Sir Percy Simmons
1922–1923	Francis R. Anderton
1923–1924	Henry C. Gooch
1924–1925	J. Herbert Hunter
1925–1926	Sir Oscar Warburg
1926–1927	Sir George Hume
1927–1928	J. M. Gatti
1928–1929	Lieutenant-Colonel Sir Cecil Levita
1929–1930	Lord Monk Bretton
1930–1931	Sir Robert Tasker
1931–1932	Ernest Sanger
1932–1933	Angus N. Scott
1933–1934	Ernest M. Dence
1934–1938	Lord Snell
1938–1939	Ewart G. Culpin
1939–1940	Eveline M. Lowe
1940–1941	A. Emil Davies
1941–1942	C. G. Ammon
1942–1943	J. P. Blake
1943	Sir Alfred Baker
1943–1944	Richard Coppock
1944–1945	Somerville Hastings
1945–1946	Charles Robertson
1946–1947	John Cliff
1947–1948	Lady Nathan
1948–1949	Walter R. Owen
1949–1952	J. W. Bowen
1952–1953	Edwin Bayliss
1953	Sir Arthur Middleton
1953–1954	Mrs. Douglas Boulton
1954–1955	Victor Mishcon
1955–1956	Norman G. M. Prichard
1956–1957	Helen Bentwich
1957–1958	R. McKinnon Wood
1958–1959	A. E. Samuels
1959–1960	Sidney J. Barton
1960–1961	Mrs. F. E. Cayford
1961–1962	Harold Shearman
1962–1963	Olive G. Deer
1963	A. Reginald Stamp
1963–1964	Arthur E. Wicks

CHAIRMEN OF THE GREATER LONDON COUNCIL

1964–1966	Harold C. Shearman
1966–1967	Herbert Ferguson
1967–1968	Sir Percy Rugg
1968–1969	Sir Louis Gluckstein
1969–1970	Leslie Freeman
1970–1971	Peter Black
1971–1972	Robert Mitchell
1972–1973	Frank Abbott
1973–1974	Arthur E. Wicks
1974–1975	Lord Pitt
1975–1976	Dame Evelyn Denington
1976–1977	Lord Ponsonby
1977–1978	Lawrence Bains
1978–1979	H. T. Mote
1979–1980	Robert Vigars
1980–1981	Bernard Brook-Partridge
1981–1982	John B. Ward
1982–1983	Sir Ashley Bramall
1983–1984	Harvey Hinds
1984–1985	Illtyd Harrington
1985–1986	Tony Banks

LONDON'S POPULATION GROWTH, 1801–1996

	London (millions)	**Greater London** (millions)
1801	0.959	1.096
1811	1.139	1.303
1821	1.379	1.573
1831	1.655	1.878
1841	1.949	2.207
1851	2.363	2.651
1861	2.808	3.188
1871	3.261	3.840
1881	3.830	4.713
1891	4.227	5.571
1901	4.536	6.506
1911	4.536	7.160
1921	4.484	7.386
1931	4.397	8.110
1951	3.347	8.193
1961	3.200	7.992
1971	3.031	7.452
1981	2.497	6.713
1991	2.627	6.890
1996	2.708	7.074

Notes: Data for London are for the area now known as Inner London, whose boundaries are similar to those of the former London County Council. Data for Greater London are for the area defined by the London Government Act of 1963.

Statistics for 1801–1991 are taken from official census returns (no census was held in 1941). Statistics for 1996 are taken from Office for National Statistics publications.

Introduction

London, like other cities, is part bricks, part mortar, part state of mind. Too large and complex for any individual to comprehend, it is often described as a collection of villages, each with its own personality. The working-class East End is only four miles, but a cultural universe, away from aristocratic Belgravia. Bangladeshi Spitalfields has little in common with West Indian Brixton except that it is part of the same urban area. Financiers rub shoulders, often uneasily, with civil service mandarins as they pass from the complex of government offices in Whitehall to the banks, insurance companies, and money exchanges of the City of London.

PHYSICAL GEOGRAPHY

The metropolitan area lies in the southeast of the United Kingdom at latitude 51° 30' north and (at Greenwich) on the prime meridian of longitude. Most of the built-up area is on the north bank of the River Thames, which meanders eastward to the North Sea across the London Basin, a structural downfold known to geologists as a syncline. The underlying rock is chalk, initially formed in oceanic conditions then buckled by the same tectonic forces that created the Alpine mountain chain in southern Europe some 40 million years ago, during the mid-Tertiary period. Later, the chalk was covered by a complex of sands, gravels, pebbles, and clays, which reach over 400 feet in depth and reflect changing environmental conditions.

Under natural conditions, the soils would be covered by deciduous woodland (notably beech, oak, and alder), with marshes along the waterways, but apart from a few remnants (as at Epping Forest) the trees and sedges have been replaced by concrete and pavement. The climate is mild, with January temperatures in the central city averaging about 42° F (5° C) and July temperatures about 65° F (18° C). Suburban areas are a few degrees cooler at all seasons because lower building densities and greater provision of park land facilitate dissipation of heat. Annual rainfall totals vary from 25 inches (about 635 millimeters) on the east of the metropolitan area to 31 inches (about 787 millimeters) on higher parts of the urban fringe, such as the Chiltern Hills and the North Downs. Most of the precipitation is cyclonic in origin, with an autumn maximum and spring minimum.

EARLY SETTLEMENT

Although archaeological studies indicate that prehistoric communities used the Thames as a source of wildfowl and fish, London's history really begins with the Romans. These invaders from the Mediterranean arrived in 43 A.D. and, utilizing patches of stable sediment, built a bridge across the waterway in order to facilitate the movement of troops and supplies. A settlement, known as Londinium (for reasons still unknown) developed at the northern bridgehead and, despite pillaging by Boadicea's Icenian followers in 61 A.D. and damage by fire about 120 A.D., grew into a substantial city.

Modern excavations have revealed that a basilica, the largest north of the Alps, was built at the site now occupied by Cornhill and connected to the bridge over the Thames by a road that followed the line of modern Gracechurch Street. Fortifications were constructed in the northwest (the area now known as Cripplegate) about 100 A.D. and a protective wall completed by 140 A.D.

Secure in the knowledge that they were technically superior to the indigenous peoples and that their frontier was moving north and west, thus making Londinium increasingly secure from attack, the Romans built a thriving commercial center that, according to some scholars, may have housed as many as 100,000 citizens during the third century. Places of worship, administrative buildings, baths, and meeting places were erected to meet religious, recreational, and organizational needs.

The clays of the London Basin provided few sources of stone, so most of these early structures were fashioned from timber, with thatched roofs, and have long since decayed. However, evidence of occupation remains in remnants of the defensive wall (as at Noble Street), the outline of the Temple of Mithras (off Queen Victoria Street), and the lines of routes that led to the city gates (for example, Cannon Street and Cheapside adopt the same routes as the Roman streets built some 2,000 years ago). Excavations of cemeteries and finds of weapons and pottery have added further knowledge of changing military, social, and economic life as Londinium became the capital of the new province, with increasingly complex financial institutions and a burgeoning port trading with continental Europe.

However, during the fourth century the power of the Roman Empire declined. In 410, the legions marched off to defend the Holy City and Londinium was left to the mercies of Anglo-Saxon migrants from the North German Plain. Until recently, many scholars believed that these newcomers, essentially agricultural peoples lacking a tradition of urban life, simply allowed the city to decay because archaeologists had found no convincing evidence of building before the middle of the ninth century. On the other hand, some writers claimed that there must have been a considerable urban population during what was once known as the Dark Ages because St. Augustine had ordained Mellitus as the settlement's first bishop in 604 and Bede (writing in 730) had described Lundenwic as a town trading with many nations.

Since 1985, the story has been clarified as a result of archaeological work carried out largely by teams from the Museum of London, who have discovered evidence of a significant settlement between the site of Whitehall and the banks of the River Fleet, beyond the Roman walls. Moreover, coins and other artefacts suggest that, for most of the period from 670 until 870, the area was part of the Kingdom of Mercia, which had strong commercial links with continental Europe. For 15 years from 871, there was a lengthy period of political instability, when the city was ruled by Danish invaders, but in 886 King Alfred regained the territory and laid out a new town stretching from just east of the site of St. Paul's Cathedral to London Bridge (between the modern Cheapside and Thames Street, and inside the area of Londinium).

Significantly, documents dated from the late eighth and early ninth centuries refer to London as Lundenburh, the *-burh* suffix indicating that it had become a fortified settlement, but it is not known whether the defenses were simply the old Roman walls or whether these were augmented by new construction. Resources were certainly devoted to other forms of construction because quays were erected along the north bank of the Thames to facilitate trading, and there is documentary evidence of a significant trade in farm produce, timber, and textiles.

The Scandinavians returned in 1016 and demanded, from London's citizenry, an annual tribute that amounted to one-eighth of the entire payment from the whole English realm, an indication of the city's wealth and importance at the time. The tribute undoubtedly had a serious impact on the economy, but the invaders remained only until 1042, when Edward the Confessor assumed the English throne and built a church and palace on the site of a former monastery at Westminster. Although undoubtedly born of piety, the decision was to have long-lasting political impact because it established, away from the Roman city, a focus of urban growth that evolved into the nation's center of political power as the church grew into Westminster Abbey and the location became the site of the Houses of Parliament.

Edward, however, had little time to make a real impact on London. He died in January 1066, just a week after his new church was consecrated and only months before the Normans changed the landscape of England. William the Conqueror, with an invading force technically superior to anything the Anglo-Saxon peoples could muster, was well aware that he would have to take command of London's wealth and trade in order to exert his influence over the remainder of the British Isles. His first attempt to enter the city failed but civic leaders, accepting that defeat was inevitable, eventually surrendered, acknowledging William as king at a coronation ceremony in Westminster Abbey on Christmas Day, 1066.

The arrival of the Normans emphasized the city's importance. It was the largest town in the country, with an established system of courts administering justice and maintaining law and order within urban boundaries. Strategically, it controlled movements along the Thames and, therefore, influenced naval and commercial transport to the interior of England and to the European mainland. However, the new regime had comparatively little effect on London's social and economic institutions because the new monarch confirmed rights of male inheritance, placed London's citizens under his protection, and agreed to maintain the laws that were in place during Edward's rule. As a result, commerce experienced no serious long-term interruption, and civic government remained largely unchanged. The physical fabric was also little altered, the most significant innovation being a considerable strengthening of the settlement's defenses, partly because of fear of attack but also to remind a subjugated people that the invaders were in charge. In particular, work began on the Tower of London; initially a wooden structure but, from 1078, rebuilt in stone, it was greatly enlarged over succeeding centuries to become the principal fortress in the capital.

The Norman peace, uneasy though it was at times, brought a prosperity that encouraged trade, the spread of services, and urban expansion. By the end of the 12th century, the city had 126 churches, many of the streets were paved, and stone was usurping wood as a building material for the homes of richer merchants as well as for public structures, such as the replacement for London Bridge begun in 1176. Harbor facilities were spreading further along the riverside, and goods were arriving from regions as far apart as Scandinavia and the eastern Mediterranean. Guilds (now known as livery companies) were forming to represent the interests of manufacturers and traders, sheriffs presided over the courts, a lord mayor was accepted as head of local government by at least 1189, and immigrants were arriving from all over Europe to seek a future in one of the most powerful kingdoms in the known world.

THE MEDIEVAL CITY

During the 13th century, the City of London used its financial might to manipulate, and sometimes even oppose, monarchs. In return for payments to royal coffers (particularly during the reigns of kings, such as John, who engaged in lavish spending or needed funds to support large armies), the lord mayor and his advisory committee of aldermen were able to negotiate privileges that enhanced the wealth of individuals and confirmed the community's commercial supremacy in England. Thus, about 1130 (the exact date is not known), Henry I issued a charter giving London the right to conduct its financial affairs without fear of intervention from the Crown and granting Londoners the freedom to trade throughout England without paying tolls or taxes. Such favored status inevitably facilitated the growth of a sizable and affluent merchant class, which vied with courtiers as the richest in the realm.

Moreover, as the royal household spent increasingly lengthy periods of time in London dealing with the financiers, Parliament met in the city more and more frequently, and a plethora of courts and offices was created to meet its needs. Specialist administrators, lawyers, and accountants were drawn to Westminster, and London increasingly became the pivot of national affairs, its development shaped as much by matters of state as by local conditions.

As a capital city, London had considerable strategic advantages. It was far from the frontiers with the warring Scots and Irish and was readily defended against European invaders, who would have to brave the might of a growing navy in the Thames estuary or fight their way through 50 miles of forest and marsh from landings on the English Channel coast. The main threat came from internal uprisings, but those that did occur, such as the Peasants' Revolt of 1381, were limited in scale and duration. As a result, the City operated in a more stable economic climate than that of other towns, so it was better able to maximize trading advantages and ride out recession.

The wealth generated was evident in the extent and opulence of the urban fabric. The size of the medieval St. Paul's Cathedral (one of the largest buildings in the country), the Gothic splendor of the medieval Guildhall (built in 1411–39 as the focus for local government), and the mansions of men such as Sir John de Pulteney (who made a fortune as a draper) bear testimony to years of successful commerce. But the citizens who lived in material comfort and had funds to spend on fine buildings, luxurious furnishings, and donations to religious charities were, in fact, a small proportion of the city's population. Most people lived in cramped, overcrowded homes that doubled as workshops and where infection spread easily. Rats fed on garbage left to decay in the streets because concepts of hygiene and knowledge of the causes of disease were limited. Water supplies were increasingly scarce as rivers were polluted with sewage, and fire spread rapidly through the timber buildings in which most of the poor were housed.

For the most deprived, Roman Catholic religious houses were a major source of food, health care, and comfort. Benedictines, Carthusians, Cistercians, Dominicans, Franciscans, and others owned large tracts of land in, and close to, the City, benefiting from the gifts of wealthy patrons hoping to buy themselves a place in Heaven. That source of succor vanished, however, when King Henry VIII reformed the Church of England, removing it from Vatican jurisdiction and dissolving the monasteries. In London, Holy Trinity Priory (founded during the 12th century by secular followers of St. Augustine) was the first to go, Parliament approving its acquisition by the monarch in 1532. Within a decade, all the others had disbanded, their inhabitants scattered to the four winds and their estates transferred to private ownership. Some buildings (like the chapel at Holy Trinity) were demolished to provide stone for new structures, some were granted to followers from whom the king wanted continued support (Sir Edward North, Chancellor of the Court of Augmentations, received Charterhouse, for instance), and much land eventually fell into the hands of entrepreneurs, who laid out housing for a growing population (as at Covent Garden).

The demise of the monasteries was a disaster for the indigent, who became an increasingly common sight on the streets of Elizabethan London. The City fathers helped by distributing grain at times of famine, introduced measures for relief of the poor in 1547, and provided medical care in new facilities. Also, wealthy private citizens made a contribution by building almshouses, schools, and hospitals, but, even so, the problems were sufficiently great to convince aldermen that continued urban expansion might lead to widespread hunger and that, in turn, could result in civil disorder, threatening the stability of the City (and, of course, their own sources of income). Their response, from 1580, was a series of attempts to control suburban growth, but those efforts failed to stem the tide.

Deprived of charitable support, the poor increasingly congregated in the East End, employed in dirty, noisy trades that were considered a nuisance by City merchants and therefore unwelcome in the urban core. Suburbs such as Whitechapel (a center of metal working, including bell making) and Wapping (with a variety of waterfront activities) grew larger and acquired reputations as rough, drunken, crime-ridden communities—reputations they were to carry, in many cases, into the 21st century. Also, many tradesmen found employment at Woolwich and Deptford, on the south bank of the River Thames, as the Royal Dockyards (originally established in 1512 and 1513 respectively) expanded, creating a second industrial focus. On the other side of the financial quarter, developers laid out Lincoln's Inn Fields and other prestigious residential estates, providing the beginnings of the fashionable West End.

The continued commercial expansion fueled immigration, and the newcomers brought skills that established new trades (and thereby caused further expansion). Silk, glass, novel forms of pottery (such as majolica ware), and other manufactured goods were produced outside the City walls and therefore beyond the control either of local government officials or of the livery companies, which restricted entry into trades and controlled their activities. Moreover, that same spirit of economic freedom encouraged the growth of service provision, as at Bankside, on the south side of the Thames in Southwark, which emerged as London's main entertainment center during the late 16th century because theaters such as the Rose and the Globe could operate without fear of censorial interference by the City Corporation.

This new competitive ethos was accompanied by a growth in materialism at the expense of religious commitment. Church building declined (in fact, the nave of St. Paul's Cathedral became a market place and its courtyard a crowded hive of print shops and book publishers). On the other hand, building for mercantile interests provided a constant stream of jobs as Thomas Gresham funded the construction of the Royal Exchange (which opened as London's first meeting place for traders in 1568), the Muscovy Company (founded in 1555), the East India Company (created by royal charter in 1600), and other powerful concerns established imposing headquarters.

At the same time, the Tower of London was losing its status as a royal residence. King Henry VIII converted York Place into Whitehall Palace and a former leper hospital into St. James's Palace, moving the court out of the City of London into the suburbs beyond. Initially, the departure of the royal family seemed to cause little resentment: most Londoners remained loyal to Henry's successors, even forming local troops to help repel a Spanish invasion anticipated in 1588. However, the reign of Charles I proved more difficult because, shortly after succeeding to the throne in 1625, he was involved in a series of confrontations with City leaders, threatening to overturn many of their long-standing rights and privileges. Naturally, the merchants resisted and threw their lot in with the parliamentarian cause when the civil war began in 1642, using their considerable financial resources to reject a royal authority they greatly disliked.

Even so, rejection of the individual was not rejection of the concept of monarchy, and, as Oliver Cromwell's Puritan supporters closed more and more places of entertainment, Public sympathy for the king returned, so news of his restoration on terms that allowed Parliament to control his excesses was received with much rejoicing in 1660. However, the concentration on political matters had diverted attention from growing infrastructural problems that were to alter the face of the city radically within a few years.

THE EMERGENCE OF MODERN LONDON

In the middle of the 17th century, London had a population of about a half a million inhabitants, more than any other settlement in Europe and some 15 times greater than the port of Bristol, which, with 30,000 people, was the next largest settlement in England. That created opportunities for the acquisition of wealth but was an enormous threat to public health and safety because the unsanitary conditions were favorable breeding grounds for rats. These, in turn, provided the ideal environment for fleas infested by *Yersinia pestis*, a bacillus that causes plague.

Plague was no stranger in London. In the middle years of the 14th century, it may have killed as many as 100,000 citizens (half the resident population), and in 1625 it wiped out 40,000. In the fall of 1664, it returned, appearing first in St.-Giles-in-the-Fields then sweeping through Clerkenwell, Cripplegate, Shoreditch, Stepney, and Westminster—the poorest, most overcrowded sectors of the urban area—but sparing no class or neighborhood. Over the next 18 months, at least 70,000 people died and business activity was devastated.

Then, from 2–5 September 1666, the weakened economy was further crippled by the worst fire in the city's history. Flames gained a foothold in the timber-framed bakery that made bread for the king and spread rapidly along the narrow streets, leaping across alleys from one thatched roof to another. The blaze raged for four days, destroying 80 percent of the urban area (all but parts of the west and northeast); 13,200 houses, 89 churches, and most major public and commercial structures (including the Guildhall and the Royal Exchange) were destroyed or seriously damaged.

The effects can hardly be overestimated. Concepts of insurance for buildings and belongings were rudimentary so many people became homeless, with neither funds nor welfare payments to help them recover. Merchants lost their stores and their records, manufacturers lost their workshops and factories, printers lost their presses, and livery companies lost their halls. But rebuilding began immediately. King Charles and the City Corporation each appointed three architects to draw up plans for reconstruction, with a specification that housing densities should be lower than those of earlier years.

Inevitably, the renewal plans were compromised by political and financial realities but, even so, the new London looked very different from the old. Brick replaced wood as the primary building material for all social groups. Confined streets and tortuous lanes were replaced by wide roads designed to prevent the spread of fire. Markets were moved and expanded, new places of worship were erected for expanded parishes, harbor facilities were improved, and the Fleet River was canalized. The churches, in particular, helped to tie the new city together because over 50 of them (including a rebuilt St. Paul's Cathedral) were designed by Christopher Wren, who was appointed surveyor general for London in 1669.

The Great Fire also proved a spur to physical expansion. Many of the estimated 100,000 residents who lost their homes and workplaces relocated outside the City walls in formerly independent settlements such as Clerkenwell, binding them into the built-up area. In addition, it allowed commercial and administrative communities to restructure and innovate. The Bank of England was founded in 1694 and, within 50 years, had helped reestablish the City as England's major financial center. Over the same period, investment in harbor facilities confirmed the port's status as the largest in the country.

Also, the union of the Scottish and English parliaments in 1707 added to Westminster's prestige as the fulcrum of national government and gave administrative emphasis to the growing civil service in nearby Whitehall. Burgeoning interest in the arts made London the literary capital of Europe during the 18th century. The Royal Academy of Arts, founded in 1768, boasted painter Joshua Reynolds as its first president. Dr. Samuel Johnson, lionized by James Boswell, his sycophantic biographer, was lauded in the drawing rooms of Piccadilly and Pall Mall. David Garrick attracted throngs of playgoers to see his performances at Drury Lane, and the piano was heard for the first time in public at the Royal Opera House in 1767.

Fashionable Georgians lounged in City coffee houses, traveled to business in sedan chairs, and bought their goods at high-class stores such as

Dodsley's bookshop and Vulliamy's clock workshop in Pall Mall. In Bloomsbury and Mayfair, speculative builders laid out gracious squares lined by houses that were adorned with colonnades and porticos reminiscent of ancient Greece and Rome. In the process, they shifted the city's center of gravity westward as affluent residents deserted the formerly desirable Soho and Covent Garden for newer, more spacious properties.

But the darker side of urban life remained. Coal fires polluted the air, and sewage polluted water supplies. Open rivers, such as the Fleet, were blocked with garbage, and the poor, crammed into overcrowded hovels, sought refuge from their sorrows in gin. Conditions were made worse by an influx of immigrants, who helped raise London's population from an estimated 670,000 in 1700 to 959,310 at the time of the first official census in 1801. Many of these new residents came from abroad: for example, Soho had a growing French population, filling the homes abandoned by the rich, and Heneage Lane had significant numbers of Spanish and Portuguese residents. But many came from rural areas of the British Isles, where agricultural change, and notably the enclosure of fields, had produced an army of landless, homeless laborers who drifted to the towns to find work. Many of them, not surprisingly, headed for London and found homes with family or friends who had traveled before them. Thus, ethnic neighborhoods became common, and services were founded specifically to meet their needs (a charity school for children of Welsh immigrants was founded at Clerkenwell in 1737, for instance).

Immigrant numbers continued to rise throughout the 19th century, driven by events such as the Irish potato famines of the 1840s and a growing industrialization, which concentrated manufacturing jobs in urban areas. As the first industrial society, Britain benefited from the creation of jobs in engineering, road construction, port industries, and the services that supplied them. All of these were labor intensive and the limited transport systems of the time required workers to live near their work; thus, in the East End, businesses and homes jostled for space in a smoky, grimy environment that lacked any provision for personal privacy or any semblance of green space. The combined rigors of long hours in an exhausting job, a poor diet, and a lack of living space took their toll, some research studies suggesting that life expectancy in Bethnal Green, during the 1840s, was as low as 16 years.

It is arguable that individual deprivation was part of the price to be paid for London's metamorphosis from an important but nonetheless regional trading city to the capital of the largest empire the world had ever known. Colonial expansion was driven as much by business opportunities as by desire for political status, and the wealth created by that new commerce helped subsidize demand for the expensive homes built by John Nash at Regent's Park, by Thomas Cubitt in Belgravia, and by other developers in north, west, and south London. It also provided funds for a great range of educational and scientific institutions, such as the British Museum (which moved to its present headquarters in stages from 1826 to 1881), London Zoo (opened in 1828), and the complex of facilities (including the Victoria and Albert Museum) at south Kensington.

On the other hand, public awareness of the plight of the poor was being raised by the works of writers such as novelist Charles Dickens and social commentator Henry Mayhew. Some individuals, including Thomas Barnardo (founder of a chain of children's homes) and William Booth (who created the Salvation Army), devoted most of their lives to improving living conditions in the East End and providing opportunities for the indigent to raise their living standards through access to education, vocational training, and better diets. Also, growing numbers of philanthropists, following the example of American-born George Peabody, invested in housing provision in return for reasonable rents.

In one sense, the railroads exacerbated the problems, pushing their way through the most crowded areas of London on their way to the city center because it was easier to dispossess the poor than to move the rich. In another, they alleviated it by breaking the vise that bound dwelling place to workplace. From the 1840s, people could live in the suburbs and journey to office or factory by train, so employment opportunities widened and businesses could relocate closer to sources of labor. Then, from 1863, the expanding tentacles of the underground railway system widened the transport network further. As a result, inner-city populations began to decline and slums were replaced by stores, banks, and other services.

The growing wealth of London's residents, coupled with the redistribution of population, allowed local government to invest in projects designed to increase quality of life within the city. In 1855, a Metropolitan Board of Works was created and appointed Joseph William Bazalgette to build a new, and much needed, system of sewers. Embankments were erected along the River Thames to contain the high tides, which sometimes caused flooding, and new streets, including Charing Cross Road and Shaftesbury Avenue, were driven through the core of the metropolis to improve communications.

As these improvements were being made, other ventures helped make London a safer and more pleasant environment. Streets were first lit by the Gas Light and Coke Company in 1807. The Metropolitan Police was formed in 1829, replacing a multitude of independent law enforcement agencies with a single unit. A citywide fire service was established in 1833 and an ambulance service in 1867. In 1870, a London School Board was formed, providing education for children aged five to 13, and in 1888 the Metropolitan Board of Works was replaced by a London County Council, which was given greater powers than its predecessor to demolish substandard properties, build homes for the working classes, and lay out park land.

By the end of the century, London had increased its population fivefold and radically altered its physical structure, engulfing formerly independent villages, such as Hampstead, under planning policies prepared by new and more democratic forms of local government. A framework of emergency services was in place, young people were increasingly literate and numerate, and provision for the poor was improving. Essentially, the city had taken its modern form.

LONDON SINCE 1900

In 1901, London was the world's largest city, with a population of some 6.5 million, compared with 4.0 million in New York and 2.7 million in Paris. However, despite the advances of previous decades, it still faced enormous social problems, largely related to poor housing and a lack of national welfare policies directed at low earners and the unemployed. London County Council responded by building the Boundary Street Housing Estate in the East End, providing homes for over 5,500 Shoreditch slum dwellers at a density of 200 people to the acre and supplying medical and educational facilities. The five-story buildings were built of good quality brick, with high gables, and are claimed by some critics to be among the most outstanding legacies of the arts and crafts movement.

Elsewhere, and notably in Hampstead Garden Suburb, private developers were attempting to relieve the monotony of paved roads by designing neighborhoods that incorporated parks, hedges, and trees, with houses as few as eight to the acre.

The First World War did little to curb urban expansion, and the 1920s and 1930s brought continued growth as the private car made commuting ever more easy. Industry, too, contributed to the outward spread as Handley Page built an aircraft manufacturing plant at Cricklewood, Hoover erected a new factory in Western Avenue, Guinness constructed a brewery at Park Royal, and other businesses took advantage of the growing pool of labor London was able to offer.

In 1938, fearing the consequences of uncontrolled metropolitan incursion into the countryside, national and local politicians promoted the establishment of a Green Belt—a broad ring of farmland that would contain the city through strict building controls and would also provide recreational amenities for urban residents. However, before the measure had much impact, the Second World War intervened, bringing devastation to the dockland areas of the East End in particular. From 7 September 1940, central London was bombed on 57 consecutive nights, and over the eight-month period of the Blitz, from then until May 1941, more than 15,000 people were killed, an estimated 3.5 million homes destroyed or made uninhabitable, and many major public buildings (such as the Houses of Parliament) seriously damaged.

The end of hostilities, in 1945, heralded a lengthy period of reconstruction accompanied by the gradual reorientation of the economy to peacetime conditions and a national austerity relieved only by the Festival of Britain, which was held, in 1951, on the south bank of the River Thames and included construction of a major arts complex in an attempt to raise public spirits. In 1956, however, the Clean Air Act introduced smokeless zones to London and put an end to the pea soup fogs that had previously plagued the city, particularly during early winter. Then, in the 1960s, a new age of affluence, coupled with greater independence for young people, ushered in an era during which swinging London was the pop capital of the world. Condemned by many residents as a time of permissiveness and decadence, it nevertheless promoted the establishment of countless small businesses as the clothes boutiques and cafés of Carnaby Street and King's Road attracted thousands of visitors.

Local government, too, changed to meet new postwar conditions. The London Government Act of 1963 swept the London County Council away and replaced it with a Greater London Council responsible for comprehensive planning over a much enlarged area. It was clear that large-scale measures were necessary to deal with the traffic congestion generated by increasing leisure and business travel within the city, the growing number of visitors arriving by air, and the decaying docks. The last of these posed particularly intractable problems as, one after another, port facilities closed down from 1967, unable to contend with crowded sites and competition from more modern facilities on the European mainland and around the British coast.

Eventually, in 1981, the London Docklands Development Corporation was created to manage the world's largest urban regeneration scheme. The result was a major investment of public and private funds, which led to new housing and commercial development programs, the creation of a marina at St. Katharine's Dock (near the Tower of London), and the transfer of many City offices to new sites at Canary Wharf on the Isle of Dogs.

The Greater London Council also promoted the construction of new road arteries (designed, in part, to enhance access to the Docklands from the city center) and the movement of inner-city residents to purpose-built new towns such as Crawley and Basildon, beyond the urban fringe. However, from 1979, it was more and more evident that the council, led by left-wing politicians, and Prime Minister Margaret Thatcher's Conservative government did not see eye to eye on economic and social reform. National policies, the council members claimed, inflicted unnecessary hardship on Londoners by creating unemployment and limiting the local authority's freedom to raise income through property taxes.

In many ways, the protests were justified. In the 30 years from 1945 until 1975, London's adult male unemployment rate had rarely exceeded 1 percent. By 1984, after Mrs. Thatcher's first five years in office, it had risen to over 10 percent and the lack of jobs was felt most sorely by the immigrant communities, undoubtedly contributing to street violence experienced in Brixton and elsewhere. Mrs. Thatcher, however, was unmoved. In 1986, exasperated by the failure of London's leaders to accept her view of the world, she abolished the council and created a complex of 33 independent local government units with identical statutory responsibilities. In a stroke, comprehensive planning had been eliminated and, for 14 years, individual areas of the city went their own way.

The result was a boom in office building but a lack of investment in public infrastructure and social welfare, which led to maintenance problems on the underground railway, an increase in begging, and greatly reduced programs of house building for the low paid. By the mid-1990s, it was evident to all political parties that continued absence of funding, combined with a lack of strategic planning, would lead to serious diseconomies, which might discourage private investment in the city, so in 1997, the newly elected Labour government announced plans for a London Assembly, headed by a mayor, to reintroduce citywide schemes for educational provision, transportation, sewage control, and other services. The members were elected three years later, with Ken Livingstone (a socialist politician running as an independent candidate) winning the mayoral poll by a considerable majority over official representatives of the Conservative, Labour, and Liberal Parties. For city residents, the new leadership brought hope that their voice would be heard in the corridors of power and that steps would be taken to ensure that London could continue to attract the economic and human capital necessary to retain its position as one of the world's preeminent financial, commercial, and cultural capitals.

The Dictionary

– A –

ABBEY ROAD. Abbey Road, which runs northwest for just under a mile from **St. John's Wood** towards **Kilburn**, was made famous in the 1960s by the Beatles, who named one of their albums after the street, where the EMI recording studios were located. In medieval times, it was a country lane leading to a convent but, during the 19th century, it was gradually built up as affluent Londoners constructed villa homes with large gardens. Most of these houses are now subdivided into flats or have been replaced by apartment blocks.

ABBEYS. *See* ABBEY WOOD; BARKING; COVENT GARDEN; DULWICH; EPPING FOREST; HYDE PARK; MONASTERIES; REGENT'S PARK; ST. MARYLEBONE; STRATFORD; STREATHAM; WESTMINSTER; WESTMINSTER ABBEY; WOODFORD.

ABBEY WOOD. A working-class residential area consisting largely of former local authority **housing** built during the 1950s, Abbey Wood lies in the **London Borough of Greenwich** on the southeastern fringes of the city. Originally marshland, which was first reclaimed by the monks of Lesnes Abbey during the 13th century, it became a testing ground for armaments manufactured at nearby Woolwich Arsenal (*see* **Royal Arsenal**) in the 1700s and 1800s. The **railway** arrived during the last years of the 19th century, and construction of homes began with the development of the Bostall Estate in the years prior to the outbreak of the First World War.

ACTON. Formerly an agricultural settlement lying some five miles west of **Marble Arch**, Acton became a suburb of London as the city expanded during the late 19th and early 20th centuries. A center of royalist support during the Civil War (1642–49), it developed a reputation as a spa during the Georgian period and, as a result, attracted affluent visitors seeking health and recreation. Many of these visitors built homes in the area, seduced by the rural environment and the proximity to the capital (the Rothschild family—one of the wealthiest in the country—bought the medieval mansion at Gunnersbury Park in 1835, for example). However, the idyll was destroyed by industrialization during the reign of Queen Victoria as brick-making companies and engineering firms transformed both the economy and the landscape, aided by a developing **transport** infrastructure, which included the **Paddington** Canal (opened in 1801), the **railways** (which arrived in 1839), and an increasingly dense network of roads. Rows of terraced housing were built to accommodate the influx of workers, even covering the golf course in 1920. Now forming the eastern fringe of the **London Borough of Ealing**, Acton is a predominantly working-class area, providing local employment in manufacturing and service companies and relatively cheap accommodation for inner-city workers. Its name is probably derived from the Old English *actun*, meaning "the settlement among the oak trees."

ADAM, ROBERT (1728–1792). Widely considered the leading neoclassical architect in Georgian Britain, Adam was responsible for the design (or redesign) of a large number of country mansions (notably **Kenwood House**, **Osterley House**, and **Syon House** in London) but also for many smaller-scale works, such as the screen in front of **The Admiralty** building in **Whitehall**. Born in Kirkcaldy (Fife), Adam learned the basic elements of his trade from his father, William, who was Master Mason to the Ordnance in north Britain and designer of such important homes for Scottish gentry as Hopetoun House and House of Dun. He was educated at Edinburgh High School and Edinburgh University then, in 1754, went to Italy, where he studied classical **architecture** at Rome, Florence, Naples, Vicenza, and Split, and cultivated the friendship of wealthy English travelers who, he felt, might provide him with commissions.

Soon after his return to Britain in 1758, Adam established a business in London, where the combination of an affable personality, contacts in aristocratic society, and the successful publication of his book *The Ruins of the Palace of the Emperor Diocletian at Spalatro in Dalmatia* (1764) made him the most sought-after architect in the city. In 1761 (jointly with Sir **William Chambers**, a great rival), he was appointed architect to King George III, but royal acceptance did not prevent him from undertaking visionary projects. In 1768, along with his brothers James and John (both architects) and William (a financier), he leased a slum property, south of the **Strand** and north of the **River Thames**, from the Duke of St. Albans and set about turning it into an area of fashionable residences. The development, known as Adelphi (from the Greek *adelphoi*, meaning "brothers"), consisted of a main terrace with two groups of 11 brick houses built back to back and a single house at each end. All were tall, thin structures typical of the period, but no expense was spared on the decoration. The steep slope to the river was counteracted by a series of arches, topped by streets. Unfortunately for the Adams, the government refused to hire the vaults as storage space for gunpowder because they flooded at high tide. Also, because of their remoteness from the fashionable **West End**, the finished houses were difficult to sell (though actor **David Garrick** took No. 5). The resultant financial problems threatened completion of the project but, in 1773, Parliament passed an act permitting the brothers to hold a lottery that offered the homes as prizes, and the work was finished soon afterwards. Most of Royal Terrace, the centerpiece, was demolished just before the outbreak of the Second World War, so few houses remain, but the concept was replicated by the more conservative Chambers at nearby **Somerset House**, which was begun in 1776.

At the time of the Adelphi project, Adam was at the height of his powers. He went on to design many other London buildings, such as Apsley House (constructed between 1771 and 1778 and now known as the **Wellington Museum**) and the homes in **Portland Place** (c. 1774–80) before his death on 3 March 1792. He was buried in **Westminster Abbey**, close to several monuments constructed to his own drawings. (*See also* CHELSEA HOSPITAL; ST. JAMES'S SQUARE; SIR JOHN SOANE'S MUSEUM.)

ADDINGTON PALACE. From 1808 until 1897, Addington Palace was the official residence of the Archbishop of Canterbury. Located at the eastern edge of the **London Borough of Croydon**, towards the south of the metropolitan area, the three-story building was originally designed by Robert Mylne and built between 1773 and 1779 for Barlow Trecothick, **Lord Mayor** of London. In 1807, the 3,500-acre estate was purchased by the Church of England and, through most of the 19th century, occupied by six successive primates. However, in 1897, Archbishop Frederick Temple decided that the cost of occupying the property was too great and opted to base himself in Canterbury. The building and grounds were bought by Frederick English, a South African millionaire who had made his fortune as a diamond merchant, and remodelled internally at the considerable cost of £70,000. During the First World War, the house was put to use as a hospital, then, when hostilities ended, was converted to a country club. In 1951, it was purchased by the local authority, which leases it to the Royal School of Church Music. The gardens, laid out by Capability Brown, have been converted to golf courses.

ADELPHI. *See* ADAM, ROBERT.

ADMIRALTY, THE. The site at the northwest end of **Whitehall**, which is occupied by the Admiralty building, has been a site for conducting naval business for some 400 years. At the beginning of the 17th century, it was occupied by Wallingford House, home of George Villiers, first Duke of Buckingham and Lord High Admiral of England. In 1694, however, the structure was damaged in a fire and replaced by an edifice, designed by **Christopher Wren**, which provided accommodation for the First Sea Lord (the head of the Royal Navy's administrative staff) and his principal officers but had only a single meeting room and limited office space. Between 1722 and 1726, that was demolished and the present brick building, designed by Thomas Ripley, erected in its place. The screen, topped by seahorses, which hides it from the street, was designed by **Robert Adam** and built in 1759–61. In 1786–88, Admiralty House, a new home for the First Lord of the Admiralty (a senior government post held by statesmen such as Winston Churchill and Arthur Balfour) was added to the south, and in 1894–95 an extension (now known as the New Admiralty) was constructed to the rear during a period of extensive public works in the city. With the exception of the Adam screen, the buildings are considered architecturally undistinguished by most critics, but the fireplace in the Board Room is decorated with outstanding wood carvings (possibly by **Grinling Gibbons**) that incorporate nautical instruments as well as flowers and fruits. Bomb damage to the property during the Second World War and a fire in 1955 necessitated much reconstruction, which was completed in 1958. In 1964, the Board of Admiralty, formerly responsible for the management of British naval affairs, was merged with the Air Ministry and the War Office to form the Ministry of Defence, which still uses offices in the building. (*See also* ADMIRALTY ARCH.)

ADMIRALTY ARCH. Admiralty Arch, built in 1906–11 as part of a national memorial to Queen Victoria, forms the eastern entrance to **The**

Mall, separating the relative quiet of **St James's Park** and the approach to **Buckingham Palace** from the turmoil of **Trafalgar Square**. Designed by Sir Aston Webb, it is a stolid structure of three deep arches that takes its name from **The Admiralty** building to the south. The arches are fitted with wrought iron gates, the central arch being opened only to allow ceremonial processions to pass through. Rooms within the structure were vacated by the Ministry of Defence in 1994, but two years later Prime Minister John Major vetoed a proposal by Defence Minister Michael Portillo to sell the arch to a private contractor who might develop its office potential.

AIR POLLUTION. Complaints about the quality of London's air have a long history, dating from as early as the 13th century, when the lime industry burned large quantities of coal during the production process. From the late 1700s, the city's physical expansion (due to the combined effects of the Industrial Revolution, the growth of overseas trade, and the increasing number of administrative tasks carried out in the nation's capital) compounded the problems as more people and more firms consumed more fuel. Smog (combinations of smoke and fog) became increasingly common and, for many people, proved lethal; in December 1873, for instance, a week of breathing polluted air caused 700 more deaths than expected in London for the time of year, with the elderly and people suffering from respiratory diseases particularly affected. Several pressure groups formed (such as the Coal Smoke Abatement Society in 1881) in an attempt to force companies to introduce smoke treatment policies, but successes were limited until after the Second World War.

The City of London (Various Powers) Act of 1946 allowed local authorities to create smokeless zones, which now cover about 90 percent of the built-up area, but failed to prevent a four-day smog, from 5 to 9 December 1952, which resulted in 4,700 more deaths than anticipated for the period. That episode prompted further action and culminated in Parliament's approval of the 1956 Clean Air Act—legislation that introduced tighter controls on emissions and affected, in particular, domestic fires, producing an 80 percent reduction in smoke levels by the late 1990s. Faced with the stringent laws, consumers switched increasingly from coal to electricity, gas, and oil, with the result that, during the second half of the century, transport superseded industry and private households as the major source of air pollution; vehicles with petroleum engines became the major cause of high carbon monoxide levels in the atmosphere, and planes landing at the city's five **airports** added nitrogen compounds and hydrocarbons. Moreover, as smoke levels decreased, the amount of sunlight reaching London rose, increasing photooxidation of pollutants (particularly the nitrogen gases) and causing photochemical smog. Most authorities now argue that further improvements in air quality will only be achieved through a combination of technical improvements (which would limit emissions from vehicles) and legislation that would encourage travellers to use public rather than private transport. (*See also* ALBERT MEMORIAL; BATTERSEA POWER STATION; EAST END; KENSINGTON PALACE; LONDON PLANE; REGENT'S PARK; WATER POLLUTION; WEST END; WHITEHALL PALACE.)

AIRPORTS. London is served by five major airports—Gatwick, Heathrow, London City, Luton, and Stansted. The first civil aerodrome in the United Kingdom, designated in 1919, was located at the western edge of the city on **Hounslow** Heath and provided daily service to Paris. The following year, however, it was closed and facilities developed at **Croydon**, which had been built in 1915 as a base for the aerial defense of southern England during the First World War. On 2 May 1928, Croydon was formally named London Airport, but the title passed to the twin runways at Heathrow on 31 May 1946, when the first direct scheduled passenger service left for the United States. Six years later, as air traffic increased, the Conservative government approved the development of Gatwick, on the farmlands of Sussex some 25 miles south of **Charing Cross**, and, on 9 June 1958, it was opened by Queen Elizabeth II. Croydon, increasingly hemmed in by urban encroachment, was closed the following year and its flat land converted into a factory site.

In 1966, the British Airports Authority assumed responsibility for the administration of both Heathrow and Gatwick, initiating programs of expansion and improvement. During the 1970s, the Gatwick runway was lengthened and a second terminal building constructed, increasing the airport area to nearly 1,900 acres. In 1977, the Piccadilly Line of the **London Underground** was extended to Heathrow, offering the prospect of speedy transport between the airport and the central city for the first time (during the first 22 years of its existence, passengers had to make the 15 mile journey in buses or cars on roads clogged by other traffic). Then, in 1986, a fourth terminal was added to the three that had served Heathrow for nearly 40 years.

Despite these improvements, the increasing demand for air travel in southeast England encouraged the government to seek a site for a third

London airport. In 1985, after considerable heart searching, it designated Stansted, about 30 miles northeast of the city center. Two terminals were opened and, by 1998, it had become Britain's fourth-biggest airport with 6.8 million passengers and 24 airlines serving 65 scheduled destinations. In the expectation of continued expansion in passenger numbers, a program of improvements involving extensions to the terminal buildings and the construction of additional departure gates was begun in 1999.

Luton's airport, 32 miles north of central London, opened in 1938, two years after aircraft production began in the area, but has developed largely since the 1980s. It is a private concern, owned by Luton Borough Council, and has proved popular with tour companies using charter flights (Britannia, the world's largest charter airline, is based there). In 1997, it announced a 10-year expansion program, at an estimated cost of £170 million, which would involve new administrative arrangements, a new terminal, and a new **railway** station, allowing it to handle up to 8.5 million passengers a year.

London City Airport, the youngest and smallest of the city's air foci, was built by the John Mowlem construction company as part of the development of **Docklands**, opening in 1987. Although only six miles east of the **City of London** and the heart of Britain's business community, it suffered from poor accessibility until a road link was opened in 1993. In addition, the cramped urban site limits the size of the aircraft that can use the single runway. In 1995, Mowlem sold the airport to Dermot Desmond, a flamboyant Irish businessman, for £14.5 million, less than a third of the £50 million it is estimated to have spent on the project. That combination of new management and better access appeared to improve fortunes because, by 2000, 10 airlines were operating scheduled services to 26 destinations in the United Kingdom and Europe.

In 1999–2000, Heathrow was the busiest of the five centers, with 63.6 million passengers. Gatwick had 31.3 million, Stansted 11.2 million, Luton 5.5 million, and London City 1.5 million. In 1999, the British Airports Authority, which wants to build a fifth terminal at Heathrow, forecast that combined annual demand at London's airports would rise to 138 million passengers within a decade, far outstripping the capacity of existing facilities. Environmental groups, however, fiercely opposed any expansion. (*See also* AIR POLLUTION; BIGGIN HILL; HENDON.)

AIR RAIDS. During the First and Second World Wars, London suffered greatly as a result of air raids, which caused much loss of life and damage to property. The first attack was made by a Zeppelin airship, which flew over the **East End** on 31 May 1915, in full moonlight, and dropped 120 high explosive bombs, killing seven people. A further 11 Zeppelin incursions over the next 29 months, all at night, were supported by daytime bombing raids, which began on 6 May 1916 and continued until 19 May 1918. Some Londoners sought refuge in the stations and tunnels of the **Tube** system, others left the city altogether, but even so, the German bombardment killed 670 people, injured 1,960, and caused damage estimated at £2 million. The most lethal raid was on 13 June 1917, when bombs dropped by 14 Gotha biplanes caused the deaths of 160 East Enders, including 17 children who were sheltering in the basement of a **Poplar** school.

The first aerial assault on London during the Second World War occurred on 24 August 1940, when German pilots lost their bearings and dumped explosives on the inner city. Britain's Royal Air Force retaliated by bombing Berlin, and German leader Adolf Hitler, who claimed that such attacks on his capital city could never happen, responded by ordering reprisals. The period from 7 September 1940 (when 320 bombers attacked the city, supported by over 600 fighter aircraft) until 11 May 1941 became known as the **Blitz**. Within five months, over 250,000 people were homeless, and by the end of the barrage over 15,000 Londoners were dead (some scholars suggest that the true figure was closer to 30,000). On the very last raid (during the night of 10–11 May 1941), the chamber of the House of Commons (*see* **Palace of Westminster**) was destroyed, along with **St. Clement Danes Church** on the **Strand**, the medieval **Temple Church**, and Queen's Hall (home of the Henry Wood Promenade Concerts [*See* **Proms, The**]). The **British Museum**, **Lambeth Palace**, **Mansion House**, the **Central Criminal Court**, **St. James's Palace**, and **Westminster Abbey** were all badly damaged.

Sporadic attacks occurred over the following months, but the city was spared further serious raids until 12 June 1944, when a V1 flying bomb killed six people at **Bethnal Green**. The V1s (the V stood for *Vergeltung*, German for "vengeance") caused considerable fear because they were pilotless, flew at 470 miles an hour, and carried a one-ton warhead. Known as buzz bombs and doodlebugs because of their noise ("doodlebug" was first used as a term for a cheap, noisy automobile), they were arriving at the rate of about 60 a day in mid-June, killing some 1,600 people and causing significant damage in suburbs south of the River Thames, such as **Greenwich** and **Lambeth**. After the Allied troops invaded the European mainland, the V1 launch sites were destroyed, and from the middle of August the raids declined in number and destructiveness, but they were replaced by the threat of V2 rockets, which first reached **Chiswick** and Epping on 7 September 1944. These new missiles carried explosives no greater than the V1, and their capacity to inflict damage was limited because they hit the ground with great speed, forming large craters rather than causing widespread destruction. Nevertheless, they were dreaded because they were launched from mobile pads, could not be tracked by radar, and were difficult to stop in the air. A total of 518 hit London between September 1944 and March 1945, most crashing down on the East End, which had suffered so much in earlier bombardments. An estimated 2,511 people died. (*See also* BIG BEN; CABINET WAR ROOMS; CLEOPATRA'S NEEDLE; CRAYFORD; GUILDHALL; IMPERIAL WAR MUSEUM; ST. JAMES'S CHURCH, PICCADILLY.)

ALBERT, PRINCE (1819–1861). Prince Albert, husband to Queen Victoria for 21 years, was never widely popular with Londoners, who distrusted his Germanic background and intellectual interests, but he used his influence to contribute enormously to the city's development. The second son of Ernest, Duke of Saxe-Coburg-Gotha, and Princess Louise of Saxe-Gotha-Altenburg, he was born in Rosenau on 26 August 1819 and christened Franz Albrecht August Karl Emmanuel. He first met Victoria when he was visiting Great Britain in 1836 and wrote to her regularly thereafter. In October 1839, during a second visit, Victoria proposed marriage, he accepted, and the wedding was held on 10 February the following year.

A hard-working consort, Albert invested considerable effort in finding out about his adopted country and had a growing influence on the Queen as she learned to depend on his diplomatic skills and organizational abilities. He also took great interest in the arts, encouraging **Charles Barry** and **Augustus Welby Northmore Pugin** to decorate the walls of the rebuilt **Palace of Westminster** with frescoes depicting great scenes from British history and literature. Also, he lent his patronage to sculptor Thomas Thorneycroft, who worked for 15 years on the statue of **Boadicea** and her daughters, which stands at the north end of **Westminster Bridge**, and served as President of the Society for the Encouragement of Arts, Manufactures, and Commerce (*see* **Royal Society of Arts**) for 18 years from 1843.

His major impact on London stemmed from his enthusiastic support for the **Great Exhibition** of 1851. The idea of an event celebrating Britain's position as the greatest industrial power the world had ever seen was the brainchild of civil servant Henry Cole, an assistant keeper at the

Public Record Office, but it would never have happened without Albert's belief that it was the country's mission, duty, and interest "to put herself at the head of the diffusion of civilization and the attainment of liberty." Overcoming the objections of critics who believed that such an exhibition would merely stimulate competition from other nations, he persuaded Prime Minister Lord John Russell to appoint a Royal Commission that he would preside over and that would raise money for the project. A **Crystal Palace** was built for the exhibits in **Hyde Park**, attracting over six million visitors, many of whom also patronized the stores in **Knightsbridge** and **Oxford Street**, thereby helping to establish the **West End** as a fashionable shopping area. The popular appeal of the venture generated a profit of £186,000, which the Prince and his committee used to purchase 87 acres of land in south **Kensington** as a location for a complex of institutions that would extend "the influence of Science and Art upon productive industry." The result was the construction of buildings for some of the nation's principal museums, educational institutions, and learned societies, including the **Natural History Museum**, the **Royal College of Music**, and Imperial College (now part of the University of London).

Albert, however, did not live to see the site fully developed. In 1861, he contracted typhoid during a visit to Cambridge and died on 14 December. His monuments in London include the Albert Embankment (*see* **Bazalgette, Joseph William**), the **Albert Bridge**, the **Albert Hall**, the **Albert Memorial**, the **Victoria and Albert Museum**, and some 50 Albert Roads, Mews, Terraces, and Closes. (*See also* LANCASTER HOUSE; NATIONAL PORTRAIT GALLERY; PADDINGTON STATION; RAILWAYS; ROYAL HORTICULTURAL SOCIETY.)

ALBERT BRIDGE. One of several London landmarks named in honor of **Prince Albert** (1819–61), husband of Queen Victoria (see, for example, **Albert Hall** and **Albert Memorial**), the bridge links **Chelsea** (on the north bank of the **River Thames**) with **Battersea** (on the south). An ornamented mixture of cantilever and suspension designs, with three spans, it was opened in 1873 and strengthened in 1973 so that it could cope with the increasing volume and weight of traffic. (*See also* BRIDGES; TRANSPORT.)

ALBERT HALL. In 1852, at the suggestion of **Prince Albert** (1819–61), Queen Victoria's consort, profits from the **Great Exhibition** were used to purchase a site in south **Kensington** that could be developed as a focus of **museums** and educational institutions. The Prince proposed a hall with libraries, exhibition rooms, and lecture facilities as a centerpiece of the complex, but nothing was achieved until, in 1863, Henry Cole (Chairman of the Society of Arts) suggested that money for a building could be raised by selling 999-year leaseholds of seats. The scheme proved attractive (over 1,300 were purchased at £100 each). Queen Victoria laid the foundation stone on 20 May 1867, and formally opened the building, which had been designed by Captain Francis Fowke and Lieutenant-Colonel Henry Darracott Scott, on 29 March 1871 (in the process, she surprised her audience by adding Royal Albert to the proposed name of Hall of Arts and Sciences). An oval structure, it is 272 feet long, 238 feet wide, and more than 150 feet high, with a roof of glass and iron. On the exterior, a frieze by students of the South Kensington School of Art illustrates "The Triumph of Arts and Sciences."

The auditorium, which can house audiences of 8,000 people, produced an echo, which made listening to music a form of purgatory (for many years, it was said that the Albert Hall was the only place where a British composer could be sure of hearing his work twice), but despite that, it became one of London's major concert venues. Organist and composer Anton Bruckner (1824–96) played at the opening event, Richard Wagner (1813–83) conducted orchestras playing his own operatic works in 1877, and in 1886 a dance floor was laid. Since 1941, the Sir Henry Wood Promenade Concerts (*see* **Proms, The**) have been held there every summer (with the audience's enjoyment much enhanced by saucer-shaped objects hung from the ceiling in 1968 to improve the acoustics). The facilities are also much used for other activities (boxing matches began in 1919, for example).

In 2000, the Hall management began a £66 million refurbishment program that included new foyers, a restaurant, improved seating, and an air conditioning system.

ALBERT MEMORIAL. A 175-foot-high structure located at the southern edge of **Kensington Gardens**, opposite the **Albert Hall**, the memorial commemorates **Prince Albert** (1819–61), the husband of Queen Victoria. A public appeal (which attracted less than the trustees had anticipated) raised funds for the edifice, which was designed by George Gilbert Scott, erected between 1863 and 1876, and decorated in multicolored stonework, gilding, mosaics, and statuary with typical Victorian exuberance. The corners are adorned with large marble representations of Europe, Asia, Africa, and America. Agriculture, manufactures, commerce, and engineering—the foundations of Britain's 19th-century industrial might—decorate the podium, and 169 life-sized figures of prominent scientists and artists form a frieze around the pedestal. A statue of Albert himself sits under a canopy, holding a copy of the catalogue of the **Great Exhibition** (which he supported with much enthusiasm) and surrounded by statues of the sciences (such as Chemistry and Astronomy), the arts (such as Poetry and Sculpture), and the personal qualities expected of Victorian Britons (such as Fortitude and Temperance). A flight of steps, 121 feet wide, leads from street level to the base. During the early 1990s, there was much debate about the future of the memorial, which had been seriously affected by the weather and **air pollution**. Some critics recommended demolition because of the cost involved in making repairs to the stonework, but the conservationist argument prevailed and an £11.2 million refurbishment program was completed in 1998.

ALDERMAN. Aldermen are elected by the people of the **City of London** to carry out duties related to the keeping of law and order (presiding over certain courts, for example), the administration of the **livery companies**, and certain ceremonial responsibilities (such as signing the documents that proclaim a new monarch). References to Aldermen (or elder men) date from Saxon times. In 1200, during the reign of King John, a Court of Aldermen was formed in **The City**; for the next 500 years, it acted as the center of local government, but gradually that role has been taken over by the **Court of Common Council**. Now, each **ward** elects one Alderman, who can remain in office until the age of 70 (from 1377 until 1975, they held office for life). Candidates must have previously received the **freedom of the city** and be approved by the aldermanic court. Aldermen act as Justices of the Peace (that is, as lay judges presiding over the lower courts), serve on **Corporation of London** committees, act as school governors, carry out duties as trustees of hospitals, and perform other civic services in addition to their ceremonial commitments. On official occasions, they wear either a scarlet gown trimmed with sable or an indigo gown trimmed with bear fur. (*See also* LORD MAYOR.)

ALDERSGATE. Although it was the site of one of the northern entrances to the Roman city (*see* **London Wall**), *Aldersgate* is a corruption of the Saxon *Ealdred's Gate.* In 1603, James VI and I entered London by this route as he arrived from Scotland to claim the English throne, and **Samuel Pepys** records that he saw the legs of traitors hung on the walls in 1660. It was damaged in the **Great Fire** of 1666, repaired four years later but demolished in 1761. Aldersgate Street, which ran past the entry, survives (the gate stood opposite No. 62).

ALDGATE. Situated at the eastern edge of the **City of London**, Aldgate was the point at which the road from the Roman port of Camulodunum (now Colchester) entered the capital, and gets its name from the Saxon *Ealdgate,* meaning "old gate." It was rebuilt during the first half of the 12th century and, from 1374 until 1385, a room in the walls above it was occupied by poet Geoffrey Chaucer (author of *The Canterbury Tales*) while he earned a living as a customs officer. Reconstruction work was carried out in 1606–9, but it was eventually demolished in 1761. During the 1980s and 1990s, the neighborhood experienced much office development as financial institutions built new premises close to London's traditional business area. (*See also* LONDON WALL.)

ALEXANDRA PALACE. Standing on **Muswell Hill**, overlooking an extensive park some six miles north of central London, Ally Pally (as it is known to local people) was built in 1873, named after the Princess of Wales, and intended to rival the **Crystal Palace** as an exhibition center. Sixteen days after it was opened, it was burned to the ground when some coal fell out of a workman's brazier, but it was immediately rebuilt to a design by architects Meeson and Johnson, with an auditorium, concert room, theater, reading rooms, and office space. Commercially, it was not a success even though it provided a focus for a variety of events, including musical performances, dog shows, horticultural competitions, and various sports. During the First World War, the seven-acre complex was converted into a camp for refugees from Belgium, then for German prisoners of war (who were put to work landscaping the 480-acre park). In 1936, a section of the building was acquired by the **British Broadcasting Corporation**, which built the world's first television transmitter on the site; the first program (*Here's Looking at You*, a variety show) was broadcast on 26 August 1936 and regular transmissions began on 2 November. Most of the studios were moved to **Shepherd's Bush** in 1956, and much of the structure was unused before being destroyed by another fire in July 1980. Following restoration, it reopened eight years later and now functions as a sports, exhibition, and leisure center administered by the **London Borough of Haringey**.

ANCHOR INN. Located in **Bankside**, south of the **River Thames** close to **London Bridge**, the Anchor is one of the most popular of London's older **public houses**. Built in the late 18th century on a site overlooking the water, where there had been an inn for at least 300 years, it still has a minstrels' gallery and nooks where runaways from the **Clink Prison** could hide. An exhibition of artifacts dating from the reign of Queen Elizabeth I, which were found during renovations, is on display, as is a model of the original **Globe Theatre**, which stood nearby. A raised terrace outside provides views across London to **St. Paul's Cathedral** and is the ideal place to drink a pint of English beer on a warm July evening.

ANGEL, THE. Located at the junction of Goswell Road and St. John Street, **Islington**, where travellers from the north diverged as they headed either for the finance houses of the **City of London** or the butchers' businesses at **Smithfield Meat Market**, The Angel flourished as a coaching inn from the early 17th century. It was rebuilt in 1819 and again in 1899, when it was converted to Lyons' Corner House, but closed in 1960 and was unoccupied until it was refurbished as a bank in 1981–82. The area is still a focus of routeways into London (five major thoroughfares meet at the site, a major traffic bottleneck despite repeated attempts by planners to improve the flow) and has experienced much rebuilding in recent years.

ARCHITECTURE. Although most of London's urban fabric dates from no earlier than the 18th century, parts of the Roman wall (completed by the second century of occupation) can still be seen and all periods from the time of the Norman invasion in 1066 are represented. The Normans brought the Romanesque to Britain, employing it in St. John's Chapel in the **Tower of London**. By the late 12th century, however, Gothic architecture was becoming more fashionable, with vaults, flying buttresses, and increasingly elaborate floor plans. In its initial form (known as Early English), it was characterized by a lack of decoration (the Lady Chapel at **Southwark Cathedral** is a much quoted example), but, as builders experimented and became more confident, the plainness was superseded by intricate tracery work, such as that of the west window at **St. Etheldreda's Church** in **Holborn**. Then, from about 1350, new designs led to more robust structures (a phase known as the Perpendicular); **St. Olave's Church** in Hart Street was typical of the period and Henry VII's Chapel in **Westminster Abbey** one of its finest legacies.

During the 16th century, Renaissance (also known as Classical and Palladian) influences from Italy began to shape building styles, but they had a major impact on the urban skyline only after **Inigo Jones** completed the **Queen's House** at **Greenwich** in 1635. The success of that commission led to further patronage by courtiers and, in particular, to the planning of the Earl of Bedford's estate at **Covent Garden**. However, much of the **City of London**'s domestic architecture and most of its Gothic parish churches were destroyed in the **Great Fire** of 1666, leaving the residents with a major rebuilding project. New regulations, intended to prevent a repeat of the tragedy, required replacement houses to be erected in brick and stone (rather than wood) and to have tiled (rather than thatched) roofs. **Christopher Wren** was given the task of redesigning **St. Paul's Cathedral** and planning some 50 other churches, using a rich imagination to make the most of awkward and confined sites. Forty years later, **Nicholas Hawksmoor** (Wren's assistant) left his own, baroque, mark with six individualistic designs for places of worship, notably **Christ Church, Spitalfields**, but, by then, fashions were changing again and Palladianism reappeared, initially in **Chiswick House** then in the work of **Robert Adam**. At the same time, there was a growing vogue for medieval styles, a trend that was later to be known as the Gothic Revival (or neo-Gothic). Although difficult to date, it is normally considered to begin with writer Horace Walpole's conversion of **Strawberry Hill** and include, as one of its finest examples, the rebuilding of the **Palace of Westminster** by **Charles Barry** and **Augustus Welby Northmore Pugin**.

The late 18th century brought a period of planned expansion that allowed squares and crescents to be designed as units (see, for example, **Bedford Estates**). Essentially, these were constructed on the conveyor-belt principle, with standard railings, window sashes, and other fittings for the houses. That principle was extended following the Industrial Revolution by builders such as **Thomas Cubitt**, who erected suburban terraces for the middle class, and then by a legion of entrepreneurs who covered the countryside with concrete as the **railways** expanded, allowing a burgeoning workforce to live at the urban fringe and commute to clerical jobs in the city center. One of the consequences was the growth, around the inner city and in the **East End**, of a large slum population living in conditions that were only alleviated following the introduction of welfare state policies in the 1940s and 1950s; local authorities undertook comprehensive redevelopment programs, housing many of the least affluent Londoners in skyscraper blocks on cleared land and moving others to estates on the fringe of the built-up area. However, attempts to keep expenditure down, perhaps inevitable at a time of postwar economic reconstruction, resulted in poor quality buildings and poor quality design, which successor authorities had to correct at a much greater cost. More recently, although some plans have aroused controversy and others have been criticized as unimaginative (see, for example, **Barbican**), greater freedom from planning restrictions has encouraged architects to return to the earlier practice of designing buildings as individuals. As a result, the modernist jostles with the traditional, as at the **Docklands**, where new buildings (such as the **Canary Wharf** tower) mix with converted 19th-century warehouses. (*See also* BANQUETING HOUSE; BRIDGES; BURLINGTON ARCADE; BURLINGTON HOUSE; CHAMBERS, WILLIAM; CHELSEA; GIBBS, JAMES; DANCE, GEORGE (1700–1768); DANCE, GEORGE (1741–1825); HOUSING; KENWOOD HOUSE; LANCASTER HOUSE; MANSION HOUSE; MARBLE ARCH; MARBLE HILL HOUSE; NASH, JOHN; OSTERLEY HOUSE; PUTNEY; ROYAL EXCHANGE; ST. DUNSTAN IN THE WEST CHURCH, FLEET STREET; ST. MARTIN-IN-THE-FIELDS CHURCH, TRAFALGAR SQUARE; ST. STEPHEN WALBROOK CHURCH; SCOTT, GILES GILBERT; SELFRIDGE'S; SURBITON; SYON HOUSE.)

ARCHWAY. The viaduct by which Hornsey Lane (running from east to west) crosses Archway Road (running from south to north) solved a serious transport problem. The main road from the **City of London** to the towns of northern Britain had a steep inclination in order to pass Highgate Hill, straining horses that dragged wagons and coaches. In 1809, Parliament approved the construction of a 750-foot-long tunnel that would allow traffic to avoid the gradient, but, on 13 April 1812, it collapsed after only about 130 feet had been built. A cut was suggested as an alternative but necessitated construction of a bridge that would carry Hornsey Lane across the gap. **John Nash** prepared plans for the structure, whose four arches resembled those of a Roman aqueduct. Archway Road opened in 1813 but the scheme was not completed until 1829, after Scottish engineer Thomas Telford had prepared a satisfactory drainage system. Storyteller Hans Christian Andersen, on a visit to **Charles Dickens**, saw "the great world metropolis mapped out in fire" when he looked from Nash's viaduct, which was replaced, in 1897, by a cast iron arch designed by Sir Alexander Binnie.

ASSOCIATION OF LONDON AUTHORITIES (ALA). The ALA was founded in 1983, when 13 Labour-dominated authorities withdrew from the **London Boroughs Association (LBA)** following that body's recommendation to the national government that the left-wing **Greater London Council (GLC)** should be abolished. The disagreement was particularly bitter because, until the rift, the LBA had functioned as a politically nonpartisan organization representing the **London boroughs** in negotiations with the government and other parties. As a result, mutual antipathy initially inhibited cooperation between the two bodies, although their interests were similar (both declared that their objectives were to protect and promote the interests of the boroughs). Also, there was an added undercurrent of animosity because the ALA acted as an avowedly Labour grouping whereas the LBA claimed that, because its membership was open to all boroughs, whatever their political leanings, it was more truly representative of the whole city. Initially, the ALA proved to be more radical than its parent, campaigning on social issues such as domestic violence, but, during the second half of the 1980s and the early 1990s, as Conservative Party supporters became increasingly disenchanted with the administrations led by Prime Ministers Margaret Thatcher (1979–90) and John Major (1990–97), common concerns led to more numerous contacts between the organizations' officials and ultimately to joint activity on a range of issues. As the antagonism decreased, the case for remerger strengthened, and in 1995 the ALA and the LBA reunited as the **Association of London Government**. (*See also* LONDON HEALTH EMERGENCY [LHE]; LONDON PRIDE PARTNERSHIP.)

ASSOCIATION OF LONDON GOVERNMENT (ALG). The ALG was formed in 1995 through the merger of the **Association of London Authorities** and the **London Boroughs Association**, providing a forum in which representatives of the 32 **London borough**s and the **Corporation of London** (the local authority for the **City of London**) could discuss matters of common interest. Also, it acts as a pressure group, attempting to win funds and policy concessions from bodies such as the national government and the European Union. Following the election of the **Greater London** Assembly in 2000, the organization was restructured to include (in addition to the **local government** representatives) members of the Greater London Employers' Association (which advises boroughs on policies relating to training and job creation), the London Boroughs Grants Committee (which contributes some £28 million a year to the funds of voluntary bodies in an attempt to reduce poverty), the London Housing Unit (a pressure group advocating improved housing conditions), and the Transport Committee for London (which facilitates the use of public transport by the elderly and disabled). It has a staff of about 150.

ATHENAEUM, THE. Among London's **gentlemen's clubs**, The Athenaeum has a reputation as a meeting place for the city's intellectuals. It was founded in 1824 at **Somerset House** by John Wilson Croker, who called it The Society and encouraged scientists, artists, and writers to join. Six years later, it moved to the premises that it still occupies at 107 **Pall Mall** and renamed itself after the center for the study of literature and science which Hadrian, Emperor of Rome, established c.135 A.D. The rooms, designed by Decimus Burton and built of Bath stone, incorporate a frieze based on decoration of the Parthenon in Athens and (above the Doric entrance porch) a gilt statue of Pallas Athena, goddess of wisdom. An attic was added in 1899. Members this century have included prime ministers and other politicians as well as senior figures from London's literary establishment. In 2001 the club voted to admit ladies to membership.

AVERY HILL. In 1902, the **London County Council (LCC)** purchased a private estate in the southeastern section of the city, some nine miles from **Charing Cross**. The 86 acres of open space were turned into a public recreation area, known as Avery Hill Park, and the mansion house, built in 1889, which became a teachers' training college, is now used by the University of Greenwich. A conservatory, damaged by a flying bomb during the Second World War, was restored in 1962 and houses an outstanding collection of plants, complementing exotic tree species that adorn the rest of the site.

– B –

BAGNIGGE WELLS. During the Georgian period, it was fashionable to visit spas, either to bathe or to drink waters believed to have therapeutic properties. In London, Bagnigge Wells, in King's Cross Road, was one of the most popular because of its accessibility and facilities. It developed during the late 1750s after Thomas Hughes, a local tobacconist, discovered that his best efforts to grow garden flowers were being undermined by the iron content of the ground water. That water proved to be an efficient purgative, and Hughes, cashing in on the leisure activities of the age, opened his property to the public, charging threepence for entry. The morning was devoted to those wanting to taste the water alone, the afternoon to those preferring tea. Games such as skittles and bowls were made available and concerts provided regular entertainment. In *Bon Ton*

(1775), **David Garrick** suggests that the well-to-do enjoyed "Drinking tea on summer afternoons, at Bagnigge Wells with china and gilt spoons," but, increasingly, the lower classes infiltrated the gardens, and, by the early 19th century, the affluent had deserted them. The venture went bankrupt in 1813; attempts to resurrect it were only partially successful, so it closed its doors for the last time in 1841. The site was quickly developed for other, more urban, purposes, but a plaque at 61–63 King's Cross Road marks the location of Bagnigge House.

BAKER STREET. Famed largely because of its associations with **Sherlock Holmes**, Baker Street runs northwest for about two-thirds of a mile from **Oxford Street** (in the heart of the city's retail area) to **Regent's Park**. Its housing was originally developed by builder William Baker on land leased from the Portman Estate in 1755. Holmes, the fictional detective created by Arthur Conan Doyle, lived at No. 221B, a site now occupied by the Abbey National Bank, which employs a full-time member of staff to reply to letters addressed to its illustrious predecessor and erected a statue in Holmes's honor during 1999. Nearby, at 239 Baker Street, there is a Sherlock Holmes Museum (which calls itself 221B Baker Street). During the 19th century, the road was a fashionable part of the city (Prime Minister William Pitt the Younger lived at No. 120 in 1802–6 and actress Sarah Siddons at No. 27 in 1817–31), but many of the houses have since been demolished or converted into shops and offices. (*See also* MADAME TUSSAUD'S WAXWORKS.)

BALHAM. Although it is now an unprepossessing, largely working-class, suburb of Victorian and early-20th-century housing, Balham probably emerged as a Saxon hamlet on Stane Street, a Roman road leading to London from the port at Chichester (some 65 miles to the southeast). It remained an agricultural area until, in the late 18th and early 19th centuries, it attracted wealthy London businessmen, who built large houses in which they could entertain their friends in the countryside. The potential for an affluent market encouraged the **railway** developers to open a station in 1856 and, after that, the area was transformed. Ease of access to jobs made the area desirable to workers who could not afford the high cost of central-city accommodation, so the green fields and woodlands quickly disappeared under bricks and mortar. Shops and other services were established for the newcomers as the developed area spread outwards and ultimately merged with neighboring settlements, such as **Clapham** (to the north) and **Tooting** (to the south). As a result, the district suffers from a lack of park land and other recreational space. The rich businessmen have long gone and their former homes have been subdivided into flats, many of which are rented rather than owned. Much of the housing built in the past 60 years is on sites damaged by bombs during the **Blitz**.

BALTIC EXCHANGE. The Baltic Exchange is the world's largest shipbroking market, accounting for more than half of global business in ship sales and 60 percent in wet bulk cargo. In addition, the 600 or so members have a growing influence on the organization of air passenger charter flights. It is located in St. Mary Axe, a street on the northeast edge of the **City of London** named after a church that housed an axe used by Attila the Hun when, according to legend, he slaughtered 11,000 virgin ladies who waited on the daughter of the King of England. In the early Georgian period, tallow (used to make candles, soap, and lubricants) was an important commodity shipped from the Baltic states, and traders who had goods to transport to northern Europe knew that in **Threadneedle Street**, at the Virginia and Maryland **Coffee House** (which renamed itself the Virginia and Baltick in 1744), they could meet captains looking for cargoes that would fill their holds during the return journey. In 1810, the premises had become so crowded that dealers moved to the nearby Antwerp Tavern (which became known as the Baltic Coffee House), then, in 1823, as Britain's world trading connections expanded, a formal association—the Baltic Club—was founded, with standardized trading regulations. In 1900, the club merged with the London Shipping Company (which had been founded in 1891 specifically to serve the growing ocean liner industry) as the Baltic and Mercantile Shipping Exchange Limited and, in 1903, occupied a new granite-faced building on the site of St. Mary Axe Church, which had been destroyed by fire 12 years earlier. By 1920, the brokers (whose word was considered binding when deals were made) represented nearly all the world's shipowners and cargo interests. Moreover, the concentration of interests led to the formation of related organizations, such as the Institute of Chartered Shipbrokers. In 1987, the **Corn Exchange** also occupied the building. On 10 April 1992, a bomb, planted by the Irish Republican Army, caused much damage to the structure but had little effect on trading. The exchange moved temporarily to **Lloyd's of London**, in Lime Street, while repairs were carried out, then moved back to its former base. In 1994, however, it transferred next door to new premises—an art deco building internally refurbished for trading in the computer age.

BANK OF ENGLAND. As the central bank of the United Kingdom, the Bank of England is responsible for designing, printing, and issuing currency notes circulated in England and Wales (and used throughout the country, though the Scottish and Northern Irish banks also issue notes). It also advises the Chancellor of the Exchequer (the United Kingdom's principal finance minister) on the impact of proposed government policies, attempts to maintain stability in domestic markets, and intervenes in foreign exchange dealings to protect sterling. It was given a royal charter, entitling it to operate, on 27 July 1694, after William Paterson (a Scot) and Michael Godfrey (like Paterson, a wealthy merchant) had suggested that a bank should be created to help King William III fund a war against France by lending its share capital to the government. A total of 1,268 individuals subscribed £1.2 million, which was loaned to the state at an interest rate of 8 percent per annum, with an additional £100,000 payable for expenses each year. The new bank was given permission to issue notes based on the security of the loan, but its early days were not easy. London's goldsmiths resented it because it stole much of their trade, rival institutions were established, and the government pressed it to supply more and more capital. However, legislation in 1708 prohibited companies with more than six partners from issuing notes, thereby greatly reducing the competition and enabling it to become banker to government departments. The management of government securities was added to its duties in 1717 and, in 1751, it assumed responsibility for administering the national debt.

The last two decades of the century brought new problems. In 1780, during the **Gordon Riots**, the Bank of England was attacked by a mob, which was beaten back by clerks who melted their ink wells to make bullets. (After that incident, the government sent guards to maintain security every night; known as the Bank Picquet, they acted as watchmen until 1973, when the bank replaced them with its own employees). Then there was a run on funds as investors panicked during the French Revolution (which began in 1789) and, in 1797, reacted to rumors that a French force had invaded Wales. Regulations were passed to prevent cash withdrawals of more than £1, and Spanish dollars, taken from captured vessels, were circulated to meet the public's need for coinage.

The Bank of England during the 19th century was, in effect, the Bank of the British Empire, meeting the needs of a country expanding its commitments abroad whilst experiencing major social and economic upheaval through industrialization. In 1833, its notes became legal tender (that is, they had to be accepted in payment of a debt), and, 11 years later, the Bank Charter Act allowed it to issue notes up to a total value of £14 million; issues over that sum had to be backed by gold. By the end of the century, all commercial banks had considerable deposits. These could be withdrawn on demand in the form of gold, at the Bank of England, which therefore became the keeper of the nation's gold reserve and, as a result, responsible for the control of credit.

Changing conditions after the First World War led, in 1928, to the ending of the requirement to pay in gold and, in 1946, to the institution's conversion from private to public ownership. A new royal charter provided for a governor, deputy governor, and 16 directors, all appointed by the Crown on the advice of the prime minister. In 1979, further legislation made the bank responsible for supervising all banks operating in the United Kingdom so that depositors would be protected, and, in 1997, it was given sole authority to alter interest rates, a task formerly reserved for government ministers.

The Bank of England's first premises were at Mercers' Hall in **Cheapside**, but it stayed there for only a few months before moving to Grocers' Hall in Princes Street. In 1734, it transferred to **Threadneedle Street**, in the heart of the **City of London**, and it has remained there for more than 250 years, on a site covering 3.5 acres. Much reconstruction work was carried out in the 1780s and 1790s to designs by Sir John Soane (*see* **Sir John Soane's Museum**), but only the outer wall remains. The present building dates from 1925–39, when it was replanned by Sir Herbert Baker. Its nickname—The Old Lady of Threadneedle Street—probably dates from a late 18th-century James Gillray cartoon, titled "Political Ravishment, or the Old Lady of Threadneedle Street in Danger," which mocks government attempts to affect the Bank of England's decision-making processes (an outline of the old lady is sculpted on the facade of the bank entrance). Visitors are not allowed beyond the entrance hall, but the bank maintains a **museum**, in Bartholomew Lane, which contains examples of modern banking technology and offers a video presentation explaining its functions and day-to-day operations.

BANKSIDE. During the late 16th and the early 17th centuries, Bankside, at the northern tip of **Southwark**, was the center of London **theater** and one of the most dissolute parts of the city. In 1988, archaeologists discovered the site of the Rose, the first of the playhouses, built in 1586–87 and still remembered in the street name Rose Alley. The Swan opened in 1596 and, according to John de Witt, who made a sketch of the building, could hold audiences of over 3,000. At the same time, **William Shake-**

speare was treading the stage at the **Globe Theatre**, originally built in 1598–99 and demolished in 1644 but now reconstructed on its original site. Actors, writers, and theater managers all lived in the area and helped to support other forms of entertainment, such as bear baiting. There were also many brothels, with rules of conduct and opening hours regulated by the Bishops of Winchester, whose London palace estate included Bankside. After the pleasure palaces were closed by Oliver Cromwell and his morally strict, Sabbath-observing Puritans during the 1640s and 1650s, much of the land was devoted to gardens, but these were gradually replaced by small industrial premises, notably **breweries**, glassmaking works, dyers' yards, and small foundries. **Public houses**, such as the **Anchor Inn**, were established to serve thirsty workers, and wharves and warehouses were built along the **River Thames**, providing facilities for ships trading with other parts of Britain and with Europe. The area is now dominated by the tall chimney of Bankside Power Station, designed by **Giles Gilbert Scott**, opened in 1963, decommissioned in 1981, and refurbished to provide a home for part of the **Tate Gallery**'s collection of modern art in 2000. As part of the development, a new footbridge (known as the **Millennium Bridge**) was built across the Thames, linking Bankside to the **City of London** and **St. Paul's Cathedral**. (*See also* CLINK PRISON; HENSLOWE, PHILIP.)

BANQUETING HOUSE. Considered by critics to be one of the finest examples of Renaissance **architectiure** in Britain, the Banqueting House was designed by **Inigo Jones** and built at the command of King James VI and I as part of a planned extension of **Whitehall Palace**. Opened in 1622 with a performance of **Ben Jonson**'s play *Masque of Angers*, it stands on the east side of **Whitehall**, on a site occupied by earlier structures built in 1572, 1581, and 1608. Originally, the exterior was masonry brought from Northampton and Oxford but, in 1829, it was faced with more durable **Portland stone**. Inside, spectators could watch events from a gallery under a ceiling that was commissioned by King Charles I in 1635 and painted by Peter Paul Rubens, who depicted the advantages of James's rule in nine allegorical settings. The hall was used for varied functions, including royal feasts, the reception of foreign dignitaries, and state ceremonies (Charles was hanged on a scaffold just outside one of the windows, and William of Orange and his wife, Mary, were formally offered the throne by an assembly of aristocrats and commoners held in the building on 13 February 1689). After a fire destroyed much of the interior in 1698, the Banqueting House was converted into a chapel royal, designed by **Christopher Wren**. For 20 years from 1809, it was the horse guards' chapel, then, from 1829 until 1890, it reverted to its status as a chapel royal before becoming the museum of the Royal United Services Institute for Defence Studies. In 1962, it was reclaimed by the government, which redecorated it in its original color scheme and returned it to its initial use as a setting for state functions.

BARBICAN. Although it is largely occupied by a controversial post–Second World War development, the Barbican area gets its name from the medieval fortifications that surrounded London (a *barbican* is a watchtower projecting over a gate in a city's defensive wall). During the 16th and 17th centuries, it was a fashionable part of the city (poet John Milton lived there from 1645 until 1649, for example, probably writing *L'Allegro* and *Comus* while in residence), but in the 1700s it became more working class and by the end of the Victorian period it was a run-down mix of houses and small businesses. In 1940 and 1941, it suffered greatly from German bombs (*see* **Blitz**), so it was ripe for new construction as London rebuilt after the conflict ended. Rather than simply allow offices to take over the site, however, Duncan Sandys (minister of housing and local government in the Conservative government) appealed, in 1956, for planners to design "a genuine residential neighborhood, incorporating schools, shops, open spaces, and amenities, even if this means foregoing a more remunerative return on the land."

In part, Sandys's view reflected a widely held fear that a flight of middle-class groups from Britain's inner cities would take retail and related services with it, leaving the poor behind and creating problems similar to those that had evolved in the United States. His plea, therefore, fell on receptive ears and, in 1958, the site was bought by the **City of London** through a compulsory purchase order. The architectural firm of Chamberlin, Powell, and Bon was commissioned to prepare plans and designed a complex that included 2,100 apartments for over 6,500 people (some of them in three skyscrapers over 400 feet high, taller than any other in Europe at the time). In addition, there were shops, offices, the **Museum of London**, a new **Guildhall School of Music and Drama**, accommodation for two City **livery companies**, a girls' school, and an arts center. The dense concentration of buildings was, in some ways, reminiscent of Europe's medieval walled cities, but the homes were designed to maximize privacy and many have small gardens. Open space and water features were also built into the plan in an attempt to alleviate the harshness of the masonry and feelings of confinement.

Opinions about the development were sharply divided, some critics praising its imaginative provision of homes on a confined site in the inner city, others repelled by the functionalism of the rough-tooled concrete **architecture**. Many of the complaints were directed at the Barbican Centre for Arts and Conferences, London's equivalent of the Lincoln Center in New York. Opened in 1982, it cost £153 million, covers 20 acres, and has 10 levels. Inside, there are an art gallery, three cinemas, a library, restaurants, conference facilities, a 2,026-seat concert hall, and a 1,166-seat theater with rehearsal rooms. The **London Symphony Orchestra** uses the Centre for performances, as did the Royal Shakespeare Company until 2001, when it moved out following actors' complaints about the subterranean auditorium, the "concrete jungle" design, and its distance form London's theater heartland on the **West End**.

BARBICAN CENTRE FOR ARTS AND CONFERENCES. *See* BARBICAN.

BARINGS BANK. In 1762, John and Francis Baring established a merchant bank in Queen Street, trading internationally in the commodity markets. Forty-three years later, the business moved to Bishopsgate, then, in 1890, it became a limited company. By the late 20th century, it was the oldest merchant bank in the **City of London**, with interests in corporate finance and investment management. However, in 1994–95, Nick Leeson, who managed its futures trading operation in Singapore, took excessive risks with the firm's funds. Betting that the Tokyo stocks would rise, he invested heavily and, when the market fell in the wake of an earthquake at Kobe, doubled his commitments. Faced with mounting losses, he fled to Europe on 23 February 1995. Barings collapsed four days later, with debts of £830 million, and was purchased by the Internationale Nederlanden Groep (ING) for £1. Leeson, arrested at Frankfurt Airport, returned to Singapore, where he received a six-and-a-half-year jail sentence after facing trial for fraud and forgery. Following a **Bank of England** inquiry, which concluded that Barings had failed to supervise its Far Eastern operations properly, several of the firm's senior staff were disqualified from holding posts as company directors. In 2001, ING sold Barings, which it had used as the American end of its investment banking operations, to rival ABNAMRO for US $275 million.

BARKING. A largely working-class suburb on the eastern edge of London, Barking is bounded by the **River Thames** in the south, the Roding River in the west, the community of **Ilford** in the north, and **Dagenham** in the east. It originated as a Saxon settlement (its name is derived from the Old English *Berecingum*, which means "Berica's people"), developing on marshy land around Barking Abbey, which was founded by St. Erkenwald around 666 A.D. By the time of its dissolution by King Henry VIII in 1539, the abbey, located at the head of Barking Creek (which forms the mouth of the Roding), had became the largest Benedictine nunnery in England, and its inhabitants provided local people with a ready Roman Catholic market, as did the relatively large population of London, so, unsurprisingly, a considerable fishing industry developed. By the mid-19th century, some 4,000 people and about 220 vessels were employed, with, in addition, others involved in tasks such as processing and distribution of the catch.

During the second half of the century, the fishing fleet moved to Great Yarmouth, in Norfolk, and Barking's economy became increasingly industrial, particularly after the **railway** arrived in 1854. Green fields were speedily replaced by buildings as the population more than tripled between 1901 (when it totalled 21,547) and 1951 (when it reached 78,170). One of the largest electricity generating stations in Europe was built in 1926, providing jobs for employees with the considerable number of construction and engineering companies that flourished in the area. In addition, extensive areas were earmarked for local authority **housing**, including the 27,000-home Becontree estate, which straddled Barking, Dagenham, and Ilford and, when it opened in the 1920s, was one of the largest public residential developments in Europe. Many of Barking's citizens work at the Ford Motor Company's Dagenham works, in distribution companies located along the main road between London and Tilbury, in chemical and pharmaceutical firms (such as Rhone Poulenc), or with manufacturing concerns such as the GPT telephone cable business. In addition, over two miles of riverfront along Barking Creek are being redeveloped for a mixture of commercial, recreational, and residential purposes. In 1965, part of Barking was merged with East Ham as the new **London Borough of Newham**. The remainder was united with its eastern neighbor as the **London Borough of Barking and Dagenham**.

BARKING AND DAGENHAM, LONDON BOROUGH OF. In 1965, the formerly independent settlements of **Barking** and **Dagenham**, located on the marshy north bank of the **River Thames** some 10 miles east of the city center, were merged into a single authority as part of a wide-ranging reorganization of London's **local government** (*see* **Greater London Council; London borough**). It covers some 14 square miles and has a population of about 155,600 (1998). Since its creation, the largely white working-class population has ensured consistent Labour Party control of the council even though substantial numbers of skilled manual workers flirted with Margaret Thatcher's Conservative Party during the 1980s. Economically, the area is dominated by manufacturing companies such as the Ford Motor Company (which began production at Dagenham in 1931 but announced early in 2000 that it intended to close much of its plant, retaining only the engine-making facility) and the Rhone Poulenc chemical and pharmaceutical group. Service employment is limited although Coral (a betting firm that has diversified successfully into other branches of the leisure industry) has its headquarters in the area. About half of the **housing** is rented from the local authority or from a housing association, most of it built between the two world wars in the form of long terraces. The Borough Council, based at a civic center in Dagenham, operates through eight departments that carry out statutory responsibilities, including town planning, provision of education (the borough has 53 primary and eight secondary schools), and maintenance of social services.

BARNARDO, THOMAS JOHN (1845–1905). The founder of a nationwide network of homes for abandoned and poor children, Barnardo was born in Dublin (now in the Republic of Ireland) on 4 July 1845. The ninth son of a German father and an Irish mother, he was raised as a Roman Catholic but converted to Protestantism in 1862 and became an evangelical preacher. In 1866, he travelled to London, intending to study medicine before undertaking missionary work in China. However, while based at the London Hospital, in the city's **East End**, he became deeply involved in attempts to improve the lot of homeless young people, initially founding a juvenile mission (1867) then (with financial help from Lord Shaftesbury) opening a boys' home at **Mile End** in 1870. Three years later, he bought an inn at **Limehouse**, converting it into a headquarters for his charity work, a church, and a meeting place for laborers in the nearby docks. In 1874, he began to provide facilities for girls, ensuring that vocational training was made available for both sexes so that young people could break the cycle of poverty by finding steady jobs. Barnardo's insistence that the children in his care should be brought up according to the tenets of the Protestant faith plunged him into frequent conflict with Roman Catholic authorities, but his homes met a real need in a city that had a high proportion of lowly paid manual workers, many of whom suffered from long spells of unemployment and had large families. Working on the principle that no destitute youngster should ever be turned away, he probably helped about 250,000 individuals before he died at **Surbiton** on 19 September 1905. In 1899, his properties became the responsibility of the National Incorporated Association for the Reclamation of Destitute Waif Children, but they have always been popularly known as Dr. Barnardo's homes. In recent years, the charity he founded has placed increasing emphasis on care in the community, rather than on residential provision, in order to meet changing social needs.

BARNES. Lying south of the **River Thames**, about six miles southwest of **Charing Cross**, Barnes was considered remote from the **City of London** before the 19th century because the village's only access was by water or by traversing the marshy common land that separated it from **Putney**, its eastern neighbor. However, a road linked the settlement to **Hammersmith** in 1827 (*see* **Hammersmith Bridge**) and the **railway** arrived in 1846, making the area attractive to businessmen wanting a substantial suburban home in keeping with their status. The demand led to much **housing** development but the large green and its pond survived, as did the common (though it was drained during the second half of the century). Brewing (*see* **breweries**) was once a significant local industry but the area is now essentially a middle-class dormitory suburb. The railway crossing of the Thames west of Barnes is the oldest **bridge** over the river downstream of **Richmond**. Erected for the London and South Western company and opened in 1849, it is made of cast iron. A wrought iron structure was added on the eastern side in 1891–95.

BARNET, LONDON BOROUGH OF. When London's **local government** was reorganized in 1965, Barnet was created through the amalgamation of the formerly independent boroughs of **Hendon** and **Finchley**, with the addition of Chipping Barnet, East Barnet, and Friern Barnet, all of which previously had urban district status. The authority covers some 34 square miles in the northwest of the city and had a population of 331,500 in 1998. Although there is some light industry in the west, the area is largely residential, with the protected land of the green belt helping to keep house prices in northern neighborhoods high and attracting wealthy (and largely white) families. The communities around **Mill Hill** and Hendon have relatively high proportions of council accommodation and a significant Asian presence, whereas the south (which includes

Hampstead Garden Suburb) is heavily dominated by nonmanual workers and Jewish **immigrants**. The affluence of the borough is reflected in the number of retail establishments (Barnet has more shops than any other part of the city except the **City of Westminster** and the **London Borough of Camden**). Several major office developments (including the British headquarters of McDonald's fast-food chain) provide important sources of employment, as do such educational institutions as Middlesex University and the Police Training Centre at Hendon. (*See also* CRICKLEWOOD; EDGWARE; GOLDERS GREEN.)

BARNSBURY. The Barnsbury area of the **London Borough of Islington**, some two miles north of **Charing Cross**, developed around Bernesbury Manor. Until the early 19th century, it was a rural community, dependent largely on dairy farming and market gardening. However, from about 1820 fields were dug up for clay by the brick-making companies and built over by developers. Initially, the new houses were acquired by skilled working-class and lower-middle-class families but, by the beginning of the 20th century, these groups had taken advantage of the growing network of **railway** lines to move farther into the suburbs. Their homes were subdivided to provide rented flats for single people seeking cheap accommodation close to the city center so, by the end of the Second World War, many properties were shabby and poorly maintained. Since then, local authorities have undertaken improvement schemes, demolishing older premises to make way for council estates and small open spaces. In addition, new owner-occupiers have refurbished many of the terraces.

BARRY, CHARLES (1795-1860). Although Barry is best known as the architect of the Houses of Parliament (*see* **Palace of Westminster**), he was also responsible for the design of several other important buildings in London and a major influence on the growth of the Gothic Revival movement in English **architecture**. The son of a stationer, he was born in Bridge Street, **Westminster**, on 23 May 1795, and began his career at the age of 15 as a trainee with Middleton and Bailey, a firm of surveyors and architects based in Paradise Row, **Lambeth**. In 1815, his father died, leaving Barry an inheritance that he used to finance a three-year tour of the Mediterranean lands, including France, Italy, Greece, Turkey, Egypt, and Cyprus. On his return, he set up his own business in **Ely Place**, **Holborn**, and made a successful living by designing churches for the rapidly expanding populations of London and other cities. In 1829–32, he prepared plans for the

Travellers' Club in **Pall Mall**; the first London building to be erected in the style of an Italian Renaissance palace, it is two stories high with a plain stucco facade and an entrance set to one side. Next door, his even grander **Reform Club** (1837–41) is constructed of **Portland stone**, with the rooms gathered around a central cloistered courtyard.

Barry also built several private homes, the most notable of which is Bridgewater House (1845–54) in Queen's Walk on the eastern edge of **Green Park**. Outside London, he designed King Edward VI School, Birmingham (1833–37), the Royal Institution of Fine Arts, Manchester (1824–35), and Halifax Town Hall (opened in 1863). While working in Birmingham, he made the acquaintance of **Augustus Welby Northmore Pugin**, who was to collaborate with him on the rebuilding of the **Palace of Westminster**. After the palace had been destroyed by fire on 16 October 1834, architects were invited to compete for the commission to erect a replacement on the same site, with the stipulation that the new building must be designed in either Elizabethan or Gothic style. Barry, eschewing his Italianate past, won, his proposals greatly enhanced by Pugin's meticulous drawings. The palace was officially opened by Queen Victoria in 1852, and Barry was knighted shortly afterwards. However, the stress generated by a project of such size took its toll. Worn out, he died at his home beside **Clapham Common** on 12 May 1860 and was buried in **Westminster Abbey**. (*See also* ALBERT, PRINCE; LIVERPOOL STREET STATION; TRAFALGAR SQUARE; TREASURY BUILDINGS; WESTMINSTER BRIDGE.)

BARTHOLOMEW FAIR. In 1133, King Henry I gave St. Bartholomew's Priory, at Smithfield, a charter entitling it to hold an annual fair for three days from St. Bartholomew's Eve (24 August). Very quickly, the event evolved into the largest cloth fair in England, but by 1604, when the **Corporation of London** became responsible for its organization, it had become better known for its fire eaters, theater groups, and other entertainers than for the goods on sale. During the 19th century, it gained a reputation for drunkenness and disorder, so the authorities closed it down in 1855, but it was resurrected on a small scale in 2000 as a means of raising money for the Butchers and Drovers Charitable Institute. (*See also* SMITHFIELD MEAT MARKET.)

BATTERSEA. Located on the south bank of the **River Thames** some three miles southwest of **Charing Cross**, Battersea has been settled since prehistoric times (the evidence includes a magnificently decorated Iron

Age shield, found in 1857 and now in the **British Museum**). It is mentioned in a charter of 693 A.D. that acknowledges that *Batrices Ege* (or Badric's Island) was owned by the Abbess of Barking, has been served by St. Mary's Church since before England's conquest by the Normans in 1066, but retained a distinctiveness throughout the Middle Ages because the river and its marshes made access difficult. Fertile soil led to the growth of a market gardening industry, selling produce to the ever increasing London population, and from the 17th century, local industries developed, notably copper making, lime production, dockyard activities, and pottery (from 1753 to 1756, John Brooks perfected the art of printing transfers on china at his premises in York House, selling the products as Battersea Enamels). However, the transfer from agricultural to urban settlement stemmed largely from the opening of the London and Southampton **railway**'s terminus at **Nine Elms**, on the eastern fringe of the area, in 1838. The station, and its associated engine repair facilities, provided jobs in numbers that greatly exceeded the limited local labor supply, so houses had to be built for incoming workers and services were established to meet their needs. In addition, ancillary industries (such as candle making, chemical production, and gas manufacture) sprang up, attracting additional migrants.

Between 1801 and 1901, Battersea's population increased from just over 3,000 to nearly 170,000 lowly paid and ill-educated manual workers and their families. Much of the formerly open land was covered in rows of terraced housing, as large estates in the south of the area were sold off to developers and the fields and market gardens in the north were snapped up by builders. As a result, little of the older, pre-industrial Battersea remains apart from St. Mary's Church (built in 1775–77 but incorporating elements of its predecessors, such as the 17th-century glass in the east window and the pre-Reformation bells). During the 20th century, the area has retained its reputation as a working-class community, but local authorities have made considerable improvements to the housing stock and provided more extensive community services, including libraries. The area is now part of the **London Borough of Wandsworth**. (*See also* BATTERSEA BRIDGE; BATTERSEA DOGS' HOME; BATTERSEA PARK; BATTERSEA POWER STATION; HARDIE, JAMES KEIR.)

BATTERSEA BRIDGE. The first bridge over the **River Thames** at **Battersea**, linking the small settlement to **Chelsea** (on the north bank of the river), was a wooden structure erected in 1771–72 to Henry Holland's plans. As the only road crossing between **Putney** and **Westminster**, it attracted a considerable volume of traffic but proved difficult to navigate, so it was demolished in 1881. Its cast iron replacement, built in 1886–90, had five arches and was designed by **Joseph William Bazalgette**, better known for his considerable contribution to London's 19th-century **sewage disposal** system. Houseboats have congregated at the northern end, some of them fetching as much as small apartments in neighboring blocks when they are placed on the market. The wrought iron **railway** bridge (sometimes known as the West London Extension Bridge), which also connects the two communities, was erected a few yards upriver in 1861 to allow the West London Railway to run services into the station at **Clapham Junction**.

BATTERSEA DOGS' HOME. A charitable organization originally founded by Mary Tealby in 1860, the home is London's main rescue center for unwanted dogs and cats. It was initially based in **Holloway** but generated so much noise that Mrs. Tealby had to move her 200 animals to a more accommodating site at **Battersea** in 1871. Thirteen years later, the Prince of Wales became the institution's patron, setting a precedent for royal support, which was followed by Queen Victoria (1885) and Queen Elizabeth II (1956). Critics scoffed at the concept of an institution dedicated to the care of strays, but through high health standards and sustained publicity it has done much to shape a more responsible approach to pet ownership. As a result, it has some 500 dogs and cats to offer to visitors every day at its premises in Battersea Park Road.

BATTERSEA PARK. During the early 19th century, the common lands along the south bank of the **River Thames** at **Battersea** earned a raffish reputation. Fairs attracted thousands of visitors who lost their money gambling, drank too much at the Red House Tavern, and patronized dubious fortune tellers. Fights were common (the Duke of Wellington and Lord Winchelsea fought a duel there in 1829), so the government was eventually forced to take action and, in 1846 (following a suggestion from **Thomas Cubitt**), encouraged Parliament to pass legislation establishing a park on the site. Under James Pennethorne's direction, a total of 198 acres was laid out, then opened to the public in 1853. Seven years later, a lake was added and, in 1864, a subtropical garden was created. An oasis of green space in a predominantly working-class area, the grounds were immediately popular. They were redesigned by Osbert Lancaster for the **Festival of Britain** in 1951 and now include tennis courts, a running track, playing fields, and a pagoda built in 1985 by Buddhist monks.

BATTERSEA POWER STATION. One of London's best-known landmarks, the coal-fired **electricity** generating plant on the south bank of the **River Thames** little more than a mile southwest of the Houses of Parliament (*see* **Palace of Westminster**) was designed by **Giles Gilbert Scott** (who was also responsible for the repair work to the **Guildhall** after the Second World War). It opened in 1933, with one 300-foot-high chimney at each end, but doubled in size during the 1940s, when two additional chimneys were built. In an attempt to limit **air pollution**, sulfur and other contaminants were removed before the smoke issued into the atmosphere, but, even so, local residents suffered much inconvenience from the large industrial site on their doorsteps. The plant closed in 1983, superseded by more efficient means of producing power, and was taken over by the Roche Consortium, a development company that intended to convert it into a theme park but ran out of funds in 1991. In 2000, however, the **London Borough of Wandsworth** approved plans by Parkview Holdings to redevelop the 35-acre site as a restaurant and leisure complex at an estimated cost of £500 million.

BAYSWATER. The area bounded by **Kensington Gardens** and **Hyde Park** (to the south) and **Paddington** (to the north) takes its name from Bayard's Watering Place, a spring where riders allowed their horses to drink. It developed as London expanded during the early 19th century, with wealthy City workers buying large houses with adequate room for servants and family. However, after the First World War, economic circumstances changed and the more affluent social groups moved to smaller homes in suburban locations. Many of their former properties in Bayswater were demolished to make way for tower blocks or townhouses, others converted for use as guest houses and small **hotels** or subdivided into rented apartments.

BAZALGETTE, JOSEPH WILLIAM (1819–1891). Bazalgette, engineer to the **Metropolitan Board of Works**, was responsible for providing the framework of the **sewage disposal** system, which still serves central London. Born in **Enfield** on 28 March 1819, he was the son of Joseph William Bazalgette (whose father had arrived from France 25 years earlier) and his wife, Theresa. Educated privately, he became a pupil of civil engineer John McNeill in 1836 then established his own business in **Westminster** in 1842. He was appointed Assistant Surveyor to the Metropolitan Commission of Sewers in 1849, promoted to Engineer in 1852, and employed by the Metropolitan Board of Works in 1856 with responsibility for street improvements and lighting, river bridges, tunnels, road building, and **flood control** over 117 square miles of London. The board's principal concern at the time was public health, so plans to deal with the growing problem caused by sewage had a high priority (Bazalgette reported to a Royal Commission in 1888 that effluent "kept oscillating up and down the river, while more filth was being constantly added to it, until the Thames became absolutely pestilential"). Despite the difficulty of constructing pipelines in a densely populated area, 80 miles of brick intercepting sewers were laid (with a fall of two feet per mile from west to east) and connected to outfall sewers attached to pumping stations. Work began in 1859 and was completed south of the river in 1864, but the system on the more urbanized north bank was not fully operational until 1875.

Bazalgette was also responsible for the Albert, **Chelsea**, and Victoria Embankments. Construction of the Victoria Embankment, which runs for 1.25 miles along the river eastwards from **Westminster Bridge** to Blackfriars Bridge, was preceded by tortuous negotiations with coal wharf operators, railway authorities, the City Gas Company, and other interests. The building process (which began in 1864) was complex, involving incorporation of a low-level sewer, difficulties in acquiring granite for facing stone, and problems with contractors (who were unwilling to use material dredged from the Thames as fill behind the new wall) but was completed in 1870. On the south side of the river, the one-mile Albert Embankment, between Westminster Bridge and Vauxhall Bridge, was begun in 1865 and finished three years later, with the project producing sufficient reclaimed marshland to provide a site for St. Thomas's Hospital. The 0.75-mile Chelsea Embankment, between **Chelsea Bridge** and **Battersea Bridge**, was built between 1871 and 1874, covering the main sewer for the area. In addition, Bazalgette supervised work on 12 river **bridges** bought by the board from private owners from 1877 and designed replacement crossings at **Battersea**, **Putney**, and **Hammersmith**. Also, he worked with architects to plan new roads: Queen Victoria Street (opened in 1871), Northumberland Avenue (1876), **Shaftesbury Avenue** (1886), **Charing Cross Road** (1887), and several other important thoroughfares, still much used, greatly facilitated travel in the growing metropolis.

In addition to his commitments in London, Bazalgette also contributed to improvements in other cities, reporting on drainage at Oxford, Glasgow, and other centers, as well as preparing plans for schemes at Odessa (in Ukraine) and Port Louis (Mauritius). A man with great technical ability and considerable diplomatic skill, he was made a Companion of the Bath in 1871, awarded a knighthood in 1874, and elected President of the Institution of Civil Engineers in 1884. He retired in 1889 and died at his home in **Wimbledon** on 15 March 1891.

BECKENHAM. A predominantly middle-class residential area lying to the northwest of the **London Borough of Bromley**, Beckenham derives its name from the Old English *Beohha* (probably one of the individuals who farmed the land) and *ham* (meaning "village"). Although the 13th-century lich gate at St. George's Church is claimed to be the oldest in England, most of the buildings were erected during the 19th and 20th centuries, as **railways**, **buses**, and automobiles enabled workers to commute to jobs in the inner city. Local employment is largely in service industries, including **local government**, education, retail provision, and professional concerns (such as those of accountants, lawyers, and realtors). (*See also* BEDLAM.)

BECKTON. In 1870, the Gas Light and Coke Company built a new plant, intended to serve the whole of London, on the north bank of the **River Thames** some 10 miles east of **Charing Cross**. The site was named after the company's Governor, Simon Adams Beck, who had a distinctively humane view of employer/employee relationships, building a village with two churches and a meeting hall for his workers. Within a few years, a sizeable manufacturing complex had developed, converting the by-products of gas production into fertilizer, ammonia, and other commodities. Further construction took place after the opening of the Royal Albert Dock in 1881 (the new estate was called Cyprus to commemorate Britain's capture of that Mediterranean island in 1878), but residential development was restricted because most of the land was used for industrial purposes by the **Port of London Authority**. However, after the introduction of natural **gas** had caused the closure of the town gas plant in 1969 and the Royal Albert Dock had followed 12 years later as harbor services were rationalized, the London Docklands Development Corporation (*see* **Docklands**), formed in 1981, prepared plans for additional homes and improved **transport** infrastructure, as well as two secondary schools. The major source of employment now is sewage treatment (the Beckton plant is one of Europe's largest).

BEDFORD ESTATES. During the 16th century, the Russell family was given title to the earldom of Bedford. In succeeding centuries, it acquired extensive estates in London, notably at **Covent Garden** (which was gifted to John, the first Earl, in 1552 in return for services to King Edward VI) and **Bloomsbury** (which was acquired through marriage in 1669). The former was sold in 1914 and the latter greatly reduced as educational institutions (such as the **British Museum** and the University of London) bought or leased the land from 1755, but the owners are remembered in many of the street names (Bedford Place, for example, links Bloomsbury Square with **Russell Square**). Bedford Square is one of the city's finest Georgian designs. Laid out by builders William Scott and Thomas Crewer in 1755–80, and probably planned by Thomas Leverton, it consists largely of brick houses, but the central building on each side is emphasized by its stucco finish. Residents have included two Lord Chancellors (Lord Loughborough at No. 6 from 1787 to 1796 and Lord Eldon at the same address from 1804 to 1819) and former Prime Minister Herbert Asquith (at No. 44 from 1921 to 1924). Most of the former homes have now been converted into office space.

BEDLAM. During the late 14th century, the hospital at St. Mary Bethlehem Priory, outside the **Bishop's Gate**, began to provide accommodation for the mentally ill (that provision was basic and hardly humane by modern standards; patients were chained to walls and whipped when they caused problems). In 1547, following the dissolution of the English **monasteries**, the **Corporation of London** bought the buildings (by that time known as Bedlam) from King Henry VIII, converting them into an asylum for lunatics. The hospital moved to Moorfields in 1557 and proved a popular attraction for city residents, who strolled along walkways as they viewed inmates housed in cages. Donations from the visitors provided the institution with a large proportion of its funds until 1770, when changing public attitudes encouraged the management to provide greater privacy for the people in their care. In 1800, the structure of the old hospital was declared unsafe so, 15 years later, the 122 patients were transferred to newly constructed premises in **Lambeth**. Provision for the criminally insane was added in 1816, then in 1835 the building was extended again, but changing medical standards led to further moves, after the First World War, to suburban sites. The Royal Bethlehem is now located at **Beckenham**, at the southeastern edge of London, and is linked to the nearby Maudsley Hospital, founded in 1916 and now the United Kingdom's major center of psychiatric research. The **Imperial War Museum** occupies part of the former Lambeth site. (*See also* PUGIN, AUGUSTUS WELBY NORTHMORE.)

BEEFEATER. Although the men who guard the **Tower of London** are formally termed Yeomen Warders of the Tower, they are usually known as Beefeaters. Founded by King Edward VI in the mid-16th century, they still wear the red uniform that distinguished them in Tudor times. Their popular name may derive from a partiality for roast beef, but some writers have suggested other sources for the word. For example, "eater" (derived from the Old English *oeta*) was employed as a synonym for "servant" 50 years after the corps was established; beefeater may have been a derogatory term used with reference to well-fed members of the royal household who performed menial duties. Now, all appointees are former warrant officers in the army or the Royal Air Force and modern security systems have rendered their duties largely ceremonial. (*See also* CEREMONY OF THE KEYS.)

BEEFSTEAK CLUB. In 1735, John Rich (founder of the **Covent Garden** theater now known as the **Royal Opera House**) and George Lambert (a scenery painter) formed a society for 24 gentlemen of noble birth. From November until June, they met every Saturday for a beefsteak dinner and convivial conversation. The society disbanded in 1866 but was succeeded by a club that intended to keep the name alive. It formed on 11 March 1866 and moved to its present home (one room above a shop in Ingram Street) 30 years later. Members include representatives of politics, the arts, and education. As they arrive for their meal, they sit at a single long table in the order in which they appear. All the waiters are called Charles.

***BELFAST,* HMS.** At 11,000 tons, the *Belfast* was the largest cruiser ever built for the Royal Navy. Launched in 1938, she saw service during the Second World War guarding Arctic convoys, took part in the Battle of North Cape on 26 December 1943 (when the German battle cruiser *Scharnhorst* was sunk), and assisted at the D-Day landings on the Normandy beaches in 1944. Her last action was in the Korean War (1950–53). After being taken out of service, she was berthed on the **River Thames** at Symon's Wharf (upstream of **Tower Bridge**) in 1971 and opened to the public, the first naval vessel to be preserved since the *Victory*, Horatio Nelson's flagship at the Battle of Trafalgar in 1805. She was refitted at Portsmouth in 1999.

BELGRAVIA. An affluent residential area between **Victoria** and **Hyde Park**, Belgravia was developed by the Grosvenor family (*see*

Grosvenor Estate), taking its name from Belgrave, their Leicestershire home. Construction began during the 1820s, with development regulated by **Thomas Cubitt**, who erected rows of terraced houses focusing on Belgrave Square at the same time as **John Nash** was building **Buckingham Palace** immediately to the east. By the second half of the 19th century, it was extremely fashionable with wealthy Londoners, a status that has been retained despite the incursion of embassy buildings and conversion of some dwellings to offices for bodies such as the Country Landowners' Association and the Royal College of Veterinary Surgeons. Belgravia forms part of the **City of Westminster**.

BERKELEY SQUARE. Lying in the heart of **Mayfair**, the square takes its name from Lord Berkeley of Stratton, a supporter of King Charles II who acquired land to the north of **Piccadilly** after the English monarchy was restored in 1660. It was laid out from 1739 as a quadrilateral, rather than a square, preserving the views from Berkeley House, which had been built 70 years earlier. During the 20th century, however, the architectural integrity of the Georgian development was destroyed. The buildings on the east side were removed and replaced by a car showroom. The gardens of Lansdowne House, to the south, are now an office block, and much of the north is also commercial accommodation. A glimpse of the original setting is gained only in the west (where No. 44 was described by architectural historian Nikolaus Pevsner as "the best terraced house of London") and in the center, which is dominated by 30 fine **London plane** trees planted in 1789. There is no recent record of a nightingale's song.

BERMONDSEY. Bermondsey forms the northern part of the **London Borough of Southwark**, stretching along the banks of the **River Thames** from **London Bridge** (in the west) to **Rotherhithe** (in the east). Settlement began in 1082, when a priory, dedicated to St. Saviour, was founded amidst the marshlands. The Cluniac monks built embankments to prevent the river from flooding, grew crops on the reclaimed land, established a monastic school, and cared for the needy, so, by 1536, when King Henry VIII began to close the English **monasteries**, a sizeable community had developed. During the 17th century, pleasure gardens were laid out, then, in 1770, the discovery of a chalybeate spring with allegedly health-giving properties led to the development of a spa, but within half a century, the area was totally transformed by the growing **dock** trade, which converted it into a warren of industrial premises, including **breweries**, warehouses, and manufacturers of leather goods. In 1836, the first **railway** line in the metropolis opened, running from Bermondsey to **Deptford** on a four-mile viaduct with 878 arches. A branch to **Croydon** was completed three years later, emphasizing the district's importance as a transport focus. After the Second World War, however, the harbor activities declined, allowing public and private concerns to initiate major land use changes, with offices, retail facilities, and **housing** replacing the 19th-century slums. The modern complex—known as London Bridge City—incorporates Hay's Wharf, the oldest in the **Pool of London**, where the dock has been filled in, creating a piazza that is covered by a glass roof and lined with restaurants, specialty stores, and wine bars. A pier has been built to facilitate passenger transport along the river, and **HMS *Belfast*** and the **London Dungeon** provide foci for tourists. (*See also* TOWER BRIDGE.)

BETHLEHEM ROYAL HOSPITAL. *See* BEDLAM.

BETHNAL GREEN. Bethnal Green is the archetypal **East End** suburb—working-class, with a high proportion of local authority **housing** and heavy dependence on social services. At the beginning of the 18th century, it was largely agricultural land, but the growth of the textile industry (expanding from its base in **Spitalfields**) initiated a process of urbanization, so by 1743 there was an estimated population of 15,000 weavers, dyers, and their families. Incomes were low (after a visit in 1777, John Wesley, founder of the Methodist faith with his brother Charles, wrote of "such poverty as few can conceive without seeing it"). As a result, the declining demand for silk from about 1840 caused much distress, leading **Charles Booth** to allege, in 1889, that 45 percent of the inhabitants were living in circumstances below subsistence level. Victorian philanthropists attempted to alleviate the worst effects by building blocks of apartments that could be let at affordable rents, providing educational facilities (*see*, for example, **Bethnal Green Museum of Childhood**) and introducing recreational facilities, such as **Victoria Park**. Major improvement, however, did not begin until the **London County Council** initiated a slum clearance project shortly after its creation in 1888, beginning with the construction of the Boundary Street Estate in the area known as Old Nichol, which was notorious for both its high **crime** rate and its poor living conditions. Over the next century, local authority building programs replaced the substandard 19th-century properties and the population declined as residents were moved to new homes on the outskirts of the city. Since the 1970s, there has been a process of gentrification, as the older properties that remain have been improved and purchased by young people or by others looking for relatively inexpensive accommodation close to central London. Bethnal Green is now part of the **London Borough of Tower Hamlets,** but incomes are still low, so family spending power is limited and retail services reflect the lack of wealth. (*See also* AIR RAIDS.)

BETHNAL GREEN MUSEUM OF CHILDHOOD. The museum—one of the largest of its kind in the world—contains model trains, dolls (some straight from the box, others clearly much loved), dolls' houses (the earliest dating from 1673), teddy bears, and some 4,000 other playthings. In addition, there are displays focusing on changing fashions in children's clothes, books (there are over 100,000 examples), and educational toys. The exhibits (which form part of the **Victoria and Albert Museum**'s collections) are housed in a prefabricated iron structure originally erected at south **Kensington** in 1856 but moved to the **East End** a decade later and clothed in brick. For the next century, its galleries emphasized agricultural products and art works but, since 1974, it has concentrated solely on aspects of childhood. (*See also* BETHNAL GREEN.)

BEXLEY, LONDON BOROUGH OF. When **local government** within the metropolitan area was reorganized in 1965, Bexley was created from the formerly independent boroughs of Bexley and **Erith**, along with **Crayford** and parts of Chislehurst and Sidcup, all of which were previously in the County of Kent. Covering 23 square miles, it had a population of some 217,800 in 1998. The north of the borough, fronting the **River Thames**, is dominated by industrial sites and the large **Thamesmead** housing development, which was built on reclaimed marshland from 1967 and planned by the **Greater London Council** as an integrated community with schools, shops, and businesses, as well as homes. However, at the end of the century, unemployment was high and racist attacks on nonwhite groups (who comprised about 15 percent of the residents) were common. Crayford, too, has a large working-class community, with chemical works and plastics factories forming an important element of the local economy, but the rest of the borough is relatively affluent, with large numbers of professional workers and high rates of home ownership. Major road and **railway** links from central London to the Kent coast connect the east and west of the borough but transport from north to south is slower, limiting communication.

BIG BANG. In the autumn of 1986, a series of reforms radically altered the operation and structure of financial institutions in the **City of London**. For some time, the City had been experiencing a relative decline in its securities trade compared with New York and Tokyo. Moreover, Prime Minister Margaret Thatcher's government was concerned about restrictive practices in the major money markets, and computerized dealing was threatening the tradition of face-to-face transactions on the **Stock Exchange**. The Financial Services Act of 1986 introduced legislation that altered the United Kingdom's system of regulating investment business, increasing competition and allowing foreign interests greater access to British commerce. Although many of the new ways of working were introduced gradually, most became effective from 27 October. On that date, the Stock Exchange converted to electronic dealing from the offices of member firms, which, for the first time, could be owned by outside corporations, enabling them to build a larger capital base. Fixed-rate commissions were abolished (thus enabling dealers to compete with one another), the distinction between brokers (who bought and sold shares on behalf of clients) and jobbers (who acted as middlemen between brokers) ended, and banks were permitted to buy stock-broking firms. The impact on employees' duties and lifestyles was considerable, but, for the firms and their customers, the overall effect was beneficial. The market expanded smoothly, average commissions lowered, and securities firms were considerably strengthened by an influx of funds. As a result, by the mid-1990s, London was clearly the major center of European investment banking, although many of its major institutions were wholly, or partly, controlled from abroad.

BIG BEN. Although the nickname "Big Ben" is usually given to the 320-foot-high clock tower at the eastern end of the **Palace of Westminster**, it is more properly applied to the 13.5-ton bell that is housed inside the tower. The clock, designed by E. J. Dent and completed in 1854, has a six-hundredweight pendulum regulated by a scape wheel weighing just one-quarter of an ounce. Each of the four dials is 23 feet in diameter, with figures two feet high. The hour hands are nine feet long and the minute hands 14 feet long. The bell, cast at **Whitechapel** in 1858 after an earlier attempt by Warner of Stockton-on-Tees had proved unsatisfactory, is decorated with the Royal Arms and the Portcullis of Westminster. An inscription around the rim reads, "This bell was cast by George Mears of Whitechapel for the clock of the Houses of Parliament under the Direction of Edmund Becket Denison QC in the 21st year of the reign of

Queen Victoria in the year of our Lord MDCCCLVIII." There is some controversy about the means by which it got its name. Some writers claim that, during a debate on the naming of the bell in the House of Commons, Sir Benjamin Hall (Chief Commissioner for Works) was speaking when an MP shouted out, "Why not call it Big Ben?" The story is attractive but, unfortunately, there is no corroborating evidence in *Hansard,* the official record of Parliamentary proceedings. A second theory suggests that it is named after the 250-pound prize fighter Benjamin Caunt, who retired at the time the bell was being made.

The clock was started on 31 May 1859, but the bell developed a crack after only a few months and had to be fitted with a smaller hammer. Automatic winding gear was installed in 1913 (until then, it took two men 32 hours to wind it manually) and the operating mechanism was overhauled in 1956, when three of the faces were reglazed. It has proved remarkably accurate; even the air raid that destroyed much of the Parliament building on 10 May 1941 knocked it awry by only one and a half seconds.

BIGGIN HILL. Located on the southeast fringe of London, about 15 miles from **Charing Cross**, Biggin Hill is an indirect result of the invention of the airplane. During the first decade of the 20th century, there was little urban development in the area, so John Westacott, a local farmer, allowed pilots to land aircraft on one of his fields. However, when the First World War began, the strip was commandeered for emergency landings, a wireless testing station was built, and courses in telegraphy were established. As a result, the strategic importance of the aerodrome was enhanced, necessitating improved road access and **housing** for employees. Further expansion was undertaken in the 1920s, causing the settlement to increase both in extent and in population, but, although Royal Air Force Spitfires and Hurricanes based at Biggin Hill played a prominent role in the Battle of Britain (1940), most of the planes left after the Second World War ended in 1945. The aerodrome still operates, primarily for private flights, although there are some scheduled services to France, and the community (now housing many commuters who work in central London) has experienced significant growth as a result of public and private investment since the 1950s. (*See also* AIRPORTS.)

BILLINGSGATE FISH MARKET. In the early ninth century, fishing boats were tied up at the Billingsgate quays, on the north bank of the **River Thames** just downstream from **London Bridge**, and captains sold their catch on the street. More than a millennium later, despite the importance of the market, facilities amounted to little more than a series of sheds, where wholesalers and retailers could inspect the fish and strike deals. However, growing sales, fuelled by rapidly increasing urban populations, required better premises so, in 1877, the **Corporation of London** opened a trading hall (designed by Horace Jones) on the site. It was never satisfactory. During the 20th century, commercial conditions became increasingly difficult because the large refrigerated lorries that took the fish throughout Britain had problems negotiating the confined streets in the **City of London**, closely packed buildings made expansion of parking space impossible, the pervasive smell annoyed owners of nearby businesses, and the colorful language of the porters offended many workers commuting to the finance houses in the **Square Mile**. As a result, in January 1982 the market was moved to a 13.5-acre site on the **Isle of Dogs** and the old brick building, with its arcades of cast iron pillars, was bought by the London and Edinburgh Investment Trust for conversion into offices. The market has been open to visitors, as well as commercial interests, since 1698, when an Act of Parliament put an end to control of sales by a small group of retailers.

BIRDCAGE WALK. With buildings on one side only, Birdcage Walk runs along the southern edge of **St. James's Park** in central London, getting its name from the aviaries that King James VI and I maintained on the site. Until 1828, the only person, apart from members of the royal family, who could use the street was the Duke of St. Albans, Hereditary Grand Falconer to the monarch. Much of the southern side is occupied by Wellington Barracks (home of the Foot Guards); the remainder is largely garden space at the rear of the 18th-century houses in Queen Anne's Gate. (*See also* CHANGING OF THE GUARD.)

BISHOP'S GATE. One of the northern entrances to the Roman city of **Londinium**, Bishop's Gate was the point at which Ermine Street, one of the invaders' principal routes to their British frontier, left the settlement. It stood where the modern road that bears its name meets Camomile Street, just south of **Liverpool Street Station**, and gets its appellation from Eorconweald, Bishop of London, who rebuilt it during the seventh century. In the 15th and 16th centuries, the area around the gate was a fashionable neighborhood for wealthy merchants, but the structure was demolished in 1760 and the traders' homes were replaced, over the next two hundred years, by offices and shops. (*See also* LONDON WALL.)

BLACK DEATH. From 1347 until 1351, much of Europe was ravaged by an epidemic of bubonic plague, which took a toll of life greater than that in any previous outbreak of disease (or war) on the continent. The illness was caused by a bacillus (*Yersinia pestis*) carried in the bloodstream of rats. Fleas that fed on the rats transferred the infection to humans, who suffered swellings (known as buboes), fever, thirst, hemorrhages, and delirium before dying. The plague reached London during the late summer of 1348 and spread rapidly through the city's overcrowded, densely packed homes, where sanitation was primitive. In January 1349, meetings of Parliament were cancelled because of the danger that members would fall ill, and by February the burial grounds were full. However, from the middle of the year, mortality levels decreased and, by the early 1350s, the epidemic had run its course (though there were recurrences in 1361 and 1368–69). Scholars have produced varying estimates of the death toll, with figures ranging from 50,000 to 100,000 people (as much as half of the city's total); in many cases, whole families were wiped out, along with many members of religious foundations who had tried to help the sick (all but one of the monks and nuns in the Hospital of St. James died, for example, as did the Abbot and 27 monks at the Monastery of Westminster). The impact of the disease was profound, affecting labor supply, wage structures, and food availability as well as the demography of the population. (*See also* GREAT PLAGUE; HAMPSTEAD; PEASANTS' REVOLT.)

BLACKFRIARS. The Blackfriars area of the **City of London**, lying about a mile east of **Charing Cross**, takes its name from the Dominican monks who, in 1221, established a **monastery** in Shoe Lane. For more than three centuries, the settlement benefited from the patronage of royalty and, frequently, was the setting for events that shaped the history of England (Parliament met there in 1311, 1450, and 1529, for example, and, in 1382, a council summoned by the Archbishop of Canterbury convened at Blackfriars to consider the allegedly heretical teachings of John Wycliffe, who had argued that there was no biblical basis for the Pope's authority over the Roman Catholic Church). In 1538, however, it was dissolved during King Henry VIII's campaign to establish a Church of England free of Catholic influences and most of the buildings were demolished. (Part of the site is now occupied by an art nouveau style **public house**—the Black Friar—which was built in 1875; the bars are decorated with marble and with bronze figures of the monks at work.) In 1577, a **theater** opened in Playhouse Yard, attracting the city's literati, so, by the early 17th century, the area had acquired a reputation as a fashionable place to live (playwrights **Ben Jonson** and **William Shakespeare** had homes there, as did artist Anthony van Dyke).

Puritan zealots, more Calvinist and less tolerant of lax lifestyles, put an end to the entertainments in 1642, initiating a lengthy period during which industrial and commercial activities increasingly dominated residential uses (in *David Copperfield,* published in 1850, author **Charles Dickens** describes the miserable conditions in which boys washed and labelled bottles in a Victorian warehouse in Blackfriars). Those land uses, in turn, attracted growing amounts of traffic and led to the evolution of a significant route focus. In 1760, work started on a **bridge**, only the third to link the north and south banks of the **River Thames** in the immediate vicinity of London. It opened to traffic in 1769 but was replaced exactly a century later by the present wrought iron structure, faced with cast iron and standing on piers of Aberdeen granite, which was designed by Joseph Cubitt. In 1864, a wrought iron **railway** bridge carried the London, Chatham and Dover, company's lines across the river to meet the Metropolitan Railway at Blackfriars. A second was built a few yards downriver for the Holborn Viaduct Station Company in 1886, and a terminus, originally known as St. Paul's but renamed Blackfriars in 1937, was opened by the London, Chatham, and Dover the same year and substantially remodelled in 1977.

Because of its economic importance, the area suffered considerably during the **Blitz** and was substantially redeveloped afterwards (St. Andrew by the Wardrobe, **Christopher Wren**'s last church in **The City**, built in 1685–95, was damaged by bombs in 1940 and reerected, to plans prepared by Marshall Sisson, in 1959–61, for instance). (*See also* PRINTING HOUSE SQUARE; *TIMES, THE.*)

BLACKHEATH. Lying south of **Greenwich Park**, Blackheath straddles the main road from London to the cathedral city of Canterbury and the port of Dover. It derives its name either from the color of the soil or from a corruption of *bleak heath*. Because of its strategic location, it has a long history of settlement and of involvement in national affairs; the Romans and the Saxons built bases in the area, the Danes had an encampment during the early 11th century, Wat Tyler assembled his supporters there at the start of the **Peasants' Revolt**, Henry VIII welcomed Anne of Cleves (his fourth wife) to England at the heath in 1540, the country's first golf club was formed on the heath in 1608 (after King James VI and I had brought the sport from Scotland five years earlier), Charles II was hailed when he returned from the continent at the end of the period of Puritan rule in 1660, John Wesley attracted hundreds of Christian worshippers to revivalist meetings during the 17th century, and Blackheath Football Club (the oldest public rugby union club in London) was formed in 1858. Urban development did not really begin until the **railway** arrived in 1849 and was primarily residential in nature, with wealthy Victorians acquiring large houses for their families and servants close to the open space and woodland. Schools, a Literary Institution, a roller skating rink, a concert hall, and other social facilities followed, promoted by an educated population willing to support community growth. During the 20th century, many of the bigger homes have been converted into apartments, but the area has retained its reputation as a relatively affluent suburb, with local interest groups (such as the Blackheath Preservation Trust) providing effective lobbies for the conservation both of the heath and of the buildings that surround it. The suburb is part of the **London Borough of Greenwich.**

BLACKWALL. A district of the **London Borough of Tower Hamlets**, Blackwall is located on the north bank of the **River Thames** some five miles east of **Charing Cross**. A harbor was established by the late 16th century, proving popular because it afforded easy road access to the **City of London**, allowing travellers to avoid the lengthy journey around the **Isle of Dogs** in a sailing vessel. In 1606, the Virginia Settlers (led by Captain John Smith) left the port to found the first permanent English colony in North America; in 1661, the **East India Company** established a small wet **dock** (the first with gates to the Thames) to refit its fleet of trading vessels; and, in 1841, a **railway** augmented traffic by carrying passengers from London to the new steamer berths. In 1897, a 4,000-foot-long tunnel was opened under the river, connecting Blackwall to the south bank (70 years later, a counterpart was built a few yards downstream so that northbound and southbound traffic could be separated), then, during the last two decades of the 20th century, road access was further improved. However, the passenger pier was removed in 1956 to make way for an electricity generating station (demolished in 1991), and the docks were closed in 1980. The people who live in the area are almost entirely manual workers, although a few employees from Reuters news agency and other offices located nearby in the Isle of Dogs have found homes close to their work.

BLITZ. From 7 September 1940 until 11 May 1941, an estimated 18,800 tons of explosive were dropped on London by German bombers. According to conservative estimates, over 15,000 people were killed and 3.5 million homes damaged during the attacks, which became known as the Blitz (from the German *Blitzkrieg,* meaning "lightning war"). Some historians suggest that the number of deaths was closer to 30,000. The areas affected worst were industrial sectors of the city (such as the **East End** and the **docks**), transport nodes, and locations that had a psychological significance to the British people (including **Buckingham Palace**, which was hit on the night of 15–16 October).

Many children were evacuated to temporary homes in the countryside for the duration of the raids. At the sound of the sirens that signalled the start of an attack, those who stayed behind took refuge in communal shelters or in the **London Underground** system. For most of the time, they were safe, but occasionally bombs penetrated the defenses with devastating effect, as at Bank station in January 1941, when more than 100 people died. The economic and social impact of the bombing was enormous, with gas and electricity supplies disrupted, transport services at a standstill, offices demolished, and industrial premises destroyed, but the common experience bound Londoners together, promoting a sense of unity that helped to overcome the disasters. In 1999, Queen Elizabeth and the Queen Mother unveiled a memorial in the churchyard of **St. Paul's Cathedral** in honor of civilians who died in the Blitz (when the bomb struck Buckingham Palace, she responded with a comment that at least now she could look the East End in the face). (*See also* AIR RAIDS; BALHAM; BARBICAN; BIG BEN; BLACKFRIARS; BRITISH BROADCASTING CORPORATION [BBC]; CANNON STREET STATION; CHARTERHOUSE; CHELSEA; CLEOPATRA'S NEEDLE; COLE ABBEY CHURCH, DISTAFF LANE; CORN EXCHANGE; CRAYFORD; CROYDON; DEPTFORD; ELEPHANT AND CASTLE; GREYFRIARS MONASTERY; GUILDHALL; HOLLAND HOUSE; HOXTON; IMPERIAL WAR MUSEUM; KNIGHTS HOSPITALLER; LANGHAM HOTEL; LEYTON; MADAME TUSSAUD'S WAXWORKS; MILE END; PALACE OF WESTMINSTER; PROMS, THE; PUGIN, AUGUSTUS WELBY NORTHMORE; ST. ALFEGE'S CHURCH, GREENWICH; ST. ANDREW'S CHURCH, HOLBORN; ST. BRIDE'S CHURCH, FLEET STREET; ST. CLEMENT DANES CHURCH, STRAND; ST. ETHELDREDA'S CHURCH, HOLBORN; ST. JAMES'S CHURCH, PICCADILLY; ST. MARY ABCHURCH CHURCH, ABCHURCH LANE; ST. OLAVE'S CHURCH, HART STREET; SHAFTESBURY AVENUE; SHEPHERD'S BUSH; STEPNEY; TEMPLE CHURCH; WATERLOO.)

BLOOMSBURY. In 1545, Thomas Wriothesley, Lord Chancellor of England, purchased the Manor of Blemonsbury (located just outside the western walls of the **City of London**). His descendant—the fourth Earl of Southampton—rebuilt the manor house in 1660, then laid out a square (now known as Bloomsbury Square) to the south. Gradually, the urban area spread as other large properties were constructed nearby. Bloomsbury became a fashionable place in which to establish a home, with access to the court and business community but also with views of the countryside. By the early 18th century, the land had been acquired by the Russell family, who also owned **Covent Garden** and had an entrepreneurial approach to its estates. Wide routeways (such as Great Russell Street, Bedford Square, and Gower Street) were constructed and lined with homes for the wealthy, but narrower roads, with smaller houses, provided links between them, attracting writers, musicians, and artists who enjoyed the sense of intimacy (*see*, for example, **Bloomsbury Group**). Lawyers, too, were attracted to the area because of its proximity to the **Inns of Court**. However, the **British Musem** was established in Montague House in 1759, the buildings of University College began to rise above Gower Street in 1827, and Bedford College opened its doors to women students in 1849. The gradual encroachment of institutions encouraged most affluent residents to seek homes elsewhere, leaving their houses to be converted into small **hotels**, restaurants, bookshops, and educational facilities. During the 20th century, many of the Georgian buildings were demolished to make way for purpose-built academic premises, so the **architecture** of Bloomsbury is an often ill-matched mixture of styles. (*See also* BEDFORD ESTATES; PUGIN, AUGUSTUS WELBY NORTHMORE; RUSSELL SQUARE.)

BLOOMSBURY GROUP. In 1904, the Stephen family—Vanessa (who married art critic Clive Bell), Thoby, Virginia (who married socialist writer Leonard Woolf) and Adrian—moved into 46 Gordon Square, **Bloomsbury**. They became the core of a group of artists, authors, and others who earned a reputation for their bohemian lifestyle and radical approach to philosophical issues. The underlying ethic, outlined by G. E. Moore, was that "by far the most valuable things . . . are . . . the pleasures of human intercourse and the enjoyment of beautiful objects. . . . It is they . . . that form the rational ultimate end of social progress." Members of the clique (most of whom had studied at Cambridge University) included novelist E. M. Forster, biographer Lytton Strachey, economist John Maynard Keynes, and artist Duncan Grant. For a quarter of a century, they met to discuss agnosticism, the nature of beauty, and other philosophical issues but, by the 1930s, they had merged with London's literary mainstream and lost their identity. The Bloomsberries, as they were nicknamed, did not form a distinct school but were significant because of the high number of richly talented individuals involved.

BLUE PLAQUES. Many London buildings bear a blue plaque, erected to commemorate some significant individual or event associated with the property. The first, mounted by the Society for the Encouragement of Arts, Manufactures, and Commerce (*see* **Royal Society of Arts**) to honor poet Lord Byron, appeared in 1866, but English Heritage (funded by the government) now assumes responsibility for their erection. About 400 individuals have been deemed worthy of recognition, including inventor John Logie Baird (who first demonstrated television transmissions at 22 Frith Street), author **Charles Dickens** (who lived at 48 Doughty Street), actor Charlie Chaplin (who lived at 287 Kensington Road), and Prime Minister Winston Churchill (whose home was at 34 Eccleston Square). In 1971, the **Greater London Council** approved recognition of foreigners, allowing plaques to be placed on 28 Dean Street, 36 Craven Street, and 23 Tedworth Square, the houses of political philosopher Karl Marx, United States's consitutionalist Benjamin Franklin, and author Mark Twain respectively. The only bases for selection are that individuals must have been dead for 20 years, eminent in their chosen fields, well known to the lay public, and deserving of recognition—criteria that have resulted in a dominance of plaques commemorating politicians and literary figures.

BOADICEA. Boadicea (or Boudicca) was Queen of the Celtic Iceni tribe, which occupied much of East Anglia during the first century A.D. When her husband, King Prasutagas, died in 60 A.D., he left part of his estate to Nero, the Roman emperor, hoping that the bequest to his imperial master would ensure protection for his family. That gesture was in vain because the Romans publicly flogged Boadicea and raped her two daughters, provoking a revolt. The Iceni pillaged the countryside and marched on **Londinium**, from which Suetonius Paulinus, the governor, withdrew his armies in the face of overwhelming numbers, leaving the settlement and its residents to their fate. Wreaking revenge for her humiliation, Boadicea led her people on an unrestrained rampage, killing 30,000 citizens and burning the city (modern archaeologists have identified a layer of reddish soil, over a foot thick, which consists of debris from the fires). The victory celebrations were short-lived, however. Gathering his forces, Suetonius pursued Boadicea northwards and, at an as yet unidentified site named Mandessum, destroyed 80,000 of her followers in battle. According to Tacitus, the Roman historian, Boadicea poisoned herself rather than submit to the enemy. A bronze of the Queen, standing in a chariot, her daughters beside her, was cast by Thomas Thorneycroft and erected at the north end of **Westminster Bridge** in 1902.

BOAT RACES. *See* DOGGETT'S COAT AND BADGE RACE; UNIVERSITY BOAT RACE.

BOND STREET. Housing some of the most expensive shops in London, Bond Street crosses **Mayfair** from north to south. Old Bond Street, between **Piccadilly** and Burlington Gardens, was developed during the late 17th century as a speculative development funded largely by Sir Thomas Bond, from whom it gets its name. The rest of the street (known as New Bond Street) was built while London was experiencing a period of considerable westward expansion in the 1720s. Mayfair's growing population attracted jewelers, art dealers, auctioneers, hosiers, tobacconists, and a chocolatier, all selling luxury goods to an affluent clientele, as well as such distinguished residents as essayist **James Boswell**, Emma Hamilton (Horatio Nelson's mistress), and Victorian actor Sir Henry Irving. Much rebuilding and reconstruction has taken place during the 20th century, but the narrow road has retained its fashionable status with Asprey's (founded in 1781) selling gold and silver at 165–166 New Bond Street, the Fine Arts Society (established in 1876) specializing in British paintings at 147 New Bond Street, H. M. Rayne (in business since 1889) offering handcrafted shoes at 16 Old Bond Street, and Truefitt and Hill (wigmakers to King George IV) cutting gentlemen's hair at 23 Old Bond Street.

BOODLE'S. Founded as an apolitical **gentlemen's club** by Edward Boodle in 1762, Boodle's now has a membership consisting largely of non-Londoners who visit the city on business. Its first premises were in **Pall Mall** but, in 1783, it moved to its present premises in St. James's Street. Members have included dandy Beau Brummell, anti-slavery campaigner William Wilberforce, and Prime Ministers William Pitt the Elder and William Pitt the Younger.

BOOTH, CHARLES (1840–1916). During the second half of the 19th century, writers and political activists voiced growing concern about the condition of London's poor (*see*, for example, **Thomas John Barnardo**, **William Booth**, and **George Peabody**). The force of their arguments was given added strength by the work of Charles Booth, who combined detailed observation with sound statistical methodology to present a depressing picture of the living conditions of the city's most destitute residents. Booth was born in Liverpool on 30 March 1840, the third son of corn merchant Charles Booth and Emily (his first wife). He was educated at the Royal Institution School then, in 1862, joined Alfred, his eldest brother, as a partner in a steamship company. Over the next 50 years, his business affairs flourished, giving him both the wealth and the time to pursue an interest in the impact of the Industrial Revolution on the British labor force. Although opposed to socialism because it implied that commercial transactions would not be "tried in the court of profit and loss," he was deeply concerned about the welfare of his employees, so, during the 1880s, he began a study of people in the **docks** area of the city's **East End**.

The fruits of Booth's efforts were the 17 volumes of *Life and Labour of the People in London*, which were published between 1889 and 1903. Relying partly on visits to deprived communities, partly on official data, and partly on information from charitable organizations, he attempted to demonstrate "the numerical relation which poverty, misery, and depravity bear to regular earnings and comparative comfort," using a series of colored maps to show the extent of poverty street by street. The work was essentially descriptive, making little attempt to identify the causes of poverty or to advance an agenda for reform, but its detail provided fuel for proponents of change, such as Beatrice Webb (a cousin of Booth's wife, Mary). His scientific contributions were rewarded with the presidency of the Royal Statistical Society (1892–94) and a Fellowship of the **Royal Society** (1899). Also, he was made a Privy Councillor in 1904, appointed to the Royal Commission on the Poor Law in 1905 (becoming a strong advocate of the introduction of pensions for the elderly), and given the first honorary degree awarded by the University of Liverpool in 1906. Booth died at his home in Whitwick (near Leicester) on 23 November 1916.

BOOTH, WILLIAM (1829–1912). During the second half of the 19th century, several social reformers were attempting to improve the standard of living of London's poor (*see*, for example, **Thomas John Barnardo** and **George Peabody**). Booth was one of that group, motivated by Christian principles to alter social and moral conditions through the foundation of a Salvation Army. Born in Nottingham on 10 April 1829, the only son of an unsuccessful pawnbroker, he received little schooling but was much affected by the oratory of Methodist preachers who delivered sermons in local halls and chapels. In 1844, he committed himself to the Christian faith and, two years later (still only 17), began to organize services. His religious activities brought no financial reward so, in 1849, he moved to London, where he found a job at a Walworth pawn shop. Booth hated the work, arguing that it exploited those people least able to help themselves, but he used the income to support his mother and sisters and his free time to study for the ministry. In 1855, he married Catherine Mumford, who persuaded him to become an itinerant evangelist. Working from a base in **Whitechapel**, where he established a mission in 1865, he held tent meetings in an attempt to reach the unchurched masses. The success of his fiery oratory forced him to create an administrative structure for his growing band of volunteers, whom, in 1878, he described as a Salvation Army (a phrase that became popular and led—despite Booth's objections—to the adoption of military titles for the leadership and a distinctive uniform for members). Recruits were ridiculed, assaulted, and jailed for preaching their Gospel but appeared to meet a genuine need.

In 1890, along with W. T. Stead (a campaigning journalist), Booth published *In Darkest England and the Way Out*—a radical agenda for social reform that advocated programs of house building, provision of training centers for the unemployed, introduction of legal aid for the poor, construction of residential accommodation for abused women, and other measures that gained widespread public acceptance. Other countries provided similar support so, by the end of the century, the movement was international, expanding from London's **East End** to the European mainland, the United States, Australia, and South Africa.

Despite his campaign for change, Booth was, in many ways, an unremitting conservative; he had a narrow set of religious convictions, condemned the acquisition of wealth (although he cultivated the acquaintance of gamblers and millionaires in order to obtain funds for his missionary work), fulminated against study of the sciences, and opposed sports such as cricket. But he was a gifted orator, deeply affected by the degradation in which many of London's children were forced to live, and was instrumental in altering attitudes towards the poor. Towards the end of his life, he was much affected by family dissension over the way the Salvation Army was run and by his declining eyesight, but he received many accolades, including an invitation to the coronation of King Edward VII in 1902. He died in London on 20 August 1912, handing over the organizational reins to his son, Bramwell.

The Army's Whitechapel headquarters was destroyed by German bombs in 1941 but replaced, 22 years later, by a purpose-built building in Queen Victoria Street (in the **City of London**). It also has training bases in south London, at **Denmark Hill** and Sydenham Hill, and coordinates work in over 90 countries around the world. (*See also* BURIAL GROUNDS).

BOROUGH MARKET. Some researchers have suggested that the Borough Market in the **London Borough of Southwark** is the oldest fruit and vegetable market in the city. A map of 1542 shows it was established by that time, and documents dating from 1671 confirm its trading boundary. In 1754, it was causing such traffic congestion that it was moved from Borough High Street to its present location in Stoney Street, near **Southwark Cathedral**. (*See also* MARKETS; STREET MARKETS.)

BOSWELL, JAMES (1740–1795). Boswell's *Life of* ***SAMUEL JOHNSON****, LL.D.*, published in 1791, provides scholars with a colorful picture of manners and personalities in late 18th-century London society. The son of advocate Alexander Boswell and Euphemia, his first wife, Boswell was born in Edinburgh on 29 October 1740. In 1760, after attending the Universities of Edinburgh and Glasgow (but graduating from neither), he travelled to London, eager to share in "the happiness of the beau monde and the company of men of genius" (*Letters Between the Honourable Andrew Erskine and James Boswell, Esq.*, 1763). The city lived up to expectations. A sociable, high-spirited young man who enjoyed the company of ladies (and was clearly attractive to them), he spent much time drinking and womanizing, catching, in the process, gonorrhea, which was to plague him for the rest of his life. Although, under pressure from father and friends, he was forced to go back to Edinburgh after only 12 months to attempt to qualify as a lawyer, he nursed an affection for the south that was "as violent as the most romantic lover ever had for his mistress" (*Letters*, 1763). Returning in 1762, he found lodgings in **Downing Street** and, on 16 May the following year, met Johnson at the **Covent Garden** premises of actor and bookseller Thomas Davies.

Initially, Johnson was cool but the friendship ripened and survived Boswell's exile to Utrecht, where he studied civil law in order to pacify his father, who, driven to distraction by his son's hedonistic lifestyle (which included the siring of an illegitimate son to a servant girl), had threatened to disinherit him. He studied through the winter and spring then moved on to Berlin, Geneva, Naples, and Corsica before returning to Scotland, where he was admitted to the Faculty of Advocates on 26 July 1766. For the next 20 years, he practiced law in Edinburgh but made regular trips south to meet Johnson and his cronies. In 1773, he was elected to The Club, a group of well-known literary figures, and spent three months travelling the west coast of Scotland with Johnson. By the end of the decade, however, he was suffering from self-doubt; an attempted entry into politics was unsuccessful, his legal practice was not flourishing as he had hoped, his debts were mounting, his wife (Margaret Montgomerie, a first cousin, whom he had married in 1769) was pregnant and ill with tuberculosis, and he believed himself susceptible to a range of diseases. He consoled himself with several women, asserting that he could "unite little fondnesses with perfect conjugal love" (*Letters of James Boswell to the Rev. W. J. Temple*, 1857), and attempted to forget the quarrels with his father by drinking "a large quantity of strong beer" (ibid.).

A few months after Johnson died on 13 December 1784, Boswell published the diary of their Scottish tour as a first installment of a biography of his friend. *Journal of a Tour of the Hebrides, With Samuel Johnson, LL.D.* was enormously successful but made the author a laughing stock because it emphasized his weaknesses (including his vanity) without making any mention of his strengths. *The Life of Samuel Johnson, LL.D.* followed in 1791 and was similarly received; 1,200 copies sold in the 12 weeks after the two-volume work appeared, but Boswell became the target of society jokes because he lionized his friend to an absurd degree, reporting personal rebuffs without quoting rejoinders, and exuded pride in his own arrogance. Moreover, after the work appeared, he found that people became less talkative when he was around, fearing that their gossip would be reported in future publications. However, because of Boswell, Johnson's witticisms are widely known, a new standard was set for biographical writing, and scholars have a rich set of descriptions of London society in the last years before the Industrial Revolution changed it utterly.

Boswell moved permanently to London in 1786 but, although called to the bar that year, failed to establish a legal practice. He was grief-stricken when his wife died in 1789 and financial difficulties added to his woes. He complained constantly of depression, was knocked down and robbed while drunk in 1793, and died at his home in Great Portland Street on 19 May 1795. For over a century, it was believed that his papers were destroyed after his death, but they were found at Malahide

Castle (near Dublin) during the 1920s and 1930s then acquired by Yale University, which initiated a publication program. (*See also* STRAND.)

BOUDICCA. *See* BOADICEA.

BOW. An **East End** suburb, Bow developed as a bridging point where the main road from London to Essex crossed the **River Lea**, some five miles east of **Charing Cross** (the bridge looked like a bow, hence the name). Before the days of surfaced roads, goods could be more easily transported by water than by land, so a small harbor grew up at the site, allowing grain to be unloaded. Industries, such as flour milling and dye works, were established close to the port, providing the basis for a small manufacturing complex. From about 1860, the pace of that industrialization increased, with soap makers, rubber producers, and others building factories. The largest plant was erected by Bryant and May, who, in 1875, employed over 5,600 workers (most of them female) to make matches: in 1888, the "match girls" withdrew their labor and brought production to a halt—the first British attempt to organize women in trade union activity. In 1902, the **London Underground** arrived, expanding horizons by providing local residents with an opportunity to commute to work in the city center. During the 20th century, the area experienced much redevelopment as many of the older factories closed (for example, the Bryant and May plant shut down in 1979 and was converted into flats), but the essentially working-class nature of the community has not changed. (*See also* LANSBURY, GEORGE.)

BOW BELLS. A **cockney** is defined as "a person born within the sound of Bow bells," probably because, in the 15th century, a curfew was rung at nine o'clock each night on the bells of St. Mary-le-Bow Church (also known as the Church of Sancta Maria de Arcubus) in **Cheapside**. The church was burned down during the **Great Fire** of 1666 but rebuilt seven years later by **Christopher Wren**, who modelled the new structure on the Basilica of Maxentius in Rome. In 1941, it was greatly damaged by German bombs, which destroyed the peal, but it reopened in 1962. During the Second World War, the **British Broadcasting Corporation (BBC)** regularly broadcast the sound of Bow bells to occupied Europe in order to boost morale by assuring listeners that Britain had not succumbed to Nazi armies. (*See also* COURT OF ARCHES; WHITTINGTON, RICHARD "DICK.")

BOW STREET RUNNERS. In 1748, novelist Henry Fielding (who had trained as a barrister) was appointed magistrate at the Bow Street courts. In order to supplement the efforts of the local constables, he established a squad of six thief catchers, who, by the end of the century, were known as the Bow Street Runners. John Fielding (Henry's blind half brother) continued to support the group after he took over the magistrate's post in 1751, but the Runners were eventually disbanded in 1839, 10 years after the creation of the Metropolitan Police.

BRENT, LONDON BOROUGH OF. When London's **local government** was reorganized in 1965, Brent was created through the amalgamation of the formerly independent boroughs of **Wembley** and **Willesden**. It covers 17 square miles, had a population of some 253,200 in 1998, and takes its name from the small River Brent, which separates the two communities. Ethnically, it is one of the most diverse authorities in the United Kingdom, with about 17 percent of its residents from the Indian subcontinent, 10 percent from the Caribbean, 9 percent from the Republic of Ireland, and 4 percent from Africa. The south is typical of inner-city environments, with high rates of deprivation (as measured by indicators such as overcrowding and unemployment) but, farther north, the proportion of citizens in professional and managerial posts is well above the national average. Although the number of manufacturing jobs in the borough declined markedly from 1981, industry still plays a significant role in the local economy; commercial giants such as the Guinness brewing company, the Heinz food processing firm, and United Biscuits provide much employment, notably at industrial parks in Alperton and Park Royal. (*See also* CRICKLEWOOD; KENSAL GREEN; KILBURN; NEASDEN.)

BRENTFORD. Legend has it that Julius Caesar crossed the **River Thames** at Brentford when he brought his Roman armies to Britain in 55 B.C., but there is no evidence to support the story. The settlement developed at a point where the land route from London to the west of England crosses the River Brent some eight miles west of **Charing Cross**. It is mentioned in records (as Breguntford) by 705 A.D. and, in 1016, was the site of a battle between Edmund Ironside (leader of the native forces) and Canute (King of the invading Danes). In 1642, there was further conflict when royalist forces defeated parliamentarian troops and advanced, albeit temporarily, on London. During the 19th century, the settlement experienced considerable industrialization, with a **gas** works built in 1821,

railways spreading their tentacles in the middle years of the period, a water pumping station opened in 1835, and a fruit and vegetable market established in 1893. During the past hundred years, these have all closed but, although many of the sites have been built over (much of the railway yard was replaced by housing and a marina, for example), the area remains rich in Victorian industrial archaeology. In particular, the waterworks (located near Kew Bridge) was converted into a **museum** in 1975; its steam engines (which were installed in 1820, supplied west London until 1944, and never needed a replacement part) are on display, along with a working forge.

BREWERIES. Brewing has a long history in London. An association of brewers was in existence by 1292 and, by the early 15th century, had become one of the **livery companies**. The Industrial Revolution of the 19th century initiated a series of amalgamations, and the second half of the 20th century brought closures as new technology and the need for increased accessibility led many firms to seek sites beyond the city limits (for example, the Albion Brewery in Whitechapel Road closed in 1979 after 171 years of production, the Anchor Brewery in Mile End Road shut its gates in 1975 after 218 years, and the Stag Brewery in **Westminster** was sacrificed to urban redevelopment in 1959 after 318 years). Only two big producers survive—Fuller, Smith and Turner at the Griffin Brewery in **Chiswick** (where beer has been produced since the days of Elizabeth I), and Young and Company in **Wandsworth**. However, since the 1980s, there has been growth in the popularity of microbreweries—tiny producers making small amounts of beer, sometimes as an addition to running a single **public house**. (*See also* BARNES; BERMONDSEY; SPITALFIELDS.)

BRIDEWELL. In 1515–20, King Henry VIII erected a brick palace beside the River Fleet, close to **Blackfriars**, naming it Bridewell in recognition of a nearby holy well dedicated to St. Bride. The **City of London** accepted the building as a gift from Edward VI in 1553, converting it into a **prison** for people found guilty of minor offenses. Most were punished by public flogging, but, given the standards of the day, treatment was relatively humane; a doctor was appointed to tend to the prisoners' medical needs in 1700 (75 years before any other London prison made similar provision), straw was provided for their beds from 1788, and flogging of women was abolished in 1791. The premises were burned down by the **Great Fire** of 1666, rebuilt the following year, closed when inmates were transferred to the new accommodation at **Holloway Prison** in 1855, and demolished eight years later. The site is now occupied by an office block.

BRIDGES. London's principal bridges straddle the **River Thames** between **Kingston Upon Thames** (in the west) and Dartford (in the east). **London Bridge**, the first of the 20 road bridges, was erected between 100 A.D. and 400 A.D. and, until the 18th century, remained the only means of crossing the river in the immediate vicinity of the city, other than by ferry (although **Kingston Bridge**, 12 miles to the southwest, had been opened by 1193). **Westminster Bridge**, built in 1738–50, reflected the growth of the western edge of the settlement and was followed by others over the next two centuries. However, despite the **docks**' industrial importance, **Tower Bridge**, which first carried traffic between the **City of London** and **Bermondsey** in 1894, was the most easterly crossing until 1991, when the Queen Elizabeth II Bridge was constructed some 20 miles downriver in an effort to alleviate congestion at the Dartford Tunnel. The 11 **railway** bridges were all built between 1846 and 1889 as lines spread from the city center to the suburbs and surrounding countryside. Barnes Bridge, erected in 1846–49 for the London and South Western Railway, was the first, bringing services from the west into **Clapham Junction** and **Waterloo**, but direct access by train to central London was not possible before the construction of the Grosvenor Bridge (also known as Victoria Bridge) by the London, Chatham, and Dover Railway. Opened in 1860, it served the station at **Victoria**. There are only three Thames bridges in London designated solely for pedestrians, one (built in 1884) at Teddington, a second attached to the Hungerford Railway Bridge (which was completed in 1864), and the third (opened in 2000) linking **The City** to **Bankside** (*see* **Millennium Bridge**). London's other major bridges include the cast iron **Archway** viaduct (completed in 1897) and the 1,400-foot-long **Holborn** viaduct, which crossed the valley of the River Fleet in 1869. (*See also* ALBERT BRIDGE; BATTERSEA BRIDGE; BAZALGETTE, JOSEPH WILLIAM; BLACKFRIARS; CANNON STREET STATION; CHELSEA BRIDGE; CHISWICK BRIDGE; HAMMERSMITH BRIDGE; KEW; LAMBETH BRIDGE; PUTNEY BRIDGE; RICHMOND BRIDGE; SERPENTINE; SOUTHWARK BRIDGE; TWICKENHAM; VAUXHALL; WANDSWORTH BRIDGE.)

BRITISH ACADEMY. At the end of the 19th century, the **Royal Society** was Britain's leading association of scholars, but its activities focused very strongly on the natural sciences so, in 1902, the British Academy was founded to accommodate those whose interests lay in the humanities. Initially, meetings were held at the **British Museum** but, in 1926, Winston Churchill (then Chancellor of the Exchequer) facilitated a move to **Mayfair**'s Burlington Gardens. The organization transferred to **Burlington House** in 1968 and then to Cornwall Terrace (**Regent's Park**) in 1982. The membership consists of up to 350 resident Fellows elected because of their distinction in the arts or social sciences (past recipients of the honor include philosopher Bertrand Russell, archaeologist Mortimer Wheeler, and socialist writer Beatrice Webb). A further 250 individuals who live overseas are designated Corresponding Fellows. Much of the academy's work is concerned with administration of schools and institutes abroad, presentation of a lecture series, awards of medals to those who have made outstanding contributions to knowledge and, through the publication of its *Proceedings*, dissemination of academic knowledge.

BRITISH BROADCASTING CORPORATION (BBC). The BBC was founded in 1922, with Lord Reith as its first Director-General. In 1926, it became a public service corporation financed by license fees paid by listeners. The first radio transmissions were made from Savoy Hill (near Waterloo Bridge) on 14 November 1922 but, in 1932, the organization moved to larger premises at Broadcasting House in Langham Place. Although the corporation very quickly outgrew its new home, opening ancillary studios in other parts of London and in provincial cities, Broadcasting House was identified by the British public as the heart of the BBC because of its importance as a source of information during the Second World War. As a result, it was a prime target for German attacks during the **Blitz** and, on 15 October 1940, was struck by a bomb that killed seven people; undeterred, Bruce Belrage continued to read the nine o'clock news to the nation while the building disintegrated around him. The World Service, much threatened by financial cuts in recent years, broadcast from Bush House (in Aldwych), a 1930s building that the BBC first occupied in 1940. However, late in 2000, the corporation announced that it would vacate the property and base all its journalists at Broadcasting House. The first television programs were transmitted from **Alexandra Palace** in 1936 but, in 1956, operations were transferred to a 3.5-acre site (known as Television Centre) at **Shepherd's Bush**. In 2000 the Centre was bombed by the Real Irish Republican Army, a terrorist group, but damage was limited and only one person was injured. (*See also* BOW BELLS; GOLDERS GREEN; LANGHAM HOTEL; PROMS, THE.)

BRITISH EMPIRE EXHIBITION. As Britain recovered from the austere conditions of the First World War (1914–19), the government considered plans for a great exhibition that would boost morale and celebrate the glories of an empire on which, according to national belief, the sun never set. A 219-acre site was chosen at **Wembley**, a new sports stadium was erected as a centerpiece, and hundreds of pavilions, devoted largely to industry and commerce, were built amidst flower beds and fountains to designs representing the architectural traditions of the dominions and colonies. When the event was opened on 23 April 1924, King George V's speech was heard around the country on radio, the first time that a sovereign had addressed his people using the new technology. Over the next 18 months, a total of 27,102,498 visitors viewed the exhibits. Some of the buildings survived into the late 20th century as industrial warehouses, notably the Palace of Arts (which told the story of art over the previous 200 years) and the Palace of Industry (which displayed products as different as cotton and chemicals).

BRITISH LIBRARY. In 1973, the British Museum Library, the National Central Library, and the National Lending Library for Science and Technology were merged to create a single British Library. It is divided into four units: a Reference Division (which has some 10 million printed books as well as newspapers, maps, government papers, sheets of music, stamps, and other documents), a Science Reference Library (the major British repository of current scientific literature), a Lending Division (which supplies books to other institutions), and a Bibliographical Division (which prepares catalogues and other records of published material). For most of its existence, the library has had no central home, operating from various locations in London, but from 1995 its collections were moved to a site close to **St. Pancras**. Initially, the new building was intended to hold 18 million books and documents, but cost increases resulted in a scaling down of the project, so about one-third of the library's stock is stored 200 miles away in Yorkshire. The brick structure itself also proved controversial. Prince Charles likened it to "an academy for secret police," and the architect, Colin St. John Wilson, claimed that, as a result, he lost so much business he had to close his practice. (*See also* LIBRARIES.)

BRITISH MUSEUM. The foundations of the United Kingdom's major **museum** were laid by physician **Hans Sloane**, who suggested that, when he died, his library and natural history collections should be purchased by the nation for £20,000, less than half their true worth. Following his death in 1753, the necessary funds were raised by a lottery, Montague House (in **Bloomsbury**) was adapted to hold the exhibits, and the displays were opened to the public in 1759 (though only to those people who applied for permission in writing). Other purchases and gifts augmented the Sloane exhibits, including a collection of manuscripts amassed by Robert Harley, Earl of Oxford, and his son, Edward. George II presented books amassed by monarchs of England since Tudor times, Sir William Hamilton's Greek vases were bought in 1782, sculptures removed from the Parthenon (in Athens) by Lord Elgin were added in 1816, and George III's library was donated by his son (George IV) in 1820.

As distinguished 18th-century figures made large donations (actor **David Garrick** handed over a collection of plays, for example, and Captain James Cook offered material he had brought home from his explorations of the Pacific Ocean islands), the available space dwindled and temporary structures were erected around the main galleries to display exhibits. In 1823, however, work began on a new building, designed by Robert Smirke. Initially, it had a central courtyard but, during the 1850s, that was roofed over to provide a reading room (where socialist revolutionary Karl Marx wrote *Das Kapital,* the philosophical rationale for early Soviet communism).

The transfer of the natural history collections to south **Kensington** in 1881 (*see* **Natural History Museum**) and of the newspaper library to Colindale in 1904–5, the building of the Edward VII galleries in 1914, the addition of the North Library in 1937, the construction of the West Gallery (for the Parthenon sculptures) in 1938, the opening of a gallery for horological material in 1975, and the move of the **British Library** to **St. Pancras** from 1995 have also relieved congestion, but the museum still has much more material than it can put on display. Currently, more than four million exhibits are presented on the 14-acre site, including coins, medals, prints, and Egyptian, Greek, Roman, and Japanese antiquities. Important additions during the 20th century included the Sutton Hoo treasure (buried in a ship on England's east coast as a memorial to a seventh-century Anglo-Saxon ruler), a hoard of Roman silver found at Mildenhall (near Cambridge), and a Roman pavement discovered (in almost perfect condition) in Devonshire. The former British Library reading room was redesigned by architect Norman Foster and reopened as the Great Court (the largest covered square in Europe) in 2000. The following year new galleries, financed by the Sainsbury family, allowed the African exhibits to be displayed more effectively. Over five million people visit the museum every year. (*See also* MUSEUM OF MANKIND.)

BRITISH TELECOM TOWER. One of London's tallest buildings, the tower, located in the city center west of Totenham Court Road, rises to 620 feet above ground level (including the 40-foot mast that supports a radar aerial). Formerly known as the Post Office Tower and the London Telecom Tower (a changing nomenclature that reflects the fortunes of the formerly nationalized telecommunications industry), it was designed by Eric Bedford and built in 1963–66. Its primary purpose is to enable radio and television waves to travel effectively above surrounding buildings in the city center, but it also serves as a very effective landmark. A viewing platform and revolving restaurant were closed in 1975 following a bomb incident.

BRIXTON. The Brixton area, lying some three miles south of **Charing Cross**, consisted largely of sparsely settled, uncultivated land until the early 19th century. The construction of a bridge over the **River Thames** at **Vauxhall** proved the spur to development, improving access to the **City of London** from 1816. Initially, the buildings housed middle-class and professional families with their servants, but, after the **railway** arrived during the 1860s, smaller homes were constructed for less wealthy commuters, and the older premises were subdivided for use as apartment blocks or lodging houses. Many of the rented rooms were acquired by **music hall** entertainers and **theater** performers, attracted by low prices, local concert rooms, and easy access to the **West End** (former Prime Minister John Major, son of a trapeze artist, spent part of his childhood in Brixton). From 1948, Caribbean **immigrants** began to settle in the area, initially in Somerleyton Road, close to the **London Underground** station. At that time, local authorities were attempting to improve the **housing** stock by replacing old buildings with modern structures, but, in doing so, they broke up communities, contributing to feelings of insecurity and unrest that were manifested in tension with incomers.

By the 1970s, the **London Borough of Lambeth** had adopted policies of housing improvement (rather than demolition and rebuilding), but continued expansion of the colored population contributed to the growth of a self-assertive black community with a distinctive lifestyle; many young people adopted the outward trappings of Rastafarianism (though only a small proportion fully accepted the religious tenets of the movement), reggae music was popular, and specialty shops opened to meet the demands of the expanding Jamaican population. Riots in 1981 sparked off similar violence in other English inner-city locations, forcing Prime Minister Margaret Thatcher to appoint a committee of enquiry, chaired by Lord Scarman. Since that time, Brixton has become less of a focus for London's black citizens, and race relations have improved. Tourists as well as local people visit the **street market**, which is centered on Electric Avenue (opened in 1888 as one of the first shopping streets in the city to be lit by the new power source) and consists of a colorful array of stalls selling a range of goods, with those in Granville Arcade concentrating on Caribbean foods, African clothes, and Jamaican music. The area also houses a **prison**, opened in 1820 and designed for convicts sentenced to hard labor. Concerns about its security were voiced in 1972, when 20 prisoners escaped, and again in 1980, when another three (including an alleged Irish Republican Army terrorist) disappeared. The building now houses about 1,000 men awaiting trial or serving short sentences. (*See also* DEPARTMENT STORES; MORRISON, HERBERT STANLEY.)

BROADCASTING HOUSE. *See* BRITISH BROADCASTING CORPORATION (BBC).

BROMLEY, LONDON BOROUGH OF. When **local government** in the metropolitan area was reorganized in 1965, several communities previously located in the County of Kent were incorporated within the **London Borough** of Bromley. Covering some 59 square miles, the new authority (the largest in the **Greater London Council** area) was created by the merger of the boroughs of **Beckenham** and Bromley, the Urban Districts of **Orpington** and Penge, and parts of Chislehurst and Sidcup. Although largely residential, there is a significant concentration of light industry towards the northeast in the valley of the River Cray (a tributary of the Darenth, which meets the **River Thames** at Dartford) and open farmland in the **Green Belt** to the southeast. The population of about 297,100 (1998) is heavily concentrated in professional and managerial families, with many workers commuting daily to jobs in **The City**. Over 81 percent of homes are privately owned (compared with a London average of 72 percent), and unemployment rates tend to be lower than for the city as a whole. (*See also* BIGGIN HILL.)

BROMPTON. The Brompton area, lying south of **Kensington**, was one of the last extensive areas of present-day central London to be covered with urban development, primarily because, from the 17th century, it developed a considerable reputation for its market gardens and plant nurseries. That semirural landscape eventually attracted wealthy businessmen (who built large homes for their families) and institutions such as the Brompton Hospital, which was established in 1842 to care for patients with chest and lung diseases. From the 1850s, much land was acquired for educational buildings (the **Victoria and Albert Museum** occupies much of the 100-acre site formerly used by the Brompton Park Nursery, for example). Also, in 1880–84, the baroque Brompton Oratory was built as a church for the priests of the Institute of the Oratory, established by St. Philip Neri in Rome in 1575 and introduced to London in 1848. One of the few remaining open spaces is the 40-acre Brompton Cemetery, consecrated in 1840 and laid out to plans prepared by Benjamin Baud; it provides a final resting place for writer George Borrow and architect Francis Fowke (who designed the **Albert Hall**). In 1998, house prices in parts of the SW1 postal district averaged £496,726 per property, a reflection of Brompton's continuing residential status.

BROWN'S HOTEL. Located in Dover Street (near **Piccadilly**), Brown's is one of London's most exclusive **hotels**. It was established in 1837 by James Brown (who had worked as a manservant) and his wife, Sarah (a maid in Lady Byron's household). Alexander Graham Bell made the first telephone call in England from the building in 1876 and, in 1905, Franklin Roosevelt (President of the United States to 1933 to 1945) and Eleanor (his wife) spent their honeymoon there. Other former patrons include statesman Cecil Rhodes and author Rudyard Kipling.

BUCKINGHAM PALACE. Buckingham Palace, at the western end of **The Mall**, has been the principal residence of Britain's royal family since Queen Victoria succeeded to the throne in 1837. In 1702–5, John Sheffield, Duke of Buckingham, built a residence on a site at the western end of **St. James's Park**. The building was purchased by King George III in 1762, but his eldest son, who succeeded to the throne as George IV in 1820, decided that a more imposing London home was needed for Britain's royal family. Moreover, he insisted that **John Nash** should be responsible for the design. Parliament, although unhappy about the projected costs, allocated £200,000 to the project, and Nash produced plans for a courtyard enclosed on all sides except the east. George, however, demanded Carrara marble, Bath stone, and other expensive building materials, which pushed up the expense of construction, so the architect was twice called before House of Commons committees to explain why the bills were three times greater than funds apportioned. In the end, the government's patience ran out. When the King died in 1830, Nash was dismissed and Edward Blore was commissioned to complete the work.

When Victoria moved in, the place was hardly fit for the servants let alone a Queen. Bells would not ring, doors would not close, windows would not open, and many fittings (such as sinks) had not been installed. Nevertheless, by 1843 she was able to write, "I have been so happy here," a sentiment echoed by all later monarchs with the exception of Edward VIII, who hated the place and spent only a few nights there during his short reign. In 1913, the eastern frontage was replaced by a facade of **Portland stone** designed by Sir Aston Webb. In addition, considerable renovation and refurbishment were carried out after the Second World War (when parts of the structure, including the chapel, were badly damaged by bombs).

The present building has about 600 rooms, most of which are used as offices or as accommodation for staff. Queen Elizabeth II and the Duke of Edinburgh occupy twelve rooms in the north wing, facing the 40-acre gardens. The State Apartments (including the Ballroom, Music Room, and Throne Room) are reserved for events such as banquets honoring foreign dignitaries and ceremonies conferring knighthood on the great and the good. Since 1993, they have been open to the public from August until early October (while the royal family is at Balmoral, in Scotland); the admission charges contribute towards the rebuilding of the rooms at Windsor Castle, which were damaged by fire in November 1992. Charles, Prince of Wales and heir to the throne, was born in Buckingham Palace (1948), as were his brothers Andrew (1960) and Edward (1964). Their sister—Anne—was born in **Clarence House** in 1950. In 1998, the palace authorities announced plans to double the size of the Queen's Gallery so that more of the royal art collection could be placed on display to the public. (*See also* CHANGING OF THE GUARD; CUBITT, THOMAS; ROYAL MEWS.)

BUNHILL FIELDS. From 1658 until 1855, Bunhill Fields, lying just outside the northern boundary of the **City of London**, was a principal **burial ground** for nonconformists (that is, Protestants who adhered to sects other than the Church of England). Under the terms of an 1867 Act of Parliament, the City Corporation is responsible for managing the cemetery, which contains the graves of authors John Bunyan (who published *The Pilgrim's Progress* in 1678) and Daniel Defoe (who wrote *Robinson*

Crusoe in 1719), artist William Blake, hymn writer Isaac Watts (remembered for *When I Survey the Wondrous Cross*), and Susanna Wesley (mother of Charles and John, founders of the Methodist Church). George Fox, who formed the Society of Friends, lies in the adjacent Quaker graveyard.

BURIAL GROUNDS. By the 17th century, space to bury London's dead was in short supply. The grounds of the churches had nearly filled so graves were being dug only a few inches apart and bodies were interred under the floors of chapels, causing an unbearable stench in hot weather. In order to alleviate the problem, some parishes obtained land at the edge of the city and used it as burial grounds, which remained in use until about 1850 (since then, many have been converted into public **parks** and gardens). These were replaced by seven large commercial cemeteries (authorized by government legislation during the 1830s and 1840s and located in a ring around the major residential area), but it was clear by midcentury that they, too, would quickly run out of space. Conscious of an increasing demand for nonprofit-making burial grounds, Parliament made provisions for the establishment of locally elected Burial Boards charged with obtaining land for funerals.

Since then, most of London's 3,000 acres of cemetery have been managed by local authorities. Many have become tourist attractions, sometimes because of their **architecture** (*see*, for instance, **Highgate Cemetery**) but often simply because pilgrims (and the curious) are attracted to the graves of the famous. Members of the Salvation Army visit Abney Park Cemetery in **Stamford Hill**, where **William Booth** (founder of the movement) is buried. Engineer Isambard Kingdom Brunel and author Wilkie Collins lie in **Kensal Green**, sculptor Jacob Epstein in Putney Vale, and Henry Bessemer (who invented the process for making steel from cast iron) in West Norwood. However, the problem of finding space for burials remains. Although over 70 percent of the 60,000 Londoners who die each year are cremated, it was estimated, in 2000, that within eight years all the ground available for interments would be filled. (*See also* BROMPTON; BUNHILL FIELDS; GREEN PARK; HUGUENOTS; ST. BOTOLPH'S CHURCH, ALDGATE; ST. JAMES'S CHURCH, PICCADILLY; STANMORE; WILLESDEN.)

BURLINGTON ARCADE. A precursor of the modern shopping mall, the arcade houses 72 small but exclusive shops along a covered passageway between **Piccadilly** and Burlington Gardens. It was constructed in 1815–19 as a means of preventing passersby from throwing rubbish into Lord Cavendish's garden and, although much altered, remains a classic piece of Regency **architecture**. Liveried beadles patrol the passageway and have authority to apprehend anybody who runs, whistles, sings, or carries an open umbrella.

BURLINGTON HOUSE. The last survivor of the noblemen's mansions that once lined the north side of **Piccadilly**, Burlington House was partly built in 1664–65 by architect John Denham as his London residence. Before it was completed, it was acquired in 1667 by the first Earl of Burlington, who finished the construction. In 1715, the third Earl commissioned **James Gibbs** to erect baroque colonnades at the edges of the forecourt but then changed architectural tack and, in 1717, employed Colem Campbell to redesign the building in Palladian style. When Burlington died in 1753, the house was inherited by Charlotte, his only child and wife of the Duke of Devonshire. In 1813, it was bought by Lord Cavendish (the sixth Duke's uncle), who carried out considerable internal modification, including the installation of a grand staircase. The government purchased the property in 1854 and, after much heart searching, converted it into a headquarters for the **Royal Academy of Arts**, the **Royal Society**, and other learned organizations. (*See also* SAVILE ROW.)

BURNT OAK. During the 1920s, **London County Council** promoted the establishment of a community on sparsely settled agricultural land at Burnt Oak (some nine miles northwest of **Charing Cross**) in an attempt to alleviate **housing** pressures in the inner city. A **railway** link to **St. Pancras** was completed in 1925, and residents from **Islington** arrived three years later to homes constructed of metal, wood, and brick. By 1931, over 40,000 houses and flats were available, attracting further immigrants who pushed the resident population up to some 20,000 by the outbreak of the Second World War. Initially, there was some friction between the working-class incomers (who had brought their inner-city customs, including an open air **market**, with them) and families in nearby middle-class areas, but the two cultures learned to coexist, with the white-collar groups drawing on blue-collar skills. Since the 1950s, the expansion of the urban area has turned Burnt Oak into a metropolitan suburb close to the M1 motorway.

BUSES. The precursors of the familiar red double-decker London bus were the horse-drawn carriages with which, on 4 July 1829, George Shillibeer introduced a service transporting up to 20 passengers at a time from **Paddington** to **The City**. By 1851, a two-deck version of the wagon had appeared. Passengers on the roof sat back to back, exposed to all that the weather could throw at them, but, even so, the new conveyances proved popular with businessmen travelling to and from their offices. For some years, competition became increasingly fierce as more and more operators tried to attract customers, but from 1855 a French firm—the Compagnie Générale des Omnibus de Londres—bought up existing businesses so rapidly that three years later, when the directors registered in Britain as the London General Omnibus Company, it controlled most of the 800 vehicles on the streets. By the end of the century, commuting had become an accepted way of life for many Londoners and the 3,500 horse buses were the chief form of public road **transport**. However, motorized vehicles became increasingly common from 1897, and the internal combustion engine challenged the dominance of the horse, which finally disappeared from the streets in 1916, superseded by the mass-produced B-type double-decker (affectionately known as Old Bill).

The years between the two world wars (1919–39) brought further technological and administrative developments. Pneumatic tires, introduced in 1925, resulted in a more comfortable ride for customers, as did the roofs over the upper deck, which became common at the same time. Then, in 1933, the whole system was taken into state control, along with the **London Underground** and the **trams**, presenting possibilities for a coordinated route network within the capital (*see* **London Transport**). For the next 52 years, investment was shaped by income from fares and government subsidies. Diesel engine vehicles went into service in 1949, to be followed in the mid-1950s by 2,800 Routemaster buses. Wider and lighter than their predecessors, they carried more passengers but also, because they had a door at the front, allowed the driver to collect fares, making conductors redundant and therefore reducing operating costs.

In 1985, London Transport created a subsidiary company—London Buses Ltd.—to run the services. That company was required to compete against private contractors for the right to operate along specified routes and found the going hard because large garages, expensive to maintain, and restrictive work practices pushed costs beyond those of small local firms. London Buses responded by subdividing into 13 area-based units, each responsible for its own budget and able to compete against both the private sector and sister units. In 1994, all were privatized through management and employee buyouts or sales to outside interests. London Transport (renamed Transport for London in 2000) acts as a contracting agency but owns none of the 5,000 public service vehicles that, every day from Monday to Friday, carry 1.2 million passengers along the 700 routes it offers for tender.

In addition to the transport within the metropolitan area, there are bus connections to all major regions of the United Kingdom from Victoria Coach Station, which is managed by London Transport but used by independent firms. Services to and from the city were deregulated in 1985, introducing a free market in provision (any operator can apply for a license to run buses between centers even though the route is identical to that used by an existing service).

BUSH HOUSE. *See* BRITISH BROADCASTING CORPORATION (BBC).

BUSHY PARK. The 1,100 acres of Bushy (sometimes spelled Bushey) Park and neighboring Hampton Court Park, in the **London Borough of Richmond Upon Thames**, were enclosed as a hunting forest by King Henry VIII in 1538. Access to the public has been available since his death nine years later. Bushy Park's outstanding feature is an avenue of 274 chestnut trees, flanked by lime trees, which were planted during the 17th century by **Christopher Wren** and stretch for a mile over the grass. A statue, believed to be of Diana the huntress, stands at the southern end and the 18th-century Bushy Park House near the northern end (Lord North occupied the premises while he was Prime Minister in the 1770s). Towards the western edge of the park, 100 acres have been converted into a woodland garden alongside the Longford River (an artificial inlet cut by command of King Charles I in 1639 in order to draw water from the River Colne). Hampton Court Park (separated from Bushy Park by Hampton Court Road) is more formally laid out because of its proximity to **Hampton Court Palace**. In addition to the landscaped areas, the parks have sports pitches, horse riding facilities, a swimming pool, and a pond for sailing model boats. The land is still owned by the Crown and is managed by the **Royal Parks** Agency.

– C –

CABINET WAR ROOMS. In 1938, as conflict between the United Kingdom and Germany seemed increasingly likely, civil service buildings at Clive Steps, off King Charles Street, were adapted for use by the British government during hostilities. Between 1940 and 1945, while the Second World War raged, Prime Minister Winston Churchill directed operations from the Map Room, accompanied by his Chiefs of Staff. When **air raids** made travel in London dangerous, he slept in a nearby room, from which he broadcast several of his radio addresses to the nation. His Cabinet congregated in a meeting place soundproofed to keep out the noise of enemy attacks and close to an anteroom containing a telephone with a direct link to the President of the United States. The remainder of the three-acre facility consisted of a canteen, a hospital, a shooting range, and tiny sleeping quarters for the 528 workers. The rooms are now open to the public, looking much as they did in the 1940s, with colored pins sticking into the wall maps and the cabinet room arranged as if ministers were expected for a meeting.

CABLE STREET. Cable Street, built in London's industrial **East End** in the late 18th century, was originally 200 yards long (the length of a cable) and lined by rope manufacturing companies. It has since been extended from the **City of London** in the west to **Limehouse** in the east and now has a variety of commercial buildings. On 5 October 1936, it formed part of the route chosen for a march by supporters of the fascist movement, led by Sir Oswald Mosley. Left-wing opponents and local residents built barricades that would disrupt the procession but became involved in scuffles with the police, who were attempting to dismantle the obstacles and preserve the movement's right of assembly. As the struggles became more frequent, Fenner Brockway (Secretary of the Independent Labour Party) was injured by a police horse and, realizing that there would be serious violence if the fascists and their opponents confronted each other, telephoned government officials. Mosley was ordered to cancel the demonstration but, over the next week, many Jewish properties in the area suffered damage as the thwarted marchers took their revenge.

CAFÉ ROYAL. In 1865, Daniel Nicolas Thévenon opened a café at 15–17 Glasshouse Street, near **Piccadilly Circus**. The business was successful, expanding into property in **Regent Street** and, by the turn of the century, attracting the fashionable members of London's bohemian artistic set (including playwright Oscar Wilde and artists Aubrey Beardsley and Augustus John) as well as nobility such as brothers Edward and George Windsor (later King Edward VIII and King George VI). Most met amid the red velvet seats and marble tables of the domino room, but there was also a billiard room, a lunch bar, and space for private meetings. Although the property was rebuilt in 1923–24 to Sir Henry Tanner's designs, it retained its attraction for writers into the 1930s (T. S. Eliot and J. B. Priestley were frequent visitors). The main entrance is now at 68 Regent Street, where the rococo decoration in the grill room preserves the opulent atmosphere.

CAMBERWELL. In the 18th century, Camberwell (which lies east of **Brixton** and about 2.5 miles southeast of **Charing Cross**) was a country village best known as the place where the now extinct Camberwell Beauty butterfly was first identified in 1748. Development began about 1820, with buildings constructed along the main roads for wealthy men who wanted a rural home for their families but daily access to their offices in the **City of London** (Joseph Chamberlain, advocate of social reform and an end to free trade, was born in Camberwell Grove, a tree-lined row of Georgian houses, in 1836). In 1844, a new cathedral-like church was built to replace the 12th-century stone chapel destroyed by fire three years earlier; designed by George Gilbert Scott and dedicated to St. Giles, it has a remarkable east window planned by John Ruskin. In 1868, William Rossiter founded an art gallery in Peckham Road. Then, in 1896, a technical school was established to teach design skills to local apprentices. Rossiter's gallery flourished; now known as the South London Art Gallery, it houses over 300 works by Victorian artists (including John Everett Millais, founder of the Pre-Raphaelite Brotherhood). In addition, since 1953 (using funds provided by the local council in celebration of the coronation of Queen Elizabeth II) it has built a significant collection of paintings by such 20th-century artists as Duncan Grant (a member of the **Bloomsbury Group**) and John Piper. The technical school, which is located next door, has been renamed Camberwell College of Art and has concentrated on teaching the fine arts, as well as design, since 1908. However, Camberwell Green, site of a fair that survived until 1855, is a busy road junction devoid of any trace of the rural peace that Felix Mendelssohn discovered when he visited in 1842 and, moved by the tranquillity, wrote *Spring Song* (which was originally titled *Camberwell Green*).

CAMDEN, LONDON BOROUGH OF. When the **Greater London Council** replaced the **London County Council** in 1965, the pattern of **local government** in the city was transformed as authorities were merged to form larger units. Camden was a product of the reorganization, created by the amalgamation of the Borough of **Hampstead**, the Borough of **Holborn**, and the Borough of **St. Pancras**. Covering an area of eight square miles, it has a population of 186,000 (1998) and takes its name from Charles, Marquess of Camden, whose family owned much of the land during the 18th and 19th centuries. The south has a large working-class population, who find jobs in nearby city center commercial firms (Camden has more square feet of shop and office space than any borough other than the **City of Westminster**), with institutions such as London University, or with the **transport** industries, though a few neighborhoods (such as **Camden Town**) are popular with young professionals and many properties are rented to students. Further north, Hampstead and **Highgate** retain their image as foci for artists and writers with an affluent lifestyle. Levels of owner-occupation in the borough are low (40 percent of homes are rented from the local authority, twice the London average), and there is a considerable ethnic mix, with Irish residents in **Kilburn**, Asian communities around **Euston Station**, Greek Cypriots in Camden Town, and a growing black presence off Camden High Street. The Holborn area has a particularly heavy concentration of educational, legal, and religious organizations, including the **British Museum**, **Sir John Soane's Museum**, Lincoln's Inn (one of the **Inns of Court**), and **St. Etheldreda's Church** (the oldest Roman Catholic church in the country). (*See also* BEDFORD ESTATES; BLOOMSBURY; CAMDEN TOWN; DICKENS' HOUSE MUSEUM; GOSPEL OAK; HAMPSTEAD GARDEN SUBURB; HAMPSTEAD HEATH; KEATS'S HOUSE; KENTISH TOWN; KING'S CROSS; LINCOLN'S INN FIELDS; PRIMROSE HILL; SPANIARDS, THE; SWISS COTTAGE.)

CAMDEN TOWN. The area north of **Euston Station** takes its name from Earl Camden, who acquired the land by marriage in 1749. Although the Earl gave developers permission to build 1,400 houses in 1791 and the Veterinary College of London (now the Royal Veterinary College) was founded during the same year, there was little urban encroachment until the second decade of the 19th century. In 1816, the construction of the **Regent's Canal** (designed to link the **River Thames** to the Grand Junction Canal at **Paddington**) introduced coal companies and other small industries to the area. Then, in 1837, the opening of Euston Station added to the pressures on land so, by the end of the century, farms had given way to uniform rows of terraced houses. Irish **immigrants** began to move in around 1880, taking advantage of the relatively low rents, and they were followed from about 1930 by Greek Cypriots, who set up small businesses in the catering and textile industries. (In 1948, the Cypriot community acquired the vacant All Saints Church, converting it for use by Greek Orthodox worshippers, but became involved in controversy eight years later when Kallinikos Macheriotis—one of the priests—was deported for supporting armed resistance to British rule in Cyprus.)

After the Second World War, much of the area east of Camden High Street was redeveloped, attracting a growing number of middle-class families to what had been a predominantly blue-collar area. From the 1960s, Camden Passage developed as an important antique market and Camden Lock as a center for more general bric-a-brac, both attracting significant numbers of tourists. Camden Town also has important associations with the arts. Novelist **Charles Dickens** lived at 16 Bayham Street in 1823–24 and drew on his expertise of the area when he depicted the homes of characters such as Bob Cratchit in *A Christmas Carol* (1843) and Mr. Micawber in *David Copperfield* (1850). Also, in 1911 a coterie of painters (including Augustus John, Wyndham Lewis, and Walter Sickert) formed a Camden Town Group whose work consisted largely of informal portraits, north London street scenes, and nude figures in depressing apartments. It merged with others two years later to form a London Group, which thrived until the Second World War.

CANARY WHARF. The development of Canary Wharf, on the **Isle of Dogs**, has been marred by controversy ever since plans were first proposed in 1985. Initially, a consortium of banks backed the major urban renewal project, attracted by a package of government concessions that included relative freedom from planning controls and a 10-year moratorium on property taxes. However, the group's suggestions for a complex of offices, shops, and **hotels**, based in three high towers, did not meet with universal acclaim, critics pointing out that other buildings in the **East End** were low rise, that the **transport** infrastructure was limited, and that the towers would block the view across the river to **Greenwich Park**. Faced with opposition and national financial recession, several of the partners withdrew but, in 1987, Olympia and York (owned by the Canadian Reichman Brothers) took charge of the scheme. Appointing architects Cesar Pelli and I. M. Pei as design consultants, they constructed a single 850-foot tower (the tallest in the United Kingdom) and incorporated a concert hall and a railway station on the 71-acre site. Local authorities tackled problems of access by preparing plans for the extension of the Jubilee Line of the **London Underground**, road improvements, and the extension of the **Docklands** Light Railway to provide a direct link with **The City**. Despite Olympia and York's collapse in 1992, the development proceeded, with Paul Reichman finding new sponsors and buying control back from the banks for a reputed £800 million three years later. With 4.7 million square feet of commercial space available, a further 8.8 million planned, and rental costs lower than those in The City, the venture stimulated office decentralization from central London, led by *The Daily Telegraph* newspaper and such finance houses as Barclays Bank and Morgan Grenfell. On 19 February 1996, the Irish Republican Army bombed the tower, killing two people and injuring 100, but the incident had no effect on the wharf's attraction for investors.

CANNING TOWN. From 1846, when a **railway** station was opened, Canning Town developed on the north bank of the **River Thames** some six miles east of **Charing Cross**. The new settlement, probably named after Lord Canning (Governor General of India), housed manual workers from the Royal Victoria Dock (which was completed in 1855), the Thames Ironworks and Shipbuilding Company (which built naval vessels at its base on Bow Creek from 1846 until 1912), the coal wharves, and other industrial premises that lined the waterways. It was one of the most deprived areas in London's **East End** during the late 19th and early 20th centuries, then suffered greatly from bombing during the **Blitz**. After 1945, however, successive local authorities implemented major regeneration plans that included the demolition of much low-quality Victorian **housing**, and construction of homes with modern amenities (as at the **Keir Hardie** estate). **Transport** improvements included provision of integrated interchange facilities for passengers on the **buses**, the **Docklands** Light Railway, and the **London Underground**. The new Underground station is built on the site of the Thames Ironworks, where the HMS *Warrior*, Britain's first iron-hulled battleship, was built in 1859. Employees at the works formed their own soccer club, which was renamed West Ham United in 1895 and has become one of England's leading teams.

CANNON STREET STATION. The **railway** station in Cannon Street, which opened in 1866, is located on a site of considerable historical importance. Excavations have revealed a sizeable Roman building, with reception rooms, private apartments, and painted walls, suggesting that the Governor of the province built his principal base there between 80 A.D. and 100 A.D. During the Middle Ages, the Hanseatic League's **steelyard**, headquarters of its trading empire, dominated the area and candlemakers sold their products nearby (the street's name—*Cannon*—is derived from "candlewick"). The station, designed by John Hawkshaw and opened in 1866, was built as the terminus of the South Eastern Railway at the southern edge of the **City of London**. Due to the steep slope of the shoreline, the tracks, brought over the **River Thames** on a five-span bridge with cast iron Doric piers, required a 60-foot-high viaduct, built of 27 million bricks, to carry them onto the platforms. The station was a cavernous structure covered by a 680-foot-long roof, which formed a single arch reaching a height of 106 feet at its highest point. Twin towers dominated the riverfront entrance and a **hotel** to accommodate travellers was erected facing Cannon Street. The building, badly damaged during the **Blitz**, was extensively renovated during the 1960s, when the roof was replaced and shops, office accommodations, and a walkway were incorporated. Since then, further commercial facilities have been added but the original walls, and the towers, remain. Much of the Victorian ornamentation on the bridge, which was also designed by Hawkshaw (along with John Wolfe-Barry), was removed when the structure was upgraded in 1979.

CANONBURY. Now part of the **London Borough of Islington**, the area acquired its name because the canons of St. Bartholomew's Priory, (*see* **Smithfield Meat Market**), held the land from 1253 until the dissolution of the **monasteries** by King Henry VIII in 1536–41. Some early development focused on the tower built by Prior William Bolton in the early 16th century and the mansion erected by Sir John Spencer (a cloth merchant and later **Lord Mayor** of London) in 1593–97 but, by the late 1700s, the economy was still essentially agricultural. In 1820, however, Henry Leroux obtained a building lease for 19 acres and laid out Canonbury Square, hoping that it might evolve into a second **Bloomsbury**. Further urban expansion occurred to the east during the 1840s and 1850s as the Marquess of Northampton laid out Canonbury Park, encouraging further construction of villas and substantial homes for relatively wealthy citizens. During the early part of the 20th century, the area was engulfed by the expansion of the inner city but, though it became a little shabby, it retained its attraction for some middle-class groups (George Orwell lived at 27 Canonbury Square in 1945, for example, and Duncan Grant with Vanessa Bell at 26A during the 1950s). After the Second World War, considerable regeneration work was undertaken (both by local authorities and by private interests) to repair bomb damage and upgrade **housing** standards. As part of that process, the tower has been restored and converted into a **theater**.

CARDBOARD CITY. During the 1970s, homeless people began to congregate in the network of subways outside Waterloo Station. By the mid-1980s, over 200 men and women slept there regularly, building homes with discarded boxes and earning the area the nickname "Cardboard City." Although the noisome assembly, many of whom were mentally disturbed, made some passersby nervous, the police and social services tolerated the shanty town until 1991, when it was discovered that residents' fires were damaging the fabric of the tunnels. A concerted effort to clear the area was partially successful, but many of those who moved filtered back after repair work was finished, so the community reformed, albeit with fewer members. In 1997, however, the British Film Institute began construction of a seven-story IMAX cinema (the largest in Europe) on the site, and, the following year, the **London Borough of Lambeth** won a High Court order compelling the remaining 35 or so occupants to leave.

CARLTON CLUB. The Carlton has been the social headquarters of the Conservative Party since it was formed in 1832, two years after a General Election had returned the Liberals to the **House of Commons** (*see* **Palace of Westminster**) with a 300-seat majority. Conservatives anxious to rebuild their strength leased rooms at 2 Carlton House Terrace, forming an association that would admit no more than 700 like-minded individuals. Membership was much sought after (so much so that the number accepted was raised to 900 in 1857) and has included most leading members of the party in the 19th and 20th centuries, including Prime Ministers Benjamin Disraeli, William Gladstone, Winston Churchill, and Harold Macmillan. The Carlton Club is now based at 68 St. James's Street. (*See also* GENTLEMEN'S CLUBS.)

CARLYLE'S HOUSE. From 1834 until his death in the drawing room on the first floor in 1881, Thomas Carlyle lived at 5 (now 24) Cheyne Row, one of a row of brick properties built in 1708. During that time, he wrote *The French Revolution* (3 volumes, 1837), *On Heroes, Hero-Worship and the*

Heroic in History (1841), and *The History of Friedrich II of Prussia, Called Frederick the Great* (6 volumes, 1857–65) while entertaining other leading authors, including John Ruskin, **Charles Dickens**, Charles Kingsley, and Alfred Lord Tennyson. The house, now maintained by the National Trust, is much as Carlyle left it; his hat perches on a peg, the pictures are those he owned, and Nero, his dog, lies buried in the garden.

CARNABY STREET. During the 1960s, Carnaby Street (one of a maze of small, narrow streets east of **Regent Street**) was as much a part of swinging London as the Beatles and Mick Jagger. John Stephen, John Vince, and Andreas Spyropoulos had opened a boutique selling men's clothes in 1957 and their success attracted similar retailers to the site. Within a decade, the road was lined with shops catering to both sexes in an era when fashion focused on colorful, outrageous garments. Businesses emphasized the arcade-like atmosphere by laying bright paving and erecting ornamental arches but, by the 1970s, young people's tastes had changed and stores were sold, so there is now little evidence of the street's considerable influence on popular culture.

CATFORD. Catford, located some 6.5 miles southeast of **Charing Cross**, is a residential area of the **London Borough of Lewisham**. Until the middle of the 19th century, it was little more than a hamlet with an economy based almost entirely on agriculture, largely because of the distance from London and the problems caused by regular flooding when the water level rose in the River Ravensbourne. However, the arrival of the **railway** in 1857 encouraged builders to erect homes for commuters and, within a few years, the fields had been replaced by rows of houses. In half a century, the village was transformed into a metropolitan suburb. Since the end of the Second World War, redevelopment has resulted in the demolition of many older properties (including the original Town Hall, completed in 1875, and St. Laurence's Church, opened in 1886) to make way for office accommodation and retail facilities. Catford is now a busy shopping and administrative center, with the headquarters of the Borough Council and regionally important recreational facilities at the ABC Cinema, Lewisham Theatre, and the greyhound racing stadium.

CATO STREET CONSPIRACY. In 1820, a group of political dissidents met in a stable loft at 6 Cato Street (near **Marble Arch**) to plot the death of the entire British Cabinet while the members were dining at Lord Harrowby's **Grosvenor Square** residence on 23 February. They planned to behead Lord Sidmouth (the Home Secretary) and Lord Castlereagh (one of his allies) but were betrayed, probably by George Edwards. On the day set for the killing, a detachment of Coldstream Guards, accompanied by policemen, broke into the loft and arrested several of the dissidents. Others (including Arthur Thistlewood, who killed one of the policemen with his sword) escaped. Thistlewood was taken into custody the next day and, on 1 May, was hanged at **Newgate Prison**, along with John Brunt, William Davidson, James Ings, and Richard Tidd. Five of their colleagues were exiled to penal colonies overseas. Public sympathy for the men was considerable—so much so that the executioner was attacked in the street and narrowly escaped castration. Cato Street was renamed Horace Street in 1827 but reverted to its original appellation early in the 20th century. It has been redeveloped to provide apartment dwellings but the loft has been incorporated into No. 1A.

CAVENDISH SQUARE. The square, laid out by John Prince, was the first urban development on land owned by Edward Harley, Earl of Oxford, on the north side of **Oxford Street**. It was named in honor of his wife, Lady Henrietta Cavendish Holles. Building began in 1717 and (although it proceeded in fits and starts for financial reasons) provided a focus for other construction as a gridiron pattern of streets was built around it, each named after a member of the Oxford family, one of their titles, or one of their estates. In 1741, the property was inherited by the Earl's daughter, Margaret, who married William Bentinck, Duke of Portland (*see* **Portland Place**), and, by 1800, was almost entirely developed. Distinguished residents have included Horatio Nelson (*see* **Trafalgar Square**) in 1791 and H. H. Asquith from 1895 until his appointment as Prime Minister in 1908. During the 20th century, the substantial homes have been replaced by offices and apartments and, in 1971, a parking garage was built under the garden in the center of the square. (*See also* ST. MARYLEBONE.)

CEMETERIES. *See* BURIAL GROUNDS.

CENOTAPH. The United Kingdom's memorial to service men and women of the British Empire and Commonwealth who were killed during the First and Second World Wars stands in the middle of **Whitehall**. Designed by Sir Edward Lutyens, it is built of **Portland stone** and was erected in 1919–20. The dedication to those who fell during the Second World War was added in 1946. A simple structure, it carries no religious motif and is decorated only by the flags of the army, the Merchant Marine, the Royal Air Force, and the Royal Navy. At 11 o'clock on the morning of the Sunday closest to 11 November (the hour and date on which hostilities ceased at the end of the First World War) a remembrance service is held, with the royal family and leaders of the major political parties in attendance. The word *cenotaph* is derived from the Greek *kenos* (meaning "empty") and *taphos* ("tomb").

CENTRAL CRIMINAL COURT. The trials of people from the London area accused of major **crime**s are normally held at the Central Criminal Court in the **City of London**. The first courthouse on the site was built in 1539 beside **Newgate Prison** in a street named Old Bailey. The present structure, designed by Edward Mountford, was erected in 1902–7. Faced with **Portland stone**, it is surmounted by a 12-foot-high gilded statue of Justice holding a sword in one hand and a set of scales in the other. An extension was added in 1970–72, allowing 19 hearings to take place simultaneously. On the first two days of every session, the judges carry posies of flowers, a reminder of the stench associated with the old prison. Those tried at the court (which is commonly known as the Old Bailey) include writer Oscar Wilde (found guilty of homosexuality in 1895), William Joyce (condemned to death as a traitor in 1945 for broadcasting in support of Nazi Germany), poisoner Hawley Harvey Crippen (1910), and multiple murderers John Reginald Halliday Christie (1953, *see* **Rillington Place**) and Peter Sutcliffe (1981). (*See also* KRAY TWINS.)

CENTRAL HALL. The headquarters of the Methodist Church in England were opened in 1912 on a site in Storey's Gate (near **St. James's Park**). The main hall, which can hold a congregation of 2,700 people, hosts concerts and public gatherings as well as church services. In 1946, it was used for the first meeting of the General Assembly of the United Nations.

CEREMONY OF THE KEYS. Every night, the **Tower of London** is closed with a 700-year-old ritual known as the Ceremony of the Keys. A **Beefeater**, accompanied by an escort, locks the West Gate, the Middle Tower, and the Byward Tower (the main entrance). At the Bloody Tower, challenged by a sentry, he replies that he brings Queen Elizabeth's keys. The Chief Warder raises his hat with a shout of "God preserve Queen Elizabeth," and the guard responds with "Amen" just before the clock strikes 10, then a bugler sounds the Last Post before the Chief Warder carries the keys to the Resident Governor for safekeeping until the tower is opened the next day.

CHAMBERS, WILLIAM (1723–1796). Chambers, architectural rival of **Robert Adam**, and designer of the ornamental buildings (including the pagoda) at the **Royal Botanic Gardens** in **Kew**, was born in Göteborg (Sweden) on 23 February 1723, the son of a merchant of Scottish descent. The family moved to England in 1728. After leaving school at the age of 16, he found work as a supercargo (the officer on a merchant ship in charge of the cargo) with the Swedish East India Company, collected material for a book on *Designs of Chinese Buildings* (published in 1757) during a voyage to Canton and, after only two years, gave up his career at sea to study **architecture**, initially in Paris and later in Rome. When he returned to Britain in 1755, he established himself in London's Poland Street (close to **Soho**) and was given a commission to design a villa for Lord Bessborough at **Roehampton** (now known as Manresa House, the building is used as a training center for Jesuit priests). Through mutual acquaintances, he was introduced to Augusta, Princess Dowager of Wales, who invited him to design gardens for her palace at Kew, where he used his knowledge of the Orient to construct replicas of a Chinese temple (1760), a Turkish mosque (1761), and a 163-foot-high pagoda (also 1761), only the last of which survives. The project was well received by the royal family, resulting in Chambers's appointment (jointly with Adam) as Architect of Works to King George III in 1772. The success also led to other commissions for distinguished individuals and organizations, notably for the building of Melbourne House (now The Albany) in **Piccadilly** (1770–74) and **Somerset House** (1776–86), and for alterations to Marlborough House in **The Mall** (1770–72).

As Chambers's fame grew, he moved from Poland Street to Berners Street (north of **Oxford Street**), then to Norton (now Bolsover) Street in Marylebone and associated with the great artists and writers of the day, including actor **David Garrick**, poet Oliver Goldsmith, and painter Joshua Reynolds. In 1768, he helped to found the **Royal Academy of Arts** and, in 1770, was dubbed a Knight of the Polar Star by King Adolphus Frederick of Sweden. He died on 8 March 1796 and was buried in **Westminster Abbey**. A pillar of the London establishment, he was an architectural conservative (criticizing Adam's Adelphi scheme, for example) but, even so, took the prevailing Palladian fashion and remolded it in a way that influenced building design on an international scale. (*See also* OSTERLEY HOUSE.)

CHANCERY LANE. Chancery Lane, which connects High Holborn and **Fleet Street**, got its name in 1377, when King Edward III acquired a property for the Keeper of the Rolls of Chancery. That building was demolished in 1896, but the street still houses several public buildings, notably the former **Public Record Office** and the Law Office (the principal professional organization for solicitors, one of the two branches of the legal profession, in England and Wales). The entrance to Lincoln's Inn (*see* **Inns of Court**) is on the west side of the road and that to the Royal Commission on Historical Manuscripts in Quality Court, an alley on the east side. When a new sovereign ascends the throne, Chancery Lane is one of the places where a formal announcement of the succession is made by heralds.

CHANGING OF THE GUARD. The ceremony of changing the guard at **Buckingham Palace** is one of London's most popular tourist attractions. The guard is normally mounted by one of the five regiments of Foot Guards in the **Household Division**. At 11:27 A.M., the new guard marches from Wellington Barracks and, accompanied by bandsmen, makes its way along **Birdcage Walk** to the palace forecourt, where it relieves the old guard. The ceremony is held every day from April until mid-August and every other day for the rest of the year. The mounted guards at **Horse Guards Parade** are also ceremonially changed at 10:00 A.M. on Sundays and 11:00 A.M. during the remainder of the week. At both locations, less formal changes of personnel take place throughout the day.

CHARING CROSS. When Eleanor, wife of King Edward I, died at Harby (Nottinghamshire) in 1290, she was carried to London for burial. At each place where her coffin rested en route, her husband erected a cross in her memory, the last being built at Charing Cross, now a busy junction where the **Strand** and **Whitehall** meet, close to **Trafalgar Square**, in the heart of London. (Some authorities claim that the area's name is derived from the French *chère reine*, which means "dear queen," others that it comes from *cierran,* the Old English word for "turn," and refers to a bend in the road on the northern shore of the **River Thames**). Edward's cross, suffering from the ravages of weather, was demolished in 1647, by which time Charing Cross had become a bustling community (during the 18th century, **Samuel Johnson** remarked that "the full tide of human existence" was to be found there). In 1818, Benjamin Golding established a small hospital in Villiers Street, but seven years later it was superseded by a larger building, designed by Decimus Burton and funded by subscriptions that included donations from the Duchess of Kent (mother of Queen Victoria). During the 1860s, the South Eastern **railway** built a **bridge** across the Thames in order to bring trains into the heart of London (*see* **Hungerford Bridge**) and constructed a station (designed by John Hawkshaw) on the site of the Hungerford fruit, vegetable, and meat **market**. Above the terminus, a lavishly furnished **hotel** (one of the first buildings in the city to be faced with artificial stone) was erected to plans prepared by E. M. Barry, and a replica of the Eleanor Cross was placed in front of it. The hospital moved to more spacious accommodation at **Fulham** in 1973, but the station survives, bringing commuters from Kent and the boroughs of southeast London to jobs in the central city. **London Underground** stations at Embankment and Trafalgar Square, along with the frequent **buses**, make the area one of the most important traffic hubs in the modern metropolis. The area forms part of the **City of Westminster**. (*See also* REGENT STREET.)

CHARING CROSS BRIDGE. *See* HUNGERFORD BRIDGE.

CHARING CROSS ROAD. During the 1880s, a thoroughfare was constructed between **Charing Cross** and **Bloomsbury** in an attempt to improve traffic flow in the central city. The work (planned by **Joseph William Bazalgette** and George Vulliamy, engineer and architect, respectively, of the **Metropolitan Board of Works**) involved the widening of Crown and Castle Streets and the demolition of some of the worst slums in the city. Architecturally, the road has little to commend it, but it is a busy route lined with shops, restaurants, and **theater**s. Foyle's (which claims to be the largest book shop in the world) is at Nos. 119–125. In 1949, Helen Hanff began a 20-year correspondence with another bookshop—Marks and Co.; the letters, published in one volume under the title *84 Charing Cross Road* (1970), became a bestseller but the shop is now closed, replaced by a café-bar.

CHARING CROSS STATION. *See* CHARING CROSS.

CHARLTON. Charlton, in the **London Borough of Greenwich**, has managed to maintain some semblance of its former village atmosphere despite its absorption into the city during the 19th century. There is evidence of settlement in the area from pre-Roman times and of the existence of a village when William the Conqueror carried out his property survey of England in 1085–86. Since 1612, the principal building has been Charlton House, built by Adam Newton and considered to be

Charing Cross Station, 1864 (Museum of London)

one of the best examples of Jacobean **architecture** in the country. Constructed of red brick, with white stone dressings and quoins, it is owned by the borough, which uses it as a community center and library. The green close to the mansion was the site of Charlton Horn Fair on 18 October each year. The origins of the event are unclear, but the local tradition is that King John (who ruled from 1199–1216) granted land to a miller as compensation when the monarch seduced his wife during a hunting expedition. Horns are the emblem of a wronged husband. Other writers have suggested that the name may be derived from pictures of St. Luke in a preliterate, God-fearing society (18 October is dedicated to the saint, who is often depicted writing beside a cow and an ox). At its height during the 18th and 19th centuries, the fair attracted thousands of visitors (many of whom wore horn headbands), but allegations of drunkenness, violence, and indecency caused the authorities to close it down in 1872. During the 20th century, much former open space in the area has been covered with houses and industrial estates, but areas of **park** land (including Horn Fair Park) have been preserved as a recreational resource.

CHARTERHOUSE. In 1348, when the **Black Death** was ravaging London and corpses lay for days awaiting burial, Sir Walter Manny bought 13 acres of land in **Clerkenwell** and donated it to the **City of London** for use as a cemetery. A chapel was built on the site of what is now Charterhouse Square so that Masses could be said for the souls of the dead. Twenty-two years later, the pious Sir Walter founded a Carthusian **monastery** on the site, converting the chapel for use as the foundation's place of worship. It thrived until 1536, when six of the monks were hanged at **Tyburn** for refusing to accept King Henry VIII as head of the Church of England. The monarch assumed control of the property, which passed through a succession of aristocratic owners before being acquired, in 1611, by Thomas Sutton (reputedly the richest commoner in England). Sutton had no children, so he used his wealth to establish Charterhouse as a school for 40 boys and a hospital for 80 poor gentlemen. The school flourished, becoming one of England's most prestigious educational institutions and numbering essayist Joseph Addison and preacher John Wesley among its old boys. It moved to Godalming (Surrey) in 1872, turning its buildings over to Merchant Taylors' School, which occupied them until it ran out of space and transferred to more commodious premises at Sandy Lodge (Middlesex) in 1933. The buildings suffered badly from incendiary bombs dropped by German planes on the night of 10–11 May 1941, but they were sympathetically restored by Lord Mottistone and Paul Paget. A medical school for St. Bartholomew's Hospital was erected on the site of the Great Cloister in 1949, but elderly pensioners to this day occupy rooms in the older part of the complex.

CHEAM. Cheam, an outer London suburb located 11 miles southeast of **Charing Cross**, was probably settled by Saxon migrants during the sixth century. It developed an important pottery industry during the Middle Ages but remained primarily agricultural until the 1920s, when an increasing demand for houses close to the rural fringe encouraged developers to line spacious streets with detached homes for affluent office workers. The focus of the community is a Tudor Revival-style shopping area, with black and white timbered stores, built just before the Second World War, but several 18th-century houses survive as reminders of the old village. The area was included in the **London Borough of Sutton** when **local government** in the metropolitan area was reorganized in 1965.

CHEAPSIDE. During the early Middle Ages, Cheapside was the **City of London**'s largest **market** (its name is derived from the Old English word *ceap*, which means "to barter"). Country people crowded into the town to sell their wares, each in their own sector of the retailing area—the poulterers were in Poultry, the bakers in Bread Street, and the dairymen in Milk Street, for example. Those found guilty of attempting to cheat customers were put into stocks (in 1382, for instance, one man was found guilty of selling a rotten conger eel and was clamped while the fish was burned in front of his face). However, during the 13th century, a competing market was established on the site of the present **Mansion House**. From then, trade declined. Most buildings were made of wood so the **Great Fire** of 1666 ravaged the area, but properties were speedily rebuilt in stone and, by the early 19th century, the district was known for its trade in precious metals and linens. For much of the Victorian period, Cheapside was an important shopping area but, over the past 100 years, offices and warehouses have replaced many of the stores. Few of the older buildings survive, but the market's legacy is evident in the number of **livery company** headquarters that cluster around the street. (*See also* BANK OF ENGLAND; BOW BELLS; JONSON, BEN; LONDINIUM.)

CHELSEA. Chelsea lies on the north bank of the **River Thames** some two miles southwest of **Charing Cross**. The origins of the settlement are obscure but it was certainly in existence by 787 A.D., when Offa, King of

Mercia, held a synod at the site. By the 16th century, it had become a popular haunt of the aristocracy, with King Henry VIII, the Duke of Norfolk, the Earl of Shrewsbury, and others owning residences in the area. In 1528, Sir Thomas More (who was to become Henry's Lord Chancellor) rebuilt the south chapel of Chelsea Old Church, which was founded at least by 1157. (The church, previously known as All Saints, was badly damaged during the **Blitz** in 1941 but restored by Walter Godfrey after the Second World War; it contains some of England's finest Tudor monumental **architecture** and, in work by Hans Holbein the Younger, the earliest Renaissance architecture in the country.) **Chelsea Hospital**, established by King Charles II in 1682 as a home for elderly soldiers, spurred further development, then, in 1745, a porcelain works (founded by Nicholas Sprimont) introduced manufacturing activity and attracted artists seeking commissions to decorate the china. Over the years, the artistic colony grew, so, by 1891 (when Frank Brangwyn and James Abbott McNeill Whistler were local residents), it was able to constitute itself as a club and rent premises in **King's Road**. One of its principal events was an annual Chelsea Arts Ball, which was held at the **Albert Hall** but became so riotous that it was discontinued after 1959. During the late 19th and early 20th centuries, population increased as a result of the opening of an army barracks (designed for 1,000 infantrymen) in 1861, the South Western Polytechnic (later Chelsea College) in 1891, Chelsea Football Club in 1905, and other institutional and public employers.

Chelsea was made a metropolitan borough within the **London County Council** structure in 1900 but amalgamated with **Kensington** in 1965 to form the **Royal Borough of Kensington and Chelsea**. Since then, there has been much redevelopment, but the Chelsea Society, an influential group of local residents, exerts pressure to retain the best of the older buildings and promote a sense of identity. (*See also* BATTERSEA BRIDGE; CARLYLE'S HOUSE; CHELSEA BRIDGE; CHELSEA PHYSIC GARDEN; NATIONAL ARMY MUSEUM; ROYAL HORTICULTURAL SOCIETY.)

CHELSEA BRIDGE. In 1851–58, a suspension **bridge**, designed by Thomas Page and incorporating cast iron towers, was built across the **River Thames** to improve access between **Chelsea** and **Battersea**. Weapons uncovered during the building work revealed evidence of a battle fought between the Roman invaders and native Britons at the site. The present bridge dates from 1934.

CHELSEA FLOWER SHOW. *See* ROYAL HORTICULTURAL SOCIETY.

CHELSEA HOSPITAL. Established in 1682 and formally known as the Royal Hospital because it was founded by King Charles II, **Chelsea** Hospital was established to provide accommodation for soldiers no longer able to undertake military duties. The brainchild of Sir Stephen Fox (England's first Paymaster General), who modelled it on French and Irish provision, it was designed by **Christopher Wren** and completed in 1689, when 476 "pensioners" took up residence. Their home, planned around three courtyards, has changed little over the past three centuries apart from a series of minor works carried out, under the supervision of **Robert Adam**, in 1765–82 and a stable block added by Sir John Soane (*see* **Sir John Soane's Museum**) in 1814. Pensioners dine in the Great Hall, where the Duke of Wellington (who commanded British troops during the Napoleonic Wars) lay in state after his death in 1852. The panelled hall contains a large mural, by Antonio Verrio, of Charles II on horseback and a painting of one pensioner who married for the third time at the age of 100). A nearby chapel is decorated with flags captured during battle and a painting, by Sebastiano Ricci, that shows Christ's resurrection. Most resident pensioners (who number about 420) are over 65 years of age, though men up to 10 years younger may be admitted if they are unable to work. Divided into six companies, each under an officer, they receive board, lodging, clothing, a weekly allowance, and medical care. Everyday dress is a navy blue uniform with a peaked cap bearing the initials R. H. but, on ceremonial occasions, required dress is a scarlet frock coat and three-cornered hat. Many out-pensioners receive financial help from the hospital. In May each year, the Chelsea Flower Show is held in the grounds (*see* **Royal Horticultural Society**). (*See also* GIBBONS, GRINLING; HAWKSMOOR, NICHOLAS.)

CHELSEA PENSIONER. *See* CHELSEA HOSPITAL.

CHELSEA PHYSIC GARDEN. The garden was established in 1676 by the Apothecaries' Company (one of the **livery companies**) so that its members could conduct research into the properties of medicinal plants. Although initially the land was leased, the property (in Swan Walk on the north bank of the **River Thames**) was gifted to the company in 1722 by **Hans Sloane**. In 1732, seed sent to James Oglethorpe in Georgia stimulated the growth of the cotton industry in North America. There is, in addition to the herb garden, a wide range of shrubs and trees (the first cedars in England were planted at the site in 1684).

CHESSINGTON. Located at the southern tip of the **Borough of Kingston Upon Thames**, Chessington is a predominantly residential area that developed, between the First and Second World Wars, around a medieval village core. Although the 13th-century church of St. Mary the Virgin is of interest to architectural historians, the community's major attraction is the World of Adventures theme park, an extension of a zoological garden that opened in 1931 and was, for a time, the largest privately owned collection of animals in the world. In 1997, the park was bought for a reported £377 million by Charterhouse Development in a deal that also involved the purchase of **Madame Tussaud's Waxworks**.

CHIEF COMMONER. In the **City of London**, the leader of the **Court of Common Council** acts as Chairman of the **Corporation of London**'s City Lands and Bridge House Estates Committee, which was formed in 1592 and administers many of the corporation's accounts. Because of the importance of the chairmanship, the individual holding the post became known, in 19th-century parlance, as the Chief Commoner, a title that gradually entered official records of office-bearers.

CHILTERN HILLS. The Chilterns form the northwest rim of the **London Basin**, stretching for some 60 miles from the **River Thames** at Goring to the Luton area of Bedfordshire. They reach a maximum height of only 852 feet (at Coombe Hill) but culminate in a chalk escarpment that dominates the low plains of central England. Large sections of the hills are covered with beech woods, which once provided the basis of a local furniture industry, but are now more important as recreational space for city dwellers.

CHINATOWN. During the Second World War, a number of Chinese restaurants opened in the Gerrard Street area, south of **Shaftesbury Avenue**, to cater to servicemen who had acquired a taste for East Asian food while serving abroad. Property was cheap and rents low, so, as Britain returned to peacetime conditions in the 1950s, several striptease clubs were established and the Chinese community (most of its members from Hong Kong) capitalized on visitors by opening shops selling foods, crafts, music, herbal medicines, and other goods. From 1973, annual New Year's celebrations have generated considerable tourist interest, and local authorities have deliberately emphasized the Far Eastern imagery by erecting oriental arches and placing Chinese characters on street signs. As a result, the streets are normally busy with shoppers, particularly on weekends, when Chinese people from all over southeast England arrive to stock up with foods not readily available elsewhere. (*See also* LIMEHOUSE.)

CHINGFORD. Chingford lies on the northeast edge of London, some 10 miles from **Charing Cross**. Saxon immigrants established a settlement in the marshes along the sides of the Bourne River but, by the 12th century, the community had moved to nearby hillsides and was clearing the oak and beech forest to provide pastureland and timber. Although brickmakers and potters provided employment during the Medieval period, the economy was essentially agricultural until, in 1873, the arrival of the Great Eastern **Railway** encouraged urban development. The impact of the builders was more restricted than in other parts of the city, however, because, in 1878, the **Corporation of London** took control of **Epping Forest** in order to maintain it as recreational space. Also, during the first half of the 20th century, the Metropolitan Water Board (*see* **water supply**) built a series of dams in the valley of the **River Lea**, forming a string of reservoirs and preserving much of the marshland. Chingford was included within the **London Borough of Waltham Forest**, created in 1965, primarily because many of its residents commute to work in the city center.

CHISWICK. A predominantly residential area lying six miles west of **Charing Cross**, Chiswick evolved at a point on the north bank of the **River Thames** where the currents facilitated development of a small quay and where it was possible to ford the waters to the southern shore. Until the **railway** arrived in 1849, it was essentially a village that focused on several large estates (*see*, for example, **Chiswick House**) and on the production of fresh fruit and vegetables for the London market. The new transport system, however, attracted commuters wanting to work in the city but live in the countryside. The estates were sold, subdivided, and built over as developers raised flats and terraced homes to meet the needs of the incomers (in the 1920s and 1930s, the Duke of Devonshire's lands, south of Chiswick High Road, were the last to succumb). After the Second World War, much of the area was the focus of regeneration and improvement programs that incorporated office development, local authority **housing**, and upgrading of the A4 road, leading to the M4 motorway and the west of England. Chiswick was included in the **London Borough of Hounslow** when that authority was created in 1965. (*See also* AIR RAIDS; ROYAL HORTICULTURAL SOCIETY.)

CHISWICK BRIDGE. The road bridge connecting **Chiswick** (on the north bank of the **River Thames**) to **Mortlake** (on the south) was opened in 1933. Its three concrete arches, faced with **Portland stone**, are the finishing point for the annual boat race between Oxford and Cambridge Universities (see **University boat race**).

CHISWICK HOUSE. In 1714–15 and in 1719, Richard Boyle, the third Earl of Burlington, made lengthy visits to Italy. A gifted architect, he was much influenced by the building styles he saw there and modelled Chiswick House (erected in 1725–29) on one of Andrea Palladio's villas near Vicenza. His friend, William Kent, was responsible for the interior and for the garden (which departed from the tradition of formal topiary by adopting a more natural look). The structure (two suites of apartments around an octagonal domed saloon) proved highly influential, sparking a revival of interest in the classical style and influencing **Robert Adam**'s work. However, Burlington never lived in it, preferring to use it as a gallery for his art collection and for entertaining his friends, who included poet Alexander Pope, author Jonathan Swift, and composer George Frideric Handel. In 1892, it was converted for use as a mental hospital and in 1928 was purchased by the Middlesex County Council in order to prevent the land from being acquired by developers. The property is now managed by English Heritage, the government's conservation agency.

CHOLERA. *See* SNOW, JOHN.

CHRIST CHURCH, NEWGATE STREET. *See* GREYFRIARS MONASTERY.

CHRIST CHURCH, SPITALFIELDS. Considered by many critics to be one of architect **Nicholas Hawksmoor**'s masterpieces, Christ Church was consecrated in 1729. Representing a brief flirtation with the baroque building style before the flowering of Palladianism (*see* **Chiswick House**), it has four pillars to mark the entrance, which is surmounted by a tower and spire. The interior is spacious, with Corinthian columns and aisles overlooked by two tiers of gallery. However, after over two centuries of use, it was declared unsafe in 1957 and closed to worshippers. Planners proposed demolition in order to allow new development in the area, but a campaign led by poets John Betjeman and T. S. Eliot forced them to back down. During the 1990s, Friends of Christ Church, **Spitalfields**, obtained grants from English Heritage (the government's conservation body) and from the National Lottery to enable a start on renovations, which included restoration of the organ and replacement of features destroyed by the Victorians.

CHRISTIE'S. One of the leading auction houses in London, Christie's International plc was established in 1766 by James Christie, a former midshipman in the Royal Navy, who sold a wide range of goods from his base in **Pall Mall**. In 1823, his son (also James) transferred the business to 8 King Street, where it has remained ever since (although the premises were reconstructed following bomb damage during the Second World War). During the 20th century, the firm has become renowned for its Eton-educated experts, whose social contacts with wealthy families have sustained a flow of art to the salerooms. The 1980s and 1990s, in particular, were marked by high profile auctions, including a bid of £24.75 million for Vincent Van Gogh's painting *Sunflowers* in 1987. In 1997, worldwide sales exceeded £1.2 billion, surpassing those of arch rival **Sotheby's** for the first time since 1954. The following year, Frenchman François Pinault bought the firm for a sum of over £900 million, taking it out of British control for the first time. Sales are held on five days each week from October until July.

CHRIST'S HOSPITAL. *See* GREYFRIARS MONASTERY.

CHURCH OF THE IMMACULATE CONCEPTION, WESTMINSTER. The church, in Farm Street, is the English headquarters of the Jesuit movement. Built to plans prepared by J. J. Scoles and opened in 1849, it has a nave flanked by red granite pillars and a high altar designed by **Augustus Welby Northmore Pugin**. After 1963, when it was made a parish church, it became very fashionable and hosted many society weddings.

CITY, THE. As a form of shorthand in speech and writing, "The City" can refer either to the distinctive **local government** and urban landscape of the **City of London** or to the business community based in the area.

CITY AND GUILDS OF LONDON INSTITUTE. The institute, based in Giltspur Street, was founded in 1878 by the **livery companies** and the

Corporation of London to promote technical and scientific education, with an emphasis on technology and on fine art as applied to industry and commerce. It has become England's principal examining body for craft skills, testing students in over 400 subjects as disparate as communications skills, flour confectionery, and radio operation. In addition, it provides a consultancy, research, and training service.

CITY CHAMBERLAIN. The Chamberlain, whose post dates from 1237, is the **Corporation of London**'s principal finance officer.

CITY CORPORATION. *See* CORPORATION OF LONDON.

CITY LIVERY COMPANIES. *See* LIVERY COMPANIES.

CITY OF LONDON. The City covers 677 acres (or slightly over one square mile) at the heart of the capital and has a permanent population of only about 5,400 people (1998), most of whom are residents in the **Barbican** development or security workers in offices. The date of the earliest settlement is unknown, but excavations clearly indicate that the Romans established a substantial community during the first century A.D., maintaining a presence until 410 (*see* **Londinium**). The Saxons arrived during the fifth century (Ethelbert, the first Christian King of Kent, founded **St. Paul's Cathedral** in 604) and ruled through **Aldermen**, a system that was retained after the Norman conquest in 1066. In 1067, William the Conqueror, the Norman leader, granted the City a charter recognizing the rights and privileges it had enjoyed under Saxon rule (but cannily built the **Tower of London** just outside the eastern wall of the town so that the citizens were constantly reminded who was in charge). During the Medieval period, the accumulation of wealth and prestige associated with the presence of royalty made London the richest city in England, an affluence that often resulted in funds being loaned to monarchs so that they could pursue military campaigns (or other policies) both at home and abroad. Astute civic leaders used that financial dependence to win concessions from the Crown, ultimately developing a unique system of **local government** (*see* **Corporation of London**), with a **Lord Mayor**, attended by **Sheriffs**, supported by the weekly Court of Husting (composed of the Aldermen) and, from 1285, advised by groups of respected residents who became known as the **Court of Common Council**.

Financial dealings have remained the principal economic activity and a major (albeit declining) source of employment in the City, which has

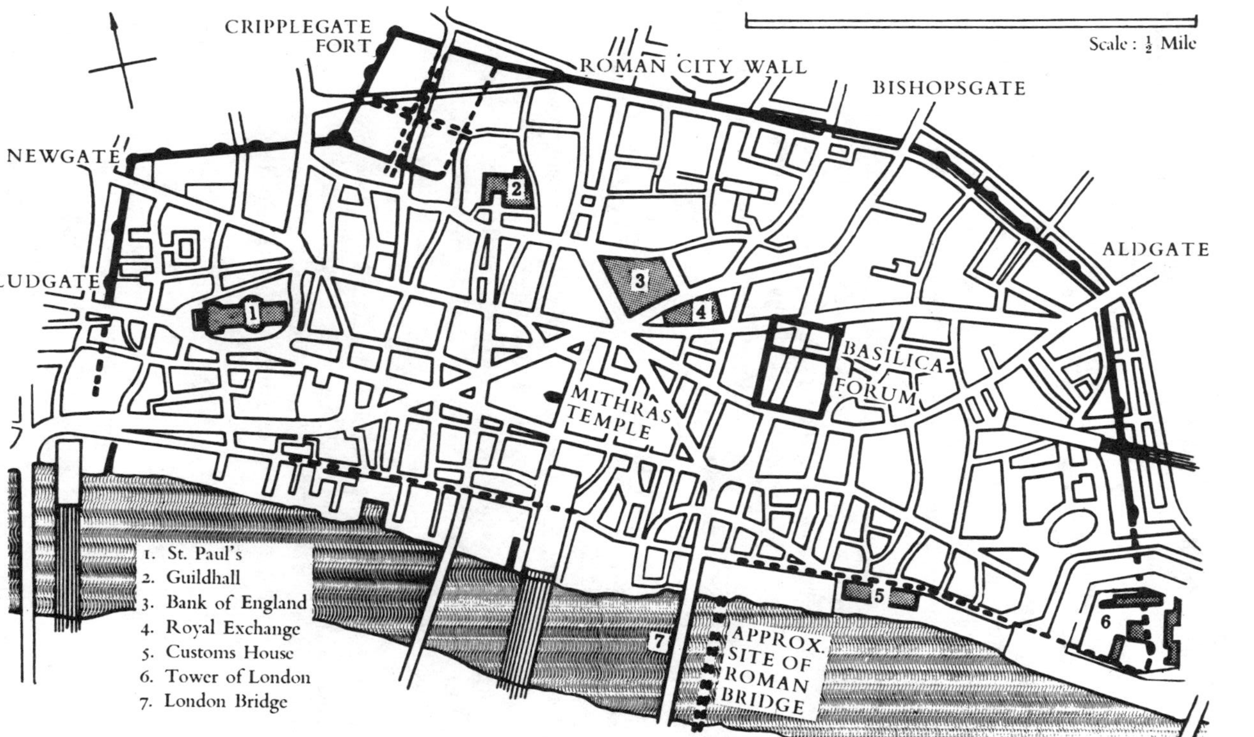

Map of Londinium superimposed on a modern map of the City of London (Museum of London)

become one of the world's leading trading centers. During the early 1970s, some 500,000 men and women commuted, every weekday, from suburbs to the offices that line the narrow streets, virtually excluding all other businesses except those (such as the **public houses**) that serve them. By the late 20th century, however, the tide had lessened, with only about 280,000 people arriving each day, a reflection of changing technology (notably the introduction of computers) and changing employment practices (particularly a trend towards working at home). About 75 percent of the employees work for financial concerns and about 40 percent for foreign companies (there are some 560 non-British banks in the City).

In terms of domestic and foreign earnings, the influence of the "**Square Mile**" is enormous. City-based banks invest more capital abroad than those of any other country, accounting for about 18 percent of global foreign loans. The foreign exchange market is by far the world's largest, with a daily turnover in 1996 of US$464 million, more than that of New York and Tokyo combined (nearly twice as much trading in the dollar takes place in London as in the United States). Also, the City is the world's largest insurance market, accounting for nearly 30 percent of world marine insurance and nearly 40 percent of aviation insurance. In addition, it is the global center for forward trading in gold and (through the **London Metal Exchange**) sets world prices for nonferrous metals. (*See also* BALTIC EXCHANGE; BANK OF ENGLAND; BARBICAN; BEDLAM; BIG BANG; BLACKFRIARS; BRIDEWELL; CANNON STREET STATION; CHEAPSIDE; CITY CHAMBERLAIN; CITY REMEMBRANCER; COLE ABBEY CHURCH, DISTAFF LANE; COMMON CRYER AND SERJEANT AT ARMS; COMMON HALL; COMPTROLLER AND CITY SOLICITOR; CORN EXCHANGE; CORNHILL; CUSTOM HOUSE; EASTCHEAP; FLEET STREET; FREEDOM OF THE CITY; GREAT FIRE; GREAT PLAGUE; GUILDHALL; HOUNDSDITCH; INTERNATIONAL PETROLEUM EXCHANGE [IPE]; LEADENHALL MARKET; LIVERY COMPANIES; LLOYD'S OF LONDON; LOMBARD STREET; LONDON BRIDGE; LONDON FIRST; LONDON INTERNATIONAL FINANCIAL FUTURES AND OPTIONS EXCHANGE [LIFFE]; LONDON INTERNATIONAL INSURANCE AND REINSURANCE MARKET ASSOCIATION [LIRMA]; LONDON METAL EXCHANGE [LME]; MANSION HOUSE; NEWGATE; NEWGATE PRISON; POLICE; ST. ANDREW UNDERSHAFT CHURCH, LEADENHALL STREET; ST. BARTHOLOMEW-THE-GREAT CHURCH, SMITHFIELD; ST.

BENET'S CHURCH, PAUL'S WHARF; ST. BOTOLPH'S CHURCH, ALDGATE; ST. BRIDE'S CHURCH, FLEET STREET; ST. DUNSTAN IN THE WEST CHURCH, FLEET STREET; ST. ETHELBURGA-THE-VIRGIN WITHIN BISHOPSGATE CHURCH, BISHOPSGATE; ST. ETHELDREDA'S CHURCH, HOLBORN; ST. MARY ABCHURCH CHURCH, ABCHURCH LANE; SOUTHWARK BRIDGE; STOCK EXCHANGE [LSE]; TEMPLE BAR; TEMPLE OF MITHRAS; THREADNEEDLE STREET; TOWER BRIDGE; WALBROOK; WARD; WARDMOTE; WHITEFRIARS.)

CITY OF LONDON POLICE. *See* POLICE.

CITY PRIDE INITIATIVE. *See* LONDON PRIDE PARTNERSHIP.

CITY REMEMBRANCER. The Remembrancer, whose office dates from the reign of Queen Elizabeth I, is a senior law officer of the **Corporation of London**. The holder of the post, who is elected by the **Court of Common Council**, advises the corporation on parliamentary matters, communicates its views to the government and the monarch, and organizes ceremonial occasions at the **Guildhall**.

CLAPHAM. A largely working-class suburb some three miles southeast of **Charing Cross**, Clapham was probably founded during the Anglo-Saxon period (its name may be a corruption of the Old English *clopeham*, which means "the homestead on the hill"). From 1664 to 1666, Londoners seeking to avoid the **Great Plague** and the **Great Fire** settled in the area, then, in 1690, a coach service was established to Gracechurch Street, giving regular access to the **Royal Exchange** and other trading institutions. Wealthy citizens, such as diarist **Samuel Pepys** and poet Percy Bysshe Shelley, set up homes as the village became increasingly fashionable during the 18th and early 19th centuries, but the arrival of the **railway** in 1838, and industrial development in nearby **Battersea**, wrought changes to the social structure as workers in the new candle factories, **gas** works, and chemical manufactories encouraged developers to build properties more in keeping with their employees' limited means. Although these sources of income are gone, much of the Victorian character remains in the rows of closely packed terraces that still characterize the neighborhood. In 1965, Clapham was incorporated into the new **London Borough of Lambeth**. (*See also* CLAPHAM COMMON; CLAPHAM JUNCTION; CLAPHAM SECT; LONDON TRANSPORT MUSEUM.)

CLAPHAM COMMON. Until the early 18th century, Clapham Common (about four miles southwest of **Charing Cross**) was undeveloped, frequented only by highwaymen who preyed on the stage coaches carrying travellers to the **City of London**. From 1722, however, the boggy areas were drained and the land improved, so by 1855 author William Makepeace Thackeray was able to claim in *The Newcomes* (1853–55) that "of all the pretty suburbs that adorn our metropolis there are few that exceed in charm Clapham Common." Many of the houses that line the edge of the 200-acre open space were built by wealthy merchants and writers (diarist **Samuel Pepys** died at his home on North Side in 1703 and historian Lord Macaulay was born at 5 The Pavement), but the only building on the open space itself is a **public house** (The Windmill) where drinkers lounge on the grass through long summer evenings. Clapham Common, unlike some of the more staid city center **parks**, is a regular site for circuses, evangelist campaigns, reggae festivals, and other boisterous events. (*See also* BARRY, CHARLES.)

CLAPHAM JUNCTION. Britain's busiest **railway** junction lies close to the industrial communities of **Battersea** and **Clapham** at a point where tracks from **Victoria** Station and **Waterloo** Station converge. From Monday through Friday, about 1.4 million travellers and over 2,000 trains arrive every day. The first services were routed through the area in 1838, then, in 1863, a station was built. Commuters bought homes nearby and facilities were established to serve them as the community grew. Also, because of its accessibility, the area developed a reputation as an entertainment and shopping center with **music halls**, **theater**s, cinemas, and a large **department store**. By the end of the 20th century, Clapham Junction had evolved into the commercial heart of Battersea, with a shopping center located alongside the station, which was the scene of a major accident on 12 December 1988, when two passenger trains collided, killing 35 people. (*See also* BATTERSEA BRIDGE; BRIDGES.)

CLAPHAM SECT. In the early 19th century, a group of wealthy evangelical Anglicans (including William Wilberforce, the anti-slavery campaigner) argued that commitment to the Christian faith must be evidenced by efforts to improve the situation of the poor and oppressed. Most lived close to **Clapham Common**, where they worshipped at Holy Trinity Church, so they were christened the Clapham Sect. As well as organizing financial help for the needy, they placed much stress on the importance of education as a means of improving living standards, supported missionary work at home and abroad, and founded *The Christian Observer* to propagate their views. Several members had seats in the House of Commons (*see* **Palace of Westminster**), where they worked for prison reform and the suppression of cruel sports. The focus of activity was the Thornton family, who provided hospitality as well as encouragement; one of its principal members is commemorated in the name of Henry Thornton School in South Side, near Clapham Common.

CLARENCE HOUSE. The southwest suite of state rooms in **St. James's Palace** is joined by a passage to Clarence House, designed by **John Nash** and built for William, Duke of Clarence (later King William IV). The original construction work was completed in 1828, but an additional story was added in 1873 and much restoration undertaken following bomb damage incurred during the Second World War. Although, for much of the war, the building was the headquarters of the Red Cross and St. John's Ambulance Brigade, it has been used primarily as a residence for members of the royal family. Princess Elizabeth (now Queen Elizabeth II) lived there from 1947 until 1950, giving birth to Princess Anne (her only daughter) shortly before she left. In 1953, the Queen Mother moved into Clarence House following the death of her husband, King George VI, the previous year.

CLARIDGE'S HOTEL. Claridge's is one of London's most exclusive **hotels**, patronized by royalty and heads of state. It was founded in 1855 when William Claridge (a butler) used his savings to purchase Mivart's Hotel in Brook Street, **Mayfair**, acquired by the Savoy Company in 1890 and rebuilt in red brick in 1895–99. A £42-million refurbishment, carried out in 1996–97, retained the best of the interior (including the art deco restaurant designed by Basil Ionides in 1926) and helped boost operating profits. In 1998, the Savoy Group was taken over by Blackstone and Colony, an American investment firm, at a cost of £520 million. The hotel's 420 staff service 198 rooms, with a single-bed apartment costing over £2,000 a night.

CLEOPATRA'S NEEDLE. A granite obelisk some 65 feet high and 186 tons in weight, the Needle was carved from a quarry at Aswan (Egypt) about 1475 B.C., erected at Heliopolis, and carved with dedications to various gods. Later, it was moved to Alexandria, where it stood for hundreds of years before falling over. In 1819, it was presented to Britain by

Mohammed Ali, the Turkish Viceroy of Egypt, but nobody was able to suggest a means of moving it until engineer John Dixon designed a special pontoon in 1877. It left Alexandria in September that year and, after surviving a storm in the Bay of Biscay, reached London the following January. Initially, it was destined for a site near the Houses of Parliament (*see* **Palace of Westminster**), but the location suffered from subsidence, so instead it was erected on the Victoria Embankment between **Hungerford Bridge** and Waterloo Bridge. A set of coins, four Bibles in different languages, a razor, a box of pins, Bradshaw's *Railway Guide*, and copies of daily newspapers were buried beneath it, along with photographs of 12 of the most beautiful ladies of the time. The obelisk, which has no known connection with Cleopatra, was slightly damaged in one of the early **air raids** on London during the **Blitz**.

CLERKENWELL. Clerkenwell lies about 1.5 miles northeast of **Charing Cross**, north of the **City of London**. It developed as a village around the Benedictine nunnery of St. Mary and the Priory of St. John of Jerusalem (*see* **Knights Hospitaller**), which were founded during the 12th century on land gifted by Jordan de Briset. When King Henry VIII dissolved the **monasteries** between 1536 and 1541, most of the religious buildings were demolished and the land was given to aristocratic families, who are remembered in such road names as Albemarle Way and Aylesbury Street. During the 16th century, however, many of these wealthy groups moved to accommodations closer to the royal court, and their homes were taken over by merchants and craftsmen. Clerkenwell was transformed into an industrial community, with skilled tradesmen employed in **breweries**, gin distilleries, print works, jewelry manufacturing, and clock makers' shops. The discovery of medicinal springs brought additional sources of income, leading to the establishment of **Sadler's Wells** in 1683 and Islington Spa in 1685.

By 1740, the area was a popular recreational focus, but the urban expansion that accompanied the Industrial Revolution consumed most of the open space, replacing grassy banks with textile workshops, small metal plants, and rows of cheap terraced houses. The situation was exacerbated by road and **railway** construction, which destroyed many of the worst slums but added to the number of homeless people. Poverty led to political unrest as Clerkenwell Green became a regular meeting place for protest groups.

During the early 20th century, economic decay and slum clearance programs resulted in population decline, but the national economic resurgence of the 1980s was reflected in an expansion of office accommodation and restoration of some of the best of the older **housing**, such as the Woodbridge Estate, originally erected in the late 18th century. Little of the original religious houses survives, but the **museum** of the Order of St. John, in St. John's Gate, outlines the history of the knights and their modern successors, the St. John Ambulance Brigade, which has 250,000 members around the world. (*See also* CHARTERHOUSE.)

CLIMATE. The weather experienced by the first Londoners must be inferred from archaeological and other indirect sources (see, for example, **London Clay**), but records of rainfall have been kept since 1697 and of wind direction since 1723. Over the past 300 years, climatic variations have followed a cyclical pattern, with cold winters during the 1740s and 1770s, and in 1809–17, 1836–45, and 1875–82. Since 1919, there has been a lengthy warming trend, with January temperatures averaging about 42° F (5° C) in the 1990s and July temperatures averaging 65° F (18° C). The inner city tends to be warmer in all months because of the heat retained by buildings, emitted by vehicle engines, and dispersed by central heating equipment. Rain falls on an average of 165 days each year, amounting to 23 inches annually and is spread fairly equally throughout the seasons. The prevailing wind is from the west-southwest. (*See also* AIR POLLUTION.)

CLINK PRISON. A small jail located south of the **River Thames** near the **Globe Theatre**, Clink Prison was used during the 16th and early 17th centuries to lock up troublemakers from the brothels and drinking houses of the **Bankside** area. Documentary evidence indicates that it was in use by 1509, but that, by the 1760s, it housed only a few debtors. The prison was destroyed during the **Gordon Riots** in 1780 and never replaced. Its name is commemorated in Clink Street (where it was located) and in the vernacular phrase "in the clink," meaning "in prison." The site now houses a museum that displays instruments of torture. (*See also* ANCHOR INN.)

CLUBS. *See* GENTLEMEN'S CLUBS.

COADE STONE. During the 1760s, Eleanor Coade improved the weatherproof qualities of terracotta by adding materials such as glass and ground quartz. Because of its resistance to the elements, Coade stone became very popular as an ornamental material on buildings and for making statues during the late 18th and early 19th centuries. The company, based in **Lambeth**, went out of business in 1840, but its product can still be seen on such buildings as the **Royal Opera House** in **Covent Garden** and the lion at the south side of **Westminster Bridge**.

COCKNEY. By tradition, a Cockney is an individual born within the sound of **Bow Bells**. The term (derived from the Middle English *cokeney*, which means "a misshapen egg" or "cock's egg") was applied during the Middle Ages to weak or effeminate men, but by the 17th century was widely used as a denigrating synonym for "Londoner." More recently, Cockneys have been depicted, by filmmakers and novelists, in a romanticized fashion, as happy-go-lucky working-class people with a distinctive dialect (using rhyming slang such as "plates of meat" for "feet," for example) and an accent that makes much use of the glottal stop. (*See also* EAST END; LAMBETH WALK.)

COFFEE HOUSES. In 1652, Pasqua Rosee (a Greek immigrant) opened London's first coffee house in St. Michael's Alley, close to the **Royal Exchange**. Although the smell of coffee was sometimes considered a public nuisance, the new drink quickly became fashionable, so within 10 years there were 82 establishments in **The City**, with other businesses serving cocoa and chocolate. The houses were important foci for gossip and transmission of news, so patrons selected the ones most suited to their business and social needs; those in **Pall Mall** were favored by wealthy aristocrats, the St. James's Coffee House (at 87 St. James's Street) was known as the haunt of Whig supporters, Will's (at 1 Bow Street) was frequented by scholarly writers such as John Dryden, the Bedford (in **Covent Garden**) attracted a theatrical clientele, including **David Garrick,** and Child's (in Warwick Lane, close to **St. Paul's Cathedral)** was preferred by clergymen (and the frequently less than morally upright **James Boswell**). In order to preserve their distinctiveness, and keep out unwanted guests, many coffee houses began to charge subscriptions and ultimately evolved into **gentlemen's clubs** (White's, at 37–38 St. James's Street, originated at White's Chocolate House, for example) or gaming rooms. Lloyd's Coffee House, originally located in Tower Street, became the insurance market now known as **Lloyd's of London**.

Reductions in the tax on coffee in 1808 and 1825 led to an enormous growth in the number of coffee houses during the 19th century and to an increase in coffee drinking by less affluent members of the community. Fashionable society moved on to other pursuits, but the 17th- and 18th-century businesses (which also sold wine and spirits) left a legacy in the language and habits of modern **public houses**. The buxom, cheerful barmaid made her first appearance in early coffee houses as proprietors used her charms to attract male custom (César de Saussure noted that he was waited on by "beautiful, neat, well-dressed, and amiable, but very dangerous nymphs," and essayist Sir Richard Steele commented that "These Idols receive all day long the admiration of the Youth"). The bar, a term now applied to a drinking establishment as well as to the counter at which drinks are sold in a pub, was the place, close to the fire, where the coffee pots were kept warm in the coffee houses. (*See also* BALTIC EXCHANGE; CORNHILL; HAMPSTEAD; KNIGHTS HOSPITALLER; STOCK EXCHANGE [LSE]; THEATRE ROYAL, DRURY LANE.)

COLE ABBEY CHURCH, DISTAFF LANE. After the **Great Fire** of 1666, Cole Abbey (then known as St. Nicholas Cole Abbey) was the first church to be rebuilt to designs prepared by **Christopher Wren**. Its name is probably a corruption of *Coldharbour*, a Middle English term for "shelter," but may also be derived from a moorage on the **River Thames** where fishermen landed their catches. The original chapel was founded at least by 1144, when it is mentioned in written records, and was the site of the first Roman Catholic Mass to be said in London after Queen Mary I succeeded to the throne in 1553 and reestablished the papal authority rejected by King Henry VIII 19 years earlier. Wren's replacement, completed in 1677, is built of red brick, with stone facing on the south side. It was damaged by bombs on 11 May 1941 (the last heavy attack of the **Blitz**), but many of the furnishings (including the pulpit and font) were saved and returned to their original sites when restoration work (using Wren's plans) was completed by Arthur Bailey in 1962.

COLLEGE OF ARMS. The college, which regulates the conferment of armorial bearings throughout the United Kingdom (except Scotland) and in the Commonwealth of Nations, was founded by King Richard III in 1484 and has occupied its present site in Queen Victoria Street since 1555. Its original building was destroyed by the **Great Fire** of 1666 but replaced in 1671–78 by a structure designed by Morris Emmett, Master Bricklayer to the Office of Works. The Earl Marshal (a hereditary title held by the Dukes of Norfolk since 1672) is the chief official, responsible for organizing major state ceremonials, such as coronations. He is assisted by three kings of arms, six heralds, and four pursuivants. All are members of the royal household rather than civil servants.

COMMON CRYER AND SERJEANT AT ARMS. The Common Cryer carries the mace that precedes the **Lord Mayor** of the **City of London** on ceremonial occasions, opens meetings at **Common Hall**, and organizes the Lord Mayor's daily activities. The origin of the office is unknown but it was certainly established by 1338.

COMMON HALL. The assemblies that choose candidates for the post of **Lord Mayor** and elect the **Sheriff**s of the **City of London** are known as Common Hall. Traditionally, they are held on Midsummer's Day (24 June) to vote for the Sheriffs and on Michaelmas Day (29 September) to select two **aldermen** to contest the mayoral position. The franchise is limited to members of the **livery companies**.

COMMONWEALTH INSTITUTE. The institute, located in Kensington High Street, acts as an information center for members of the Commonwealth of Nations, offering conference facilities for business interests, hosting art exhibitions, providing extensive library facilities for researchers, and working with schools to provide material for classroom projects. Originally founded to commemorate the golden jubilee of Queen Victoria's rule in 1887 (when it was known as the Imperial Institute), it is housed in a pagoda-like building designed by Sir Robert Matthew, Johnson-Marshall and Partners and was opened in 1962. Most of the organization's funding is provided by the British government through the Foreign and Commonwealth Office.

COMPTROLLER AND CITY SOLICITOR. A senior official of the **Corporation of London**, the Comptroller and City Solicitor is principally responsible for the conduct of the authority's legal business but also participates in many of the **City of London**'s ceremonial activities and carries out other traditional duties (such as ensuring the security of the keys to the City Seal, which is used to authenticate formal documents). The duties are an amalgamation of tasks previously held by individual officers of the corporation (for example, the post of City Solicitor dates from 1545).

CONNAUGHT HOTEL. In 1891–93, Carlos Place was built to improve movement between **Grosvenor Square** and **Berkeley Square** in **Mayfair**. The Connaught was erected on the west side of the street in 1897, occupying a site that had provided accommodations for visitors to the city since 1815. Initially, Auguste Scorrier, the proprietor, called it "The

Coburg," but the name was changed in 1917 because of anti-German feeling in Britain. During the Second World War, it served as a headquarters for Charles de Gaulle's Free French forces. The Connaught was once known as London's home for landed families because many wealthy individuals rented permanent suites. Now part of the Savoy Group, it is one of the capital's leading **hotels**, recognized for its discreet service and outstanding restaurant.

CONSTITUTION ARCH. *See* HYDE PARK CORNER.

CONSTITUTION HILL. A tree-lined avenue connecting **The Mall** with **Hyde Park Corner**, Constitution Hill separates the gardens of **Buckingham Palace** from **Green Park**. It was the site of unsuccessful attempts to assassinate Queen Victoria in 1840, 1842, and 1849, and the location where Sir Robert Peel (founder of the Metropolitan Police force) met his death after falling from his horse in 1850. Nobody knows how the street got its name, but some scholars suggest that King Charles II exercised there in order to improve his constitution.

CORN EXCHANGE. London's first Corn Exchange was erected in 1747 at Mark Lane, the location of a **City of London** market founded during the late 13th century. Initially, it was little more than a walled courtyard open to the elements, but extensions and improvements were made at various stages during the 19th and early 20th centuries. The building was severely damaged in 1941, during the **Blitz**, but reopened in 1954. In 1987, business transferred to the **Baltic Exchange**, where dealers trade in such commodities as fertilizer and animal feed as well as in cereals.

CORNHILL. One of eight streets that meet at the **Bank of England**, Cornhill got its name from the medieval grain **market** that was held on the site. It was well known both for its stocks, where merchants caught cheating were clamped, and (from the 16th to the 19th centuries) for the **coffee houses** that flourished in its alleyways. Although the present buildings, dating from the late 1800s, are now occupied mainly by finance firms, the area once had important literary associations. Thomas Guy, who founded Guy's Hospital in 1721, had a bookshop at the junction with **Lombard Street** and poet Thomas Gray was born in a house on the site where No. 39 now stands. Smith and Elder ran a publishing business at No. 65 (now No. 32) from 1816 until about 1868 (Charlotte and Anne Brontë caused Mr. Smith much consternation when they appeared at his office in 1848 to prove that they were the authors he knew as Currer and Acton Bell) and **Charles Dickens**'s Mr. Pickwick stayed on several occasions at the **George Inn** and Vulture Inn in Castle Court, attended by Sam Weller. There are two churches—St. Peter-upon-Cornhill and St. Michael—both of which were designed by **Christopher Wren** but have since been much restored. St. Peter's is allegedly built on the site of the Roman basilica constructed in 179 A.D. (*See also* GREYFRIARS MONASTERY.)

CORPORATION OF LONDON. Local government within the **City of London** is organized by a corporation whose powers and procedures are determined as much by precedent as by statute. It consists of a **Lord Mayor** (who serves for one year), two **Sheriff**s (who are junior only to the Lord Mayor in status), **Aldermen** (whose responsibilities are largely administrative), and a **Court of Common Council** (an elected body representing residents). From the 13th until the 18th centuries, the Aldermen carried out most duties, but the Court of Common Council has been the effective governing body for the past 200 years, meeting in the **Guildhall**. Much of the work is done by committees that have specific areas of responsibility, such as the management of **Epping Forest**, educational provision, and the conduct of **Leadenhall Market**. (*See also* CHIEF COMMONER; CITY AND GUILDS OF LONDON INSTITUTE; CITY CHAMBERLAIN; CITY REMEMBRANCER; COMMON CRYER AND SERJEANT AT ARMS; COMMON HALL; COMPTROLLER AND CITY SOLICITOR; FREEDOM OF THE CITY; GUILDHALL SCHOOL OF MUSIC AND DRAMA; LONDON PRIDE PARTNERSHIP; MANSION HOUSE; MUSEUM OF LONDON; ROYAL NAVAL DOCKYARDS; THAMES, RIVER; THEATER; WARD; WARDMOTE; WATERMEN; WATER SUPPLY.)

COUNTY HALL. In 1905, the **London County Council** (LCC) decided to build a new headquarters on a site south of the **River Thames** opposite the Houses of Parliament (*see* **Palace of Westminster**). Construction at the location, formerly occupied by a complex of lumber yards and small factories, began in 1909, was halted in 1916 because of the First World War, and resumed in 1919. The building, designed by Ralph Knott following an international competition, was formally opened by King George V on 17 July 1922 but not fully completed for another 11 years. A six-story structure finished in **Portland stone** and granite, it has a series of internal courtyards as well as office space, rooms for committee meetings, and a debating chamber. Additional premises to the south (built to plans prepared by the LCC's own staff of architects) were added in 1963. County Hall became the main base of the **Greater London Council** in 1965 and lay empty for several years after that body was abolished in 1986. In 1993, however, it was bought by a Japanese company and converted into a family entertainment complex with **hotels** and restaurants attached. The major attractions are a large aquarium and a soccer **museum**.

COURT OF ARCHES. The court is the principal court of appeal for the Church of England's Province of Canterbury. It gets its name because it originally met at St. Mary-le-Bow Church (*see* **Bow Bells**), which was also known as the Church of Sancta Maria de Arcubus. From 1660 until about 1800, it stood at the center of the ecclesiastical judicial system, handing down judgments on marriage, inheritance, and moral issues, but in the 19th century most of its rights were transferred to the secular courts. Reports (known as Process Books) of about 10,000 of its cases are held at **Lambeth Palace**, providing historians with much information about life in southern England during the late 17th and 18th centuries.

COURT OF COMMON COUNCIL. On the first Friday in December, voters in each of the 25 **ward**s (local electoral areas) in the **City of London** elect freemen (*see* **Freedom of the City**) to serve on the Court of Common Council, which, since the 18th century, has been the principal decision-making body in the **Corporation of London**'s local government structure. Most of the candidates are members of the **livery companies**; those who are successful are known as Common Councilmen, hold office for one year, and are eligible for reelection at the end of their term. Meetings of the court are held at the **Guildhall** every third Thursday (except during the summer and Christmas holidays). The **Lord Mayor** presides over debates, which are different in context from those in the council chambers of the **London borough**s because the participants have not been elected on the basis of their allegiance to a political party. Common Councilmen form the bulk of the corporation's numerous committees, which deal with matters as distinct as management of open spaces and the conduct of **markets**. On formal occasions, they wear a mazarine (light blue) gown with short, fur-trimmed sleeves.

COURTAULD INSTITUTE OF ART. In 1931, the institute was founded by textile manufacturer Samuel Courtauld (at the suggestion of Viscount Lee of Fareham) as a college of the University of London (*see* **universities**) and a center for the study of Western art. Both men, anxious to provide the university with facilities equivalent to the Ashmolean Museum in Oxford and the Fitzwilliam Museum in Cambridge, bequeathed their collections of paintings to it when they died in 1947. These gifts were augmented by donations from the estates of Robert Witt (1952), William Spooner (1967), and others. The Courtauld (the first educational institution in Britain to award degrees in art history) was originally based in Portman Square, with its galleries in Woburn Square, but moved to **Somerset House** in 1990. It houses one of Europe's most important collections of impressionist and post-impressionist paintings and makes its library of 130,000 books available to scholars, along with an archive of three million photographs. In addition, it supports research centers studying illuminated manuscripts and Romanesque sculpture in Britain and Ireland.

COUTTS AND COMPANY. Although Coutts is best known as Queen Elizabeth II's banker, it can also claim the distinction of being one of the oldest finance houses in London. It was founded in 1692 by John Campbell but became particularly well established during the second half of the 18th century, largely through the business skills of Edinburgh brothers James and Thomas Coutts, who were made partners in the firm in 1755 and 1760 respectively. King George III placed his account in their hands, a practice followed by every British monarch since. Now part of the National Westminster group, Coutts has 15 branches in London, with its headquarters at 440 Strand in a building designed by Frank Gibberd and Partners and opened in 1978 (the structure retained elements of the site's early-19th-century developments planned by **John Nash**). Traditions that all male employees must wear a frock coat and eschew beards are still observed.

COVENT GARDEN. Following King Henry VIII's dissolution of the English **monasteries** in 1536–41, the Covent Garden area—an open space owned by **Westminster Abbey**—was acquired by the Crown, then, in 1552, granted to John Russell, first Earl of Bedford, as a reward for his services to King Edward VI (*see* **Bedford Estates**). In 1630, Francis Russell, the fourth Earl, was granted a development license by King Charles I and commissioned **Inigo Jones** to design one of London's first extensive planned estates. Jones drew on his knowledge of Leghorn (Italy) and Paris to prepare a scheme that incorporated a piazza (measuring 316 feet from north to south and 420 feet from east to west) with, on the west side, **St. Paul's Church**, which was intended to provide a focus for the new community. The southern aspect, fronting the Earl's gardens, was left open, but the northern and eastern fringes of the square were lined by tall, terraced houses more typical of continental European **architecture** than of English styles. Conservative critics voiced their opposition but, after the buildings were erected, Russell found no difficulty commanding high rents from tenants such as poet William Alexander, dramatist Thomas Killigrew, and courtier Sir Edmund Verney.

The harmony of Jones's design lasted only a few decades, however. In 1670, William Russell, fifth Earl (and later first Duke) of Bedford obtained a royal charter to hold a daily fruit and vegetable **market** in the piazza and to collect tolls from traders. With a growing urban population located nearby and 15,000 acres of market gardens within a radius of 10 miles, the market expanded rapidly, changing the social and economic context of the area in the process. **Coffee houses**, turkish baths, and brothels were opened to meet the needs of the newcomers, and the formerly patrician houses were subdivided into small apartments, many of which were taken over by actors.

In 1828, faced with increasing congestion and consistent flouting of the trading rules, Parliament approved legislation intended to reorganize the buying and selling of goods. The temporary booths were replaced, during the 1830s, by permanent halls, which were designed by Charles Fowler and described in the *Gardener's Magazine* as of "great beauty and elegance," but which also completely obliterated Jones's piazza. In 1874–75 and 1888–89, these halls were covered by glass and iron roofs, but that did nothing to reduce complaints from residents as more and more people flocked to the area and traders spread into nearby streets. In 1918, the Duke of Bedford (finding that most of the income from Covent Garden was being spent on upkeep of the buildings and regulation of trade) sold the concern to the Covent Garden Estate Company, owned by the Beecham family, then, in 1962, an Act of Parliament established the Covent Garden Market Authority to manage the complex, paying the Beechams £3.9 million for the business.

In 1974, trading transferred to a new, purpose-built site at **Nine Elms**, a move that destroyed a traditional way of life in inner London, spelled the end for many small local businesses (such as **public houses** and newsagents) that relied on the market workers for income, and left a large city-center site unused. As early as 1969, the **Greater London Council**, following the prevailing fashion for commercial development, had indicated that it intended to demolish most of the older buildings and

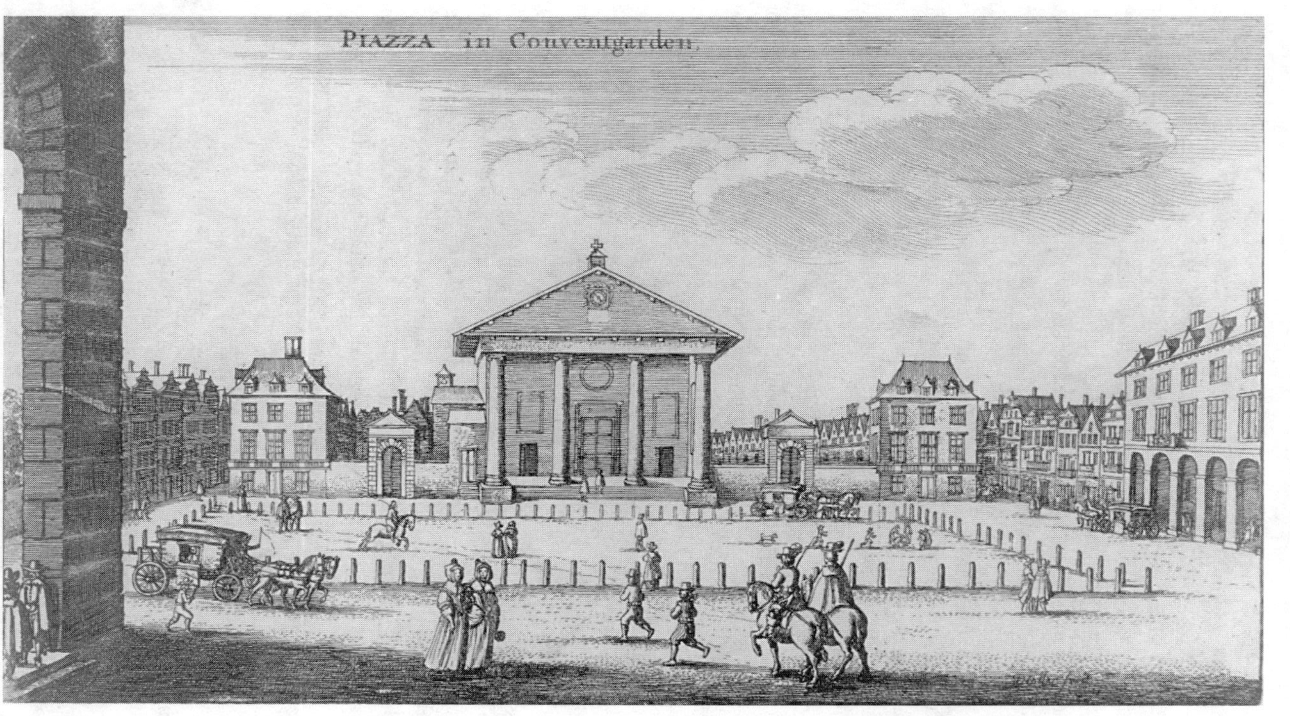

The Piazza, Covent Garden, circa 1647 (Museum of London)

erect office blocks in their place, but public protests were so vehement and so sustained that, in 1971, a public inquiry sent the planners and politicians back to their drawing boards. New, and more widely acceptable, proposals were prepared for conversion of the market hall into small units, primarily specialist shops, boutiques, wine bars, and restaurants, with offices on the top floor. Booths now line the open areas and street entertainers provide music, juggling, and puppet shows, attracting hundreds of thousands of visitors to one of London's newer tourist attractions.

Covent Garden lies within the **City of Westminster**. (*See also* LONDON TRANSPORT MUSEUM; ROYAL OPERA HOUSE; THEATRE MUSEUM; THEATRE ROYAL, DRURY LANE.)

CRAYFORD. Crayford is located south of the **River Thames** at a point, some 15 miles east of **Charing Cross**, where invading Jutes defeated the Britons in 457 A.D. and where the main road from London to Dover crosses the River Cray. It developed as an industrial center during the 17th century, when Cresheld Draper, the local landowner, established linen bleaching and textile printing processes. The manufacture of chemicals, optical instruments, carpets, bricks, and knife handles was added following the Industrial Revolution, then, in 1888, Hiram Maxim introduced production of machine guns. Also, the first Wolseley cars were built at Crayford in 1903. Many of the commercial buildings were destroyed in **air raids** during the **Blitz**, but St. Paulinus's Church, which dates from the decades following the Norman Conquest in 1066, still stands, its chancel located between twin naves and its altar hidden by the piers of the arcade. Since the area was incorporated within the **London Borough of Bexley** in 1965, a series of business parks have been developed, attracting such major companies as Burmah Castrol Chemicals, British Telecom, and Allied Mills.

CRICKET. *See* MARYLEBONE CRICKET CLUB (MCC); OVAL, THE.

CRICKLEWOOD. A suburb to the northeast of **Willesden**, Cricklewood is a largely residential area that straddles Edgware Road, where most commercial development is located. The arrival of the Midland **Railway** stimulated growth from 1868, resulting in the construction of terraces of small homes for the labor force and the building of large goods and coal sidings. The availability of **transport** and a pool of skilled manual workers attracted aircraft manufacturer Handley Page to the area in 1913, then, after the First World War, motor company Armstrong Siddeley provided additional employment. However, limitations of space restricted technological change and, in 1930, these businesses moved out, leaving the land (including Handley Page's aerodrome) for conversion into playing fields, **housing** estates, and premises for small light engineering firms.

CRIME. Changes in definitions of crime, alterations to urban boundaries, fluctuating approaches to sentencing policy, and the lack of accurate statistics make comparisons of lawbreaking at different historical periods impossible, though some scholars argue that economic depression leads to an increase in the level of offending in London. Theft, burglary, and crimes against the person have always been common, though their causes and nature have changed with time. During the 19th century, reaction to the changes wrought by the Industrial Revolution led to considerable social unrest, which was sometimes manifest in violence when opposing groups met. Also, advocates of social change often deliberately broke the law in order to draw attention to their causes, as with the Chartists and the suffragettes, both of whom campaigned for electoral reform. Poverty played a major role as well, particularly in the period prior to the introduction of welfare state policies after the Second World War, with many children turning to begging, pick-pocketing, and prostitution in order to survive. In the 1940s and 1950s, criminal activities were dominated by gangs who controlled gambling, fraud, and protection rackets in different geographical areas of the city (which they termed their "manors"). Most, such as the **Kray Twins**' network in the **East End**, were ultimately broken up by the **police**, but the late 1960s brought new problems, notably an increase in drug-related offenses. From the 1970s, the violence wrought by terrorist groups such as the Irish Republican Army became a major focus of law enforcement.

Between the late 1930s and the early 1990s, the number of serious crimes committed in London rose from just under 100,000 a year to over 850,000, but, by 1997, had declined to 798,169. Almost half of all offenses now relate to theft or the handling of stolen goods. Violence against individuals accounts for only about 6 percent of all offenses and sexual crimes for less than 1 percent. Young people aged 14–20 are five times more likely to be convicted of these offenses than are their seniors. Comparison with national figures indicates that the overall rate of crimes against households is lower in London than in the rest of England and Wales but that the incidences of vehicle theft and of burglary are higher.

(*See also* BOW STREET RUNNERS; CABLE STREET; CENTRAL CRIMINAL COURT; JACK THE RIPPER; PRISONS; RILLINGTON PLACE; ROOKERIES; ROYAL COURTS OF JUSTICE; SOUTHWARK; TYBURN; WHITECHAPEL.)

CRIPPLEGATE. Cripplegate was built by the Romans as a northern entrance to **Londinium** (*see* **London Wall**). The derivation of its name is uncertain, some scholars claiming that cripples once begged there, others that it comes from the Old English *crepel* (which means "covered way" and may refer to the invaders' defenses), and some that lame sightseers were cured when the body of Edmund the Martyr passed through in 1010. The structure was rebuilt by the Brewers' Company (one of the **livery companies**) in 1244 and served as a prison during the 14th century. Further reconstruction was carried out in 1491, but in 1760, the gate was demolished so that improvements could be made to the road system. (*See also* GREAT FIRE; SHAKESPEARE, WILLIAM.)

CROWN JEWELS. England's crown jewels, and other items used during the coronation of a new monarch, are permanently on display in the **Tower of London**. The oldest items are an ampulla (dating from about 1399) and a spoon (dating from the 12th century), both of which are used when a new ruler is anointed. The other elements of the regalia date from the mid-17th century or later because, after the execution of Charles I in 1649, the earlier symbols of majesty were destroyed by parliamentarians. St. Edward's crown was probably fashioned from one of the older crowns for the coronation of Charles II in 1661; weighing five pounds, it is used for the crowning ceremony but, because of its weight, immediately replaced by the lighter Crown of State, which was made for Queen Victoria. In addition, there is a jewelled sword and golden spurs (both of which represent knighthood), an orb (symbolizing Christianity's dominance of the globe), a ring (celebrating Dignity), and a scepter (standing for regal power and justice). All are made of precious metals and richly adorned with precious stones (the Crown of State, for example, has a frame of fine gold inset with over 3,000 jewels, mainly diamonds and pearls but including a ruby presented to the Black Prince during the 14th century). Other items on display include the crown made for the coronation of Queen Elizabeth (consort of George VI) in 1937; it includes the 109-carat Koh-i-Noor diamond, which is supposed to bring good luck to a woman who wears it but bad luck to a man.

CROYDON. A suburb lying some 10 miles south of **Charing Cross**, Croydon is located at a point where the Roman road from London to Portsmouth followed a dry valley into the **North Downs**. The settlement was established by Saxon times, developed partly due to the patronage of the Archbishops of Canterbury (it was the last stop on the journey from the ecclesiastical capital of England to the nation's center of government), and, by the 17th century, had become a significant market and administrative town. In 1803, the Surrey Iron **Railway** (the world's first public rail service, provided by horse-drawn carriages) linked the town to **Wandsworth**, then the arrival of the steam railway in 1839 encouraged further urban growth and, in 1920, the local aerodrome became London's first significant civil **airport**. Serious bomb damage during the **Blitz** allowed local authorities to undertake a wholesale reconstruction of the central business area from 1954, deliberately promoting accessibility as a means of attracting office firms and building shopping and entertainment complexes in order to encourage in-migration of labor. As a result, the modern townscape is more typical of the American central city than the British, with more than 50 skyscrapers dominating the street pattern.

CROYDON, LONDON BOROUGH OF. Croydon, with 338,200 residents (1998) has the largest population of all the **London borough**s. Covering 33 square miles, it was formed in 1965 through the amalgamation of the County Borough of **Croydon**, the Rural District of Coulsdon, and the Rural District of Purley. Since then, the local authority has vigorously pursued a policy of attracting commercial and retail development. As a result, central Croydon alone has some 2.7 million square feet of office space and one of the most popular shopping complexes outside the **West End**. Although many people travel by train to central London for work, the borough itself provides significant employment in financial services, the retail sector, and health care. The south of the area is archetypal commuterland, with communities such as Cousldon and Purley living in detached and semidetached houses close to golf courses and the open land of the **Green Belt**. Farther north, there are fewer professional and managerial workers, a larger **immigrant** presence, and greater residential mobility, but owner-occupation rates are high and scores below average on deprivation indices (Croydon's figures for single-parent families and loneperson households are below the London norm, for example). (*See also* ADDINGTON PALACE; AIRPORTS.)

CRYSTAL PALACE. One of the principal features of the **Great Exhibition** in 1851 was the structure designed by Thomas Paxton and built in **Hyde Park** to house some of the principal exhibits. Two thousand workmen used 400 tons of glass, 4,000 tons of iron, 200 miles of wooden sash bars, and 30 miles of guttering to build the palace, then, when it was completed, troops of soldiers were told to jump and shout inside to make sure that it would stand up to the wear and tear of visitors. When the exhibition ended, the building was reerected south of the **River Thames** on a hilltop at Sydenham, where it served as **theater**, concert hall, and exhibition center at the hub of an amusement park. On the night of 30 November 1936, however, it burned to the ground. The site was redeveloped during the 1960s to provide a National Sports Centre, with an Olympic standard swimming pool, a dry ski slope, an athletics stadium, and facilities for indoor activities. Two hundred acres of surrounding land were landscaped to provide **parks**, gardens, and boating lakes.

CUBITT, THOMAS (1788–1855). Until the early 19th century, anyone wanting to find labor to erect a building had to contract with individual craftsmen. Cubitt was the first businessman to tackle the whole task, from site clearance to interior fixtures, and so was responsible for many of the London properties that were completed during the construction boom of the Regency and early Victorian periods. The son of Jonathan Cubitt, he was born in Buxton (Norfolk) on 25 February 1788 and trained as a carpenter before setting up business on his own in 1809. Faced with the economic necessity of keeping his workforce busy, he purchased vacant land, built houses, then sold the properties—a speculative approach to commerce that was to become his hallmark. His first projects were in **Highbury** and the **St. Pancras** area, but he realized that wealthy individuals were seeking property to the west, rather than the north, of the **City of London** and, from 1825, turned his attention to **Belgravia**. In addition, he undertook much work for the royal family, including the construction of the east front of **Buckingham Palace**. Cubitt was one of the principal advocates of the establishment of **Battersea Park** and of improvements in urban environmental quality (he limited the output of smoke from his Thames Bank factory, for instance). He made significant donations to educational and religious organizations and negotiated the purchase of a property for the **Great Exhibition** without charging any fee. He also made sure that his employees were treated fairly; when his premises were destroyed by fire in 1854, he refused to lay off any of his men and allocated finances to replace their tools. Cubitt died, a self-made millionaire, at his home near Dorking on 19 November 1855. (*See also* ISLINGTON; PIMLICO; STOKE NEWINGTON; VICTORIA.)

CUBITT TOWN. During the 1840s and 1850s, the land at the southeast of the **Isle of Dogs** was developed by William Cubitt (**Lord Mayor** of London in 1860–61 and brother of builder **Thomas Cubitt**) to provide an industrial complex of sawmills, brickworks, timber wharves, and a cement factory as well as homes for dock workers. Most of these sources of employment no longer exist, but the area remains largely working-class, consisting primarily of local authority **housing** estates, although some private homes were built along the **River Thames** during the 1970s in an attempt to diversify the social composition of the community.

CUPER'S GARDENS. During the late 17th and early 18th centuries, these long narrow gardens were a popular place of recreation for middle-class Londoners. They were opened in about 1683 by Abraham Boydell Cuper, gardener to Thomas Howard, Earl of Arundel, and located on the south side of the **River Thames** in **Southwark** on a site now covered by the southern approaches to Waterloo Bridge. During the summer months in particular, visitors arrived by boat to follow winding paths, lined with trees and shrubs, towards a landscaped lake at the west end of the property. Further attractions were added in 1738, when Ephraim Evans took over the business and established a band, which played during the evenings. Servants in livery were not allowed to enter, and watchmen were employed to keep potential troublemakers out. In 1753, new legislation designed to reduce the incidence of theft resulted in the conversion of much of the area into a tea garden, but in 1760, the facilities closed down and the land was developed as a vinegar distillery.

CUSTOM HOUSE. London's first center for the collection of import and export duties was erected at Old Wool Quay, on the north bank of the **River Thames** near the **Tower of London**, in 1273. It was rebuilt in 1378 then again in 1559 (after being burned down), 1669 (following damage in the **Great Fire**), 1717 (three years after it was destroyed by an explosion in a nearby gunpowder store), and 1817 (after another conflagration). The present structure, in Lower Thames Street, was designed by David Laing and is located a few yards west of the 13th-century premises.

The name is also applied to an area of south **Newham** near the Royal Victoria Dock where customs were collected during the 19th century. It developed as an area of working-class **housing** close to employment in riverside industries but suffered greatly from bombing during the **Blitz** and was extensively redeveloped, largely for residential purposes, after the end of the Second World War. A research unit, founded by Sir Patrick Manson at a seamen's hospital close to the Royal Albert Dock in 1890, evolved into the London School of Tropical Medicine, which is now part of the University of London (*see* **universities**).

CUTTY SARK. One of the last, and one of the fastest, of the tea clippers that sailed between Britain and the Far East, the *Cutty Sark* (212 feet 5 inches long, 36 feet wide, and weighing 921 tons) was built at Dumbarton (Scotland) in 1869 for John Willis, a London shipowner. The construction work bankrupted the builders (Scott and Linton), so the final fitting was carried out by William Denny and Brothers. After a period carrying cargoes of Australian wool, the vessel plied between Portugal and North America before undergoing a complete refit in 1922. She served as a training ship for young sailors until after the Second World War then was restored to her original state. Since 1954, she has lain in dry dock at **Greenwich**, housing an exhibition of ships' figureheads and maritime prints. Her name is taken from Robert Burns's poem *Tam O' Shanter*, which includes a reference to a shapely young witch wearing only a cutty sark, or short shift. Alongside her lies the 54-foot-long ketch *Gipsy Moth IV*, in which Francis Chichester made a solo circumnavigation of the world from 27 August 1966 to 28 May 1967. In recognition of the achievement, Queen Elizabeth II knighted Chichester using the sword with which Elizabeth I had conferred the same honor on Francis Drake 387 years earlier.

– D –

DAGENHAM. Lying on the marshy north bank of the **River Thames**, about 12 miles east of the city center, Dagenham developed as a working-class suburb of London during the 20th century. It was founded during Saxon times (its named is derived from the Old English *Deccanhaam*, which means "Decca's home") and remained a predominantly agricultural settlement until the end of the First World War. From then, however, it became increasingly residential and industrial, with the population rising from about 9,000 in 1921 to over 114,000 in 1951. In part, the change was due to provision of local authority **housing** on sites away from the congested inner-city core (for example, over half of the 27,000-home Becontree Estate—the largest public development of its kind in Europe at the time—was in Dagenham). Also, industrialists found the extensive areas of flat land inviting: the Ford Motor Company began production there in 1931 and May and Bryant (makers of matches) followed three years later. Other manufacturing companies produced goods as diverse as telephone cables, armaments, and popcorn. The trends continued into the second half of the century, obliterating all of the early rural settlement except parts of the medieval church and an inn dating from about 1500. In 1965, most of the community was united with **Barking**, its western neighbor, in the **London Borough of Barking and Dagenham**, although some territory in the north was incorporated within the **London Borough of Redbridge**.

DANCE, GEORGE the Elder (1700-1768). During the middle years of the 18th century, George Dance the Elder designed the **Mansion House**, several churches, and numerous other public buildings in the **City of London**. The son of a mason, he joined his father's business in 1717 and was responsible for the refurbishment of the stonework at the South Sea Company's headquarters as well as in the Carshalton home of Sir John Fellows, its Governor. In 1732, he worked with surveyor James Gould, his father-in-law, on designs for a development at the Minories then, in 1735, was appointed Clerk of Works to the **Corporation of London**. Dance's new post carried no salary but conferred the prestige he needed in order to attract private commissions from wealthy clients and organizations. Over the next 15 years, he prepared plans for the Mansion House (1739), St. Leonard's Church, Shoreditch (1736), **St. Botolph's Church, Aldgate** (1741–44), St. Matthew's Church, Bethnal Green (1743–46), a new corn market in Mark Lane (1747), a headquarters for the Surgeons (one of the **livery companies**) in 1748, and a replacement (which was never built) for **Newgate Prison**. Then, from 1756 until 1760, he collaborated with Robert Taylor on the renovation of **London Bridge**, a task that involved demolition of housing and replacement of the two arches with a single span. Although some writers have praised his ability to maximize the use of cramped sites, modern architects often consider his designs clumsy and uninspired. Dance died on 8 February 1768 and was buried at St. Luke's Church, Old Street.

DANCE, GEORGE the Younger (1741–1825). The son of **George Dance the Elder** (who designed the **Mansion House**), Dance was responsible for the rebuilding of **Newgate Prison** (1770–78), the neoclassical design of All Hallows Church at **London Wall** (1765–67), the oval layout of **Finsbury** Square (1777), and the unusual mixture of Gothic, Greek, and Indian elements on the front of the **Guildhall** (1788–89). However, most of the structures were swept away in subsequent redevelopment programs, leaving only street patterns and a few properties (such as the group of five-story houses in the Crescent, near **Tower Hill**) as a legacy. Born in Chiswell Street, Moorfields, he studied in Italy from 1758 until 1764 then trained as an architect in his father's office, eventually succeeding him as Clerk of Works to the **Corporation of London** in 1768. He was elected a Fellow of the Society of Antiquaries in 1794 and was a founding member of the **Royal Academy of Arts**, with which he held the post of Professor of Architecture from 1798 until 1805. As he aged, he tended to forsake building design for art, contributing several chalk portraits to academy exhibitions. He died at his home in Gower Street (now No. 91) on 14 January 1825 and was buried in **St. Paul's Cathedral**.

DENMARK HILL. A south London suburb, lying east of **Brixton**, Denmark Hill is named after Prince George of Denmark, whose wife (Queen Anne) had a house in the area. Development in the 19th century was largely residential and middle-class, with writer John Ruskin living at 163 Denmark Hill from 1843 until 1872 and engineer Henry Bessemer (inventor of the steel manufacturing process that bears his name) maintaining a mansion on a site now occupied by a **housing** estate. During the early 20th century, the combination of a semirural environment and easy access to central London attracted a number of institutional interests, notably King's College Hospital (1913), Maudsley Hospital (1915), and the Salvation Army's William Booth Training College (designed by **Giles Gilbert Scott** and opened in 1932).

DEPARTMENT STORES. In the mid-19th century, most goods in London were sold in specialist stores or in bazaars, such as that established by John Trotter at **Soho** in 1816. During the 1860s and 1870s, however, William Whiteley (following trends in Paris) bought up shops in middle-class Westbourne Grove, **Bayswater**, and advertised himself as a "Universal Provider." **Harrods**, founded in 1853 as a grocery store, followed suit in equally fashionable **Knightsbridge**, then, over the next 30 years, drapers in **Oxford Street**, **Regent Street**, and **Piccadilly** expanded their premises, making businesses such as Debenham's, Dickens and Jones, and Swan and Edgar household names.

The first purpose-built department store in the city was Bon Marché, opened by James Smith at **Brixton** in 1877 and backed by money he won gambling on horse races. Others followed in the early years of the 20th century, most notably **Selfridge's**, which brought American sales methods to Britain. In succeeding decades, some retailers (such as Marks and Spencer) became international concerns, but by the 1990s most were feeling the sharp edge of competition from low-cost discount stores and some (such as C&A) were forced to close.

DEPTFORD. Located on the south bank of the **River Thames** between **Rotherhithe** and **Greenwich**, Deptford was a convenient fording point across the River Ravensbourne, so it became the last stop for coaches travelling from Dover to London and developed as a village with an inn serving the passengers. In 1513, however, King Henry VIII established a **Royal Naval Dockyard** at Deptford Creek, transforming the small settlement into a burgeoning industrial center and attracting ancillary services such as the victualling yard, which became the British Navy's most important supply depot. **Trinity House**, which ensures that Britain's coastal waters can be navigated safely, was based at Deptford during the 16th century, and the **East India Company**, formed in 1600, developed shipbuilding facilities and warehouses on the west side of the creek. For over 300 years, the port was a major focus of Britain's maritime development—Francis Drake set sail from the harbor in 1577 on the start of his circumnavigation of the world, James Cook left to search for the continent of Terra Australis in 1768, and, in 1820, the General Steam Navigation Company became one of the first firms in the world to offer scheduled services in coal-powered vessels.

The emphasis on the sea and ships continued to flourish until 1869, when the dockyard closed, a victim of silting by the Thames currents and lack of space for expansion. The victualling yard survived until 1961, but its site has since been developed as a large local authority **housing** estate named after **Samuel Pepys**, who, during the 17th century, was Secretary to the Navy Board, which managed the docks. Little of the medieval fabric of the area remains, with the exception of the 15th-century ragstone tower of the parish church, dedicated to St. Nicholas, the patron saint of sailors (the church itself was severely damaged by an incendiary device, dropped by German bombers in 1940, but was subsequently restored). However, Albury Street retains some early Georgian houses, with elaborately carved door cases, which were occupied by sea captains during the early 1700s. The modern community is working-class and multicultural (about 20 percent of the population is of Afro-Caribbean descent) but has suffered little from ethnic tensions. In 1992, the government provided funding for a regeneration program designed to improve the quality of the urban area and attract new employment. The University of Greenwich has a campus in the town, which forms the northeast corner of the **London Borough of Lewisham**. (*See also* EVELYN, JOHN; GIBBONS, GRINLING.)

DESIGN MUSEUM. The **museum**, which opened in 1989 at a former warehouse on Butler's Wharf, was funded by the Conrad Foundation as part of the London **Docklands** regeneration project. It has two main galleries, one showing how design affects the way commercial products look and how they are used, the other displaying examples of contemporary design from around the world. Exhibits range from children's toys to household furniture and from kitchen appliances to artwork.

DIANA, PRINCESS OF WALES (1961–1997). Princess Diana, former consort of Prince Charles, heir to the British throne, spent much of her life in London and is linked, in particular, with **Kensington**, where she lived before and after her marriage. Born Diana Frances Spencer, she was the third child of Edward, Viscount Althorp, and Frances, his first wife. The family lived at Park House, on the royal estate at Sandringham in Norfolk, so Diana grew up with Queen Elizabeth II's children (and particularly Prince Andrew and Prince Edward) as playmates. She attended West Heath School in Kent but did not distinguish herself academically, perhaps because of the stresses imposed by her parents' separation when she was only six years old. After a short period at the Institut Alpin Videmanette finishing school in Switzerland, she returned to London, where she found a part-time job at the Young England Kindergarten in **Pimlico** and shared an apartment in Coleherne Court (on the corner of Old Brompton Road and Redcliffe Gardens) with three other young women.

Perhaps inevitably, given her social contacts, she renewed her acquaintance with the Queen's children and, apparently, fell in love with Prince Charles in November 1977 when they met in a ploughed field at Althorp (Northamptonshire), where the Prince was staying as the guest of Lady Sarah, Diana's elder sister (rumor suggested that, at the time, there was a mild romance between Charles and Sarah). The couple were married in **St. Paul's Cathedral** on 29 July 1981 and settled in **Kensington Palace**, where Diana bore two children (Prince William on 21

June 1982 and Prince Harry on 15 September 1984). She assumed her public duties with vigor, undertaking lengthy foreign tours with her husband and involving herself in a wide range of charities, including Dr. Barnardo's Homes (*see* **Barnardo, Thomas John**), **Great Ormond Street Hospital for Sick Children**, the **Royal Academy of Dramatic Art (RADA)**, the **Royal Academy of Music**, and groups helping those who suffered from AIDS, leprosy, cancer, and other illnesses.

From the mid-1980s, however, stories circulated of a less than happy relationship between the couple. Undoubtedly, many of the problems stemmed from their differing personalities. Charles was introspective and reflective, diffident in contacts with the public, and happiest away from the city, where he could pursue his interests in organic farming and other countryside pursuits. Diana, 13 years his junior and only 20 when she married, was more outgoing and less constrained by royal protocol. Determined that her sons would grow up knowing how most of the population live, she took them to the Odeon Cinema in Phillimore Gardens and to the neighborhood McDonald's in High Street, Kensington. Inevitably, the press made much of the differences, forcing the family to deal with their problems in the full glare of publicity. Charles spent more and more time at Highgrove, his country estate in Gloucestershire, where he found a soul mate in former girlfriend Camilla Parker-Bowles. Diana lived mainly in Kensington Palace but was linked romantically with other men, notably James Gilbey and James Hewitt. Eventually, in 1992, they separated and, four years later, divorced.

There is little doubt that Diana had problems coping with a crumbling marriage and the consequences of the parting. The press pursued her wherever she went, following her to the **Earl's Court** gymnasium, where she attempted to keep fit, and to the doctors whom she consulted about eating disorders. Reports appeared hinting at affairs with such married men as England rugby captain Will Carling and art dealer Oliver Hoare. But, in many ways, Diana deliberately courted publicity, as when she appeared on a **British Broadcasting Corporation** television program in 1995 to talk about her unhappiness and when she used the media to gain publicity for her charity work. She did, however, maintain her very close relationship with her sons throughout the difficulties and spent much time in their company.

Princess Diana died in Paris on 31 August 1997, when the car in which she was travelling with Dodi Al Fayed (son of the owner of **Harrods**) crashed in Paris while being pursued by photographers. In the immediate aftermath, the Royal Family was much criticized for failing to mourn immediately and in public. Critics argued that the lack of response indicated that the Queen was out of touch with the feelings of her subjects and that Diana's major contribution had been to give royalty a human face. Since the death, however, advisers have made considerable effort to change public perceptions, Prince Charles's attributes have been presented in a more positive light, and retrospective press articles have suggested that Diana was as much sinner as sinned against.

DICKENS, CHARLES (1812–1870). Dickens, one of the greatest English novelists, used his vast knowledge of London to weave tales of city life that fascinated Victorian Britain. The eldest son of civil servant John Dickens and his wife, Elizabeth, he was born in Portsea (near Portsmouth) on 7 February 1812. The family moved to the London area two years later, settling, in 1816, at Chatham, which features in the partly autobiographical *David Copperfield* (1849–50) and other stories. John Dickens, on whom Charles modelled Mr. Micawber (one of the characters in the novel), was, apparently, an affectionate father, but he had little financial sense. As a result, the family frequently suffered hard times, notably in 1824, when Mr. Dickens was committed, as a debtor, to the **Marshalsea Prison** and Charles was withdrawn from school so that he could earn an income making up parcels in a warehouse. The experience was undoubtedly humiliating for a middle-class boy, but it provided a wealth of material for his literary work; the impoverished landlady from whom he rented a room in **Camden Town** was the model for Mrs. Pipchin in *Dombey and Son* (1848), the Marshalsea features in *Little Dorrit* (1857), and scenes involving vulnerable young people appear frequently in other writings. In 1825, as his fortunes improved, he obtained a job as a legal clerk, then, after learning shorthand (as described in *David Copperfield*), he found employment as a reporter in the law courts before becoming a journalist specializing in Parliamentary matters.

In 1833, using Boz as a pen name, Dickens began to submit articles to periodicals. The success of these essays led to an invitation from publisher Chapman and Hall to write a narrative that would accompany a series of engravings. The result—*The Pickwick Papers* (1836–37)—was an outstanding success, largely through the creation of a kindly, street wise **Cockney** whom Dickens named Sam Weller. On the strength of that reception, he gave up his newspaper job, wrote *Oliver Twist* (1837–39) as a series for *Bentley's Miscellany* (which he edited), then followed with *Nicholas Nickelby* (1839), *The Old Curiosity Shop* (1840–41), and *Barnaby Rudge* (1841), creating a series of humorous characters but stressing the problems of the poor and needy in 19th-century cities. As fame and fortune increased, he moved from 48 Doughty Street in **Holborn** (1836–39), to 1 Devonshire Terrace (1839–51), then to Tavistock House in Tavistock Square, **Bloomsbury** (1851–60), and finally to Gad's Hill, Rochester (1860–70). His output was enormous as he edited weekly periodicals, wrote stories, commented on political affairs, designed amateur theatricals, and gave public readings. However, by the 1850s his spirits were at a low ebb; his marriage was crumbling and disillusionment with the politics of Viscount Palmerston's Liberal government was evident in novels such as *Bleak House* (1852–53) and *Little Dorrit* (1857), which were much less effervescent than their predecessors, with heavier symbolism and more complex characterization. After his wife left him in 1858, he turned increasingly to public appearances, undertaking lengthy tours to provincial towns, as well as to France and the United States, but the rigors of travelling, coupled with perpetual brooding, wore him down. He collapsed suddenly on the evening of 8 June 1870, after working on *Edwin Drood*, and died the following day.

During the late 19th and early 20th centuries, critics were condescending about his work (in 1948, for example, F. R. Leavis wrote that Dickens was an entertainer rather than a serious writer) but, more recently, scholarly opinion has elevated him to a position second only to **William Shakespeare** in the canon of English literature. (*See also* ARCHWAY; BLACKFRIARS; CARLYLE'S HOUSE; CORNHILL; DICKENS' HOUSE MUSEUM; GEORGE INN; HAMPSTEAD HEATH; HIGHGATE CEMETERY; HOLLAND HOUSE; JACK STRAW'S CASTLE; KENSAL GREEN; NEWGATE PRISON; OLD CURIOSITY SHOP; ROOKERIES; ST. DUNSTAN IN THE WEST CHURCH, FLEET STREET; ST. PANCRAS; SPANIARDS, THE; TWICKENHAM.)

DICKENS' HOUSE MUSEUM. The **museum** is based at 48 Doughty Street, the sole surviving London home of author **Charles Dickens** (1812–70). He moved in during March 1837, along with Kate (his wife) and Charles (their baby son). During his stay, he wrote *Oliver Twist* (1837–39), *Nicholas Nickleby* (1839), parts of *The Pickwick Papers* (1836–37), and *Barnaby Rudge* (1841). By 1839, however, Mrs. Dickens had given birth to two daughters and the terraced house had become cramped, so, in October, the family moved to 1 Devonshire Terrace (near **Regent's Park**). In 1924, the property was acquired by the Dickens Fellowship, which displays many first editions of the writer's work alongside such personal possessions as the velvet covered desk he used for public readings.

DOCKLANDS. The 8.5 square miles of former **docks**, which comprise the world's largest urban regeneration scheme, are known as Docklands. During the late 1960s, the **River Thames** shipping business moved downstream to Tilbury, leaving an extensive area close to the city center derelict as port facilities closed. In 1971, initial plans to convert the area to office and commercial purposes were rejected by the Conservative government in the face of public outcry but, 10 years later, the London Docklands Development Corporation (LDDC) was established to secure long-term physical, social, and economic regeneration of the area by creating an attractive environment, providing **housing** that would enable people to live on the site, and encouraging businesses to open up. By 1998, it had built over 20,000 homes, virtually doubled the population (from 39,400 to 77,000), and spent £1.75 billion of public money. The private sector had invested £6.27 billion, constructed 14.7 million square feet of office space, and provided 43,000 new jobs, with major international companies such as News International and Citibank moving in. The social infrastructure also improved as 11 new primary schools were built, specialty stores opened, and £116 million was spent on community programs, health centers, and other amenities. Critics complained that **transport** provision was limited and that the lack of strict planning control had resulted in a disjointed landscape. Also, in times of recession, speculators had difficulty selling property, but most observers felt that the benefits of change outweighed the weaknesses. In 1994, the LDDC began to wind down its activities and hand its properties and responsibilities to the **London Borough**s of **Newham**, **Southwark**, and **Tower Hamlets**, finally closing its offices in March 1998. (*See also* DESIGN MUSEUM; ExCEL; INTERNATIONAL PETROLEUM EXCHANGE [IPE]; LONDON COMMODITY EXCHANGE; PORT OF LONDON AUTHORITY [PLA].)

DOCKS. London's docks date at least from the days of the Romans because archaeological evidence shows that the invaders tied their galleys to posts on the north bank of the **River Thames**, close to their base along the Walbrook Stream. By the 1720s, according to Daniel Defoe, there were "about two thousand sail of all sorts, not reckoning barges, lighters or pleasure boats or yachts" using the harbor facilities, which, before the end of the century, became thoroughly congested. The commerce

London Docks, 1827 (Museum of London)

promoted by the Industrial Revolution added to the problems but also encouraged several companies to invest in construction schemes designed to stimulate trade. Between 1802 and 1921, a series of enclosed docks were built along both sides of the river in a 10-mile stretch from the western end of the **Pool of London** downstream to Gallions Reach. The most westerly was St. Katharine's (opened in 1828 beside the **Tower of London**) and the most easterly the 245-acre Royal Group (the largest area of impounded dock water in the world). The establishment of a **Port of London Authority** in 1909 provided a means of comprehensive planning, boosting commerce significantly, so, by the early 1960s, a labor force of about 100,000 was handling over 60 million tons of cargo each year.

The period between 1965 and 1981 brought a change of fortune. Faced with competition from foreign ports, outdated equipment, and a growth in container ships that required deep water berths closer to the mouth of the Thames, dock companies located near the city center went out of business, closing yards that were later to be redeveloped as office, leisure, and **housing** complexes (*see* **Docklands**). The main focus of activity is now at Tilbury, some 20 miles downstream from **Tower Bridge**. Originally opened in 1886, its wharves and warehouses have been much modernized in recent years, with new provision for containers, bulk cargoes (such as steel and grain), and roll-on, roll-off ferry traffic. The improvements have allowed London to maintain its position as Britain's largest British port (and the eighth largest in Europe) in terms of annual cargo tonnage processed. In addition, a cruise terminal has been constructed to handle the growing leisure traffic. (*See also* BERMONDSEY; BLACKWALL; BLITZ; BOOTH, CHARLES; EAST INDIA COMPANY; LIMEHOUSE; LONDON DOCK STRIKE; MILLWALL; POPLAR. Opening and closing dates for individual docks are listed in the Chronology of Historical Events on pages xxiii–lxix.)

DOGGETT'S COAT AND BADGE RACE. In 1713, Thomas Doggett, manager of the **Drury Lane** Theatre (*see* **Theatre Royal**), left a will ensuring that part of his estate would provide a coat and silver badge for the winner of a boat race to take place every year on the **River Thames**. The oldest annual sporting event in the country, it is held on 1 August over a 4.5-mile course from **London Bridge** to Cadogan Pier at **Chelsea**, with participants sculling against the ebb tide.

DORCHESTER HOTEL. The Dorchester, one of London's leading **hotels**, stands on the site of the former home of the Earl of Dorchester in

Park Lane. Opened in 1931, it is built of reinforced concrete and, for that reason, became General Dwight Eisenhower's British headquarters after the United States entered the Second World War in 1941. It has 244 rooms, furnished in the style of an English country house, and a ballroom, panelled in black Spanish glass, which has hosted state as well as private functions. Prince Philip held a stag party in the hotel before his marriage to Princess Elizabeth (now Queen Elizabeth II) in 1947.

DOWNING STREET. About 1680, Sir George Downing built a cul-de-sac of brick-terraced houses along a short street leading from **Whitehall**. In 1720, part of the property was acquired by the Crown and, since 1732, No. 10 has been the official residence of the British Prime Minister (though early holders of the office often preferred to live in more spacious premises elsewhere). No. 12, which was purchased in 1803 and became the Judge Advocate General's residence, is now used by the government Whips, and No. 11, bought in 1805, is the home of the Chancellor of the Exchequer. All of the structures have been much altered internally since they were erected, No. 10 by William Kent in 1732–35, Sir John Soane (*see* **Sir John Soane's Museum**) in 1825, and Raymond Erith in the 1950s and 1960s. The last of these improvements revealed evidence of Roman occupation of the site, the remains of a Saxon hall, and part of the **Whitehall Palace** tennis court, built for King Henry VIII in 1533. For security reasons, gates were placed across the entrance to the street in 1990, preventing public access. (*See also* GORDON RIOTS; TREASURY BUILDINGS.)

DRAIN. The 1.4-mile **London Underground** connection that links **The City** to **Waterloo** railway station is known affectionately as the Drain by the thousands of commuters who use it every weekday; everyone who has watched the street-level entrances swallow up the jostling, bumping flow of rush hour humanity knows how appropriate that nickname is. The line, opened in 1898, was built by the London and South Western Railway. In 1947, it became the only underground link in the national rail network following nationalization of the system by the Labour government, but, in 1994, it was handed over to **London Transport**. It carries some 12 million passengers each year.

DRURY LANE. The street, which connects Aldwych and the **Strand** to High Holborn, takes its name from Sir Thomas Drury, who built a house beside the roadway during the 16th century. It became a fashionable neighborhood for over a hundred years, with residents including the Earl of Stirling (1634–37), Oliver Cromwell (1646), and the Earl of Clare (1683). However, during the Georgian period it declined in status and, by 1900, contained some of the worst slums in the city. Road-building programs in the early 20th century resulted in the clearance of many properties and the construction by the Peabody Trust (*see* **Peabody, George**) of solid homes for some 1,500 working-class Londoners. (*See also* THEATRE ROYAL, DRURY LANE.)

DULWICH. The former hamlet of Dulwich lies at the southern tip of the **London Borough of Southwark**. It has a lengthy history; records show that King Edgar granted the land to one of his supporters in 967, the Cluniac monks at Bermondsey Abbey held it from the early 12th century until the 16th, and King Henry VIII sold it to Thomas Calton in 1544 (following the dissolution of the **monasteries**). In 1605, it was bought by actor and theater-owner Edward Alleyn, who used part of his fortune to endow a "College of God's Gift in Dulwich," which provided education for 12 poor scholars and an almshouse for six poor brothers and six poor sisters. During the 18th century, the area developed a reputation as a spa, but development was limited until the enclosure of common land (which followed parliamentary legislation in 1805 and 1808) allowed wealthy Londoners to acquire property and build country villas. The opening of a **railway** station at nearby **Crystal Palace** provided a spur to growth from 1856, so homes for the middle classes and for manual workers replaced woods, market gardens, and farmland during the final decades of the 19th century. Further construction during the 20th century made Dulwich an integral part of the metropolitan area, but sensitive planning preserved much open space. In particular, the 72 acres of Dulwich **Park** attract visitors to the displays of azaleas and rhododendrons. The Alleyn Foundation now supports three educational establishments—Alleyn's School, James Allen's Girls' School, and Dulwich College. The college also administers Dulwich Picture Gallery, Britain's oldest public art gallery. Opened in 1814, it is housed in a building designed by Sir John Soane (*see* **Sir John Soane's Museum**) and extensively refurbished by Rick Mather Associates in 1998–2000. It contains an impressive representative collection of the major periods in the evolution of painting in Europe, including William Hogarth's *A Fishing Party* (c. 1730), Anthony Van Dyck's *Portrait of Emanuel Philibert* (1624), and Watteau's *Le Bal Champêtre* (1714–15). Many of the works were collected by Alleyn himself; others formed a bequest by Sir Francis Bourgeois in 1811.

– E –

EALING. The suburb of Ealing, some nine miles from **Charing Cross**, is an important retail center on the western side of London. It was probably founded in Saxon times but experienced little development until the 18th century, when it became very fashionable with aristocrats and wealthy merchants (in 1761, for example, Princess Amelia, the youngest daughter of King George III, set up home in Gunnersbury House). These residents maintained a semirural environment until, in the 1870s and 1880s, builders constructed, piecemeal, terraces of middle-class **housing** and turned Ealing into the "Queen of the Suburbs," with no significant industrial employment and, therefore, few manual workers except in the west at Stevens Town. The opening of **railway** stations from 1879 encouraged further building (particularly during the first decade of the 20th century) but, even so, the area has retained its predominantly residential character, with commercial activity concentrated on Ealing Broadway, which formed part of the main road from London to Oxford until the 1980s. (*See also* PUGIN, AUGUSTUS WELBY NORTHMORE.)

EALING, LONDON BOROUGH OF. Ealing is a diverse collection of formerly independent villages that coalesced as the urban area expanded westwards. Merged under a single authority in 1965, they cover some 21 square miles and have a resident population of 302,100 (1998). Uxbridge Road, Western Avenue, and Westway, running from east to west across the borough, attracted light industry and commercial developments that (along with job opportunities in the central city, a relatively low proportion of public sector **housing**, and the availability of rented properties) encouraged the growth of large concentrations of **immigrants**. **Southall**'s Asian community is one of the largest in the country and there is a large Polish group in the north of the area. (*See also* ACTON; HANWELL; NORTHOLT.)

EALING STUDIOS. In 1904, film producer George Barker bought West Lodge at The Green, in **Ealing**, and went into business as Barker Motion Photography Ltd. The firm was bought by Union Studios in 1929 then acquired by Associated Talking Pictures, which updated the facilities and began filmmaking in 1931. In 1938, Michael Balcon took control of the company, changed its name to Ealing Studios Ltd., and, until the early 1950s, made a series of highly successful movies—such as *Kind Hearts and Coronets* (1949) and *Whisky Galore* (also 1949)—which starred such distinguished actors as Alec Guinness and became known as the Ealing Comedies. The premises were sold to the **British Broadcasting Corporation** in 1955 then, in 1992, were acquired by the National Film and Television School, which leased the stages to independent producers. In 2000, they were taken over by Fragile Films, which spent £10 million upgrading technology and announced plans for a new series of comedies.

EARL'S COURT. The Earl's Court area of west London gets its name from the Earls of Zetland, Warwick, and Holland, who were Lords of the Manor during medieval and early modern times. It remained agricultural until, during the 1860s, the building of the Metropolitan **Railway** attracted urban development that, within two decades, covered the fields with rows of houses. In the 20th century, wealthier residents moved farther into the countryside, leaving their properties to be converted into small **hotels** or subdivided for rent to young **immigrants** seeking jobs in the central city (in particular, Australians arrived in large numbers, leading outsiders to refer to the neighborhood as Kangaroo Valley). The principal building is the Earl's Court Exhibition Hall, which, when it opened in 1937, was Europe's largest reinforced concrete structure. Designed by Chicago architect C. Howard Crane, its 450,000 square feet are used for events such as boat shows and travel fairs. A smaller hall, adding 17,000 square feet, was completed in 1992.

EASTCHEAP. Eastcheap, located to the northeast of **London Bridge**, was the location of the **City of London**'s meat **market** during the Medieval period. Its western end was demolished in 1829–31 to facilitate the construction of King William Street (which links the **Monument** area to the **Bank of England**) and the roadway widened in the mid-1870s while the Metropolitan **Railway** was built. The street is now occupied by banks, offices, and small shops. (*See also* ST. CLEMENT DANES CHURCH, STRAND.)

EAST END. In the northern hemisphere, the prevailing winds blow from the west. As a result, in Britain's 19th-century industrial cities they carried **air pollution** to the east of the built-up area. As manufacturing increased, wealthy citizens, unwilling to suffer the problems caused by dirt, soot, and dust, bought homes in the more pleasant westerly parts of the metropolitan area, where the cleaner air supported trees, **parks**, and gardens. Working-class citizens, without the funds to compete for the desirable properties, had to remain amidst the grime, particularly so because factories, mills, and **docks** increasingly congregated in the east, near the potential labor force. In some usages, London's East End stretches from the eastern boundary of the **City of London** to the metropolitan boundary with the County of Essex, a distance of some 10 miles. More frequently, the term is applied to inner-city areas such as **Bethnal Green**, **Bow**, and **Hackney**. In the public's imagination, these communities are characterized by deprivation—limited shopping facilities (a reflection of low incomes), high levels of local authority **housing** and terraced properties, and low levels of educational attainment. There is also a distinctive accent (for example, the East End is one of very few areas in Britain to use the glottal stop) and a strong family structure. In practice, however, these stereotypes have decreasing validity.

Much of the East End is cosmopolitan because the cheap housing attracted many **immigrants** (particularly Jews, Bangladeshis, and Chinese) and, towards the end of the 20th century, a process of gentrification (part of it a deliberate policy on the part of local authorities, as at **Cubitt Town**) took young professionals to the working-class neighborhoods. In turn, many East End families have moved out of the city to homes on green-field sites in Essex, a trend encouraged, until the 1970s, by the government's post–Second World War New Towns policy. (*See also* BARKING; BARKING AND DAGENHAM, LONDON BOROUGH OF; BARNARDO, THOMAS JOHN; BETHNAL GREEN MUSEUM OF CHILDHOOD; BLACKWALL; BLITZ; BOOTH, CHARLES; BOOTH, WILLIAM; BOW BELLS; CABLE STREET; CANARY WHARF; CANNING TOWN; COCKNEY; DOCKLANDS; DOCKS; EAST HAM; EDMONTON; HACKNEY, LONDON BOROUGH OF; HARDIE, JAMES KEIR; ISLE OF DOGS; JACK THE RIPPER; KRAY TWINS; LANSBURY, GEORGE; LIMEHOUSE; MILE END; NEWHAM, LONDON BOROUGH OF; PEABODY, GEORGE; PETTICOAT LANE; POPLAR; POPLARISM; REGENT'S CANAL; STEPNEY; STRATFORD; TOWER HAMLETS, LONDON BOROUGH OF; TOYNBEE HALL; VICTORIA PARK; WHITECHAPEL.)

EAST HAM. An **East End** suburb some eight miles from **Charing Cross**, East Ham was probably settled during Roman times but remained a village until the second half of the 19th century. Between 1851 and 1911, its population grew from 1,750 to over 133,500 as **immigrants** flooded in, most of them working-class or lower-middle-class families who had skills that could be used at the **docks** on the north bank of the **River**

Thames, the **gas** works at **Beckton**, or other industries on the fringes of the area. They successfully resisted incorporation within the **London County Council**'s jurisdiction in 1889, remaining in the County of Essex until 1965, when East Ham became part of the **London Borough of Newham** as the **local government** of the metropolitan area was reorganized. It forms a parliamentary constituency that consistently produces majorities for Labour Party candidates and sometimes displays a radical streak, as when, in 1923, it chose Susan Lawrence, one of the first two women elected to represent Labour in the **House of Commons**.

EAST INDIA COMPANY. The company was formed in 1600, when Queen Elizabeth I granted a charter giving a group of merchants exclusive rights to trade with India and with east and southeast Asia. The prime focus of the commerce was spices, which commanded a high price in Europe, but cotton, indigo, porcelain, saltpeter (used both to preserve meat and to make explosives), silks, and tea were also important. In 1661, the firm established its own **docks** at **Blackwall**, expanding them in 1806 in order to cope with the increasing volume of imports. Trade was organized from a headquarters in Leadenhall Street (in the **City of London**) and goods were stored at warehouses in Cutler Street. In addition to its business activities, the company wielded enormous political influence, acting as the government's agent and greatly extending the area absorbed within the British Empire. However, alleged maltreatment of native peoples, coupled with financial irregularities, led, in 1784, to legislation that transferred control from shareholders to a regulatory board answerable to Parliament. The monopoly rights were removed in 1813, then in 1873, 16 years after the Indian Mutiny demonstrated that a private concern could not adequately represent British interests in the subcontinent, the company was terminated. (*See also* DEPTFORD; WANSTEAD.)

EDGWARE. Edgware lies at the northwest fringe of London, astride Watling Street, which connected the Roman settlements of **Londinium** and Verulamium (now St. Albans). The hamlet, which is first mentioned in written records dating from 978 A.D., was owned by religious interests (including the Priory of St. Bartholomew, the Knights of St. John of Jerusalem, and All Souls College, Oxford) for much of the Medieval period. Despite the arrival of the **railway** in 1867, it retained its rural character until extensions to the **London Underground**'s Northern Line connected it to the central city in 1924. It is now a residential suburb, although there have been some institutional developments, notably the North London Collegiate School (located in Canons Park, a Georgian residence built for the Duke of Chandos) and the National Orthopaedic Hospital. Elements of Edgware's age are evident in the 15th-century tower of St. Margaret's Church and the White Hart, a 17th-century coaching inn in High Street.

EDMONTON. Edmonton lies on the west bank of the **River Lea**, some eight miles northeast of **Charing Cross** on the main road from London to Cambridge. During the 18th and early 19th centuries, the Bell Inn was a favorite **public house** with city dwellers because of its attractive rural location and accessibility. Essayist Charles Lamb (who lived in Church Street) entertained visitors at the hostelry, and in *John Gilpin* (1782) poet William Cowper tells how Gilpin's wife recommended the place for a wedding anniversary celebration (with unfortunate results, because Gilpin's horse bolted). In 1872, the arrival of the Great Eastern **Railway** changed the character of the area, attracting developers, who built low-quality **housing** for manual workers from the **East End**. These quickly turned into slums, most of which were replaced by higher quality local authority housing in the years after the Second World War. The suburb was incorporated within the **London Borough of Enfield** in 1965.

EDUCATION. London had no formal educational provision for its young people until the second half of the 19th century. Prior to that time, schooling was available only from religious organizations, charitable foundations (see, for example, **Charterhouse** and **Dulwich**) or private teaching establishments of varying quality. In 1870, however, a London School Board was appointed to introduce classes for children between the ages of five and 13. The first accommodation (in Berners Street, north of **Oxford Street**) was ready two years later and, by 1900, places were available for 531,500 boys and girls. Younger pupils received instruction in religious education, reading, writing, arithmetic, and music; older scholars had a broader curriculum, which included history, geography, mathematics, and sciences. In 1904, statutory responsibility for tuition passed to the **London County Council (LCC)**, which established an Education Department (headed by Scotsman Robert Blair) to ensure that its duties were properly carried out. Over the next decade, Blair formulated the policies that would shape the city's education for more than 40 years, integrating the board schools with the voluntary (mainly church-run) institutions, renovating properties, establishing in-service training courses for teachers, providing scholarships, expanding provision for the older age groups, introducing welfare services (such as health care), and supporting technical education.

During the Second World War, about half of the capital's children were evacuated to rural areas (some 200,000 of them during the first 10 days of September 1939). Only 50 of the city's 1,200 school buildings escaped bomb damage, making replacement a priority when peaceful conditions returned in 1945. Government commitments, made in the 1944 Education Act, to extend the period of compulsory schooling added pressure on existing provision, as did the baby boom of the late 1940s and early 1950s. Between 1948 and 1957, over 100 new schools were opened, while the number of children aged five to 11 rose from 150,000 in 1945 to 247,000 in 1954. Inevitably, demands on scarce resources resulted in inequities, with children in some neighborhoods benefiting from up-to-date facilities while others were receiving an education in classrooms designed for Victorian standards.

Changing social attitudes also affected the nature of the education service. In particular, high school selection procedures, which involved assessment of academic ability at age 11 and direction of the brighter children into grammar schools, were largely replaced by a system that required schools to take children of all abilities.

In 1965, when the LCC was disbanded, the administration of education in the central city passed to an **Inner London Education Authority (ILEA)**, with the 20 newly created outer **London borough**s assuming responsibility for their own schools. The ILEA, which deliberately attempted to use education as a means of compensating for children's impoverished home backgrounds, made generous provision of resources but, in 1990, was abolished by a Conservative government with whom it had often found itself at odds. Responsibility for provision was given to the 12 member boroughs.

In 1996, there were some 301,000 children in London's public sector schools. A further 32,000 attended independent schools. Because of the multiethnic nature of the city's population, about 18 percent of high school pupils lacked fluency in English. In national examinations, students in the outer boroughs performed as well as those in the rest of the country, but those in inner London gained fewer university entry qualifications. Funding varied greatly between boroughs, with high schools in the **London Borough of Lambeth** receiving £3,800 for each student while those in the **London Borough of Bromley** received £1,850. (*See also* CITY AND GUILDS OF LONDON INSTITUTE; LONDON

SCHOOL OF ECONOMICS AND POLITICAL SCIENCE [LSE]; MILL HILL; ROYAL ACADEMY OF DRAMATIC ART [RADA]; ROYAL ACADEMY OF MUSIC; ROYAL BALLET; ROYAL COLLEGE OF ART; ROYAL COLLEGE OF MUSIC; ROYAL SOCIETY OF ARTS [RSA]; UNIVERSITIES.)

ELECTRICITY. Electricity began to challenge **gas** as a source of lighting from 1882, when parliamentary legislation authorized the use of overhead and underground cables as a means of providing power. The world's first electricity generating station was opened at Holborn Viaduct the following year, supplying energy that lit the **Central Criminal Court** and the Post Office, but it was quickly followed by others, so, by the outbreak of the First World War, there were over 70 in operation. Competing interests installed prepayment meters and offered customers cut-price wiring, operating with little government regulation and creating a complex pattern of provision as public and private interests adopted both alternating and direct current delivered at a range of voltages. **London County Council** made consistent attempts to reduce the confusion but, although improvements were made as small undertakings merged, rationalization was limited until 1948, when the Labour government nationalized the industry and created a London Electricity Board authorized to distribute power throughout the city. The Electricity Act of 1989 returned the industry to private hands in 1991, reintroducing competition but retaining standards of supply.

In 1890, electricity was first used on the **London Underground**, providing power for the line from Stockwell to King William Street (in the **City of London**). The innovation was extremely popular (because it eliminated the discomfort caused by smoke and dirt from coal-fired engines) and, as its use spread, led to rapidly increasing use of the system. (*See also* BANKSIDE; BATTERSEA POWER STATION; BRIXTON; STREET LIGHTING.)

ELEPHANT AND CASTLE. A busy road junction about one mile south of **Southwark Bridge**, the Elephant and Castle was an important coaching station during the 18th and 19th centuries and later became a **railway** terminus. Nearby properties were badly damaged by bombs during the **Blitz**, but the area was redeveloped, during the early 1960s, to include a covered shopping mall, a cinema, a sports center, government offices, and premises for the London College of Printing. A further regeneration scheme, costing £1.5 billion, was announced by the **London Borough of**

Southwark in 2000. The origin of the area's name is unclear, but it is certainly taken from a **public house** that had adopted it in 1760. Some scholars claim that it is a corruption of *L'Enfant de Castile* (a term used to describe the daughter of King Philip III of Spain, with whom Prince Charles, son of King James VI and I, attempted to arrange marriage in 1623), but an elephant with a castle on its back was a relatively common feature in medieval European heraldry (possibly to emphasize strength), and the enterprising landlord may simply have copied the device onto a sign and hung it outside his inn in order to attract custom.

ELTHAM. The suburb of Eltham lies in the **London Borough of Greenwich**, some nine miles southeast of **Charing Cross**. Archaeological excavations reveal that it was probably settled during Roman times, but its growth focused on Eltham Palace, which was presented to Prince Edward (later King Edward II) by Anthony Bek, Bishop of Durham, in 1305. For 200 years, it was a favorite royal residence; according to tradition, Edward III established the Order of the Garter (the oldest knighthood in Europe) at a meeting there in 1348, and it was the site of the marriage, by proxy, of Henry VII to Joan of Navarre in 1402. However, Henry VIII preferred **Greenwich Palace,** and by the middle of the 17th century it had fallen into disrepair. The Great Hall, with an imposing hammer-beam room, completed in 1480, was restored by Stephen Courtauld (*see* **Courtauld Institute of Art**), who obtained a lease on the property in 1931, but little else remains. The proximity of the palace and the availability of rural land encouraged the establishment of other large houses, such as Eltham Lodge (a Restoration building designed by Hugh May for Sir John Shaw and completed in 1664). More recent urban expansion is largely the result of 19th- and early 20th-century improvements to road and **railway** links with central London. Entertainer Bob Hope was born at 44 Craigton Road on 29 May 1903.

ELY PLACE. From 1290 until 1772, the Bishops of Ely retained a London mansion in Ely Place, **Holborn**. In 1327, Phillippa of Hainault resided there before her wedding to King Edward III, and John of Gaunt (her fourth son and the real ruler of England during her husband's last years) lived in the building from 1381 until 1399. It served, during the civil wars of the 1640s, as a prison for royalist captives and a hospital for parliamentary supporters injured in battle, and then, in a state of considerable disrepair, was acquired by the Crown in 1772. The clergy moved to Dover Street and the building was demolished, but the neighboring

St. Etheldreda's Church, built in the late 14th century as a chapel for the Bishops, survives. (*See also* BARRY, CHARLES.)

EMBANKMENTS. *See* BAZALGETTE, JOSEPH WILLIAM.

EMERGENCY SERVICES. *See* LONDON AMBULANCE SERVICE; LONDON FIRE BRIGADE; POLICE.

ENFIELD. The suburb of Enfield lies on the northern fringe of London on the west bank of the **River Lea** some 3.5 miles northeast of **Charing Cross**. Utilizing the fertile alluvial soils, it developed as a significant agricultural area before the Normans invaded England in 1066 and remained rural until the Industrial Revolution stimulated economic change during the 18th century. Before the construction of surfaced roads, the river was the major transport link. During the 1760s, it was canalized so that barges could be used to carry grain from Hertfordshire to London. Flour mills were built at Ponders End during the early 19th century and, in 1804, a small arms factory was constructed nearby; muskets were manufactured from 1816 and, in 1854, the premises were expanded to allow production of the Enfield rifle. The Edison Swan Electric Light Company (which pioneered the manufacture of valves for radios) opened in 1886, the Northmet **electricity** generating station in 1903, and other manufacturing concerns following the completion of the Cambridge Road after the First World War. These sources of employment attracted workers from throughout the country, generating a building boom (particularly during the 1930s). When the **Greater London Council** was formed in 1965, the community united with neighboring areas to form the **London Borough of Enfield**.

ENFIELD, LONDON BOROUGH OF. The most northerly of the **London boroughs**, Enfield was formed in 1965 by the amalgamation of the Borough of **Edmonton**, the Borough of **Enfield**, and the Borough of Southgate. Covering 31 square miles (about one-third of it **green belt** land, upon which development is strictly controlled), it has a population of 264,900 (1998). The southwest is largely residential, with a high proportion of the employed population in professional, managerial, or skilled technical jobs. Elsewhere, however (and particularly in the east, along the valley of the **River Lea**), there is more industrial activity, including chemical production, food processing, and printing. In recent years, the local authority has made successful attempts to attract high tech firms producing optical products, photographic goods, and biotechnology. As a result, some 17 percent of the workforce is employed in manufacturing and many businesses with household names—such as the Ford Motor Company and Coca-Cola Schweppes—have plants in the area. The conversion of the Lea Valley from an industrial wasteland into London's first regional **park** has also helped entice employers to the borough, as has access to good road communications to the rest of the country.

EPPING FOREST. A remnant of the woods that once swathed southeast England, Epping Forest covers over nine square miles and lies about eight miles northeast of **Charing Cross**. After the Norman invasion in 1066, England's kings used the land for hunting, often finding accommodation at nearby Waltham Abbey, which had been founded as a collegiate church of secular canons in 1030. From the late 18th century, however, monarchs became less attached to the chase, much of the woodland was cut down for fuel (or used as building material), and the cleared land was plowed. The 9,000 acres of trees cleared between 1771 and 1871 left only 3,000 acres untouched, encouraging campaigners to press for legislation that would prevent further encroachment. In 1874, the **Corporation of London** won a court ruling that all enclosures of land since 1851 had been illegal. Four years later, Parliament awarded it control of 6,000 acres, enabling it, in 1882, to proclaim the forest "an open space for the enjoyment of the people for ever." Much used for recreation by residents in the working-class areas of east London, where **parks** are relatively limited, it is now the largest hornbeam woods left in England and has a population of several hundred deer. There are **museums** at Queen Elizabeth's Hunting Lodge (originally built for Henry VIII in 1543) and in Sun Street, Waltham Abbey; the former concentrates on natural history and the latter on daily life in the area from early settlement to the present day.

ERITH. Records show that a settlement existed at Erith, on the marshy south bank of the **River Thames** 4.5 miles east of **Charing Cross**, as early as 695 A.D. During the Medieval period, the community focused on Lesnes Abbey, an Augustinian foundation established in 1178 by Richard de Luci as a penance for supporting King Henry II in a dispute that led to the murder of Thomas Becket, Archbishop of Canterbury. (The buildings are now in ruins, but the surrounding lands have been converted into a 200-acre woodland **park** renowned for spring displays of bluebells and daffodils.) During the early 16th century, King Henry VIII built a naval dockyard at Erith to fit out warships built upstream at **Woolwich**, stimulating the growth of port facilities. The combination of these industries and the transport potential of the North Kent **Railway** (which arrived in 1849) encouraged further manufacturing growth during the second half of the 19th century, including the opening of the Callender Cable Company in 1880 and the Maxim-Nordenfelt Gun Company (which later became known as Vickers) in 1887. The area suffered greatly from bombing during the **Blitz** and was much redeveloped after the Second World War. It became part of the **London Borough of Bexley** in 1965. In 1998, archaeologists found the remains of a prehistoric forest in the mud of the Thames shoreline at Erith. The soggy remains of alder, ash, oak, and (unexpectedly) Scots pine and yew allowed specialists to refine their understanding of the natural vegetation of the river estuary 12,000 years ago, as the last Ice Age ended.

ERMINE STREET. Built by the Romans, Ermine Street ran north for over 200 miles from London to York. Some scholars suggest that it may also have extended south of the city, crossing the **River Thames** near the site of **London Bridge**. It is named after Arminus, a Saxon leader who defeated Roman troops at Winfeld, on the River Weser in Germany, in 9 A.D.

EROS, STATUE OF. *See* PICCADILLY CIRCUS.

ETHNIC GROUPS. Although London has a long history of immigration (*see* **immigrants**), the lack of official records on ethnic background has created problems for social scientists studying the city's changing population. Until recently, the best available sources of information were the tables on place of birth published every 10 years in the national census results, but these did not allow researchers to differentiate between, for example, black people born in London and white people born in London. In 1991, however, the census included a question on ethnic origin, permitting more accurate analysis. Respondents were asked to place themselves in one of a specified number of categories, based partly on color and partly on regional affiliation. The results showed that about 1.35 million people (about 20 percent of the resident population) identified with a nonwhite group (the corresponding proportion for the whole country was 5 percent). The principal minorities were the Indians (who formed 5.2 percent of the city's population), black Caribbeans (4.4 percent), black Africans (2.4 percent), Bangladeshis (1.3 percent), Pakistanis (1.3 percent), and Chinese (0.8 percent). These communities tended to settle in different parts of the city (for example, 43 percent of the Bangladeshi population lived in the **London Borough of Tower Hamlets**), so some boroughs had larger communities than others (45 percent of the population in the **London Borough of Brent** was in one or another of the minority groups, compared with only 3 percent in the **London Borough of Havering**). Government estimates indicated that, in 1997, London's ethnic minorities accounted for about 24 percent of the resident population (and for 48 percent of the minority population of the whole country). (*See also* LAMBETH, LONDON BOROUGH OF; REDBRIDGE, LONDON BOROUGH OF; WESTMINSTER, CITY OF.)

EUSTON STATION. One of London's principal **railway** stations, Euston is the terminus for trains serving northwest England and the west of Scotland. It was built by the London and Birmingham Railway in 1837, occupying a site, towards the edge of the urban area, which was dominated by market gardening businesses. In 1838, a 72-foot-high portico (designed by Philip Hardwick and incorporating four Doric columns) was erected in front of the structure; in 1839 two **hotels** were opened alongside; and then, 10 years later, the concourse and waiting rooms were redesigned. Over the next century, the complex changed little, although the area around it developed a landscape of bed and breakfast establishments, **public houses**, restaurants, and retail services catering to travellers. During the 1960s, however, British Rail (the nationalized company that operated train services and managed the station) demolished the Victorian edifice, despite howls of protest from conservationists who wanted the portico retained, and replaced it with a new building, which has 18 platforms and a 30,000-square-yard piazza designed by R. L. Moorcroft to meet 20th-century needs. Further office accommodation was opened in 1976.

EVELYN, JOHN (1620–1706). Evelyn's diary, written over a period of 75 years, provides historians with a rich source of information about 17th-century London. Although less personal than the writings of **Samuel Pepys**, it covers a much longer period and describes conditions during such major events as the Civil War (1642–49), the Restoration of the monarchy in England (1660), the **Great Plague** (1664–66), and the **Great Fire** (1666). Evelyn was born in Wotton (Surrey) on 31 October 1620, the fourth child of wealthy landowner Richard Evelyn and his wife, Eleanor. A staunch royalist, he joined the army of King Charles I at the outbreak of the Civil War but left for home after only three days, noting that his continued presence with the troops would expose him to financial ruin "without any advantage to his majesty." In 1643, after some months spent making improvements to the family estate, he embarked on a European tour, travelling to Italy and France, then, on 27 June 1647, marrying Mary, the only daughter of Sir Richard Bourne, the King's ambassador to Paris. In 1652, he moved into his father-in-law's property in **Deptford**, where he lived quietly throughout the period of Puritan government but nevertheless enjoyed the entertainments London offered. In 1657, for example, he reported seeing a bearded lady, and there are details of visits to pleasure gardens, near **Charing Cross**, where "the thickets seem to be contrived to all advantages of gallantry."

Evelyn also corresponded with many of the educated men of the day, including scientist Robert Boyle, to whom, in 1659, he addressed a letter proposing the foundation of a college that would be dedicated to "the promotion of experimental knowledge." That vision eventually took practical form as the **Royal Society**, to whose council he was nominated in 1662 by King Charles II. Although shocked by the conduct and lavish spending of Charles's followers after the King was restored to his throne in 1660, Evelyn was much respected by the monarch and served on several important committees, including those formed to consider improvements to London streets (1662), regulate Gresham College (*see* **Gresham, Thomas**) in 1663, and repair **St. Paul's Cathedral** (1666). He was also consulted regarding the founding of **Chelsea Hospital** in 1681 and served as treasurer at Greenwich Hospital (*see* **Royal Naval College**) from 1695 until 1703.

In many ways, Evelyn was typical of the gentry of the period, his religious and political opinions reflecting the prevailing loyalist landowning orthodoxy, but he was unusually curious about the world around him, conducting his own research into matters that intrigued him. He is remembered as one of the fathers of arboriculture because he advocated the planned planting of woodlands and in *Sylva, Or a Discourse of Forest-Trees, and the Propagation of Timber* (produced in 1664 for the Commissioner of the Navy and still in use during the 19th century), described methods of pruning, pest control, and transplanting that were based on work carried out on the family lands. He also developed a new form of etching, known as the mezzotint, and wrote a moving biography of Margaret, wife of Lord High Treasurer Sidney Godolphin. Evelyn died in his home at Wooton on 27 February 1706. (*See also* GIBBONS, GRINLING.)

ExCEL. The ExCel conference center, built on the site of the Royal Victoria Dock, opened its first 65,000 square meters of space for business in November 2000. Further development will increase its size to 155,000 square meters, making it the largest building of its type in Britain. Designed as the focal point of a small waterfront town on the north bank of the **River Thames**, it is equipped with technology intended to attract futuristic international exhibitions and will be served by a complex of **hotels** and restaurants. Estimates suggest that by the time the project is complete it will have created about 14,000 jobs, many of them in the **London Borough of Newham**, one of the poorest parts of the city. Many jobs, however, may be at the expense of employment in older locations, such as the hall at **Earl's Court**.

EYRE REPORT. In 1997, Chris Smith, Secretary of State for Culture, asked Sir Richard Eyre to chair a committee charged with preparing a report on government proposals to make the English National Opera share the **Royal Opera House** facilities in **Covent Garden** with the Royal Opera and the **Royal Ballet**. The document, published the following year, was a damning indictment of management at the opera house, where three chief executives, two chairmen, and the entire board had resigned within a year. Alleging overspending, arrogance, and elitism, Eyre proposed that a new artistic director should be appointed, that top salaries should be cut, that financial controls should be tightened, and that public funding should be increased. Within weeks, the chairman was replaced and the Arts Council (the government's agency for dispensing grants to drama, literary, and music groups) had promised higher levels of financial support.

– F –

FAIRS. Annual fairs were held regularly in England from Anglo-Saxon times, providing opportunities for larger-scale trading than was possible at weekly **markets**. Many survived until the Victorian period, when increasing drunkenness and civil disorder encouraged local authorities to discontinue them. There are records of a two-week fair taking place in **Peckham** in late July and early August each year from the early 13th century until 1827. Other events were held at **Croydon**, **Pinner**, and **Tower Hill** from the 14th century, at **Stepney** from the 17th, and at **Mitcham** from the 18th. A number still survive, including that on

Hampstead Heath every August bank holiday weekend. (*See also* BARTHOLOMEW FAIR; CHARLTON; FROST FAIRS; ST. JAMES'S FAIR.)

FAMILY RECORDS CENTRE. *See* PUBLIC RECORD OFFICE (PRO).

FENCHURCH STREET STATION. In 1841, the London and Blackwall **Railway** opened the **City of London**'s first train station at Fenchurch Street. It was replaced, in 1854, by a new terminus (also used by the London, Tilbury, and Southend Railway), which was extensively redesigned in 1935. During the 1980s, a £1.6 million development, known as Broadgate and financed by Stanhope Properties, integrated the station with new office premises. Rail services bring some 30,000 commuters from east London and Essex into **The City** each weekday.

FESTIVAL OF BRITAIN. In 1951, Prime Minister Clement Atlee's Labour government promoted a Festival of Britain in an effort to boost public morale at a time of food rationing and economic reconstruction following the end of the Second World War. The principal focus in London was a dockside area of **Lambeth**, between **Waterloo Bridge** and **Hungerford Bridge**, where derelict buildings were demolished and a series of pavilions, which told the story of Britain's land and its people, were erected in their place. Murals, water sculptures, and a skylon (a vertical structure that could be lit up at night) provided additional attractions. The intent was to create a relaxed, funfair atmosphere, but the only structure designed to be permanent was the **Royal Festival Hall**, which became the focus for the development of an arts complex on the **South Bank** of the **River Thames**. Farther west, **Battersea Park** was redesigned by Osbert Lancaster and John Piper to incorporate new walks and a fountain.

FINCHLEY. The suburb of Finchley lies some seven miles northwest of **Charing Cross**. Although it was settled by the Saxons, it experienced little growth until the Great Northern **Railway** provided a train link to central London in 1867. The increased accessibility attracted speculative builders, who erected homes for middle-class commuters, ultimately covering the fields with houses and linking formerly independent villages. The local authority has established conservation areas to protect the best of these Victorian and Edwardian neighborhoods. Finchley was incorporated within the **London Borough of Barnet** when London's **local government** was reorganized in 1965. (*See also* JEWISH MUSEUM.)

FINSBURY. Until the 17th century, Finsbury was an extensive area of moorland lying outside the northern wall of the **City of London**. Victims of the **Great Plague** were buried there in communal graves in 1664–65 and refugees from the **Great Fire** found safety on the open space beyond the flames in 1666. Building began in about 1670 and increased during the Georgian period, with the Finsbury Estate, planned by **George Dance the Elder** (1700–1768), laid out as a residential suburb between 1777 and 1800 and Finsbury Circus (designed by his son, **George Dance the Younger** [1741–1825]) constructed in 1815–17. Office developments appeared in the early 20th century, so, by the end of the Second World War, the area had become an extension of London's financial district. It was incorporated within the **London Borough of Islington** in 1965.

FLEET MARRIAGES. During the first half of the 18th century, marriages were conducted, without proper authority, by clergymen sent to **Fleet Prison** for failure to pay debts. Many of the ceremonies took place in nearby hostelries, which displayed signs showing male and female hands clasped, but Parliament declared the unions void in 1753.

FLEET PRISON. There is documentary evidence of a **prison** on the east bank of the **Fleet River** in 1170, but some scholars suggest that it may have been erected a century earlier soon after the Norman invasion (1066). Conditions for the inmates were appalling but, for the Keeper, very lucrative because he could claim customs dues from vessels arriving at the Fleet and fees from prisoners for lodging, food, and privileges. The system was open to great abuse (many of the men who paid for a day outside the jail simply vanished), but it survived until the institution was closed in 1842. The building was demolished in 1846 and the site acquired by the London, Chatham, and Dover Railway in 1864. (*See also* GORDON RIOTS.)

FLEET RIVER. The Fleet rises in **Hampstead** and flows southwards to enter the **River Thames** east of **Charing Cross**. Although its name is probably derived from a Saxon word for "tidal inlet," it is not mentioned in records until the 12th century, when ships unloaded cargoes on its banks. It attracted a number of small industries, including tanneries, cutlery makers, and wharf facilities where butchers could dump waste. Nearby residents complained of the smell but, although the waterway was cleaned up in 1502 and 1606, it was inaccessible to boats by 1652, partly because of the rubbish covering its surface. During the 18th century, it was covered over and now runs underground as part of the city's **sewage** system.

FLEET STREET. Fleet Street (named after the **Fleet River**) extends eastwards for a third of a mile from **Temple Bar** to Ludgate Hill. During the Medieval period, it was a major thoroughfare where senior figures in the Catholic Church built their residences. That coterie of learned citizens helped to attract booksellers and printing shops, which congregated in the area from the late 15th century. On 11 March 1702, the first newspaper—the *Morning Chronicle*—began to publish from premises in Fleet Street. By the mid-20th century, most of the major English dailies had their headquarters there, news agencies such as Reuter's and the Press Association maintained offices, and the regional press rented rooms for London representatives. From the early 1980s, however, hot metal succumbed to computerized printing technologies and business managers became increasingly frustrated by congested inner-city conditions that prevented easy delivery of newsprint and fast distribution of papers. Most big publishers moved out (for example, News International built premises at **Wapping** for ***The Times*** and *The Sun*, and the *The Daily Telegraph* relocated, with the *Guardian*, to the **Isle of Dogs**). The pubs, legal practices, and other businesses that relied on the newspapers for trade suffered with the departure of customers, but most have survived, finding new clients in the offices that replaced the presses. (*See also* ROTHMAN'S OF PALL MALL; ST. BRIDE'S CHURCH, FLEET STREET; ST. DUNSTAN'S IN THE WEST CHURCH, FLEET STREET; SWEENEY TODD; WAPPING DISPUTE.)

FLOOD CONTROL. Flooding has long been a problem in London. The *Anglo-Saxon Chronicle* reports that, in 1099, the **River Thames** "sprung up to such a height and did so much harm as no man remembered that it ever did before." Records indicate that, during the 16th century, one incursion of water left fish dying on the floor of **Westminster Hall**, and **Samuel Pepys** noted in his diary that, on 7 December 1663, "There was last night the greatest tide that ever was remembered in England to have been in this river, all Whitehall having been drowned." Large-scale attempts to limit damage and loss of life followed the passage of the Thames Flood Act in 1879; embankments were built along much of the river (*see* **Bazalgette, Joseph William**) heightened between 1930 and 1935 (following a flood in 1928) and raised again in 1971–72. However, by the time of the last construction work, scientists had provided convincing evidence that the defenses would have only limited effect if meteorological and marine conditions combined in a form predicted to occur once every 200 years. Troughs of low pressure moving from the western Atlantic could push surges of high water southwards through the North Sea. As those surges reached the narrow entrance to the English Channel, they would back up into the Thames estuary and be carried towards London with the high tide. When the inevitable flooding occurred, 45 square miles of the city would be inundated (including the major government offices in the vicinity of **Whitehall**), the **London Underground** would be unable to function, more than a million people would drown, gas and electricity supplies would be cut off, and damage to property would cost billions of pounds to repair. Moreover, according to the researchers, the likelihood of such floods was increasing every year because global warming was melting the polar ice caps, the southeast of Britain was tilting downwards at the rate of about 12 inches every century, and the weight of buildings was causing the metropolis to sink into its foundation of **London Clay** and other sediments.

Faced with the facts, the Conservative government decided, in 1972, to authorize construction of a flood barrier across the river at **Woolwich**, where the waterway was comparatively straight and the subsurface of clay-with-flints suitable for building. Completed in 1982, the barrier (designed by Charles Draper) is a 570-yard-long machine rather than a dam. It has 10 moveable gates, four of which are wide enough to allow seagoing vessels through. In normal conditions, these gates sit on the river bed, but, when high water levels threaten, they can be raised to stem the tide (by 1998, they had been used on more than 20 occasions). The cost of installation amounted to about £500 million, of which one-quarter was funded by the **Greater London Council** and the rest by government. At current conditions of sea-level rise (just under three feet per century), the Thames barrier is expected to protect the capital from flooding until the year 2030; at that time, new solutions will be required. Its operation is the responsibility of the National Rivers Authority, which has provided a visitors' center on the south bank.

FOOTBALL. The game of football (known to Americans as soccer) has been played in Britain for centuries under a variety of local rules.

Frequently, matches ended violently, so, in 1846, a nationally agreed set of regulations was negotiated then in 1863, the Football Association (now based in Lancaster Gate) was established to administer the sport. During the second half of the 19th century, several teams were formed in industrial areas of the city, where the game was most popular (*see*, for example, **Canning Town** and **Royal Arsenal**). The creation of an English League in 1888 furthered calls for payments to players, the growth of professionalism, and, since the end of the Second World War, increasing commercialization. Of the 13 London clubs currently playing in the four major divisions, the oldest are Fulham (formed in 1879), Leyton Orient (1881), and Tottenham Hotspur (1882). Hundreds of other teams play in semiprofessional, amateur, and school leagues. (*See also* OVAL, THE; WEMBLEY.)

FOREST HILL. A residential suburb in the **London Borough of Lewisham**, some six miles southeast of **Charing Cross**, Forest Hill was largely undeveloped until the early 19th century, when canal and **railway** building brought an influx of population. During the 1880s, German **immigrants** established a community in the area, building a church in Dacres Road where theologian Dietrich Bonhoeffer (who was executed in 1945 for plotting against Adolf Hitler) was pastor from 1933 until 1935. In the 20th century, many of the Victorian homes have been subdivided into apartments and others have made way for local authority **housing** developments. (*See also* HORNIMAN MUSEUM.)

FORTNUM AND MASON. London's best-known grocery store was founded in 1707, when William Fortnum resigned from his post as footman in Queen Anne's household and set up business as a supplier of provisions in partnership with Hugh Mason. The pair was ideally suited to commerce because Mason had a quick commercial mind (he established stables near the store in order to facilitate deliveries to customers, for example) and Fortnum was able to use his experience with the royal family to stock high-value goods he knew would appeal to the moneyed classes. In 1808–14, during the Peninsular War, British officers used Fortnum and Mason as a source for luxuries they could not find while on campaign and, in 1819, Sir William Edward Parry bought two hundredweight of cocoa to take on his unsuccessful attempt to find a northwest passage from the Atlantic Ocean to the Pacific Ocean. For three centuries, the business has supplied groceries to reigning monarchs and it still stocks a vast range of unusual and expensive foods. Despite updating its premises at 181 Piccadilly and adding furniture, clothing, and other goods to its wares, it has retained elements of the shopping experience of bygone eras by keeping chandeliers and red carpet in the food hall and insisting that sales assistants must wear morning coats.

FOUNDLING HOSPITAL. In 1742, master mariner Thomas Coram, disturbed by the number of infants abandoned on the streets by their parents, persuaded a group of wealthy Londoners to help him build a children's hospital at Lamb's Conduit Fields. Demand for admission was so great that a ballot was instituted and strict rules were established (only the first child of an unmarried mother could be accepted, for example). William Hogarth supported the venture by encouraging other painters (including Thomas Gainsborough and Joshua Reynolds) to donate works of art that were put on display, attracting members of the public who made donations when they went to view the pictures. George Frideric Handel also contributed by presenting an organ and holding performances of his oratorio *Messiah*. The hospital moved out of London and the site was redeveloped, but the Thomas Coram Foundation for Children continues its charitable work (and still displays its pictures) from offices in Brunswick Square.

FREEDOM OF THE CITY. In medieval times, as apprentices of the craft guilds (*see* **livery companies**) gained experience, they had to appear before a court of their seniors in order to prove their competence. If they were successful, they were considered free of the guild and entitled to practice on their own. That status achieved, they then had to be made free of the **City of London** in order to set up business. The custom of awarding the Freedom of the City has continued into modern times and can be earned by redemption (that is, by being sponsored by two members of livery companies), by servitude (which involves completion of an apprenticeship to a Freeman), or by patrimony (children of Freemen may be awarded the Freedom of the City if they were born after their parent's admission and are over 21 at the time of application). Each successful candidate pays a fee, which is used to further the **Corporation of London**'s educational work. Approval of applications is vested in the **aldermen** (when the applicant is a member of a livery company) and the **Court of Common Council** (in all other cases). British nationals who have given outstanding service to the country may be awarded Honorary Freedom of the City. Formerly, Freemen had the right to certain educational and other privileges, but these were largely superseded by welfare state legislation after the Second World War.

FREEMAN. *See* FREEDOM OF THE CITY.

FREUD'S HOUSE. In 1938, psychoanalyst Sigmund Freud fled to London from his native Austria, where the Nazis condemned his work as being "Jewish science." He moved into a house at 20 Maresfield Road, in **Swiss Cottage**, and died there on 23 September the following year. Anna, his daughter and also a psychoanalyst, occupied the property until her own death 43 years later, keeping her father's study and library as it was during his last months. The building is now a **museum** where visitors can see Freud's prototype couch, his letters, and other personal effects.

FROST FAIRS. Until **London Bridge** was demolished (and replaced by John Rennie's structure in 1823–31), its narrow arches impeded the flow of the **River Thames**, causing the water to freeze in particularly cold winters. Londoners seized the opportunity to hold celebrations that became known as frost **fairs** (though, technically, they were not fairs because these required a royal charter). In 1564–65, for example, archery tournaments were held on the ice, and in 1683–84 (when King Charles II attended with his family) an ox was roasted. Similar events took place in 1715–16, 1739–40, 1788–89, and 1813–14, with merchants setting up stalls and musicians leading dances.

FULHAM. Early in the eighth century, Bishop Tyrhtilus of Hereford granted land in Fulanhum, on the north bank of the **River Thames**, to Waldhere, Bishop of London. Some three centuries later, Waldhere's successors built a summer home (which became known as Fulham Palace) on the site, and a small community grew around the building, with a second focus developing at a ferry landing site nearby. By 1500, the people were utilizing the fertile alluvial soils to grow vegetables for the London market, an enterprise so successful that it prevented significant urban development from encroaching until the second half of the 19th century, even though the central city lies only four miles to the northeast (the last farm in the area was sold in 1910 and the land converted to a housing estate). Ultimately, however, the pressure from builders became too great to resist. The arrival of the **railways**, the construction of a workhouse and infirmary (now the site of Charing Cross Hospital) in 1849, the erection of a **gas** plant, the provision of facilities for travellers along Fulham Palace Road (the main highway from London to the naval base at Portsmouth, on the south coast of England), and the opening of an **elec-**

Frost fair on the River Thames, 1814 (Museum of London)

tricity generating station in 1936 all created compelling demands for space where workers and commuters could establish homes. The new residents, in turn, provided a market for shops, entertainments, and other services, so, by 1950, Fulham's character had changed and the community had become a metropolitan suburb. In 1965, when the city's **local government** was reorganized, it was incorporated within the **London Borough of Hammersmith and Fulham**. (*See also* HURLINGHAM CLUB; PUTNEY BRIDGE; WANDSWORTH BRIDGE.)

– G –

GARRICK, DAVID (1717–1779). David Garrick revolutionized 18th-century London **theater**, replacing a very affected style of acting with more natural characterization. He also greatly influenced other aspects of the stage, writing, producing, and promoting playhouses. His entry into the world of entertainment happened by chance rather than design because his family had no background in the profession. Peter, his father, was an army officer descended from **Huguenot** immigrants and Arabella, his mother, was the daughter of a clergyman at Lichfield Cathedral. He was born at the Angel Inn, Hereford, on 19 February 1717, while his father was on a recruiting trip, and initially educated at Lichfield Grammar School. In 1736, he transferred to the academy that **Samuel Johnson** had opened at Edial but that venture was unsuccessful, so, in March 1737, the two men set off to seek their fortunes in London.

Initially, Garrick intended to study law, but a legacy from an uncle allowed him to set up business as a wine merchant. The work led to contacts with the bohemian world of the theater, in which he thrived. Turning his hand to playwriting, he drafted *Lethe, Or Esop in the Shades*, a comedy that received its first performance in the Drury Lane Theatre (*see* **Theatre Royal, Drury Lane**) in April 1740. Then, in March 1741, when the actor playing Harlequin at a theater in Goodman's Fields fell ill, Garrick stepped in to play the part. A series of relatively minor appearances followed over the next few months, earning him a growing reputation, but in October of the same year he shot to fame when he appeared in the leading role in **William Shakespeare**'s *Richard III* and was lauded by a public who loved his realistic portrayal of a king killed in battle. Over the next six years, theatergoers in London and Dublin flocked to see him in Shakespearean dramas, including *Hamlet* and *King Lear*, and in works by **Ben Jonson**, Thomas Otway, and other popular writers. In 1747, in partnership with James Lacy (a failed actor but a canny businessman), he bought a lease on the Drury Lane Theatre, carrying his inventiveness into theater organization by moving the orchestra from the gallery to the front of the stage and refusing to reduce admission prices for playgoers who arrived late. His repertoire, strongly biased towards works by Shakespeare, turned the theater into the most successful of its time and made him a rich man, able to employ **Robert Adam** to enlarge his country villa on the **River Thames**, near **Hampton Court Palace**, and entertaining lavishly both there and at 27 Southampton Street, his townhouse north of the **Strand**.

In 1776, Garrick sold his interest in the Theatre and retired. Three years later, he took ill while celebrating the New Year with Lord and Lady Spencer at Althorpe Park, Northamptonshire, and on 20 January, shortly after returning to London, died at his home in the Adelphi (*see* **Adam, Robert**) development. He was buried at Poet's Corner in **Westminster Abbey**. In 1831, the Duke of Sussex founded the Garrick Club (for actors, writers, painters, and other artists) in his memory. Now located at 15 Garrick Street, its membership is still heavily drawn from workers in theater and other branches of entertainment, including television and film. Three London theaters (and one in New York) were also named after him. (*See also* BAGNIGGE WELLS; BRITISH MUSEUM; CHAMBERS, WILLIAM; ST.-GILES-IN-THE-FIELDS CHURCH, ST. GILES HIGH STREET; STREATHAM.)

GAS. In 1807 Frederick Winsor presented a display of gas street lighting in **Pall Mall** as a celebration for the birthday of George, Prince of Wales, but its use for that purpose on a permanent basis did not begin until 1814, when the Gas Light and Coke Company provided lamps on **Westminster Bridge**. Other firms soon followed so, by 1850, major streets (such as Tottenham Court Road) were lit, as were **Buckingham Palace** and the House of Commons (*see* **Palace of Westminster**). Over the next two decades, companies divided much of the urban area among themselves so that each had a monopoly in some districts, but from 1870 the Gas Light and Coke Company increasingly dominated the north London market, providing a cheap product through underground mains from its riverside plant at **Beckton**, where the coal needed for the production process arrived by barge. Gradually, it merged with its competitors to become the largest gas manufacturing company in Europe.

On the other side of the river, the South Metropolitan Gas Company was becoming similarly dominant from its base in **Greenwich**. From the

1880s, both firms, threatened by the growth of **electricity** supply companies, put much effort into the marketing of gas as a source of power and heat rather than light, placing an emphasis on fires and kitchen equipment in an attempt to maintain profits, but after the Second World War the Labour government eliminated competition by nationalizing supply companies and creating regional boards with responsibility for providing gas to different parts of the metropolitan area. As a result, manufacture was concentrated at a smaller number of sites and, with changing technology, converted from coal to oil-based supplies. The discovery of natural gas in the North Sea in 1965 caused further change, leading to the closure of all town gas plants by the end of the 1970s. The last gas street lamps to be lit by hand every evening survived in the Temple area (*see* **Inns of Court**) until 1986. (*See also* **Street Lighting.**)

GATWICK AIRPORT. *See* AIRPORTS.

GEFFRYE MUSEUM. The **museum**, located in Kingsland Road, Haggerston, houses a series of furnished rooms depicting the development of interior design in London from the 15th until the 20th centuries. Exhibits include Georgian shop fronts, wood paneling (which originally graced city mansions), a carpenter's shop from **Limehouse**, and the plastered ceiling from the hall of the Company of Pewterers (one of the **livery companies**). The building was erected in 1715 as an almshouse and paid for with funds from the estate of Sir Robert Geffrye, a former **Lord Mayor** of London and Master of the Ironmongers' Company (another livery organization). It was bought by the **London County Council** and opened as a museum in 1914.

GENTLEMEN'S CLUBS. The first gentlemen's clubs in London were informal groups that met in **coffee houses** or taverns to gossip during the late 17th century. As the gatherings increased in size, some of these groups took over entire properties (particularly in the St. James's area close to **Pall Mall**) and paid fees to the proprietor in return for rights to dine, read newspapers, and socialize. Inevitably, men associated with friends and colleagues who shared their interests, so the clubs developed distinct identities; for example, **The Athenaeum** (formally founded in 1824) became popular with intellectuals, the Garrick (*see* **David Garrick**) with writers, the **Carlton Club** (1832) with the Tory Party, and the Reform (1836) with Whigs. Many of the organizations eventually built imposing premises in central London and often had long waiting lists of potential members. During the 20th century, they became less popular but many still survive, though most have now admitted women to membership. (*See also* BARRY, CHARLES; BEEFSTEAK CLUB; BOODLE'S; BOSWELL, JAMES; HURLINGHAM CLUB; JERMYN STREET; JOHNSON, SAMEUL; MARYLEBONE CRICKET CLUB [MCC]; PICCADILLY; STOCK EXCHANGE [LSE].)

GEOLOGICAL MUSEUM. The Geological **Museum** was founded in 1837 to educate the public about Britain's mineral resources. It moved to its present building in Exhibition Road in 1935, became part of the **Natural History Museum** in 1985, and now houses over one million specimens, including a reference collection of building stones that is used often by conservation workers attempting restoration projects. A £12 million refurbishment, completed in 1998, allowed the museum to develop an innovative approach to exhibitions, adopting modern technology to mount eye-catching displays of fossils and gems and to demonstrate the story of the earth's evolution. In addition, it provides offices for the British Geological Survey, formed in 1835 to prepare geological maps of Great Britain.

GEOLOGY. *See* CHILTERN HILLS; GEOLOGICAL MUSEUM; LONDON BASIN; LONDON CLAY; NORTH DOWNS.

GEORGE INN. There is evidence that the site where the George Inn stands in Tooley Street, south of **London Bridge**, was occupied by a hostelry in 1542. The present building, dating from 1642, is the last galleried coaching inn left in London. Originally, it enclosed three sides of a courtyard, but the central and northern wings were demolished in 1899 to make way for **railway** developments. Author **Charles Dickens** knew the place well, describing it in several of his novels, including *Little Dorrit* (1857). Scenes from his works (and from the plays of **William Shakespeare**) are performed in the yard during the summer.

GIBBONS, GRINLING (1648–1721). One of the finest in a long line of London woodcarvers, Gibbons was born in Rotterdam on 4 April 1648, the son of an English emigrant. While working in **Deptford** in 1671, he was discovered by diarist **John Evelyn**, who introduced him to King Charles II and the royal court. His finely crafted reproductions of flowers, fruits, and game, carved in lime wood, were well received by wealthy aristocrats and merchants, who inundated him with commissions, many of which had to be carried out by other people, albeit to Gibbons's designs. He had considerable talent as a sculptor as well; Dalkeith House (in East Lothian) has a marble chimneypiece by Gibbons and several churches (such as Exton, in Rutland) have monuments on which he worked. In London, his versatility is clearly evident. He carved the choir stalls, thrones, and organ screen for **St. Paul's Cathedral** in oak and most of the exterior panels below the lower windows in stone. In **St. James's Church, Piccadilly**, he completed the reredos in lime and the font in marble. At **St. Mary Abchurch**, his altar screen incorporates four Corinthian pillars, which support a pediment decorated with urns. His monuments are seen in **Westminster Abbey** and his statuary in the bronzes of King Charles II at **Chelsea Hospital** and of King James VII and II in front of the **National Gallery**. Gibbons died at his home in Bow Street on 3 August 1721 and was buried in **St. Paul's Church, Covent Garden**. (*See also* ADMIRALTY, THE; ST. JAMES'S PALACE.)

GIBBS, JAMES (1682–1754). Gibbs, best known for his design of **St. Martin-in-the-Fields Church**, was born on 23 December 1682 to Aberdeen merchant Peter Gibbs and his wife, Isabel. After graduating from the city's Marischal College, he studied at the Scots College in Rome, intending to train as a missionary, but turned his attention to **architecture**, with Carolo Fontana (Surveyor General to Pope Clement XI) as his tutor. In 1709, funded by John Erskine, Earl of Mar (whom he had met in Holland), he set up a practice in London and won the commission to design St. Mary-le-Strand Church (1714–23), which critic Simon Jenkins describes as the finest 18th-century ecclesiastical building in the city. In 1719, he added two stories and a steeple to the tower of **St. Clement Danes Church** (designed by **Christopher Wren**) then, in 1722, began work on St. Martin-in-the-Fields, incorporating a steeple and classical portico, which were reproduced in countless later buildings throughout Britain and North America. In addition, he was responsible for the design of several of the memorial sculptures in **Westminster Abbey**, including that of John Holles, Duke of Newcastle (1723). His best known works outside London are the Senate House in Cambridge (1722–30), Allhallows Church, Derby (1723–25), and the Radcliffe Library, Oxford (1737–49). Although never the most fashionable of architects (his Italian experiences led him to adopt elements of the baroque that were never fully appreciated by a society in love with Palladianism), Gibbs had a distinctive style that won many admirers and influenced successors for nearly a century after his death in London on 5 August 1754. (*See also* BURLINGTON HOUSE.)

GIPSY HILL. During the 17th century, the relatively remote area of hilly land west of present-day **Crystal Palace** became an increasingly popular gathering ground for the gypsy community, who earned an unsavory reputation as troublemakers in nearby communities. Efforts to remove them proved unsuccessful until, early in the 19th century, parliamentary legislation allowed landowners to enclose previously open fields with walls and hedgerows. The arrival of the **railway** in mid-century completed the dispersal process as speculative builders destroyed the last remnants of the encampments by erecting houses for middle-class commuters who had jobs in the central city but were prepared to travel to them from homes near the countryside.

GIPSY MOTH IV. *See CUTTY SARK.*

GLOBE THEATRE. In 1598–99, Cuthbert and Richard Burbage built a round **theater** at **Bankside**, then the center of London's entertainment district. It took its name from the sphere on its sign and (because it had no roof) was used only during the summer months. Although many writers had works performed on its stage, it has become most closely associated with **William Shakespeare**, many of whose plays—including *Romeo and Juliet*, *Macbeth*, *Othello*, *The Taming of the Shrew*, and *The Winter's Tale*—were presented to London audiences there. The theater was destroyed by fire in 1613, rebuilt, but closed by Puritan authorities in 1642. In 1970, Sam Wanamaker (the Chicago-born actor and film director) established a Shakespeare Globe Playhouse Trust with the intention of raising funds to build a replica. Construction began, 17 years later, on a site some 200 yards from the location of the original theater and was greatly aided by archaeological excavations that, in 1989, revealed details of the 16th-century building. The modern structure presented its first season in 1997 and forms the core of a growing artistic and educational complex, with a library, an archive of audiovisual material, and other resources.

GOLDERS GREEN. Although Golders Green lies only some five miles northwest of **Charing Cross**, it survived as a predominantly agricultural area until the early 20th century. The catalyst for change was the extension to the Northern Line of the **London Underground** system, which was tunnelled under **Hampstead Heath** in 1905. Its arrival greatly improved accessibility to the central city and sparked a frenzy of speculative house building by private developers. Many of those who bought the new homes were second generation Jewish **immigrants** moving from **Whitechapel** and other areas of the **East End**, taking with them distinctive foods and religious practices. The Jews' College (founded in 1855) contains the largest library on Judaism in Europe, the Jewish Cemetery (opened in Hoop Lane in 1895) buries Sephardic Jews under flat stones in its eastern section and Reform Jews under upright stones in the west, and both Finchley Road and Golders Green Road have competing kosher butchers, bagel shops, and booksellers. The Hippodrome Theatre, originally opened as a **music hall** in 1914, became the home of the **British Broadcasting Corporation**'s Radio Concert Orchestra in 1968 and, in 1974, Ivy House (where dancer Anna Pavlova lived from 1913 until her death in 1931) was converted into a **museum** of ballet. Golders Green was incorporated within the **London Borough of Barnet** when **local government** in the metropolitan area was reorganized in 1965.

GORDON RIOTS. In 1780, Lord George Gordon led a series of protests designed to coerce Lord North's Tory government into dropping its plans to repeal legislation that discriminated against Roman Catholics. On 2 June, he marched to Parliament at the head of a mob of supporters intent on presenting a petition of protest. The action provoked a week of rioting across the city. Chapels in **Spitalfields** and Moorfields were set ablaze, jails (including **Fleet Prison** and **Newgate Prison**) were ransacked and inmates released, official government residences in **Downing Street** were attacked, and the **Bank of England** was stormed (albeit unsuccessfully). Estimates of the number of people killed range from about 250 to over 800. Gordon was tried on a charge of high treason but acquitted on the grounds that he had no treasonable intent. Twenty-one other men were hanged. (*See also* CLINK PRISON; LAMBETH PALACE; POLICE.)

GOSPEL OAK. A largely working-class residential suburb lying between **Kentish Town** and **Hampstead Heath**, some 3.5 miles north of **Charing Cross**, Gospel Oak gets its name from the practice of reading passages from the Bible under a tall oak tree during the ceremonial beating of the parish boundaries just before Ascension Day (40 days after Easter) each year. Until the middle of the 19th century, the area was used primarily for grazing, but the gradual extension of London's urban area encouraged developers to purchase land and erect rows of terraced houses, particularly after the Midland **Railway**, the North London Railway, and the Tottenham and Hampstead Junction Railway improved accessibility to other parts of the city. Brickfields, train shunting yards, a **tram** depot, and small factories provided local employment. After the Second World War, much of the poorer quality property was demolished and replaced by large local authority **housing** estates, particularly in the Lismore Circus area. Gospel Oak was incorporated within the **London Borough of Camden** in 1965.

GRAND UNION CANAL. The first Grand Union Canal was opened in 1814, linking London to Leicestershire and Northamptonshire in the East Midlands of England. It was taken over, in 1894, by the Grand Junction Canal Company, which completed a second Grand Union Canal 35 years later by connecting **Regent's Canal** with other waterways so that barges could travel as far as Birmingham. Management responsibility passed to the British Transport Commission in 1948 (when the Labour government placed all of Britain's canals under state control) then, in 1963, to the British Waterways Authority.

GRAY'S INN. *See* INNS OF COURT.

GREATER LONDON. The 32 **London borough**s, along with the **City of London**, are together known as Greater London. Greater London has a total population of 7.19 million people (1998) and covers an area of 610 square miles (a population density of 11,782 people per square mile). Fourteen central authorities—**Camden**, **City of London**, **Hackney**, **Hammersmith and Fulham**, **Haringey**, **Islington**, **Kensington and Chelsea**, **Lambeth**, **Lewisham**, **Newham**, **Southwark**, **Tower Hamlets**, **Wandsworth**, and **Westminster**—are collectively termed Inner London by the Office of Population Censuses and Surveys (though other bodies, such as the **Inner London Education Authority** [ILEA] have used different groupings. Inner London has 2.76 million residents on 116 square miles (a population density of 23,798 people per square mile). The remaining authorities—**Barking and Dagenham**, **Barnet**, **Bexley**, **Brent**, **Bromley**, **Croydon**, **Ealing**, **Enfield**, **Greenwich**, **Harrow**, **Havering**, **Hillingdon**, **Hounslow**, **Kingston Upon Thames**, **Merton**, **Redbridge**, **Richmond Upon Thames**, **Sutton**, and **Waltham Forest**—comprise Outer London. Outer London has 4.43 million people on 494 square miles, a density of 8,960 people per square mile.

GREATER LONDON AUTHORITY (GLA). The abolition of the **Greater London Council (GLC)** in 1986 removed a powerful critic of Mrs. Margaret Thatcher's Conservative government but left the metropolitan area with no single authority responsible for overall planning and resulted in much uncontrolled development. During the 1990s, advocates of a new citywide authority attracted growing numbers of supporters, particularly in the Labour Party, which, within weeks of its General Election victory in 1997, produced a consultation paper that outlined proposals for a full-time elected mayor who would act as the voice of the city, run new transport and economic development bodies, initiate projects designed to improve the environment, and hold the urban purse strings. The Mayor, along with 25 elected representatives of a London Assembly, would form a Greater London Authority, which would take over many of the former duties of the GLC but avoid interfering in matters of purely local concern within the **London borough**s. The plans were clarified in a White Paper published in March the following year and were supported by 72 percent of the city's residents in a referendum held on 7 May 1998. The first elections were held on 4 May 2000, with 14 of the assembly members selected to represent geographical areas and the remainder chosen to represent political parties. **Kenneth Robert Livingstone** was appointed first Mayor of London, heading the authority.

GREATER LONDON COUNCIL (GLC). The GLC was established by the London Government Act of 1963 and met for the first time two years later, when its predecessor—the **London County Council (LCC)**—was disbanded. Its creation was essentially the result of population movements because, during the 1950s, middle-class groups had fled the city, effectively leaving the LCC permanently under the control of the Labour Party. The new authority—covering an area of about 610 square miles, more than five times that of its predecessor, and encompassing many of the affluent suburbs—would, the Conservative government believed, provide right-wing politicians with an opportunity to take over. That belief was justified; for 10 of its 21 years' existence the Conservatives were in the majority. The council was composed of 92 members, each elected for four years. A Leader (the political head) was chosen by the party with the most seats and a Chairman (the ceremonial head) by the whole body. Responsibilities were wide ranging (though not as wide ranging as those of the LCC), including strategic planning of road networks, traffic control, financial control of **London Transport**, education in the central-city boroughs (*see* **Inner London Education Authority**), and the administration of the **London Fire Brigade**.

Given the impact of its decisions on the day-to-day lives of Londoners (and on outsiders who commuted to work), the authority was unsurprisingly dogged by controversy. At the 1970 council elections, most areas had candidates running solely to protest the priority given to roads over **housing**. In the mid-1970s, the Labour camp was riven by internecine strife stemming from disagreements about the social implications of plans to reduce the authority's £1.6 billion debt. In the late 1970s, Horace Cutler, the Conservative Leader of the Council, gained a reputation for outspoken criticism of transport workers and erratic changes of policy. When Labour gained control in 1981 and appointed a clique of left wingers to important positions, with **Kenneth Robert Livingstone** as Leader, matters came to a head. Despite critical articles in many newspapers, Livingstone and his supporters proved to be very popular with city residents and thus provided a focus of dissent against the free market policies of Prime Minister Margaret Thatcher and her followers in Parliament. Right-wing groups called for the abolition of the authority (*see*, for example, **London Boroughs Association**) and Mrs. Thatcher listened. Her substantial Conservative Party majority approved a House of Commons bill abolishing the Greater London Council, which ceased to exist on 31 March 1986, leaving London as the world's only major metropolitan area without a citywide planning authority. Many of the GLC's responsibilities and assets were devolved to the 32 boroughs. Others were transferred to government-appointed bodies. (*See also* LONDON AMBULANCE SERVICE; LONDON HEALTH EMERGENCY [LHE]; LONDON RESIDUARY BODY [LRB]; MARBLE HILL HOUSE; THAMESMEAD.)

GREAT EXHIBITION. The suggestion that an exhibition of achievements in the arts and the sciences should be held in London was first proposed by Henry Cole, an assistant keeper at the **Public Record Office**. It was enthusiastically endorsed by Lord John Russell's Liberal Party government, which, in 1850, appointed a Royal Commission to raise money for the event. **Prince Albert** (Queen Victoria's husband and a staunch supporter of the project) presided over a committee consisting of such distinguished national figures as Russell himself, former Prime Minister Robert Peel, William Gladstone (who had been President of the Board of Trade in Peel's administration), and builder **Thomas Cubitt**. A site was chosen at **Hyde Park** (much to the chagrin of ***The Times***, which forecast that the open space would disappear under "a bivouac of vagabonds"), and Joseph Paxton was invited to build a **Crystal Palace** to house the exhibits after a competition that attracted over 200 entries had failed to produce a satisfactory design. Most of the objects on display reflected Britain's technological expertise (including engines, textiles, domestic utensils, and other products of the industrial age), but there were many other treasures to make the six million visitors gasp with wonder, including the Koh-i-Noor diamond (which had been brought to Britain from the Punjab in 1849 and added to the **crown jewels**), the largest pearl ever discovered, a bronze statue of Richard the Lionheart (King of England from 1189 to 1199), and a glass fountain 27 feet high. The success of the venture, which was opened by Queen Victoria on 1 May 1851 and ran for 14 weeks, earned Paxton a knighthood and produced profits sufficient to purchase 84 acres of land in south **Kensington**, which were developed as an educational complex incorporating the **Albert Hall**, the **Geological Museum**, the **Natural History Museum**, the **Royal College of Art**, the **Royal College of Music**, the **Science Museum**, the **Victoria and Albert Museum**, and other institutions.

GREAT FIRE. Early in the morning of 2 September 1666, fire broke out in the premises of Thomas Farynor, the Royal Baker in **Pudding Lane**, close to the **River Thames**. It spread rapidly through the closely packed wooden houses that lined the narrow streets of the **City of London**, raging for more than three days before it was fully extinguished. Diarist **Samuel Pepys** records that, while he sat in an alehouse in **Bankside**, he saw "one entire arch of fire from this to the other side of the bridge and in a bow up the hill about a mile long." Seeking safety for his wife and belongings, he fled to **Woolwich** but returned within hours to find King Charles II trying to help soldiers put out the flames at **Cripplegate**. Only nine lives were lost (including a maid in the building where the conflagration started), but over 460 acres were blighted, with 89 churches burned down and more than 13,000 other structures destroyed. In the aftermath, owners had to prove title to land before they could reerect properties, a Fire Court was established to settle disputes, and new regulations required builders to use brick and stone, rather than wood, for construction. Many of the designs for new public buildings were prepared by **Christopher Wren**, who was the architect of 50 City places of worship in addition to **St. Paul's Cathedral**. (*See also* GREYFRIARS MONASTERY; GUILDHALL; HAMPSTEAD; LEADENHALL MARKET; LONDON FIRE BRIGADE; MONUMENT; NEW-

GATE PRISON; ST. BRIDE'S CHURCH, FLEET STREET; STEELYARD; THREADNEEDLE STREET.)

GREAT ORMOND STREET HOSPITAL FOR SICK CHILDREN. Even by the middle of the 19th century, London had few hospital facilities for children, who were excluded from most institutions caring for the sick. Determined to improve medical care for the young, Dr. Charles West rented a property at 49 Great Ormond Street in 1851, providing 10 beds for patients aged from two to 12 (it was felt that those under two should be treated as outpatients because they needed the care and comfort of their mother). In 1877, a larger hospital was built on the same site, and in 1893 a further extension was opened, allowing doctors to look after 240 youngsters. Further rebuilding was carried out during the 1930s. The hospital became part of the National Health Service system when the Labour government introduced its program of welfare state policies in 1946 and has undertaken extensive refurbishment in recent decades, increasing provision to 305 beds. In 1994, it converted to National Health Service Trust status in order to give its management greater control over finances and, by the end of the century, it employed 1,760 medical and administrative staff to look after 18,800 inpatients and 66,000 outpatients each year. The institution benefits significantly from J. M. Barrie's gift of the copyright of his play *Peter Pan* in 1927. Under English law, those benefits would have expired in 1987 (50 years after Barrie's death), but a special Act of Parliament passed that year extended the rights to all royalties in perpetuity. After the Second World War, an Institute of Child Health was developed at the hospital. Now Britain's leading research center focusing on childhood diseases, it merged with University College (part of the University of London) in 1996.

GREAT PLAGUE. From the winter of 1664–65 until the spring of 1666, London suffered an epidemic of plague. The disease, carried by fleas that had fed on the blood of infected rats, was first detected in St. Giles-in-the-Fields (a suburb lying west of the **City of London**) but spread quickly through the closely packed, overcrowded, and unsanitary houses of the capital. Slum areas such as **Shoreditch** and **Stepney** bore the brunt of the deaths, but no section of society was spared. King Charles II and his royal court fled to **Hampton Court Palace** on 29 June 1665, lawyers deserted the **Inns of Court,** and employers closed their factories because coal boats would not call at the **docks**. Houses whose members had fallen victim to the infection were marked with a red cross and guards were placed at the door to prevent residents from leaving for 40 days after the sufferer had died or recovered. Given the high mortality rate (725 in the week before the King left, for example), **burial grounds** filled, bodies lay in piles awaiting interment, and the stench of death permeated all corners of the city. The **Lord Mayor** ordered that all dogs and cats should be killed because they might spread the disease; some 200,000 of the latter were destroyed, thereby removing one of the rat's most effective predators and adding to the incidence of the disease. However, in December 1665, the mortality rate fell and stayed low so, on 1 February of the following year, the court returned, encouraging other refugees to follow. The official total of people who died was 68,577, but public records were inaccurate (and probably falsified to prevent alarm) so scholars suggest that the actual number was closer to 100,000 (out of an estimated population of some 460,000). One children's nursery rhyme recalls the event:

> Ring-a-ring o' roses,
> A pocket full of posies,
> Atishoo! Atishoo!
> We all fall down.

The ring of roses is the rash that was one of the early symptoms of the illness, the posies were bunches of flowers carried to ward off the smell of decay, and the "atishoo" represents the sneezing fits that characterized the later stages of the affliction. The last line refers to the mass deaths. (*See also* FINSBURY; HAMPSTEAD; ST. BOTOLPH'S CHURCH, ALDGATE; ST. GILES-IN-THE-FIELDS CHURCH, ST. GILES HIGH STREET; ST. OLAVE'S CHURCH, HART STREET.)

GREAT STINK. During the exceptionally hot summer of 1858, the sewage carried by the **River Thames** emitted a stench that became known as the Great Stink. Pleasure boats cancelled trips and the windows of the Houses of Parliament (*see* **Palace of Westminster**) were draped in sheets soaked in chloride of lime in an attempt to alleviate the smell. Tons of chalk lime and carbolic acid were poured into the river but had little impact, so the stink continued until cooler, wetter weather arrived in the early autumn. (*See also* WATER POLLUTION.)

GREEN BELT. In the period between the two world wars, politicians, academics, and local authority planners voiced increasing concern that London's physical expansion might lead to a continuous sprawl of urban development as far south as the English Channel and as far north as Birmingham. The result was an Act of Parliament that, in 1938, designated a "Green Belt" of protected land around the city. Building was restricted, preventing existing settlements from growing and stopping the encroachment of metropolitan influences. The results were not wholly satisfactory. The Green Belt undoubtedly provided an area where Londoners could escape into the countryside, particularly on weekends, but it also drove house prices higher as buyers competed for homes in environmentally attractive areas, thus preventing the young and the poor from finding places to live (for that reason, parts of the area were christened "the gin and Jaguar belt" by the press). Also, much development simply leaped the protected area, so urban influences actually reached well beyond the city. In recent decades, population growth in southeast England has led construction firms to demand a relaxation of the building restrictions. (*See also* NORTH DOWNS.)

GREEN PARK. Green **Park** gets its name from the color of the grass and trees that dominate; traditionally, there are few flowers because the site was used as a **burial ground** for lepers during the Middle Ages. Its 53 acres, which form a triangle bounded by **Piccadilly**, **Constitution Hill**, and **St. James's Palace**, were enclosed by King Henry VIII during the first half of the 16th century and converted into a **Royal Park** during the second half of the 17th by King Charles II, who laid out walkways and built a snow house for cooling drinks during the summer (the mound where the house stood can still be seen opposite 110 Piccadilly). During the Georgian period, it was popular both for duelling and for ballooning. Now, it provides a green oasis, close to the heart of the city, where office workers and shoppers can relax over a picnic lunch. It is still owned by the Crown and is maintained by the Royal Parks Agency. (*See also* BARRY, CHARLES.)

GREEN PARK ARCH. *See* HYDE PARK CORNER.

GREENWICH. The suburb of Greenwich, on the eastern edge of London south of the **River Thames**, dates at least from Anglo-Saxon times (its name is derived from the Old English *grone* and *wic*, meaning "green dwelling place"). It developed, initially, as a small port close to **Greenwich Palace** and the Franciscan **monastery** established by King Edward IV in 1480, but the establishment of a **Royal Naval Dockyard** at Deptford Creek in 1513 hastened expansion, introducing craftsmen skilled in the industrial tasks of shipbuilding and repair and providing a foundation for other institutions, such as the **Royal Observatory**, which was created by royal warrant in 1675 and had close links with the navy because navigation on the high seas depended heavily on a knowledge of the disposition of the stars. Greenwich Hospital (a home for disabled seamen, which was later converted into the **Royal Naval College**) added to the complex during the 1690s and, with the other employment sources, stimulated residential development (Crooms Hill, for example, is largely Georgian). The **railway**, which arrived in 1878, brought the settlement within commuting range of the **City of London,** then, in 1902, a pedestrian tunnel built under the Thames allowed residents easy access to jobs in the burgeoning **docks** on the north bank of the river. Greenwich now has a flourishing tourist trade, with more than 2.5 million visitors arriving each year to look at the buildings, picnic in the **park**, and scramble on to the tea clipper, ***Cutty Sark***, which is preserved in dry dock at King William Walk. Numbers were boosted in 1997, when the United Nations made Greenwich Britain's 17th **World Heritage Site**. (*See also* GREENWICH, LONDON BOROUGH OF; GREENWICH MEAN TIME [GMT]; GREENWICH PARK; MILLENNIUM DOME; NATIONAL MARITIME MUSEUM; PRIME MERIDIAN; QUEEN'S HOUSE; RANGER'S HOUSE; ST. ALFEGE'S CHURCH, GREENWICH.)

GREENWICH, LONDON BOROUGH OF. The borough was formed in 1965 through the amalgamation of the previously independent local authorities of **Greenwich** and **Woolwich**. Covering 18 square miles, it has a population of some 215,100 (1998) and very contrasting environments. The south of the area, around **Eltham**, is primarily residential with some 40 percent of residents living in public sector **housing** and over half working in manual posts. The northeast, too, has a high proportion of local authority homes but also provides job opportunities at industrial estates in **Abbey Wood** and in Woolwich, which has a long history of dockyard work. Elsewhere, **tourism** provides a significant income, with visitors attracted by the ***Cutty Sark***, **Greenwich Observatory**, the **National Maritime Museum**, and related sites. Nevertheless, unemployment is higher than in many other parts of the city and, by the end of the century, with nearly one-quarter of the adult population claiming social security benefits because of low incomes, problems associated with poverty were placing significant strains on local government finances. (*See also* AVERY HILL; BLACKHEATH; CHARLTON; PLUMSTEAD; ROYAL NAVAL DOCKYARDS.)

GREENWICH HOSPITAL. *See* ROYAL NAVAL COLLEGE.

GREENWICH MEAN TIME (GMT). Since 1884, mean solar time at the **prime meridian** (0° longitude), which passes through the **Royal Observatory** at **Greenwich**, has been used as the international basis for chronometry in order to avoid the confusion arising from a multiplicity of local systems. Until 1925, the start of the solar day (denoted by 00:00 hours GMT) was noon but, since then, it has occurred at midnight in order to accord with the beginning of the civil day. In 1928, the International Astronomical Union changed its nomenclature, replacing the term Greenwich Mean Time with Universal Time. The original phrase, however, is still much in use, particularly in English-speaking countries (with reference to time zones, for example).

GREENWICH MERIDIAN. *See* PRIME MERIDIAN.

GREENWICH PALACE. For three centuries, Greenwich Palace was a favorite residence of England's monarchs and particularly of the Tudors, who ruled from 1485 until 1603. The building, initially known as Bella Donna, was erected in 1426 by Humphrey, Duke of Gloucester and brother of King Henry V, who made provision for a large **library**; the first substantial collection of books to be formed by an individual rather than an institution, it became the foundation on which Oxford University created the Bodleian Library after his death. Henry VI acquired the property in 1447 and Henry VII rebuilt it in 1500–1506, renaming it Placentia (meaning "the pleasant place"). Henry VIII, born there in 1491, greatly enjoyed hunting in the extensive grounds (*see* **Greenwich Park**) and became very fond of the residence, adding a banqueting hall, armories, and a tiltyard for jousting. His daughters, Mary (later Mary I) and Elizabeth (later Elizabeth I), were also born at Greenwich; Mary was never greatly enamored of the place but Elizabeth spent many summers there after she became Queen (during one visit Walter Raleigh allegedly spread his cloak over a puddle so that she would not get her dainty shoes dirty and during another she signed the warrant sending Mary, Queen of Scots, to her death after asking that it be hidden amongst other documents so that she would not know what she was doing). Following the execution of Charles I in 1649, Oliver Cromwell's parliamentarian supporters tried to sell the palace but, in grimly Puritan England, could find no purchaser. Instead, they turned it into a biscuit factory, then (in 1653–54) into a prisoner of war camp holding captives taken during the war with Holland. After the restoration of the monarchy in 1660, Charles II undertook some rebuilding work, but his successors, William III and Mary II, had little interest in the house, preferring **Hampton Court Palace**

and **Kensington Palace**, so, in 1694, it was demolished and the Royal Naval Hospital (later adapted as the **Royal Naval College**) was erected in its place.

GREENWICH PARK. The first of the **Royal Parks** to be enclosed, Greenwich Park was created in 1433 by Humphrey, Duke of Gloucester and brother of King Henry V, when he built walls around his residence at Bella Donna, which became **Greenwich Palace**. King Henry VIII held regular sporting events at the site on May Day (and an oak tree that he danced around with Anne Boleyn, his second wife, survived until 1991, when it was blown down in a gale). In 1662, King Charles II employed André Le Nôtre, the French landscape gardener renowned for his work at the Palace of Versailles, near Paris, to lay out the grounds anew, constructing tree-lined avenues and introducing a series of terraces (*see also* **St. James's Park**). In particular, he made a focal point of the **Queen's House**, designed by **Inigo Jones** and erected in 1616–35 for Anne of Denmark, wife of James VI and I. Additional trees were planted during the 1660s, then in 1675, the **Royal Observatory** was built on a site formerly occupied by the Duke of Gloucester's castle. The public was admitted during the 18th century, the **railway** arrived at Greenwich in 1838, and steamer trips from central London began in 1854. Ready access turned the **park** into a popular recreational resource, with Londoners bringing their children on day trips, particularly on weekends and holidays, to look back at the city from Greenwich Hill. It remains popular with tourists, who visit the **National Maritime Museum** (at its northern edge) and the 18th-century **Ranger's House** (to the southeast). There are also sports pitches, a boating pond, a deer enclosure, and regular puppet shows for children in the summer. The 200-acre estate is still Crown land managed by the Royal Parks Agency.

GRESHAM, THOMAS (1519–1579). Founder of the **Royal Exchange**, Gresham was the second son of Sir Richard Gresham and Audrey, his first wife. In 1535, after a period of study at Cambridge University, he was apprenticed to his merchant uncle, Sir John Gresham (**Lord Mayor** of London in 1547), who traded principally with the Levant and ensured that his nephew gained a thorough knowledge of international commerce. From 1551 until 1574, he was a royal agent, basing himself in Antwerp for much of the year while he negotiated loans for the English Crown, provided his government with information about political conditions in Europe, and arranged the provision of supplies for the army. Gresham's trading practices were often highhanded, sometimes downright illegal (he was not averse to bribery, for example, and, at one point, prepared a scheme to smuggle currency from Holland to London in bags of pepper), but he was regarded favorably at court and, in 1559, was knighted on his appointment as Ambassador to the Court of the Duchess of Parma, Regent of the Netherlands. His activities were well rewarded financially, allowing him to purchase several fine residences (including a country home at **Osterley House** and a town mansion in Bishopsgate Street) and to invest in schemes designed to bring benefits to London and its citizens. One of these projects was the construction, at his own expense, of a central meeting place for exchange dealers in the **City of London**. Known as the Royal Exchange, it opened in 1568 and soon became a focal point for wealthy merchants. He also supported eight almshouses close to his city home and, in 1579, endowed Gresham College, creating seven lectureships in the arts and sciences. Gresham died suddenly on 21 November 1579 after leaving a meeting at the exchange. Allegedly the richest commoner in England, he was followed to his grave in St. Helen's Church, Bishopsgate, by 200 poor men and women clothed in black gowns.

GREYFRIARS MONASTERY. In 1224, four Franciscan friars established a base at a **Cornhill** property gifted to them by John Travers, **sheriff** of London. The following year, textile merchant John Ewin offered them land in Newgate Street, where they built a **monastery**. The settlement flourished for 300 years, attracting many wealthy patrons after the heart of Queen Eleanor (wife of King Edward I) was buried before the high altar of the monks' church in 1291, but was broken up in 1538 as a result of King Henry VIII's anti-Catholic campaign. The church was retained, initially as a store for wine taken from captured French ships but then (renamed Christ Church) as the religious focus for a local parish. In 1553, just 10 days before he died, King Edward VI established a hospital and school for fatherless boys in the building, which was destroyed in the **Great Fire** of 1666 but rebuilt in 1667–87 to **Christopher Wren**'s designs. The school (known as Christ's Hospital) remained on the site until 1897, when it moved out of London to Horsham (Sussex). Five years later, most of the buildings were demolished to make way for Post Office facilities. With the exception of the steeple, the church was destroyed by bombs during the **Blitz**. (*See also* PUGIN, AUGUSTUS WELBY NORTHMORE.)

GROSVENOR ESTATE. In 1677, Sir Thomas Grosvenor acquired, through marriage to Mary Davies (the 12-year-old heiress of a scrivener), 400 acres of land in **Belgravia** and **Pimlico**, with a further

100 acres in **Mayfair**. At the time, the estate lay west of the urban area of the city, but expansion during the Georgian and Victorian periods converted it into some of the most highly valued property in the **City of Westminster**. Building in Mayfair began in the 1720s and in Belgravia 100 years later, with development concentrating on substantial terraced houses that would appeal to the affluent. Despite suffering heavy estate taxes during the 20 century, much of the original inheritance is still intact although large parts of the less fashionable Pimlico area have been sold. In 1979, Grosvenor Estate Holdings was formed to combine the various elements of the property (which now include land in Australia, Canada, and the United States and contribute significantly to the wealth of the Duke of Westminster, who owns the estate) under a single management group. The family name is also retained in many of the local road names, including Grosvenor Street (which links **Hyde Park** to New Bond Street) and **Grosvenor Square** (where the **United States's embassy** is located).

GROSVENOR SQUARE. The second largest square in London (after **Lincoln's Inn Fields**) was built between 1725 and 1731 as the focus of the **Grosvenor Estate**'s 100-acre development in **Mayfair** because Sir Richard Grosvenor wanted to emulate the success of Hanover Square, laid out by Richard Lumley (Earl of Scarborough) a decade earlier. None of the schemes for architectural symmetry was realized (with over 30 building groups leasing sites, uniformity was always unlikely), but the area did attract high-status residents, including three Prime Ministers—the Marquess of Rockingham (who lived there from 1750 to 1782), Lord North (at various times between 1753 and 1792), and Henry Addington (1792–95). The square has a long association with the United States; John Adams (first U.S. Ambassador to Britain and later President of the United States) lived at No. 9 from 1785 to 1788, financier John Pierpoint Morgan occupied No. 12 from 1902 to 1943, and No. 20 was the U.S. army's headquarters during the Second World War. However, of the original houses, none remains (the last was demolished in 1968). The **United States's embassy**, constructed in 1958–61, occupies the west side and much of the remainder has been rebuilt in neo-Georgian style as **hotels** and offices. (*See also* STREET LIGHTING.)

GRUB STREET. According to **Samuel Johnson**'s *Dictionary of the English Language*, published in 1775, Grub Street was "originally the name of a street in Moorfields in London, much inhabited by writers of small histories, dictionaries, and temporary poems; whence any mean production is called grubstreet." The name (probably originally taken from a resident known as Grubbe) was changed to Milton Street in 1830, but has lingered in the English language as a general term for the world of literary hacks (some scholars attribute its first use in that sense to satirical poet Andrew Marvell, who lived at **Highgate** and was buried at **St. Giles-in-the-Fields Church** in 1678). Tobias Smollett describes a Grub Street dinner party in *Humphrey Clinker* (1771), and George Gissing deals with the vicissitudes of London literary life in *New Grub Street* (1891).

GUILDHALL. For nearly 900 years, the Guildhall has been the center of **local government** in the **City of London**. It probably originated as the place where Saxons went to hand over their taxes (the Old English *gild* means "payment"), but there is no documentary reference to a building until 1128, when a Guildhall is included in a survey of property owned by **St. Paul's Cathedral**. The present structure was begun in 1411, largely completed in 1439. Apart from the exterior walls, it was destroyed in the **Great Fire** but was rebuilt immediately afterwards and survived the **Blitz** even though it was set on fire in an **air raid** in December 1940. Its central feature is the Great Hall, 150 feet long and 89 feet high (one of the largest in the country and, therefore, a popular location for entertaining visiting dignitaries and mounting showpiece events). Lady Jane Grey (Queen of England for only nine days) was tried for treason there in 1553, Archbishop Thomas Cranmer defended himself (equally unsuccessfully) against a similar charge in 1555, and in 1606, Henry Garnet (a Jesuit priest) was found guilty of an attempt to blow up the Houses of Parliament (*see* **Gunpowder Plot**; **Palace of Westminster**). Today, its stained glass windows and statues of national heroes, including Admiral Horatio Nelson and Sir Winston Churchill, provide a setting for civic and state functions such as the **Lord Mayor**'s banquet. The Old Library housed a reference library and **museum** from 1873 until 1974, when the collections were moved to a newly constructed west wing and to the **Museum of London**. Both now serve as reception halls. The biggest medieval crypts in London lie underneath.

Over the years, the building has been much altered to meet changing needs. Following the Great Fire, a flat roof was installed, the work probably supervised by **Christopher Wren**. In 1862, the **Court of Common Council** decided to replace it with a hammer beam ceiling more in keeping with the medieval style of the rest of the Guildhall, sanctioned the reconstruction of much of the interior, and built a minstrels' gallery. A further roof (designed by **Giles Gilbert Scott** and with arches of stone) and new stained glass windows were needed following the 1940 air raid, and the Lady Mayoress's Gallery (originally erected in 1910) was rebuilt in 1953. More recently, a hall for City **livery companies** who do not have their own premises was added (again to Scott's plans) in 1957, an ambulatory giving access to offices and kitchens was built the same year, six new commemorative windows were placed in the west crypt in 1973, and the west wing was opened in 1974. In 1987–88, excavations revealed a Roman amphitheater under the Guildhall Yard. (*See also* DANCE, GEORGE [1741–1825].)

GUILDHALL SCHOOL OF MUSIC AND DRAMA. The school, one of Britain's leading arts colleges, was founded by the **Corporation of London** in 1880 to promote the teaching of music (**theater** studies were added in 1937). Classes were initially held at an unused warehouse in Aldermanbury but transferred to **Blackfriars** in 1887 then, in 1977, to the **Barbican**, where students have access to a 300-seat auditorium, a music hall, and other facilities. By the end of the 20th century, over 700 students, from 40 countries, were studying such disparate topics as early music, music therapy, and technical theater. The school's graduates (who include actor Ewan McGregor) find work with orchestras and in films and television drama as well as on the stage.

GUNPOWDER PLOT. In 1605, a group of Roman Catholics devised a plan to kill King James VI and I, along with his advisers, by blowing up the Houses of Parliament in the hope that sympathizers would seize power while the country was leaderless and give Catholics rights denied them by the government. However, Francis Trenshaw, one of the men involved, tried to save his brother-in-law, Lord Monteagle, by sending him an unsigned note warning him to stay away from the **Palace of Westminster** on 5 November. Monteagle informed the authorities, who searched the building and found Guy Fawkes (the group's explosives expert) in a cellar stacked with 20–30 barrels of gunpowder. Under torture in the **Tower of London**, he revealed the names of his coconspirators, all of whom were put to death (Fawkes himself was hanged, drawn, and quartered on 31 January 1606). The incident led to further repression of Catholicism and is still celebrated, on the anniversary of the event, by the burning of effigies of Guy Fawkes on bonfires throughout the country.

GWYN, ELEANOR "NELL" (1650–1687). The most popular actress in late 17th-century London, Eleanor "Nell" Gwyn (or Gwynn) was born on 2

February 1650, allegedly in an alley off **Covent Garden**. Her father is unknown (according to tradition, he died in a debtor's prison while she was still an infant) and her mother (Helena) ran a brothel where, as a child, Nell sold brandy to patrons. At the age of 14, while selling oranges to audiences at the King's Theatre (on the site now occupied by the **Theatre Royal, Drury Lane**) she attracted the attention of actor Charles Hart, became his mistress, and, through his connections, launched herself into a career on the stage. A fine dancer and singer, she was ideally suited for the female roles in Restoration dramas, starring as the King's Company's leading comedienne and appearing as Florimel in John Dryden's *Secret Love* and Mirida in James Howard's *All Mistaken*. Diarist **Samuel Pepys** was captivated, referring to her as "pretty, witty Nell." In 1669, she was introduced to King Charles II, who added her to his list of mistresses. For the rest of her life, she was faithful to the monarch, bearing him two sons and entertaining his aristocratic friends. Small and slender, she was greatly loved by the English public, who saw her as the antithesis of the Puritan ethos, but, by the time of the King's death in 1685, she was deeply in debt. Charles's last wish was that she should not starve and his brother, King James VII and II, respected the request, paying off her creditors and granting her a pension of £1,500 a year. In March 1687, she was stricken by apoplexy and partially paralyzed. She died on 14 November and was buried, as she had asked, at **St. Martin-in-the-Fields Church**, **Trafalgar Square**.

– H –

HACKNEY. Hackney lies on the west bank of the **River Lea**, some four miles northeast of **Charing Cross**. The area was rural until the middle of the 19th century, providing country homes for noble families (for example, Lady Margaret Lennox, the mother of Henry Darnley, Mary Queen of Scots' first husband, lived in Brooke House) and open spaces (such as Hackney Marshes) where less wealthy residents could enjoy hare coursing and fishing. However, as London's urban area expanded, fields and market gardens were superseded by small industries, particularly woodworking, textile manufacturing, and shoemaking, so by the beginning of the 20th century, the land was covered with terraces occupied mostly by manual workers. After the Second World War, many of these properties were demolished to make way for local authority **housing** estates. In 1965, Hackney was amalgamated with **Shoreditch** and **Stoke Newington** to form the **London Borough of Hackney**.

HACKNEY, LONDON BOROUGH OF. The borough was formed in 1965 through the amalgamation of the borough of **Hackney**, the Borough of **Shoreditch** and the Borough of **Stoke Newington**. Stoke Newington, which has a common boundary with the northeastern edge of the **City of London**, has some commercial activity, but the remainder of the area is largely residential, with pockets of industry along the **River Lea**. The 194,700 population (1998), spread over eight square miles of London's working-class **East End**, is one of the most deprived in the country. Over half of all families live in public sector **housing**, incomes are low, and unemployment is higher than average for the metropolitan area. Moreover, there is considerable ethnic diversity (one in three residents is of nonwhite ancestry), and the quality of the urban environment is poor. During the 1990s, the local authority initiated a series of efforts to improve the quality of life, attracting over £1 billion of funding for regeneration projects from organizations such as the European Union. As a result, tower blocks on municipal estates such as those at Nightingale and Holly Street were replaced by more traditional homes, with local labor employed on the construction sites. Also, small parks were built to alleviate the urban drabness. But considerable social problems remain (Hackney Downs School was closed by the government in 1996 because of its low educational standards, for example), there are few sites suitable for large business premises, and transport links are poor. (*See also* CLAPTON; HOXTON; STAMFORD HILL; VICTORIA PARK.)

HAM HOUSE. In 1610, Sir Thomas Vavasour (Knight Marshal to King James VI and I) built a country mansion on the south bank of the **River Thames**, within easy riding distance of **Richmond Palace**. Sixty-two years later, John, Earl of Lauderdale, embarked on a reconstruction program that turned the house into one of the most luxurious in the land, with a marble staircase, leather wall hangings, satins on the beds, and furniture upholstered to coordinate with the decor. After that, the structure of the building was comparatively unaltered for nearly 300 years, so when it was acquired by the National Trust in 1948 the **Victoria and Albert Museum**, managers of the property, were able to use Lauderdale's records to re-create the rooms' 17th-century sumptuousness and open the building to the public. In addition, the formality of the garden has been retained, forming a contrast with the "natural" plantings of early 18th-century properties.

HAMMERSMITH. Hammersmith lies on the north bank of the **River Thames** some five miles west of **Charing Cross**. The fertile alluvial soils favored the growth of a market gardening industry, with vegetables and flowers going to the London market from the 15th century and urban development restricted to the main roads that traversed the area, connecting **Bayswater** to **Uxbridge** and **Kensington** to **Brentford**. During the second half of the 19th century, however, the metropolitan area's westward expansion combined with the improvements in accessibility wrought by the **railway** to force land prices up, encouraging owners to sell to speculative builders, who built terraces of small homes for working-class and lower-middle-class families. Partly because of the social structure of its new population, the area acquired a reputation as an entertainment complex, with cinemas, a film studio, the **Olympia** exhibition hall (erected in 1884), Queen's Park Rangers **Football** Club (founded in 1885), the Lyric Theatre (built in 1890), the Palais de Danse (opened in 1919 and, two years later, the first British dance hall to have a jazz band on stage), and the **British Broadcasting Corporation**'s Television Centre (which produced its first programs in 1960). In 1965, Hammersmith was united with neighboring **Fulham** to form the **London Borough of Hammersmith and Fulham**. (*See also* HAMMERSMITH BRIDGE; KELMSCOTT PRESS.)

HAMMERSMITH AND FULHAM, LONDON BOROUGH OF. One of the smallest of the **London borough**s, **Hammersmith** and **Fulham** houses 157,500 people (1998) on only six square miles. It was formed in 1965, when the two communities were united under a single local authority as part of a reorganization of **local government** in the metropolitan area. Good transport links to Heathrow Airport, and the national motorway system, have attracted major employers such as Coca-Cola and Disney, both of whom have their British headquarters on Hammersmith Broadway. There is also a large media presence, with the **British Broadcasting Corporation**'s Television Centre, record companies (such as EMI), film businesses (such as United International Pictures), and publishers (such as HarperCollins) all providing employment. As a result, property prices are high and there are pockets of considerable affluence (as in Fulham). However, amidst the wealth, the borough has some of Britain's poorest neighborhoods, including **White City** and **Shepherd's Bush**, which were targeted for employment and training initiatives during the 1990s. (*See also* HAMMERSMITH BRIDGE.)

HAMMERSMITH BRIDGE. The first suspension **bridge** in London, Hammersmith Bridge links the **London Borough of Hammersmith and Fulham** (on the north bank of the **River Thames**) to the community of **Barnes** (on the south). Its 422-foot central span was completed in 1827 but replaced in 1883–87 by a new structure designed by **Joseph William Bazalgette**. In 1939, the Irish Republican Army attempted to blow up the bridge, but the bomb was discovered and thrown into the river by a passerby. Improvements were made to the load-bearing girders in 1973–76, but, in January 1997, cars were banned from using the crossing, although buses, cyclists, and pedestrians continued to enjoy access.

HAMPSTEAD. The 443-foot-high hill on which Hampstead has developed, some 4.5 miles north of **Charing Cross**, was settled in prehistoric times and became a refuge for Londoners fleeing the **Black Death** of 1348–50 and the **Great Plague** of 1664–66. However, it did not experience significant urban growth until after the **Great Fire** (1666) when its trees were felled so that the **City of London** could be rebuilt. From 1701, fashionable London society arrived to sample the allegedly health-promoting waters that emerged from a chalybeate spring, encouraging entrepreneurs to open **coffee houses**, a bowling green, an assembly room for concerts, and other facilities for genteel entertainment on the southern slopes of the incline. By 1725, according to author Daniel Defoe, Hampstead was being transformed "from a little village almost to a city," and by 1801 (the year of the first British census) the population numbered 4,300. During the 19th century, the area became popular with wealthy businessmen, politicians, writers, and artists who sought escape from the growing pollution of the central city and who confirmed its reputation as a high-status neighborhood (author Wilkie Collins lived in Church Row, for example, architect George Gilbert Scott in Admiral's Walk, and poet John Keats in Wentworth Place). The literary set continued to be move in during the 20th century (even though the arrival of the **Tube** in 1900 made Hampstead more attractive to commuters); poet Edwin Muir lived in Downshire Hill during the 1930s, and in his autobiography, published in 1954, claimed that the flats of the day were "filled with writing people and haunted by young poets despairing the poor and the world, but despairing together, in a sad but comforting communion." When **local government** was reformed in 1965, Hampstead was absorbed by the **London Borough of Camden**, which has treated the area sensitively, preserving its essentially residential nature. (*See also*

HAMPSTEAD GARDEN SUBURB; HAMPSTEAD HEATH; JACK STRAW'S CASTLE; KEATS'S HOUSE; SPANIARDS, THE.)

HAMPSTEAD GARDEN SUBURB. When, in 1907, Wyldes Farm (located immediately northwest of **Hampstead Heath**) was put on the market by Eton College, Henrietta Barnett (whose husband had founded **Toynbee Hall** in 1884) suggested that some 160 acres of the land could be used to develop a residential area in which people from all social classes would live together in an integrated, stable community. A trust—the Hampstead Tenants' Association—was formed to buy the property, Raymond Unwin and Barry Parker (who had designed Letchworth Garden City a few years earlier) were invited to prepare plans for the layout, and architects such as Edward Lutyens (who thought Mrs. Barnett "a nice woman but a Philistine") were commissioned to work on individual buildings. The result was a suburb of secluded closes, roads that curved with the contours of the hillside, tree-lined streets, and a mix of **housing** types. Flats for skilled manual workers predominated to the north of the area, semidetached villas for the middle class to the west, and large detached homes for affluent families to the south, at the edge of the Heath. The relatively high ground rents paid by the rich were intended to reduce those levied on poorer residents, with housing for vulnerable groups (such as the disabled and the elderly) built in special quadrangles amidst other residences. The First World War interrupted progress, and afterwards, though the suburb was considerably extended, pressure on accommodation forced up prices. As a result, the community became increasingly middle class and the planners' ideal was never realized. Hampstead Garden Suburb has been criticized because it has no shopping facilities (and no **public house**) at its core but, even so, most modern scholars consider it a good example of sensitive urban planning. In 1996, the government placed 500 of the buildings (mainly the artisans' houses) on a list of structures it considered of national architectural or historic interest, thereby limiting the extent to which they can be altered.

HAMPSTEAD HEATH. The 790 acres of Hampstead Heath, in the **London Borough of Camden**, have an element of wildness that contrasts with the carefully managed flower beds and lawns of central-city open spaces such as **Kensington Gardens** and **St. James's Park**. The area first began to attract attention in 1698 as stories spread of the medicinal properties of springs bubbling to the surface in the woodlands. Authors and poets wrote of their qualities (**Charles Dickens**, John Keats, and Alexander Pope were all regular visitors) and encouraged local residents who, from 1831 to 1871, fought a long-running battle with Sir Thomas Maryon, the Lord of the Manor, to ensure that the land did not succumb to urban development. Now, as many as 100,000 people turn up on bank holidays to fly kites, enjoy the view from Parliament Hill, or swim in the pools (one for men, one for women). **Kenwood House**, at the northern fringe of the Heath, is a regular venue for outdoor concerts of classical music during the summer.

HAMPTON COURT PALACE. When Thomas Wolsey, Archbishop of York, began building Hampton Court Palace in 1514, he intended that it would be the finest residence in England. Located on the north bank of a meander in the **River Thames**, about 12 miles southwest of **Charing Cross**, it became famous throughout Europe both for the splendor of its **architecture** and the sumptuousness of its furnishings. Initially, it had about 280 rooms, but King Henry VIII (to whom Wolsey gifted the property in 1529 in a vain attempt to regain the status lost by his failure to plot the monarch's divorce from Catherine of Aragon) added a library and additional kitchens as well as replacing the Great Hall and refurbishing the chapel. Such was the haste to get the work done that carpenters were employed night and day, working by candlelight after darkness had fallen. Gardens were laid out, trees planted, and deer introduced to the surrounding **park** land (*see* **Bushy Park**). Edward VI (Henry's only son) spent most of his 15 years at Hampton Court and Mary I (Edward's half sister) pined there for four years while she hoped for a child. Elizabeth I (another half sister) conducted affairs of state at the palace but also turned it into a place for festivity and entertainment, with hunts, balls, and banquets to keep her guests amused. James VI and I, her successor, continued the tradition but also, more seriously, held a Conference of Divines in 1604 in a fruitless effort to resolve theological differences between the Puritans and the Church of England (one of the results of that meeting was the authorized version of the Bible).

Between 1651 and 1658, Oliver Cromwell lived in the palace, but his simple tastes appealed little to Charles II, who, after the monarchy was restored in 1660, set about redesigning the gardens, acquiring lavish furnishings, and providing accommodation for his string of courtesans. From 1689, William III and Mary II carried out another extensive building program, using **Christopher Wren** to redesign the property in accordance with late 17th-century taste by building in the French Renaissance style. Construction and decoration work continued until George III came to the throne 1760. George broke with tradition by staying away from Hampton Court (allegedly because he harbored a grudge about being chastised there while he was a child) and his successors followed suit. In 1986, fire damaged some of Wren's south wing, but it was restored over the next six years, with some of the Tudor features he had covered up being uncovered again. Since Queen Victoria's reign, the public has been allowed increasing access to the building. Modern visitors can see many of the rooms, including the state apartments (which contain works of art by Pieter Brueghel, Tintoretto, and others), Henry VIII's Great Hall (with a hammer beam roof over a chamber 97 feet long, 40 feet wide, and 60 feet high), and the enormous Tudor kitchens. The grounds contain lawns and formal flower beds, an astronomical clock designed by Nicholas Oursian in 1540, a maze laid out for William III, and a vine planted by landscape gardener Capability Brown in 1768, which still produces grapes. (*See also* KENSINGTON PALACE; ROYAL HORTICULTURAL SOCIETY.)

HAMPTON COURT PARK. *See* BUSHY PARK.

HANWELL. The suburb of Hanwell, lying some 10 miles west of **Charing Cross**, developed during the Medieval period as a bridging point where one of the principal routes out of London crossed the River Brent (a tributary of the **River Thames**). Until the 19th century, it was little more than a hamlet, with a few houses clustered around the 12th-century St. Mary's Church and services for travellers located on the Uxbridge Road. However, in 1838 the Great Western **Railway** improved accessibility to the metropolitan area, attracting incomers (Isambard Kingdom Brunel built the Wharncliffe Viaduct to take the trains over the river, giving passengers such an impressive view of the surrounding countryside that Queen Victoria regularly told her engine driver to slow down so that she could fully enjoy the crossing). St. Mary's was rebuilt in 1842, and a school for poor children opened in 1856 (actor Charlie Chaplin was one of its pupils), providing employment in construction trades and encouraging builders to erect estates of small houses for workers. As population grew, Hanwell became increasingly urban in character but, even so, has managed to retain its village green and some semblance of former village life. It was incorporated within the **London Borough of Ealing** in 1965.

HARDIE, JAMES KEIR (1856–1915). In 1892, Keir Hardie won a parliamentary election at **West Ham** South, becoming one of the first two members of working-class political organizations to represent London in the House of Commons (*see* **Palace of Westminster**) (the other was John Burns, who took the **Battersea** seat at the same time). Born at Legbrannock (Lanarkshire) on 15 August 1856, he was the illegitimate son of Mary Keir, a servant girl who was later to marry carpenter John Hardie. With no schooling, he started work as a message boy at the age of seven then, after three years, turned to coal mining and earned a reputation as an agitator demanding improved conditions throughout the industry. In 1878, blacklisted by employers and unable to get a job, he opened a stationer's shop and wrote newspaper articles while developing his political activities as an official of groups devoted to miners' interests. Nine years later, he launched *The Miner* in order to give his views wider currency, and in 1888 he unsuccessfully attempted to win a seat in Parliament as the member for Mid-Lanark.

Keir Hardie's election victory at West Ham South was not entirely unexpected because the constituency was located in the heart of London's working-class **East End**, but it was certainly made significantly easier by the death of the Liberal Party candidate shortly before polling. Unfortunately, he and John Burns never saw eye to eye, so their cooperation at the **Palace of Westminster** was limited. After Burns's election to the **London County Council** in 1889, he helped form an alliance (known as the Progressives) between the socialists and the Liberals. Unwilling to jeopardize that sometimes uneasy association by identifying himself with Keir Hardie's hard-line policies, he rejected the Scot's suggestion that a small parliamentary grouping should be formed under Burns's leadership and later stood as a Liberal for the Battersea seat. Keir Hardie, however, continued to plow a militant furrow, earning himself the nickname "Member for the Unemployed" as a result of his impassioned speeches supporting the rights of the jobless. In 1893, he became the first Chairman of the Independent Labour Party, which had been formed through the merger of several small socialist associations, but, despite the attendant publicity, lost his West Ham seat two years later when the Liberals withdrew their support for his campaign.

For five years, he edited *The Leader* (a periodical that had developed from *The Miner*) and tried to persuade the trade unions to form a new political party that would represent working people. A Labour Representation Committee was eventually founded in 1900 and Keir Hardie, fighting at Merthyr Tydfil, was one of two candidates to win parliamentary seats on its behalf that year. In 1906, the organization changed its name, became the Labour Party, won 26 seats in the General Election and elected Keir Hardie the first Chairman of the Parliamentary Labour Party. However, he had to resign from the position after only a few months as a result of failing health and, on 26 September 1915, died in Glasgow, believing himself to be a failure because he was unable to persuade workers throughout Europe to strike in an attempt to prevent the outbreak of the First World War. (*See also* CANNING TOWN.)

HARINGEY, LONDON BOROUGH OF. When **local government** in the metropolitan area was reorganized in 1965, Haringey was formed by the merger of the formerly independent Boroughs of **Hornsey**, **Tottenham**, and Wood Green. It houses a population of 221,600 (1998) on 11.5 square miles, with significant communities of African, Caribbean, Cypriot, Irish, and Jewish extraction and a high proportion of homes rented from the municipal authority. The eastern area is largely residential, with Wood Green providing the major shopping facilities. Tottenham has a more industrial character. Most businesses in the borough are small (90 percent have fewer than 25 employees), with retailing (and the associated wholesale distribution trade) providing more jobs than any other sector of the economy, though confectionery production, clothing manufacture, and engineering are also important. Strongly working-class in composition, the local authority provides consistent majorities for the Labour Party in local and parliamentary elections. (*See also* ALEXANDRA PALACE; ARCHWAY; MUSWELL HILL.)

HARLEY STREET. Renowned as a location for doctors' surgeries, Harley Street (which runs north from Cavendish Square to the southern edge of **Regent's Park**) was built in the second quarter of the 18th century as part of the development of the Portland Estate (*see also* **Portland Place**) and named for the family of the landowner, Edward Harley, Earl of Oxford and Mortimer. It was immediately fashionable; portrait painter Allan Ramsay lived at No. 67 from 1770 to 1780, artist J. M. W. Turner at No. 64 from 1804 to 1808, and Kitty, Duchess of Wellington, at No. 11 from 1809 to 1814. Largely because of the affluent patients living nearby, the medical men moved in from around 1845 and still occupy most of the properties, offering treatments in such disparate specializations as cosmetic surgery, dentistry, dermatology, hypnotherapy, ophthalmology, and testicular implantation. By the end of the 20th century, some 1,500 physicians, surgeons, and dentists were based in Harley Street, along with eight private hospitals.

HARRODS. One of the world's most famous department stores, Harrods was founded in 1853, when tea merchant Charles Harrod opened a grocery shop in **Knightsbridge**, then a village outside London. Harrod's son (also Charles) took over the business in 1861, when the **West End** was becoming increasingly fashionable and shopkeepers were attracting customers by offering a variety of goods under a single roof rather than specializing in a particular product. Within a decade, there were 16 assistants in the store and sales were rising annually. In 1873, an extension was built, followed a year later by acquisition of additional premises, but in December 1883 the whole store was destroyed by fire. In the aftermath, Harrod wrote to every customer, explaining that "in consequence of the above premises being burnt down, your order will be delayed in the execution a day or two" but adding that "I hope, in the course of Tuesday or Wednesday next, to be able to forward it." The letter proved to be a masterstroke, laying the foundations of a reputation for quality service. Also, the fire itself brought benefits because it allowed Harrod to build a new, five-story, purpose-built shop with fittings designed to appeal to an affluent society (the additional space permitted an increase in the range of goods offered, allowing Harrods to boast that it could provide anything anybody asked for, from a mouse to an elephant). In 1889, the firm became a limited liability company and nine years later London's first escalator was installed (an assistant stood at the top, ready to administer smelling salts to customers who fainted as a result of using the new mode of transport). The main part of the present terracotta frontage was constructed between 1901 and 1905, with the Meat Hall decorated by art nouveau tiles depicting hunting scenes at the same time.

Harrods now has 300 departments, where 4,000 assistants serve 35,000 customers who spend over £1.1 million a day. There are 11 restaurants. The business was bought by House of Fraser in 1959 but sold to the Al Fayed brothers in 1985. Following the car crash that killed **Diana, Princess of Wales**, and Dodi Al Fayed in 1997, Mohamed Al Fayed (Dodi's father) claimed that the Duke of Edinburgh had planned the deaths. In 2000, the Duke withdrew his patronage from the store, and Al Fayed responded by surrendering his warrants (or privileged rights) to supply goods to Queen Elizabeth II, Queen Elizabeth the Queen Mother, and Prince Charles.

HARROW, LONDON BOROUGH OF. When London's **local government** was reorganized in 1965, Harrow, uniquely, retained its preexisting boundaries (which, in fact, had changed little since the 11th century). The borough, covering 20 square miles and housing 211,300 people

(1998), is located on the northwest fringe of the metropolitan area. Although largely residential in character, it has significant office development, with strong banking, information technology, and business service sectors whose growth is facilitated by good rail transport to the central city and by road links to the national motorway network and Heathrow Airport. Nearly 90 percent of the homes are owner-occupied, with residents heavily concentrated in the professional and managerial employment groups. There is a large Asian community, many of whom are involved in retailing and other small businesses. (*See also* HARROW-ON-THE-HILL; PINNER; STANMORE.)

HARROW-ON-THE-HILL. Harrow is one of three main areas of upland in northwest London (the others are **Hampstead** and **Highgate**). It was settled by Anglo-Saxon times (deriving its name from the Old English *hergae*, which means "shrine" or "temple") and is mentioned in documents, dating from 767 A.D., which define a grant of land by Offa (King of Mercia) to Stidberht (Abbot of St. Albans). During the Medieval period, the woods surrounding the 406-foot-high hill were popular with the monarchy as hunting grounds, so many of the buildings erected at the time were associated with visiting aristocrats (for example, the King's Head **Public House** is built on the site of King Henry VIII's hunting lodge). However, because of the steepness of the slopes and the policies of the governors of Harrow School (which owns much of the land), construction since then has been limited, leaving much open space for use as sports fields. The school was founded in 1572 by John Lyon, a local farmer, and has become one of the most prestigious in the country. Former pupils include seven Prime Ministers—Spencer Perceval, Viscount Goderich, Robert Peel, the Earl of Aberdeen, Lord Palmerston, Stanley Baldwin, and Winston Churchill—as well as such distinguished figures from other walks of life as poet Lord Byron and Second World War military commander Earl Alexander of Tunis. Modern Harrow is predominantly residential, with associated retail and administrative services. Development is restricted by conservation area legislation that protects the urban fabric, notably St. Mary's Church, whose 15th-century spire is a landmark for miles around. The suburb was included within the **London Borough of Harrow** when **local government** in the metropolitan area was reorganized in 1965.

HATTON GARDEN. Hatton Garden, the street that links Holborn Circus (at the northern boundary of the **City of London**) to Clerkenwell Road (in the **London Borough of Camden**), is one of the major centers of the world diamond trade. It takes its name from Sir Christopher Hatton, Chancellor to Queen Elizabeth I, who erected a mansion on orchard land in the area in 1576. The properties that line the roadway were popular with London's gentry during the 17th and 18th centuries (George Bate, Oliver Cromwell's physician, died there in 1688, for example) but, by the 1830s, several jewellers had established premises, and, as their number increased, private residents moved out to less commercial areas. In recent years, however, depressed trading has encouraged some firms to seek other, less expensive, locations, and De Beers, the South African–based company that dominates the production and sale of rough diamonds, has been under pressure to transfer many of its London jobs to its home country, further threatening the street's dominance in the marketing of precious stones.

HAVERING, LONDON BOROUGH OF. Havering is located on the northeast fringe of the London metropolitan area, covering 46 square miles (half of which is protected by **green belt** legislation) and housing 228,300 residents (1998). It was formed in 1965 through the merger of the Borough of Romford and Hornchurch Urban District, taking its name from the village of Havering-atte-Bower. Romford is the principal retail and administrative center, with a regionally important office complex and a predominantly white-collar workforce. Hornchurch and Upminster have large skilled manual groups, many of whom work at the Ford Motor plant in nearby **Dagenham** and have roots in the **East End**. Largely a commuter borough, Havering has a high proportion of owner-occupiers and a low proportion of **immigrants**.

HAWKSMOOR, NICHOLAS (1661–1736). Although his reputation is overshadowed by that of his mentor, **Christopher Wren**, Hawksmoor was an architect of considerable ability (albeit with a sometimes eccentric style) whose work shaped the townscape of late 17th- and early 18th-century London. Born in Nottinghamshire in 1661, he was employed by Wren as a clerk at the age of 18, working with him on the building of **St. Paul's Cathedral** and **Chelsea Hospital**. He was appointed Clerk of Works at **Kensington Palace** in 1691, adding the King's Gallery in 1695–96. At Greenwich Hospital (*see* **Royal Naval College**), where he became Deputy Surveyor in 1705, he was responsible for the architectural decoration of the hall and supervised the implementation of construction plans prepared by Wren and Sir John Vanbrugh. Hawksmoor also worked on such large country houses as Castle Howard (Yorkshire) and Blenheim Palace (Oxfordshire), as well as on buildings for the University of Oxford, but he is now best known for his London churches, particularly St. Anne's (in Commercial Road, **Limehouse**), St. Mary Woolnoth (in King William Street, in the **City of London**), and **Christ Church, Spitalfields**. He died at his home in Millbank, **Westminster**, on 25 March 1736. (*See also* ARCHITECTURE; ST. ALFEGE'S CHURCH, GREENWICH.)

HAYMARKET. Haymarket, some 400 yards long, links Coventry Street to **Pall Mall** East in central London. During the 17th century, a **market** for straw and hay was established in the area (probably because the King's horses were stabled nearby). The Queen's Theatre (opened in 1704) and the Haymarket Theatre (1720) attracted playgoers to the site so, when the market closed in 1830, the land was quickly colonized by other forms of entertainment, with taverns and prostitutes serving the clientele. During the 20th century, cinemas added to the complex, making Haymarket an important component of the city's **West End**. The Queen's Theatre (now known as Her Majesty's) has had mixed commercial fortune; during the 19th century, it was remodelled by **John Nash** (1816–18), burned down (1867), rebuilt (1869), closed because of debt (1881), then demolished (1891). The present building—a French Renaissance–style structure designed by C. J. Phipps—was erected in 1897 and, in recent years, has housed such successes as **Andrew Lloyd Webber**'s musical *Phantom of the Opera* (which had its first performance in 1986). The Haymarket was rebuilt to Nash's plans in 1821 but remodelled by Phipps in 1880. Most of the other properties lining the street were erected during the 20th century and function as shops or showrooms. (*See also* REGENT STREET.)

HAYWARD GALLERY. Although some critics have fulminated at the Hayward's concrete facade (architectural historian Ann Saunders described it as "of quite frightening ugliness" in 1988), the gallery has become an important venue for art exhibitions next to the concert halls on the **South Bank** of the **River Thames** near **Waterloo** Bridge. Designed by Hubert Bennett and built in 1968, it was named after Sir Isaac Hayward, Leader of the **Greater London Council** at the time.

HEALTH CARE. Much of London's early health care was provided by religious settlements (for example, St. Thomas's Hospital, now based near **Waterloo**, was founded at the Priory of St. Mary Overie, in **Southwark**, during the early 12th century). From the later Medieval period, specialist services became more common—apothecaries supplied drugs, barbers pulled teeth, and (in 1518) a **Royal College of Physicians of**

London was established—but medical science was primitive, death rates from infectious disease were high, and life expectancy was limited. Modern provision dates only from the 18th century, when the voluntary movement (so called because individuals supported institutions by volunteering annual payments) led to the establishment of several general hospitals in the city (Westminster Hospital was founded in 1719, Guy's in 1725, St. George's in 1733, the London in 1740, and the Middlesex in 1745). More specialist facilities followed soon afterwards, as did structured training for doctors (William Hunter provided anatomy lectures, illustrated by dissections, from 1745).

The 19th century brought further improvements in provision, such as Charing Cross Hospital (which opened in 1818), **Great Ormond Street Hospital for Sick Children** (1851), and the Hospital for Tropical Diseases (1899), but also, through the activities of campaigners such as **John Snow**, heightened awareness that poor health was linked to low standards of **housing**, limited incomes, and lack of hygiene. **Joseph William Bazalgette**, who was responsible for constructing the capital's **sewage disposal** system and demolishing slums as he built new roads, indirectly raised health standards through environmental improvements. Other measures, promoted by the General Board of Health (established in 1848) and the Medical Officer of Health to the **City of London** (a post created the same year), had similar effects (by changing conditions in factories, for instance).

The creation of a National Health Service (NHS) by the Labour government revolutionized provision in 1948, promising, for the first time, free medical and dental care for everyone, regardless of their means. An aging population and rising costs enforced radical revision of facilities during the 1990s, with amalgamations of medical schools and hospital closures, but the NHS still dominated London's health care at the end of the 20th century. Sixteen area health authorities were responsible for commissioning health services for their populations. The city had 3,838 general medical practitioners (each with an average 2,060 patients), 2,857 dentists, and 1,686 ophthalmic practitioners. In some ways, the quality of the service was declining (for example, the number of hospital beds fell by 40 percent between 1987 and 1997, leading administrators to turn away emergency cases and the press to allege that patients were dying in corridors on hospital gurneys). On the other hand, London's 61 public and 46 private hospitals had some of the finest equipment and the most advanced research units available—St. Mark's was one of only two hospitals in the world specializing in intestinal disease, the Royal Brompton had Europe's biggest cystic fibrosis unit, and the nicotine patch (now used internationally to wean smokers off cigarettes) was developed as a result of investigations carried out at the Institute of Psychiatry. (*See also* FOUNDLING HOSPITAL; HARLEY STREET; KING'S CROSS; KNIGHTS HOSPITALLER; LONDON HEALTH EMERGENCY [LHE]; ROYAL COLLEGE OF SURGEONS OF ENGLAND; ST. ANDREW'S CHURCH, HOLBORN; ST. GILES-IN-THE-FIELDS CHURCH, ST. GILES HIGH STREET.)

HEATHROW AIRPORT. *See* AIRPORTS.

HENDON. The suburb of Hendon is located in northwest London some seven miles from **Charing Cross**. Although it has a long history (the land was owned by **Westminster Abbey** as early as the 10th century and the fabric of St. Mary's Church dates from only 300 years later), the settlement remained an agricultural village until 1911, when Claude Graeme-White converted open fields into an aerodrome that earned world renown as a center of innovation during the early days of aircraft development (within months of its establishment, it had been the base for the first aerial postal delivery and the starting point of the first nonstop flight from London to Paris). Also, from 1920 until 1937, the Royal Air Force (RAF) mounted annual air displays, giving visitors an opportunity to see new military airplanes, demonstrating the pilots' skills, and raising money for charities. **Transport**-related industries, including car manufacturing, were based in premises nearby, but urban encroachment ultimately limited the airfield's potential and, after the Second World War, much of it was used for building. However, several of the hangars were retained and, in 1972, converted for use as an RAF **museum**, with exhibits showing the evolution of the service since its formation in 1918, telling the story of the Battle of Britain, and outlining the exploits of Bomber Command. Planes on display range from the Sopwith Camel to the Spitfire and the Hurricane. Since 1954, Church Farm House Museum, in Greyhound Hill, has housed displays dealing with local history in a 17th-century building where several of the rooms have been furnished in period style. In 1965, Hendon was incorporated within the **London Borough of Barnet**.

HENRY WOOD PROMENADE CONCERTS. *See* PROMS, THE.

HENSLOWE, PHILIP (c. 1550–1616). Henslowe was the principal **theater** owner during the late Elizabethan period, when **Bankside** was the center of

London entertainment and **Ben Jonson**, **Inigo Jones**, **William Shakespeare**, and others drew large crowds to masques and plays. He was born in Lindfield (Sussex), probably in 1550, to Edmund Henslowe (Master of the Game in Ashdown Forest) and his wife, Margaret. For some years, he worked as a servant of the bailiff to Viscount Montague, work that took him to **Southwark** by 1577. When his master died, he married the widow and, using her money, purchased property and invested in a range of businesses, pawn shops, lodging houses, inns, and small industries, such as dyeing and starch making. In 1587, he built the Rose Theatre (the first at Bankside), 13 years later he constructed the Fortune (the largest theater of its day), then, in 1613, he erected the Hope (which was designed for bear baiting as well as plays). Henslowe kept a tight hold on finances, buying works from authors then hiring out his theaters to groups of players but keeping writers and actors indebted to him in order to retain their services. His diary (which lists details of bills for costumes, payments to authors, loans to players, names of plays performed, and dates of performances) is a major source of information about the economics of late 16th- and early 17th-century theater management. He died in London on 6 January 1616 and was buried in St. Saviour's Church, Southwark.

HERNE HILL. The suburb of Herne Hill, bordering **Dulwich** and **Camberwell** some four miles south of **Charing Cross**, takes its name from a 17th century resident. In the later 18th and early 19th centuries, the area was semirural in character, with large detached houses providing homes for affluent families (in his autobiographical work, *Praeterita*, published in 1885–89, author John Ruskin describes the country walks around 28 Herne Hill, where he lived from 1823 to 1842). However, in the 1860s, the arrival of the **railway** transformed the area as rows of cheap houses were built to house an influx of working-class groups, turning it into part of metropolitan London within two decades. The **London County Council** and other local authorities have provided much public **housing** since the end of the Second World War, but many neighborhoods retain their Victorian character and the grounds of former Brockwell Hall (built in 1811–13 but largely destroyed by fire in 1990) have been converted into a public **park** with an 18th-century walled garden and an open air swimming pool. Herne Hill became part of the **London Borough of Lambeth** in 1965.

HIGHBURY. Although Highbury lies only three miles northeast of **Charing Cross**, it maintained an essentially rural character until the early 19th century, supplying London with dairy goods and other agricultural products. Speculative builders began to construct properties in 1774, but there was little growth in population until the 1820s, when **Thomas Cubitt** erected a row of villas at Highbury Grove. Highbury College (a theological center) followed in 1826, Park Terrace in 1830, Highbury New Park in 1853–61, and Grosvenor Avenue in the 1860s, all providing homes for relatively affluent families. Meanwhile, Highbury Barn was supplying entertainment ranging from tea and cakes to circus events, open air dances, and club dinners for as many as 4,000 people at a sitting; ultimately, however, local residents complained of the noise and the facility closed in 1871. The developers' demands and competition for property by commercial concerns (such as the Arsenal **Football** Club, which relocated from **Woolwich** in 1913) placed considerable pressure on land (the Barn vanished under bricks and mortar within 12 years), but some open space was preserved, notably the 27.5 acres of Highbury Fields, which were saved from encroachment in 1885 and 1891. Twentieth-century local authority **housing** provision has detracted from the Victorian character of the area and many of the original properties are gone, but several of the early streets survive. Highbury was included within the **London Borough of Islington** when **local government** in the metropolitan area was reorganized in 1965.

HIGHGATE. Highgate—five miles north of **Charing Cross**—takes its name from the tollhouse situated on a hill close to the village during the 14th century. Kilns dating from the first century indicate that it was occupied by the Romans, but the area remained largely undeveloped until the final decades of the 16th century, when affluent courtiers built grand homes overlooking London. A free school (which still survives as Highgate School) was established by Sir Roger Cholmley in 1565, and a nonconformist chapel opened in 1622 (these churches were banned within five miles of the **City of London;** the site in Southwood Lane lay just outside that boundary). By the late 17th century, wealthy merchants were building properties (or adapting the older mansions for their own use), beginning an expansion of population that was reflected in the later growth of institutions such as the Whittington Almshouses, built by the Mercers' Company (one of the **livery companies**) in 1822, and the Smallpox Hospital, which opened in 1850. Many of the old buildings remain (including Cromwell House, erected in 1637–38 for the Sprignell family, and St. Michael's Church, constructed in 1831–32), but new developments (including projects by the **London Borough of Camden**) have extended the settlement. At the junction of Highgate Hill and **Archway**, a stone cat sits on the pavement, allegedly at the spot where **Richard Whittington** heard **Bow Bells** calling him back to London and promising him that he would serve three times as **Lord Mayor**. (*See also* HIGHGATE CEMETERY.)

HIGHGATE CEMETERY. In 1839, the London Cemetery Company opened a 17.5-acre **burial ground**, planned by architect Stephen Geary in collaboration with landscape gardener David Ramsay and located on the south slope of **Highgate** West Hill. It very quickly became a fashionable place for funerals, attracting visitors who marvelled at the views of London as well as at the flamboyant Victorian decoration of the tombstones, so, in 1857, a 19.5-acre extension was added to the southeast. A century later, however, the firm's successor—the United Cemetery Company—was suffering from a cash shortage and its land had degenerated into a tangle of weeds where monuments were hidden by shrubbery and buildings were falling apart. Local people, determined to restore the area to its former glory, formed the Friends of Highgate Cemetery, a volunteer group that acquired the freehold in 1981 and began repair work. Eight years later, ownership was transferred to the Custodian of Charities. In recent years, many improvements have been made, attracting a growing stream of visitors (including a number of film companies). Some of the tombs fascinate simply because of their decoration—menagerie keeper George Wombwell is guarded by a sleeping, cross-pawed lion, for example, and the headstone at cricketer Frederick Lillywhite's grave displays a broken wicket, showing that he had completed his innings. Other vaults shelter the bones of the rich and famous (some of whom lived in nearby **Hampstead**); Michael Faraday (the discoverer of electromagnetic induction) rests in Highgate, as do authors **Charles Dickens** and George Eliot, philosopher Herbert Spencer, and bare knuckle fighter Tom Sayers. Dante Gabriel Rossetti committed his young wife, Lizzie Siddal, to the earth then had her coffin dug up so that he could retrieve a book of manuscript poems he had buried with her. Perhaps the most famous grave is that of Karl Marx, who died in 1883 and lies under a headstone as weighty as his writings.

HILLINGDON, LONDON BOROUGH OF. When metropolitan **local government** was reorganized in 1965, Hillingdon was created through the merger of the Borough of **Uxbridge** and the Urban Districts of Hayes and Harlington, **Ruislip** and Northwood, and Yiewsley and West Drayton. It covers 43 square miles, has a population of 251,200 (1998), and takes its name from Hillingdon village, which stands close to the center of the area. Heathrow **Airport**, located in the southern part of the borough, is a major employer that has attracted ancillary service and manufacturing industries, aided by good road links to the nationwide motorway system. However, that transport network has also raised problems of noise pollution, illegal **immigrants**, and drug smuggling, which are continuing sources of discontent among local residents. Uxbridge, further north, is a prosperous commuter suburb with low unemployment levels, and Ruislip, with a high proportion of **green belt** land, has more in common with neighboring rural communities than with the urban core.

HOLBORN. Holborn, located north of the **Strand**, takes its name from the Holebourne stream (a tributary of the **Fleet River**) and is first mentioned in a 10th-century document that records a grant of land by Edgar, King of England from 959 A.D. until 975 A.D., to **Westminster Abbey**. Its boundary with the **City of London** (which lies immediately to the east) is marked by two stone obelisks, known as Holborn Bars, which were erected in about 1130 to identify a tollbooth. The area has given its name to a number of metropolitan landmarks, including a street called Holborn, which is known to have existed as early as the 13th century, when it was an important route by which wool, corn, timber, and other products were delivered to City customers. Today, the road (now known for most of its length as High Holborn) links **Shaftesbury Avenue** to the major road junction at Holborn Circus, which was constructed in 1872 as part of a traffic improvement program. The same program included the building of Holborn Viaduct, 1,400 feet long and 80 feet wide, across the valley of the Fleet so that Holborn could be connected to Newgate Street and the neighborhood of **St. Paul's Cathedral**. In 1874, the London, Chatham, and Dover **Railway** opened a station at the southeastern end of the viaduct, providing commuters from the towns along the south bank of the **River Thames** with easy access to the city's financial district. During the **London County Council**'s jurisdiction, Holborn was the smallest of the metropolitan boroughs. Dominated by commercial properties, it was incorporated within the **London Borough of Camden** when **local government** was reorganized in 1965. (*See also* ELECTRICITY; ELY PLACE; INNS OF CHANCERY; INNS OF COURT; METROPOLITAN DRINKING FOUNTAIN AND CATTLE TROUGH ASSOCIATION; RED LION SQUARE; ST. ANDREW'S CHURCH, HOLBORN; ST. ETHELDREDA'S CHURCH, HOLBORN.)

HOLLAND HOUSE. In 1606, Sir Walter Cope, King James VI and I's Chancellor of the Exchequer, built a mansion in extensive grounds at **Kensington**. Originally known as Cope Castle, it acquired its present name after it was inherited by Lady Rich (Sir Walter's daughter), whose husband was created Earl of Holland in 1624. In the late 18th and early 19th centuries, it was one of the social centers of London as such Whig politicians as Prime Minister George Canning and Earl Grey mixed with leading literary figures of the day, including author **Charles Dickens**, playwright Richard Brinsley Sheridan, and poet William Wordsworth (*see* **Holland House Circle**). From 1866, however, parts of the estate were sold to developers, then, during the **Blitz**, most of the building was destroyed. The **London County Council** bought the property in 1952, restored the east wing, and converted it for use as a youth hostel dedicated to King George VI. Art exhibitions are sometimes held in the Orangery and the former ice house, and the **park** (which incorporates a rose garden, an iris garden, and a Dutch garden) provides an important oasis of green space in a densely populated area of west London.

HOLLAND HOUSE CIRCLE. Early in 1851, painter G. F. Watts moved into **Holland House** as the guest of Sara Prinseps. Over the next 30 years, the rambling building became the focus of a bohemian clique as the farmland it overlooked was converted into the streets and squares now known as west **Kensington**. Such young, talented artists as Frederick Leighton and Holman Hunt (attracted as much by Prinseps's three beautiful sisters as by Watts) set up studios nearby and were joined at Sunday afternoon soirees by writers as renowned as William Thackeray and Alfred Lord Tennyson, scientists as distinguished as astronomer John Herschel, and politicians as senior as Prime Ministers Benjamin Disraeli and William Gladstone. Their relationships did not accord with modern stereotypes of Victorian rectitude (Joseph Edgar Boehm actually died in a highly compromising position whilst supposedly teaching the art of sculpture to Queen Victoria's daughter, Princess Louise) but, nevertheless, they successfully established a respected status as moral exemplars by producing patriotic and morally uplifting works. Their allegorical style is now out of fashion (partly because few houses have room for 50-foot-long canvases) but, in their day, they were regarded throughout Europe as the most gifted painters of the period and some (such as Leighton) became millionaires.

HOLLAND PARK. *See* HOLLAND HOUSE.

HOLLOWAY. The area between **Highgate** and Finsbury Park, four miles north of **Charing Cross**, was owned throughout the Medieval period by the Dean and Chapter of **St. Paul's Cathedral**. It is first referred to as Holloway (meaning "sunken highway") during the 15th century and became urbanized following the building of **Holloway Prison** in 1852, the establishment of the **Metropolitan Cattle Market** on the 75-acre site of a Jacobean mansion house in 1855, and the construction of roads and **railways** during the third quarter of the 19th century. Rows of cheap houses and small industrial premises replaced fields and hedgerows, creating a suburb that earned an unenviable reputation for shabby terraces occupied by underpaid clerical workers (the lifestyle is described in George and Weedon Grossmith's *Diary of a Nobody*, published in 1892). Since the Second World War, local authorities have improved the **housing** stock (partly by building on the site of the cattle market, which closed in 1963), but Holloway is still characterized by a mixture of industry and relatively cheap residential property. It was incorporated within the **London Borough of Islington** in 1965. (*See also* BATTERSEA DOGS' HOME.)

HOLLOWAY PRISON. The first prison at **Holloway** was built in 1852 to house both sexes but, from 1902, accepted women only (including Emmeline Pankhurst and other campaigners for female suffrage). The present red brick structure, the largest women's jail in Britain, was designed by Robert Matthew, Johnson-Marshall, and Partners to meet modern standards and erected in 1970. The 500 inmates live in units of 16 or 32 people, with bedrooms housing one or four prisoners. Each unit has its own dining area and common room, but a hospital, swimming pool, and gymnasium serve the whole jail. Mothers with infant children have special facilities.

HOLMES, SHERLOCK. In 1887, Arthur Conan Doyle, unable to make ends meet as a Portsmouth doctor, turned to mystery writing in an attempt to boost his income. His first short novel—*A Study in Scarlet*—was an outstanding success, introducing amateur detective Sherlock Holmes to a middle-class public ready to suspend its disbelief and accept a romanticized world of crime in which a pipe-smoking, violin-playing, cocaine-using dilettante draws startlingly logical conclusions from scraps of evidence overlooked by plodding police officers.

Holmes (modelled on Dr. Joseph Bell, who lectured at Edinburgh University, where Conan Doyle studied medicine) lived in apartments at 221B **Baker Street**, where his adventures where chronicled by his friend Dr. John Watson (whose character is drawn from that of Dr. James Watson, President of the Portsmouth Literary and Scientific Society). Conan Doyle moved to London in 1890 and opened a medical practice at 2 Devonshire Place, **St. Marylebone**, but it attracted few patients, so he returned with vigor to his writing, publishing a series of short stories featuring Holmes in *Strand* magazine. By 1893, he was bored by the character and tried to kill him off in a struggle with his arch enemy, Professor Moriarty, but public demand forced him to bring the detective back to life in *The Hound of the Baskervilles*, published in 1902. Conan Doyle was knighted in the same year for his work at a field hospital in southern Africa during the Boer War and died at Crowborough (Sussex) on 7 July 1930, by which time Holmes had become one of the most copied characters in crime fiction, with a cult following in the United States as well as Great Britain. Many of the tales illuminate the social history of the metropolitan area at the end of the 19th century, focusing on the lifestyles of different social classes and on social distinctions between town and country.

HONOURABLE ARTILLERY COMPANY. The Artillery Company claims to be the oldest military unit in the United Kingdom. It was created in 1537, when King Henry VIII gave a body of citizen archers (known as the Guild of St. George) the formal title of Fraternity or Guild of Artillery of Longbows, Crossbows, and Handguns and made it responsible for the defense of London. The prefix "Honourable" was first applied in 1685, though not confirmed until the 19th century. Initially, the company was based in Artillery Lane, Bishopsgate (*see* **Bishop's Gate**), but, in 1642, it moved to its present location in City Road, where, on 18 June 1774, the first major cricket match held in Great Britain was played between Kent and All England. Although most of their duties are now ceremonial, members saw active service during the First and Second World Wars and, as part of the modern Territorial Army, undergo regular military training.

HONOURABLE CORPS OF GENTLEMEN AT ARMS. Officially, members of the corps, originally formed by King Henry VIII in 1509, act as bodyguards to the royal family, but their public duties are now largely ceremonial. They dress in skirted red coats, carry battleaxes, and wear helmets with white plumes at all times, even at religious services. Like the **Yeomen of the Guard**, they formerly served with the armed forces.

HORNIMAN MUSEUM. During his travels abroad, tea magnate Frederick J. Horniman amassed a large collection of objects that he made available to the public at his home in **Forest Hill** in 1890. Eight years later, the house was demolished and replaced by a stone and brick art nouveau building designed by C. Harrison Townsend. When it was completed in 1901, the **museum**, along with 21 acres of **park**land and garden, was handed over to the **London County Council**. The collection that it houses is a typically Victorian blend of natural history and ethnography, including a stuffed walrus, shrunken heads, and musical instruments.

HORNSEY. Hornsey is located some six miles north of **Charing Cross**. It was probably founded during Saxon times as a forest settlement and was owned for much of the Medieval period by the Bishops of London, who used it for hunting. Urban development began in 1850, when the Great Northern **Railway** built a station at the eastern end of the village, allowing commuters to work in **The City** and return to country homes at night; within 30 years, fields and woods had been covered by **housing** estates, small industries, and urban services. After the Second World War, many of the less sound properties were replaced by local authority residential building. In 1965, when **local government** within the metropolitan area was reformed, Hornsey was incorporated within the **London Borough of Haringey**.

HORSE GUARDS PARADE. Horse Guards Parade, located immediately east of **St. James's Park**, is built on the former tiltyard of **Whitehall Palace**. Horse Guards building, which lines three sides of the courtyard, stands on the site of a palace guardhouse; designed by William Kent in Palladian style, it was erected in 1750–60 under the direction of John Vardy. The entrance from **Whitehall** is guarded, between 10 A.M. and 4 P.M. each day, by two cavalrymen of the **Household Division** (the changing of the guard at 11 o'clock is one of London's principal tourist attractions). Every year, on the reigning monarch's official birthday, the ceremony of **Trooping the Colour** is held on the parade ground, which is marked by statues of distinguished military commanders, including Lord Mountbatten of Burma (who was murdered by the Irish Republican Army in 1979) and Lord Kitchener (who organized the British Army at the start of the First World War). (*See also* TREASURY BUILDINGS.)

HOSPITALS. *See* HEALTH CARE.

HOTELS. Hotels were slow to develop in London, partly because wealthy male visitors to the city stayed at their clubs (*see* **gentlemen's clubs**) and ladies stayed in private houses. The less affluent used inns or other lodgings. Even by the early 19th century, most of the few establishments called hotels were hired out as whole buildings rather than as separate rooms. The spur to the development of accommodation for travellers was the expansion of the **railway** network, which brought people from the provinces in increasingly large numbers from the 1830s. Railway companies themselves built hotel properties at their London termini, many of them (such as the Midland's Grand Hotel at **St. Pancras**) lavishly decorated and luxuriously furnished. The success of these ventures encouraged other entrepreneurs, including Frederick Gordon, who opened the Grand Hotel, the Metropole Hotel, and the Victoria Hotel on Northumberland Avenue during the 1870s. Later, in the period between the First and Second World Wars, many aristocratic mansions, deserted by owners who had fled to the country or found the cost of upkeep too high were demolished to make way for hotels (the Duke of Westminster's Grosvenor House in **Park Lane** was replaced by the Grosvenor House Hotel in 1926–28, for example). Also, many large townhouses in areas such as **Bloomsbury** and **Marylebone** (*see* **St. Marylebone**) were subdivided for use as bed and breakfast establishments, attracting restaurants, public houses, and other services in their wake. By the later 1990s, London had over a thousand hotels, motels, guest houses, and similar businesses. Of the total 138,000 beds available each night, the majority were concentrated in inner-city localities, notably the **City of Westminster** (48,000), the **Royal Borough of Kensington and Chelsea** (19,400), and the **London Borough of Camden** (16,600). (*See also* BAYSWATER; BROWN'S HOTEL; CANARY WHARF; CANNON STREET STATION; CLARIDGE'S HOTEL; CONNAUGHT HOTEL; DORCHESTER HOTEL; EARL'S COURT; EUSTON STATION; ExCEL; GROSVENOR SQUARE; JERMYN STREET; JOHNSON'S HOUSE, DR.; KENSINGTON; KING'S CROSS; LANGHAM HOTEL; LEICESTER SQUARE; LIVERPOOL STREET STATION; MAYFAIR; PIMLICO; PORTLAND PLACE; RITZ HOTEL; RUSSELL SQUARE; SMITH, W. H., LTD.; STRAND; VICTORIA.)

HOUNDSDITCH. The 300-yard-long street that connects **Aldgate** to Bishopsgate (*see* **Bishop's Gate**) follows the line of the moat that formed part of the northeastern defenses of the **City of London** during medieval times. It may derive its name from kennels where hunting animals were kept or (according to 16th-century historian **John Stow**) from the habit of using it as a depository for "much filth, especially dead dogges." The population plummeted during the **Great Plague** of 1664–66, when 1,100 victims were buried in a communal pit, but had recovered by the 19th century, when the area gained a reputation as a Jewish neighborhood with cheap clothes and other goods. During the 20th century, most of the properties were converted for use by banks and other financial institutions.

HOUNSLOW. Hounslow is located on the western fringe of London, 11 miles from **Charing Cross** and directly under the flight path of planes landing at Heathrow Airport. It lies on the Roman road that ran from London to the route center of Calleva Attrebatum (now known as Silchester) but developed from 1214, following the establishment of a priory by the Friars of Holy Trinity to provide accommodation for travellers and care for the sick. The heath land around the settlement became popular as a military training ground (King James VII and II maintained a standing army there from 1686, cavalry barracks were built in 1793, and accommodation for infantry was added in 1875). Also, in 1784, General William Roy established a base line for the mapping of Britain, which was retained until satellite imagery replaced conventional surveys during the late 20th century.

Despite the presence of the army, the community's prosperity relied heavily on provision of services for travellers to and from the west of England, with inns providing refreshment and rooms for coach passengers as well as facilities for changing, shoeing, and stabling horses. In 1840, the opening of the Great Western **Railway** killed the coaching trade, but **transport** retained its local economic importance, with the London and South Western Railway providing services from 1850 and the District Railway from 1883. In addition, during the early 20th century, Hounslow became a focus of **bus** routes and maintenance then, in 1919, the site of the first civil **airport** in Britain, with daily services to Paris (the first flight to Australia from England left in November of the same year). In 1932, the **London Underground** system arrived, the Piccadilly Line providing regular services to the city center. These developments encouraged house building for local workers and for commuters as well as office construction for firms requiring easy accessibility, fuelling a considerable expansion both of population numbers and of the urban area as well as an increase in the community's importance as a retail and service center. The settlement acquired Urban District Council status in 1894, became a borough in 1932 then, when London's **local government** was reorganized in 1965, gave its name to a new **London Borough of Hounslow**.

HOUNSLOW, LONDON BOROUGH OF. The **London Borough** of Hounslow was created in 1965 through the amalgamation of the Borough of **Brentford** and **Chiswick**, the Borough of Heston and Isleworth, the Borough of **Hounslow**, and the Urban District of Feltham under a single local authority. It covers 23 square miles and had a resident population of 211,600 in 1998. The area has considerable ethnic and economic diversity, with a large Asian community and a mixture of manufacturing, office, and service jobs. The proximity of Heathrow **Airport** (to the west) and the Great West Road (which bisects the area and provides links to the national motorway network) attracted light industries, particularly around Brentford, Chiswick, and Feltham, but recession and the movement of business to more spacious semirural sites resulted in higher than average rates of unemployment among manual workers during the 1990s. The Borough Council responded with a major regeneration program, focusing on Feltham, which is designed to attract 2,500 jobs through expansion of trading estates and the development of a technology park. **Chiswick House**, **Osterley House**, and **Syon House** help draw tourists to the east of the area but not in sufficient numbers to have a major impact on employment.

HOUSEHOLD CAVALRY. *See* HOUSEHOLD DIVISION.

HOUSEHOLD DIVISION. The seven regiments of the British Army's Household Division undertake numerous ceremonial tasks, including guard duties at **Buckingham Palace**, **Horse Guards Parade**, **St. James's Palace**, and the **Tower of London**. With the exception of the Irish Guards (established in the 19th century) and the Welsh Guards (formed during the First World War), all were founded during the 17th century. The mounted regiments that form the Household Cavalry are distinguished by their uniforms, the Life Guards wearing scarlet tunics and carrying white plumes on their headdress, the Blues and Royals blue tunics and red plumes. Bandsmen, led by trumpeters (on grey horses) and drummers (on skewbalds), are dressed in scarlet and gold. The five regiments of Foot Guards all wear red tunics and black bearskins; they have different collar badges, shoulder badges, and buttons but are most readily identified by the presence or color of the plumes on their headgear (the Coldstream Guards have red plumes, the Grenadier Guards white, the Irish Guards blue, the Welsh Guards green and white, and the Scots Guards no plume). All seven groups have distinguished records of active service and still undertake normal military duties. (*See also* CHANGING OF THE GUARD; KNIGHTSBRIDGE; ST. JAMES'S PARK; STATE OPENING OF PARLIAMENT.)

HOUSE OF COMMONS. *See* PALACE OF WESTMINSTER.

HOUSE OF LORDS. *See* PALACE OF WESTMINSTER.

HOUSES OF PARLIAMENT. *See* PALACE OF WESTMINSTER.

HOUSING. Until the 17th century, London extended over only a few square miles, so judge and journeyman lived in close proximity, with the great majority of the population occupying houses built of wood. After the **Great Fire** of 1666, brick and stone increased in popularity as building materials and many suburban developments were aimed specifically at an affluent market (as in **Mayfair**), but the great expansion in construction of homes occurred only in the Victorian period, as the impact of the Industrial Revolution increased. During the early 19th century, many wealthy families moved westward from the crowded city center into terraced residences erected by speculative developers, such as those constructed by **Thomas Cubitt** at **Belgravia**. Then, from the late 1830s, the spreading tentacles of the railroad system allowed the middle classes to rent or purchase detached or semidetached properties on the outskirts of the metropolitan area and commute to work. Some suburbs (such as **Surbiton**) were, in effect, created by the railroad companies, which built stations in the countryside knowing that builders would buy up land and erect houses. Elsewhere, **Dulwich**, **Lewisham**, and other formerly independent villages were encoiled in the urban embrace as fields and woods were replaced by rows of substantial villas following the railroad's arrival.

The poorer sectors of society were less able to move. Increasingly, they concentrated in central and east London slums (known as **rookeries**), close to jobs in manufacturing plants, which belched dirt and soot 24 hours a day, and in **dock** industries where pollution was widespread. Among the middle class of mid-Victorian England, there was a widespread belief that the poor deserved their fate, condemned to a miserable

London slums, 1872 (Museum of London)

life by indolence and lack of character. However, during the second half of the century, writings by **Charles Booth**, **Henry Mayhew**, and others made a wider public aware that the less well off were trapped by poverty, unable to acquire better housing because of low wages, lack of access to the education that would bring advancement, and susceptiblility to infectious diseases that flourished in overcrowded conditions. Gradually (partly because of a genuine wish to improve the lot of the worst off, partly because of a fear that illnesses such as tuberculosis would spread from working-class to middle-class areas), the clearer understanding of housing standards stimulated efforts to improve conditions. Initially, changes stemmed from the efforts of individual philanthropists (such as **George Peabody**) and by charities (known as model dwelling companies) that encouraged businesspeople to invest in housing for the deserving poor by promising a 5 percent return. Increasingly, however, pressure was placed on state and local authorities to take action.

The **London County Council (LCC)** entered the market in 1900, when the Housing of the Working Classes Act gave it power to purchase land at the periphery of the city and build low-cost homes, but became much more heavily involved after the First World War, as Prime Minister David Lloyd George promised that reconstruction would shape "a country fit for heroes to live in," with residential provision at the core of social policy. New parliamentary legislation required local authorities to satisfy their area's housing needs and provided subsidies so that rents could be kept low. As a result, over 27,000 homes were made available in London from 1919 to 1921, when funding was suspended as the cost to the nation's exchequer rose. The period from 1924 to 1933 brought further building (again supported by central government), which added another 64,000 properties. Most of the construction took place on green field sites or at inner-city areas made available by slum clearance, and it turned the state into London's largest landlord (the Becontree development alone had 116,000 tenants).

Initially, house building for owner-occupation lagged behind council building in the period between the two world wars because material costs were high, but subsidies to potential buyers with building society mortgages (a policy introduced in 1923) boosted construction and, by the 1930s, low prices and a rising market combined to produce steady employment for bricklayers, carpenters, and other tradesmen. Two-storied, semidetached houses, with small gardens and bow windows (described by novelist George Orwell as "brick doll's houses" in *Coming Up for Air*, published in 1939), bordered tree-lined streets in **Harrow**, Purley,

Croydon, Morden, **Wembley**, Finsbury Park, and other outlying areas as buyers leapfrogged existing suburbs in the search for a home close to the country but with access to city jobs.

During the Second World War, labor and resources were directed to military ends, so house building was severely restricted. Moreover, during the **Blitz**, an estimated 116,000 homes were destroyed in the Greater London area. As a result, the city faced a critical housing deficit as service men and women returned to civilian life and evacuees moved back from the countryside in 1945. Inevitably, at a time of supply shortage, the bulk of the construction program relied on local authority investment. London's councils refurbished over 100,000 damaged properties in 1945–47, built over 10,000 new homes within the city every year from 1948 to 1963, and acquired land on which to develop estates in surrounding counties, such as Essex and Kent. About one-quarter of these new dwellings were skyscraper apartments, many erected in the densely populated **East End**.

Despite the efforts, however, high-standard housing was still at a premium in the mid-1960s. The parliamentary *Report of the Committee on Housing in Greater London* (usually known as the Milner Holland Report, after the committee's Chairman) pointed out that, in 1965, demand exceeded supply, much of the stock was of substandard quality (some 200,000 families had no fixed bath, for example), and the tenure of many people renting from private landlords was insecure. Moreover, at the same time, doubts were cast on the success of high-rise developments as residents, academics, and architects made allegations of shoddy workmanship and claimed that skyscrapers were inappropriate for people who had spent much of their lives in two-story homes with gardens. In 1968, the collapse of the 23-floor Ronan Point block in the **London Borough of Newham** after a gas explosion fuelled concerns, persuading authorities to eschew further "streets in the sky" and concentrate on low-density developments.

From 1979, policies changed further as the new Conservative government questioned the principles underlying the provision of council housing. Legislation limiting local authorities' ability to raise funds through property taxes restricted the funds available for construction, and the introduction, in 1980, of legislation giving council tenants the right to buy their homes resulted in a reduction of publicly owned housing stocks as part of a national policy to encourage the growth of a property-owning democracy. The effects were not wholly beneficial, however. Those tenants who opted to buy their homes tended to be the ones living in better-quality structures, so councils were saddled with responsibilities for low-standard buildings but had limited cash with which to make improvements. New **immigrants**, young people without the resources to get a mortgage, and low-income families were forced to live on the streets, and many private houses were subdivided into apartments as landlords attempted to meet the demand for accommodation. As a result, by 1996 the number of homeless families, according to official government figures, was more than twice that of a decade earlier, and house prices in London were increasing at nearly twice the national average (by 1999, the average price of a home in London was £193,000). About 57 percent of the three million properties were owner-occupied, 22 percent rented from local authorities, 15 percent rented from private landlords, and 7 percent rented from housing associations.

Eight percent of the properties were considered unfit for human habitation, many of them in the privately rented sector, but, increasingly, low-standard homes are being bought by people who invest in refurbishment, sell at a profit, and move on. This gentrification is led by young professionals, leading to complaints that working-class people in inner-city communities such as **Spitalfields** and **Paddington** are unable to get accommodation in their home areas but also reversing the process of decay and, frequently, resulting in conservation of parts of the urban fabric that might otherwise have vanished in development programs. (*See also* ABBEY WOOD; ACTON; BAKER STREET; BALHAM; BARBICAN; BARKING; BARKING AND DAGENHAM, LONDON BOROUGH OF; BARNES; BARNET, LONDON BOROUGH OF; BARNSBURY; BATTERSEA; BAYSWATER; BEDFORD ESTATES; BELGRAVIA; BERMONDSEY; BETHNAL GREEN; BEXLEY, LONDON BOROUGH OF; BIGGIN HILL; BLACKHEATH; BRENTFORD; BRIXTON; BURNT OAK; CANNING TOWN; CANONBURY; CAVENDISH SQUARE; CHISWICK; CLERKENWELL; CRICKLEWOOD; CUBITT TOWN; CUSTOM HOUSE; DAGENHAM; DENMARK HILL; DEPTFORD; DOCKLANDS; DRURY LANE; EALING; EALING, LONDON BOROUGH OF; EDMONTON; FINCHLEY; FOREST HILL; FULHAM; GOSPEL OAK; GREATER LONDON COUNCIL (GLC); GREENWICH, LONDON BOROUGH OF; HACKNEY; HACKNEY, LONDON BOROUGH OF; HAMPSTEAD GARDEN SUBURB; HERNE HILL; HIGHBURY; HOLOWAY; HORNSEY; HOXTON; ILFORD; IMMIGRANTS; ISLINGTON; ISLINGTON, LONDON BOROUGH OF; KENTISH TOWN; KIDBROOKE; LAMBETH; LAMBETH, LONDON

BOROUGH OF; LEWISHAM, LONDON BOROUGH OF; LOCAL GOVERNMENT; LONDON BOROUGHS ASSOCIATION [LBA]; LONDON PLANNING ADVISORY COMMITTEE [LPAC]; LONDON PRIDE PARTNERSHIP; MERTON, LONDON BOROUGH OF; METROPOLITAN BOARD OF WORKS; MILLWALL; NASH, JOHN; NORTHOLT; NOTTING HILL; ORPINGTON; PECKHAM; PENTONVILLE; PICCADILLY; POPLAR; REDBRIDGE, LONDON BOROUGH OF; RED LION SQUARE; ROEHAMPTON; ROYAL NAVAL DOCKYARDS; ST. MARYLEBONE; SHEPHERD'S BUSH; SHOREDITCH; SOUTHWARK, LONDON BOROUGH OF; SPITALFIELDS; STEPNEY; SYDENHAM; TOTTENHAM; TUFNELL PARK; VAUXHALL; WALTHAM FOREST, LONDON BOROUGH OF; WALTHAMSTOW; WANDSWORTH, LONDON BOROUGH OF; WAPPING; WHITECHAPEL; WOOLWICH.)

HOXTON. Hoxton is a largely working-class area lying some 2.5 miles northeast of **Charing Cross**. Until the 17th century, it was a rural village that produced vegetables and flowers for the London market, but as building land in the capital became increasingly scarce its open fields attracted developers. **Livery companies** erected almshouses for their members (for example, in 1692, the Haberdashers Company constructed a property that would provide accommodation for 20 men unable to provide for themselves and schooling for the sons of another 20) and business interests opened **music halls** to supply entertainment for the growing urban population (the Britannia Theatre, in High Street, held its first performances in 1850, catering to audiences of up to 3,000 people). By the end of the 19th century, the suburb was one of the poorest in the city, with infectious disease spreading readily in the overcrowded homes, but the extensive damage suffered during the **Blitz** (when the Britannia Theatre was destroyed) allowed local authorities to restructure **housing** provision in municipal developments. Hoxton was incorporated within the **London Borough of Hackney** when London's **local government** was reformed in 1965.

HUGUENOTS. In the last years of the 17th century, London's population was augmented by an estimated 30,000 Huguenots, who were persecuted in France because of their Protestant beliefs. Skilled silk weavers, they settled primarily in **Spitalfields** and **Soho**, earning a considerable reputation for their craftsmanship. The large windows that allowed light into their attic rooms can still be seen at Fournier Street (near **Christ Church,**

Spitalfields), where floor joists were packed with silk waste to deaden the sound of the looms. A smaller group established a community at **Wandsworth**, where they built up a hat-making industry sufficiently respected to attract orders from the Roman Catholic clergy at the Vatican. At East Hill, many of the **immigrants** were buried in a tiny cemetery close to their church. The **burial ground** was closed in 1854 and converted into a public garden; many of the inscriptions on the gravestones are now too eroded to read easily, but a memorial erected in 1911 lists some of the families represented. (*See also* MERTON; MORTLAKE; PADDINGTON; STREATHAM.)

HUNGERFORD BRIDGE. The first Hungerford **Bridge**, designed by Isambard Kingdom Brunel and built in 1841–45, provided access from the south bank of the **River Thames** to Hungerford **Market**, which sold fruit, vegetables, meat, and fish. However, the market closed in 1860, unable to compete with **Covent Garden**, and the site was developed by the South Eastern **Railway** as Charing Cross Station. Brunel's suspension bridge was demolished (the rail management argued that nobody used it because of the stench of sewage in the river) and replaced, in 1864, by the present wrought iron lattice girder structure built to John Hawkshaw's designs. The bridge (also known as Charing Cross Bridge) has a footbridge (one of only two across the Thames in central London) on its eastern side and was subject to a major overhaul in 1979, when new cross girders were installed.

HURLINGHAM CLUB. In 1875, the rules of polo were formalized by the Hurlingham Club at its Ranelagh Gardens premises in **Fulham**. The club was formed in 1867, when Frank Heathcote leased land at Hurlingham House (built in 1760) so that members could indulge in pigeon shooting, but the organization rapidly developed into a more general association for people with sporting interests as facilities were provided for cricket, croquet, golf, lawn bowls, skittles, squash, swimming, tennis, and other activities. The site on which the first polo match was played, in 1874, was converted into a municipal **housing** estate by the **London County Council** in 1946.

HYDE PARK. Hyde Park covers 340 acres of central London, stretching from **Bayswater** in the north to **Green Park** in the south and from **Kensington Gardens** in the west to **Mayfair** in the east. During the Middle Ages, it was owned by **Westminster Abbey** but, when that **monastery**

was dissolved in 1540, the land was acquired by King Henry VIII as a hunting forest. The public was admitted from the early 17th century and on May Day, in particular, fashionable London paraded itself in the grounds (in 1663, diarist **Samuel Pepys** records buying new clothes before going to Hyde Park in the hope of being noticed by King Charles II). After dusk, however, it was a dangerous place, haunted by highwaymen and a popular location for settling disagreements by duel; the Duke of Hamilton and Lord Mohun killed each other in one contest there in 1712, for example. In 1730, Queen Caroline, wife of King George II, added a boating lake, known as the **Serpentine**, increasing the area's recreational attractions, then, during the 19th century, the park became the setting for large public gatherings, such as the **Great Exhibition** in 1851. From 1860, the Victorians introduced flower beds, fountains, and statues, formalizing, managing, and taming the landscape. Modern usage reflects these traditions. Protagonists disagree verbally, rather than violently, at **Speakers' Corner**. Horse riders still use **Rotten Row** (where King William III exercised his animals), the Serpentine is popular with canoeists and young couples in paddle boats, the crowds still gather for big events (the Rolling Stones have played there), and, on a summer Sunday, as many as 50,000 people will use the facilities for quiet recreation—jogging, dog walking, swimming, or listening to concerts at the bandstand. The park is still owned by the Crown and maintained by the **Royal Parks** Agency. (*See also* LANSBURY, GEORGE; PARKS.)

HYDE PARK CORNER. At the southeast corner of **Hyde Park**, five roads meet at one of London's busiest traffic junctions, used by more than 150,000 vehicles every weekday. In the 18th century, the site was the location of a tollgate, where fees were charged to travellers making their way from the west into **Piccadilly**. The entrance to the **park** is now marked by a three-arched classical screen designed by Decimus Burton and erected in 1825 to provide a suitably regal approach from **Buckingham Palace**. Burton was also responsible for Wellington Arch (also known as Constitution Arch and Green Park Arch), which stands at the center of the junction. Intended as a triumphal entry to Hyde Park, it was erected outside Apsley House in 1828 but moved to its present position in 1883 so that it would dominate the western end of **Constitution Hill**. The structure houses a police station (the second smallest in London after that at **Trafalgar Square**) and is surmounted by *The Quadrigia*, a bronze statue (completed by Captain Adrian Jones of the Third Hussars in 1912) that shows the angel of peace descending into a chariot drawn by four horses.

Apsley House, on the north of Hyde Park Corner just east of the former tollgate, was known as No. 1 London because of its position. It was designed by **Robert Adam** and built in 1771–78 for Lord Chancellor Henry Bathurst but, in 1817, became the home of the Duke of Wellington, who lived in it until his death in 1852. The property was presented to the nation by the seventh Duke in 1947 then converted into the Wellington Museum, which opened in 1952. The interior has been retained much as it was when the first Duke was in residence, with exhibits (depicting both his army and his political career) focusing on the Waterloo Gallery, where he held an annual banquet to celebrate his victory over Napoleon Bonaparte's army on 18 June 1815. The front of the building is marked by a bronze statue of Wellington, mounted on Copenhagen, the horse that carried him to victory at Waterloo; designed by Joseph Edgar Boehm, it was cast from captured French guns and erected in 1888. Nearby, there are memorials to men of the Machine Gun Corps and the Royal Regiment of Artillery who died during the First World War.

In 2001 English Heritage (a government-funded conservation agency) revealed plans (prepared by Kim Wilkie, one of Britain's leading landscape architects) to remodel Hyde Park Corner at a cost of £20 million. (*See also* MAYFAIR.)

– I –

ILFORD. A residential suburb lying on the east bank of the River Roding, some nine miles northeast of **Charing Cross**, Ilford has a lengthy history, with archaeological investigations revealing evidence of an Iron Age encampment. About 1140, Adeliza, Abbess of Barking, established a leper house that was enlarged 40 years later by Abbess Mary Becket in memory of her brother Thomas, who had been murdered at Canterbury Cathedral in 1170. Nearby, a village developed at the limit of navigation on the river, with commodities such as timber, gravel, and coal imported and exported, but significant population growth dates from 1839, when the arrival of the **railway** promoted a construction boom, attracting families willing to commute to city center jobs in order to have ready access to semirural environments on weekends. Present-day homes date mainly from the 1930s and 1950s and are located in large local authority estates, including the 27,000-unit Becontree development, begun in 1921 by the **London County Council** and shared with neighboring **Barking** and

Dagenham. Ilford was incorporated within the **London Borough of Redbridge** when London's **local government** was reformed in 1965, becoming the new authority's principal administrative base.

IMMIGRANTS. London's development has been shaped by immigrants. It was founded by the Romans (*see* **Londinium**), developed by the Normans, and influenced by people from around the world who were attracted by the city's wealth and prestige. During the 19th century, the expansion of sea-borne trade with a growing empire brought foreign sailors to the **docks** along the banks of the **River Thames**; many settled, forming distinctive communities, such as that of the Chinese in **Limehouse**. In the 1920s and 1930s, significant numbers of migrants (including some professional groups, such as doctors and lawyers) arrived from the Asian subcontinent, and the early years of the Second World War brought large numbers from central and eastern Europe.

The bulk of foreign immigration, however, took place in the late 1940s and the 1950s, when organizations such as British Railways, London Transport, and the National Health Service conducted recruitment campaigns in the Caribbean and Africa in an attempt to reduce labor shortages. Jamaicans, in particular, arrived in large numbers, but groups also travelled from other West Indies islands and from Ghana and Nigeria. These newcomers tended to settle in different parts of the city (Anguillans in Slough, for example, and Trinidadians in **Notting Hill**), forming readily identifiable concentrations that were often the focus of racial tension. In an attempt to avoid conflict, Prime Minister Harold Macmillan's Conservative government passed legislation that restricted immigration from Commonwealth countries after 1 July 1963. Even more stringent measures were approved in 1968, 1971, 1981, and 1988, reducing the number of people admitted to the United Kingdom on a permanent basis.

Returns from the 1991 census showed that some 1.4 million Londoners (about 20 percent of London's population) were of foreign immigrant background. Of these, about 362,000 were Indian, 304,000 black Caribbean, and 170,000 black African. Estimates based on likely growth rates suggested that, by 2011, the ethnic minorities would account for 28 percent of the residents in the metropolitan area and for over 50 percent of those in the **London Borough**s of **Brent** and **Newham**.

London also acted as a magnet for immigrants from other regions of Britain, fuelling a growing population until after the end of the

Second World War. In the 1960s, however, academics and politicians expressed concern that increasing numbers were placing a strain on **housing**, **sewage disposal**, **transport**, and other services. Successive governments adopted policies designed to persuade businesses to relocate outside the city and encourage the construction of new towns on green field sites to attract metropolitan residents. As a result, London experienced a net migration loss of about 100,000 people annually from then until the late 1980s. Since 1991, that outflow has lessened, averaging about 50,000 each year (in 1996, for instance, 168,000 people moved to London from other parts of Britain and 213,400 left London for other areas). Most of the out-migrants relocated in economically buoyant areas, particularly southeast and southwest England and East Anglia, all of which received more people than they sent. Every other area of the country, with the exception of Northern Ireland, experienced a net outflow of population to the capital. In 1996, about 80 percent of those arriving in the city were in the 16–44 age range, compared with 63 percent of those who left. Every other age category in the capital suffered a net migration loss. (*See also* BARNET, LONDON BOROUGH OF; BRIXTON; BURNT OAK; CAMDEN TOWN; CHINATOWN; CHINGFORD; EALING, LONDON BOROUGH OF; EARL'S COURT; EAST END; EAST HAM; ETHNIC GROUPS; FOREST HILL; GOLDERS GREEN; HARINGEY, LONDON BOROUGH OF; HUGUENOTS; JEWISH MUSEUM; KILBURN; MILE END; MORTLAKE; OLD JEWRY; PADDINGTON; RAG FAIR; SHEPHERD'S BUSH; SPITALFIELDS; STAMFORD HILL; STOKE NEWINGTON; TOWER HAMLETS, LONDON BOROUGH OF; VAUXHALL; WESTMINSTER, CITY OF; WHITECHAPEL.)

IMPERIAL WAR MUSEUM. The **museum** was established by Act of Parliament in 1920. Originally based at **Crystal Palace**, it moved to **Kensington** in 1924 then to its present location—the Lambeth Road site of **Bedlam**—in 1935. During the 1980s, it was completely rebuilt in order to improve its displays of material relating to the two world wars and to improve visitors' understanding of the conflicts. One area, for example, is designed as a First World War trench, where the sounds of battle reverberate beyond barbed wire. Elsewhere, an **East End air raid** shelter receives a severe jolt as a bomb lands nearby. The museum also has a large collection of 20th-century British art and an extensive collection of artefacts, including tanks and fighter planes.

INNER LONDON. *See* GREATER LONDON.

INNER LONDON EDUCATION AUTHORITY (ILEA). The ILEA was established in 1965 as a committee of the **Greater London Council (GLC)** charged with provision of **education** at all levels (with the exception of the universities) in the **City of London** and 12 inner-city **London boroughs—Camden**, **Greenwich**, **Hackney**, **Hammersmith and Fulham**, **Islington**, **Kensington and Chelsea**, **Lambeth**, **Lewisham**, **Southwark**, **Tower Hamlets**, **Wandsworth**, and **Westminster**. The largest authority of its kind in the world, it wielded considerable power, arguing that providing high-quality education, with good resources for libraries and related learning facilities, could help overcome the problems created by deprived homes and neighborhoods. In addition, it supported a research unit that made an important academic contribution to scholars' understanding of the dynamics of education in Britain's metropolitan areas, particularly among immigrant groups. The ILEA survived the GLC's abolition in 1986, becoming an elected body in its own right, but agitation among its constituent boroughs for the right to govern their own affairs led to its dismemberment on 31 March 1990.

INNER TEMPLE. *See* INNS OF COURT.

INNS OF CHANCERY. Although the original reason for their foundation is not clear, the Inns were probably created during the Medieval period to train Chancery Clerks, who prepared writs for the English courts. By the 15th century, they had become schools for aspirant lawyers but, over the next 300 years, students increasingly turned for tuition to the **Inns of Court**, which had the sole right to decide whether individuals could be admitted as barristers and therefore prosecute or defend cases in the senior courts of England and Wales. The Inns of Chancery gradually became more important as meeting places for lawyers (who could appear only in the lower courts) but the formation of the Law Society, which began to regulate standards for these legal representatives in 1825, rendered them obsolete. During the 19th century, they closed down and their property was taken over by other interests. The eight principal Inns were Clifford's (founded in 1345 but closed in 1903), Thravies (formed in 1348 and dissolved during the 1760s), Staple (which survived from 1378 until 1884 and whose building in **Holborn** has been converted for use as offices), Furnival's (named after Lord Furnival, who rented the property to law students in 1383, but dissolved in 1817), Lyon's (which originated as a tavern, became an Inn of

Chancery in 1420 and was dissolved in 1863), Barnard's (which was functioning by 1435 but whose dilapidated property was purchased by the Mercers, one of the **livery companies**, in 1892), Clement's (founded by 1480 and named after **St. Clement Danes Church**, located nearby on the **Strand**, its property was sold in parcels between 1868 and 1891), and New Inn (formed in 1485 but taken over by the **London County Council** in 1899 and demolished to facilitate road improvements).

INNS OF COURT. The four Inns are legal societies that have the exclusive right to admit law students as barristers, a title that confers the right to prosecute or defend cases at the senior courts in England and Wales. Lincoln's Inn dates at least from 1422, Middle Temple from 1501, Inner Temple from 1505, and Gray's Inn from 1569, but all were probably founded in the 14th century to protect the rights of lawyers and teach the principles of English law (music, dancing, and history were also on the curriculum so that students could be prepared for a place in the higher strata of professional society). Each Inn is independent of the others and of central government apart from a Council of Legal Education (established jointly in 1872 to regulate training practices) and a Senate (formed in 1974 to carry out certain administrative duties related to law reform and maintenance of standards). The term "Inn" arose because each body provided accommodation for students and their teachers.

Lincoln's Inn is named after either Henry de Lacy (Earl of Lincoln and adviser to King Edward I during the later 13th and early 14th centuries) or Thomas de Lyncoln (King's Serjeant at **Holborn** during the early 1400s). It moved to its present location on the west side of **Chancery Lane** between 1422 and 1522. The early records of the Inner and Middle Temples were destroyed during the **Peasants' Revolt** in 1381, but it is known that both occupy sites formerly owned by the **Knights Templar**. The two Inns, neighbors on the south side of **Fleet Street**, were given the property in perpetuity by King James VI and I in 1608 provided they maintained the **Temple Church** (which was consecrated in 1185 and is one of only five round churches in England), but the estate was not formally divided until 1732, when the Middle Temple took the west side and the Inner Temple the east. That part of the Knights' land outside **Temple Bar** was known as Outer Temple but never had any association with the legal profession. Gray's Inn occupies the site, in Gray's Inn Road, of the London home of Sir Reginald le Grey, who died in 1308. It has extensive gardens that were laid out in 1606 by Sir Francis Bacon, a distinguished lawyer who, 12 years later, became Lord

Chancellor, one of the most powerful positions in the land. (*See also* RED LION SQUARE.)

INTERNATIONAL PETROLEUM EXCHANGE (IPE). The IPE, based in a redeveloped area of the **Docklands** at the southeastern edge of the **City of London**, is Europe's principal energy futures and options exchange, trading over US$1 billion daily. It lists contracts for three major commodities—Brent crude (which establishes the benchmark price for two-thirds of the world's crude oil), gas oil (the price of which is used to value heating oil, diesel, and aviation fuel throughout Europe), and natural gas (launched in 1997 as Europe's first natural gas futures contract). Trading of the first two is by "open outcry," with dealers facing each other on the market floor (known as a pit), but natural gas negotiations are computerized. The exchange is owned by its members, most of whom are finance, energy, and brokerage companies. Plans to demutualize the market were blocked in 1999. (*See also* LONDON CLEARING HOUSE [LCH].)

ISLE OF DOGS. Some four miles east of **Charing Cross**, the **River Thames** curves sharply south, creating a peninsula known as the Isle of Dogs. The name has never been satisfactorily explained, though some writers have claimed that royal dogs were once kennelled there. The marshy land lay undeveloped until, in 1802, the West India Docks were built in the north of the area. During the 1840s and 1850s, **Cubitt Town** and **Millwall** were established in the south, creating communities whose economic health relied largely on warehousing and shipbuilding. The declining importance of these activities during the 20th century resulted in high rates of unemployment and consequent poverty. Following the closure of the **docks** in 1980 and the creation of the London **Docklands** Development Corporation the following year, attempts were made to revitalize the area by changing the industrial structure. **Billingsgate Fish Market** was transplanted from **The City**, printing works were built by *The Daily Telegraph* and *The Guardian*, the London Arena (a venue for major spectator events) was constructed on the site of Millwall Dock, the controversial **Canary Wharf** complex included office provision for commercial concerns, road access was improved, and the Docklands Light Railway was linked to the **City of London**. However, although the landscape was transformed, the jobs created in the new light industries were very different from those in the docks, so most were taken by outsiders and the local unemployment rate remained high. In addition, the majority of workers commute from suburban homes, so the Isle's residents are mainly working-class despite attempts to diversify the social structure by building homes attractive to professional groups.

ISLINGTON. Islington, located two miles northeast of **Charing Cross**, developed during the Medieval period, when it passed through the hands of a series of landowners and was popular with English monarchs, who hunted in the surrounding forest (and, in the case of King Henry VIII, built mansions for mistresses). Later, it became fashionable with religious nonconformists (Charles Wesley, cofounder of the Methodist Church, was educated at Charles Morton's Academy, for instance) and earned a reputation for tea gardens that, along with other recreations, attracted affluent visitors from the **City of London** during the 18th century. However, road building, the construction of the **Regent's Canal** (which opened in 1820), and the arrival of the **railway** (in 1850) encouraged speculative developers (such as **Thomas Cubitt**) to convert market gardens and other open space into **housing** estates. Many of these were sensitively designed to suit educated office workers but, during the first half of the 20th century, as families moved to more suburban sites, the properties were converted for use as efficiency apartments by a more transient and impoverished population. From the early 1960s, parts of the area regained their fashionable status (Prime Minister Tony Blair lived in Islington while he was Leader of the Opposition in the **House of Commons**) but, despite the gentrification and the spread of trendy restaurants, the area remains one of the most deprived in London. In 1965, it merged with **Finsbury** to form the **London Borough of Islington**. (*See also* MARYLEBONE CRICKET CLUB [MCC].)

ISLINGTON, LONDON BOROUGH OF. The borough was created in 1965 by the amalgamation of the formerly independent **local government** authorities in **Finsbury** and **Islington**. Lying immediately north of the **City of London**, it forms a long strip of land that covers some six square miles and has a resident population of 179,000 (1998). Islington has little manufacturing industry, although there is some light engineering. **Tourism** is important near the boundary with **The City**, where finance firms and other commercial concerns also provide employment. Although some neighborhoods (such as **Canonbury**) have significant representation of professional and managerial groups, most are largely working-class. The borough ranks as the fourth most deprived local government district in England, according to government surveys based on the 1991 census. Almost 60 percent of the **housing** is provided by the local authority and only 36 percent of households consist of married couples. One in seven families is headed by a single parent, nearly one of every two births is illegitimate, and one in three residents is in the dependent age groups. Politically, the community leans to the left, with a council dominated by the Labour Party, which also holds the two parliamentary constituencies. (*See also* ANGEL, THE; BARNSBURY; BUNHILL FIELDS; CHARTERHOUSE; CLERKENWELL; HIGHBURY; HOLLOWAY; PENTONVILLE; TUFNELL PARK.)

– J –

JACK STRAW'S CASTLE. One of London's best-known **public houses**, the Castle, once a coaching inn, was extensively redesigned in 1964. Some writers argue that it is named after one of the leaders of the **Peasants' Revolt** against high taxation in 1381. However, although the building was certainly a rallying point for the rebels, "Jack Straw" was also a generic name for farm workers, so the pub may simply have gotten its title from the agricultural laborers who frequented it. Its historical associations and its location in North End Way, close to **Hampstead**, made it popular with the literary set during the 19th century; Wilkie Collins, **Charles Dickens**, and William Makepeace Thackeray were regular imbibers. (*See also* SPANIARDS, THE.)

JACK THE RIPPER. On 7 August 1888, 35-year-old Martha Taylor was found murdered in a building near Whitechapel Road. Over the next three months, five other women were killed in the same area of the **East End**; all had their throats cut, all were mutilated, and all but one were prostitutes. Mary Ann Nicholls was found on 31 August, Anne Chapman on 8 September, Elizabeth Stride and Catherine Eddowes on 30 September, and Marie Kelly (the nonprostitute) on 9 November. The press, assuming that one person was responsible for all the deaths, nicknamed the murderer Jack the Ripper and fuelled public fascination with the case. Police investigations, conducted in the glare of publicity and taunted by letters from an individual who claimed to be responsible, involved interviews with hundreds of suspects but failed to identify a culprit. The mystery remains unsolved, but Jack the Ripper has become a minor industry, with walking tours of the square mile where the bodies were found a regular element of London's tourist season and a steady stream of books claiming to unmask the killer. The suspects include Prince Albert (Duke of Clarence) and his Cambridge University tutor, James Stephen.

JACKSON'S OF PICCADILLY. During the 17th and 18th centuries, the Jackson family established a series of businesses in London, notably candle-making and tallow merchandizing. In the 1820s, Richard Jackson merged all of the enterprises into a single concern based at 190 **Piccadilly** then, in 1840, opened larger premises at Nos. 170–72 so that the shop could stock a wider range of goods, including fruit, game, poultry, soaps, and wine. Jackson's built a considerable reputation with affluent **West End** residents, but closed its retail outlet in 1980 in order to concentrate on the supply of teas (and other commodities) to stores, such as **Harrods**, that have a large trade in luxury foods.

JERMYN STREET. Famed for its men's clothing shops, Jermyn Street parallels the south side of **Piccadilly** for some 600 yards from **Haymarket** to St. James's Street. It was built during the late 17th century on land owned by Henry Jermyn, Earl of St. Albans, and, by Queen Victoria's reign, was lined with fashionable **hotels**. None of the early properties survive, and the hotels (with the exception of the Cavendish) have closed, replaced by shirt-makers, shoe retailers, and hatters, who began to infiltrate from about 1840, taking advantage of the affluent clientele in nearby residential areas and **gentlemen's clubs**. Former residents include scientist Isaac Newton (who lived in a house on the site now occupied by No. 87) and Thomas Wall (inventor of a distinctively British form of ice cream and founder of a large food processing group), who was born at No. 113, which is now a restaurant.

JEWISH MUSEUM. The **museum**, founded in 1932, was based at Woburn House (in Tavistock Square) until 1995, when it moved to more spacious premises at Nos. 129–31 Albert Street (north of **Euston Station**). It owns one of the world's finest collections of Jewish ceremonial art and presents a series of exhibits detailing the history of Jews in Britain since the time of the Norman conquest in 1066. An annex at the Sternberg Centre (a Jewish community center at 80 East End Road, **Finchley**) houses the organization's social history collections, including some 400 tape recordings and 12,000 photographs. In addition, displays outlining the Jews' place in London life incorporate reconstructions of a tailor's workshop and a cabinet-maker's business.

JOHNSON, SAMUEL (1709–1784). Although Samuel Johnson would earn more than a footnote in histories of English literature because of his contributions as poet, critic, essayist, and lexicographer, he is best remembered for his witticisms and his role in London social life as documented by **James Boswell**. The son of bookseller Michael Johnson and his wife, Sarah, he was born in Lichfield on 18 September 1709 and educated at the local grammar school. He attended Oxford University but left in 1729 without completing his degree, took a teaching post at a school in Market Bosworth, then, in 1736, set up his own academy for young gentlemen at Edial. The venture collapsed after only a few months, encouraging Johnson to seek his fortune in London along with pupil **David Garrick**, who was later to achieve fame as an actor. From 1738, he contributed regularly to the *Gentlemen's Magazine* and, in 1744, published *An Account of the Life of Mr. Richard Savage, Son of the Earl Rivers* (the biography described the impoverished conditions in which his poet friend lived and which Johnson knew firsthand, partly because of his own difficult circumstances and partly because he and Savage spent much time together). In 1750, he introduced *The Rambler*, a twice weekly periodical, to London society. Published by John Payne, each of the 208 issues was a single anonymous article, 203 of which were written by Johnson himself. Most were moralistic, including themes such as *The Frequent Contemplation of Death Necessary to Moderate the Passions*, but tell much about the issues debated in mid-18th-century intellectual circles.

Johnson's *Dictionary of the English Language*, published in two volumes in 1755, cemented his growing reputation. The work was not the first of its kind, but it was well received because of its polished definitions and the wide range of quotations used to demonstrate nuances in the usage of words listed. However, fame was not accompanied by fortune. Most of the income from sales of the *Dictionary* paid helpers and defrayed expenses, with neither publication of *The Idler* (a periodical reminiscent of *The Rambler*) in 1758–60 nor returns from *Rasselas, Prince of Abyssinia* (his only lengthy work of fiction, which was finished in 1759) helping to augment finances. Only in 1762, when he accepted a pension of £300 a year from the government, did his circumstances improve (ironically, in the *Dictionary*, Johnson notes that, in England, the word pension is "generally understood to mean pay given to a state hireling for treason to his country").

In 1763, he was introduced to Boswell and formed a friendship that would last until his death. Many of the aphorisms that make Johnson probably the most quoted author after **William Shakespeare** are carefully noted in Boswell's writings, as are his assessments of friends, acquaintances, and other authors. For example, in his *Life of Samuel Johnson, LL.D.* (1791), Boswell refers to Johnson's opinion of politician Edmund Burke, with whom he had founded The Club (a group of influential figures, including artist Joshua Reynolds and writer Oliver Goldsmith) in 1764. "In private life he is a very honest gentleman," he says, "but I will not allow him to be so in publick life." The same work also includes the assertion that "when a man is tired of London, he is tired of life; for there is in London all that life can afford." Elsewhere, in Boswell's *Journal of a Tour of the Hebrides* (1784), Johnson remarks that "By seeing London, I have seen as much of life as the world can shew."

Johnson continued to publish after meeting Boswell, editing an eight-volume edition of William Shakespeare's works (1765), preparing political tracts (including one that defended the right of the British government to tax colonists in North America on the grounds that the emigrants had freely left a country where they had parliamentary representation for a land where they had none) during the early 1770s, and (1778 and 1781) writing a series of biographies of English poets. He was awarded doctorates by Trinity College, Dublin, in 1765 and Oxford University in 1775 but never referred to himself as Dr. Johnson; Boswell's *Life* popularized that usage.

From his childhood, Johnson suffered from physical infirmities that affected his relationships and his behavior. He was shortsighted, hard of hearing, frequently afflicted by depression, debilitated by chronic bronchitis, and limited in mobility by dropsy (swelling of the lower limbs). He suffered a stroke in June 1783 and died on 13 December the following year. His body lies in **Westminster Abbey**. (*See also* CHARING CROSS; GRUB STREET; JOHNSON'S HOUSE, DR.; KNIGHTS HOSPITALLER; OLDE CHESHIRE CHEESE, YE; ROYAL NAVAL COLLEGE; VAUXHALL.)

JOHNSON'S HOUSE, DR. From 1748–59, **Samuel Johnson** lived at 17 Gough Square, near **Fleet Street**. In 1750, he began to publish *The Rambler*, a twice weekly periodical, but by the time his wife, Tetty, died in the house in 1752, he was deeply involved in the compilation of a *Dictionary of the English Language*, which had been commissioned by a consortium of booksellers. Converting his attic (which ran the whole length of the property) into a workroom, he employed six clerks (five of whom were Scots) to help with the preparation of the work, which was published in 1755 and immediately made him a household name in fashionable London. After Johnson left, the building became a somewhat shabby **hotel**, but, in 1910, it was purchased by Lord Cecil Harmsworth, who restored it and presented it to the nation three years later. Now owned by the Dr. Johnson's House Trust and open to the public, it contains several of the writer's personal belongings, paintings of him and his acquaintances, and a first edition of the *Dictionary*.

JOINT LONDON ADVISORY PANEL. *See* LONDON PRIDE PARTNERSHIP.

JONES, INIGO (1573–1652). The spread of Palladianism in England during the early 17th century was largely due to Jones's influence, which was strongly felt in London. The son of an impoverished cloth worker, also named Inigo, Jones was baptized at the Church of St. Bartholomew the Less in Smithfield, but further information about his early years is limited. There is some evidence that he worked for a while as a joiner's apprentice and that he showed some skill as an artist. By 1604, he had certainly visited Italy (probably financed by William Herbert, Earl of Pembroke, who had learned of his ability as a landscape painter) and attracted the patronage of King Christian IV of Denmark. Christian's sister, Anne, wife of King James VI and I, introduced him to the London court, where he designed the scenery and costumes for a series of masques, the words for which were very often written by **Ben Jonson**. He also worked for the Earl of Salisbury, for whom he designed his first building, the New Exchange (now demolished) in the **Strand**. In 1610, he was appointed Surveyor of Works to Henry, Prince of Wales, then, five years later, became Surveyor to the King.

In 1613, Jones made a second journey to Italy, where he studied the works of the country's greatest architects, including Andrea Palladio (1508–80), who had revived classical styles. When he returned to London the following year, he introduced these ideas into his plans for the **Queen's House** at **Greenwich** (1616–35) and, more particularly, at the **Banqueting House** (1619–22), which is regarded as his masterpiece. Faced with **Portland stone**, which Jones introduced to London **architecture** (possibly because Palladio had used light-colored exteriors in his Italian structures), the Banqueting House marked the beginning of the King's redesign of the **Whitehall** area and consists of a single chamber standing above a vaulted crypt. It has only two facades, suggesting that it was originally designed as part of a much larger palace.

Of Jones's other buildings, only the Queen's Chapel at **St. James's Palace** remains intact, but the architect's influence is clearly evident elsewhere in the city and notably at **Covent Garden**, where he introduced London to the formally planned town square (1630). From 1633 to 1642, he worked on **St. Paul's Cathedral**; his repairs to the nave and his replacement to the west front of the church were destroyed in the **Great Fire** of 1666, but scholars believe that the designs helped to shape **Christopher Wren**'s work on **City of London** churches. He died, unmarried, on 21 June 1652 and was buried in **St. Benet's Church, Paul's Wharf**, which was also destroyed in the 1666 fire, but his Renaissance style dominated English building practices until the middle of the 18th century. (*See also* SYON HOUSE.)

JONSON, BEN (1572–1637). The most important Jacobean playwright after **William Shakespeare**, Jonson is best known for his comedies, particularly *Every Man in His Humour* (1598), *Volpone* (1606), *The Alchemist* (1610), and *Bartholomew Fair* (1614). The son of a clergyman (who died two months before Jonson was born on 11 June 1572), he was educated at Westminster School, spent some months working as a bricklayer, then fought with the English forces in Flanders. By 1592, he was back in London and, by 1595, was working in the **theater** trade. In 1597, he was writing for **Philip Henslowe**, the most important playhouse proprietor of the day, and, in 1598, had a major success with *Every Man in His Humour*, which was given its first performance by the Lord Chamberlain's Company at the **Globe Theatre**, with Shakespeare in the cast.

Jonson's fame was such that, in 1603, the new King, James VI and I, commissioned him to provide entertainment for the court as it stayed at Althorpe during its journey from Edinburgh to London. Such events usually took the form of masques, relatively simple affairs in which players danced and sang for the audience. Jonson, however, made them much more extravagant, introducing dialogue and dramatic action, employing sumptuous costumes, and using complicated scenic effects designed by **Inigo Jones**. Enticed by the novelty, people flocked to the performances and lauded the author, praising him for his characterization and his skillfully composed plots.

However, although the public acclaimed him, he was constantly in trouble. In 1597, he was imprisoned because of his involvement in a production of *The Mask of Dogs*, which the courts considered seditious. The following year, he killed actor Gabriel Spencer in a duel fought at **Shoreditch** and escaped being hanged only by pleading benefit of clergy (the ability to read the Latin Bible). He got into trouble again in 1603 when his classical tragedy, *Sojanus*, was considered treasonable and, in 1604, when *Eastward Ho!*, to which he had contributed, was condemned for its anti-Scottish sentiment. Such a boisterous lifestyle, lived on the edge of the law, earned the condemnation of many upright citizens but made him a role model for young artists, particularly writers (including Robert Herrick and Richard Lovelace) who gathered at the Mermaid Tavern in **Cheapside** and were later to become known as the Cavalier Poets.

In 1618–19, Jonson embarked on a walking tour to Scotland and was made an Honorary Burgess of Edinburgh but, by that time, his powers and popularity were waning. Plays such as *The Staple of News* (1625), although still demonstrating his mastery of language, had only moderate success and, from 1627, the court masques were organized by other writers. In 1628, he suffered a stroke, after which he was virtually confined to his house until his death on 6 August 1637. In his last years, he was a poor man. At one point, the Dean of Westminster Abbey asked if he could help. Jonson allegedly responded by telling him that "Six feet long by two feet wide is too much for me. Two feet by two feet will do for all I want," so he was buried upright in Poet's Corner (*see* **Westminster Abbey**). The epitaph on his tombstone reads simply "O Rare Ben Jonson." (*See also* BANQUETING HOUSE; BLACKFRIARS.)

– K –

KEATS'S HOUSE. In 1818, poet John Keats was invited to move into a house at Wentworth Place, **Hampstead**, by fellow writer Charles Armitage Brown. During his two years there, he wrote much of his best work, including *Ode to a Nightingale*, which was inspired by a bird singing in the garden. In 1819, Fanny Brawne, Keats's fiancée, moved into the adjoining cottage with her widowed mother, but the two never married because, in 1821, the poet died, at only 25 years of age, of tuberculosis in Rome. Both properties were purchased in 1838–39 by Eliza Chester, a retired actress, who converted them into one unit and added a drawing room on the east end of the building. Restoration work was carried out in 1974–75 and major structural repairs in 1998. The house is open daily as a **museum** displaying some of Keats's personal effects, including letters.

KELMSCOTT PRESS. In 1891, William Morris founded the Kelmscott Press close to Kelmscott House, his **Hammersmith** home. Convinced that a return to the values and practices of the past would improve society and that workers should strive for the highest standards of craftsmanship, he commissioned handmade paper like that used in the 15th century and designed three new type faces (Chaucer, Golden, and Troy) for use with dark inks. Books were pressed and bound by hand. Over the next seven years, Kelmscott published 53 titles in 66 volumes, the best known of which is *The Works of Geoffrey Chaucer*, which appeared in 1896. The quality of the publications greatly influenced competing printers, leading to considerable improvements in design and production. (*See also* WILLIAM MORRIS GALLERY.)

KENNINGTON. An inner-city suburb lying some two miles southeast of **Charing Cross**, Kennington benefited from royal patronage during the Medieval period (Edward the Black Prince, son of King Edward III, had a palace there during the 14th century, for example) and the Prince of Wales is still ground landlord in several parts of the area. It remained a village until well into the 18th century, but improvements in **transport**, such as the opening of **Westminster Bridge** in 1750, led to urban development during later Georgian and Victorian times (many of the terraces built then still survive, notably in Cleaver Square, Kennington Road, and Kennington Park Road). Kennington Park, formerly a 20-acre common, was the principal place of execution for the County of Surrey (several supporters of the Second Jacobite Rebellion, in 1745–46, were hanged, drawn, and quartered there) and, from the 17th until the 19th centuries, it was an important meeting place for religious and political groups (John Wesley, cofounder of the Methodist Church, preached to congregations of over 50,000). From 1818, however, it was eroded by road improvements, church building, and other developments; the remnant that survives provides sports and recreational facilities in a part of the city otherwise lacking such amenities. The area was incorporated within the **London Borough of Lambeth** when London's **local government** was reorganized in 1965. (*See also* OVAL, THE.)

KENSAL GREEN. The Kensal Green suburb, five miles northeast of **Charing Cross**, developed after the first of London's commercial **burial grounds** was laid out by J. W. Griffiths on a 54-acre site in 1833 (39 acres were allocated to adherents of the Church of England, the rest to nonconformists). Built to relieve pressure on overcrowded church properties, the burial ground became fashionable after the Duke of Sussex and Princess Sophia, son and daughter of King George III, were interred in 1843 and 1848 respectively. Actor Charles Kemble (1854), engineer Isambard Kingdom Brunel (1859), and writers W. M. Thackeray (1863), Anthony Trollope (1882), and Wilkie Collins (1889) all followed over the next 50 years. Several of the terraced streets built at the time still survive, but many of the larger properties (including Kensal Lodge, where W. Harrison Ainsworth entertained fellow novelist **Charles Dickens** and other literary figures) have been demolished. Kensal Green was incorporated within the **London Borough of Brent** when **local government** in the city was reorganized in 1965.

KENSINGTON. Kensington lies about three miles west of **Charing Cross** on land that rises from the north bank of the **River Thames**. It is first mentioned as Chenesit (or Cynesige's estate) in William the Conqueror's Domesday survey of England, carried out in 1085–86. During the Medieval period, the land was increasingly used for agriculture and, by the late 16th century, was supplying hay and vegetables to the London market, then, from about 1600, courtiers and merchants built large mansions in the area, attracted by the advantages of large estates relatively close to the city (*see*, for example, **Holland House**). After 1689, when King William III instructed **Christopher Wren** to convert Nottingham House into **Kensington Palace**, the immigration intensified, with the royal court attracting aristocratic neighbors and providing a market for local traders, but the most significant rise occurred during the 19th century, with the resident population leaping from 8,556 in 1801 to 176,628 in 1901 as rural estates were leased or sold to developers. In addition, land originally acquired for the **Great Exhibition** of 1851 was used to provide space for a variety of national educational institutions, including the **Victoria and Albert Museum** (established at its present site in 1857), the **Royal College of Art** (1863), the **Natural History Museum** (1881), and the **Royal College of Music** (1883). These, in turn, attracted numerous private schools, which have continued to flourish, and shopping facilities, along with other service-oriented businesses, opened to cater to the newcomers. In the 20th century, the trend continued, with an important retail focus developing in Kensington High Street, former family homes converted into **hotels** and rented apartments, and foreign governments purchasing properties for use as embassies. In 1901, Queen Victoria (who had been born at Kensington Palace) granted the area the title of Royal Borough, then, when **local government** was reorganized in

1965, it was incorporated within the **Royal Borough of Kensington and Chelsea**. (*See also* ALBERT HALL; ALBERT MEMORIAL; DIANA, PRINCESS OF WALES; KENSINGTON GARDENS.)

KENSINGTON AND CHELSEA, ROYAL BOROUGH OF. The borough was formed in 1965 through the amalgamation of previously independent authorities. It covers an area of about 4.5 square miles, stretching from the **River Thames** north to the **London Borough of Brent** and from the **London Borough of Westminster** in the east to the **London Borough of Hammersmith and Fulham** in the west. In 1901, **Kensington**, which forms the northern half of the borough, was granted the title of Royal Borough by Queen Victoria, but associations with the monarchy go back to 1689, when King William III bought a country house and commissioned **Christopher Wren** to convert it into **Kensington Palace** (where Victoria was born in 1819). Partly because it has long been populated by aristocrats, who built substantial residences, about 70 percent of the borough is covered by conservation area legislation, which restricts redevelopment but promotes **tourism**. Some 10,000 firms provide employment in the leisure industry (including **hotels**, which provide about 14 percent of all bed spaces available to London's visitors), manufacturing (and associated distribution facilities), pharmaceuticals and cosmetics, and media services. Together, these companies generate about 86,000 jobs, of which one-quarter are filled by local people. The resident population in 1998 numbered 169,900. Nearly half of all households were made up of single people and accommodation was more expensive than anywhere else in the country (in 2000, the average cost of a home was £491,354, compared with £71,749 in Northern Ireland). The Borough Council is dominated by the Conservative Party, but there is strong minority representation by Labour Party voters both in working-class and in middle-class areas. (*See also* CARLYLE'S HOUSE; CHELSEA; CHELSEA PHYSIC GARDEN; COMMONWEALTH INSTITUTE; GEOLOGICAL MUSEUM; HARRODS; HOLLAND HOUSE; KENSINGTON GARDENS; NATIONAL ARMY MUSEUM: NATURAL HISTORY MUSEUM; VICTORIA AND ALBERT MUSEUM.)

KENSINGTON GARDENS. The gardens, covering 275 acres and lying immediately to the west of **Hyde Park**, were originally part of the private grounds of **Kensington Palace**, but King George II (who reigned from 1727 to 1760) opened them for public use on Saturdays when the royal family was not in residence. The Round Pond (now a popular place for sailing model boats) was built in 1728, access was extended in the 1830s by King William IV, a flower walk was laid out towards the southern edge of the estate in 1843, then, from the 1860s, the Victorians and Edwardians used the **park** to indulge a passion for statues. The **Albert Memorial** was erected in 1863, a granite obelisk commemorating John Hanning Speke's identification of the source of the River Nile was built the following year, and sculptures of Queen Victoria and William III were added in 1893 and 1907 respectively. A representation of Physical Energy (by G. F. Watts) was completed in 1904, but children (including those of advancing years) are much more likely to be captivated by George Frampton's whimsical bronze of Peter Pan (the little boy who never grew up, created by author J. M. Barrie), which was placed near the **Serpentine** in 1912, and the tree trunk, carved with small animals by Ivor Innes, located in the playground at the northern end of Broad Walk in 1928. In summer, the park is a popular place for kite flying and puppet shows. It is also a haunt of one of Britain's endangered species—the nanny, wearing sensible shoes and conservative dress, who pushes an infant in a perambulator and trails an older brother or sister at her heels; their concentration in the park reflects the suitability of the habitat, a large diplomatic community in nearby **Knightsbridge**. The gardens are still owned by the Crown and are maintained by the **Royal Parks** Agency.

KENSINGTON PALACE. Originally a country mansion, the palace, located in the southwest corner of **Kensington Gardens**, has experienced several phases of development. The first building on the site was erected early in the 17th century by Sir George Coppin and purchased in 1689 by King William III, who instructed **Christopher Wren** to supervise its extension. Following the death of his wife, Queen Mary, at the house in 1694, the King (who disliked central London, where the **air pollution** exacerbated his asthmatic condition) became increasingly attached to the place, lavishing much attention on the landscaping of the gardens. After suffering serious injuries when he fell from his horse at **Hampton Court Palace** in 1702, he begged to be taken back so that he, too, could die there. In 1714, Queen Anne—his sister-in-law and successor—also passed away at **Kensington** (a result of apoplexy caused by overeating). She had treated the residence as a pleasant country escape, but King George I wanted greater comfort and a building more in keeping with his royal status, with new state rooms, improved kitchen facilities, and additional courtyards built in 1718. George II made Kensington his main residence, but George III, who succeeded him in 1760, preferred a home nearer the corridors of power.

Since that time, no reigning monarch has lived at the palace, but it has been much used by other members of the royal family. Queen Victoria was born in a ground floor room in 1819 and held her first Privy Council meeting in the Red Saloon in 1837. In 1867, Princess Mary Adelaide gave birth to a daughter, also Mary, who was to become the consort of King George V, and, in recent years, Prince Charles, **Diana, Princess of Wales**, Princess Margaret, the Duke and Duchess of Gloucester, Princess Alice, the Duke and Duchess of Kent, and Prince and Princess Michael of Kent have all had homes there (it is Princess Margaret's principal residence). Victoria opened the state apartments (designed by Colen Campbell and decorated by William Kent) to the public in 1889; access to further rooms (including Queen Victoria's bedroom and nursery) was granted in 1933. There is an exhibition of court dress as well as numerous mementoes of Victoria's reign. Press reports in 1998 suggested that Queen Elizabeth II wanted to turn the whole building into a gallery, holding paintings from the royal collection (which is currently scattered at sites around the country) as a memorial to Princess Diana. The public would be charged for entry and the money used to reduce the royal family's dependence on state funds to run other palaces. (*See also* HAWKSMOOR, NICHOLAS.)

KENTISH TOWN. The village of Kentish Town grew around a daughter chapel of **St. Pancras** Church, which was built, in 1449, on a major routeway out of London to the north. Some three miles from **Charing Cross** and outside the urban area of the **City of London**, it developed a reputation as a healthy place to live, so wealthy families erected country houses in which to entertain their friends. Around the end of the 18th century, however, the pace of construction accelerated and the area was transformed from a small agricultural settlement into a desirable London suburb. For 70 years, it maintained its status but, in the 1860s, the arrival of the Midland **Railway**, with its attendant smoke and grime, encouraged most of the affluent residents to leave. The railway company bought large areas of land for sheds and sidings, craftsmen opened small industrial premises, and laborers flooded in to find jobs, turning the community into a typically poor working-class district. During the 20th century, the social composition of the area has changed little, with many properties subdivided to provide efficiency apartments for students and others needing cheap accommodation. Kentish Town was incorporated within the **London Borough of Camden** when London's **local government** was reorganized in 1965.

KENWOOD HOUSE. One of **Robert Adam**'s finest works, Kenwood lies in wooded **park** land at the northern fringe of **Hampstead Heath**. The first building on the site was erected in 1616, but the present structure dates from 1764, when William Murray (Attorney General and later Lord Chief Justice) commissioned Adam, then a very fashionable architect, to remodel the property. When Murray died in 1793, the estate passed to David Murray, his nephew, who added wings (of white Suffolk brick) designed by George Saunders. The property was retained by the family until 1922, when the Kenwood Preservation Council purchased 120 acres to prevent building developments and vested the land in the **London County Council (LCC)**. In 1924, Edward, Lord Iveagh, bought the house and remaining grounds. Upon his death, three years later, the building (which housed an extensive art collection) and the parks also passed into LCC hands. The whole area is now managed by English Heritage, established by the government in 1983 to preserve historic buildings and enhance public enjoyment of them. The north frontage of the house is a stucco block with a portico, surmounted by a pediment, rising to the top of the building. Inside, the major architectural feature is the library, which has a tunnel vaulted ceiling painted by Antonio Zucchi, but there is also a collection of paintings, donated by Lord Iveagh in 1927 and including works by Thomas Gainsborough, Rembrandt, and Joshua Reynolds. The estate, landscaped by William Murray, includes a lakeside concert venue.

KETCH, JACK. In 1685, Jack Ketch bungled the execution of the Duke of Monmouth, failing to sever the unfortunate aristocrat's head even with five blows of his axe and ultimately sawing it off with a knife. After that incident, all London executioners were known in the vernacular as Jack Ketch.

KEW. A fashionable, middle-class suburb on the south bank of the **River Thames** about seven miles west of **Charing Cross**, Kew was probably settled before the Roman invasion of Britain in 43 A.D. Its status, however, dates from the 16th century, when its accessibility by boat and its proximity to **Richmond Palace** made it an attractive location for the homes of the aristocracy (Mary Tudor, sister of King Henry VIII, had a house there, for example). Queen Anne donated the site for St. Anne's

Church, which was built on Kew Green in 1710–14 (but extended in 1770, 1836, and 1884), and that encouraged further construction during the 18th century, as did the erection of a wooden **bridge** across the Thames to Gunnersbury in 1758–59. (A structure of Purbeck stone replaced that edifice in 1784–89 and it, in turn, was superseded by the present granite bridge, opened in 1903). In 1869, the London and South Western **Railway** also built a link across the river, using a lattice girder bridge set on cast iron piers; that added to the pressures on land for development, but Kew retained its essentially residential nature, partly because so much of the open space was owned by the Crown. The modern focus of the area is the **Royal Botanic Gardens**, which were established by Princess Augusta (widow of Frederick, son of King George II) and donated to the nation by Queen Victoria in 1841. Nearby, in a 1970s building in Ruskin Avenue, many of the documents relating to the history of Britain are stored in the **Public Record Office**, which makes its archives available to researchers.

KEW BRIDGE MUSEUM. *See* BRENTFORD.

KEW GARDENS. *See* ROYAL BOTANIC GARDENS.

KEW PALACE. *See* ROYAL BOTANIC GARDENS.

KIDBROOKE. For much of the Medieval period, a small village thrived at Kidbrooke, some five miles southeast of **Charing Cross**. However, by the end of the 15th century—and for reasons still unclear—it had been abandoned, its church derelict. From then until the 1930s, when suburban development spread outwards from the metropolitan area (aided by improvements in the road from central London to the port of Dover, on the English Channel), a small population earned a living from farming. The area, incorporated within the **London Borough of Lewisham** in 1965, is now predominantly residential, with a mixture of local authority and private **housing** developments.

KILBURN. A largely working-class residential suburb within the **London Borough of Brent**, Kilburn lies some four miles northwest of **Charing Cross** alongside Watling Street, built by the Romans to connect Dubris (now Dover) with Verulamium (now St. Albans). Even by the early Medieval period, the well-travelled road had attracted settlement, including a priory (established in 1130), inns, and lodging houses. From 1742, the

Bell Tavern (which had been functioning since about 1600) capitalized on Georgian tastes by encouraging affluent Londoners to venture out and taste the bitter, milky waters diverted from a local spring into its pump room, but the establishment of a **railway** connection with **Euston Station** in 1852 resulted in construction of houses for less wealthy commuters. The opening of Brondesbury Station (on the North London Railway) in 1860 and the arrival of the Metropolitan Line (now part of the **London Underground** system) in 1879 added impetus to that development, increasing the population and thus fuelling demand for shops and other services along Edgware Road (which follows the line of Watling Street); the Gaumont State Cinema (built to designs by George Coles, which included a tower and a richly decorated foyer) was the largest movie theater in Europe when it opened in 1937. During the 20th century, many of the houses were subdivided into single-room apartments, which became popular with Irish **immigrants** seeking cheap accommodation. The cinema, too, has changed, now serving as a bingo hall.

KING'S CROSS. King's Cross lies at the edge of central London, about 1.5 miles north of **Charing Cross**. Until the early 19th century, it was the site of a small village, known as Battle Bridge, located beside the **Fleet River**. During the 18th century, the settlement was renowned as a spa, attracting hundreds of visitors every week. Also, in 1746 it became the site of a hospital for victims of smallpox, then one of the major deadly diseases in the city. In 1836, a memorial to King George IV was erected at the junction of Euston Road, Gray's Inn Road, Pentonville Road, and St. Pancras Road. Designed by Stephen Geary, it incorporated a statue of the monarch atop a pillar. The column, 60 feet high, stood on an octagonal base and was guarded by replicas of Britain's four patron saints (St. Andrew for Scotland, St. David for Wales, St. George for England, and St. Patrick for Ireland). Initially, the base was used as a police station, but later it was converted into a **public house**. Public reaction to the structure was so negative that it was removed in 1842–45. In 1851–52, the Great Northern Railway built its terminus on the site of the hospital (*see* **King's Cross Station**), greatly affecting local land uses. **Hotels**, cafeterias, boarding houses, small shops, and other businesses were established to provide services for travellers and still dominate the local economic scene. The area was included within the **London Borough of Camden** when **local government** in the metropolitan area was reorganized in 1965. (*See also* KING'S CROSS FIRE.)

KING'S CROSS FIRE. At about 7:30 on the evening of 18 November 1987, towards the end of the rush hour, a fire broke out underneath one of the escalators connecting **King's Cross Station** with **London Underground**'s Piccadilly Line. The fire burned for about 15 minutes, then swelled quickly into a major conflagration, sending a ball of flame up the escalator to the ticket hall. Emergency procedures proved inadequate as escalators carried people to the heart of the blaze, trains disembarked passengers onto smoke-filled platforms, and station staff were unable to evacuate tunnels. As a result, 31 people died. Twenty firemen (including one who was killed) received commendations for bravery. Following the tragedy, a public inquiry heard evidence over a period of 91 days, concluding that the cause was probably a cigarette, dropped by a passenger, which fell on grease-impregnated dirt, spawning flames that spread to the timber of the escalator. The members made 150 safety recommendations and the Underground banned smoking throughout the system. Litigation continued in the courts for many years: in 1996, for example, a guitarist who was unable to resume his career satisfactorily won damages totalling £650,000.

KING'S CROSS STATION. When the station was opened on the site of the Whittington Smallpox Hospital at **King's Cross** in 1852, it was the largest **railway** terminus in the country. Built by the Great Northern Railway, it was planned by Lewis Cubitt (younger brother of **Thomas Cubitt**), who prepared a design that, he said, depended for its effect "on the largeness of some of its features, its fitness for its purpose, and its characteristic expression of that purpose." The result was a widely admired building consisting of two train sheds (each 800 feet long and 105 feet wide) that had a yellow brick frontage at the south end. Underneath one of the platforms, there was stabling for the 300 horses that delivered goods to and from the station (the granary held 60,000 sacks of corn) and the coal stores held 150,000 tons of fuel for the steam engines. In 1973, major reconstruction work was completed on the concourse, providing modern shops and ticket offices, with improved access to the **London Underground** system, but the essence of the Victorian structure is still evident. Most services from the station connect London to the suburbs north of the city, the east coast of England, and Scotland. (*See also* KING'S CROSS FIRE.)

KING'S ROAD. King's Road runs for 2.5 miles from **Belgravia** to **Fulham**, forming the main routeway through **Chelsea**. Until 1830, it was a private thoroughfare, allowing King Charles II access to **Hampton Court Palace** and King George III to his residence at **Kew** (*see* **Royal Botanic Gardens**). Although some 18th-century residential properties remain (as at Nos. 211–15, which were built during the 1720s), the street is now best known for its fashionable boutiques, **public houses**, and restaurants.

KINGSTON BRIDGE. The present **bridge** connecting **Kingston Upon Thames** (on the east bank of the **River Thames**) to Hampton Wick (on the west) was built of brick, faced with stone, in 1825–58. However, the crossing, some 12 miles southwest of central London, was in use at least by 1193, when William de Coventry was appointed Master of the Bridge. Because it and **London Bridge** provided the only roads over the Thames until the 18th century, Kingston Bridge became a focus of land routes and therefore contributed significantly to the growth of settlement in the area. The remains of that medieval structure have been incorporated in the John Lewis Department Store. The London and South Western **Railway** constructed a cast iron bridge a few yards downriver, in 1860–63, to provide a connection between Kingston and **Twickenham**. It was superseded, in 1907, by a replacement made of steel.

KINGSTON UPON THAMES. Kingston lies on the east bank of the **River Thames** some 10 miles southwest of **Charing Cross**. It was settled during Saxon times (when it was the site of crowning ceremonies for seven monarchs, including Edward the Elder, son of Alfred the Great, in 900 A.D.) but became particularly important in the Medieval period because it provided the first crossing upriver from **London Bridge**. The settlement benefited from its location close to several royal residences, such as **Hampton Court Palace** and **Nonsuch Palace**, but also developed an important **market** because it was a natural focus of land and river transport routes. Ancillary industries, such as boat building, brewing, and milling, provided additional sources of income and diversified the local economy. When **Putney Bridge** opened in 1729, Kingston lost some of its traffic, but it retained its regional influence and is still a significant market town with other employment in aviation, chemicals, engineering, plastics, and printing. Although the central area has been redeveloped, much of the medieval street pattern has been preserved and the **architecture** dates from the 15th century. (*See also* KINGSTON UPON THAMES, ROYAL BOROUGH OF.)

KINGSTON UPON THAMES, ROYAL BOROUGH OF. The Borough of Kingston Upon Thames was formed in 1965 through the amalgamation of the formerly independent authorities of **Kingston Upon Thames**, Malden and Coombe, and **Surbiton**, all of which were previously located in the County of Surrey. Its regal prefix, originally earned through the 30 royal charters awarded to Kingston between 1200 and 1685, was confirmed by Queen Elizabeth II. Covering some 12 square miles, it stretches from **Richmond Park** in the north to Ashtead Common in the south and from the **River Thames** in the west to Motspur Park in the east. Although most of the land is devoted to residential uses, the construction of a relief road around Kingston in 1989 helped to reduce traffic congestion and attracted several large stores to the area. These were augmented, during the 1990s, by the expansion of the Eden Walk shopping center into one of the largest retail complexes in southeast England. The local authority and the University of Kingston are major employers, but the opening of seven business parks has attracted several multinational companies, including Samsung Electronics and Nikon, adding to the range of clerical and manufacturing jobs. In 1998, the borough had a population of 147,300, the smallest of all the London authorities. (*See also* CHESSINGTON; WORCESTER PARK.)

KNIGHTSBRIDGE. Knightsbridge runs for three-quarters of a mile along the south side of **Hyde Park** from Kensington Road to **Hyde Park Corner**, taking its name from a bridge across a tributary of the **River Thames** where, according to legend, two knights fought a battle to the death. It was developed during London's 19th-century expansion and now has a variety of land uses, including **hotels**, offices, and apartments. In 1998, house prices in some postal districts were the highest in the United Kingdom, averaging £530,484 in part of the SW7 area. Knightsbridge Barracks are the headquarters of the Household Cavalry (*see* **Household Division**), with stabling for nearly 300 horses and the same number of men. The barracks was established in the late 18th century, but the modern buildings, designed by Basil Spence (who prepared the plans for Coventry Cathedral), were erected in 1966. The area was included in the **City of Westminster** when London **local government** was reshaped in 1965.

KNIGHTS HOSPITALLER. The Hospitallers (also known as the Knights of Malta, the Knights Hospitaller of St. John of Jerusalem, and the Most Venerable Order of the Hospital of St. John of Jerusalem) were established in the 11th century as a religious community dedicated to caring for the sick. In London, it was based at the Priory of St. John of Jerusalem in **Clerkenwell**, where travellers could seek temporary shelter. The property was destroyed in 1381, during the **Peasants' Revolt**, but reerected shortly afterwards, incorporating a church (now known as St. John, Clerkenwell), which was famed for its soaring bell tower. In 1536–41, when the **monasteries** in England were dissolved, many of the Knights fled, leaving the church to King Henry VIII, who used it to store the tents he needed when hunting. In 1547–50, much of the stone was removed to build **Somerset House**, and by the 18th century most of the Priory had vanished. The chapel chancel survived, however, despite serving at various times as a playhouse, a private place of worship for Lord Burleigh, and a nonconformist meeting hall. It was repaired in 1721–23 and became a parish church before being returned to the Hospitallers in 1929. During the **Blitz**, it was damaged by German bombs but restored, under the supervision of Lord Mottistone, after the Second World War. The Priory Gatehouse, built of Kentish ragstone and erected in 1504, also escaped demolition. Its rooms provided offices for Queen Elizabeth I's Master of the Revels in the 16th century, a **coffee house** during the late 17th century, and a printing works (where **Samuel Johnson** was provided with writing accommodation) in the 18th century. It was reacquired in 1874 by the Knights and now houses a **museum** of exhibits describing the order's history (St. John's Ambulance Brigade, founded in the Gatehouse in 1877, has more than 250,000 members around the world). The suburb of **St. John's Wood** is built on formerly forested land owned by the Hospitallers prior to the Reformation. (*See also* KNIGHTS TEMPLAR.)

KNIGHTS OF MALTA. *See* KNIGHTS HOSPITALLER.

KNIGHTS TEMPLAR. The Order of the Knights Templars was formed in 1119 to defend pilgrims travelling to the Holy Land. Initially, it had provincial headquarters near **Chancery Lane** but, in 1165, it moved to a new site on the north bank of the **River Thames**, three-quarters of a mile east of **Charing Cross**, where it built a circular church (some scholars claim that the design was chosen in honor of the Church of the Holy Sepulchre in Jerusalem, others that the Dome of the Rock, in the same city, was a more likely model). In the early 14th century, members were accused of irreligious practices, the order was dissolved (1312), and its property in London was acquired by arch rival the **Knights Hospitaller**, which leased the land to lawyers. The site is now occupied by the Inner and Middle Temples of the **Inns of Court**. (*See* TEMPLE BAR; TEMPLE CHURCH.)

KRAY TWINS. During the 1960s, London's criminal underworld was organized by a small number of gangs, each of which controlled a geographical area. In the **East End** of the city, the principal figures were twins Reginald and Ronald Kray, who ran a protection racket, enforced by violence, while maintaining a public image of respectable businessmen who contributed to local charities. Police investigations of their activities were hampered by threats to potential witnesses, but, eventually, some associates agreed to give evidence in return for their own freedom. In January 1969, the Krays and several of their closest henchmen were put on trial at the **Central Criminal Court**. Ronnie was sentenced to life imprisonment for the shooting of George Cornell (a member of the Richardson gang, which was based in south London) at the Blind Beggar public house in **Whitechapel** in March 1966. Reggie, found guilty of being an associate, was jailed for 10 years. In addition, both were imprisoned for life (with the judge's recommendation that they serve at least 30 years) for the murder of Jack McVitie, a small-time criminal who was stabbed to death in a basement flat in **Stoke Newington** in October 1966. In 1979, Ronnie, a homosexual with a history of mental problems, was certified insane. He died in Broadmoor maximum security psychiatric hospital on 17 March 1995 (over 60,000 people lined the streets of east London to watch the funeral procession). His brother was released, on compassionate grounds five years later, when doctors discovered that he was suffering from terminal cancer of the bladder, and passed away in his sleep at a hotel in Thorpe St. Andrew, near Norwich, on 1 October 2000.

– L –

LAMBETH. Lambeth lies on the east bank of the **River Thames** between **Waterloo** and **Clapham**. Until the early 18th century, it was largely marshland though a few industrial premises were located in the area, notably the Vauxhall plate glass works, a factory making **Coade stone**, and a pottery producing tin-glazed earthenware. After the opening of **Westminster Bridge** facilitated access in 1750, industrial activity increased (the Doulton and Watts porcelain company was founded in 1815, for instance) and houses were built to accommodate the inflow of workers.

Following the Second World War, most of the poorer-quality residential developments were replaced by local authority **housing** estates and manufacturing gave way to offices. In 1965, when the capital's **local government** was reformed, the area gave its name to the **London Borough of Lambeth**. (*See also* BEDLAM; LAMBETH BRIDGE; LAMBETH PALACE; LAMBETH WALK.)

LAMBETH, LONDON BOROUGH OF. Formed in 1965 through the amalgamation of **Clapham**, **Lambeth**, and **Streatham**, the borough covers some 11 square miles. Shaped like a trapezium, it stretches for seven miles from the **River Thames** in the north to Streatham Vale in the south but at its broadest (between Streatham and West Norwood) is only three miles wide. Close to the Thames, commercial and administrative interests have pushed out residential land uses, with government offices, the **South Bank** arts complex, and the transport hub of **Waterloo** Railway Station using most of the space. Elsewhere, extensive undeveloped areas provide facilities for recreation, notably on the commons at Clapham, Streatham, and Tooting Bec. Over most of the borough, however, **housing** dominates, much of it (in suburbs such as **Brixton** and **Vauxhall**) small apartments rented by individuals and families with low incomes. Deprivation levels are high; 37 percent of homes (nearly twice the London average) are provided by the local authority, for example, and over half of all households consist of single people or single-parent families. In addition, about one in three of the resident population belongs to an ethnic minority, usually black Caribbean. The population (1998) is approximately 269,500. (*See also* CARDBOARD CITY; DENMARK HILL; GIPSY HILL; HERNE HILL; KENNINGTON; OVAL, THE; TULSE HILL; WANDSWORTH, LONDON BOROUGH OF.)

LAMBETH BRIDGE. The first **bridge** to cross the river between **Lambeth** (on the east bank) and **Westminster** (on the west) was opened in 1862 at a site that had been used by ferrymen from at least 1513 until 1750. The suspension design, with three 268-foot spans, was proposed by P. W. Barlow. In 1932, it was replaced by the present five-span steel arch structure, built to plans prepared by George Humphreys.

LAMBETH CONFERENCE. *See* LAMBETH PALACE.

LAMBETH PALACE. The palace is the official residence of the Archbishop of Canterbury, ecclesiastical head of the Church of England. One of very few domestic buildings surviving in London from the Medieval period, it was originally constructed in the early 13th century but was extended and renovated on several occasions, notably in 1434–35 (when the Lollards' Tower was built to improve water supplies), 1486–1501 (when a gatehouse was erected), 1553 (when Queen Mary authorized a refurbishment), the 1630s (when Archbishop Laud renovated the chapel), the 1660s (when the Great Hall and the Guard Room were rebuilt), and 1828–34 (when Edward Blore added offices and redesigned the living quarters). The first primate to occupy the palace was Stephen Langton (whose consecration as Archbishop in 1207 precipitated a crisis between King John and Pope Innocent III). John Wyclife was called to the chapel to defend himself against charges of heresy in 1377, Wat Tyler's supporters burned furnishings and beheaded the Archbishop during the **Peasants' Revolt** in 1381, Thomas More was taken to the guard room and questioned about his refusal to accept King Henry VIII as head of the Church in 1534, and during the **Gordon Riots** in 1780 the building was placed under siege. In 1610, Archbishop Bancroft bequeathed his books to his successors, forming the nucleus of an extensive library that includes manuscripts dating from the ninth century.

Since 1867, the Bishops of the Church of England have met at irregular intervals to debate matters of common interest at the Lambeth Conference. The 1888 convention accepted four matters of principle (known as the Lambeth Quadrilateral) to be used as the basis for discussions about union with other Christian groups; three of these (acceptance of the Holy Scripture as the rule of faith, of the Apostles' and Nicene Creeds, and of the sacraments of baptism and the Lord's Supper) have caused few problems, but most Protestant denominations have proved unwilling to adopt an episcopacy, as required by the fourth principle. In 1900, nine acres of the palace grounds were donated to the **London County Council** for use as a public **park**, providing a significant area of green space in a largely developed area of the inner city.

LAMBETH WALK. Lambeth Walk, which parallels the course of the **River Thames** for about half a mile in the **London Borough of Lambeth**, gives its name to a dance supposedly representing the strutting walk of the local **Cockneys**. Performed with walking steps in march time, it was first popularized in 1937 by Lupino Lane in the musical *Me and My Gal* and, according to young people of the time, was often used in dance halls as a relatively gentle item to follow the more exhausting jitterbug. The street had a popular **market**, established during the early

19th century, and was renowned for its stoicism during the worst days of the **Blitz**.

LANCASTER HOUSE. The foundations of the house, in Stable Yard on the west side of **St. James's Palace**, were laid in 1825 and building begun to designs prepared by Benjamin Wyatt for Frederick, Duke of York (of nursery rhyme fame). The structure (originally named York House) was still unfinished when the Duke died, deeply in debt, two years later, so the government took over the mortgage and leased the property to the Marquess of Stafford (the income from the deal was used to purchase ground for **Victoria Park** in the **East End**). When the Marquess passed away in 1833 (shortly after being created first Duke of Sutherland), the building was still incomplete, so the second Duke commissioned Wyatt to plan the interior, with **Charles Barry** hired as adviser and Robert Smirke appointed to implement the proposals. The exterior of the building was plain—a three-story rectangle of Bath stone with a simple, two-story Corinthian portico at the entrance. The inside, however, was ebulliently decorated in the style of Louis XV of France, with a grand staircase rising the full height of the building and lit from a clerestory. For the remainder of the century, York House was one of the pivots of London's social life, with the Sutherlands entertaining the major social reformers of the day, including Lord Shaftesbury (who promoted legislation designed to improve conditions for factory workers) and William Garrison (the American advocate for the abolition of slavery), as well as Queen Victoria (who came with **Prince Albert** and the Duke of Wellington to hear Frédéric Chopin play the piano in 1848). In 1912, the fourth Duke sold the building to industrialist Sir William Lever (later Viscount Leverhulme), who renamed it Lancaster House after his native county and presented it to the nation. Until 1946, it housed the London **Museum** (*see* **Museum of London**) but is now used largely for government conferences and receptions.

LANGHAM HOTEL. The Langham was the first of London's luxury **hotels**. Built in **Portland Place** in 1864–65, it had seven floors reminiscent of a Florentine palace, with 600 rooms decorated in scarlet and gold and mosaic flooring laid by Italian craftsmen. For 80 years, its private suites housed the rich and famous, including Emperors Napoleon III of France and Haile Selassie of Ethiopia, but in 1940, during the **Blitz**, a land mine fractured its 38,000-gallon water tank and flooded the building. The **British Broadcasting Corporation**, which provided radio services from nearby Broadcasting House, later adapted it for use as offices and studios, but in 1991 it returned to its original use as the 350-room Langham Hilton.

LANSBURY, GEORGE (1859–1940). George Lansbury led the Labour Party from 1931 to 1935, campaigning for the rights of the poor and for improvements in the living conditions of citizens in London's **East End**. The son of railwayman George Lansbury and Mary, his Welsh wife, he was born near Lowestoft (Suffolk) on 21 February 1859 but moved to the capital with his family when he was nine, eventually setting up home in **Whitechapel**. At 14, he left school for work in the Great Eastern Railway's coal depot but, in 1890, married the daughter of a local sawmill owner and became a partner in his father-in-law's business. He was deeply influenced by Christian socialist philosophies, taking up the cause of the deprived in local politics, helping to find jobs in rural areas for the urban unemployed, and serving as a member of the Royal Commission on the Poor Laws in 1905–9. He first entered Parliament in 1910, representing **Bow** and Bromley for the Labour Party, but resigned after two years in order to contest the seat as an independent and draw attention to his support for women who demanded the right to vote. He failed to win reelection but continued to espouse the socialist cause, helping to found the *Daily Herald* (the Labour movement's first daily newspaper) in 1912 and defending the rights of conscientious objectors during the First World War.

A man of great charisma, he drew large crowds to hear his speeches, moving listeners with a rhetoric that emphasized the importance of brotherly love as the foundation on which all political action should be based. Turning words into deeds, he led a campaign designed to win financial support for the unemployed, ultimately serving a jail sentence as a result of his activities (*see* **Poplarism**) but returning to the House of Commons (*see* **Palace of Westminster**) in 1922 with great local support.

When Prime Minister Ramsay MacDonald formed his second government in 1929, Lansbury was made Commissioner of Works, approving many projects (such as the construction of the Lido in **Hyde Park**) that brought benefits to London citizens. Following Labour's defeat in the General Election in 1931, he was made Leader of the Party, but his pacifist beliefs were increasingly at odds with the philosophies of the times and, after four years, he gave up the post, unable to approve of the use of force against Italian troops that had invaded Abyssinia. As war clouds darkened over Europe in the late 1930s, he found few who would support his belief that Britain should adopt a policy of disarmament and was politically marginalized. He died in London on 7 May 1940.

LAW COURTS. *See* ROYAL COURTS OF JUSTICE.

LEA, RIVER. The Lea (or Lee) rises in Bedfordshire and flows southwards for 46 miles, through east London, to meet the **River Thames** at **Poplar**. It has long been used for navigation, the Romans employing it as a means of access to Verulamium (now St. Albans) and King Alfred chasing an invading Danish force up it in 896. In 1767, a series of locks was built to improve shipping movements (particularly for vessels carrying cargoes of grain from Hertfordshire and Essex), and during the 19th century it was the focus for many industrial premises, including flour mills at Ponders End and a small arms factory at Enfield Lock. In 1967, a major rehabilitation scheme was introduced in an attempt to reverse the effects of pollution, resulting from centuries of use, by turning the area into a regional **park**. Local authorities have combined to clean up some 2,000 acres along 25 miles of river and construct a chain of reservoirs that supplies London with about one-sixth of its water needs as well as provides facilities for bird watching, fishing, sailing, and other activities. In 2001 the government announced plans to build an £87 million stadium in the park for track and field events. (*See also* STRATFORD.)

LEADENHALL MARKET. Based on the south side of Leadenhall Street, which stretches from **Aldgate** to **Cornhill**, in the **City of London**, Leadenhall **Market** stands on the site of the basilica (or town hall) that marked the center of Roman **Londinium**. It has been offering provisions since the 14th century, when the Neville family allowed people from outside London to sell poultry, cheese, and butter from the grounds of their lead-roofed mansion house. In 1445, a granary was built and the market widened its range of produce, adding goods such as grain and eggs. Later, wool and leather were also made available. The buildings (including the mansion) were destroyed in the **Great Fire** of 1666 but replaced by three courtyards; one sold beef (along with leather and wool), one concentrated on veal, mutton, and lamb (with fish and cheese as sidelines), and one dealt in fruit, vegetables, and herbs. In 1881, these were replaced by a flamboyant, glass-roofed market designed by Horace Jones. Foodstuffs are still the most common goods on sale but, in recent years, book shops and other stores have begun to infiltrate. The **public houses** are popular with office workers from nearby finance houses, such as **Lloyd's of London**.

LEE, RIVER. *See* LEA, RIVER.

LEICESTER SQUARE. In 1631–35, the Earl of Leicester erected a mansion on the northern side of what is now Leicester Square. By the end of the 17th century, the gardens laid out in front of the new building were lined on all sides by the homes of aristocrats, artists, and merchants, creating a very fashionable, affluent neighborhood. For nearly 150 years, despite the encroachment of some commercial activity, the area retained its very desirable status but, during the 1840s, the opening of New Coventry Street brought increased traffic, so the wealthy citizens moved out to quieter suburban locations. Their large homes were converted to **hotels**, shops, and **museums**. These, in turn, attracted other activities, particularly restaurants and **theater**s (the Alhambra playhouse opened in 1858, the Empire in 1884, and the Hippodrome in 1900). As a result, the character of the square changed radically within a few decades, becoming, by the early years of the 20th century, a center of London nightlife (particularly male nightlife, hence the nostalgic farewell reference in *It's a Long Way to Tipperary*, the First World War soldiers' song). Since then, it has remained at the heart of the **West End**, close to a number of London's largest cinemas, as well as the theaters. Some semblance of the Earl's gardens has survived, however, largely through the efforts of Albert Grant, a larger than life financial speculator whose business dealings eventually took him to the bankruptcy courts but who had sufficient sensitivity to purchase the remaining open land in 1874 and refurbish the space, which has statues of three former Leicester Square residents—surgeon John Hunter (*see* **Royal College of Surgeons of England**) and artists William Hogarth and Joshua Reynolds.

LEWISHAM. Lewisham lies south of the **River Thames** between **Blackheath** (to the north) and **Catford** (to the south) about six miles from **Charing Cross**. It was settled during Anglo-Saxon times, focusing on St. Mary's Church, and, for 1,000 years, survived as a small farming and industrial center, with much of the industry (such as the mill that produced metal for armor during the 16th century) depending on water power supplied by the River Ravensbourne. During the 17th century, when the village became a fashionable place for country homes, a number of substantial houses were erected, a grammar school founded, and almshouses established, then, in 1774–77, the church was rebuilt in neoclassical style to designs by George Gibson. In 1849, however, the **railways** arrived and the community was transformed as builders erected terraces for commuters prepared to trade the time spent travelling to work for a residence in a semirural environment. By 1900, Lewisham was a middle-class residential suburb, and by the end of the 20th century most of the early properties had disappeared to make way for new developments, including a shopping center and sports complex. In 1965, when London's **local government** was reorganized, the town gave its name to the new **London Borough of Lewisham**.

LEWISHAM, LONDON BOROUGH OF. Created, in 1965, by the amalgamation of the previously independent authorities at **Deptford** and **Lewisham**, the borough covers 14 square miles. It has a narrow frontage (about one-third of a mile) on the **River Thames**, but broadens to the south, reaching a maximum of five miles between Upper Sydenham and Grove Park. Largely residential, with extensive public and private **housing** estates, Lewisham houses 248,000 citizens (1998) who focus on central London for employment. Incomes are generally below the urban average, reflecting relatively poor levels of educational attainment and consequent high rates of unemployment. Deptford, to the north, has all the social characteristics of the inner city, with fewer than two of every five homes owner-occupied and one in three of the population in a non-white ethnic group. Other areas are more typically suburban, though there is a significant concentration of light industry in the west, where the major shopping facilities are located. The borough is crossed by several major roads and rail routes, which connect London to settlements on the Thames estuary and the English Channel coast. (*See also* BECKENHAM; BLACKHEATH; CATFORD; FOREST HILL; KIDBROOKE; SYDENHAM.)

LEYTON. Leyton lies six miles northeast of **Charing Cross** on marshland east of the **River Lea**. It was probably settled in Roman times and farmed by the Saxons, remaining predominantly agricultural until the Industrial Revolution. In 1840, the Eastern and Northern **Railway** built a station at Lea Bridge and, with the Great Eastern Railway (which arrived in 1856), acquired large amounts of land for use as sidings and maintenance depots. Immigrants flooded in to seek work, turning the settlement into a working-class suburb towards the edge of the metropolitan area. Leyton suffered badly during the **Blitz** and was extensively redeveloped after the Second World War. In 1965, it was incorporated within the **London Borough of Waltham Forest** when the capital's **local government** was reorganized.

LIBERTY'S. In 1875, Arthur Lasenby Liberty, son of a Buckinghamshire draper, opened a shop at 218A **Regent Street**, selling Indian silk to an affluent clientele. The business was an immediate success, allowing him to expand into a wider variety of oriental goods and take over additional premises. In 1924, a major redevelopment allowed the firm to acquire Nos. 210–20 and build an entrance from Great Marlborough Street using timbers from the men-of-war HMS *Hindustan* (launched in 1824) and HMS *Impregnable* (launched in 1865 and the largest ship of its day). The flamboyant Regent Street frontage incorporated a 115-foot-long frieze, showing the wealth of distant lands, and a clock on which St. George fights a battle with a dragon every hour. Liberty's has exerted enormous influence on the tastes of the wealthy ever since its establishment, promoting (at various times) hand-printed fabrics, art nouveau designs, pre-Raphaelite lines, and countryside imagery in a range of furniture, wallpaper, and jewelry as well as textiles. At the beginning of the 21st century, however, its sales were affected by new discount retailers and its future was in doubt. A fire in November 2000 that gutted the basement and destroyed thousands of square feet of floor space added to the uncertainties. Then, early the following year, Liberty announced plans to scrap its high-fashion ready-to-wear collection, pull out of mail order and e-commerce business, concentrate on core retail activities, and spend £4 million refurbishing its store. (*See also* MERTON.)

LIBRARIES. Although educational, religious, and professional institutions such as the **Royal College of Physicians of London** and the **Royal Society** provided libraries for the use of their members, Londoners had no facilities for borrowing books until rising levels of literacy and changing fashions led to an increase in reading for pleasure during the 18th century. As demand for access to the works of writers such as Daniel Defoe, Charles Dickens, and Walter Scott mounted, entrepreneurs established commercial lending libraries for the leisured middle classes, particularly during the reign of Queen Victoria. By 1900, the largest of these enterprises was Mudie's, which held a stock of nearly one million volumes on its site at the corner of New Oxford Street and Museum Street. **W. H. Smith** had also acquired a considerable share of the market as a branch of its newspaper distribution and retailing business. In 1844, the London Library (founded through the efforts of writer Thomas Carlyle, politician William Gladstone, and political philosopher John Stuart Mill) opened in **Pall Mall** with the aim of providing texts that could be loaned to scholars of the humanities, and, in 1855, the Public Libraries Act gave **local government** bodies power to fund public libraries from property taxes, so by 1900 Londoners had wide access to reading material. That access increased throughout the 20th century, particularly following the introduction of welfare state policies by the Labour government after the Second World War, so by 2001 the libraries in the **London borough**s had lending stocks of about two books per resident, with extensive collections for children and ancillary newspapers, periodicals, compact discs, and videos. In addition, changes in technology have led to investment in computers with Internet access as methods of information gathering focus on electronic media, and reciprocal arrangements allow London libraries to meet readers' demands for the esoteric by obtaining books for short periods from other collections. (*See also* BARBICAN; BRITISH LIBRARY; BRITISH MUSEUM; CHARLTON; COMMONWEALTH INSTITUTE; COURTAULD INSTITUTE OF ART; FREUD'S HOUSE; GLOBE THEATRE; GOLDERS GREEN; GREENWICH PALACE; GUILDHALL; HAMPTON COURT PALACE; KENWOOD HOUSE; LAMBETH PALACE; LONDON SCHOOL OF ECONOMICS AND POLITICAL SCIENCE [LSE]; NATIONAL ARMY MUSEUM; NATURAL HISTORY MUSEUM; ORPINGTON; ROYAL ACADEMY OF MUSIC; ROYAL BOTANIC GARDENS; ROYAL COLLEGE OF SURGEONS OF ENGLAND; ROYAL FESTIVAL HALL; ROYAL GEOGRAPHICAL SOCIETY; ROYAL HORTICULTURAL SOCIETY; RUISLIP; SCIENCE MUSEUM; SLOANE, HANS; SWISS COTTAGE; WIMBLEDON; WOOLWICH.)

LIFFE. *See* LONDON INTERNATIONAL FINANCIAL FUTURES AND OPTIONS EXCHANGE (LIFFE).

LIGHTERMEN. Traditionally, lightermen have had the sole right to carry goods from ship to shore on the **River Thames**. They united with the **watermen** in 1700 (following a dispute over the transport of passengers) and thrived until the 19th century, when the construction of enclosed **docks** (where ships could berth alongside quays) greatly reduced their numbers. The progressive closure of London's harbor facilities after the Second World War caused further unemployment but a few individuals keep the trade alive.

LIMEHOUSE. Limehouse, located on the north bank of the **River Thames** some 3.5 miles east of **Charing Cross**, takes its name from the production of lime, which was an important industry in the area during the Middle Ages, but its economic development was more closely linked to London's rising importance as a maritime center. During the 16th and 17th centuries, many seafarers (such as Sir Humphrey Gilbert, who established England's first North American colony at Newfoundland in 1583) acquired homes there, and, by the 18th century, it had an important shipbuilding industry. The opening of the West India **Docks** in 1802 brought an influx of manufacturing and importing companies, stifling the former seagoing atmosphere but offering new sources of employment and tying Limehouse into the **East End** as open spaces between formerly independent communities were urbanized. Many of the new residents were from abroad, particularly Chinese sailors who arrived on **East India Company** ships. Relations between the incomers and the local people were often strained because British seamen claimed that Chinese mariners were undercutting their wages, so several violent clashes occurred (especially in 1908). However, the **immigrants** stayed, settling in Limehouse Causeway and Pennyfields, where they were operating about 30 shops and restaurants by 1914 (and were portrayed in the somewhat sensationalist novels of Sax Rohmer, who based the evil Fu Manchu on a tall well-dressed Chinese man he saw getting into a car in Limehouse Causeway on a foggy night in 1911). During the 20th century, Limehouse shared in the decline of the docks and suffered in the bombing of the **Blitz**. The former resulted in the closure of most of the industrial premises and the latter in large-scale rebuilding programs by local authorities. As a result, the area is now predominantly residential, albeit still largely working class. Also, the Chinese community has vanished, dispersing during the 1950s when nearly all the buildings in Pennyfields and the Causeway were demolished and replaced by council flats. The only sign of their existence remains in road names such as Canton Street and Peking Street. Limehouse was included within the **London Borough of Tower Hamlets** when metropolitan **local government** was reorganized in 1965. (*See also* BARNARDO, THOMAS JOHN.)

LINCOLN'S INN. *See* INNS OF COURT.

LINCOLN'S INN FIELDS. Lincoln's Inn Fields, in **Holborn**, form central London's largest open square. Originally common land (known as Cup Field and Purse Field), they were initially used as animal pasture, then became a place of execution during the 16th century, and ultimately were developed from 1638, when William Newton was given permission by King Charles I to build houses around the perimeter (despite the objections of Lincoln's Inn). The area immediately became fashionable; Edward Montagu (Earl of Sandwich), Thomas Pelham-Holles (Duke of Newcastle), **Eleanor "Nell Gwyn"** (mistress of King Charles II), and Prime Ministers William Pitt the Younger, Spencer Perceval, and William Gladstone all had homes there at various times over the next two centuries. Most of the early properties are gone, replaced by buildings dating from 1730 to 1960. The gardens became a public **park** in 1894. (*See also* SIR JOHN SOANE'S MUSEUM.)

LITTLE VENICE. *See* REGENT'S CANAL.

LIVERPOOL STREET STATION. The station was opened in 1874, on the site of **Bedlam**, as the terminus of the Great Eastern **Railway**. It was extended in 1891 (shortly before the Great Eastern **Hotel**, designed by **Charles Barry**, was added on the eastern side) and, with 18 tracks, was the biggest in London until Victoria Station was enlarged in 1908. In 1986, a major redevelopment program was undertaken, with refurbishment of the station concourse involving improvements in shopping and restaurant facilities and the construction of the Broadgate office complex above platforms 11–18.

LIVERY COMPANIES. The **City of London**'s livery companies (also known as guilds) were founded as tradesmen's organizations from the 12th century onwards and got their name because members wore a distinctive livery (or uniform). Initially, their prime purpose was to protect the interests of their crafts by supervising standards of workmanship, controlling the entry of apprentices, and regulating prices. However, they also had an important welfare role, looking after members who had fallen on hard times (by arranging funerals, for instance). In the process, many became very wealthy, building opulent premises and meeting regularly for lavish meals. Rivalry was intense (in 1267, the Tailors and the Goldsmiths had a pitched battle, the Clothworkers and Cordwainers added to the melee, and the leading protagonists were later hanged). So, in 1514, the Court of Aldermen (*see* **Alderman**) was forced to intercede and establish an order of precedence based primarily on the capital resources of the guilds, with the Mercers (dealers in high quality textiles) at the top, followed by the Grocers, Drapers, Fishmongers, and Goldsmiths. The sixth rung of the ladder posed problems because the Skinners and the Merchant Tailors both claimed the position, so the **Lord Mayor**, showing all the qualities of diplomacy for which Britain is renowned, decreed that the two contestants should alternate sixth and seventh place each year, a decision that led to the phrase "at sixes and sevens" (meaning "confused," or "uncoordinated"). The Haberdashers, Slaters, Ironmongers, Vintners, and Clothworkers, respectively, were allocated the next five positions. These high-ranking organizations were known as the Great Twelve; the other 36 were considered minor companies.

During the 17th and 18th centuries, the companies found themselves under pressure, partly because of differences with the Crown (in 1608, for example King James VI and I forced them to finance the settlement of immigrant farmers in Ulster) and partly because changing demands for services reduced the membership of some guilds. The Industrial Revolution brought a change in fortunes, however, as craft skills increased in economic importance, and the later 20th century has seen the establishment of a series of new companies representing modern ways of earning a living (the Launderers' Company, open to people employed in the dry cleaning business, was formed in 1960, for instance).

By the late 1990s, there were about one hundred companies, ranging in size from groups such as the Basketmakers' Company (which was formed in 1569 and has a livery of 500) to those such as the Cooks' Company and the Fan Makers' Company (formed in 1311 and 1709 respectively and with liveries of fewer than 100). All are ruled by annually elected courts, headed by a Master, but membership criteria vary; some companies accept only individuals who have connections with their trade, some respect entry by patrimony (accepting a son born while his father was a liveryman), and some have a policy of redemption (being sponsored by two members). Although they still seek to maintain the status of their crafts and have a role in the government of the City of London (*see* **sheriff**, for instance), much of their modern work is charitable. The Haberdashers' Company (formed in 1327 by men who made tents and padded tunics worn under battle armor) supports schools in several parts of England, the Spectacle Makers (founded in 1629) grants funds for research projects dealing with optical issues, and the Clothworkers (created by an amalgamation of guilds in 1528) has shown particular concern for the blind. (*See also* BREWERIES; CHEAPSIDE; CHELSEA PHYSIC GARDEN; CITY AND GUILDS OF LONDON INSTITUTE; COMMON HALL; COURT OF COMMON COUNCIL; CRIPPLEGATE; DANCE, GEORGE [1700–1768]; FREEDOM OF THE CITY; GUILDHALL; HIGHGATE; HOXTON; ROYAL COLLEGE OF SURGEONS OF ENGLAND; ST. ANDREW'S CHURCH, HOLBORN; WATERMEN.)

LIVINGSTONE, KENNETH ROBERT (1945–). In May 2000, Ken Livingstone—a politician with political views significantly to the left of Prime Minister Tony Blair's Labour Party—won London's first mayoral election contest despite the best efforts of the British government to engineer his defeat. The son of Robert Livingstone and his wife, Ethel, he was born on 17 June 1945 and educated at Tulse Hill Comprehensive School in south London before working as a technician at the Chester Beatty Cancer Research Institute, then, in 1973, taking a teacher's certificate at the Phillippa Fawcett College of Education. He joined the Labour Party in 1969 and gained a seat on the Council of the **London Borough of Lambeth** two years later, serving as vice chairman of the Housing Committee in 1971–73. In 1978, he moved to the **London Borough of Camden**, sitting as a Council member until 1982 and acting as Chairman of the Housing Committee in 1978–80.

It was with the **Greater London Council (GLC)**, however, that Livingstone became a household name. First elected to represent Norwood (1973–77), he later campaigned successfully in **Hackney** North (1977–81), and **Paddington** (1981–86). In 1981, the Labour Party, led by the politically moderate Andrew McIntosh, gained control of the council with a nine-seat majority. Under party rules, an election for Leader of the GLC Labour group (and, by implication, of the GLC itself) had to be held immediately and Livingstone, aided and abetted by fellow left-wingers, mounted a successful challenge. As a result, London got a far more militant administration than it had bargained for. Within weeks, Livingstone was annoying Prime Minister Margaret Thatcher with announcements that, in order to tackle London's problems, property taxes would have to rise by 120 percent and that the authority's multimillion-pound art collection would have to be sold. As unemployment in the city increased, he hung a giant banner, chronicling the rise, on **County Hall**, located on the south bank of the **River Thames** directly opposite the House of Commons (*see* **Palace of Westminster**) and clearly in Mrs. Thatcher's view. When he invited the mother of an Irish Republican Army member to tea and held a republican party on the day Prince Charles married **Diana, Princess of Wales**, a rash of press editorials accused him of insensitivity.

The Conservative government eventually decided that enough was enough and abolished the GLC in 1986. Livingstone remained in politics, however, winning the Brent East constituency for Labour at the 1987 General Election. In the House of Commons, he specialized in economic affairs, kept a comparatively low profile, and, over the next decade, acquired a reputation as a champion of London among those who regarded the early 1980s as the GLC's golden era, in which it fought a war of attrition with a Prime Minster who was driven by concepts of financial gain rather than social concern.

When plans for a **Greater London Authority (GLA)** were announced shortly after Labour won the 1997 General Election, Livingstone sought selection as the party representative but was rejected because of his left-wing views. Undeterred, he entered the contest as an independent and won, taking over 38 percent of the vote (some 12 percent more than his closest challenger). His success was hailed as a victory for the people over the Labour machine, which had done its best to derail the Livingstone campaign, expelling him from the party and issuing statements claiming that it would be a disaster for London if he topped the poll.

Livingstone has control over an annual budget of about £3.3 billion (more than that of many members of the United Nations) and is a good media performer, presenting Prime Minister Blair with a political opponent who has real clout and a clear mandate from the people he represents. Outside politics, he is recognized as an authority on amphibians, particularly newts, and served as vice president of the Zoological Society of London from 1991 to 1998.

LLOYD'S OF LONDON. Lloyd's is the world's leading insurance exchange, writing about one-third of all airline insurance and reinsuring the liability risks of nearly all of the ships. It is not itself an insurance company; members traditionally have consisted of individuals and syndicates, who accept liability for the losses incurred by claims. These members are known as "names" because, when the insurance is arranged through a syndicate, the parties sign their names to the contract. The practice of insuring ships and cargoes against loss became common during the 16th century. By the 1680s, Edward Lloyd's **coffee house** in Tower Street—a favored haunt of ship masters and merchants and, therefore, a source of reliable, up-to-date information about vessel movements and cargoes—had become accepted as the best place in London to arrange an insurance deal. The business flourished but, during the 1700s, increasingly attracted speculators willing to take wild gambles so, in 1769, a new coffee house was opened in Pope's Head Alley by the more sober financiers. Five years later, by which time the group had developed formal rules of procedure and appointed a governing committee, it transferred to the **Royal Exchange**, where it remained until it moved to Leadenhall Street in 1928. By that time, its horizons had broadened well beyond the shipping industry and its importance as a center for the insurance of nearly all types of risk was recognized abroad, particularly in the United States (which accounted for about 30 percent of its total business by the 1990s).

In 1957, a large extension for the underwriters was opened in Lime Street but, in 1978, needing additional space, Lloyd's commissioned architect Richard Rogers to redevelop the Leadenhall site. The result was a controversial glass and steel structure, first used in 1986, which some commentators thought was more suited to Dallas than London but others felt was an imaginative break from traditional styles. The heart of the building is a large chamber (known as The Room) where trading is done. Around it rise 12 floors, including a gallery for spectators. The total space available for underwriters is about 200,000 square feet.

Lloyd's membership rose steadily from 79 in 1771 to nearly 13,000 in 1997. Foreigners were admitted as names in 1968, women the following year. In 1982 an Act of Parliament (Lloyd's Act) gave its directors immunity from lawsuits and enabled it to become an entirely self-regulating body, but those principles were challenged soon afterwards when the institution's existence was threatened by cumulative losses of more than £8 billion from 1987 to 1992. The immediate cause was claims on policies involving asbestos poisoning and environmental pollution, but critics alleged that many names had taken unacceptable risks and that unsupervised expansion, coupled with poor management of trading, meant that those who ran Lloyd's had to accept some of the blame. Court cases followed in the United Kingdom and elsewhere, leading to a settlement offer that cost £3.1 billion but was accepted by 91 percent of members in 1996. Two years earlier, corporate capital had been introduced for the first time in an attempt to shore up the market and very quickly overtook the names in underwriting Lloyd's total risk of £10 billion.

Lloyd's is managed by a Council of 18 people, including representatives of names and corporate capital as well as nominated members approved by the Bank of England. In addition, a 12-member Regulatory Board is responsible for enforcing standards. Since 1998, the organization's activities have been subject to review by the Financial Services Authority, a nongovernment agency created by Parliament and charged with maintaining public confidence in Britain's financial institutions. (*See also* LUTINE BELL.)

LLOYD WEBBER, ANDREW (1948–). During the last three decades of the 20th century, the imaginative sets, catchy tunes, and emotional lyrics of Lloyd Webber's work breathed new vigor into the London musical **theater**. Born on 22 March 1948, he was raised in Harrington Court, **Kensington**, by a family for whom music was a way of life. His father (William) taught at the **Royal College of Music** before taking the post of Director at the London School of Music, his mother (Jean) was a piano teacher, and his younger brother (Julian) is a celebrated cellist. At Westminster School, he showed a considerable talent for history and, in 1964, won a scholarship to Oxford University, but the pull of the stage was greater than the lure of the library. A chance meeting with fellow student Tim Rice led to a successful collaboration, with Lloyd Webber writing the music for songs and Rice writing the lyrics, so, after only a few months, the two dropped out of higher education to concentrate on making musicals. Their first venture (*The Likes of Us*, staged in 1968) was not well received, but it was followed by a string of successes, including the biblical pop opera *Joseph and the Technicolour Dreamcoat* (also 1968), the rock opera *Jesus Christ Superstar* (1971), and the more political *Evita* (1978). After the partnership broke up in the late 1970s, Lloyd Webber branched out on his own with *Cats* (1981), which set verses by T. S. Eliot to music and, in 1997, became the longest running show on Broadway after 6,138 performances. *Song and Dance* appeared in 1982, *Starlight Express* in 1984, *The Phantom of the Opera* in 1986, *Aspects of Love* in 1989, *Sunset Boulevard* in 1993, and *Whistle Down the Wind* in 1997.

Many of the productions proved controversial: *Jesus Christ Superstar* was condemned by Jews as anti-Semitic and by right-wing Christians as irreverent, *Jeeves* (which appeared in 1975 and was based on the stories of novelist P. G. Wodehouse) received poor reviews, *Aspects of Love* was rejected by many columnists as pretentious, the original stagings of *Sunset Boulevard* and *Whistle Down the Wind* were plagued by problems with the sets, and *Evita* was considered by some observers to be a glorification of the pro-fascist Eva Perón, wife of Argentinean dictator Juan Perón. But audiences loved the music, flocking to the shows in large numbers so that Lloyd Webber, on occasion, had three musicals running simultaneously in New York and in London. He has won numerous awards, including six Tonys and three Grammys, and was recognized for his services to music with a knighthood in 1992 and a peerage (as Lord Lloyd-Webber of Sydmonton) in 1997.

In 2000, Lloyd Webber paid £87.5 million for the Stoll Moss theater company because, he said, there was a real possibility that theaters would fall into the hands of "pen-pushers and number crunchers" who did not realize that "the thing about the theater is you have got to take risks." The acquisition added 10 London venues (including such famous locations as the Lyric, the London Palladium, and the **Theatre Royal, Drury Lane**) to the three he already owned and gave him control of over half the theater seats in the **West End**, although, under a preexisting arrangement, two halls (the Gielgud and the Queen's) were due to pass to impresario Cameron Mackintosh when the leases expired in 2004.

LOCAL GOVERNMENT. The first citywide local government authority was the **Metropolitan Board of Works**, appointed in 1855. Its powers were confined mainly to civil engineering projects so, although it made considerable improvements to London's **sewage disposal** system as well as building many roads, by the 1880s reformers were advocating the creation of a new body that would have wider powers. In 1898, the **London County Council (LCC)** was formed and, over the next 77 years, had a major impact on **housing** provision and on services such as **education**. Twenty-eight Boroughs were created in 1898, partly in an attempt to limit the power of the new authority, but criticism of its policies mounted, particularly as the migration of middle-class groups from the inner city to the suburbs gave the Labour Party a monopoly of control from 1934. Conservative governments of the 1950s and early 1960s determined to institute change and, in 1965, replaced the LCC with a **Greater London Council (GLC)**, which covered a wider area than its predecessor and included some of the city's wealthy suburbs. At the same time, 32 **London borough**s were formed and given responsibility for local services, leaving strategic planning to the GLC. In addition, an **Inner London Education Authority (ILEA)** was established as a committee of the GLC to administer educational services in the 12 central city boroughs and also in the **City of London**.

Frequently, the GLC was at loggerheads with the national government, and, in 1986, having proven too painful a thorn in Prime Minister Margaret Thatcher's flesh, it was abolished (although the ILEA survived for another four years). The individual boroughs became unitary authorities, and London earned an unenviable reputation as the only major world city without an overall planning authority. By the end of the 20th century, it was clear that some centralized control of essential services (such as **transport**) was needed if London were to continue to attract investment, so, soon after winning the General Election in 1997, the Labour Party announced plans for a new **Greater London Authority**. The first elections were held in 2000. Throughout the period, the **City of London** maintained its own local government system, administered by the **Corporation of London**. (*See also* ALDERMAN; ASSOCIATION OF LONDON AUTHORITIES [ALA]; ASSOCIATION OF LONDON GOVERNMENT [ALG]; COUNTY HALL; COURT OF COMMON COUNCIL; GUILDHALL; LIVINGSTONE, KENNETH ROBERT; LONDON BOROUGHS ASSOCIATION [LBA]; LORD MAYOR; SHERIFF; WARD; WARDMOTE.)

LOMBARD STREET. One of eight highways that meet at the **Bank of England**, Lombard Street has been at the center of London's banking industry since merchants arrived from Lombardy, in north Italy, during the 12th century and now provides offices at No. 10 for the Institute of Bankers (the leading British organization training financial service workers). The wealth generated by the firms located in the buildings that line the street's 300 yards has given rise to the assertion that anyone who wagers "All Lombard Street to a china orange" is convinced that the bet is safe. The church of St. Edmund the King, on the north side of the street, was founded in the 12th century and dedicated to an East Anglian monarch who was killed by Viking invaders for refusing to renounce Christianity. The building, destroyed in the **Great Fire** of 1666 was replaced by a structure designed by **Christopher Wren** and Robert Hooke in 1670–79.

LONDINIUM. When the Romans arrived in Britain in 43 A.D., led by Aulus Plautius, they landed near the site of modern town of Deal, in Kent, and made their way northwest. The **River Thames** formed a barrier to their advance, with marshlands on both shores, but the invaders were able to build a bridge at a point where a sandbar on the southern side stood opposite a gravel patch on the north. A port, known as Londinium, developed on the north bank, surviving the ravages of an attack by **Boadicea** in 61 A.D. to become the capital of the new colony. Ultimately, the settlement expanded to over 300 acres, with city walls, the largest basilica north of the Alps built east of the **Walbrook**, a Governor's Palace erected on the site of **Cannon Street Station**, baths constructed where **Cheapside** and Upper Thames Street now stand, and places of worship founded so that soldiers and administrators could pay homage to their gods (*see*, for example, **Temple of Mithras**). By the second century, when the frontier had moved far to the north, the city was a thriving commercial center, with quays and warehouses where goods were imported and exported. However, from 408 A.D., Rome's defenses were threatened by groups from the north German Plain and, two years later, the legions were withdrawn from Britain. It is unclear what happened to Londinium after they left, but almost certainly the population dwindled when the Anglo-Saxons (an agricultural, rather than an urban people) arrived in Britain shortly afterwards. Only fragments of the fabric remain, although the **Museum of London** has a large collection of artefacts dating from the period. (*See also* ALDERSGATE; ALDGATE; BISHOP'S GATE; CITY OF LONDON; CRIPPLEGATE; ERMINE STREET; GUILDHALL; HIGHGATE; LEADENHALL MARKET; LONDON WALL; LUDGATE; NEWGATE.)

LONDON, CITY OF. *See* CITY OF LONDON.

LONDON, TREATY OF. On several occasions since the mid-14th century, negotiations have led to the signing of documents known as the Treaty of London.

1. Edward, the Black Prince, captured King John II of France at the Battle of Poitiers on 19 September 1356 and carried him back to London, where he was forced to sign a treaty surrendering much of his land to the English monarch, Edward III. The French refused to honor the document.
2. In 1373, England and Portugal negotiated a mutual aid pact that is still in force.
3. Meetings between representatives of England and Spain in 1604 led to cessation of hostilities between the two nations after 16 years of war.
4. In 1718, Britain, France, the Netherlands, and the Holy Roman Empire (sometimes known as the Great Powers) determined that, on the extinction of the male line of the Medici family, the Grand Duchy of Tuscany would pass to Don Carlos de Bourbon (later King Charles III of Spain). Also, Victor Amadeus II, Duke of Savoy and sovereign ruler of Piedmont, was forced to yield Sicily to the Hapsburg empire in exchange for Sardinia (then a Spanish possession).
5. Britain, France, and Russia signed an understanding to support the Greeks' campaign for independence from Ottoman rule in 1827. The pact is sometimes known as the London Convention.
6. Five years later, the same powers allied with Bavaria to guarantee Greek independence within prescribed boundaries but retained rights of intervention and insisted that the new country should be ruled by a monarchy.

7. In 1840, Mohammed Ali, the Ottoman empire's viceroy in Egypt, forfeited his control over Syria and Adana in return for the right to pass his Egyptian sovereignty to his children. The treaty established a family dynasty that survived for over a century.
8. Prussia agreed to withdraw from Luxemburg in 1867, allowing the Grand Duchy to become an independent nation whose neutrality was guaranteed by Britain and other European powers. Sovereignty was vested in the Nassau family.
9. The Balkan Wars were ended by a treaty signed in London in 1913. The document prescribed much reduced boundaries for the Ottoman empire.
10. In 1914, some months prior to the outbreak of the First World War, Britain, France, and Russia formed an alliance against Germany, the Austro-Hungarian empire, and Turkey (often known as the Central Powers).
11. Italy joined the alliance against the Central Powers in 1915 in return for the right to control Trentino, part of the South Tyrol, Trieste, part of Dalmatia, Albania, Libya, and areas of German East Africa and Asia Minor after the war. In addition, Britain agreed to pay Italy 1.25 billion lira. Under pressure from the United States, Britain and France reneged on the treaty in 1918.
12. In 1946, Transjordan was given full independence from the United Kingdom.

LONDON AMBULANCE SERVICE. London's first ambulance service was established by the Metropolitan Asylums Board, which was created in 1867 and used carriages to take sick and mentally ill patients to its hospitals. Responsibility for provision passed to the **London County Council** in 1930 and then, in 1965, to the newly formed **Greater London Council**, which merged parts of nine different units to create a single London Ambulance Service. In 1974, a restructuring of health service provision transferred control to the South West Thames Regional Health Authority and, in 1996, the service took advantage of legislation introduced by the Conservative government to convert to self-governing National Health Service Trust status, giving its managers fuller control over policy and resource allocation. Day-to-day activities are in the hands of a Chief Executive (assisted by a group of Directors) who reports to a London Ambulance Service Trust Board consisting of a Chairman, the Chief Executive and eight other members. The service employs about 3,000 people and takes about 1.6 million patients to hospital each year.

Accident and emergency units respond to some 1,500 calls every day and the Patient Transport Service deals with 3,800 nonurgent transfers over the same period. The 70 ambulance stations, with 700 vehicles (including motorbikes designed to make their way quickly through congested city traffic), are controlled from a single center at **Waterloo**.

LONDON ASSEMBLY. *See* GREATER LONDON AUTHORITY (GLA).

LONDON BASIN. London lies in a geological trough drained by the **River Thames** and its tributaries. The sides of the syncline are formed by chalk initially laid down under the seas of the Cretaceous period (144–66.4 million years ago) then folded by later orogenic activity. They rise to just under 1,000 feet in the **North Downs** (at the southern edge of the city) and to about 850 feet in the **Chiltern Hills** (to the northwest). The floor of the basin, which opens towards the east, is a complex of sands, gravels, and clays deposited as the oceans advanced and retreated during the Tertiary period (66.4–1.6 million years ago). More recent alluvial materials overlie some of these sediments. Much of the material has been removed for brick making and road infill, leaving large holes that have been utilized for refuse disposal, nature reserves, and recreation such as water skiing. London is built mainly on three gravel terraces above the Thames—the Boyn Hill terrace (which average 100–130 feet above sea level and are the base for settlements such as **Richmond** and **Islington**), the Lynch Hill terrace (which average 75–80 feet and provide a foundation for the **City of London**), and the Taplow Terrace (which at only about 30 feet above sea level, lies under Trafalgar Square and Stepney). For most of their history, the low-lying lands in the basin have been liable to flooding. (*See also* LONDON CLAY.)

LONDON BOROUGH. The first 28 boroughs in London were created in 1898, partly in order to limit the power of the **London County Council (LCC)**, which had been established 10 years earlier. Boroughs were territorial divisions of the LCC area (now essentially the inner city) and exercised responsibilities over local matters, leaving strategic planning to the citywide authority. The geographical nature of the boundaries caused problems because affluent boroughs were able to provide more extensive, and better quality, services than the poor boroughs could do. Also, in the years following the end of the Second World War, as many people left the central city for new homes in the suburbs, it was clear that many of the authorities were too small (in terms both of population and of size) to carry out their duties properly. In 1965, the system was reorganized, with the **Greater London Council (GLC)** replacing the LCC and covering a much wider area. Thirty-two new boroughs were established, each with an elected council charged with carrying out duties intimately affecting the daily lives of citizens, such as in refuse disposal, library provision, and administration of certain personal social services. The 20 outer boroughs also had responsibility for state supported **education** (with the exception of **universities**) but, in the inner 12 boroughs, that task was given to the **Inner London Education Authority (ILEA)**, operating as a committee of the GLC, which also had statutory responsibility for citywide strategic planning. Following the GLC's abolition on 31 March 1986, the outer boroughs became unitary authorities, with a statutory duty to provide all local government services. The ILEA continued to supervise inner-city education until 1990, when it, too, was disbanded and its responsibilities handed over to the constituent boroughs. (*See also* ASSOCIATION OF LONDON AUTHORITIES [ALA]; ASSOCIATION OF LONDON GOVERNMENT [ALG]; LONDON BOROUGHS ASSOCIATION [LBA].)

LONDON BOROUGHS ASSOCIATION (LBA). In 1964, the LBA was created as a forum in which representatives of the **Corporation of London** (the local authority for the **City of London**) and the 32 newly established **London boroughs** could discuss common problems, coordinate activities, and act as a pressure group on government. It avoided internal political conflict until 1982, when its Conservative Party majority proposed that the Labour-led, and socially radical, **Greater London Council** (the strategic planning body for the city as a whole) should be abolished. Incensed, most of the Labour boroughs withdrew the following year to form their own organization, the **Association of London Authorities (ALA)**. For the next decade, the LBA's rump of 19 boroughs and the corporation was dominated by Conservative councillors, reflecting the political complexion of the national government, so policies tended to be reactive rather than confrontational or proactive. Five committees dealing with policy and finance, **education** and training, environment, **housing**, and social services each met five times a year and representatives had frequent discussions with Cabinet ministers, senior civil servants, and trade unions in an attempt to influence decision making. Successes included concessions from the government on issues such as management of local authority housing and the financial arrangements for schools that opted out of borough control. These activities, and the salaries of the 15 officers, were funded by the subscriptions paid by the member authorities. Increasingly, however, the lobbying was carried out in conjunction with the ALA, particularly during the early 1990s, as the LBA became disillusioned with the administrations of Prime Ministers Margaret Thatcher and John Major. The two groups cooperated closely on the preparation of London Local Authority Bills, which allow Parliament to introduce legislation tackling specific problems common to certain boroughs (such as control over all-night cafés and powers to deal with faulty burglar alarms). Also, they worked together to obtain grants from the European Union's Social Fund, winning some £10 million in 1993–94. Over the years, the bitterness of the 1983 dispute faded as a sense of common purpose reemerged and, in 1995, the two bodies reunited as the **Association of London Government**. (*See also* LONDON PRIDE PARTNERSHIP.)

LONDON BRIDGE. The first **bridge** linking the banks of the **River Thames** was erected by the Romans between 100 A.D. and 400 A.D. It was rebuilt several times but, until **Westminster Bridge** opened in 1750, remained the only direct route into the city from the south. In 1014, the wooden structure was deliberately destroyed by King Ethelred for military reasons and, in 1091, its replacement was blown away by a gale. Fire ravaged the third bridge in 1136, encouraging citizens to begin work on a stone crossing in 1176. Twenty-five years later, the new edifice was lined by houses and had room for a small chapel, dedicated to St. Thomas Becket, at the center. From then, it featured in many major episodes in English history: Simon de Montfort used it to enter London while he held King Henry III captive in 1264, the head of William Wallace (the Scottish freedom fighter) was displayed on it in 1305 (initiating a singularly grisly custom that lasted until 1661), Henry V's body (accompanied by over 800 retainers) was brought back to the capital over it after he died of typhus in France in 1522, and in 1660 Charles II rode back over it to reclaim his throne after the restoration of the English monarchy.

The bridge also had a significant effect on London life. Its 19 narrow arches made navigation difficult and greatly impeded the flow of the Thames, causing the river to freeze over in winter (*see* **frost fairs**) and concentrate sewage (*see*, for example, **Great Stink**). From 1758 to 1762, the houses were removed and the arches strengthened but, by the early 19th century, it was clear that a new structure was needed to meet the needs of the industrial age. Built by John Rennie in 1823–31, the replacement had five arches and was sited a few yards upriver of its venerable predecessor. In 1970, it was sold to American interests for £1 and transported stone by stone to Lake Havasu City in Arizona (there is an enduring belief in London that the Americans thought they were buying **Tower Bridge**). The present bridge, built of prestressed concrete and with three arches, opened in 1973; it is functional but lacks the architectural interest of the earlier crossings. *London Bridge Is Falling Down*—the children's nursery rhyme—probably dates from the days of Ethlered's demolition though the words did not take their present form until the 17th century. (*See also* TRANSPORT.)

LONDON BRIDGE CITY. *See* BERMONDSEY.

LONDON CITY AIRPORT. *See* AIRPORTS.

LONDON CLAY. A marine sediment deposited during the Eocene period (from approximately 57.8 to 36.6 million years ago), the London Clay underlies most of the metropolitan area, reaching a thickness of about 600 feet in places. Brown, gray, or bluish in color, it has yielded fossils of mollusks, worms, crabs, fish, brachiopods, crocodiles, and other animals, along with the fruit of palm trees and conifers. That assemblage suggests that, while the clays were being laid down, the **London Basin** was experiencing climatic conditions similar to those of the modern tropics.

LONDON CLEARING HOUSE (LCH). A limited company founded in 1888, the Clearing House guarantees deals struck on the **International Petroleum Exchange** of London, the **London International Financial Futures and Options Exchange**, the **London Metal Exchange**, and Tradepoint Financial Networks. After a contract has been agreed at one of these centers, it is substituted by two new ones between LCH and each of the parties involved (a process known as novation). If one side defaults, the other is compensated from the Clearing House's default fund, to which each member contributes £150 million. It has been used on only three occasions.

LONDON COMMODITY EXCHANGE. The exchange was formed in 1954 through the merger of a number of organizations marketing soft commodity futures and conducted business at its premises on Mincing Lane (in the **City of London**), where Mediterranean produce had been bought and sold as early as the 10th century. In 1987, it transferred to

St. Katharine's Dock (at the western end of the **Docklands** redevelopment area), renaming itself London Fox, the Futures and Options Exchange, and concentrating on cocoa, coffee, grain, potatoes, meat, rice, rubber, and soybean meal. Nine years later, it was absorbed by the **London International Financial Futures and Options Exchange**.

LONDON CONVENTION (1827). *See* LONDON, TREATY OF.

LONDON COUNTY COUNCIL (LCC). The LCC was the first of the city's local authorities to be directly elected by residents. It was established by the Local Government Act of 1888, replacing the **Metropolitan Board of Works** and exercising its jurisdiction over an area of some 117 square miles covering the center of modern London. A total of 126 councillors were elected to serve for three years. In addition, the councillors themselves elected 21 **Aldermen**, who held office for six years. Their duties and responsibilities were extensive and expanded during the 77 years of the body's existence, covering **housing**, **transport**, **sewage disposal**, **education**, **health care**, and other services that affected the daily lives of citizens.

From the LCC's inception, its policies were determined by political ideologies. The Progressives (essentially supporters of the Liberal Party) were in overall control for most of the period from 1889 until 1907 and the Moderates (allied to the Conservative Party) from 1907 until 1934, when Labour became the majority grouping. After the Second World War, middle-class families increasingly left the inner city for new homes in suburbs established by counties beyond LCC boundaries. As a result, the increasing concentration of manual groups in the inner city effectively guaranteed socialist control of the metropolis. That proved popular with the voters but, during the 1950s, was a constant thorn in the flesh of Conservative governments, so, in 1957, a Royal Commission, chaired by Sir Edwin Herbert, was appointed to investigate alternative forms of local provision. Its report, presented to Parliament in 1960, recommended creation of new boroughs (*see* **London borough**) exercising more limited powers than those acquired by the LCC. In addition, it envisaged a **Greater London Council** with responsibility for strategic planning and covering a wider territory. The proposals were welcomed by the predominantly Conservative **House of Commons**, which passed the necessary legislation in 1963. The LCC met for the last time two years later. (*See also* AVERY HILL; BETHNAL GREEN; BLUE PLAQUES; BURNT OAK; CHELSEA; COUNTY HALL; EAST

HAM; EDUCATION; ELECTRICITY; GEFFRYE MUSEUM; HARDIE, JAMES KEIR; HERNE HILL; HOLBORN; HOLLAND HOUSE; HORNIMAN MUSEUM; HURLINGHAM CLUB; ILFORD; INNS OF CHANCERY; KENWOOD HOUSE; LAMBETH PALACE; LONDON AMBULANCE SERVICE [LBA]; LONDON FIRE BRIGADE; LONDON SCHOOL OF ECONOMICS AND POLITICAL SCIENCE [LSE]; LONDON TRANSPORT [LT]; MARBLE HILL HOUSE; MORRISON, HERBERT STANLEY; NATIONAL WESTMINSTER TOWER; OLD VIC; POPLARISM; QUEEN ELIZABETH HALL; RANGER'S HOUSE; ROEHAMPTON; ROYAL NATIONAL THEATRE; SEWAGE DISPOSAL; TOOTING; TRAMS; WATERLOO; WATER SUPPLY.)

LONDON DISCOUNT MARKET ASSOCIATION (LDMA). Bills of exchange (documents that merchants use to confirm that payments for goods will be made on a specified date) are marketable commodities. They are exchanged for cash, at a discount, thereby facilitating acquisition of funds that can be applied where liquid capital is needed. In London, the trades are carried out by "bill brokers" attached to discount houses, which are members of the LDMA and were founded, in most cases, during the first half of the 19th century. With the volume of business amounting to several billion pounds for a single house every working day, the significance of the deals is considerable, so the firms work closely with the **Bank of England**, which uses the relationship to influence interest rates and thus shape national monetary policies.

LONDON DOCK STRIKE. On 19 August 1889, workers in London's **docks** went on strike in support of a pay rate of a "tanner" (sixpence) an hour. Led by John Burns, Tom Mann, and Ben Tillett, and buoyed by £79,000 contributed by well wishers in Australia and Britain, they forced the port managements to accept their demand at negotiations chaired by Cardinal H. E. Manning, Archbishop of Westminster. The men returned to work on 16 September, buoyed by a success that brought more than their "docker's tanner." Encouraged by a victory for organized labor, unskilled laborers throughout the country formed new trade unions in the hope of improving their working conditions.

LONDON DOCKLANDS DEVELOPMENT CORPORATION (LDDC). *See* DOCKLANDS.

LONDON DOCKS. *See* DOCKS.

LONDON DUNGEON. Located in Tooley Street, **Bermondsey**, the London Dungeon is a **museum** that concentrates on torture and death. Realistic life-sized exhibits show, in graphic detail, religious martyrs burning at the stake and a Jacobite supporter being hanged, drawn, and quartered. Instruments designed to cause mutilation are featured, along with a reconstruction of the gallows at **Tyburn** and a description of conditions in **Newgate Prison**. Despite its gruesome theme, the museum is one of city's most successful tourist sites, attracting more than 600,000 visitors every year.

LONDON EYE. Also know as the Millennium Wheel, the London Eye is located beside **County Hall** and allows visitors a view of the city from 450 feet above the **River Thames** as it carries them on a 30-minute trip in 32 capsules, each holding 25 people. The £20 million project was funded by British Airways to celebrate the beginning of the 21st century. The conditions set by urban planners allow it to remain in place for five years.

LONDON FIRE BRIGADE. London had no organized means of defending life and property against flames until after the **Great Fire** of 1666. That experience persuaded insurance firms that their interests would be best served by forming private fire brigades, which would only attempt to put out blazes at properties that the parent company insured. Over the years, the brigades increasingly cooperated, a process that ultimately led to their amalgamation as the Fire Engine Establishment in 1833. The resources of the new organization were frequently stretched, however, as when much of the **Palace of Westminster** was destroyed in 1834 and when, in 1861, a warehouse fire in Tooley Street took two days to extinguish. Eventually, in 1865, Parliament was persuaded that a citywide service should be provided at public expense, and it approved legislation creating the Metropolitan Fire Brigade, controlled by the **Metropolitan Board of Works**. Responsibility for the service (which formally changed its name to the London Fire Brigade in 1904) was taken over by the **London County Council** in 1899, the **Greater London Council** in 1965, and the London Fire and Civil Defence Authority (which consists of one member from each of the 33 local authorities in the metropolitan area) in 1986. It has a staff of about 7,300 (of whom 6,100 are firemen), 114 stations, and 650 engines operating from three major bases in **Lewisham**, **Stratford**, and **Wembley**, with an emergency control center in **Lambeth**. Members attend nearly 200,000 incidents annually, with the stations at **Brixton**, **Paddington**, and **Peckham** averaging over 3,000 calls every year. Towards the end of the 20th century, much of the brigade's work concentrated on fire prevention, rather than on fire fighting, allowing it to devote an increasing amount of time to other incidents, such as rail accidents, motorway crashes, and animal rescues.

LONDON FIRST. From its headquarters in Tothill Street (near the Houses of Parliament [*see* **Palace of Westminster**]), London First coordinates public and private interests in an effort to promote investment in the city, improve the quality of **transport**, reduce **air pollution**, and encourage **tourism**. Established in 1992, the organization has a membership of more than 250 businesses, whose financial contributions support a small staff and pay for project costs, and is governed by a board composed of commercial and **local government** interests. In 1994, it established the London First Centre to provide a free consultancy service to companies interested in opening premises in the city. By the end of 1997, the Centre had helped over 100 firms from 17 countries to locate in the capital, providing some 5,400 jobs. London First also co-chairs the **London Pride Partnership** with the **Association of London Government**.

LONDON FOX, THE FINANCE AND FUTURES EXCHANGE. *See* LONDON COMMODITY EXCHANGE.

LONDON GAZETTE. The *Gazette*, published by the British government, carries official announcements (such as the award of military decorations). It first appeared on 5 February 1666, promoted by King Charles II, and is printed at premises in **Printing House Square**.

LONDON HEALTH EMERGENCY (LHE). Britain's largest pressure group dedicated to the preservation of the National Health Service (the United Kingdom's system of socialized medicine), London Health Emergency was founded in 1983 to campaign against the Conservative government's plans to close hospitals in the city. Initial funding was provided by the **Greater London Council** and, after that body was disbanded in 1986, by the Labour-dominated members of the **Association of London Authorities**. By the late 1990s, it had over 200 affiliated organizations (including labor unions and community groups) linked by a quarterly newspaper with a print run of over 10,000 copies. As well as providing a resource base for activists and the media, LHE carries out research and publicity work for local authorities and other bodies. It advocates abolition of the market system in **health care** and proposes the establishment of a single health authority to coordinate services in the capital.

LONDON INTERNATIONAL FINANCIAL FUTURES AND OPTIONS EXCHANGE (LIFFE). LIFFE, based at Cannon Bridge, in the **City of London**, opened in 1982 as a trading base for over 200 companies and individuals dealing in financial transactions involving an element of risk. In essence, traders who have contracts that depend on changing share prices, variations in interest rates, or altering asset values may transfer the risk to others willing to accept the consequences of upswings and downswings in the market. As a result, banks, insurance companies, and other institutions can protect pension funds, offer fixed rate mortgages to house buyers, and lend funds at specified rates to small businesses. Most trading was done by the traditional "open outcry" method, with dealers facing each other across a "pit" floor, but there were facilities for computerized deals in low-volume commodities, such as financial futures, options, and sugar futures. A statistical service provided historical data on activities to traders, financial institutions, and other bodies (such as **universities**).

The exchange absorbed the London Traded Options Market in 1992 and London Fox, the Futures and Options Exchange (*see* **London Commodity Exchange**) in 1996, by which time it was the largest of its kind in Europe, with an average daily volume of 660,000 contracts valued at £160 billion. However, it failed to respond to changes in trading methods, holding onto open outcry when others were moving to electronic trading. As a result, competitors (especially the German futures exchange in Frankfurt, which was fully automated) rapidly encroached on LIFFE's business and in 1998 the 210 members voted to computerize their dealings. The following year, a link was developed with the Chicago Mercantile Exchange, allowing traders access to business on both sides of the Atlantic, and in 2001 a joint venture with NASDAQ (the North American exchange for high-technology shares) aimed at forming a market for stock futures. (*See also* LONDON CLEARING HOUSE [LCH]; ROYAL EXCHANGE.)

LONDON INTERNATIONAL INSURANCE AND REINSURANCE MARKET ASSOCIATION (LIRMA). LIRMA, based in Mincing Lane in the **City of London**, is one of the world's largest representative organizations for insurance and reinsurance companies. Formed in 1991 through the merger of a number of preexisting groups, it has 96 full members located in London and the European Economic Area, with a further 87 associate members in other parts of the globe. Trading is almost exclusively in nonlife business, with an emphasis on catastrophic risks such as earthquakes and hurricanes. In the mid-1990s, the association accounted for about two-thirds of all nonmarine treaty insurance business on the London market (the largest in the world) and underwrote more than £3 billion of premium income each year (most of it contributing to Britain's invisible earnings). A company limited by guarantee, it is managed by a council of 16 individuals (mainly company chairmen or chief executives) elected annually by the full members.

LONDON METAL EXCHANGE (LME). The Metal Exchange, based in Leadenhall Street, in the **City of London**, is the world's largest nonferrous futures exchange. It has its origins in the **Royal Exchange**, where metal dealers first met regularly during the late 16th century, but was formally constituted in 1877 to trade in copper and tin. Lead and zinc were added in 1920 (though they had been the subject of earlier unofficial deals), primary aluminum in 1978, nickel in 1979, and aluminum alloy in 1992. The system of buying and selling is unique. At 11:45 A.M., the trading floor (known as the Ring) opens and the metals trade in sequence for five minutes each. At 12:30 P.M., the process is repeated, with the metals in a different order. Following the announcement of the prices agreed, a period of more general trading (termed the Kerb) is held, with all seven metals on the market simultaneously. A second session of Ring trading is held between 3:20 P.M. and 5:00 P.M. The value of the deals, which amount to over US$2,000 billion a year, sets the global reference price for each commodity. By the late 1990s, LME had a membership of over 100 firms in five categories but only the 15 in the most senior group could trade in the Ring. In 1987, the exchange was constituted as a limited company with a Board of Directors responsible for managing the institution and a Ring Committee ensuring that trading rules are observed. In 2000, it began moves toward demutualization. (*See also* LONDON CLEARING HOUSE [LCH].)

LONDON PASSENGER TRANSPORT BOARD (LPTB). *See* LONDON TRANSPORT (LT).

LONDON PHILHARMONIC ORCHESTRA (LPO). The London Philharmonic was formed in 1932 by Sir Thomas Beecham, a sometimes cantankerous conductor who railed against the standard of music in the United Kingdom. It quickly earned a reputation for high quality performances, so, when Beecham went to the United States in 1939, it was able to continue as a self-governing group of musicians, a status that it has maintained ever since. It experienced a difficult financial period during the 1950s but survived to become the resident orchestra at the Glyndebourne opera season (from 1964), work with conductors of the caliber of Sir Adrian Boult and Sir George Solti, and undertake major foreign tours (including, in 1956, the first visit to the Soviet Union by a British orchestra and, in 1973, the first to China by a Western orchestra). In 1990, the LPO was made resident symphony orchestra at the **Royal Festival Hall**. Plans for a merger with the **Royal Philharmonic Orchestra** were dropped in 1995 after a report by management consultants indicated that any financial savings would not justify the artistic turmoil involved.

LONDON PLANE. A hybrid of *Platanus orientalis* (a native of western Asia and southeast Europe) and *Platanus occidentalis* (a North American species), the London plane tree was introduced from Virginia in 1636. It became popular as a decorative species from the mid-18th century, and particularly after the Industrial Revolution, because it sheds its bark and, therefore, survives in areas where **air pollution** is high. It gets its name because it is common in the central city (*see*, for example, **Berkeley Square** and **The Mall.**)

LONDON PLANNING ADVISORY COMMITTEE (LPAC). LPAC is the statutory planning committee for London. Created by the same parliamentary legislation that dissolved the **Greater London Council** in 1986, it advises government and the **London boroughs** on strategic planning matters and major development proposals, represents the capital's interests in discussions dealing with regional planning in southeast England, and makes recommendations relating to vehicle parking policy. At the end of the 1990s, its major priorities included the balancing of **housing** needs with job creation, and improving the quality of the urban environment (particularly along the **River Thames**). The committee consists of one representative from each of the 33 local authorities in the city and has a staff of 22.

LONDON PRIDE. The pink flowers of this saxifrage (*Saxifraga umbrosa*) light up the corners of basement patios and window boxes throughout

London's inner suburbs. The plant gets its name because it survives in relatively dark conditions, where other species wither and die.

LONDON PRIDE PARTNERSHIP. In 1993, John Gummer, Secretary of State for the Environment, launched a City Pride Initiative, which invited London, Birmingham, and Manchester to produce plans combining a vision for each city's future with realistic policies for achieving it. In the capital, **London First** was given responsibility for producing the documents and responded by forming a partnership of public and private organizations, including the **Association of London Authorities**, the **Corporation of London**, the **London Boroughs Association**, and the London Chamber of Commerce. The blueprint that these bodies published in 1995 identified five priorities—business growth, improved **transport**, better **education** and training, more good-quality **housing** at affordable prices, and higher standards of environmental quality. It also suggested three aims—creation of a robust economy, greater social cohesion, and provision of a high-quality service infrastructure. Gummer responded by inviting the consortium leaders to meet regularly with the government's Cabinet Sub-Committee for London, under the title of the Joint London Advisory Panel, to discuss issues of strategic importance to the metropolitan area and move towards implementation of the proposals.

LONDON REGIONAL PASSENGERS' COMMITTEE (LRPC). Established by the 1984 **Transport** Act, the LRPC considers complaints and suggestions from individuals or groups concerned about **bus** and **railway** services in and around London, making recommendations to **London Transport**, the government, and other bodies when necessary. In addition, it reviews objections to plans involving withdrawal of rail services and reports to the Secretary of State for Transport on any hardships likely to result from the closures. London Transport is required by law to consult with LRPC over bus service alterations, fare changes, and other planning proposals. The LRPC, based in Gresham Street (in the **City of London**), consists of a Chairman and up to 30 members chosen to represent a cross section of public transport users, including the disabled, ethnic minorities, and commercial concerns. All of the appointments are made by the Secretary of State.

LONDON REGIONAL TRANSPORT (LRT). *See* LONDON TRANSPORT (LT).

LONDON RESIDUARY BODY (LRB). The seven-member LRB was appointed to wind up the affairs of the **Greater London Council**, which was abolished on 31 March 1986. The prime tasks were disposal of the authority's assets (such as **County Hall**) and reallocation of its responsibilities to other bodies. Following the breakup of the **Inner London Education Authority** four years later, it carried out similar redistribution procedures. Most of the work was completed by 1994.

LONDON SCHOOL OF ECONOMICS AND POLITICAL SCIENCE (LSE). When Henry Hunt Hutchison, a left-wing sympathizer, died in 1894, he left instructions that the funds generated by his estate should be utilized for socially progressive purposes. Five trustees agreed that the finances should found an educational institution, modelled on L'École Libre des Sciences Politiques in Paris, which would be known as the London School of Economics and Political Science and would study major social problems. In 1896, LSE founded the British Library of Economic and Political Science (now one of the finest collections of social texts in the world) and, in 1900, became a college of the **University** of London. Initially based in **Robert Adam**'s Adelphi development, it moved, in 1900, to a Clare Market site donated by the **London County Council** and remained there throughout the 20th century, building new premises and converting neighboring properties in the 1920s, 1930s, 1960s, and 1970s. It has an international reputation for academic excellence and, through consultancy work and published research, has had a major impact on economic and political decision making. (*See also* EDUCATION.)

LONDON STOCK EXCHANGE. *See* STOCK EXCHANGE (LSE).

LONDON SYMPHONIES. In 1790, Johan Peter Saloman, a violinist and impresario who presented regular concerts at rooms in Hanover Square, commissioned six symphonies and 20 other pieces from Austrian composer Joseph Haydn. Haydn arrived in London to begin work in 1791 and was so impressed (both by his reception and by the musical atmosphere) that he remained until June of the following year then returned for a second visit in 1794. During his stays, he wrote 12 symphonies (Nos. 93–104), which are considered by many scholars to be the greatest of his works (particularly Symphony No. 102 in B-flat Major) and are collectively known as the London Symphonies.

LONDON SYMPHONY ORCHESTRA (LSO). The LSO is the capital's oldest orchestra, formed when the Queen's Hall Orchestra disbanded (amidst considerable friction) in 1904. It has toured widely, worked with most major 20th-century conductors (including Hans Richter and Edward Elgar), and made many recordings, becoming resident, in 1981, at the Barbican Centre, where it plays about 80 concerts every year. Administration is in the hands of a Board of Management, which has 13 members, nine of whom play with the orchestra.

LONDON TEA AUCTIONS. Tea, imported from India and the Far East, was first auctioned in London during 1679. The sales became an accepted method of setting a fair price for a commodity that varied greatly in quantity but, during the 20th century, were increasingly replaced by deals conducted over the telephone and by e-mail. The last auction was held at the Chamber of Commerce in Queen Victoria Street on 29 June 1998. Since then, major purchasing companies (such as Tetley and Unilever) have worked through brokers, who pass orders directly to consumers.

LONDON TELECOM TOWER. *See* BRITISH TELECOM TOWER.

LONDON TRANSPORT (LT). Public **transport** provision in London suffered from considerable managerial instability throughout the 20th century. In 1929, faced with competition from independent operators, the managers of the city **trams** (run by the **London County Council**), the **London Underground**, and the London General Omnibus Company announced that they intended to coordinate their services. Implementation of the plan was prevented by critics who interpreted the proposals as a scheme by Lord Ashfield, Chairman of the Underground, to enhance his personal power but, on 1 July 1933, Prime Minister Ramsay MacDonald's national government formed a London Passenger Transport Board (LPTB), taking all **buses**, trams, trolleybuses, and Underground trains into public ownership in order to facilitate integration of provision. That body, like its successors, became known as "London Transport" in popular speech. Following the outbreak of the Second World War in 1939, the government assumed control of the LPTB for strategic reasons and remained in charge until the board was replaced by the London Transport Executive (LTE) on 1 January 1948. The Transport Act of 1969 denationalized the city's transport, handing responsibility for financial control and overall policy to the **Greater London Council (GLC)** but leaving the LTE in charge of day-to-day management.

In 1984, however, the service was nationalized for a second time, London Regional Transport (LRT) was created as a statutory corporation answerable to the Secretary of State for Transport, and a Board consisting of three full-time members, supported by part-time members with business expertise, was appointed to oversee provision. LRT organized its activities by establishing a series of wholly owned subsidiaries. Two of these (London Underground Ltd. and Victoria Coach Station Ltd.) have been retained, but London Transport Advertising and London Buses Ltd. were sold to the private sector in 1994 and 1995 respectively. Also, Docklands Light Railway was transferred (at the government's insistence) to the London **Docklands** Development Corporation in 1992 and London Transport International (a consultancy company) ceased trading the same year.

The scale of London Transport's operation is enormous. Every working day, the system copes with an influx of about one million people from the suburbs between 7 A.M. and 10 A.M. and a similar exodus between 4 P.M. and 7 P.M. A workforce of over 18,000 enables 470 underground trains to serve 267 stations located along 254 miles of rail and 5,000 buses to operate on 700 routes. Capital expenditure exceeds £1.1 billion each year. In July 2000, London Transport was renamed Transport for London. (*See also* DRAIN; LONDON REGIONAL PASSENGERS' COMMITTEE [LRPC]; LONDON TRANSPORT MUSEUM; MORRISON, HERBERT STANLEY.)

LONDON TRANSPORT EXECUTIVE (LTE). *See* LONDON TRANSPORT (LT).

LONDON TRANSPORT MUSEUM. In the years between the two world wars, the London General Omnibus Company built up a small collection of its vehicles. Following the establishment of the **London Transport Executive** in 1948, the **Museum** for British Transport was opened at a disused bus garage in **Clapham**, using that collection as a nucleus but incorporating additional paintings and models. From 1973, it was based at **Syon House**, where it was known as the London Transport Collection. Then, in 1980, it moved to a converted flower market building at **Covent Garden** and, renamed the London Transport Museum, concentrated on 150 years of public transport in the capital. The displays include a reconstruction of the first city omnibus, operated by George Shillibeer in 1829, and a knifeboard horse **bus**, on which passengers on the roof sat back to back. In addition, there are several early steam locomotives and features showing the early days of the **London Underground**. (*See also* TRANSPORT.)

LONDON UNDERGROUND. Initially, underground railways were a means of reducing road congestion and of allowing businesspeople easy access to suburban homes. The first, operated by the Metropolitan **Railway** Company, opened on 10 January 1863 and ran for just under four miles from **Paddington** to the **City of London**. It was successful from the start, encouraging a flurry of proposals for similar developments, including an Inner Circle Line (completed in 1884) and extensions to settlements at the urban fringe. Using a refinement of the system introduced by Marc Brunel earlier in the century, James Greathead constructed the world's first underground electric **tube** railway from King William Street (near the **Bank of England**) to Stockwell (south of the **River Thames**) in 1890. A connection between **Waterloo** and **The City** opened eight years later (*see* **Drain**) and the "twopenny tube" (which got its nickname from the flat 2d fare) followed in 1900. During the first decade of the 20th century, much of the finance for new lines came from Charles Tyson Yerkes, an American who funded the **Baker Street** and Waterloo (quickly abbreviated to "Bakerloo") Railway and the Great Northern, Piccadilly, and Brompton Railway, both of which introduced services in 1906. His Charing Cross, Euston, and Hampstead Railway followed in 1907.

After the First World War ended in 1919, there was a further phase of activity that, by 1932, had extended the system as far afield as Watford (20 miles northwest of central London) and Morden (10 miles south). In 1933, the lines were nationalized and a single body, formally known as the London Passenger Transport Board but always referred to as **London Transport**, was created to provide a planning authority that could develop the underground railways as a single unit. The outbreak of the Second World War in 1939 put a temporary stop to developments (many stations were used as shelters during the **Blitz**), but work very quickly resumed after the conflict, bringing extensions to the Central Line by the end of the 1940s. In 1962, construction began on the **Victoria** Line—the first new tube line in the inner city for 50 years—which opened in stages from 1969 until 1971. In 1977, the Piccadilly Line reached Heathrow **Airport** and, in 1979, a new Jubilee Line (named to celebrate Queen Elizabeth II's 25 years on the British throne) linked **Bond Street** to **Charing Cross**. An extension through the **Docklands** to **Stratford**, in the **East End**, was completed in 2000.

Technological innovation also brought changes to the rolling stock and increased comfort for passengers. The early steam trains had equipment that converted spent steam into water but, even so, were unsuitable for the deep tube lines. Greathead's electric system, therefore, greatly enhanced potential for development, though the steam engines remained in service until 9 September 1961. In 1936, technical improvements to the carriages allowed motors to be housed under the floor of compartments, adding significantly to seating capacity. Air doors replaced metal mesh gates at about the same time, making travel less hazardous, but the major improvements in safety over the past 50 years have followed harrowing accidents. On 28 February 1975, a train crashed into a wall at the end of Moorgate Station, killing 35 people and injuring 74; speed controls and other preventive measures were introduced soon afterwards. Also, in the aftermath of a blaze that killed 31 commuters and rescue workers at **King's Cross Station** in 1987, a major investment was made in improvements to escalators and refuse disposal arrangements (*see* **King's Cross Fire**). The Underground now operates daily services as far afield as Amersham, 27 miles northwest of the city center. It maintains 267 stations, 254 miles of track, and 470 trains that carry 2.5 million passengers every weekday. Oxford Circus (*see* **Oxford Street**) and Victoria are the busiest stations, with some 86 million travellers a year.

By the end of the century, lack of investment had resulted in considerable deterioration of the system, which used elderly carriages and needed much maintenance so, shortly after its election in 1997, the Labour government announced plans for partial privatization, with commercial interests taking responsibility for track and signalling within three years, but internal disagreements over funding led to postponements. Robert Kiley, who had redesigned the New York subway, was appointed commissioner of the newly established Transport for London body in 2000, and the following year the government agreed to invest £4 billion in the network.

In addition to operating a railway, London Underground (despite consistently difficult financial circumstances) has been a significant supporter of the arts. Its headquarters in Broadway, built in 1927–29 over **St. James's Park** station, was designed by Charles Holden, who incorporated sculptures by the then controversial Jacob Epstein, Eric Gill, and Henry Moore in the facade. Even earlier, in 1908, Frank Pick (a publicity officer) had started to commission advertising posters by Graham Sutherland and other artists—a policy that London Transport still pursues. Also, since 1986, passenger compartments have featured short poems among the sales literature on the walls. The idea was the brainchild of American novelist Judith Chernaik, who wanted to take poetry to the captive audience of commuters, and has been a considerable success. (*See also* BOW; BRIXTON; BUSES; CANARY WHARF; CANNING TOWN; EDGWARE; ELECTRICITY; FLOOD CONTROL; GOLDERS GREEN; HOUNSLOW; MERTON; MERTON, LONDON BOROUGH OF; MILL HILL; MORRISON, HERBERT STANLEY; NEWHAM, LONDON BOROUGH OF; PICCADILLY CIRCUS; ROTHERHITHE; SOUTHWARK, LONDON BOROUGH OF; SWISS COTTAGE.)

LONDON UNIVERSITY. *See* UNIVERSITIES.

LONDON WALL. Towards the end of the second century, the Romans built a wall to protect **Londinium**. Some two miles long and enclosing an area of about 330 acres, it was composed of ragstone, which had to be imported from Kent because the clays on which the settlement was located were wholly unsuitable for large-scale construction work. Entry points were provided at **Aldersgate**, **Aldgate**, **Bishop's Gate**, **Cripplegate**, **Ludgate**, and **Newgate**. The structure (now known as London Wall) served as the boundary of London's urban area until the 16th century but was increasingly breached as the settlement spread outwards, particularly during the late 18th and the 19th centuries (in several places, it was incorporated into the foundations of the new buildings). Parts can still be seen (for example, in the small garden at the **Museum of London** and at **Tower Hill**).

LONDON ZOO. In 1828, the Zoological Society of London (founded three years earlier) opened its collection of animals to the public in gardens laid out by Decimus Burton at the northern end of **Regent's Park**. The royal menagerie (previously housed at Windsor Castle) augmented the exhibits in 1830 and additional beasts were brought from the **Tower of London** in 1832–34. The first chimpanzee, displayed in 1835, was an immediate sensation, as were the four giraffes that arrived the following year (these created a fashion for ladies' clothes with patterns resembling those on their skins). The world's first reptile house was opened in 1843, the first aquarium in 1853, and the first insect houses in 1881. As the number of animals increased, the zoo was redesigned and refurbished, with eminent architects preparing many of the plans for new buildings, such as the Mappin Terraces for bears and goats (designed by John Belcher and J. J. Joass, erected in 1913, and representing an important step away from cages to more natural settings for animals), the aviary (constructed under Lord Snowdon's supervision in 1963–64), and the elephant house (brainchild of Hugh Casson and opened in 1965). In the early 1990s, changing social attitudes, declining attendances, and the elimination of government support threatened the institution's existence, but changes in management, coupled with large donations, ensured its survival. Much effort is now concentrated on conservation of threatened species and on education. A children's zoo opened in 1995, for example, and four years later a new building with 65 live animal exhibits, designed to tell visitors about the Web of Life, was added.

LORD MAYOR. The Lord Mayor is the leader of the **Corporation of London**, the local authority for the **City of London**. Records first mention a Mayor of London (Henry FitzAilwyn) in 1189, but it was not until 1215 that King John gave **The City** a charter permitting it to elect an official of its own choice. The title "Lord Mayor" began to be used during the 16th century but was never formally granted. Over 700 men and a single woman have held the post, which confers certain rights as well as a number of duties. Within the City, the holder ranks second in status only to the monarch (and therefore ahead even of the heir to the throne). He is entitled to style himself "Right Honourable" and can, if necessary, seek an audience with the sovereign. The Lord Mayor is elected annually from, and by, a Court of **aldermen**, not by the City's residents, and must have previously served as a **sheriff**. The election is held on Michaelmas Day (29 September), when members of the **livery companies** nominate two individuals for the post, one of whom will normally be the most senior alderman who has not held the position. It is that person who is usually appointed by the Court of Aldermen, but the decision requires the monarch's approval.

On the Friday preceding the second Saturday in November, the new Lord Mayor is admitted to office at a ceremony known as the Silent Change because the trappings of authority, including a sword and a mace, are handed from the retiring Lord Mayor to his successor without a word being exchanged by the principals or any of the attendants. The following day, he drives to the **Royal Courts of Justice** to take the oath of office. Formerly, the procession (known as the Lord Mayor's Show) allowed citizens to present addresses along the route, but, from the 16th century, pageants became popular elements of the event and now participants decorate lorries according to a theme chosen by the incoming Lord Mayor (topics such as natural resources, transport, and education have been featured in recent years).

Two days after being sworn in, the Lord Mayor hosts a banquet at the **Guildhall**, the Corporation of London's headquarters, in honor of his predecessor. The event has been held annually, except during wartime, for more than 400 years and is attended by senior politicians, representatives of the member countries of the Commonwealth of Nations, religious leaders, and the heads of major commercial concerns. Traditionally, the Prime Minister makes a major speech surveying the United Kingdom's role in international affairs. For the next 12 months, the Lord Mayor officially resides at the **Mansion House** and undertakes numerous ceremonial engagements. He also acts as the corporation's chief magistrate, chairing meetings of the Court of Aldermen and the **Court of Common Council**. In addition, he holds several *ex officio* appointments, such as the Chancellorship of City University, which have their own obligations. Although the Lord Mayor is paid by the Corporation of London for performing his or her duties, holders of the office meet many of their own expenses. By implication, only the affluent can aspire to the position. (*See also* PEASANTS' REVOLT; TEMPLE BAR; WARD; WHITTINGTON, RICHARD "DICK".)

LORD MAYOR'S BANQUET. *See* LORD MAYOR.

LORD MAYOR'S SHOW. *See* LORD MAYOR.

LORD'S CRICKET GROUND. *See* MARYLEBONE CRICKET CLUB (MCC).

LUDGATE. According to legend, King Lud built an entry to the western edge of London in 66 B.C. Archaeological evidence suggests, however, that the original structure was erected by the Romans to allow passage through **London Wall** to a **burial ground** located near the present site of **Fleet Street**. The gate was rebuilt in 1215 and 1586 but demolished in 1760.

LUTINE BELL. Traditionally, the Lutine Bell was rung at **Lloyd's of London** to signal important announcements for insurance underwriters and brokers. It was originally carried by *La Lutine,* a French frigate that surrendered to Britain in 1793, became part of the Royal Navy, but was sunk off the coast of Holland in 1799, taking a cargo of gold and silver bullion in its holds. Lloyd's met claims of £1 million as a result of the loss. Several salvage attempts were mounted, one (in 1858) recovering the ship's bell, which was hung in the underwriting room at the **Royal Exchange** and sounded whenever news of overdue ships was received. Normally, when vessels were late, underwriters attempted to limit their potential loss by asking brokers to reinsure some of their liability. When reliable information was received, the bell was rung once if the news was bad (as when a ship had gone down), twice if it was good (if there had been a positive sighting, for example). The chimes eliminated the possibility of unprincipled trading by ensuring that everybody got the details at the same time. Modern communications have rendered the Lutine Bell redundant, however. Last rung to announce a lost ship in 1979 and a safe arrival in 1981, it is now used only on ceremonial occasions.

LUTON AIRPORT. *See* AIRPORTS.

– M –

MADAME TUSSAUD'S WAXWORKS. As a child, Marie Groszholtz, born in Strasbourg (France) in 1761, learned the art of making wax figures from her uncle, Dr. Phillippe Curtius. In 1780, she was appointed art tutor to Élisabeth (sister of King Louis XVI). Because of her position she was considered an enemy of the people during the French Revolution and required to take death masks of prominent individuals who died on the guillotine, including Louis and his Queen, Marie Antoinette (both of whom were killed in 1793). She inherited her uncle's collection of figures in 1794 then, the following year, married engineer François Tussaud, but the relationship foundered and, in 1802, as conditions in France worsened, she moved to Britain, taking an exhibition of her work around major cities before settling at a permanent site in **Baker Street** in 1835.

In 1884 (by which time there were 400 figures on display), her grandsons moved the galleries to their present site around the corner in Marylebone Road. Much of the material was damaged by fire in 1925 and by bombs during the **Blitz**, but the casts from which the models were made survived. The oldest figure on display (known as the Sleeping Beauty) is that of Madame du Barry (mistress of King Louis XV of France), which was modelled in 1765. Others, often now displayed as tableaux, include Maximilien Robespierre (architect of France's Reign of Terror in 1793–94), King George III of Britain, poet Lord Byron, American statesman politician and inventor Benjamin Franklin, and Prime Minister Winston Churchill. Some are permanently on view to the public; others (such as entertainers) appear and disappear as fashions change. Most subjects, who are usually modelled from life, supply clothes for their figure.

In 1958, a planetarium was added to the business, built on the site of the Madame Tussaud's cinema, which had been destroyed by a bomb in 1940. Initially, the displays of star systems were accompanied by live commentaries, but most are now automated in order to accommodate a range of special effects, including a virtual reality, three-dimensional journey through the cosmos. A gallery depicting the history of astronomy was opened in 1980. The complex is one of the most popular tourist attractions in London, Madame Tussaud's alone admitting over 2.7 million visitors annually. In 1998, it was acquired by Charterhouse Development from Pearson, the media group, for a reported cost of £377 million, a price that included the World of Adventures theme park at **Chessington**.

MAIDA VALE. In 1806, British troops, led by General Sir John Stuart, defeated a French force at Maida, in southern Italy. Not long afterwards, a **public house** named Hero of Maida opened in northwest London near the **Grand Union Canal**. As more and more homes were erected during the 1840s and 1850s, the area became known as Maida Hill and then as Maida Vale. By the 1860s, brick buildings were more common than the stucco mansions constructed 20 years earlier, and by the 1880s apartments had superseded individual homes. The area is still largely residential, though many of the older houses have been subdivided and local authority **housing** has replaced many of the poorer structures in the east of the area, as at the Mozart Estate, erected in 1975. The suburb forms part of the **City of Westminster**.

MALL, THE. The Mall forms a processional route from **Admiralty Arch** to **Buckingham Palace**. Just under three-quarters of a mile long, it was originally laid out as part of a scheme of improvements to **St. James's Park** shortly after King Charles II was restored to the throne in 1660, replacing **Pall Mall** as the major location for the game from which that thoroughfare took its name, and becoming, until late in the 17th century, a fashionable place for wealthy Londoners to promenade. In 1903–4, the line of the road was moved a few yards to the south as part of plans, prepared by Aston Webb, for a national tribute to Queen Victoria. The street was built 65 feet wide, with walkways, 25 feet broad, on either side. **London plane** trees and decorated lamp posts lined the route. The **Queen Victoria Memorial** lies at the western end, statutes dedicated to the Royal Marines and to explorer

Captain James Cook in the east, and a memorial to men of the Royal Artillery who died during the Boer War of 1899–1902 in the southeast. (*See also* CHAMBERS, WILLIAM.)

MANSION HOUSE. The official residence of the **Lord Mayor** of the **City of London** was built in 1739–52 to designs by **George Dance the Elder**. Standing opposite the **Bank of England** on a site where criminals were once clamped in the stocks, it is constructed of **Portland stone** in the Palladian style, with a portico of six Corinthian pilasters topped by a richly sculptured pediment. The banqueting room (known as the Egyptian Hall because it was based on a description of the home of the pharaohs published by the Roman architect Marcus Vitruvius Pollio during the first century B.C.) has columns on all sides, with an ambulatory separating them from the walls. Originally, a clerestory allowed light to enter from above, but it was removed in 1794–95. The apartments on the second floor include a ballroom, originally known as the Dancing Gallery. Furnishings are opulent, with ornamental wood and plaster work, a large collection of statuary depicting British historical figures and characters from English literature, paintings of London scenes, displays of gold and silver plate, and the Lord Mayor's insignia of office (which include a scepter of crystal mounted in gold and a chain of gold, onyx, and diamonds). Since it was constructed, the building (which also functions as a court house) has been much altered, detracting somewhat from the sense of space generated by the original design.

MARBLE ARCH. The Arch stands on an island at the intersection of Bayswater Road, Edgware Road, **Oxford Street**, and **Park Lane**. Designed by **John Nash**, it is built of marble and, like the Arch of Constantine in Rome, has three archways flanked by Corinthian columns. The reliefs on the north side are by Richard Westmacott and those on the south by Edward Baily; a statue of King George IV should have crowned the parapet but was located at **Trafalgar Square** instead. In 1828, the structure was erected as a gateway to **Buckingham Palace**, but it proved too narrow for the state coach and so was moved, in 1851, to its present position, where it sits in the middle of one of the busiest traffic junctions in the city.

MARBLE HILL HOUSE. Regarded as a classic example of an 18th-century English country house, Marble Hill (near **Twickenham**) was designed by Lord Henry Herbert for Henrietta Howard (Countess of Suffolk and mistress of the Prince of Wales, who later succeeded to the throne as King George II). Erected under the supervision of Roger Morris in 1724–29, it is built in Palladian style and set in **park** land (laid out by Charles Bridgman) that stretches down to the **River Thames**. From 1734, the Countess used the mansion to entertain her friends (who included poet and dramatist John Gay, poet Alexander Pope, and novelist Horace Walpole), but, following her death in 1767, it passed through a variety of hands, becoming increasingly dilapidated until it was bought by the **London County Council** in 1902. After the Second World War, it was restored by the **Greater London Council** and, in 1966, opened to the public as a **museum** of 18th-century furnishings and paintings.

MARKETS. London's status as England's preeminent trading center, coupled with its relatively large population, led to the growth of urban markets during the Medieval period. **Cheapside** was the principal location, leaving a legacy of modern street names (such as Honey Lane and Bread Street), which bear testimony to the goods sold there. Livestock became increasingly concentrated at Smithfield (*see* **Smithfield Meat Market**), fish at **Billingsgate Fish Market**, meat at **Eastcheap**, and butter, cheese, and poultry at **Leadenhall Market**. As demand increased, the quality of produce grew and the range expanded. New markets, such as **Covent Garden**, were established to meet the needs and, from the 1830s, the spreading **railway** network allowed goods to be brought from throughout Great Britain and Europe. However, by the second half of the 20th century, escalating rents, the problems of operating in cramped facilities, and competing demands for inner-city space forced most of the big sites to move to more suburban locations (thus Covent Garden's vegetable market was relocated at **Nine Elms** in 1964 and Billingsgate on the **Isle of Dogs** in 1982). Vacated premises were redeveloped as office and retail accommodation. (*See also* BOROUGH MARKET; BRENTFORD; BURNT OAK; CHARING CROSS; CORN EXCHANGE; CORNHILL; COURT OF COMMON COUNCIL; FAIRS; HAYMARKET; HUNGERFORD BRIDGE; LONDON TRANSPORT MUSEUM; METROPOLITAN CATTLE MARKET; PECKHAM: PETTICOAT LANE; PINNER; PORTOBELLO ROAD MARKET; RAG FAIR; ROYAL NAVAL DOCKYARDS; SHADWELL; SHEPHERD'S BUSH; SPITALFIELDS; STRATFORD; STREATHAM; STREET MARKETS; THEATRE MUSEUM; WHITECHAPEL.)

MARLBOROUGH HOUSE. The house, immediately east of **St. James's Palace**, was designed by **Christopher Wren** and built in 1709–11 for Sarah, Duchess of Marlborough, who had obtained a lease on the land from her friend, Queen Anne. Ironically, Frenchman Louis Laguerre was commissioned to paint the walls and staircases with scenes from the Duke of Wellington's victories over the armies of King Louis XIV of France. Although Sarah died in 1744, the building remained in the hands of the family until 1817, when it reverted to the Crown. For over a century, until the death of Queen Mary in 1953, it was used as a residence for members of the royal family, but in 1959 it was presented to the government for conversion into a Commonwealth of Nations conference center.

MARSHALSEA PRISON. In the 16th century, Marshalsea **Prison** in **Southwark** was one of London's most important jails. Its name is derived from the court convened by the Steward and Marshal of the King's Household, but the date of its foundation is unknown (though it was certainly built by 1381, when it was stormed during the **Peasants' Revolt**). By the 18th century, the condition both of the structure and of the inmates, most of whom were debtors, was causing serious concern, and in 1842 it was closed. In *Little Dorrit* (1857), author **Charles Dickens** (whose father was incarcerated in the cells in 1824) describes the place as "an oblong pile of barrack building, partitioned into squalid houses standing back to back, so that there were no back rooms; environed by a narrow paved yard, hemmed in by high walls spiked at the top."

MARYLEBONE. *See* ST. MARYLEBONE.

MARYLEBONE CRICKET CLUB (MCC). In 1752, a group of wealthy individuals who regularly played cricket at White Conduit Fields in **Islington** formed themselves into the White Conduit Club. Some years later, feeling that public playing fields were beneath their dignity, they asked Thomas Lord, one of their employees, to find a place where they could enjoy their sport in private, so, in 1787, Lord took a lease (in his own name) on the piece of land now occupied by Dorset Square (to the southwest of **Regent's Park** near Marylebone Road). Shortly afterwards, some of the club members reconstituted themselves as the Marylebone Cricket Club (they played their first match against a White Conduit team the following year, winning by 83 runs). In 1811, facing a rent increase, Lord moved his turf to a site at

Marylebone Bank then, five years later (just before the **Regent's Canal** was driven through the area), picked it up again and relaid it at its present location in **St. John's Wood** Road.

Partly because its membership consisted largely of affluent and distinguished gentlemen, the MCC gradually became recognized as the ultimate authority on the rules of cricket and thus as the international headquarters of the sport. A **museum** of cricket was established in 1865, the club acquired the freehold of Lord's Ground in 1866, a new grandstand was erected the following year, and the Tavern was rebuilt the year after that. Middlesex County Cricket Club (formed in 1864) made the pitch its home base in 1877. During the 20th century, major reconstruction work turned the venue into a modern stadium, which became a regular venue for test matches against other countries. The MCC is now run by a committee headed by a President, who is appointed by his predecessor and holds the post for an indefinite period. In 1999, after a lengthy campaign, women were admitted as members.

MAYFAIR. Recognized for its affluence and gracious living, Mayfair is bounded by **Oxford Street** (to the north), **Park Lane** (to the west), **Piccadilly** (to the south), and **Regent Street** (to the east). It lies within the **City of Westminster** and gets its name from a fair held near **Hyde Park Corner** from 1686 until 1735. From the 1660s until the 1770s, the area developed as an aristocratic suburb close to the royal court at **St. James's Palace**, moving the heartland of affluent London west from **Covent Garden** and **Soho** in the process. Most of the building was undertaken by great landholders (particularly the **Grosvenor Estate**) whose names are remembered in the roads that cut through their property—the widowed Lady Berkeley of Stratton in **Berkeley Square**, Sir Nathaniel Curzon in Curzon Street, Lord Grosvenor in **Grosvenor Square**, and Lord Burlington in Burlington Gardens, for example. Wealthy residents attracted services, leading to the growth of exclusive retail facilities such as jewelry in **Bond Street** and tailoring in **Savile Row**, so commercial premises have always been present. During the 20th century, however, these infiltrated further as families found large homes increasingly difficult to maintain, particularly as they could no longer afford servants. Many people moved out, leaving their successors to turn houses into small **hotels**, night clubs, restaurants, offices, banks, and other activities that wanted the social cachet of a Mayfair address. In addition, large international hotel groups opened premises (such as the 228-room Inn on the Park) at the fringe of the area. As a result, few of the great houses survive in their original state (even though planners have affected the pace and nature of change by controlling the facades and heights of properties), but the aura of wealth is still clearly evident.

MAYHEW, HENRY (1812–1887). One of several authors who drew attention to the living conditions of the city's manual workers during the second half of the 19th century (*see*, for example, **Charles Booth**), Mayhew is best remembered for *London Labour and the London Poor*, a series of letters and articles that originally appeared in the *Morning Chronicle*. The son of solicitor Joshua Dorset Joseph Mayhew, he was born in London and educated at **Westminster** School but ran away to sea rather than complete his studies. After a period in Calcutta (India), he returned to England to work with his father for three years before turning his hand to writing. In 1831, he launched (with Gilbert à Becket) a weekly journal entitled *Figaro in London*, then, in 1834, wrote his first play—*The Wandering Minstrel*—which was performed at the Royal Fitzroy Theatre. In 1841, he launched the satirical magazine *Punch*, which he coedited with Mark Lemon for two years, then, until his death in **Bloomsbury** on 25 July 1887, published a variety of stories, biographies, dramas, and songs. Mayhew's articles on London were written in a lively but sympathetic prose that demonstrated more than superficial understanding of the men and women he described. Focusing on city tradesmen and their families, he drew partly on experience and partly on anecdote in an attempt to conform with the *Chronicle*'s policy of covering the important social issues of the day. The writings were collected in three volumes published in 1851, with a fourth (written with John Binny and concentrating on the prison system) added in 1862. A single revised volume appeared in 1864.

MAYOR OF LONDON. *See* GREATER LONDON ASSEMBLY.

MEDICINE. *See* CHARING CROSS; CUSTOM HOUSE; GREAT ORMOND STREET HOSPITAL FOR SICK CHILDREN; HEALTH CARE; LONDON HEALTH EMERGENCY [LHE]; ROYAL COLLEGE OF PHYSICIANS OF LONDON; ROYAL COLLEGE OF SURGEONS OF ENGLAND.

MERTON. Merton lies towards the outskirts of London, some seven miles southeast of **Charing Cross**. The land was acquired in 1114 by Gilbert the Knight, who established an Augustinian priory; there, in 1236, the English barons met to sign the Statute of Merton, which allowed Lords of the Manor to enclose common lands and is sometimes said to be the first Act of Parliament. The priory was dissolved in 1538 and the masonry carried off to build **Nonsuch Palace**, but the secular community survived and was later augmented by **Huguenot** immigrants, who established a calico bleaching and printing industry. In the early 19th century, Edmund Littler founded a textile printing business that was acquired by **Liberty's** in 1904 and printed that company's fabrics until 1974. Also, William Morris, one of the leaders of the arts and crafts movement, worked from premises he set up in Merton in 1881. The only home Lord Horatio Nelson ever owned was at Merton Place (south of the present High Street), where he lived with his mistress, Emma Hamilton, and her husband from 1801 until his death at the Battle of Trafalgar in 1805. However, most building has occurred since 1871, when horticulturalist and businessman John Innes began to lay out streets in which **architecture** and trees blended to produce a pleasing urban landscape. The arrival of the **London Underground** in 1926 added to the pace of development, turning the area into a residential suburb. The settlement was part of the County of Surrey until 1965, when it gave its name to the new **London Borough of Merton**.

MERTON, LONDON BOROUGH OF. Merton's 15 square miles are covered largely by suburban **housing**. The borough was formed in 1965 through the merger of **Merton**, **Mitcham**, Morden, and **Wimbledon**, all of which were previously part of the County of Surrey. The Wimbledon area is one of the most affluent parts of London, with high proportions of professional and managerial workers who use the southern terminus of **London Underground**'s District Line to commute to jobs in the central city (nearly two of every three employed people living in Merton have jobs outside the borough, reflecting the limited industrial and commercial base). Elsewhere, manual and clerical workers in transport, retailing, and public service predominate, with about one in every five citizens drawn from nonwhite ethnic groups. The population numbered 184,300 in 1998.

METROPOLITAN BOARD OF WORKS. By the 1850s, a number of services (such as policing and **sewage disposal**) were administered on a London-wide basis, but many others were organized locally. More than 300 bodies (some with very vague powers) exercised authority in a wide variety of areas, including road maintenance and **health care**. **St. Pancras** alone had 16 different committees dealing with street paving and carrying out duties required by 29 Acts of Parliament. Arguments favoring centralization were frequently countered by local leaders, frightened of losing power, who claimed that the city was too diverse to be ruled by one council because people in the suburbs had little in common with those in the center of the urban area, but the case for reform was compelling and, in 1855, the Metropolitan Board of Works was established by Parliament under the terms of a Metropolis Management Act.

The board had 45 members, appointed by the **City of London**'s **Court of Common Council** and by 38 newly created District Boards (defined on a territorial basis) rather than by city residents. Its powers were limited (in deference to the critics) and concerned largely with civil engineering matters. The requirements that all projects costing over £50,000 should get government approval and all those over £100,000 parliamentary approval greatly inhibited its freedom of action, but the **Great Stink** from the **River Thames** during the summer of 1858 proved a powerful ally, and the go-ahead was given for construction of a new drainage system. In less than 10 years, Chief Engineer **Joseph William Bazalgette** supervised the laying of 82 miles of sewer that would carry the city's effluent to outlets east of the city. Also, a major road building program was undertaken, involving construction of lengthy sections of the embankment along the Thames and the building of streets, including **Charing Cross Road** and **Shaftesbury Avenue**. The new thoroughfares undoubtedly improved access and introduced opportunities for a variety of new businesses, but their introduction required the demolition of much inexpensive **housing** and thereby added to problems of overcrowding in other slum areas. As the evidence of the interrelationship between housing and poverty mounted, radical pressure groups maintained that private enterprise could not solve the problems of London's poor on its own, and, by the 1880s, they had convinced the politicians of the need for a new authority with wider powers and responsibilities. As a result, in 1888 the Board of Works was superseded by the **London County Council**. (*See also* LONDON FIRE BRIGADE; PLUMSTEAD.)

METROPOLITAN CATTLE MARKET. In 1855, trading in live cattle was moved from Smithfield (*see* **Smithfield Meat Market**) to a new location, known as the Metropolitan Cattle **Market**, in Copenhagen Fields at **Holloway**. Animals were bought and sold on Mondays and Thursdays, leaving the rings available for a more general market on Fridays. As animal sales declined, the other business (known as "The Caledonian" because of its proximity to Caledonian Road) increased, with over 2,000 stalls present during the 1930s, but the Second World War brought trading to an end for good. For over 25 years, the site was unused, then, in 1965, it was covered by a local authority **housing** estate.

METROPOLITAN DRINKING FOUNTAIN AND CATTLE TROUGH ASSOCIATION. The association was founded, in 1859, by Member of Parliament Samuel Gurney, who hoped that it would decrease the incidence of **cholera** and drunkenness in the city. The first fountain was erected outside the Church of the Holy Sepulchre (in **Holborn** Viaduct), where it still stands. Drinking troughs for animals were built from 1867 and are still maintained by the organization.

METROPOLITAN POLICE. *See* POLICE.

MIDDLE TEMPLE. *See* INNS OF COURT.

MILE END. Mile End is a largely working-class suburb lying four miles east of **Charing Cross**. Open land until the late Middle Ages, it was built over from the 15th century. The western section, close to **Spitalfields**, developed particularly rapidly during the late 1600s and became known as Mile End New Town. During the 18th and 19th centuries, it was an important focus of small industrial and processing activities, including sugar refining, fish curing, saw milling, and dyeing. To the east, Mile End Old Town became a center for Jewish **immigrants** after they were allowed into England in 1657 (the Jews' first burial ground in London was established there). Later, in the Victorian period, religious groups and individual philanthropists concentrated much of their charitable work in the area (in 1868, at Mile End Waste, **William Booth** held some of the first meetings from which his Salvation Army developed, and two years later, **Thomas John Barnardo** opened a home for orphan children near **Ben Jonson** Road). By the early 20th century, Mile End was densely populated, with residents finding employment in the **docks** and other local industries, such as brewing. The bombs of the **Blitz** caused much loss of life and damage to property but did allow local authorities to clear land and erect modern homes after the Second World War. The suburb was incorporated within the **London Borough of Tower Hamlets** when London's **local government** was reorganized in 1965. (*See also* TURNPIKES.)

MILLENNIUM BRIDGE. At the end of the 20th century, a footbridge was built across the **River Thames** in an attempt to link the open space around **St. Paul's Cathedral** (in the **City of London**) to the **Globe Theatre** and **Tate Gallery** developments at **Bankside** (on the northern edge of **Southwark**). London's first river crossing for over a century (and the sole crossing in the central city available only to pedestrians), it was designed by a consortium consisting of architects Foster and Partners, sculptor Sir Anthony Caro, and engineers Ove Arup and Partners, who won the contract in an international competition that attracted 227 entries. The structure, which cost over £14 million, was opened in June 2000 but immediately closed because it rocked violently from side to side as 100,000 people tried to cross it. Project consultants admitted that work to correct the fault could cost a further £10 million.

MILLENNIUM DOME. The dome was built on a site close to the **River Thames** at **Greenwich** to mark the beginning of the 21st century and opened on 31 December 1999. Fraught with problems from its inception, it cost £758 million, about half of which was raised through the National Lottery and the rest through private sponsorship. Much of the exhibition area consisted of 13 themed zones (including the Body Zone, Home Planet, and the Play Zone) with the remainder designed to accommodate public performances for large audiences. The plans were criticized by many people who felt that the money invested would have been better used on improvements to educational provision and health care. Also, religious leaders (including the Archbishop of Canterbury, head of the Church of England) argued that a monument built to mark the passage of 2,000 years since the birth of Christ should have a religious theme (press reports indicated that Prime Minister Tony Blair had refused to allow the Archbishop to hold a service at midnight on New Year's Eve because it would spoil the party atmosphere). Prince Charles claimed that the building looked like a monstrous blancmange, many guests invited to the opening ceremony failed to arrive because their invitations had been mailed late, and hundreds of those who did turn up waited several hours for public transport to the site because limited car parking was available. Then, after only five weeks of operation, the Chief Executive of the New Millennium Experience Company was fired because visitor numbers were well below expectations. Government plans to sell the dome to a private concern after 12 months' operation produced further complaints that the site should be used for some public purpose. The exhibitions closed at the end of 2000, with the future of the building still uncertain.

MILL HILL. Mill Hill lies on the northwest fringe of London, some 10 miles from **Charing Cross**. From the 17th century until after the First World War, it was a fashionable place in which to establish a country home; three **Lord Mayors**—John Wilkes (1774), John Anderson (1797), and Charles Flower (1808)—had houses there, as did Peter Collinson (1694–1768), the botanist who introduced the yucca and the hydrangea to Britain, and William Wilberforce (1759–1833), who campaigned in the House of Commons (*see* **Palace of Westminster**) for the abolition of slavery. Also, it attracted a number of educational institutions, including Mill Hill School (built in 1907 for the children of nonconformists) and St. Joseph's College (opened in 1871 to train Roman Catholic missionaries). During the 1920s, however, it became less exclusive as **London Underground**'s Northern Line extended into the area, attracting commuters willing to travel to office jobs in the city and encouraging developers to lay out streets of detached and semidetached homes. Although much open space remains nearby (partly as a result of the designation of the **Green Belt** in 1938), Mill Hill is a typical interwar suburb. It was incorporated within the **London Borough of Barnet** in 1965. (*See also* EDUCATION.)

MILLWALL. Millwall occupies the western half of the **Isle of Dogs**, taking its name from the structures that pumped water out of the marshes that line the north shore of the **River Thames**. It was industrialized during the 19th century, attracting port activities such as food processing and shipbuilding (when the *Great Eastern*, designed by Isambard Kingdom Brunel, was launched from John Scott Russell's yard in 1859 it was the largest ship ever built in Britain). The 36-acre Millwall **dock** opened in 1868, dealing largely in grain, and Millwall **Football** Club was founded in 1885, providing a Saturday afternoon recreational facility for the largely working-class population. As migrants moved in, looking for homes near their jobs, the area suffered increasingly from overcrowding, but extensive damage during the **Blitz** and the progressive closure of London's docks from the 1960s enabled local authorities and private interests to undertake major redevelopment programs. Much of the land is now occupied by offices and by newspaper printing works, but some **housing** has been built along the river front. The area was included within the **London Borough of Tower Hamlets** when the city's **local government** was restructured in 1965.

MITCHAM. Mitcham, eight miles southwest of **Charing Cross**, was farmed before the Roman invasion of Britain and was well populated by

Anglo-Saxon times (excavation of a graveyard near Ravensbury Park, revealed over 200 bodies interred during the period, along with numerous brooches and other artefacts). During the Middle Ages, a community developed around the Church of St. Peter and St. Paul (established during the 13th century) and wealthy Londoners acquired country estates nearby. Calico bleaching and printing developed in the 17th and 18th centuries, augmenting farming incomes, as did the growing of medicinal herbs, market gardening, and the cultivation of watercress. Also, inns were built along the road to the capital and, by 1732, an annual fair was being held every August. From the later 1800s, however, the area was converted from a rural village into a metropolitan suburb as **trams** and **railways** improved access to the central city and attracted commuters who wanted a home near the country. The area became increasingly developed, but the 460-acre common was preserved as open space and, although partially converted into sports fields, is now managed as an ecological resource. In 1934, as population rose, Mitcham was accorded borough status, but when London's **local government** was reformed in 1965 it was incorporated within the **London Borough of Merton**.

MITHRAIUM. *See* TEMPLE OF MITHRAS.

MONASTERIES. Although most monastic groups preferred the peace of rural areas to the hustle and bustle of English towns during the Medieval period, London attracted several major religious foundations, including the Benedictine community at **Westminster Abbey**, the Carthusians at **Charterhouse**, the Dominicans at **Blackfriars**, and the Franciscans at **Greyfriars Monastery**. In addition, many smaller groups dedicated themselves to the care of the urban poor, establishing **hospitals** as well as chapels. From 1532, all of these orders were required to accept the Acts of Supremacy, which recognized the Monarch (rather than the Pope) as head of the Church in England. Many refused and paid the price; their buildings were torn down, their property confiscated, their monks and nuns executed or imprisoned, and their communities dispersed. Those believers who were willing to take oaths supporting the legislation were given pensions. The dissolution of the monasteries is frequently regarded by scholars as the end of the Middle Ages in London because of its social impact, clearing the city of the cassocked clergy and leaving it with too few hospitals and places of worship for its needs. (*See also* ABBEY WOOD; BARKING; BARTHOLOMEW FAIR; BEDLAM; BERMONDSEY; CANONBURY; CLERKENWELL; COVENT

GARDEN; DULWICH; EDGWARE; EPPING FOREST; ERITH; GREENWICH; HEALTH CARE; HOUNSLOW; ILFORD; KILBURN; KNIGHTS HOSPITALLER; MERTON; MUSWELL HILL; ORPINGTON; REGENT'S PARK; ST. BARTHOLOMEW-THE-GREAT CHURCH, SMITHFIELD; ST. MARYLEBONE; SHOREDITCH; SPITALFIELDS; STANMORE; STRATFORD; STREATHAM; SYON HOUSE; WANSTEAD; WATER POLLUTION; WHITEFRIARS; WOODFORD.)

MONUMENT. In 1666, Parliament approved the rebuilding of those areas of the **City of London** that had been destroyed by the **Great Fire** and authorized the erection of a monument "to preserve the memory of this dreadful Visitation." **Christopher Wren** and his friend, Robert Hooke, prepared the plans, proposing a single shaft of **Portland stone** surmounted by a bronze urn and a gilded ball of flame. The 202-foot-high structure (still the tallest isolated stone column in the world) was completed in 1671. Inside, a spiral staircase with 311 steps leads to a balcony, which, in 1842, was enclosed in an iron cage after six people had thrown themselves to their deaths. At the base, inscriptions in Latin describe the conflagration (a sentence attributing it to "Popish frenzy" was removed in 1831), note the contribution of King Charles II and his Parliament to the rebuilding, and list the **Lord Mayor**s of the time. Also, a bas-relief by Caius Gabriel Cibber depicts the King commanding his courtiers to give help to the distressed area. If the monument toppled eastwards, the urn would land exactly at the location of the baker's premises where the fire began.

MORRISON, HERBERT STANLEY (1888–1965). Although Morrison is best remembered for his prominent role in national politics from 1945 to 1959, his work in London between the two world wars had more lasting impact. Born in **Brixton** on 3 January 1888, the youngest of seven children in the family of Police Constable Henry Morrison and his wife, Priscilla, he left school at the age of 14 and worked in a series of jobs before becoming Secretary of the London Labour Party in 1915. Realizing that electoral success depended on finding suitable candidates and training them to manipulate committees, he introduced organizational reforms that resulted in major Labour successes in the **London borough** and **London County Council (LCC)** elections in 1919. He was elected Mayor of **Hackney** the same year then, in 1922, gained an LCC seat himself. By wooing voters on the rapidly expanding local authority

housing estates, he won a surprise victory for Labour in the council elections in 1934, establishing a foundation that (aided by the movement of more wealthy residents to suburban areas beyond the LCC boundary) resulted in socialist government in the city for the next 31 years.

By creating a new Public Relations Department, Morrison skillfully fed the local press with stories and pictures that created the image of an administration bent on improving conditions for all Londoners. Work began on a new bridge at **Waterloo** in 1934, programs of slum clearance and house building were implemented within the inner city (under Morrison's direction, Labour built new homes for over 34,000 people during its first three years in office), the regulations preventing married women from working as schoolteachers were swept away in 1935, and a **green belt**, which preserved open space by restricting the outward extension of urban development, was established in 1938.

In 1923, Morrison was elected Member of Parliament for Hackney South and, six years later, was made Minister of **Transport** by Prime Minister Ramsay MacDonald. Arguing that the **London Underground** and other mass transit services in the city needed unified management, he introduced the London Passenger Transport Bill to the House of Commons (1931). The subsequent legislation created the London Passenger Transport Board (*see* **London Transport**), a public corporation that, at the time, was the world's largest transport authority.

Morrison lost his parliamentary seat in 1931 but regained it four years later and led a campaign, strongly supported in London, for new laws that would curb the activities of pro-Nazi groups in the city. The principal results—gained through the passage of the Public Order Act in 1936—were a ban on the wearing of uniforms for political ends and additional powers enabling the police to stop marches that might result in violence. When the National government was formed in 1940, some months after the outbreak of the Second World War, Morrison was initially made Minister of Supply but, after a few months, was appointed Home Secretary, forming a nationwide Fire Service to ensure coordination in efforts to reduce the effects of enemy **air raids**. In 1945, he put his experience of political party organization to good effect, receiving much of the credit for Labour's victory in the first postwar General Election. Prime Minister Clement Attlee appointed him Lord President of the Council, with responsibility for the reconstruction of the British economy, but he never fully grasped the issues involved and, after two years, concentrated solely on piloting the government's contentious legislation on the nationalization of industries through the House of Commons (a task that allowed him to make full use of his administrative skills). For a few months in 1951, he was at the Foreign Office, but, a Londoner at heart, he lacked the knowledge and understanding of other cultures necessary for such a diplomatic position and was not a success.

When Attlee retired from the post of Leader of the Labour Party in 1955, Morrison was one of the candidates for the position but, at the age of 67 and unable to win Attlee's support, lost to Hugh Gaiskell. He was awarded a peerage in 1959 then served as President of the British Board of Film Censors. Following his death at Sidcup on 6 March 1965, he was cremated and his ashes scattered on the **River Thames**.

MORTLAKE. Mortlake lies on the south bank of the **River Thames** between **Barnes** and **Kew**. It was part of the Archbishop of Canterbury's estate during the Middle Ages and, by the end of the 16th century, had evolved into a substantial village. From 1619, when King James VI and I provided premises for a community of 50 **Huguenot** weavers, the settlement earned a reputation for producing the finest tapestries in Europe, then, following the closure of the business in 1703, became widely known for its market gardens, pottery workshops, and **breweries**. It escaped the 19th-century industrialization that transformed other riverside areas of London and remains predominantly residential, with several 18th-century properties surviving (as at The Limes, built in the 1720s for the Countess of Stafford). J. F. Bentley (architect of **Westminster Cathedral**) and explorer Richard Burton are buried at St. Osmond's Roman Catholic Church, Burton in an unusual tomb resembling a desert nomad's tent fashioned in stone. Mortlake was included within the **London Borough of Richmond** when London's **local government** was restructured in 1965. (*See also* CHISWICK BRIDGE; UNIVERSITY BOAT RACE.)

MOST VENERABLE ORDER OF THE HOSPITAL OF ST. JOHN OF JERUSALEM. *See* KNIGHTS HOSPITALLER.

MOUSETRAP, THE. Agatha Christie's mystery, *The Mousetrap*, opened at the Ambassador's **Theatre** on 25 November 1952 and was still attracting audiences, after nearly 20,000 performances, at the end of the millennium, by which time it was the world's longest running play. The production, watched by a total audience of over 10 million, has starred some 350 actors and actresses, including David Raven (who appeared 4,575 times as Major Metcalfe) and Nancy Seabrooke (who understudied the role of Mrs. Boyle for 6,240 performances and appeared on only 72 occasions). In 1973, the play transferred to St. Martin's Theatre, but the set has changed only twice, in 1963 and 1999. On the latter occasion, props were auctioned to provide funds for Denville Hall, a residential nursing home for retired actors and actresses.

MUSEUM OF LONDON. In 1976, Guildhall Museum (established in 1826 by the **Corporation of London**) and the London **Museum** (founded by Viscount Esher and Viscount Harcourt in 1912) merged collections illustrating the city's history to form a single Museum of London. Housed in the **Barbican** development, the museum combines modern technology with artefacts from the past (such as a Roman pavement, Elizabethan jewelry, an 18th-century goldsmith's goods, and a Victorian barber's shop) to explain how a small settlement beside the **River Thames** evolved into a major metropolis. It also supports archaeological excavations designed to further understand the capital's development.

MUSEUM OF MANKIND. In 1970, the **British Museum**, lacking sufficient space to exhibit ethnographic material at its Great Russell Street site, opened the **Museum** of Mankind in Burlington Gardens, taking over a building erected in 1869 for the University of London. Collections from Africa, the Americas, Australasia, Eurasia, and the Pacific islands were housed in galleries that emphasize education rather than mere display, with items as disparate as a crystal skull fashioned by Aztec craftsmen and masks once worn by tribal groups in New Guinea. In recent years, some of the material has been a focus of controversy because foreign governments claim the return of artefacts which, they argue, were stolen by British colonialists (Ghana would like to see the Ashante regalia returned to West Africa, for example). From 1995 the exhibits were returned to new galleries at the main British Museum in **Bloomsbury** and in 1997 the Museum of Mankind closed.

MUSEUM OF THE MOVING IMAGE. The most recent addition to the arts complex on the **South Bank** of the **River Thames**, the **Museum** of the Moving Image is located next to the **National Film Theatre** underneath the arches of **Waterloo** Bridge (both institutions are managed by the British Film Institute, which was formed in 1933 to develop film as an art form). Opened in 1988, the museum tells the story of the evolution of moving images from the days of Javanese shadow puppets, which entertained audiences 4,000 years ago, to the computer-generated special effects of productions such as *Star Wars*. Visitors can read the news on television, submit to interviews, and, like Mary Poppins, fly over London. There are also posters, props, stills, and other illustrative material as well as space for temporary exhibitions. In the evening, the National Film Theatre takes over the premises to show full-length movies. The museum closed for refurbishment in 2000 and was expected to reopen in 2003 with considerably enlarged premises.

MUSEUMS AND GALLERIES. Although kings and courtiers amassed *objets d'art* with which to impress their subjects and aristocratic visitors, the concept of museums and galleries as centers of learning and public **education** did not develop in London until the 18th century. Visitors to the **British Museum**, when it opened in 1759, were strictly controlled; only 30 were allowed in each day and then only if they had applied in writing and received the approval of the Principal Librarian. Within a few decades, however, rich merchants and professional men were bequeathing their private (and often very eclectic) collections to the nation (*see*, for example, **Sir John Soane's Museum**) and events such as the **Great Exhibition** were fuelling interest in the unusual and exotic. Also, the need for an educated workforce encouraged investment in the dissemination of knowledge. At the instigation of **Prince Albert**, the site of the Great Exhibition in south **Kensington** was developed to extend "the influence of Science and Art upon productive industry" through the erection of museums, concert halls, and premises for learned societies; the **Natural History Museum**, the **Science Museum**, and the **Victoria and Albert Museum** became the 19th-century equivalents of Animal Planet and the Discovery Channel. At the same time, great works of art were increasingly brought from private collections and offered to a wider audience; the **National Gallery** opened in 1824 after the Tory government had purchased 38 old masters from the estate of John Julius Angerstein, the **National Portrait Gallery** followed in 1859 (also partly because of Prince Albert's enthusiastic support), and the **Tate Gallery** (the gift of sugar refiner Sir Henry Tate) widened the range of paintings further in 1897.

During the 20th century, increased leisure time and the spread of literacy widened the market for museums and galleries, but the cost of maintaining large, all-embracing collections rose markedly. Although the major institutions continued to flourish, they had to keep apace with the times by employing up-to-date technology (as with the **Blitz** Experience at the **Imperial War Museum**) and, during the 1980s (amidst great controversy), to charge admission in an attempt to defray expenses. Also, they found themselves competing with growing numbers of smaller, specialist museums such as the **Cabinet War Rooms**, the **London Transport Museum**, and the **Bethnal Green Museum of Childhood**. As a result, the city now has a great range of premises presenting exhibits of enormous variety using techniques that range from mounting artefacts in traditional glass cases to hands-on examinations and computerized multimedia experiences. (*See also* BAKER STREET; BANK OF ENGLAND; BANQUETING HOUSE; *BELFAST,* HMS; BRENTFORD; CAMBERWELL; CLERKENWELL; COURTAULD INSTITUTE OF ART; DESIGN MUSEUM; DICKENS' HOUSE MUSEUM; DULWICH; EPPING FOREST; FREUD'S HOUSE; GEFFRYE MUSEUM; GEOLOGICAL MUSEUM; GOLDERS GREEN; HAYWARD GALLERY; HENDON; HORNIMAN MUSEUM; JEWISH MUSEUM; JOHNSON'S HOUSE, DR.; KEATS'S HOUSE; KENSINGTON PALACE; KENWOOD HOUSE; KNIGHTS HOSPITALLER; LONDON DUNGEON; MADAME TUSSAUD'S WAXWORKS; MARBLE HILL HOUSE; MARYLEBONE CRICKET CLUB [MCC]; MUSEUM OF LONDON; MUSEUM OF MANKIND; MUSEUM OF THE MOVING IMAGE; NATIONAL ARMY MUSEUM; NATIONAL MARITIME MUSEUM; RANGER'S HOUSE; ROYAL ACADEMY OF ARTS; ROYAL COLLEGE OF SURGEONS OF ENGLAND; ST. BRIDE'S CHURCH, FLEET STREET; SERPENTINE; SLOANE, HANS; SOHO; SOMERSET HOUSE; SYON HOUSE; THEATRE MUSEUM; TOTTENHAM; TOWER BRIDGE; TOWER OF LONDON; TOYNBEE HALL; WESLEY'S CHAPEL; WHITECHAPEL; WILLIAM MORRIS GALLERY; WIMBLEDON; WOOLWICH.)

MUSIC HALLS. The music hall was a popular place of entertainment for working-class Londoners from about 1850 until the period between the First and Second World Wars. Drawing on the fairground performers' tradition of mixing acrobatic acts, songs, and dances, the halls developed from 1843, when the Theatres Act allowed public houses to offer cheap entertainment. By the mid-1860s, about 200 were operating, seating audiences of up to 2,000, but the introduction of increasingly strict fire prevention regulations from 1878 caused many of the smaller businesses to close and entrepreneurs to build larger auditoriums. Bawdy humor, songs with rousing choruses, and an ability to make patrons forget their troubles combined to make entertainers such as Dan Leno, Marie Lloyd, George Robey, and Vesta Tilley household names, despite efforts by the temperance movement and other protectors of moral rectitude to deplore the drunkenness and sexual license with which the halls were often associated. By the early 1900s, however, fashions were changing. Performers forsook the music halls, with their procession of individual acts and sketches, for more sophisticated musicals and revues. Then, in the 1920s, cinemas began to attract the customers who had previously frequented the halls and, although **theaters** such as the Hackney Empire, the London Palladium, and the Victoria Palace kept the genre alive, young people were looking for other forms of entertainment. The music hall tradition survives (most notably in the annual Royal Command Performance, attended by Queen Elizabeth II and other members of the royal family) but its most enduring legacy is probably the image of the **Cockney** as the archetypal, cheerful, indomitable, working-class Londoner portrayed by characters such as Eliza Doolittle in George Bernard Shaw's *Pygmalion* (first performed in 1913) and in the countless productions of the Alan Jay Lerner and Frederick Loewe musical *My Fair Lady* (1956), which is based on Shaw's play. (*See also* BRIXTON; CLAPHAM; GOLDERS GREEN; HOXTON; OLD VIC; SADLER'S WELLS; SOHO.)

MUSWELL HILL. During the 12th century, the Augustinian community at St. Mary's Priory in **Clerkenwell** acquired land at Muswell Hill, six miles north of **Charing Cross**, for pasturing cattle and producing milk. The estate included a mossy well whose waters were believed to have healing qualities and which gave its name to the area. Apart from a few villas erected in the 18th century, the land remained agricultural until, in the two decades from 1896, James Edmundson and W. J. Collins laid out a typically late Victorian suburb of solid homes and shops built with stone-dressed brick. The spire of St. James's Church (which was designed by J. S. Alder, opened in 1901, and was constructed of Ancaster stone with Bath stone facings) provides a prominent landmark. Muswell Hill became part of the **London Borough of Haringey** when the **local government** in the metropolitan area was reorganized in 1965.

– N –

NASH, JOHN (1752–1835). Nash had a major impact on London's townscape, converting the open lands of royal estates west of the **City of London** into the residential development and spacious lawns of **Regent**

Street and **Regent's Park**. Born in 1752 (possibly in London but perhaps in Wales), he was trained by architect Robert Taylor before going into business on his own account as a builder and house designer. When that venture failed in 1783, he moved to Carmarthen but continued to practice **architecture** and built up a strong list of clients as he concentrated on the preparation of plans for country houses and institutional structures (such as Cardigan jail).

When he returned to London in the late 1790s, working in an informal partnership with landscape gardener Humphry Repton, Nash's work attracted the attention of several aristocratic patrons, including George, Prince Regent, who, in 1811, commissioned him to present a scheme for the conversion of Marylebone Park into a place for public recreation. The development, now known as Regent's Park, included the **Regent's Canal**, gardens, and a lake, with shopping arcades and **housing** designed for artisan as well as for middle-class families. Regent Street, built to link the park to the Prince's residence at Carlton House, was completed between 1820 and 1825, with All Soul's Church (which has an unusual circular portico and a conical spire) erected at Langham Place to add impact to the view. Nash was also responsible for the Royal Opera Arcade (erected in 1816 and 1818 and one of the earliest arcades in the city), the layout of parts of the **Charing Cross** area (including Suffolk Place and Suffolk Street in 1820), the conversion of **Buckingham Palace** from country mansion to royal palace (1820–30), the redesign of **St. James's Park** (1827–29), and the building of the Theatre Royal, **Haymarket** (1831). His last years in business were marred by disputes over the cost and structural quality of the Buckingham Palace program. Dismissed from the project following King George IV's death in 1830, he retired to East Cowes Castle (on the Isle of Wight) which he had built in 1798 and where he died on 13 May 1835. (*See also* ARCHWAY; CLARENCE HOUSE; MARBLE ARCH; OXFORD STREET; PORTLAND PLACE; ROYAL MEWS; TRAFALGAR SQUARE; WOOLWICH.)

NATIONAL ARMY MUSEUM. The **museum**, originally located at the Royal Military Academy Sandhurst (in Surrey), was moved to its present site beside **Chelsea Hospital** in 1971. Its displays outline English and British military history from the early 16th century, with additional exhibits relating to the armies of the Commonwealth of Nations. An extensive library of books, photographs, and related material is available to researchers.

NATIONAL FILM THEATRE (NFT). In 1953, the British Film Institute (founded in 1933 and primarily concerned with the promotion of film as an art form) built a cinema on the **South Bank** of the **River Thames** near **Waterloo** Bridge. Known as Telekinema, it concentrated on demonstrating technical developments in movie production and proved so successful that a new building—the National Film Theatre—was built under the arches of the bridge five years later. A second auditorium was opened in 1970 and the screen at the **Museum of the Moving Image** commandeered for evening performances from 1988. Altogether, about 2,000 films are shown every year, including early silent movies as well as recent releases. In addition, the NFT hosts the annual London Film Festival. Shows are open only to members, but visitors can purchase day membership for a small charge.

NATIONAL GALLERY. The gallery, located on the north side of **Trafalgar Square**, holds one of the world's most important art collections. Its nucleus was the 38 paintings acquired by the government from the estate of Russian-born merchant John Julius Angerstein in 1824. As private collectors gifted other works, the gallery rapidly outgrew its initial home in Angerstein's **Pall Mall** house so William Wilkins was commissioned to design the present building, which was erected on the site of the **Whitehall Palace** stables in 1838 and has since been extended several times, most recently in 1991 when a wing (funded by the Sainsbury family) was added to the west. The gallery's principal strength is its fine selection of paintings by representatives of the various mainland European schools, including Flemish and Dutch masters such as Rembrandt and Rubens, the principal Italian Renaissance artists (Giotto and Leonardo da Vinci, for example), French painters of the 17th, 19th, and early 20th centuries (notably Poussin and Cézanne), and Spanish canvases by Velázquez, Goya, and El Greco. The gallery, which receives some five million visitors every year, has its own conservation department and presents a regular lecture program. (*See also* GIBBONS, GRINLING; TATE GALLERY.)

NATIONAL MARITIME MUSEUM. The **museum**, which opened in 1937, is based at **Greenwich** in a complex of buildings with naval connections and considerable architectural interest. Its main center is the **Queen's House**, designed by **Inigo Jones** and originally intended as a residence for Anne of Denmark, wife of King James VI and I. The museum uses it as a gallery for its Elizabethan and Stuart collections.

Other buildings, commissioned in 1807 to commemorate Lord Nelson's victory at the Battle of Trafalgar two years earlier, are connected to the Queen's House by colonnades. In addition, there are exhibits in the former **Royal Naval College** and the **Royal Observatory**. In total, the 29 galleries comprise the world's largest maritime museum and include marine art (Joshua Reynolds's early study of Commodore Keppel, painted in 1749, is on display), water transport (there is a section dealing with emigration from Britain to North America), and archaeology (with an emphasis on the replica of a 7th-century burial ship discovered at Sutton Hoo, Suffolk, in 1939) as well as naval material and biographical data on individuals such as Captain James Cook, who added many territories to the British Empire during the 18th century. One of the most popular foci for visitors is the jacket Nelson was wearing when he was shot at Trafalgar: the hole where the fatal musket ball entered his body is clearly evident.

NATIONAL PORTRAIT GALLERY. The gallery was opened in 1859 following pressure on the government from historian Philip, Earl of Stanhope, who convinced **Prince Albert**, Queen Victoria's husband, to support his cause. Its initial collection of 57 paintings was regularly augmented by gifts and purchases, necessitating a series of moves to bigger and better accommodations, which culminated in the building of its present home, behind the **National Gallery**, in 1890–95. Currently, the gallery has about 10,000 works, selected on the basis of subject rather than artistic qualities, which depict men and women who have graced the stage of English history. Some of the canvases are by renowned artists (such as Holbein, who painted King Henry VII, King Henry VIII, and Thomas More). Others are crude by any standards but important nonetheless (for example, the portrait of Jane Austen by Cassandra, her sister, is the only likeness of the novelist completed while she was alive). Since 1968, the paintings, drawings, and sculptures have been augmented by an archive of photographs, which now contains over half a million pictures. In recent years new building and refurbishment have enhanced the displays. In 2000 Queen Elizabeth II opened the Ondaatje Wing. Erected largely through funding provided by Christopher Ondaatje, it houses the Tudor galleries and incorporates a balcony with images of late 20th-century celebrities. Also, a redesign of the Victorian and early-20th-century galleries has unblocked windows and given a lighter feel to the previously enclosed space. The collection attracts about a million visitors every year.

NATIONAL THEATRE. *See* ROYAL NATIONAL THEATRE.

NATIONAL WESTMINSTER TOWER. In 1959, the National Provincial Bank (which merged with the Westminster Bank in 1968) purchased property adjoining its premises at 15 Bishopsgate and applied to the **London County Council** for planning permission to allow it to demolish the newly acquired buildings and erect offices. The council felt that the old structures had sufficient architectural and historical interest to merit retention and requested revised proposals, which were approved. However, in 1964, before work started, the government passed legislation limiting the size of office developments in London so the plan was postponed again. At the end of the decade, as opinions about urban design changed, the **Corporation of London** gave the go-ahead for a skyscraper development that would act as a focal point in the city center. Construction of the 52-story, 600-foot-high tower began in 1971 and was completed in 1981. Until **Canary Wharf** was finished a decade later, it was the tallest building in London.

NATURAL HISTORY MUSEUM. One of a complex of educational institutions in south **Kensington**, the **museum** was opened in 1881 when natural history exhibits were transferred from the **British Museum** in an attempt to relieve congestion. The building, designed by Alfred Waterhouse, has a large central hall (deliberately reminiscent of a cathedral because the museum would display the works of the Creator) and a typically Victorian ornate exterior. Several of the galleries were destroyed by bombing during the Second World War, but new accommodations were constructed after the conflict ended, providing (in 1959) facilities for the library, lecture theater, reference collections, a Botanical Gallery (finished in 1963), and an additional wing built in 1977.

Initially, the museum's core exhibits were those collected by physician **Hans Sloane** during the first half of the 18th century, but these were augmented by purchases and donations such as the botanical collection of Sir Joseph Banks (President of the **Royal Society** from 1778 to 1820). Currently, new additions are made at a rate of about 300,000 every year, so the museum can show only a fraction of its 65 million specimens. For that reason, it has concentrated, since the 1970s, on displaying a series of self-contained exhibitions in an attempt to attract more visitors; for example, computer technology is employed to enable children to find things out for themselves, and one gallery of arthropods is labelled "creepy crawlies." The resultant tension between scholars and accountants led one writer to *The Spectator* to claim, in 1991, that there were, in effect, two institutions, one consisting of the community of research scientists who have little or no influence on what is displayed in the public galleries and the other the museum, with themed displays viewed by some 1.7 million people every year.

NEASDEN. Neasden, seven miles northeast of **Charing Cross**, lies in the center of the **London Borough of Brent**. An agricultural village until late in the 19th century, it was transformed by improved accessibility to the central city. The first changes occurred in the 1880s, when the Metropolitan **Railway** Company built houses for employees laying its lines. Then, in the period between the First and Second World Wars, the construction of the North Circular Road around inner London initiated a second phase of development, turning the area into a residential suburb. Its supposed lack of individuality has made it the butt of many jokes, particularly in the satirical magazine *Private Eye*.

NELSON'S COLUMN. *See* TRAFALGAR SQUARE.

NEWGATE. Archaeological evidence suggests that Newgate was one of the principal entries in the western sector of the defensive wall built around **Londinium** by the Romans during the late second century. The gate was rebuilt in 1555–56, 1628–30, and 1672, but demolished in 1767.

NEWGATE PRISON. By the 12th century, a **prison** had been established near the **Newgate** entrance to the **City of London**, but that structure was completely destroyed during the **Great Fire** of 1666. Although a new building opened in 1672, contemporary records indicate that conditions for the inmates were primitive, with inadequate water supplies or ventilation. The smell was overwhelming, outbreaks of infectious disease were common, and warders supplemented their incomes by selling candles or letting wealthy prisoners occupy cells in the least oppressive areas. In 1770–78, a replacement jail was erected to designs by **George Dance the Younger** but damaged in 1780 during the anti-Catholic **Gordon Riots** and rebuilt in 1780–83 (one of its first occupants was Lord George Gordon, who was convicted on charges of libel in 1787 and kept in the cells until his death six years later). In 1783, public hangings were transferred from **Tyburn** to a gibbet outside the prison, continuing there until parliamentary legislation in 1868 brought them to an end. Newgate was demolished in 1902 to provide space for the erection of the **Central**

Criminal Court. Its inmates had included Quaker leader William Penn, author Daniel Defoe, and Rob Roy MacGregor (clan chief and cattle thief). Elizabeth Fry visited in 1813 and was appalled by the sight of women, many drunk and starving, lying on floors with no bedding. She proposed a series of administrative changes (including the separation of prisoners by sex, provision for religious and other **education**, employment for inmates, and female warders for female convicts), which were increasingly adopted throughout Europe during the 19th century. Novelist **Charles Dickens** also admitted to a fascination for Newgate, describing it in chilling detail in *Sketches by Boz* (1835–37). (*See also* CATO STREET CONSPIRACY; WHITTINGTON, RICHARD "DICK".)

NEWHAM, LONDON BOROUGH OF. Newham was formed in 1965 through the merger of **East Ham** and **West Ham** with parts of **Barking** and north **Woolwich**. It has all the economic and social hallmarks of inner-city areas, with high proportions of manual workers, above average rates of unemployment, significant concentrations of ethnic minorities (which together accounted for nearly half the 231,000 population in 1998), and an unenviable reputation as one of the most deprived areas in the United Kingdom. In recent years, local authorities have cooperated with national government and local businesses to invest in regeneration schemes. These focus primarily on **Stratford** (proposed as the site for a railway station that would provide a terminus for lines linking Britain to France, attracting commercial interests, and providing clerical and managerial employment) and the former Royal Docks (on the north bank of the **River Thames**), where a 56-acre business park has been developed in an effort to provide facilities for research companies. The southern part of the borough is well served by east-west road links but lacks good **London Underground** connections. (*See also* BECKTON; CUSTOM HOUSE; ExCEL; HOUSING.)

NEW SCOTLAND YARD. From 959 until the early 16th century, Scotland's monarchs occupied property close to **Whitehall Palace** during their visits to London, so the buildings in the area became known as Little Scotland Yard, Middle Scotland Yard, and Great Scotland Yard. In 1829, the headquarters of the new Metropolitan **Police** force was based at 4 **Whitehall** Place, which had been formed by merging the first two of these yards, but the rear of the premises was converted into a police station with an entry from Great Scotland Yard and, very quickly, the formal title of Metropolitan Police Office was simplified to Scotland Yard in common parlance. The name stuck, so in 1890, when office staff were moved to another site near **Westminster Bridge**, James Munro (the Commissioner of Police) decided to recognize the usage by calling the accommodation New Scotland Yard. That name was retained in 1967, when a further transfer was made to a 20-story block in Broadway that houses nearly 700 offices and covers 11 acres. Great Scotland Yard is now occupied by the Civil Service Club and the first New Scotland Yard (now renamed Norman Shaw Building, in honor of its architect) used as offices for Members of Parliament.

NINE ELMS. A working-class area on the eastern edge of **Battersea**, Nine Elms takes its name from a row of trees that grew by the roadside during the first half of the 17th century. It developed as an industrial area with brewing, flour milling, lime production, and dockyard activities all providing sources of income. The economy was boosted in 1838, when the London and Southampton Railway opened its terminus. Although the station functioned for only a decade, it attracted goods yards, sidings, and other facilities, which remained after the company moved its base to **Waterloo**, providing an attractive location for manufacturing plants until after the Second World War. During the 1950s and 1960s, reorganization of rail **transport** led to the closure of many of the yards, and economic change put several factories out of business, but the relocation of the **Covent Garden** fruit and vegetable **market** to the derelict premises in 1974 fuelled a resurgence in activity. The market (the largest wholesale source of fresh produce in Britain) occupies a 68-acre site, with the flower trade located on the site of the former station. The area forms part of the **London Borough of Wandsworth**.

NONSUCH PALACE. In 1538, King Henry VIII cleared the population from Cuddington Village, near **Cheam**, and built a hunting palace that was named Nonsuch because it was without equal. The building was small by standards of the time but opulently decorated in Renaissance style, with stucco reliefs along the south front and around the inner of two courtyards. Ornate towers, surmounted by cupolas, were erected at either end of the 150-yard-long structure and gardens laid out with the studied formality required by Tudor taste. King James VI and I continued to use the palace as a base for hunting, but his grandson, King Charles I, presented it to a mistress, Barbara, Countess of Castlemaine, who sold it to Lord Berkeley in 1682. Shortly after, the new owner demolished the structure, using some of the stone to erect a house near Epsom. The location of the building was lost until 1959, when excavations allowed archaeologists to reconstruct its ground plan. The land is now used as a public **park**. (*See also* WORCESTER PARK.)

NORTH DOWNS. A range of chalk hills, known as the North Downs, marks the southern edge of the **London Basin**. Rising to just over 800 feet in places, it is heavily wooded and characterized by steep-sided valleys. London's suburbs spread onto the northern slopes, but much of the land is protected from urban development by **green belt** and similar legislation.

NORTHOLT. The Northolt area, some 12 miles west of **Charing Cross**, was settled by Anglo-Saxon times (in the middle of the 11th century it belonged to Ansgar, who fought against the invading Norman force at the Battle of Hastings in 1066). It developed as an agricultural village, producing hay and grain for the London market, with brick making also contributing to the local economy, particularly during the 19th century. Changes began in 1907 with the arrival of the **railway**, continued with the opening of an aerodrome in 1915, and speeded up following the First World War as construction firms erected row upon row of small properties to meet the demands of office workers willing to commute daily from a home in a semirural environment to an office job in **The City**. After 1945, local authorities took advantage of green field sites to add to the stock of public **housing** and alleviate overcrowding in the inner city. In spite of the building, however, the center of the small settlement (including the village green and the church of St. Mary the Virgin, which measures only 44 feet by 25 feet) survived comparatively unscathed and is now protected by conservation legislation. When **local government** in the metropolitan area was reorganized in 1965, Northolt was included within the **London Borough of Ealing**.

NOTTING HILL. Notting Hill forms the northern section of **Royal Borough of Kensington and Chelsea**. It evolved during the Middle Ages as an agricultural village, with gravel pits providing additional employment from the 17th century. From the 1830s, however, the farmland was eroded by **housing** development as London expanded and, within 50 years, had vanished altogether. The new residents formed a heterogeneous community, with rich and poor living next door to each other. In addition, during the 1950s, the area became a focus for Trinidadian **immigrants**, who brought their festive traditions and, in 1966, founded the exuberant Notting Hill Carnival. The event, which was almost closed after groups of young black people rioted in 1976, is held each year on the Sunday and Monday of England's August Bank Holiday and, with 500,000 participants, is claimed to be Europe's largest street festival. (*See also* RILLINGTON PLACE.)

– O –

OLD BAILEY. *See* CENTRAL CRIMINAL COURT.

OLD CURIOSITY SHOP. A bric-a-brac store in Portsmouth Street (near **Lincoln's Inn Fields**), the Old Curiosity Shop was built in 1567 and claims to be the oldest in London. It takes its name from **Charles Dickens**'s novel, published in 1841 (the shop was the home of Little Nell, the story's heroine).

OLDE CHESHIRE CHEESE, YE. Throughout the 18th and 19th centuries, the Cheshire Cheese (in Wine Office Court, off **Fleet Street**) was a favorite **public house** for London's men of letters. **Samuel Johnson**, **James Boswell**, Thomas **Carlyle**, Thomas Hood, Alfred Lord Tennyson, and William Makepeace Thackeray all gathered beneath the oak beams to drink ale and dine on puddings made with beef, larks, oysters, kidneys, mushrooms, and spices. More recently, the building (erected in 1667) has become a tourist haunt, but even so, the oak panelled interior retains some of the atmosphere of the past, and steak pie is still on the menu.

OLD JEWRY. By the 12th century, the area of the **City of London** now known as Old Jewry was settled by Jewish **immigrants**, who built a synagogue where they could meet for worship but suffered greatly for their beliefs (in 1262, for example, over 500 Jews were murdered because one moneylender charged more than the legal rate of interest). Replaced as the city's chief financiers by Italian and French Christians, they were driven out of England by King Edward I in 1290 and remained in exile until Oliver Cromwell sanctioned their return in 1656. From then, they reestablished themselves in their former area and became a significant force in city finance companies, although their businesses were marginalized by the growth of the central banks during the early 20th century.

OLD VIC. In 1818, a new playhouse, designed by Rudolph Cabanel and named the Royal Coburg Theatre, opened in Waterloo Road, attracting such distinguished actors as Edmund Kean. Fifteen years later, it changed its name to the Royal Victoria Theatre in honor of the 14-year-old Princess (later Queen) Victoria, reduced prices, and staged more down-market productions for a local clientele. The interior was redesigned in 1871 then again in 1880, when Emma Cons, a champion of social reform and the first woman member of the **London County Council**, converted it into the Royal Victoria Coffee **Music Hall**, where working-class people could enjoy wholesome entertainment without the temptation of alcohol to divert them from the pleasures of the stage. After her death in 1912, the property (which became widely known as the Old Vic) was acquired by her niece, violinist and teacher Lilian Bayliss, who attempted to raise artistic standards by presenting **William Shakespeare**'s plays, along with operas and dance. In 1931, the Vic-Wells Ballet Company was formed under Ninette de Valois (*see* **Royal Ballet**), and from 1963 to 1976 the building was the home of the National Theatre (*see* **Royal National Theatre**). In 1981, the Old Vic was bought by Edwin Mirvish, a Canadian businessman, who restored it to its late Victorian splendor, then, in 1998, it was sold to a charitable trust dedicated to preserving it as a home for serious **theater** in London.

OLYMPIA. With over 500,000 square feet of display space, Olympia is one of London's major venues for exhibitions, indoor sports events, and, more recently, conferences. Designed by architect Henry E. Coe and set in 5.5 acres of garden, it opened, as the National Agricultural Hall, in 1884, assuming its present name two years later. Since then, it has staged major circus performances, motor shows, ideal home exhibitions, international show jumping competitions, boxing matches, and other entertainments. A New Hall (now known as the National Hall) was added in 1923 and was followed six years later by the art deco Empire Hall (renamed Olympia 2 in the post-colonial years after the Second World War). Conference facilities were built into the complex in 1987.

ORCHESTRAS. *See* LONDON PHILHARMONIC ORCHESTRA (LPO); LONDON SYMPHONY ORCHESTRA (LSO); PHILHARMONIA ORCHESTRA; ROYAL PHILHARMONIC ORCHESTRA (RPO).

ORPINGTON. Orpington, on the southeast outskirts of London, has been settled since Neolithic times but remained an agricultural village until the early 20th century. During the First World War, a hospital was built to treat Canadian servicemen, then, in the 1920s and 1930s, **housing**

estates were erected to meet the needs of commuters. Further private and local authority developments since the 1950s have turned the area into a metropolitan suburb. Most industry is concentrated at nearby St. Mary Cray, whose location beside the River Cray helped further manufacturing activities, such as bell making and paper works. Orpington Priory, founded during the 13th century as a hostelry for the priors of Christ Church, Canterbury, was restored with public funds in 1974–75 and converted for use as a museum, library, and office complex. When London's **local government** was reformed in 1965, Orpington was included within the **London Borough of Bromley**.

OSTERLEY HOUSE. Osterley, one of the finest country houses in the London area, lies north of **Hounslow**. It was built in 1576 for Sir **Thomas Gresham**, a wealthy merchant, but substantially remodelled from the late 1750s by brothers Robert and Francis Child, who commissioned **William Chambers**, then (from 1761) **Robert Adam**, to prepare the plans. Adam radically altered the structure, enlarging the property and changing its Tudor features to meet Georgian tastes for classical **architecture**. A double screen of Ionic columns, approached by an imposing flight of steps, was erected across the east front, and windows were moved on all four sides of the building to emphasize symmetry. In the front hall, state rooms, and long gallery, great care was invested in the selection of sumptuous furniture, paintings, carpets, and wall hangings, which would complement ceiling, frieze, and pilaster decorations. The work was completed in 1780 and the house remained a private residence until 1949, when the Earl of Jersey (a descendant of Robert Child) presented it to the nation. The National Trust manages the building and the **park**, which contains a conservatory, gardens, and butterfly house.

OUTER LONDON. *See* GREATER LONDON.

OVAL, THE. The headquarters of the Surrey County Cricket Club (which was formed in The Horns, a local **public house**, in 1845), the Oval, like much other property in the area, is leased from the Duchy of Cornwall. Until the first half of the 19th century, cricket was played on the nearby **Kennington** Common, but as that open space was converted to urban uses alternative pitches became increasingly necessary. The Montpelier Cricket Club obtained a lease on a former market garden site in 1845 and, the following year, a match between the Gentlemen and the Players of Surrey took place on the grounds. A pavilion was erected in 1858 and the first test match against Australia held on 6–8 September 1880 (England won by five wickets). The Oval has also been used for other sports, including rugby and **football** (it staged many of the Football Association Cup final matches between 1870 and 1892, for example), and was requisitioned to provide accommodation for German prisoners during the Second World War. The Long Room, in the pavilion, houses many mementoes of games and players.

OXFORD CIRCUS. *See* OXFORD STREET.

OXFORD STREET. Oxford Street, one of London's principal retailing centers, stretches westwards for 1.25 miles from the northern end of **Charing Cross Road** to **Marble Arch**, following the line of a Roman road that once ran from the south coast of England to East Anglia. It gets its name from Edward Harley, Earl of Oxford, who owned land on the north side of the street during the 18th century. Until 1739, the thoroughfare was flanked by fields, but from that year development spread from the urban area in the east, so by 1800 it was lined with houses and shops as far as **Hyde Park**. Towards the end of the 19th century, **department stores** began to oust shoemakers, furniture makers, and other specialist trades, turning the street over to mass market sales in nationwide stores such as Boots, John Lewis, and Marks and Spencer. The older tradition survives, however, partly through the fruit carts, which seem to be parked at every corner, and partly through the itinerant vendors who offer (illegally) cheap souvenirs and other low-price goods.

Oxford Circus (the intersection of **Regent Street** and **Oxford Street**) was laid out by **John Nash** in 1816–24, but the present buildings (consisting of four quadrants with identical facades) was designed by Sir Henry Tanner; the southeast sector was erected in 1913, the northeast in 1923, the southwest in 1925, and the northwest in 1928. Because of its location at the crossroads of major east-west and north-south highways in an area of considerable commercial importance, the junction generates very heavy road traffic. In addition, three **London Underground** lines (the Bakerloo, Central, and **Victoria**) interconnect below street level, disgorging a quarter of a million passengers every day and making the station one of the busiest on the network. However, pedestrian flows in the street fell by 34 percent between 1987 and 1999 as shoppers transferred their allegiance to huge new out-of-town malls, so at the turn of the century, retailers were considering plans to woo the public back by banning traffic, providing more restaurants, and offering play areas for children.

– P –

PADDINGTON. Paddington lies on the northwest edge of central London, bounded by Bayswater Road in the south, Edgware Road in the east, **Maida Vale** in the north, and **Notting Hill** in the west. Its name is probably derived from that of Padda, an Anglo-Saxon leader who settled in the area following the Roman withdrawal in 410 A.D. Until the Industrial Revolution, the economy was based on agriculture, although **Huguenot** refugees from France introduced craft industries (such as textile working) during the 18th century. Urban development began in 1801 (when the Grand Junction Canal connected London with the midlands of England and attracted commerce to its terminus at Paddington Basin) then flourished after the Great Western **Railway** opened in 1838 (*see* **Paddington Station**). Land owners and speculative builders laid out extensive estates (such as that at Ladbroke, named after a family that had held property in the area for several generations); many built expensive homes for wealthy families (in **Bayswater**, for instance), others designed more modest houses for manual workers and tradesmen (particularly near **Kilburn**). Attracted by employment in the building industry and by the cheap accommodation, **immigrant** labor arrived from other parts of the British Isles and from abroad, creating a cosmopolitan residential neighborhood (for example, Queensway, and the southern end of the Edgware Road, have become significant Arab business areas and there is a large Irish community). By the mid-20th century, however, many of the buildings had become slums, and unscrupulous landlords were charging exorbitant rents to incomers desperate for living space. Since then, redevelopment programs, coupled with laws that improved the rights of tenants, have raised living standards while retaining the best of the Victorian **architecture**. The area is now largely residential and commercial, with few industrial premises, but has retained its distinctive ethnic mix. (*See also* BUSES; LONDON UNDERGROUND.)

PADDINGTON STATION. The station at **Paddington** opened in 1838 as the London terminus of the Great Western **Railway**. Four years later, Queen Victoria arrived at the end of her first train journey; the 17-mile trip from Slough took 23 minutes at an average 44 miles per hour, a speed **Prince Albert** (her husband) felt was excessive. The present building, designed by Isambard Kingdom Brunel, was completed in 1854 and covers 13 acres, with a roof of glass and steel. The platforms are 700 feet long. However, in 2000, Railtrack (the company that operates the station) announced plans for a major redevelopment that would include a 673-foot-high skyscraper with over 900,000 square feet of office space, additional platforms, and demolition of train sheds. Paddington is still the principal London station for services to Wales and southwest England.

PALACE OF WESTMINSTER. In the middle years of the 11th century, Edward the Confessor built a palace on the north bank of the **River Thames** at **Westminster**, providing an alternative focus of development to that of the **City of London**. For 463 years (and 25 reigns), it was the center of the English court, losing its prestige only when King Henry VIII moved to **Greenwich Palace** in 1529. The King's Council met in **Westminster Hall**, which was added to the palace in 1097 and evolved into the House of Lords and the House of Commons, forming the basis of Britain's parliamentary system of government. However, on the night of 16 October 1834, most of the structure was destroyed by fire, only the Great Hall, the 13th-century undercroft of St. Stephen's Chapel, and the Jewel Tower surviving. The government immediately announced a competition to design a replacement building, which would be known as the New Palace of Westminster and constructed in Elizabethan or Gothic style. **Charles Barry**'s entry was considered the best of the 97 that were submitted, and construction began in 1837, with **Augustus Welby Northmore Pugin** commissioned to assist. Barry was most at ease with Renaissance **architecture**, Pugin with Gothic, but (despite some bickering about who should take the greatest credit) the two collaborated well, the former producing the overall plan and the latter adding the exuberant decoration of the interior. The House of Lords was opened in 1847 and the House of Commons completed four years later. Work on the Clock Tower (commonly known as **Big Ben**) ended in 1858 and the Victoria Tower (336 feet high) was roofed in 1860 (a flag flying from the Victoria Tower by day, and a light shining from the Clock Tower by night, indicate when Parliament is sitting).

Between September 1940 and May 1941, during the **Blitz**, the building was damaged by German bombs on 11 occasions, most seriously on 10 May, when the House of Commons was destroyed. It was reconstructed in 1945–50 to plans prepared by **Giles Gilbert Scott**, who retained Barry's overall design but (to the annoyance of some critics) subdued the flamboyance of Pugin's decoration. (*See also* ALBERT, PRINCE; GREAT STINK; GUNPOWDER PLOT.)

PALL MALL. When, in 1603, King James VI of Scotland succeeded to the English throne (as King James I), he moved his court south from Edinburgh, introducing to London a French game—pallo a maglio—which was similar to croquet. The sport proved popular with aristocrats, and particularly with King Charles II (James's grandson), who enjoyed playing it with his mistresses in **St. James's Park**. Unfortunately, activities were frequently disrupted by passing carriages, so in 1662 the traffic was moved to a new road built immediately to the north. Although formally named Catherine Street (after Catherine of Braganza, Charles's Queen), it was popularly known as Pall Mall and that vernacular name survived. Because of the road's royal associations, the properties that lined it were much sought after, becoming the homes of aristocratic families (and **Eleanor "Nell" Gwyn**, one of Charles's favorite paramours). During the 18th and 19th centuries, its status declined as shops and **coffee houses** were established and writers and artists moved in (Jonathan Swift, author of *Gulliver's Travels*, took up residence in 1710, writer Laurence Sterne in 1760, and artist Thomas Gainsborough in 1774, for example). Now, it is entirely commercial, best known for its **gentlemen's clubs**, notably the Travellers' Club (founded in 1819), **The Athenaeum** (1824), and the **Reform Club** (1836). (*See also* BARRY, CHARLES; GAS; MALL, THE; REGENT STREET; ROTHMAN'S OF PALL MALL; ROYAL ACADEMY OF ARTS; STREET LIGHTING.)

PARK LANE. Park Lane runs for three-quarters of a mile along the eastern edge of **Hyde Park**, linking **Marble Arch** to **Hyde Park Corner**. The first buildings were erected during the 18th century, but the area did not become fashionable until about 1820, when new properties were constructed and older ones extensively refurbished (for example Londonderry House, designed by James Stuart for the Earl of Holdernesse, was built in the 1760s but much altered in 1825–28 by Benjamin and Philip Wyatt for the Marquess of Londonderry). By 1850, its residents were all affluent aristocrats or merchants, but in the second half of the century their peace was increasingly disturbed by a growing volume of traffic and the use of Hyde Park for public assemblies, such as the demonstration against a Sunday Trading Bill that attracted 150,000 protesters in 1855. From the 1920s, as families left for more peaceful environments, homes were converted into offices or demolished and replaced by **hotels**, such as the **Dorchester Hotel**, which opened in 1931.

PARKS. London has about 400 parks of 20 acres or more and hundreds of smaller open spaces. In the central city, the largest of these were originally royal hunting grounds located outside the medieval town walls, but were engulfed by urban expansion during the 19th and 20th centuries; although still owned by the Crown, they are now open to the public (*see* **Royal Parks**). Others (such as **Victoria Park**, in the **East End**) were established as the municipal authorities in the Victorian city responded to campaigns encouraging them to provide recreational facilities in the burgeoning residential areas (and particularly in working-class communities). Also, the construction of embankments (*see* **Bazalgette, Joseph William**) along the **River Thames** during the 1860s and 1870s presented an opportunity for providing gardens, such as those at the northern end of **Hungerford Bridge** (close to **Charing Cross** and the **Strand**), which are often used by office workers on summer lunch breaks. Many common lands, where tenants had a right to collect firewood and graze animals, survived the building boom as well (although sometimes the space had to be fought for, as at **Wandsworth**, where wealthy residents attempted to enclose it for their own purposes); as a result, extensive areas of land, such as the 1,100 acres of Wimbledon Common are retained in a form that still has an element of wildness. In addition, local councils sometimes acquired formerly private estates (at **Avery Hill**, for example) and were able to make the grounds available to neighborhood residents. During the second half of the 20th century, planning policies have required inclusion of parkland within building developments so that residents are provided with sports facilities, land where children can play informally, and places where families can walk. (*See also* ALEXANDRA PALACE; BATTERSEA PARK; BURIAL GROUNDS; BUSHY PARK; CLAPHAM COMMON; CUPER'S GARDENS; DULWICH; EPPING FOREST; ERITH; GREEN PARK; GREENWICH PARK; HAMPSTEAD HEATH; HERNE HILL; HOLLAND HOUSE; HORNIMAN MUSEUM; HYDE PARK; KENNINGTON; KENSINGTON GARDENS; LAMBETH PALACE; LEA, RIVER; LINCOLN'S INN FIELDS; MARBLE HILL HOUSE; NONSUCH PALACE; OSTERLEY HOUSE; PECKHAM; PRIMROSE HILL; REGENT'S PARK; RICHMOND PARK; ROYAL BOTANIC GARDENS; ST. JAMES'S PARK; SERPENTINE; SYDENHAM; VAUXHALL.)

PARLIAMENTARY CONSTITUENCIES. The metropolitan area took its modern form in 1965, when the **Greater London Council** replaced the **London County Council**. At that time, the city sent 103 representatives to the House of Commons (*see* **Palace of Westminster**), but boundary revisions over the next three decades brought reductions as residents moved out of the urban area. The most recent change occurred in 1997, when the number of constituencies fell from 84 to 74. In the General Election that year, the Labour Party won 57 of the seats (gaining 49.5 percent of the total vote), the Conservative Party 11 (with 31.2 percent of the vote), and the Liberal Party six (with 14.6 percent of the vote). Conservative support was confined to affluent suburbs such as **Beckenham** and **Orpington** and to such wealthy inner-city areas as the **City of Westminster**. The Liberal Democrats were at their strongest in the southwest, where they had built strong bases of support at the local council level. The new Members of Parliament included 11 women, 10 representing Labour seats and one representing the Liberal Democrats.

PEABODY, GEORGE (1795–1869). In the mid-19th century, Peabody's largesse was responsible for significant improvements in the quality of life of large numbers of London's least affluent citizens. Born on 18 February 1795 into a poor Puritan family living in South Danvers (Massachusetts), he had little formal education. However, the tenets of hard work, considered use of resources, and concern for others that dominated the values of his home stood him in good stead when he began to earn a living. In 1814, along with Elisha Riggs (who provided financial backing), he opened a dry goods warehouse at Georgetown in Washington, D.C. It relocated to Baltimore the following year and, by 1822, had branches in Philadelphia and New York. In 1827, business interests took him to London, where he settled 10 years later, then, in 1843, founded a bank. From 1862 until his death at a friend's home in Eaton Square on 4 November 1869, he made gifts amounting to some £500,000 to his adopted city, with the specification that the money should be used "to ameliorate the condition of the poor and needy of this great metropolis and promote their comfort and happiness." The authorities met the condition by building "cheap, cleanly, well-drained and healthful dwellings" (known as Peabody Buildings) for the working class. The first opened at **Spitalfields** in 1864, but others followed rapidly, so by 1890 some 5,000 homes had been made available. The exteriors were austere (architectural historian Nikolaus Pevsner condemned one block as "detestable"), but they undoubtedly did much to alleviate overcrowding in central London and the **East End**. Peabody also promoted Anglo-American relations, encouraging meetings between prominent figures from both nations, and used his considerable wealth to support charitable causes in the United States (for example, from 1866 to 1869 he donated US$3.5 million to groups promoting education for all races in the Deep South). In 1868, the name of his birthplace was changed to Peabody, in his honor. The trust that now manages the properties he financed in London controls some 12,000 apartments on over 70 sites. In recent years, it has undertaken much refurbishment, improving provisions internally and renovating external brickwork.

PEABODY BUILDINGS. *See* PEABODY, GEORGE.

PEARLY KINGS AND QUEENS. During the 19th century, London's costermongers (the people who sold fruit, vegetables, and other goods from barrows in the street or at **markets**) appointed representatives to protect their rights, fend off competitors, and act as bodyguards. So that they could be identified, these individuals (who rapidly attained an elite status among the traders) decorated their clothes, in flamboyant Victorian style, with pearl buttons. Today, they still dress up for functions such as the costermongers' Harvest Festival, held in **St. Martin-in-the-Fields Church**. In 1911, they formed a Pearly Kings' and Queens' Association, which devotes much energy to charitable causes.

PEASANTS' REVOLT. In 1381, rural dwellers were provoked to rebellion by a combination of the food shortages that followed a series of bad harvests, actions taken by landowners to counteract the labor shortages caused by the **Black Death**, and taxes levied to provide funds for war with France. King Richard II decided to confront Wat Tyler (one of the rebel leaders) at **Blackheath** but was unable to reach the meeting place because of the large crowds. Frustrated, Tyler marched on London, killing a number of lawyers, destroying legal records, and setting inmates free from prisons. On 14 June, Richard made concessions, granting demands for an easing of restrictions on land sales, an end to feudal service, and the introduction of a right to rent property, but Tyler continued to terrorize the city, beheading the Archbishop of Canterbury (Simon of Sudbury) and setting fire to the **Tower of London**. Taking the law into his own hands, William Walworth, the **Lord Mayor**, attacked and killed Tyler during a meeting at Smithfield (*see* **Smithfield Meat Market**). Robbed of direction, the peasants drifted back to the countryside. The event—the first large-scale public protest recorded in England—had little long-term impact but did succeed in ending the poll tax. (*See also*

INNS OF COURT; JACK STRAW'S CASTLE; KNIGHTS HOSPITALLER; LAMBETH PALACE; MARSHALSEA PRISON.)

PECKHAM. Peckham lies south of the **River Thames** between **Camberwell** and **Deptford**. It was settled during Anglo-Saxon times and, for over a millennium, functioned as an agricultural village where incomes from farming were supplemented by market gardening and by provision of pasturage, accommodation, and refreshments for drovers taking cattle to the London **markets**. The Grand Surrey Canal, which was intended to link the Thames Docks to **Mitcham**, was the first spur to urban development, arriving in 1826, and was soon lined with houses and industrial premises such as the South Metropolitan **Gas** Company's works. An omnibus service from the Adam and Eve Inn to the West End furthered contacts with the central city from 1851, and from 1872 the London, Chatham, and Dover **Railway** allowed commuters to live in the area but work elsewhere. The improved access encouraged speculative builders to develop **housing** estates, replacing green fields with brick terraces, but some open space remained, notably the 54-acre Nunhead Cemetery (laid out in 1840), the 64-acre Peckham Rye Common (which was bought by Camberwell Vestry in 1868 and converted into sports fields), and the 49-acre Homestall Farm (which became a public **park** in 1890). After the Second World War, and particularly from 1960, many of the poorer quality Victorian properties were demolished and replaced by local authority housing. The canal, having outlived its usefulness, was closed in 1971. Peckham forms part of the **London Borough of Southwark**. (*See also* PECKHAM EXPERIMENT.)

PECKHAM EXPERIMENT. In 1935, Dr. Scott Williamson opened a three-story building in St. Mary's Road, **Peckham**, with the intention of conducting investigations into the biology of human beings. The glass and concrete structure, designed by Sir E. Owen Williams, contained a cafeteria, games rooms, a gymnasium, a swimming pool, and a **theater**. Families were encouraged to become members through payment of a weekly subscription and submission of an undertaking to attend regular physical examinations in the clinic on the site. The project was interrupted by the Second World War (when a munitions plant took over the accommodation) and abandoned in 1950 when funds were exhausted.

PENTONVILLE. The area east of **King's Cross** was one of London's first planned suburbs, laid out from 1773 on 134 acres of farmland owned by

Thomas Penton, the Member of Parliament for Winchester. Initially, it was popular with craftsmen working in the **City of London**, but during the second half of the 19th century, shops and small industrial premises infiltrated the residential area and the estate gradually turned into an urban slum. After the Second World War, local authorities demolished most of the properties, replacing them with higher standard public **housing**. Pentonville Prison, which opened in 1842, was designed as an institution where male offenders would be taught a trade then transported to work in the colonies. Modernized in the late 20th century, it now holds men convicted of civil offenses and others awaiting sentence. The area forms part of the **London Borough of Islington**. (*See also* RILLINGTON PLACE.)

PEPYS, SAMUEL (1633–1703). Pepys's diary is an important source of information on London life during the 1660s, a turbulent decade that included the **Great Plague** (1664–66), the **Great Fire** (1666), and the restoration of the English monarchy following Oliver Cromwell's Puritan rule. Pepys was born in the city on 23 February 1633, one of 11 children in the family of tailor John Pepys and his wife, Mary. He was educated in Huntingdon and at St. Paul's School (London) before entering Cambridge University, where he earned a B.A. degree in 1650 and an M.A. in 1660. The considerable influence of his cousin, Sir Edward Montagu, secured him a post as Clerk to the King's Ships, from which relatively lowly status he rose to become the most respected of the country's naval administrators, combining his talents for diplomacy and hard work with a business acumen that endeared him to Parliament and the monarchy. He survived accusations of treason and of support for Roman Catholicism in 1679 to become President of the **Royal Society** (1684) and first Master of **Trinity House** (1685), dying at **Clapham** on 26 May 1703.

Pepys's diaries are notable partly because of the writer's eye for detail, partly because of the importance of the events of the time, and partly because of his honest observation. They begin on 1 January 1660 and end on 31 May 1669, by which time failing eyesight had made recording a painful task. The pain of the plague years is clearly evident; on 16 October 1665, Pepys noted that he "walked to the town; but, Lord! How empty the streets are, and melancholy, so many poor, sick people in the streets full of sores; and so many sad stories overheard as I walk, everybody talking of this dead, and that man sick, and so many in this place, and so many in that." The following summer, he saw London burn, writing on 2 September that he went to an alehouse in **Bankside** where he watched the conflagration spread "as far as we could see up the hill of the City, in a most horrid, malicious, bloody flame, not like the fire flame of an ordinary fire." He took good care, however, to protect his own property as far as possible, because two days later he dug a pit in his garden to bury wine and parmesan cheese so that they would not be destroyed.

The diaries also tell of family joys and sorrows. On 18 March 1664, Pepys went to **St. Bride's Church** to make funeral arrangements for Thomas, his brother. The negotiations with the grave digger proved shocking. "To see how a man's tombes are at the mercy of such a fellow, that for sixpence he would, as his own words were, 'I will jostle them together but I will make room for him;' speaking of the fulness of the middle aisle, where he was to lie; and that he would, for my father's sake, do my brother, that is dead, all the civility that he can; which was to disturb other corps that are not quite rotten, to make room for him." Other days proved more pleasurable. Pepys was clearly attracted by ladies, making frequent reference to their looks; on 18 August 1667, he records that, while attending a service at **St. Dunstan in the West Church, Fleet Street**, he "stood by a pretty, modest maid whom I did labor to take by the hand and the body, but she would not, but got further and further from me, and at last I could perceive her to take pins out of her pocket to prick me if I should touch her again." Domestic arrangements, relationships with superiors, and social engagements are all faithfully recorded, providing a fertile source of material for scholars. (*See also* ALDERSGATE; FLOOD CONTROL; HYDE PARK; ROYAL NAVAL DOCKYARDS; ST. MARGARET'S CHURCH, WESTMINSTER; ST. OLAVE'S CHURCH, HART STREET; VAUXHALL.)

PETTICOAT LANE. One of London's principal **street markets**, Petticoat Lane (in **Whitechapel**) probably derived its name from the shopkeepers who sold secondhand clothes in the area during the 16th century. The road was renamed Middlesex Street in 1830 in a puritanical attempt to avoid reference to ladies' underwear, but popular usage retained the earlier title for the **market**, which was established by the mid-18th century. Attempts were made to stop trading on Sunday mornings but, in 1936, parliamentary legislation confirmed rights to operate. Although stalls are open every day of the week, they are busiest by far on Sunday, when over 800 booths are set up to sell clothes, leather goods, records, fruit, vegetables, confectionery, flowers, kitchen knives, and other goods. Buyers banter with the **East End** salesmen, who rely on crowd reaction to promote trade.

PHILHARMONIA ORCHESTRA. The Philharmonia was formed in 1945, primarily to make recordings of classical music. It made its first European tour in 1952 and visited the United States in 1955, then suffered a period of administrative disharmony before becoming a self-governing entity, administered by a Council of Management, in 1964. For some years after that, it was threatened by serious financial problems but survived to become one of the world's leading orchestras. During the 1990s, it developed major bases at Bedford, Paris, the **Royal Festival Hall** (where it became resident in 1996), Leicester, and Athens. It has played under most major conductors during the second half of the 20th century, including Herbert von Karajan, Otto Klemperer, and Richard Strauss, presenting about 40 concerts in London each year and (since 1992) making a commitment to commission works from leading composers.

PICCADILLY. Piccadilly is one of central London's principal routeways, stretching for about a mile from **Piccadilly Circus** to **Hyde Park Corner** in the **City of Westminster**. In the early 17th century, it was no more than a country lane but, as traffic from the west increased, it became the major highway to the **City of London**, attracting **housing** development. One of the first residents was tailor Robert Baker, who made picadils (a trimming for collars then very fashionable among aristocrats); he built a mansion named Piccadilly Hall, after the source of his wealth, and, over the next 150 years, the name was applied to the whole street. With the exception of **Burlington House**, the earliest buildings have been swept away by more recent developments. A number of the present properties date from 1760–1850, when wealthy citizens gained status by owning homes located close to the city but with semirural surroundings (for example, Apsley House, designed by **Robert Adam** and built in 1771–78, was the residence of the Duke of Wellington and, since 1952, has housed the **Wellington Museum** collections). Further building occurred during the late 19th and early 20th centuries, but since then, most private residents have moved away and their houses have been converted for use as **gentlemen's clubs**, shops, airline offices, and **hotels**, particularly in the east. Only **Green Park** has escaped the developers, providing an important recreational space for workers and shoppers close to the heart of the city. (*See also* CHAMBERS, WILLIAM; FORTNUM AND MASON; JACKSON'S OF PICCADILLY; RITZ HOTEL; ST. JAMES'S CHURCH, PICCADILLY; WREN, CHRISTOPHER.)

PICCADILLY CIRCUS. A busy road junction in the center of London, Piccadilly Circus was first formed in 1819, when **Regent Street** was designed to link with **Piccadilly** and the frontages at the intersection were set back to enhance the sense of space. **Shaftesbury Avenue**, constructed during the 1880s, brought further traffic, then in 1893 a statue of Eros (designed by Alfred Gilbert and placed in the center of a fountain) was erected at the crossroads as a memorial to the seventh Earl of Shaftesbury, who had advocated education for the poor and other social reforms (Eros represents the angel of Christian charity, not the god of love, and was the first statue in London to be cast in aluminum). Between 1900 and 1910, electrically illuminated billboards were placed on the buildings forming the northeast sector of the Circus, which, by midcentury, had become a brash mixture of shops, restaurants, and offices, particularly busy after dark as playgoers made their way to the nearby **theater**s. Since the end of the Second World War, there have been intermittent debates about how to improve the area, which lacks architectural impact (particularly during the day) and attracts homeless young people, but there has been little action although access to Eros has improved and the **London Underground** station was refurbished in 1989.

PIMLICO. Pimlico occupies the north bank of one of the **River Thames**'s southerly meanders, with **Belgravia** to the west and **Westminster** to the east. The origin of the name is unknown; some writers suggest that it is derived from Ben Pimlico (an innkeeper during the 16th century), others that it recognizes a connection with the Pamlaco tribe of American Indians who traded with England during the 1600s, or that it is the name of a local drink whose ingredients are now unknown. During the 17th century, the area was acquired, through marriage, by Sir Thomas Grosvenor (*see* **Grosvenor Estate**) but was undeveloped until **Thomas Cubitt** replaced the marshes and market gardens with rows of terraced houses from 1835. The properties were less grand than those in Belgravia, so Pimlico never acquired the same social status as its neighbor but, even so, became popular with the middle class. During the 20th century, many of the homes were converted into small **hotels**, and other commercial properties infiltrated the area, but it still retains a predominantly residential character with a slightly bohemian reputation stemming from its popularity with artists and literary groups. The suburb forms part of the **City of Westminster**. (*See also* DIANA, PRINCESS OF WALES; VAUXHALL.)

PINNER. Although its name is derived from Old English, the settlement is not recorded in documents until 1321. An affluent middle-class residential suburb in the northwest of the **London Borough of Harrow**, it consists largely of substantial, red brick family homes erected during the 1930s and clustering around the 15th-century flint and freestone church of St. John the Baptist. Many older buildings (including two 16th-century half-timbered **public houses** in High Street) are protected from development by conservation area legislation, but Headstone Manor (constructed in 1344 for the Archbishop of Canterbury) serves as a local history **museum** and other properties are used as shops or offices. A fair is held every spring; originally founded as a cattle **market** in 1336, it is now devoted entirely to the pursuit of pleasure, with merry-go-rounds and ferris wheels.

PLANETARIUM. *See* MADAME TUSSAUD'S WAXWORKS.

PLUMSTEAD. Plumstead, on the south bank of the **River Thames** in the **London Borough of Greenwich**, was settled before the Roman invasion and thrived as an agricultural village, noted for sheep grazing and fruit growing, until the 19th century. Then, the arrival of the **railway** (in 1849) and industrial expansion at neighboring **Woolwich** increased demands for building land and resulted in rapid population increases that transformed the area into a metropolitan suburb. The community resisted much of the development, rioting when open spaces were acquired for military training in the 1870s and forcing the **Metropolitan Board of Works** to purchase Plumstead Common and Winns Common, which were protected from further encroachment and preserved for public recreation.

POET'S CORNER. *See* WESTMINSTER ABBEY.

POLICE. Until the early 19th century, nobody had sole responsibility for maintaining law and order in London. In the **City of London**, the peacekeeping process evolved over time into a geographically based system of 200 precincts, each with its own constable. In addition, every **ward** had unpaid watchmen who were supposed to prevent illegal activities. **Westminster** adopted a similar arrangement in 1584 but, as in **The City**, each territorial unit guarded its individuality, so there was little cooperation across boundaries. By the 18th century, corruption was rife as professional thief catchers worked for rewards and posts such as Keeper of

Newgate Prison were auctioned to the highest bidder, who then attempted to recoup his expenditure by whatever means was available, including extortion. Moreover, the constables could not be relied on to carry out their duties (for example, during the **Gordon Riots** of 1780 many sympathized with the rebellion and made no attempt to prevent looting or destruction of property). In 1812, 1816, and 1818, parliamentary committees recommended change, but the public objected, fearing that reform might bring a loss of freedom; The City, in particular, mounted strong opposition because it did not want to see its police force controlled by the House of Commons (*see* **Palace of Westminster**).

In 1829, however, Home Secretary Robert Peel negotiated a compromise that allowed the **Corporation of London** to make its own arrangements but created a Metropolitan Police force to coordinate crime prevention and detection throughout the rest of London, with administrative headquarters at **Scotland Yard**. Initially, wages were low and citizens hostile, so manpower wastage was considerable, but by midcentury, the tide of opinion was changing and the police were becoming an accepted part of London life. A Criminal Investigation Department was formed in 1878 to coordinate detective work, a Special Branch in 1885 to investigate acts of terrorism, and a Central Finger Print Bureau in 1901 to provide a database of criminals. During the First World War, a women's unit was formed to carry out the work of policemen serving with the armed forces; initially, it was intended to be a temporary body but, in 1919, it was absorbed within the main force. Since then, the emphasis has been on increasing specialization to meet more sophisticated forms of crime. In part, that is reflected in the multiplication of special units, such as the Bomb Squad, Drug Squad, and Fraud Squad. Also, the force has increased its specialists in computers, video surveillance cameras, and other high-technology equipment. However, the rising cost of crime prevention, coupled with pressure on finances, was reflected in manpower. In 2000, the Metropolitan Police had 24,600 officers (over 7,000 fewer than in 1991) and, according to its commissioner, Sir John Stevens, was facing a major recruitment crisis after a series of press reports about corruption and racism.

The City of London eventually reformed its policing system in 1839 but remains a separate force. It is organized on similar lines to those of the Metropolitan Police but has only about 800 officers. Because of The City's relatively small resident population, much of its work relates to fraud and to security at the large number of financial institutions in the **Square Mile**. (*See also* BOW STREET RUNNERS; RIVER POLICE; TRAFALGAR SQUARE.)

POLLUTION. *See* AIR POLLUTION; GREAT STINK; SEWAGE DISPOSAL; WATER POLLUTION.

POOL OF LONDON. The Pool stretches along the **River Thames** from **London Bridge** downstream to Limekiln Creek. Shipping has made little use of the section above **Tower Bridge** in modern times (though some cruise liners tie up alongside **HMS *Belfast***), but the reaches provided most of the city's harbor facilities from the Roman period until the advent of large container vessels, which necessitated a move closer to the deep waters of the river mouth during the late 1960s. Faced with the decline in traffic, the East India **Docks** closed in 1967; Wapping (1968), St. Katharine's (1969), Surrey (1970), West India (1980), Millwall (1980), King George V (1981), Royal Albert (1981), and Royal Victoria (1981) all followed, leaving extensive areas of derelict land on both banks of the river. Many of the 19th-century warehouses, built to hold cargoes from around the world, were demolished as development programs were introduced, but the **Docklands** urban regeneration scheme retained some elements of the old port in its marinas, retail complexes, and offices.

POPLAR. For most of its existence, the **East End** suburb of Poplar (lying on the north bank of the **River Thames** some five miles east of **Charing Cross**) has had close links with the sea. During the Medieval period, it developed as a fishing village, then, from the 16th century, expanded as ships increasingly utilized harbor facilities at nearby **Blackwall**, attracting repair, construction, and supply businesses. The opening of the West India **Docks** in 1802, followed by the East India Docks four years later, brought an influx of merchants, administrators, seamen, craftsmen, tradesmen, and laborers who swelled the **population** from 4,500 in 1801 to over 55,000 in 1881. During the 20th century, however, the port facilities declined and the middle-class element left for more attractive residential environments, turning Poplar into one of the poorest areas in London. In such conditions, the Labour Party's socialist philosophies found fertile ground (*see*, for example, **Poplarism**) and produced a continuing stream of left-wing politicians both at the **local government** and at parliamentary levels. The area suffered greatly during the **Blitz**, but once the land was cleared of damaged properties when the Second World War ended in 1945, extensive public **housing** programs effected major improvements in living conditions. With the closure of the docks from 1967, the maritime industries disappeared. Small engineering firms and a host of small textile manufacturers and retailers (many from

Bangladesh, India, and Pakistan) provide employment, but levels of wealth are still low. In 1965, when the local authorities in the metropolitan area were reorganized, Poplar was included within the **London Borough of Tower Hamlets**. (*See also* AIR RAIDS.)

POPLARISM. During the 1920s, residents of **Poplar** (in London's **East End**) campaigned for national and **local government** policies that would ease the plight of the city's poor. Led by **George Lansbury**, the local Councillors declined to levy the property taxes that would pay the borough's contribution towards the running costs of the **London County Council**, the Metropolitan Asylums Board, and the Metropolitan **Police**. Thirty of them were imprisoned for insisting on maintaining the protest and were marched off to prison, but fear of public unrest in the East End forced the government to release them after six weeks and to introduce parliamentary legislation that transferred much of the cost of caring for the least well off to the Ministry of Health. As a result, official efforts to help the disadvantaged became widely known as Poplarism.

POPULATION. All figures for London's population prior to 1801 (when the first official census was carried out in Great Britain) are educated guesses because no authority was responsible for collating statistics of births, deaths, and population migration. Moreover, assessments of change over time are complicated by periodic revisions of local authority boundaries. It is believed, however, that numbers during the Roman occupation reached 45,000 to 50,000 in the third century but declined after the invaders' withdrawal because the economy of the Anglo-Saxon peoples who replaced them was rural, rather than urban, in character. Evidence of occupation from the fifth until the 11th centuries is limited; modern Londoners march to work along streets (such as **Cheapside**) that have Old English names, and the Venerable Bede wrote, at the beginning of the eighth century, that London was "the mart of many nations resorting to it by sea and land," but, in the absence of suitable data, few scholars venture estimates of the city's size.

Several writers claim that, in the period immediately following the Norman conquest in 1066, London had 15,000–20,000 residents, only returning to Roman levels in the middle of the 13th century at a time of considerable prosperity. From then, growth was limited until (for reasons that are still unclear but were probably related more to **immigration** from other parts of England than to changes in the birth rate or death rate) the citizenry increased from 50,000 souls to over 200,000 during the last 50 years of

Tudor rule (which ended in 1603) then to around 600,000 by the time the Hanoverian monarchs replaced the ill-fated Stuarts in 1714.

The 1801 census indicated that the area now covered by the 32 **London boroughs** had 1,096,784 residents (though some writers suggest that the real total was as much as 5 percent higher). Within 40 years, they doubled to 2,207,653, then, over the next 40, doubled again to 4,713,441 as medical and environmental improvements lengthened life expectancy and as migrants arrived in droves (as many as 30,000 a year in 1841–71) to seek work. The spread of the **railway** network from 1836 encouraged speculative builders to erect housing near **transport** links, speeding up the rate of urban growth and hastening the evolution of dormitory suburbs—a trend continued by the expansion of **bus** routes and ownership of private cars during the 20th century. Before the outbreak of the Second World War in 1939, London's population reached 8.6 million but, by 1981, numbers had fallen to 6,713,165 as parents chose to raise families in the countryside rather than the city and as government urban renewal policies resulted in the transfer of council house and slum tenants to newly built properties, with a high standard of amenity, in surrounding counties. Since then, however, the total has climbed again, reaching just under 7.2 million in 1998, largely as a result of relatively high rates of natural increase.

Population densities are highest in the inner city (where parts of the **Royal Borough of Kensington and Chelsea** have over 5,400 people per square mile) and lowest in the suburbs (where densities in parts of the **London Borough of Bromley** and the **London Borough of Harrow** fall below 1,350 per square mile). Residents in 1998 were younger than the British average (41.3 percent are aged 20–44, compared with 36.3 percent in that age group over the United Kingdom as a whole). As a result of that youthfulness, the crude birth rate (14.9 per 1,000 population) was higher than the national rate (12.5), but levels of fertility (an average of 1.75 children per woman in London and 1.72 countrywide) were very similar. Also, because of the age structure, crude death rates in the metropolitan area (9.3 per 1,000 population) were lower than the national average (10.9).

PORTLAND PLACE. Named after the Duke of Portland, who owned the land on which it was built, Portland Place was laid out to the east of **Cavendish Square** by **Robert Adam** and his brother, James, from 1774. Forty years later, **John Nash** (who believed that it was the finest road in London) used it as a northern extension of **Regent Street**, linking **Regent's Park** to **Pall Mall**. Originally entirely residential, it became increasingly commercialized after the opening of the **Langham Hotel** in

1865. As developers moved in, many of the original properties (most of which were designed by James Adam) were demolished or substantially altered, so, although it retains some of its original style, the street has lost much of its architectural impact. Modern occupants of the buildings have included several national institutions, notably the **British Broadcasting Corporation** (in Broadcasting House at No. 10), the Royal Institute of Public Health and Hygiene (No. 28), the Royal Institute of British Architects (No. 66) and the **City and Guilds of London Institute** (No. 76, once the home of novelist and Governor General of Canada John Buchan). (*See also* ST. MARYLEBONE.)

PORTLAND STONE. For centuries, Portland stone was much prized as building material for churches and other important structures in London. A strong, attractive, easily carved limestone, which rings like a bell when struck with a chisel, it consists of material laid down in a subtropical sea during the Jurassic period (some 120–140 million years ago) and now exposed in near horizontal strata off England's south coast on the Isle of Portland. The rock, first quarried by the Romans, was introduced to London architects in the early 17th century by **Inigo Jones** then used by **Christopher Wren** to rebuild **St. Paul's Cathedral** after the **Great Fire** of 1666 (he transported it to the city in a fleet of barges routed along the English Channel and up the **River Thames**) and by **William Chambers** in the construction of **Somerset House** (1776–86). It is also found in the **Banqueting House**, **Mansion House**, the **Royal Courts of Justice**, and many of the government offices that line **Whitehall**. (*See also* BARRY, CHARLES; BUCKINGHAM PALACE; CENOTAPH; CENTRAL CRIMINAL COURT; CHISWICK BRIDGE; COUNTY HALL; MONUMENT; REGENT STREET; RICHMOND BRIDGE; ST. BENET'S CHURCH, PAUL'S WHARF; ST. JAMES'S CHURCH, PICCADILLY; UNITED STATES' EMBASSY.)

PORTOBELLO ROAD MARKET. From 1870, Portobello Road (in north **Kensington**) became a popular location for trade in horses. As business increased, other merchants set up their stalls in an attempt to attract customers for other goods, so, in 1929, a formal license for street trading was issued by the local authorities. The **market** continued to flourish after the Second World War, drawing tourists as well as Londoners to the growing number of booths offering antiques. The market is open every day except Sunday but is busiest on Saturdays, when bargain hunters throng the mile-long street.

PORT OF LONDON. *See* DOCKS; POOL OF LONDON; PORT OF LONDON AUTHORITY (PLA).

PORT OF LONDON AUTHORITY (PLA). In 1902, a Royal Commission reported that London's harbor facilities were inefficient, poorly equipped, expensive, managed by too many organizations, and likely to become increasingly uncompetitive. It recommended the creation of a single authority to manage the **docks**, but because of bickering between vested interests and claims by some politicians that the proposal was a step towards socialism, the new body—the Port of London Authority—was not established until 1909. It took over responsibility for the tidal area of the **River Thames** from Teddington (west of the metropolis) to the mouth of the estuary, a distance of about 100 miles, and, by 1939, had dredged a 50-mile-long channel, 30 feet deep at low water, so that large ships could sail upriver. In addition, it had built six miles of quay and enclosed 80 additional acres of dock water. As a result, the annual weight of cargo passing through London rose by 50 percent to 60 million tons and the percentage of the United Kingdom's sea-borne trade handled by the port rose from 29 to 38. Further improvements were made immediately after the Second World War, partly in order to repair damage but also to facilitate the rebuilding of the country's economy. In particular, container handling equipment was installed at Tilbury, some 20 miles downstream of the city center. During the last quarter of the 20th century, the PLA became heavily involved in the redevelopment of the harbor area closest to **Tower Bridge** (*see* **Docklands**), occupying a site at the showpiece St. Katharine Dock as its own headquarters. Also, in 1987 it assumed responsibility for pilotage on the river.

The PLA (which moved, in 2000, to offices in Bakers' Hall, Harp Lane) is unusual amongst Britain's harbor management agencies because it is wholly independent of the commercial cargo handling operations that use the port. It functions as a public trust, funded by charges on vessels using the docks, and is governed by a board consisting of a chairman supported by seven nonexecutive members (all of whom are appointed by the Secretary of State for Transport) along with four executive members (chosen by the board itself). In addition to its general oversight of port activities, it licenses certain craft (such as tugs) and the people who work on them. Also, it can veto any proposal to build on, over, or under the river bed if navigation would be impaired.

POSTAL DELIVERIES. The first regular system of postal deliveries to private citizens began in 1635, when arrangements were made to carry letters along the main routes out of the **City of London** as part of the Royal Mail service organized by the General Post Office (GPO). Local carriage had to be arranged privately until, in 1680, William Dockwra offered to transport letters and packages within the urban area at a cost of one penny, paid by the sender. Business was so great that, in 1682, his enterprise was taken over by the government and incorporated within the GPO. During the early 19th century, reforms (initiated by Edward Johnson of the Postmaster General's Office) speeded up deliveries but, in 1801, a price increase (to twopence) put the service beyond the means of many households. Campaigns for reform resulted in the introduction of a national delivery service in 1840, with the basic penny cost reinstated. In London, the great bulk of the mail is still delivered by the Post Office, with prices based on weight, but there is also a large fleet of motorbike riders who carry parcels and documents between commercial concerns on a private basis.

POST OFFICE TOWER. *See* BRITISH TELECOM TOWER.

PRIME MERIDIAN. The meridian is the line of 0° longitude that passes through the **Royal Observatory** at **Greenwich**. Until the Observatory published the *British Nautical Almanack* in 1767, sailors tended to use the capital city of their home country as the base for calculating longitude. From the late 18th century, however, the *Almanack* was increasingly used by mariners of all nations as an aid to navigation, so, in 1884, an international conference held in Washington, D.C., confirmed the Greenwich meridian as the reference point from which all longitudes should be measured. World time zones are measured from the same place, with every 15° east or west of Greenwich representing an hour (though there are many local deviations). The meridian's location is marked by a brass rod, set in concrete, beside the Observatory. (*See also* GREENWICH MEAN TIME [GMT].)

PRIMROSE HILL. Lying just north of **Regent's Park**, Primrose Hill, which is 206 feet high, is an ideal site for viewing a city skyline extending from **Tower Bridge** in the east to beyond the Houses of Parliament (*see* **Palace of Westminster**) in the west. During the Medieval period, it was forest land (the hill probably got its name from the primroses that bloomed in the woodlands in spring), but the trees were cleared during the second half of the 16th century and the land was converted to meadow. By the 1800s, it had become a popular location for duelling and also as a gathering ground for protest groups, such as the Chartists. During the Second World War it housed an anti-aircraft battery. The hill, now an open space hemmed in by urban development, is managed by the **Royal Parks** Agency.

PRINTING HOUSE SQUARE. By the 17th century, printing shops had concentrated on the former site of the Dominican monastery at **Blackfriars** so the area became known as Printing House Square. Bonham Norton and John Bill (who produced official documents for King Charles I) had a press in operation by 1627, publishing the first edition of the ***London Gazette*** on 5 February 1666. In 1784, John Walter bought the building and, the following year, founded the *Daily Universal Register*, which changed its name to ***The Times*** in 1788. Now the longest surviving national newspaper in England, *The Times* was a financial success, expanding into neighboring properties and earning the nickname of "The Thunderer" with impassioned editorials during debates on parliamentary reform in 1830. When production moved to Gray's Inn Road in 1974, the Printing House Square premises were occupied by *The Observer* (a Sunday paper first published in 1791). *The Times* was absorbed by Rupert Murdoch's publishing empire in 1981 and is now printed at **Wapping**. *The Observer* has also left, taking over part of the **Canary Wharf** site in the 1990s.

PRISONS. *See* BRIDEWELL; BRIXTON; CLINK PRISON; CRIPPLEGATE; FLEET PRISON; HOLLOWAY PRISON; MARSHALSEA PRISON; NEWGATE PRISON; PENTONVILLE; TOWER OF LONDON; WORMWOOD SCRUBS.

PROMS, THE. In 1895, Robert Newman, manager of the Queen's Hall in Langham Place, appointed Henry Wood conductor of an orchestra he was forming and asked him to introduce a series of promenade concerts that would interest the public in classical music. At the time, the only other permanent orchestra in the metropolitan area was based south of the **River Thames** at **Crystal Palace** and Wood mixed the familiar with the innovative, presenting talented young solo performers who introduced audiences to works by new composers, so the events were a considerable success. However, by 1927 costs had risen and the future was uncertain, so the **British Broadcasting Corporation**, which had been formed five years earlier with a mandate to educate and entertain, assumed organizational control, retaining Wood as conductor but using its own symphony orchestra, founded in 1930, to provide much of the music. Following the destruction of the Queen's Hall by German bombs on 10 May 1941, during the **Blitz**, The Proms moved to the **Albert Hall** and are still held there every summer, a highlight of the city's musical season. Traditionally, the last night is a noisy, ebullient affair with a regular program of sea shanties and a promenaders' chorus of *Rule Britannia*.

PUBLIC HOUSES. Pubs have been a feature of British life ever since the Roman conquest, which began in 43 A.D. As the invaders spread through the islands, they established a series of *tabernae*—inns where travellers could be assured of food and shelter from the elements. As London grew, taverns opened up to meet the needs of city residents as well as visitors (*see*, for example, **Anchor Inn**, **George Inn**, and **Ye Olde Cheshire Cheese**) but the growth in popularity of the public house dates primarily from the 19th century, as hot and dusty labor in mills and factories produced millions of thirsty workers. Water was often unpalatable and usually polluted, so beer became the preferred alternative, particularly for the working class. Public houses became important components of the landscape of the docks, of manufacturing areas, and of the neighborhoods where the workforce lived. Often, they carried a sign that aided identification by a largely illiterate population. From the early 20th century, many of these independent businesses were acquired by **breweries** intent on providing a guaranteed market for their products, but since the 1960s, changing fashions have led to closures as patrons have found other leisure time activities. In response, many of the 7,000 pubs in the city began to provide food as well as drink and, in addition, attempted to attract a particular clientele, adapting their decor and providing entertainment (such as music, strippers, or quizzes) to meet the perceived tastes of office workers, commuters, young people, or other social groups. (*See also* ANGEL, THE; BLACKFRIARS; COFFEE HOUSES; EDMONTON; HARROW-ON-THE-HILL; JACK STRAW'S CASTLE; KRAY TWINS; LEADENHALL MARKET; MAIDA VALE; OVAL, THE; SOUTHWARK; SPANIARDS, THE; SWISS COTTAGE.)

PUBLIC RECORD OFFICE (PRO). Until the middle of the 19th century, official government documents were stored at several locations, including the **Tower of London** and **Westminster Abbey**. However, in 1838, an Act of Parliament established a Public Record Office responsible for collating and storing the papers. A mock Tudor building, designed by Sir James Pennethorne, was erected in **Chancery Lane** and records were deposited following its completion in 1856. By the end of the century, several extensions to the property had expanded storage space, but, even so, the accommodation proved inadequate, and after the First World War, administrators had to erect sheds and huts nearby in order to cope with the growing volume of paper. In 1977, however, a new facility was opened at **Kew** to hold documents from modern government departments. Legal material and state papers dated prior to 1782 remained at the central London site until an extension at Kew was completed in 1995. By the end of the following year, the Chancery Lane site was vacated, with microfilm records of births, marriages, deaths, wills, and 19th-century census material transferred to a new Family Records Centre at 1 Myddelton Street in the **London Borough of Islington**. Among its most prized documents, the PRO has copies of the Domesday Book (William the Conqueror's survey of his English estates, carried out in 1085), Magna Carta (a charter of liberties, restricting royal rights, signed by King John in 1215), and **William Shakespeare**'s will (in which he left his wife his second best bed). (*See also* GREAT EXHIBITION.)

PUBS. *See* PUBLIC HOUSES.

PUDDING LANE. The **Great Fire** of London began in Farynor's bakery, in Pudding Lane, on the night of 2 September 1666 and spread throughout the city, destroying 89 churches and 13,200 houses. The street, on the north bank of the **River Thames** east of **London Bridge**, probably got its name from the animal entrails (or puddings) carried down the road from butchers' premises to refuse disposal boats during the Middle Ages.

PUGIN, AUGUSTUS WELBY NORTHMORE (1812–1852). Although **Charles Barry** designed the exterior of the **Palace of Westminster**, Pugin was responsible for the exuberant neo-Gothic decoration that characterizes the interior. The only child of Augustus and Catherine Pugin, he was born in the family home at 34 Store Street, **Bloomsbury**, on 1 March 1812. He attended Christ's Hospital School, then worked in the architect's practice owned by his father, who had fled to London to escape the consequences of the French Revolution in 1789. In 1827, Pugin was awarded a commission to design furniture for the royal palace at Windsor, then, in 1831, he prepared the scenery for *Kenilworth*, a ballet performed at the **Theatre Royal, Drury Lane**, but he did not prosper financially and, the same year, was imprisoned for debt. He became a

Roman Catholic in 1835, a year before he published the polemical *Contrasts*, a work in which he argued that the quality of a society's **architecture** was a reflection of its cultural values.

The next decade was to be the most productive and influential period in Pugin's career. He was a prominent critic of the work of John Soane (*see* **Sir John Soane's Museum**) and James Wyatt, designers of the **Palace of Westminster**, so when the building burned down on 16 October 1834 he wept few tears. The competition to design a new meeting place for the nation's Parliament was won by Charles Barry, with Pugin preparing the drawings that accompanied the entry. In 1836, he presented further sketches of fixtures and fittings then, in 1844, was called upon to make additional plans for decoration. In all, historians suggest, he completed over 2,000 pictures of furniture, hangings, metalwork, tiles, wallpaper, and wood carvings. His involvement in such a prestigious development inevitably earned him much attention and brought many commissions, including those for St. Alban's Church (Macclesfield), St. Chad's Church (Birmingham), Downside Priory (Bath), St. Giles Church (Cheadle), St. Mary's Church (Stockton-on-Tees), St. Mary-on-the-Sands Church (Southport), and St. Oswald's Church (Liverpool). In London, he worked on St. Joseph's School (Cadogan Street, **Chelsea**), St. Thomas's Church (Rylston Road, **Ealing**), and St. George's Roman Catholic Cathedral, **Southwark** (most of which was destroyed by German bombs in 1941, during the **Blitz**). He also prepared the altarpiece for the **Church of the Immaculate Conception** in Farm Street, **Mayfair**, planned additions to Alton Towers (the Staffordshire home of the Earl of Shrewsbury), published several books, married three times, and fathered eight children. By 1851, he was suffering from overwork and the following year he spent some time in the **Bedlam** mental asylum. On 14 September 1852 (only a few months after his 40th birthday), he died at his home in Ramsgate, Kent, exhausted physically and mentally. The government awarded his widow an annual pension of £100 in recognition of his contribution to British architecture. (*See also* ALBERT, PRINCE.)

PUNK. Punk was an assertive, confrontational, fashion that took root among young working-class people during the second half of the 1970s. Although it flourished for a time in cities of the United States, it was replaced in North America by disco, leaving London as the focus of the trend. There, its followers adopted aggressive clothing (such as leather jackets emblazoned with provocative slogans), body piercing (such as nose rings and lip rings, sometimes linked by chains), and unconventional, gaudily colored hairstyles. Politically, punks were frequently associated with right-wing political movements such as the National Front and musically they favored the **Sex Pistols**, Clash, and other rock bands that challenged accepted orthodoxies through the profanity of their language and the decadence of a lifestyle focusing on sex and drugs. During the 1980s, young people turned away from the excesses of the movement, but several of its attributes (such as the acceptance of tattoos on women, ear rings on men, and lip studs on both sexes) were absorbed by mainstream society.

PURCELL ROOM. *See* QUEEN ELIZABETH HALL.

PUTNEY. Putney lies on the south bank of the **River Thames** about five miles from **Charing Cross**. Archaeological evidence suggests a lengthy period of settlement, dating from the Iron Age, but the economy was based on farming and fishing until the early 16th century, when wealthy noblemen and merchants (such as Thomas Cromwell, adviser to King Henry VIII) began to acquire property and give it an up-market reputation. Growth occurred rapidly (given the standards of the time) during the 17th and 18th centuries, and was enhanced by the opening of a bridge across the Thames to **Fulham** in 1729 (*see* **Putney Bridge**), but modern Putney is largely a product of Industrial Revolution expansion. In 1846, the opening of a **railway** station on the London and South Western company's line to **Waterloo** allowed office workers to move out of the central city and buy a terraced or semidetached home in the fashionable riverside town, which rapidly became a suburb of London as open spaces were acquired by builders. However, the cost of land and the greater attraction of areas closer to the city for commercial and industrial developers allowed Putney to retain its essentially residential nature. The lack of construction since the 1920s (by which time most of the former fields and market gardens were built over) emphasizes the Victorian and Edwardian **architecture** of the area, which is now part of the **London Borough of Wandsworth**. (*See also* UNIVERSITY BOAT RACE.)

PUTNEY BRIDGE. The first **bridge** across the **River Thames** between **Putney** and **Fulham** was a wooden edifice, designed by Jacob Ackworth and opened in 1729. Until 1750, when **Westminster Bridge** was built, it was the closest crossing to the **City of London** west of **London Bridge**, but its 26 spans (varying in size from only 14 feet to 32 feet) proved an increasingly serious impediment to navigation, so in 1882–86, it was replaced by the present granite structure, designed by **Joseph William Bazalgette**, which has five spans. The bridge has been the starting point of the annual boat race between Oxford and Cambridge Universities since 1845 (*see* **University Boat Race**). The lattice girder railway bridge, which lies a few yards to the east, was erected for the London and South Western Company in 1887–89.

– Q –

QUEEN ELIZABETH HALL. Built immediately east of the **Royal Festival Hall** in the arts complex on the **South Bank** of the **River Thames** close to **Waterloo Bridge**, and named after Queen Elizabeth II, the concert hall opened in 1967. It seats about 1,100 people and initially presented programs by small orchestras. However, the stage has recently been adapted for the performance of musicals and opera. The Purcell Room, part of the same building and erected at the same time, is more intimate, holding audiences of up to 370 for concerts by solo artists and chamber music groups. The **London County Council** Architect's Department was responsible for the design of the complex and prepared its plans at a time when stark, multilevel, concrete buildings were fashionable. The result, to modern critics, looks bare and functional, with exterior bridges and stairways that present considerable problems to elderly and physically challenged patrons.

QUEEN'S HOUSE. In 1616, King James VI and I commissioned **Inigo Jones** to build a house for his wife, Anne of Denmark, in **Greenwich Park**. Anne died, three years later, before much work was done, but the building was completed during the 1630s for Henrietta Maria, consort of Charles I. The first English residence built in the Palladian style, it was constructed in the form of the letter H, straddling the **Woolwich** to **Deptford** road, with the two sides connected by a bridge. The Queen loved it, calling it her "house of delight"; ousted when her husband was dethroned during the Civil War, she returned when the monarchy was restored in 1660 and spent most of her last years there. During the 1690s, **Christopher Wren** (at the insistence of Queen Mary II) ensured that his plans for the construction of the **Royal Naval College** maintained a clear view of the building from the **River Thames**. For the next century, it continued to serve as a home for aristocrats but, in 1806, was converted for use as a school and, by 1933, when the educators moved out, was in a dilapidated condition. After improvements had been made, it was handed over to the **National Maritime Museum** in 1937 as a gallery for its Elizabethan and Stuart exhibits, then, from 1984 to 1990, was returned to its 17th-century condition at a cost of £5 million. The first floor apartments have been furnished in the style of a royal palace of the period and are open to the public.

QUEEN VICTORIA MEMORIAL. Soon after Queen Victoria's death in 1901, a committee was formed to devise a means of commemorating her reign. Part of its plan was a program of "architectural and scenic" change in the neighborhood of **Buckingham Palace**, with a statue of the monarch forming the centerpiece. Thomas Brock was commissioned to prepare the sculpture, which consists of a 13-foot-high representation of Victoria facing eastwards down **The Mall** from a richly ornamented pedestal, which clearly demonstrates the Edwardians' passion for allegorical figures as Truth, Constancy, and Motherhood compete for attention with Charity, War, Architecture, Peace, and Manufacture. Carved from a single 2,300-pound block of marble, the statue was unveiled in 1911 by King George V (the Queen's grandson), who knighted Brock during the ceremony. Later, critic Osbert Sitwell, disrespectfully but memorably, described the sculpture as "tons of allegorical females in white wedding cake marble, with whole litters of their cretinous children." The Memorial (which is a favorite grandstand for the more athletic members of the crowds that turn out to see members of the Royal Family make public appearances on the Palace balcony) is surrounded by flower beds.

– R –

RAG FAIR. A secondhand clothes **market**, the Rag Fair was probably established during the Stuart monarchy in the 17th century and flourished during the Victorian period, when penniless slum dwellers had few options but to buy other people's cast-offs (commentators of the time refer to the goods on offer as mere "shreds and patches"). Held in Rosemary Lane (which was renamed Old Mint Street in 1905), it was managed principally by Jewish **immigrants** and thrived on the custom of poor citizens from nearby neighborhoods, many of them Irish incomers who had made their way to London to find work. The fair survived into the 20th century but disappeared before the outbreak of the First World War.

RAILWAYS. London's railways are a product of the Victorian era, with the core of the network taking shape between 1836 and 1876. The first line, from **Bermondsey** to **Deptford**, was authorized by Parliament in 1833 and ran its first services three years later. Other connections quickly followed—**Euston Station** to Birmingham in 1837, **London Bridge** Station to **Croydon** in 1839, **Fenchurch Street Station** to **Blackwall** in 1841, and London Bridge to Brighton in the same year. **Paddington Station** opened in 1838, providing connections to the west (Queen Victoria made her first rail journey, from Slough to Paddington, in 1842, averaging a speed of 44 miles an hour, which **Prince Albert**, her husband, felt was much too high). **King's Cross Station** became the terminus of the Great Northern Railway in 1852, attracting traffic from Edinburgh, Newcastle, and York. **Victoria** Station brought services from the southwest over the **River Thames** in 1860 and **Liverpool Street Station** was designated the Great Eastern Railway's base in 1874.

Most of the termini were located towards the edge of the city's urban area but provided a focus for warehouses, **hotels**, shops, and other services, thereby contributing significantly to the expansion of the metropolis. Also, the construction process drastically altered patterns of social segregation because middle-class families bought homes in environmentally attractive locations, leaving the dirty, smoky, noisy sites beside the lines to those who could afford nothing better. In addition, many homes in poorer areas were demolished to make way for track and sidings (estimates of the numbers of people made homeless vary but they were probably in the region of 37,000 from 1857 to 1869 and 76,000 from 1850 to 1900). During the last quarter of the 19th century, routes reached towards the outer suburbs as the city spread its bricks and mortar, with much of the suburban house building actively promoted by the railway companies. The **London Underground** system, which opened in 1863, complemented those lines that brought workers from the outskirts to downtown jobs.

The first half of the 20th century brought further improvements; additional connections filled gaps in provision and the nationalization of the system by the Labour government in 1947 allowed the newly formed British Railways to plan timetables as a whole. Since the 1960s, however, passenger numbers have declined, resulting in the closure of many branch lines and reductions in the frequency of services elsewhere. The only significant construction in recent years has been the **Docklands** Light Railway, which linked the southeast of the **City of London** to the redeveloped **docks** area at **Canary Wharf** in 1987. During the 1990s,

Prime Minister Margaret Thatcher's government denationalized the network, handing over the lines to Railtrack and giving individual companies the right to provide services. The result was an enormous rise in complaints about trains failing to run on time and allegations that safety was taking second place to profit. (*See also* ABBEY WOOD; ACTON; AIRPORTS; BALHAM; BARKING; BARNES; BATTERSEA; BATTERSEA BRIDGE; BLACKFRIARS; BRIDGES; CANNING TOWN; CANNON STREET STATION; CATFORD; DRAIN; EARL'S COURT; EDMONTON; KILBURN; KING'S CROSS FIRE; ST. PANCRAS; STRATFORD; SURBITON; TRANSPORT; WANDSWORTH; WATERLOO; WILLESDEN.)

RANGER'S HOUSE. One of a series of buildings associated with **Greenwich Palace**, the Ranger's House was erected in 1699–70 for Captain Francis Hosier and enlarged 40 years later by Philip, Earl of Chesterfield. In 1815, it became the official residence of the Rangers (or guardians) of **Greenwich Park** (the first holder of the post was Princess Sophia Matilda), but in 1902 was bought by the **London County Council**, which turned it into a cafeteria. Restoration work was carried out in 1959–60 then, in 1974, it was converted to an art gallery housing the Suffolk Collection of 17th-century portraits (one of the most important exhibitions of Jacobean and Stuart family paintings in the country) and the Dolmetsch collection of musical instruments. The grand salon is used regularly as a concert venue.

REDBRIDGE, LONDON BOROUGH OF. Redbridge lies on the north-eastern outskirts of the London conurbation. When **local government** in the area was reorganized in 1965, the borough was created through the merger of **Woodford** and **Wanstead** with **Ilford**, parts of **Dagenham**, and sections of Chigwell. All of the new authority (which covers just under 22 square miles and takes its name from a red brick bridge that crossed the River Roding during the 18th century) was previously within the County of Essex. About one-third (mostly in the north and west, including stretches of **Epping Forest**) is **green belt** where urban development is restricted. Elsewhere, the land is largely covered by **housing**, much of it owned by lower middle-class workers employed in public administration, banking, and retailing. The population of 231,900 (1998) includes a large Asian community (the majority of whom live in the south of the area).

RED LION SQUARE. As a result of the **Great Fire** in 1666, London suffered a chronic shortage of **housing**, so speculative developers, sensing profit, bought rights to build homes on land that had previously been open space. One of these entrepreneurs—Nicholas Barbon—laid out Red Lion Square, in 1684, on a 17-acre paddock in **Holborn**, incurring the wrath of the lawyers at nearby **Gray's Inn** (the august members of the legal profession objected to the loss of their rural vistas and attempted to take the law into their own hands, unsuccessfully attacking Barbon and his workmen). During the 18th and 19th centuries, the square became popular with the city's radicals, including pre-Raphaelite painter Dante Gabriel Rossetti, who, in 1851, rented No. 17, accepting a lease that required that "the models are kept under gentlemanly restraint as some artists sacrifice the dignity of art to the baseness of passion." William Morris, one of the founders of the arts and crafts movement and a friend of Rossetti, lived in the same house in 1856–59 and opened a showroom for his fabric designs at No. 8. The area's nonconformist links are still evident; the National Secular Society (established in 1886) has its headquarters at No. 26 and the South Place Ethical Society (which formed in 1793) is based at Conway Hall, whose rooms are rented for gatherings of left-wing political groups, gay book fairs, and similar events. John Harrison, inventor of the marine chronometer, which, from the 1770s, allowed seamen to determine longitude accurately, occupied a property on the site where the Cable and Wireless Company's offices now stand.

REFORM CLUB. The Reform Club was founded, in 1836, as a **gentlemen's club** with radical political views, attracting most leading members of the Whig Party during the 19th century. Its rooms at 104–5 **Pall Mall**, in the heart of London's clubland, were designed by **Charles Barry** and are opulently furnished (Phineas Fogg was in the smoking room when he accepted the bet that took him on the journey described by novelist Jules Verne in *Around the World in Eighty Days*, published in 1873). During the 20th century, the club gradually moved away from its roots and is now almost entirely a social organization. It amended its rules in 1981 so that ladies could join.

REGENT'S CANAL. Regent's Canal, which opened in 1820, links Paddington Basin to the **River Thames** at **Limehouse**, where a **dock** was constructed to allow ships to load and unload cargoes. It formally closed for industrial traffic in 1969, having lost the competition for trade with road and rail transport. However, large sections of the towpath still survive, providing an important recreational resource in the heavily urbanized **East End.** At Camden Lock (in **Camden Town**) a weekend

street market, popular with young people, sells antiques, books, records, and bric-a-brac. Farther east, the area around the junction with the **Grand Union Canal** is known as Little Venice (a name apparently conferred by poets Robert Browning and Lord Byron but not popularly used until the second half of the 20th century). The tree-lined walkways have attracted artists (such as Lucian Freud) as well as tourists, who take narrowboat trips through **Regent's Park.**

REGENT'S PARK. Covering 487 acres, Regent's **Park** is a major open space close to the center of London. In 1539, the land (which had been owned by Barking Abbey) was acquired by King Henry VIII, who set aside a large portion as hunting territory. A survey in 1649 showed that it still had over 16,000 trees, but these were felled soon after (partly to build ships for the Royal Navy) and the estate was converted to farm land, which provided milk and other produce for the city markets. As the urban population expanded, however, buildings increasingly encroached on the fields, so in 1811, John Fordyce, Surveyor General for Crown Lands, held a competition designed to produce a plan that would increase profits from the area. The winner—**John Nash**—presented a scheme for a garden city, with detached homes and terraced houses carefully located in a setting that emphasized countryside rather than town.

Although critics raised objections to the proposal, the Prince Regent (later King George IV) vehemently supported Nash, exerting a royal influence that enabled work to begin in 1812. Because costs rose, the architect's vision was never fully realized (only eight of the suggested 56 villas were completed, for instance) but, by 1840, a large element was in place, with the elegant terraces (such as Cumberland Terrace, named after the Duke of Cumberland, George's younger brother) greatly admired.

Unfortunately, a combination of **air pollution** and, during the Second World War, neglect led to deterioration, so, by 1945, the buildings required considerable rehabilitation, which was undertaken by the Crown under the guidance of architect Louis de Soissons, who completed the work during the 1970s. The park now includes an open air **theater** (where **William Shakespeare**'s plays have been performed on summer evenings since 1900), sports facilities (including tennis courts, football pitches, and an athletics track), bandstands, children's playgrounds, and the **London Zoo.** It is maintained by the **Royal Parks** Agency and has been used as a model for public park provision at sites around the world. (*See also* GRAND UNION CANAL; REGENT STREET.)

REGENT STREET. Designed by **John Nash** in 1813–16, Regent Street was intended to link Carlton House (home of George, the Prince Regent) to the new developments at **Regent's Park**, alleviate traffic congestion at **Charing Cross**, and increase the value of royal lands at **Haymarket** and **Pall Mall**. Just under a mile long, it involved construction of **Oxford Circus** and **Piccadilly Circus** in order to accommodate road junctions and, at its southern end, required an eastward curve (known as The Quadrant) to avoid the fashionable aristocratic area around **St. James's Palace**. Nash sought to achieve a visual balance with the buildings that would line the route, managing to preserve an element of architectural unity even though the development was funded by private individuals, who had their own views about property facades. The area north of **Oxford Street** was intended to be residential but, farther south, the plans provided for exclusive shops catering to an affluent clientele. For most of the 19th century, the stores thrived, but by 1900 an increasingly demanding public, seeking fashionable goods at low prices, was threatening the security of several of the businesses, which frequently had too many customers crowding into limited retail space. As a result, rebuilding was undertaken when leases ran out, replacing Nash's stucco frontages with more prosaic **Portland stone**. Also, in 1925 the local traders founded the Regent Street Association to promote their commercial interests and help members facing financial difficulty. As a result, the road has retained its commercial importance, with shops such as Mappin and Webb's jewelry premises and Dickins and Jones's **department store** complementing music publisher Boosey and Hawkes and the Veeraswamy Indian restaurant. All the properties are owned by the Crown Estate, which, in 1999, announced proposals to pedestrianize the street over a period of 10 years. (*See also* CAFÉ ROYAL.)

RICHMOND. During the 12th century, the Kings of England frequently moved their court nine miles from London to the manor house at Shene, on the south bank of the **River Thames**, so that they could enjoy hunting in the surrounding forests. A small village grew up around the house, which became a favorite resort for aristocrats and developed as the number of courtiers increased. When the residence burned down in 1499, King Henry VII decided to rebuild it in situ and named his new palace Rychemonde after his estates in Yorkshire (*see* **Richmond Palace**). Since then, the settlement has retained its status and evolved as a service center rather than an industrial community. The palace was largely destroyed after the execution of Charles I in 1649 but, during the early 18th century, the town continued to attract visitors, who came to drink the waters at the wells in the grounds of Cardigan House. A **theater** opened in the 1760s and, ever since, has presented productions featuring Britain's leading actors (Edmund Kean actually became lessee in 1831 and was buried in the churchyard two years later).

The road **bridge**, which opened in 1777 (*see* **Richmond Bridge**), brought additional population, as did the **railway** some 70 years later, but there are still extensive areas of public open space, as at **Richmond Park** and the **Royal Botanic Gardens**. Even the village green, where King Henry VII held a jousting tournament in 1492, has survived and is still used for sporting events by the local cricket team. During the 1980s, the riverside area was redeveloped to provide offices, shops, restaurants, and apartments. Many of the Georgian and Victorian frontages were retained and the facades of the new buildings designed to blend with the old. Some critics have claimed that the result is an unattractive pastiche, but others (such as Prince Charles) argue that it is a successful attempt to retain the best of the old in a modern townscape. Many of Richmond's residents commute to work in the **City of London**, but the quality of the urban environment has helped to attract the British headquarters of the Compaq computer company and educational institutions such as the US-based Richmond College. (*See also* RICHMOND UPON THAMES, LONDON BOROUGH OF.)

RICHMOND BRIDGE. The graceful five-span bridge of **Portland stone**, which links **Richmond** (on the east bank of one of the **River Thames** meanders) with **Twickenham** (on the west), was designed by James Paine and built in 1774–77. It is the oldest road crossing of the waterway in the London area. Downstream, the steel **railway** bridge, designed by J. W. Jacomb Hood, was erected in 1908. It replaced a cast iron structure that had carried the tracks of the Windsor, Staines, and South Western Railway from Richmond to Windsor since 1848.

RICHMOND PALACE. From the reign of King Henry I, during the 12th century, England's monarchs used the manor house at Shene, some nine miles southwest of **Charing Cross**, as a base for hunting. It became a favorite haunt of Richard II, Henry V, Edward IV, and Henry VII in particular but, in 1499 (by which time it was known as Shene Palace), was destroyed by fire. Henry VII erected a new building on the site, naming it Rychemonde Palace after his estates at Rychemonde in Yorkshire, and died there a decade later (reputedly leaving a fortune in gold hidden under the floors and in the walls). Catherine of Aragon lived at Richmond from 1502 until she married Henry VIII in 1509, Anne of Cleves received the palace as part of her divorce settlement from the same monarch, Elizabeth I entertained Walter Raleigh and other courtiers there during the summer, and the ill-fated Charles I gave it to his bride (Henrietta Maria of France) as a wedding present in 1625. Following Charles's execution in 1649, most of the structure was destroyed, but a single gatehouse (bearing the arms of Henry VII) survives and, in Old Palace Yard, part of the Tudor building (with 18th-century alterations) was converted into three houses during the 1950s.

RICHMOND PARK. The largest of the **Royal Parks** in London, Richmond **Park**'s 2,360 acres were first enclosed, in 1637, by King Charles I, who used the land as a hunting forest. Its vegetation remains seminatural, consisting largely of ancient oak woodland and acidic grassland, with areas of bog and bracken. Deer still roam the area (which was classified as a Site of Special Scientific Interest by English Nature—one of the government's conservation agencies—in 1992) but are fed in winter to ensure their survival. Pen Ponds, built during the 18th century, attract fishermen seeking pike, bream, carp, and roach. In 1894, King Edward VIII (who chose to abdicate his throne rather than give up the American divorcee he loved) was born in the White House, built in 1727–29 by the Earl of Pembroke towards the southeast of the park. The building is now used by the Royal Ballet School and closed to the public, but visitors can find refreshment at another Georgian property, Pembroke Lodge, where Lord John Russell (who derived no pleasure from London social life) lived while he was Prime Minister during the 1840s and 1850s. The park has two golf courses and is popular with horse riders. Cars are confined to the perimeter of the area so most of the estate's features are accessible only on foot.

RICHMOND UPON THAMES, LONDON BOROUGH OF. The only **London borough** to span the **River Thames**, Richmond was created in 1965 by the merger of **Twickenham** (on the western side of the waterway) with **Richmond** (on the east). Largely residential, Richmond has one of the highest proportions of professional and managerial residents of any local authority area in England and a low proportion of children. Twickenham is similarly affluent, though with a greater proportion of its workforce in technical posts. Much of the borough's 21 square miles are open space, used for recreation (see, for example, **Bushy Park**, **Richmond Park**, and the **Royal Botanic Gardens**), but there is a significant commercial and industrial presence, with retailing, publishing, and a growing high technology sector attracted by good road and rail links to central London. In 1998, the resident population was 186,700. (*See also* BARNES; KEW; MORTLAKE.)

RILLINGTON PLACE. In 1950, Timothy Evans (who had the intellectual capacity of a 10-year-old child) was executed in **Pentonville** Prison after confessing to the murder of his wife and baby daughter at 10 Rillington Place, **Notting Hill**. Four years later, the bodies of three women were found in a cupboard at the flat below, occupied by John Reginald Halliday Christie. A police search discovered the body of Christie's wife under the kitchen floorboards and the skeletons of two more women in the garden. Under questioning, Christie admitted to murdering all eight females. He was tried, then hanged at Pentonville in 1952. Evans's death fuelled the campaign for the abolition of the death penalty in the United Kingdom. He was given a full pardon (though not until 1996) and Rillington Place was demolished.

RITZ HOTEL. The Ritz has become a byword for opulent luxury, contributing *ritzy* to the vocabulary of the English language. It was erected in **Piccadilly** for the Blackpool Building and Vendor Company Ltd., on a site previously occupied by the Walsingham House and Bath Hotels, and opened in 1906. The first major steel-framed building in London, it was designed by architects Charles Frederic Mewès and Arthur Joseph Davis to the specifications of Swiss businessman César Ritz, who had made a great success of the Carlton hotel in **Haymarket**. Furnished in the style of King Louis XVI's reign in France, with rooms decorated in blue, peach, pink, and yellow, the hotel was bought from the Trafalgar House group by private individuals in 1995 and refurbished in stages using French craftsmen and suppliers. Room prices start at around £300 a night.

RIVER POLICE. By the end of the 18th century, about two-thirds of Britain's imports and exports were passing through London's **docks**, but secure facilities for storing commodities were limited so theft was common. In 1798, Patrick Colquhoun and John Harriott attempted to reduce the losses by forming a 200-strong force of river policemen, who frequently suffered violent attacks as they attempted to arrest thieves and pirates. In 1839, the force was incorporated within the Metropolitan **Police**.

ROEHAMPTON. Roehampton lies east of **Richmond Park**, some 6.5 miles southeast of **Charing Cross** in the **London Borough of Wandsworth**. It was established during the late 13th century by incomers from **Putney**, then developed, from about 1630, as a fashionable place for wealthy nobles and merchants to build a country mansion. From the Victorian period, however, many families moved farther away from the city, selling their estates to speculative builders and their homes to medical and educational interests (thus, for example, Roehampton House, which was designed by Thomas Archer, erected in 1710–12, and expanded by Sir Edwin Lutyens in 1912, was converted for use as a hospital in 1915). The **London County Council** also utilized much of the open space for public **housing** after the Second World War, diversifying the social composition of the area, which has a mix of residential and institutional uses. (*See also* CHAMBERS, WILLIAM.)

ROOKERIES. London's 19th-century slums were known as rookeries. Black from accumulations of soot, overcrowded, fetid, and noisy, they were considered by middle-class Victorians to be the hiding place of humanity's dregs, ridden with **crime** and permeated by disease. Many had a high proportion of Irish-born residents, adding to the fear of the unknown for outsiders. The most notorious was St. Giles, a zone of cramped, winding alleys bounded by Great Russell Street, Crown Street (now **Charing Cross Road**), Long Acre, and **Drury Lane**. There, according to the 1851 census, over 50,000 people lived at a density of twelve to a house (100 years earlier, artist William Hogarth had condemned it as a place of debauchery and vice in *Gin Lane* and other prints). Saffron Hill, a similarly poor environment between Smithfield and Clerkenwell Green, was made the home of the Artful Dodger and Fagin in **Charles Dickens**'s *Oliver Twist* (1838), and much of the **East End** and the areas close to the docks were also impoverished. The suggestion that these places were sources of disease was undoubtedly justified because the high-density living led to the spread of infection. However, the allegation that they were occupied by criminals may have been overstated, according to some modern scholars. They were removed by large-scale slum clearance programs (many designed to make way for the railways) from the 1840s, but the demolition simply shunted the poverty to other parts of the city as tens of thousands of people were thrown out of their homes without any compensation or alternative accommodation.

ROTHERHITHE. Four miles east of **Charing Cross**, Rotherhithe is located on the marshy southern shore of the **River Thames** in the **London Borough of Southwark**. By the 14th century, although isolated from the **City of London**, it had developed a shipbuilding industry, shaping a relationship with the sea that was to last for over 700 years. In 1620, the *Mayflower* left the harbor to carry the Pilgrim Fathers to the Americas; Christopher Jones, her captain, was a native of the community and lies buried in St. Mary's churchyard. Seventy-nine years later, the Howland, London's earliest enclosed **dock**, was opened, the first of nine that would extend over 300 acres by the beginning of the 20th century and be jointly known as Surrey Commercial Docks. In 1823, Marc Brunel began work on the first tunnel under the Thames, linking Rotherhithe to **Wapping**. He took 20 years to complete the project, assisted by his son, Isambard, but revolutionized engineering by employing a novel shield that left only a small part of the advancing excavation exposed to workers and thus reduced the danger that the soft clays would collapse as the shaft advanced. Originally used by pedestrians, the tunnel was converted for the East London Railway Company's trains in 1869 and is now part of the **London Underground** system. A second tunnel, which linked the area to **Shadwell** from 1908, involved much demolition of property as new streets were built to provide access for vehicular traffic. Following the closure of the docks in 1970, most of the harbor areas were filled in and sold to developers. By the late 1990s, over 6,000 new homes had been built, along with budget accommodation for students and young people (Rotherhithe has London's largest youth hostel as well as housing for undergraduates at the University of Westminster). In addition, some of the old warehouses were converted into flats and new bus routes integrated the area with the central city. But, in the process, the links with the sea were severed as the employment base and social composition of the community changed.

ROTHMAN'S OF PALL MALL. In 1890, Louis Rothman (an immigrant from the Ukraine) opened a tobacconist's shop at 55 **Fleet Street**. Each day, after his store closed, he sat for hours, making cigarettes for sale to the reporters who worked in the newspaper businesses nearby. Ten years later, as his reputation spread and his profits grew, he moved to a more prestigious site in **Pall Mall**. Royal warrants from King Edward VII of

Britain (1905) and King Alfonso XIII of Spain (1910) brought additional business from the courts of Europe and allowed him to develop larger factory premises, where workers continued to roll the cigarettes manually until, after the outbreak of the First World War, he introduced a machine that made Virginia blends. Rothman died in 1926 and, three years later, his business became a limited company. In 1999 (by which time it had expanded into luxury goods, with interests in Montblanc and Cartier), the firm was taken over by British American Tobacco for US$7.55 billion. The merged producer was expected to control about 16 percent of the world cigarette market.

ROTTEN ROW. During the last decade of the 17th century, King William III rode regularly between his residences at **Kensington Palace** and **St. James's Palace**. The track he followed became known as the *route du roi* (French for "the King's road"), which, in time, was corrupted into Rotten Row. The 1,500-yard path, at the southern edge of **Hyde Park**, was the first street in England to be lit at night because the King, determined to frighten off highwaymen, arranged for 300 lamps to be hung from nearby trees. A fashionable place to promenade during Georgian and Victorian times, Rotten Row is still used by horse riders, though stabling, once common, is no longer available.

ROYAL ACADEMY OF ARTS. Reputably the oldest British society devoted to the fine arts, the academy was founded in 1768. Artist Joshua Reynolds served as the first President, architect **William Chambers** was the first Treasurer, painter Thomas Gainsborough was one of the leading members, and King George III announced that he would be the institution's Patron. Originally based in the **Strand**, with exhibitions held at a property in **Pall Mall**, the academy moved to its present location in **Burlington House** in 1868. For much of its history, it has been criticized as a bastion of artistic conservatism, failing to support individualistic talent, but its elitism has made it a powerful lobby in business and political circles. It mounts frequent, often controversial, exhibitions, the best known being the summer show, which has been held annually for 200 years. The academy owns an important collection of works gifted by artists such as John Constable and J. M. W. Turner—a collection destined to grow because its regulations require each newly elected Academician to present "a picture, bas-relief or other specimen of his abilitie." (*See also* ROYAL COLLEGE OF ART; ROYAL SOCIETY OF ARTS [RSA].)

ROYAL ACADEMY OF DRAMATIC ART (RADA). The academy—the oldest school of drama in England—was founded by actor-producer Sir Herbert Beerbohm Tree in 1904. Two years later, a Council was formed to facilitate management, then, in 1908, Associates, all distinguished in aspects of the theater, were appointed as advisers. The Prince of Wales (later King Edward VIII) became Patron in 1921 and in 1931 the institution's Gower Street headquarters was remodelled to incorporate a **theater**. As RADA's activities have expanded (it has become the country's principal training ground for young actors and actresses) it has required further space, so workshops and rehearsal rooms are now housed in a Chenies Street annex.

ROYAL ACADEMY OF MUSIC. The academy was founded in 1823, largely through the influence of a group of aristocrats headed by Lord Burghersh. Although King George IV agreed to act as Patron, the institution's early years were dogged by financial problems, but fortunes improved from 1868, following a decision by Prime Minister William Gladstone's Liberal government to award an annual grant. In 1926, it moved to its present premises in Marylebone Road, adding a theater and lecture room in 1926, a library (funded by a public appeal) in 1968, and a concert hall in 1977. The academy is the oldest organization undertaking advanced musical training in the United Kingdom. (*See also* ROYAL COLLEGE OF MUSIC.)

ROYAL AIR FORCE MUSEUM. *See* HENDON.

ROYAL ALBERT HALL. *See* ALBERT HALL.

ROYAL ARSENAL. Until the early 18th century, the principal gun casting works in southeast England was located in the **City of London** but, in 1713, following an explosion that killed 17 people, it was moved to more spacious premises at **Woolwich**, close to the **Royal Naval Dockyard**. Originally known as The Warren (after the site where it was located), the depot was renamed the Royal Arsenal by King George III in 1805. By the time of the First World War, it had extended to over 1,200 acres and employed nearly 80,000 people, but output declined from the mid-20th century and the works was closed in 1967. For 30 years, the site stood derelict but, in 1996, plans were announced to develop the area as a complex of **museums**, workshops for small businesses, sports facilities, and dormitories for students at the University of Greenwich.

In 1886, a works **football** team was formed at the arsenal. In 1914, it moved to **Highbury** in north London and, as the Arsenal Football Club, has become one of Europe's leading teams.

ROYAL BALLET. The ballet was founded in 1956, when the Sadler's Wells Company (originally formed by Dame Ninette de Valois in 1931 at the **Old Vic**) was awarded a royal charter. It is based at the **Royal Opera House** (in **Covent Garden**), where it has mounted productions with most of the world's leading dancers. During the 1990s, the ballet suffered from a series of artistic and financial crises as lackluster productions led to disaffection among dancers and to the departure of leading talents. However, the refurbishment of the company's Royal Opera House headquarters in 1998–99 and the appointment of Australian Ross Stretton as Director in 2000 offered the prospect of greater stability and a return to world-class status. The Royal Ballet School (also a product of Dame Ninette's enterprise) provides both general education and dance training for young people. Those aged 11–16 are taught at White Lodge (**Richmond Park**), and older students at a property in Talgarth Road (West **Kensington**), which was originally acquired with an Arts Council grant in 1947. Most members of the country's leading ballet companies have attended the school.

ROYAL BOTANIC GARDENS. One of the world's major centers of botanical research, the gardens are located about seven miles west of **Charing Cross** in the suburb of **Kew** (and so are popularly known as Kew Gardens). They were originally laid out by Augusta, the widow of Frederick, Prince of Wales, in 1759, but extended by her son, King George III, then landscaped by Capability Brown during the 1770s. Under the unofficial direction of botanist Sir Joseph Banks (who was President of the **Royal Society** from 1778 to 1820), they built a reputation as a locus for the scientific study of plant life during the early 19th century. That reputation lay partly in the extent of the collections (as Britain acquired an empire, the gardens acquired species brought by explorers from all corners of the world), but now rests on expertise in conservation and in the economic exploitation of species (scientists from Kew introduced bread fruit trees to the West Indies and rubber trees to Malaya, for instance). In addition, researchers have access to a library of over 120,000 monographs and a seed bank, which concentrates, in particular, on wild plants of Great Britain and the arid tropics.

Since 1840, when the estate was donated to the nation following a Royal Commission report, the 300-acre grounds have also had an important recreational and educational function. Hurricane force gales on 15 October 1987 caused havoc, destroying many trees, but Kew still has an enormous collection of plants. The Alpine House alone contains over 3,000 upland species and the Grass Garden over 600. Also, many of the buildings are of considerable architectural merit. The 10-story Orangery, designed by **William Chambers** and built in 1761, has been converted into a **museum** and book stall, but Decimus Burton's glass and iron Temperate House (which was started in 1860 but took 30 years to complete) and his Palm House (the latter designed in conjunction with engineer Richard Turner during the 1840s) retain their original function (the Temperate House was restored in 1980).

Another of Chambers's buildings—the Great Pagoda, which was inspired by a visit to Canton—was built in 1761–62 in the southeast corner of the gardens, providing an easily identifiable landmark. In the north, the red brick Kew Palace (which measures only 70 feet long by 50 feet wide and is the smallest of the royal residences) dates from 1631. It was built by Samuel Fortey, a merchant of Dutch parentage (and so it is sometimes known as the Dutch House) but it was leased by Queen Caroline in 1728 and became the favorite home of King George II. The garden behind the palace (named the Queen's Garden after Queen Elizabeth II) is laid out in 17th-century style, with an emphasis on herbs.

ROYAL COLLEGE OF ART. In 1837, following a parliamentary inquiry into art education, a School of Design was established at **Somerset House**, with classes emphasizing the practicalities of industrial draughtsmanship rather than mastery of the fine arts. Four years later, the government founded similar institutions in other parts of the country so the school began a program of teacher training. In 1896, it was renamed the Royal College when Queen Victoria granted it permission to award diplomas and, in 1967, it was given a charter empowering it to grant Masters and doctoral degrees. The college is now based in Kensington Gore, housed in a stark 1960s building (designed by H. T. Cadbury-Brown, Sir Hugh Casson, and R. Y. Gooden), which contrasts with the 19th century ebullience of the **Albert Hall**, its immediate neighbor. (*See also* ROYAL ACADEMY OF ARTS.)

ROYAL COLLEGE OF MUSIC. In 1882, largely as a result of the influence of the Prince of Wales, the Royal College was established in Kensington Gore. It moved to its present site in Prince Consort Road during 1894, occupying a building (designed by Sir Arthur Blomfield) that was extended in 1964 and 1973. The college owns a collection of old musical instruments—including Joseph Haydn's clavichord—which was presented to it by Sir George Donaldson in 1894, and numbers composers Benjamin Britten and Ralph Vaughan Williams among its former students. (*See also* ROYAL ACADEMY OF MUSIC.)

ROYAL COLLEGE OF PHYSICIANS OF LONDON. The college—the oldest of England's medical organizations—was founded in 1518, largely due to the efforts of Thomas Linacre, King Henry VIII's doctor. Its headquarters in St. Andrew's Place (close to **Regent's Park**) house an important library of historical textbooks, some 140 of them survivors of the **Great Fire** of 1666, others bequeathed by the Marquess of Dorchester in 1680. Along with the British Medical Association and the **Royal College of Surgeons of England**, the college forms a powerful lobby for **health care** interests in the United Kingdom.

ROYAL COLLEGE OF SURGEONS OF ENGLAND. Although the college was founded in 1800, it can trace its roots to a Guild of Surgeons that functioned in the **City of London** during the Medieval period (*see* **livery companies**). That guild was amalgamated with the Barbers in 1540, but members sought to regain their independence in 1745, breaking away to form a Company of Surgeons. In 1797, the organization obtained property at **Lincoln's Inn Fields**, extending the premises on several occasions over the past 200 years to provide exhibition galleries, laboratories, and facilities for the Nuffield College of Surgical Sciences, which trains graduate students. The College of Surgeons has a library of over 120,000 books and houses the Hunterian **Museum**, a collection of over 6,000 anatomical specimens, most of which were acquired by Scottish surgeon John Hunter (1728–93) for use with his pupils. It has a strong research orientation and lists most of the distinguished English surgeons of the past two centuries among its membership. (*See also* ROYAL COLLEGE OF PHYSICIANS OF LONDON.)

ROYAL COURTS OF JUSTICE. Until the late 19th century, the principal English courts dealing with civil litigation had no central base they could use throughout the year, so, in 1871, an area on the north side of the **Strand** was cleared of slums and work begun on a new building that would allow all noncriminal cases to be heard at a single location. The plans were approved by 1874, but bad weather, problems over financing, and disputes with the workforce meant that the Victorian Gothic structure was not opened until 1882 (architect George Edmund Street died of a stroke in 1881, allegedly worn out by attempts to complete the project). Built of brick and faced with **Portland stone**, it has over 1,000 rooms arranged round a central hall that is 230 feet long. Initially, there were 19 courts but extensions in 1911 and 1968 added a further 16. The Supreme Court of Justice, which uses most of the facilities, consists of the Court of Appeal, the High Court, and the Crown Court, with the High Court subdivided into the Court of Chancery (which considers matters related to property issues), the Family Division (which rules on domestic disputes), and the Queen's Bench Division (which deals principally with wrongs that can be compensated by an award of damages). The Court of Appeal hears appeals on civil and criminal matters and the Crown Court hears trials on indictment. In addition, the Bankruptcy Court and Companies Court have separate premises to the north of the complex and a number of criminal trials are held there because of pressure on the space at the **Central Criminal Court**. In addition to its formal title, the building is often referred to simply as the Law Courts.

ROYAL EXCHANGE. In 1565, a group of London merchants, led by Sir **Thomas Gresham**, purchased a site at the junction of **Cornhill** and **Threadneedle Street**, with the intention of erecting a meeting place where they could buy and sell. Most of the building materials for the four-story structure were imported from Antwerp (Belgium), where the Merchant Adventurers (who controlled more than half of England's foreign trade) had their headquarters. Grasshoppers—an element of the Gresham family crest—adorned the bell tower, and the walls around the inner courtyard were decorated with statues of England's monarchs. Space was provided for about a hundred shops, including goldsmiths, milliners, and booksellers. The building was opened in 1568 and, on 23 January 1570, received a visit from Queen Elizabeth I, who decreed that it should be named the Royal Exchange "and so to be called from henceforth and not otherwise," but it survived only until 1666, when it was destroyed in the **Great Fire**.

A second Exchange, designed by Edward Jarman and built on the same site, was opened on 28 September 1669, but storekeepers proved unwilling to rent all of the sites made available to them and eventually much of the property was taken over by Royal Exchange Assurance and **Lloyd's of London**. Some offices were occupied by the **Lord Mayor**'s court, and the **East India Company** stored pepper in the vaults.

On 10 January 1838, another fire (which is thought to have begun in Lloyd's premises) destroyed the Exchange for a second time, so a third edifice, designed by Sir William Tite, was erected, with Sir **Christopher Wren**'s St. Benet Fink Church demolished to make way for it. Eight Corinthian columns support a pediment with an elaborate sculpture, by Richard Westmacott, which shows Commerce attended by the Lord Mayor and merchants from around the world. The internal courtyard contains the pavement from the original Exchange, and the walls are adorned with scenes from London's past. When Queen Victoria officially opened the building on 28 October 1844, she echoed her royal predecessor with an announcement that "It is my royal will and pleasure that this building be hereafter called the Royal Exchange." It ceased to function as a place for general business dealings in 1939, many of its original commodities having developed specialist markets, such as the **London Metal Exchange**, with their own premises. Since then, most of the facilities have lain unused, although a number of the rooms have been occupied by an insurance company, legal firms, small shops, and a restaurant. Also, for a number of years in the 1980s and early 1990s, the trading floor was occupied by the **London International Financial Futures and Options Exchange (LIFFE)**.

ROYAL FESTIVAL HALL. The Festival Hall was the first building erected at the **South Bank** arts complex near **Waterloo** and is used for concerts, ballets, choral events, and films. Opened in 1951 as part of the **Festival of Britain** celebrations, it was designed by Robert Matthew and J. L. Martin and much praised for the quality of its acoustics. The concrete exterior looks bleak to some observers but the interior is spacious, with a 3,000-seat auditorium and an open network of foyers and staircases. Since 1988, the hall has housed the Arts Council's Poetry Library, whose archives and readings are open to visitors. (*See also* PHILHARMONIA ORCHESTRA; ROYAL PHILHARMONIC ORCHESTRA [RPO].)

ROYAL GEOGRAPHICAL SOCIETY. Since its foundation in 1830, the Royal Geographical Society has fostered exploration, supporting expeditions such as those by David Livingstone to Africa in the middle years of the 19th century, Robert Falcon Scott to the polar lands in the early 20th century, and John Hunt to Mount Everest in 1953. In the process, it has accumulated the largest privately owned collection of maps in the world and a 150,000-volume library. It also has a large archive of photographs donated by travellers. In recent years, the 13,000-member society has favored interdisciplinary research studies in sparsely populated areas and small-scale projects mounted by educational organizations. During the 1990s (and not without some acrimony), it united with the Institute of British Geographers (formerly the professional academic body for geography professors and graduate students at British **universities**) in order to provide a stronger voice in public debate at a time when government policies were reducing the time available for the discipline in schools. The society's offices at Lowther Lodge in Kensington Gore were designed by Norman Shaw and built in 1874.

ROYAL HORTICULTURAL SOCIETY. The society was founded in 1804 (as the Horticultural Society of London) by a group of botanists and gardeners led by John Wedgwood (son of Josiah Wedgwood, who founded the pottery firm at Stoke-on-Trent). In 1821, it leased 33 acres of land at **Chiswick** and, 10 years later, held its first exhibition. Financial problems during the 1850s were solved by the intervention of **Prince Albert** (husband of Queen Victoria), who became President in 1858 and persuaded the Commissioners of the Great Exhibition to provide the organization with access to their south **Kensington** property. By 1882, expenses had become prohibitive, forcing the society to abandon its London gardens, but in 1903, it was gifted an extensive area at Wisley (Surrey) and established its main nurseries there. The following year, it opened a new headquarters in Vincent Square, then in May 1913, held the first of its annual shows in the grounds of **Chelsea Hospital**. The gold medals awarded to exhibitors are highly prized and the show is undoubtedly the highlight of Britain's horticultural year, but increasing numbers of visitors (including members of the royal family) place great pressures on the limited show space. The society has also organized the annual flower show at **Hampton Court Palace** since 1993 and hosts regular events at its Vincent Square site and its hall in nearby Greycoat Street. Its collection of some 50,000 books forms one of the world's leading horticultural libraries.

ROYAL HOSPITAL, CHELSEA. *See* CHELSEA HOSPITAL.

ROYAL INSTITUTE OF INTERNATIONAL AFFAIRS. After the First World War, a group of influential academics, politicians, and journalists (including Viscount Cecil and ***The Times*** Editor Geoffrey Dawson) agreed to form a British Institute of International Affairs in order to provide a forum for discussions about issues affecting the world community. In 1923, the organization purchased premises at 10 St. James's Square (the former home of Prime Ministers William Pitt the Elder, the Earl of Derby, and William Gladstone), and in 1926 it was given a royal charter by King George V. An independent body, it conducts research and encourages publication on international issues. Membership is by election.

ROYAL INSTITUTION. The institution was founded in 1799 by Benjamin Thompson as a means of "diffusing the knowledge and facilitating the general introduction of useful mechanical inventions and improvements." It acquired premises in Albemarle Street (close to **Piccadilly**), which it converted into office, laboratory, and lecture facilities, and was awarded a royal charter by King George III in 1800. In 1802, it appointed chemist Humphry Davy (inventor of the miners' safety lamp) as its first professor. Eleven years later, Michael Faraday was engaged as Davy's assistant, a position that enabled him to conduct the series of experiments that established the nature of electromagnetic induction in 1831. Since then, many influential scientists, including T. H. Huxley and Lord Rutherford, have held positions at the institution, which has restored Faraday's workroom and mounted an exhibition of his instruments. During the winter, it holds a series of lectures designed to present research findings in terms understandable by a general audience.

ROYAL MEWS. The Mews (or stables) were an integral part of **John Nash**'s plans for **Buckingham Palace** and were built in 1824–25. They still house the royal family's carriage horses and about a hundred carriages, including the Gold State Coach (built for King George III in 1762 and used at coronations ever since), the Irish State Coach (made in Dublin in 1852 and acquired by Queen Victoria for use at **state openings of Parliament**), and the Glass State Coach (bought by King George V in 1910 for royal weddings). The Mews is administered by the Crown Equerry, who is also responsible for the coachmen and grooms.

ROYAL MILITARY ACADEMY. *See* WOOLWICH.

ROYAL MINT. It seems certain that a mint was founded in London some 200 years before the Norman Conquest of 1066 and that, by the beginning of the 14th century, it was based in the **Tower of London**. In 1811, because of pressure on space, it was moved to a building in Little Tower Hill, then in 1968, as part of the Labour government's attempt to decentralize official functions to the British regions, to Llantrisant in south Wales.

ROYAL NATIONAL THEATRE. The suggestion that Britain should have a national **theater** was first made by London publisher Effingham Wilson in 1848, but no steps were taken to build one until the early 20th century. Meetings were held, appeals proposed, and sites recommended, but nothing concrete was achieved until 1944, when the **London County Council** promoted the amalgamation of the Shakespeare Memorial National Theatre Committee (formed in 1907 as a vehicle to promote works by aspiring playwrights as well as productions of classical drama) and the **Old Vic** Theatre (which opened in 1818 and, by the 1940s, was the principal stage for presentations of **William Shakespeare**'s plays in the nation's capital). Parliament approved funds for a new theater in 1949 and, two years later, the foundation stone was laid at a site just east of **Waterloo** Bridge on the **South Bank** of the **River Thames**. Little further work was done for several years but, in 1962, a National Theatre Board was established, with Viscount Chandos (formerly Oliver Lyttleton) as the first Chairman and actor Sir Laurence Olivier as artistic director. The board built up a National Theatre Company, based at the Old Vic, which presented its first production (Shakespeare's *Hamlet*, with Peter O'Toole in the leading role) the following year. Serious work on the new theater, designed by Denys Lasdun, began during the late 1960s and was completed in 1976. The building has three auditoriums. The Olivier (named after Sir Laurence) is the largest, with about 1,100 seats placed around an open stage. The Lyttleton (honoring the first Chairman of the company) is a conventional proscenium theater seating an audience of 900, and the Cottesloe (taking its name from a former Chairman of the Arts Council, which promotes drama and other arts through government grants) has 300 seats that can be removed to allow actors to mingle with paying customers in experimental theater. There are also rehearsal rooms big enough to allow actors to work with a full set, as well as costume shops and facilities for making scenery. Free performances are staged in the foyer. The company presents Shakespeare regularly but has also developed a reputation for its wide range of works by modern writers. In 1988, it was given permission by Queen Elizabeth II to add the prefix "Royal" to its title.

ROYAL NAVAL COLLEGE. The college buildings, designed by **Christopher Wren**, were built on the site of **Greenwich Palace** and originally used as a home for disabled and elderly seamen. Wren's first plans were controversial because they hid the view of the **Queen's House** from the **River Thames**, so they were redrawn at the specific request of Queen Mary II. There are four ranges: King Charles Building (completed in 1694) and King William Building (built in 1704 but with a facade on the west front, designed by John Vanbrugh, added in 1728) lie to the east, Queen Anne Building (finished in 1728) and Queen Mary Building (opened in 1742) to the west.

Writer **Samuel Johnson** was unimpressed, claiming that the structures were "too much detached to make one great whole" and the hospital residents, too, were unenthusiastic (in 1771, a Captain Baillie complained that "Columns, colonnades and friezes ill accord with bully beef and sour beef mixed with water"). However, modern scholars suggest that the complex is Wren's finest work after **St. Paul's Cathedral** and praise James Thornhill's decoration of the Great Hall, where, after his death at the Battle of Trafalgar in 1805, Lord Nelson lay in state under a painted ceiling that shows King William III and Queen Mary II delivering peace and liberty to Europe. During the first two decades of the 19th century, the hospital housed as many as 3,000 patients. However, by the 1860s the number had declined significantly, so, in 1873, the Royal Naval College was transferred to the premises from Plymouth in order to ensure that the space was fully utilized. For over a century, young officers from Britain and abroad attended lectures at the site but, in 1994, the government decided to concentrate training for all armed forces at one location. **Greenwich** was considered too small for the purpose. As a result, in 1996, arrangements were made for the buildings to be taken over by the University of Greenwich and Trinity College of Music. (*See also* HAWKSMOOR, NICHOLAS.)

ROYAL NAVAL DOCKYARDS. England's first royal dockyard was built at Portsmouth, on the south coast. That town had the advantage of a strategic location commanding ship movements through the English Channel but was a considerable distance from London, where cannons were made, so, in 1512, King Henry VIII established a second dockyard at **Woolwich**, on the south bank of the **River Thames** and therefore closer to the source of armaments. Its first task was to build *Great Harry* as the flagship for his navy. A third yard was opened three miles upriver at **Deptford** the following year. Both sites were close to **Greenwich Palace**, so the King could watch his vessels take shape. The yards, run by a Navy Board, attracted ancillary activities (such as rope-making, coopering, and sail manufacture), so they became foci for industrial development and urban expansion. Although **Samuel Pepys**, Secretary to the Board, found "much evidence of neglect" during a visit in 1661,

Woolwich and Deptford were at the center of the country's maritime activities for three centuries. Queen Elizabeth I ordered Francis Drake to Deptford to receive his knighthood in 1581 following his circumnavigation of the world in the *Golden Hind.* From Woolwich, Walter Raleigh set off for the Americas and John Franklin for the Arctic. However, during the 19th century, the yards failed to adapt to the new technologies brought by the Industrial Revolution and suffered as the river deposited silt in their harbors. **Housing** hemmed in port activities, leaving little room for expansion, so in 1869 both were closed. The **Corporation of London** purchased most of the Deptford site and converted it for use as a cattle **market** (the only original building left standing is the master shipwright's house, which was erected in 1704). At Woolwich, the yards are covered by housing, built by the **London Borough of Greenwich** during the 1970s. (*See also* ROYAL ARSENAL.)

ROYAL OBSERVATORY. Britain's oldest government-funded scientific establishment, the Royal Observatory was built in 1675 to designs prepared by **Christopher Wren**. It is located in **Greenwich Park** and was originally charged with improving navigation on the high seas by developing techniques that would allow sailors to fix their position. In 1767, it began to publish the *British Nautical Almanack*, which rapidly became so widely used that, at an international conference held in Washington, D.C., in 1884, delegates agreed that the 0° line of longitude should pass through the building (*see* **Prime Meridian**). In 1833, a large red ball was built on a turret and is still lowered at one o'clock every afternoon so that mariners in the **River Thames** can set their chronometers accurately. By the later 19th and early 20th centuries, however, the industrialization of southeast England was seriously interfering with astronomical observations, so, in 1948, the observatory's scientific work was moved to the clearer skies of rural Herstmonceux, in Sussex. The **National Maritime Museum** took over the old buildings, where visitors can see the top-floor Octagon Room, which Wren designed for Sir John Flamsteed, the first Astronomer Royal. There is also a fine collection of early astronomical equipment, including a 28-inch refracting telescope (one of the largest in the world) which was installed in 1857.

ROYAL OPERA HOUSE. In 1732, entrepreneur John Rich (*see* **Beefsteak Club**) built a lavish new **theater** in **Drury Lane** (near **Covent Garden**). It opened with William Congreve's *Way of the World*, which was followed, over the next 70 years, by a string of successes, including

George Frideric Handel's *Judas Maccabeus* (1747), Oliver Goldsmith's *She Stoops to Conquer* (1773), and Richard Sheridan's *The Rivals* (1775). In 1808, the building was destroyed by fire, but a second theater was erected the following year, presenting the first performances in English of Wolfgang Amadeus Mozart's *Don Giovanni* (1817) and *The Marriage of Figaro* (1819), and of Gioacchino Rossini's *The Barber of Seville* (1818), before experiencing financial difficulties, which were relieved only after a public appeal for funds in 1829. In 1855, that theater, too, burned down, leaving a gutted site that remained empty until 1858, when the present structure, designed by E. M. Barry, was built.

Initially known as the Covent Garden Theatre, it was renamed the Royal Opera House in 1892, reflecting the policy of the management, which mounted the English premieres of Richard Wagner's *Lohengrin* (1875), Giuseppe Verdi's *Aida* (1876), Giacomo Puccini's *Tosca* (1900), and Richard Strauss's *Der Rosenkavalier* (1913). In 1946, the Sadler's Wells Ballet and the Covent Garden Opera Company made it their base and, in 1956 and 1968 respectively, were granted royal charters. Renamed the **Royal Ballet** and the Royal Opera, they mounted a series of high-cost productions, turning the "House" into the principal British focus for both art forms but experiencing mounting criticism over costs. In particular, a £260 million refurbishment and considerable friction between management and artists fuelled press complaints that it was an over-funded institution serving a minority group (*see* **Eyre Report**). However, when Michael Kaiser (formerly of the American Ballet Theater) was appointed executive director in 1998, the Arts Council agreed to raise its annual grant to £20 million in return for introduction of policies (such as reduced price seats), which would attract larger audiences, and understandings were reached with the performers' labor unions. By 2000, when Kaiser decided to move on, media reports were suggesting that the House's public image, and its financing, had improved significantly.

ROYAL PARKS. Several of London's largest **parks** were originally land that was designated for hunting by King Henry VIII during the early 16th century or as deer farms for animals that would later be used as game. Over time, attitudes towards hunting changed and the protected ground was surrounded by urban expansion, limiting the sporting opportunities. Gradually, the public was allowed access to the expanses of grass and woodland, which are now major recreational resources in the city although still owned by the Crown. The parks are maintained by the Royal Parks Agency, which also looks after other open spaces in the city, including Parliament Square. (*See also* BUSHY PARK; GREEN PARK; GREENWICH PARK; HYDE PARK; KENSINGTON GARDENS; PRIMROSE HILL; REGENT'S PARK; RICHMOND PARK; ST. JAMES'S PARK.)

ROYAL PHILHARMONIC ORCHESTRA (RPO). The orchestra was founded in 1946 by Sir Thomas Beecham, who guided its fortunes until his death in 1961. In its early days, its finances were derived largely from recording contracts with U.S. companies, but it also played regularly in London and at the Glyndebourne summer opera season (where it was resident from 1948 until 1963). When Beecham died, the orchestra restructured itself as a limited company, with each member a shareholder. It formed its own record business in 1986, then, in 1987, created a concert orchestra to cater to audiences interested in light classical music. Plans to merge the Royal Philharmonic with the **London Symphony Orchestra** were abandoned in 1995 after a report by management consultants suggested that the likely financial savings could not justify the artistic turmoil that would ensue. The RPO now divides its time between London (where it plays at the Royal **Albert Hall**) and Nottingham. It has undertaken to provide 125 compact discs for Tring International—the largest contract ever signed between a single orchestra and a record company.

ROYAL SOCIETY. Britain's oldest scientific organization was officially established in 1660 (although scholars had been meeting informally to discuss matters of common interest since 1648). Properly known as the Royal Society of London for the Promotion of Natural Knowledge, it depended heavily on Puritan sympathizers for its early support, but, as knowledge of the natural sciences improved, it gained rapidly in influence and funds. In 1768, it organized the first scientific expedition from Europe to the Pacific in order to observe the planet Venus; led by Captain James Cook, the group also charted the east coast of Australia and claimed it for Britain. Other activities included sponsorship of the ill-fated attempt by John Franklin to find the Northwest Passage through the Arctic from the Atlantic Ocean to the Pacific Ocean in 1845 (all 130 explorers died) and, more successfully, the confirmation of Albert Einstein's Theory of Relativity through field observations in the Gulf of Guinea in 1919. It also advises the government on scientific matters when required, awards medals to those who have made particularly significant contributions to knowledge, and (since 1665) has published academic papers in its *Philosophical Transactions*. The Royal Society (based in Carlton House Terrace, near **Admiralty Arch**, since 1967) has about 1,000 members (known as Fellows) who must be proposed for election by existing Fellows prepared to attest to the candidate's scientific achievements. Former Presidents have included architect **Christopher Wren** (1681–83), physicist Isaac Newton (1703–27), and Nobel prize winning nuclear energy researcher Ernest Rutherford (1925–30). (*See also* BRITISH ACADEMY.)

ROYAL SOCIETY OF ARTS (RSA). The RSA was founded in 1754 by William Shipley, a Nottingham art teacher, as the Society for the Encouragement of Arts, Manufactures, and Commerce. It adopted its present title, by permission of King Edward VII in 1908, and occupies premises at 8 John Adam Street, which was part of **Robert Adam**'s Adelphi development. The society organized the country's first art exhibition in 1760, the first photographic exhibition in 1852, and (in conjunction with the **Royal Academy of Arts**) the first major exhibition of industrial design in 1935. Each year, it awards its Albert Medal (named after **Prince Albert**, Queen Victoria's consort and President of the society from 1843 to 1861) to an individual who has made distinguished contributions to commerce, the arts, or science; recipients have included physicists Michael Faraday (1866) and Ernest Rutherford (1928), surgeon Joseph Lister (1894), engineer Barnes Wallis (1968), actor Laurence Olivier (1976), and businessman Lord Sainsbury (1989). In 1856, the RSA introduced a series of examinations designed to enable working-class students to gain qualifications in vocational skills. The certificates gained widespread acceptance among employers, so by 1989, when the Examinations Board became an independent body with charitable status, nearly one million candidates were presented annually.

RUISLIP. Ruislip, some 13 miles northeast of **Charing Cross**, forms the northern part of the **London Borough of Hillingdon**. It was an agricultural settlement until 1904, when the Metropolitan **Railway** arrived, attracting urban development, which, by the end of the century, had turned the township into a city suburb. Many of the older buildings survived the change, however. St. Martin's Church, a flint rubble building dating from about 1250, has medieval wall paintings, a 15th-century roof, and 16th-century pews. Next to Manor Farmhouse, a timber-boarded, aisled Great Barn, erected during the late 13th century, is said by some scholars to be the oldest barn in England. Its neighbor—the Little Barn (with a roof dating from around 1600)—has been converted into a public library, and High Street has been sympathetically planned to incorporate modern shops whilst restoring older structures. In addition, much of the former open space has been preserved, including Park Wood, a source of timber for construction work in the **Tower of London** and the **Palace of Westminster** during the 14th century.

RUSSELL SQUARE. One of the principal features of the **Bloomsbury** townscape, Russell Square was laid out in 1800 and given the family name of the Duke of Bedford, owner of the property. Traditionally, it has attracted men from the professions and the arts: painter Sir Thomas Lawrence maintained a studio at No. 62 from 1805 to 1830, lawyer Lord Denman lived at No. 50 from 1818 to 1834, and Sir George Williams (founder of the Young Men's Christian Association) made his home at No. 13 from 1880 until his death in 1905. Although architect James Burton would recognize several of the houses he designed for the west side of the square, those to the north and south have been much altered and those on the east were demolished in 1898 to make way for the Russell **Hotel**. In addition, there has been significant infiltration of institutional uses associated with the University of London (*see* **universities**).

– S –

SADLER'S WELLS. Although Sadler's Wells, in Rosebery Avenue, is one of London's best-known **theater**s, it has suffered a series of vicissitudes since its foundation in 1683, when Thomas Sadler advertised the medicinal qualities of a spring flowing just beyond the northern boundary of the **City of London** and, encouraged by the response (some 500 visitors a day), provided musical entertainment for his customers. The business was acquired by Thomas Rosoman, who, in 1765, built a permanent theater where Joseph Grimaldi (later to develop a reputation as a clown) first performed (as a child dancer) in 1781 and where actor Edmund Kean appeared (while still a boy) in 1804.

During the second half of the 19th century trading conditions proved difficult, so performances ceased in 1871 and an attempt to revive fortunes by catering to **music hall** audiences was successful only from 1893 until 1906. In 1931, hopes of a more secure future encouraged construction of a new building, which would be a permanent base for ballet and opera companies. However, performances were suspended during the

Second World War. Then, in 1946, the ballet dancers left for the **Royal Opera House** in **Covent Garden**. Two decades later, the opera singers also departed, transferring to the Coliseum Theatre in 1968. In 1997–98, however, a £48 million refurbishment was undertaken, with most of the money coming from the proceeds of Britain's National Lottery and the design placing an emphasis on facilities for dance. In the process, a bore was sunk to the original well, providing water that would be sold to patrons and used in the air conditioning system. A new auditorium, with 1,600 seats, is the focus of an artistic complex, which includes a second theater (the 200-seat Lilian Baylis), an education center, a lecture room, film facilities, and space for archives.

ST. ALFEGE'S CHURCH, GREENWICH. Considered one of **Nicholas Hawksmoor**'s finest works, St. Alfege's stands in Greenwich High Road on the site where the saint (appointed Archbishop of Canterbury in 1005) was allegedly murdered by invading Danish forces in 1012 when he refused to approve payment of the ransom that would have saved his life. After an earlier building was destroyed by a storm in 1710, parishioners asked Parliament to provide them with a new place of worship. The result of their petition was legislation, passed the following year, that sanctioned the building of 50 new churches in London, with the construction financed by a tax on coal. Hawksmoor's structure was erected in 1711–18, but a tower (an early version of the pepper pot style) was added by John James in 1730. The interior was destroyed by German bombs in 1941, during the **Blitz**, but restored in 1952 under the direction of Albert Richardson. St. Alfege's was the christening place of Prince Henry (later King Henry VIII) in 1491 and of Charles Gordon (one of Britain's most distinguished 19th-century military leaders) in 1833. Thomas Tallis (sometimes referred to as "the father of English church music") was buried beneath the chancel of the old church in 1585 and General James Wolfe in the family vault at the new in 1759, following his death fighting the French at Quebec.

ST. ANDREW'S CHURCH, HOLBORN. St Andrew's is the largest of the parish churches built by **Christopher Wren**, standing on a site that was occupied by a Christian chapel in 951 A.D. Erected in 1684–90, it is 105 feet long and 63 feet wide. In 1896, the construction of Holborn viaduct, across the valley of the River Fleet, resulted in loss of the churchyard, and during the **Blitz** of 1941, German bombs caused much damage but the church was restored to its original condition by John

Seely (later Lord Mottistone) and Paul Paget in 1960–61. During the winter of 1827, Dr. Richard Marsden found a young woman dying in the precincts because she had been unable to get treatment at any of the London hospitals. Marsden was so affected that he persuaded the Cordwainers' Company (one of the City **livery companies**) to found the Royal Free Hospital, the first clinic to provide treatment to all comers, regardless of their ability to pay. Two future Prime Ministers, Henry Addington and Benjamin Disraeli, were christened in St. Andrew's in 1757 and 1817 respectively.

ST. ANDREW UNDERSHAFT CHURCH, LEADENHALL STREET. The church is first mentioned in records dating from 1147, when it was known as St. Andrew **Cornhill**. It gets its present name from the extremely tall maypole that overshadowed the steeple when it was erected during May Day celebrations in the 15th and early 16th centuries (the festivities were discontinued after 1517 following attacks by **livery company** apprentices on foreign residents). The present building, erected in1520–32, has been restored and renovated on several occasions. Its organ (by Renatus Harris) dates from 1696 and its altar rails (by Jean Tijou) from 1704. St. Andrew also contains a statue of **John Stow** (the first historian of London), who was buried in the church when he died, a pauper, in 1605. The monument is inscribed with the motto *Aut scribenda agere, aut legenda scribere* ("Either do something worth writing about, or write something worth reading") and includes a real quill pen in Stow's hand. Each year, at a memorial service, the **Lord Mayor** removes the pen, hands it to the school pupil adjudged to have written the best essay on the city, and replaces it with a new one.

ST. BARTHOLOMEW-THE-GREAT CHURCH, SMITHFIELD. The oldest parish church building in London, St. Bartholomew is the only remaining part of an Augustinian priory founded in 1123 by Rahere, a courtier of King Henry I. In 1539, during the Reformation, it was sold to Sir Richard Rich (*see* **Wanstead**), who demolished the nave. During the 17th and 18th centuries, much of the structure was put to secular use. The crypt served as a coal and wine store, and the Lady Chapel (which had been rebuilt in 1336) was redesigned as private residences, then became a print shop (where Benjamin Franklin, one of the founding fathers of the United States, worked as an apprentice in 1725). The cloisters were turned into stables, the south triforium into a school, the sacristy into a hop store, and the north transept into a blacksmith's forge. However, in

1887, the Rector (Reverend Borrodail Savory) initiated restoration work, aided by architect Sir Aston Webb. The porch was rebuilt and the west front refaced before the end of the century and a choir screen (by Frank Beresford) erected in 1932. Because of its great age, St. Bartholomew has a particularly rich collection of funeral monuments dating from the 16th century.

ST. BENET'S CHURCH, PAUL'S WHARF. St. Benet's, erected in 1683 on the site of a 12th-century chapel destroyed in the **Great Fire**, serves London's Welsh-speaking Anglican community. Built of red brick, with alternate courses of **Portland stone** at the corners, it was designed by **Christopher Wren**, who departed from his normally plain style by decorating the window frames with stone garlands. **Inigo Jones**, a fellow architect, was buried in the old church in 1652 and, in 1747, author Henry Fielding demonstrated a disdain of middle-class values by marrying Mary, his first wife's former maid, in the new.

ST. BOTOLPH'S CHURCH, ALDGATE. St. Botolph, a patron saint of travellers, has several churches dedicated to his name in London. That at Aldgate may have been founded before the Norman conquest of 1066 and was certainly in use by 1115. The present brick building was designed by **George Dance the Elder** and erected in 1741–44 but has been much altered internally since then, principally by John Francis Bentley (architect of **Westminster Cathedral**) in 1887–91. In addition, from 1958 to 1966, Rodney Tatchell supervised repairs necessitated by Second World War bomb damage and an unexplained fire in 1965. St. Botolph's organ was built by Renatus Harris in 1676 and its peal of eight bells cast by Lester and Pack in 1744. Daniel Defoe, who was married in the church in 1683, records how, at the time of the **Great Plague**, 5,136 people were interred at the **burial ground** in only 16 weeks. The crypt now serves as a center for homeless people and as a youth club.

ST. BRIDE'S CHURCH, FLEET STREET. Archaeological excavations suggest that St. Bride's occupies the site of London's first church, founded by St. Bridget during the sixth century. The building was originally designed by **Christopher Wren** and erected in 1671 after its 15th-century predecessor was destroyed in the **Great Fire** five years earlier. A spire, added in 1701, was the only substantial part of the structure to survive German bombing on 29 December 1940, during the **Blitz**, but restoration work (supervised by Godfrey Allen and financed largely by donations from the national and international press) retained much of Wren's plan, including the tunnel vaulted nave. The crypt, which incorporates a **museum** of London west of the **Fleet River**, displays remains of the earlier buildings and other relics. St. Bride's is still the parish church of London's newspaper industry even though most of the presses have moved away from the area. Its spire had been the inspiration for wedding cake designs ever since a local pastry cook hit on the idea of associating the church's dedication with the marriage ceremony in the late 18th century. (*See also* PEPYS, SAMUEL.)

ST. CLEMENT DANES CHURCH, STRAND. The origins of St. Clement's are obscure, though writers have suggested that it takes its name from a ninth-century Danish settlement in the area (some scholars believe that it may be the burial place of Harold Harefoot and other Scandinavian leaders). A church erected on the site in the late 10th or early 11th century survived the **Great Fire** of 1666 but was considered unsafe in 1679 and demolished. A new building, designed by **Christopher Wren** and completed in 1682, survived until German bombs destroyed it during the **Blitz** of 1941. It was restored in 1955–58 by Anthony Lloyd, with much of the funding contributed by the Royal Air Force (RAF), which designated it as a memorial church commemorating the 125,000 members of the service who were killed in the Second World War. Over 700 badges of RAF units were cut from Welsh slate and laid in the side aisles. Under the north gallery, a book of remembrance lists the names of American airmen who died while based in Great Britain between 1941 and 1945. The peal of bells, which was hung in 1957, sometimes plays the tune associated with the nursery rhyme *Oranges and Lemons*, but the St. Clement's Church mentioned in the verses is probably that at **Eastcheap**, where citrus fruits were unloaded from cargo boats arriving from Mediterranean countries. (*See also* GIBBS, JAMES.)

ST. DUNSTAN IN THE WEST CHURCH, FLEET STREET. Although St. Dunstan's is not mentioned in written records until 1185, it was probably founded before the Norman Conquest of 1066. William Tyndale (translator of the first Bible to be printed in English) worked there as a preacher (1523), poet John Donne was Rector (1624–31), and Izaak Walton (author of the *Compleat Angler*, published in 1653 by Richard Marriott, whose business operated from the churchyard) was scavenger, questman, and sidesman (1629–44). The building escaped destruction in the **Great Fire** of 1666 and was refurbished in 1701, but by 1829 it was so dilapidated that it had to be demolished. Its replacement (built on the site of the former **burial ground** so that nearby streets could be widened) was an octagonal structure, designed by John Shaw and opened in 1831. An early example of Gothic Revival **architecture**, it has a yellow freestone tower modelled on that at All Saints' Pavement Church in York and a clock that was originally placed on the old church in 1671. The timepiece, the first in London to have a minute hand, was a notable city landmark, mentioned in Oliver Goldsmith's *Vicar of Wakefield* (1766), Walter Scott's *The Fortunes of Nigel* (1822), and **Charles Dickens**'s *Barnaby Rudge* (1841). In 1954, St. Dunstan's was designated a Guild Church, so its parish was merged with that of **St. Bride's Church, Fleet Street**, and the building closed on Saturdays and Sundays, but during the week, it holds services and other meetings for **City of London** office workers. (*See also* PEPYS, SAMUEL.)

ST. ETHELBURGA-THE-VIRGIN WITHIN BISHOPSGATE CHURCH, BISHOPSGATE. The **City of London**'s smallest church, measuring some 60 feet by 30 feet, St. Ethelburga's is dedicated to the daughter of Aethlebert I, King of Kent from 560 to 616 and the first Anglo-Saxon ruler to accept the Christian faith. The first stone building on the site was probably erected during the 13th century, but there was considerable restructuring 200 years later and much alteration and refurbishment since then, including the addition of a south gallery in 1629 and a bell turret in 1775. St. Ethleburga's was designated a Guild Church in 1954; its parish was amalgamated with that of St. Helen Bishopsgate Church, and instead of serving a declining population of local residents on Sundays, it introduced weekday services for office workers, with special emphasis on healing. In 1993, it was badly damaged by an Irish Republican Army bomb that exploded in a nearby street, but six years later, the Bishop of London launched an appeal for funds that would support a rebuilding program using the original fabric and incorporating a center for peace and reconciliation.

ST. ETHELDREDA'S CHURCH, HOLBORN. In 1876, when St. Etheldreda's was acquired by the Fathers of Charity, it became the first place of worship in England to revert to Roman Catholic use after the Reformation. Originally built towards the end of the 13th century as a private chapel for William de Luda, Bishop of Ely (where Etheldreda had been an abbess some six centuries earlier), it was badly damaged during the **Blitz** but renovated after the Second World War. The east and west windows contain stained glass by Joseph Nuttgens and Charles Blakemen, which commemorate martyrs who refused to renounce their faith and were put to death at **Tyburn**. On 3 February each year, when a service is held in memory of St. Blaise (who saved a lad who was choking to death on a fishbone), candles are lit near worshippers suffering from throat diseases. (*See also* ELY PLACE.)

ST. GILES-IN-THE-FIELDS CHURCH, ST. GILES HIGH STREET. In 1101, Matilda (wife of King Henry I) built a leper hospital in the fields beyond the western wall of the **City of London** and dedicated it to St. Giles, the patron saint of outcasts. The hospital chapel, which also served as a parish church, was rebuilt in 1623 (largely through the largesse of Alicia, Duchess Dudley) and again (to designs prepared by Henry Flitcroft) in 1733. Since then it has changed very little apart from interior alterations made in 1875 and 1896. Henry Pelham (a future Prime Minister) was baptized in St. Giles in 1694 and actor **David Garrick** married there (to Eva Maria Veigel) in 1749. Poet Andrew Marvell was buried in the church in 1678, Luke Hansard (printer to the House of Commons [*see* **Palace of Westminster**]) in 1828, and architect John Soane (*see* **Sir John Soane's Museum**) in 1837. Because the **Great Plague** began in St. Giles Parish in 1665, the churchyard also provided a last resting place for many of its victims. (*See also* TYBURN.)

ST. JAMES'S CHURCH, PICCADILLY. St. James's, the last of the London churches designed by **Christopher Wren** and the only one built on a new site, was part of a fashionable suburban development promoted by Henry Jordan, Earl of St. Albans. The brick building, with **Portland stone** quoins and dressings, was consecrated in 1684 and designed so that everyone in a congregation of 2,000 could hear the preacher clearly. It suffered badly during the **Blitz**, but was renovated under the direction of Sir Albert Richardson after the Second World War. Fitments that had survived the damage (including the reredos and the marble font, both carved by **Grinling Gibbons**) were retained and the **burial ground** turned into a garden of remembrance to commemorate the courage of Londoners during the German **air raids**.

ST. JAMES'S FAIR. For seven days from the eve of St. James's Day, medieval Londoners held a fair outside the leper hospital at the site on which **St. James's Palace** now stands. It was clearly a boisterous event, because it was closed in 1664 on the grounds that it promoted riotous behavior and loose living, reopened in 1689, closed again (and for the same reasons) in 1708, and revived in 1738. During the 1760s, according to John Carter, there were booths for prize fighters, jugglers, and exotic animals. Moreover, "the sports under cover were mountebanks, ass-racing, dice-ditto, ups-and-downs, merry-go-rounds, bull-baiting, running for a shift, hasty pudding eaters, eel-divers and an infinite variety of other pastimes." The fair closed for good in 1764 because the Earl of Coventry, who had a residence in nearby **Piccadilly**, complained about the noise.

ST. JAMES'S PALACE. Standing at the western end of **Pall Mall**, where **Green Park** and **St. James's Park** adjoin, the palace is located on the site of a medieval leper hospital built outside the walls of the **City of London**. King Henry VIII bought the property in 1531, gave the inmates a pension, demolished the buildings, and erected a small residence in their place. It has been much used by royalty ever since. Mary Tudor died there in 1533, Elizabeth I slept there while the Spanish Armada sailed up the English Channel in 1588, Charles I stayed there in 1649 the night before he was taken to the gallows, Charles II made it his principal home (refurbishing it after Oliver Cromwell had turned it into a prison so that he could provide rooms for his several mistresses), and William III employed **Christopher Wren** to design new apartments of state. From 1698 (when **Whitehall Palace** was destroyed by fire) until 1837 (when Queen Victoria moved into **Buckingham Palace**), it was the principal royal palace in Britain (and, legally, remains so, which is why foreign ambassadors are accredited to the Court of St. James). Queen Anne and her successors (George I, George II, and George III) spent much time there and George III's son (the future George IV) was married there in 1795 (his bride, Queen Caroline, reported that he was so drunk after the wedding celebrations that he collapsed, stupefied, into a fireplace and lay there until morning).

A large part of the structure was destroyed by fire in 1814 but immediately rebuilt. It is now the London residence of Prince Charles, and of Princess Alexandra and Sir Angus Ogilvy. Also, it houses the offices of the Lord Chamberlain (who is responsible for the management of the monarch's domestic staff) and the Prince of Wales's administrative staff. With the exception of the Chapel Royal (where services are held on Sunday mornings from October until the week before Easter) and the Queen's Chapel (where they are held from Easter Sunday until the end of July), none of the rooms—which contain fine carvings by **Grinling**

Gibbons, door cases by William Kent (*see* **Kensington Palace**), and tapestries woven for Charles II—is open to the public. (*See also* ST. JAMES'S FAIR.)

ST. JAMES'S PARK. A **Royal Park** covering 90 acres in the heart of London, St. James's **Park** is bounded by **The Mall** to the north, **Buckingham Palace** to the west, **Birdcage Walk** to the south, and the government buildings of **Whitehall** to the east. It takes its name from St. James's leper hospital, which stood at the northwestern edge of the area during the 15th and early 16th centuries on the site now occupied by **St. James's Palace**. King Henry VIII bought the estate in 1531, drained the marshes where the lepers had grazed their pigs, and used the land as a deer farm. Over the next 50 years, many of the trees were cut down, so James VI and I, after his accession to the English throne in 1603, was able to lay out formal gardens, build a small zoo, and construct an aviary. During the second half of the 17th century, King Charles II (advised by André Le Nôtre, the French landscape gardener who had been responsible for the design of the grounds at the Palace of Versailles, near Paris) planted fruit trees, built an avenue surfaced with powdered cockle shells, and linked a series of small ponds into a single length of water (known as the Canal), but after his death in 1685 the grounds was little cared for, becoming a favored location for prostitutes to ply their trade. Improvements, which shaped the present structure of the area, were made in 1827 by **John Nash**, who remodelled the Canal, introduced new walks, and planted more trees. Other features (such as an iron suspension bridge across the water) were added later in the century but most have since been removed. By the late 20th century, the park had become a popular place for feeding wildfowl (which have frequented the lake since Charles II's day) and listening to summer band concerts. The views across to Whitehall are mentioned in almost every guidebook to city sights. In 1982, a bomb, planted in the bandstand by the Irish Republican Army, exploded as a detachment of the Household Cavalry (*see* **Household Division**) was passing; four soldiers and seven horses were killed.

ST. JAMES'S SQUARE. In the late 18th century, St. James's Square (north of **Pall Mall**) was the most desirable residential area in London. It was laid out in 1665 by Henry Jermyn, Earl of St. Albans and a staunch supporter of King Charles II, who had returned from exile the previous year. Plots were leased to speculative builders willing to build houses for aristocratic families seeking homes close to **St. James's Palace** and red brick residences were erected on the north, east, and west sides of a central piazza. However, over the next hundred years, most of the properties were demolished or extensively redesigned, then, during the first half of the 19th century, many were taken over by commercial interests as private individuals moved west to **Belgravia**, so little of the original fabric remains and the buildings are almost entirely devoted to business or institutional purposes. Residents have included three Prime Ministers (William Pitt the Elder, the Earl of Derby, and William Gladstone, who lived at No. 9 in 1751–61, 1837–54, and 1890 respectively). General Dwight D. Eisenhower established his headquarters at No. 31 during the Second World War, and architect **Robert Adam** considered No. 20 (built in 1771–75) one of his best works.

ST. JOHN'S CHURCH, CLERKENWELL. *See* KNIGHTS HOSPITALLER.

ST. JOHN'S WOOD. The residential area to the northwest of **Regent's Park** takes its name from the Knights of St. John of Jerusalem (*see* **Knights Hospitaller**), who owned it from 1312 until the Reformation. Largely forested until the early 19th century, it succumbed to urban development following the construction of the **Regent's Canal** in 1812–20 and an artillery barracks in 1832. The building of the Great Central **Railway** during the 1890s added to the pressures on land, then, during the 1920s and 1930s, apartment blocks were erected for city workers. "The Wood" experienced considerable damage during the **Blitz**, but since the end of the Second World War, many of the older properties have been restored and development has taken the form of town houses rather than apartments. The relatively inexpensive but well-designed semidetached villas built during the Victorian period attracted middle-class groups, including painters, authors, and scientists (for example, novelist George Eliot lived at 21 North Bank, with critic G. H. Lewes, and naturalist T. H. Huxley at 48 Marlborough Place). The artists (who became known as the St. John's Wood Clique) concentrated on dramatic, frivolous, or pathetic scenes and included W. F. Yeames, best known for *When Did You Last See Your Father?* Perhaps because of its somewhat secluded environment, the area also became a favorite place for wealthy men to provide accommodation for their mistresses (Napoleon III of France made a home for Elizabeth Anne Howard at 23 Circus Road, for instance). (*See also* MARYLEBONE CRICKET CLUB [MCC].)

ST. MARGARET'S CHURCH, WESTMINSTER. St. Margaret's—the parish church of the House of Commons (*see* **Palace of Westminster**)—was founded in the early 12th century, but the present building dates from 1486. Since then it has been altered and refurbished on many occasions. It narrowly escaped demolition in 1549, when the Duke of Somerset ordered that it be knocked down to provide stone for his new palace (*see* **Somerset House**). However, the parishioners refused to give up their chapel, attacked the workmen, and chased them away. Diarist **Samuel Pepys** was married in the church in 1655, poet John Milton in 1656, and Prime Minister Winston Churchill in 1908. Printer William Caxton was buried there in 1491 (though the site of his tomb is unknown) and the headless body of Sir Walter Raleigh was placed under the high altar following his execution in 1618.

ST. MARTIN-IN-THE-FIELDS CHURCH, TRAFALGAR SQUARE. St. Martin-in-the-Fields is located at the northeast corner of **Trafalgar Square**. A chapel stood on the site as early as 1222 (when it really was surrounded by fields), but the present structure, designed by **James Gibbs**, was erected in 1722–26 to serve the area west of **Covent Garden**, which was developing as a fashionable suburb. The building is a simple rectangular hall with a portico of six Corinthian columns, surmounted by a pediment and a high steeple—a design much copied in the United States. Church members have a long tradition of helping the homeless, dating from the days when the crypt was used to shelter soldiers returning from the First World War. They have also seen many famous men and women buried in the grounds, including courtesan **Eleanor "Nell" Gwyn** in 1687, painter Joshua Reynolds in 1762, cabinet maker Thomas Chippendale in 1779, and surgeon John Hunter (*see* **Royal College of Surgeons of England**) in 1793. In 1987, the bells (which were making the steeple structurally unstable) were sent to the University of Western Australia in exchange for 20 tons of copper and tin, which were fashioned into a new (and lighter) peal. A new organ, with 3,637 pipes, 48 stops, and three manuals, was installed in 1990, continuing the church's long tradition as a focus of fine music. (*See also* PEARLY KINGS AND QUEENS.)

ST. MARY ABCHURCH CHURCH, ABCHURCH LANE. Of all the London churches designed by **Christopher Wren**, St. Mary's is the least altered. Erected in 1686 on the site of a 12th-century chapel, it forms a square, some 63 feet long and 60 feet broad, under a shallow dome, which rests on eight arches and is lit by oval lunettes. The quality of the interior decoration is outstanding; the dome was painted by William Snow, the wood pulpit carved by William Grey, and the marble font sculpted by William Kempster. The reredos—the only one in the **City of London** known to be by **Grinling Gibbons**—was blasted into more than 2,000 pieces when the church was damaged by German bombs in 1940 but was restored between 1948 and 1953. Under the terms of legislation approved by Parliament in 1952, St. Mary's was made a Guild Church, closing its doors on weekends but providing services, and other activities, for office workers from Monday to Friday.

ST. MARYLEBONE. The St. Marylebone area lies north of **Oxford Street** (the name is derived from the Church of St. Mary by the bourne, or stream, and is often listed simply as Marylebone). During the Middle Ages, the land was held by the **Knights Templar**, **Knights Hospitaller**, and **Barking** Abbey, but it was acquired by the Crown when King Henry VIII dissolved the English **monasteries** from 1532. Much of the northern section became royal hunting forest and was later converted into **Regent's Park**. Other sections were acquired, in 1553, by the Portman family (which still owns large tracts in the area). The remainder of the estate was leased to a variety of tenants before being sold by King James VI and I to Edward Forsett (a Justice of the Peace) in 1611; after passing through several hands, it was acquired (through inheritance) by the Earl and Countess of Oxford, who developed it from 1717 in an attempt to emulate the successful **housing** ventures in **Mayfair**. The focus of building was **Cavendish Square**, the center of a gridiron pattern of streets differing markedly from the wandering alleys of the **City of London**. In 1741, the land passed to Oxford's daughter, Margaret, who later married William Bentinck, Duke of Portland, and continued the expansion process (*see*, for example, **Portland Place**). By the end of the 18th century, the area was extensively built up, with the final open spaces covered soon afterwards. Since the end of the Second World War, commercial uses have increasingly infiltrated, but distinct communities still thrive, focusing on local shopping centers such as Marylebone High Street. (*See also* HOLMES, SHERLOCK.)

ST. MARY-LE-BOW CHURCH, CHEAPSIDE. *See* BOW BELLS.

ST. NICHOLAS COLE ABBEY CHURCH, DISTAFF LANE. *See* COLE ABBEY CHURCH, DISTAFF LANE.

ST. OLAVE'S CHURCH, HART STREET. St. Olave's is the last survivor of five London churches dedicated to King Olaf of Norway, who fought alongside King Aethelred II of England against the invading Vikings in 1014 and was canonized for his services to the Christian faith. The original wooden church was erected during the 11th century, replaced 200 years later with a more substantial stone structure, then rebuilt in Perpendicular style (*see* **architecture**) in about 1450. It survived the **Great Fire** of 1666 but was badly damaged by bombs in 1941, during the **Blitz**, and restored under the supervision of E. B. Glanville, reopening in 1954. **Samuel Pepys** was a regular worshipper during the 17th century, describing several of the services in his diaries. His wife, Elizabeth, was buried there in 1669 (aged only 29 but having been married for 14 years). The parish register records that, in 1586, a Mother Goose was interred in the churchyard, which also contains the remains of Mary Ramsay, who allegedly introduced the **Great Plague** to London in 1664.

ST. PANCRAS. The St. Pancras area is one of the oldest foci of Christian worship in England, with a church established by the early seventh century, only a few years after St. Augustine arrived from Rome, charged by Pope Gregory I with the task of converting the Anglo-Saxons. Most of the land remained under the control of the Church until King Henry VIII's reign, when it was divided into a number of agricultural estates administered by rich barons. Urban development began during the Georgian period, as the **City of London** expanded, and sped up after the **railways** arrived in the 19th century. St. Pancras Station was opened in 1868 as the terminus of the Midland Railway, which had previously shared the Great Northern Railway's facilities at **King's Cross**. Designed by W. H. Barlow, it was built on the site of Agar Town, one of mid-Victorian London's worst slums, which author **Charles Dickens** described as "A complete bog of mud and filth with wretched hovels, the doors blocked up with mud, heaps of ashes, oyster shells and decayed vegetables," adding that "The stench of a rainy morning is enough to knock down a bullock." An enormous glass and iron hall, 640 feet long, 249 feet wide, and 100 feet high, it earned much praise from architectural critics of the time. Above it, the former Midland Hotel (built to George Gilbert Scott's plans, opened in 1872 and closed in 1935) presents a Gothic facade of towers and spires to Euston Road. In recent years, local authorities have swept away many of the older properties, replacing them with modern institutional buildings, such as the **British Library** (which moved to the site in 1997) and a youth hostel (opened in 1997 to provide budget accommodation for young tourists). Also, the resident population has declined as the railway industry has contracted and property values have risen.

ST. PAUL'S CATHEDRAL. St. Paul's is the cathedral church of the **City of London** and the site of most religious ceremonies of state in the United Kingdom (the major exception is the coronation of the monarch, which takes place in **Westminster Abbey**). The present building is the fifth Christian place of worship on the site, succeeding a wooden chapel erected early in the seventh century but destroyed by fire, a stone edifice that replaced it in 685 but was ransacked by Viking invaders in 962, a late 10th-century structure, and a Norman cathedral begun in 1087 after the last Saxon church burnt down. During the Medieval period, St. Paul's was more than a religious focus; Londoners met there to socialize and do business, a law school was established in the precincts, booksellers traded in the churchyard, and major public announcements were made from the steps. However, by the time King James VI and I succeeded to the throne in 1603, much of the fabric was decaying. An extensive program of renovation began in 1638 but was halted during the Civil War of 1642–49, when the nave was used as a barracks for Oliver Cromwell's anti-royalist troops. Then, in 1663, **Christopher Wren** was asked to prepare plans for further refurbishment, but in September 1666, less than a week after his proposals were approved, the cathedral was destroyed by the **Great Fire**.

Not entirely unhappy at the prospect of designing a completely new building, Wren drew up a further set of designs and began work on the construction of the present cathedral in 1675, altering details as he progressed and completing the project in 1710. The main entrance is by the steps and two-story portico of the west front. Inside, the dominating feature is the baroque dome, decorated by James Thornhill with scenes from the life of St. Paul and rising 218 feet above the floor. At its base, it is encircled by the Whispering Gallery, where softly spoken words by a visitor on one side can be picked up by a listener on the other, 107 feet away. In the crypt, one of the largest in Europe, the remains of Admiral Horatio Nelson lie immediately underneath the dome in the cask of spirits that preserved his body during the journey back to England from the Battle of Trafalgar in 1805. Wren himself is buried nearby, his tomb bearing the Latin inscription *Lector, si monumentum requiris, circumspice* ("Reader, if you seek a monument, look around you"). Despite its size, the cathedral survived the **Blitz** with little damage, partly because an army of volunteers risked their lives to defuse unexploded bombs that fell nearby. The Jesus Chapel, behind the High Altar, was struck in 1940 but refurbished as the American Chapel, a tribute to the 20,000 U.S. citizens based in Great Britain who lost their lives during the Second World War. In 1997, amidst much controversy, the cathedral appointed Lucy Winkett as its first female priest. (*See also* GIBBONS, GRINLING; HAWKSMOOR, NICHOLAS; JONES, INIGO; PORTLAND STONE.)

ST. PAUL'S CHURCH, COVENT GARDEN. The first Anglican church to be built on a new site in London after the Reformation, St. Paul's was designed by **Inigo Jones**, who had been commissioned by Francis Russell, Earl of Bedford, to plan a **housing** development at **Covent Garden** in 1627. Construction was completed in 1633, parish boundaries drawn up in 1645, and major renovations undertaken in 1788, 1795 (following a fire), and 1871. The church is located on the western side of the piazza, which formed the center of Jones's scheme, with the main entrance opening onto the square. However, the Church of England hierarchy insisted that the altar should be placed in its traditional place against the east wall, so the door at that point is a sham and entry is gained from the rear of the building. The 1795 fire destroyed most of the original structure, but it was faithfully rebuilt to Jones's designs by Thomas Hardwicke. St. Paul's is very closely associated with the entertainment community because several **theater**s are located nearby and, for three centuries, actors have found accommodation in neighboring lodgings. Thomas Arne (composer of *Rule Britannia*) was buried there in 1778, as was actress Ellen Terry in 1928. Inside there are memorials to composer Ivor Novello and others who have contributed to the London stage. George Bernard Shaw set the opening scene of *Pygmalion* (published in 1916) in the church portico, which is still used as an impromptu stage by street musicians. (*See also* GIBBONS, GRINLING.)

ST. STEPHEN WALBROOK CHURCH, WALBROOK. St. Stephens was originally founded in the second half of the 11th century. The present church, regarded by many critics as architect **Christopher Wren**'s finest achievement (David Piper claimed that it surpasses **St. Paul's Cathedral**), St. Stephen's was built during the 1670s. Its principal feature is a large Roman dome, lit centrally and supported by eight Corinthian columns. Arches, outer columns, and angled clerestory walls combine to produce changing patterns of light and shade and differing

St. Paul's Cathedral engulfed in the Great Fire of 1666 (Museum of London)

The environs of St. Paul's Cathedral after the Blitz (Museum of London)

perspectives as visitors move about the church. Furnishings survived the **Blitz**, so the pulpit, reredos, rails, and font are Wren's originals, but the altar is a highly controversial Henry Moore sculpture of travertine stone placed under the dome in 1987, following a series of bitter court battles. Property developer Peter Palumbo financed much restoration work within the building and commissioned the new altar. Traditionalists likened the rock to a lump of cheese and argued that it moved the focus of worship from the east end of the church (where the pulpit stood) to the center, but the judges ultimately ruled for the modernizers.

SALVATION ARMY. *See* BOOTH, WILLIAM.

SAVILE ROW. Connecting Burlington Gardens with Conduit Street, towards the eastern edge of **Mayfair**, Savile Row takes its name from Lady Dorothy Savile, wife of the Earl of Burlington, who developed the road on land behind his **Piccadilly** house during the 1730s (*see* **Burlington House**). Originally, the properties were occupied by families (residents included physician Richard Bright, who identified Bright's Disease of the kidney, at No. 11 from 1830 to 1858 and dramatist Richard Brinsley Sheridan at No. 14 from 1813 until his death in 1816). However, from 1843 (when Henry Poole and company started trading), gentlemen's tailors increasingly set up business, attracted by the affluent Mayfair market and willing to pay rents that private individuals could not match. By the end of the 20th century, the street was entirely commercial, its name an international byword for fine clothing. Gieves and Hawkes are at No. 1, Hardy Amies at No. 14, Welsh and Jefferies at No. 35. Maxwell and Company, the shoemaker at No. 11, was founded as a manufacturer of spurs in 1756. In 1998, Margaret Howells became the first woman to open a store in what had previously been an exclusively male domain (she stocks designer men's wear).

SCIENCE MUSEUM. The **museum** holds the scientific collections of the **Victoria and Albert Museum**, which was founded in 1857. Initially, the sciences were represented by exhibits from the **Great Exhibition** of 1851 and the museum of the Royal School of Practical Art (created in 1852), along with items acquired from a variety of other sources. In 1864, a collection of naval models, donated by **The Admiralty**, was added, then, in 1883, a science library was established. The following year, the Patent Office Museum was incorporated, bringing Richard Arkwright's spinning machine (which enabled the production of cotton yarn to become a factory industry) and George Stephenson's *Rocket* (the locomotive that revolutionized steam power and led to the expansion of the **railway** industry). As the exhibits increased in number, display space became a scarce resource, so, in stages from 1913 (when the east front was built) until 1977 (when an east block extension was completed), the acquisitions were moved to the present premises in Exhibition Road, behind the **Natural History Museum**. There, displays focus on three major themes—industry, science, and society—with a concentration on the inventions that led to Britain's 19th-century technological prowess as well as on international scientific achievement during the 20th century (including the development of computers and advances in medicine). The museum, which receives about 1.5 million visitors every year, also presents regular lectures and houses a library of over 500,000 volumes.

SCOTLAND YARD. *See* NEW SCOTLAND YARD.

SCOTT, GILES GILBERT (1880–1960). Scott, designer of several of the most important buildings erected in London during the first half of the 20th century, came from a long line of architects; his grandfather (George Gilbert Scott) prepared the plans for the **Albert Memorial** and his father (also named George Gilbert Scott) played a considerable part in promoting the Gothic Revival movement in Victorian Britain. Giles Scott was born in **Hampstead** on 9 November 1880 and educated at Beaumont College in Old Windsor. He achieved prominence in 1902 when he won the competition to design a Church of England cathedral for Liverpool, a success that caused the organizers some embarrassment because he was hardly out of his teens and, furthermore, a Roman Catholic.

Further church commissions followed (including St. Albans in **Golders Green**), but he did not restrict himself to religious structures. In 1932, he was appointed architect for **Waterloo** Bridge, proposing a five-arch combination of concrete and steel with comparatively little decoration. Also, he was responsible for the imposing brick design of **Battersea Power Station**, opened in 1933. Following the Second World War, Scott was invited to carry out remedial work on a number of old buildings. The most important was the **Palace of Westminster**, where the House of Commons had been badly damaged by bombs, so the architectural challenge was to reconstruct the debating chamber in its original form but without the exuberance of **Augustus Welby Northmore Pugin**'s decoration. Reconstruction of the **Guildhall** in the **City of London** involved replacement of the roof while maintaining such masonry and timber as remained. Scott was knighted in 1924, served as President of the Royal Institute of British Architects from 1933 to 1935, and was awarded the Order of Merit in 1944. He died in London on 8 February 1960. (*See also* DENMARK HILL.)

SELFRIDGES. One of London's largest and best-known department stores, Selfridge's stands near the western end of **Oxford Street**. It was opened in 1909 by Henry Gordon Selfridge, a native of Ripon (Wisconsin) who had worked in the retail trade in Chicago before seeking his fortune in Europe. The building, with a facade of Ionic columns, occupies a complete block on the north site of the street and is considered an outstanding example of Edwardian commercial **architecture**. Its design was the result of a transatlantic collaboration; originally conceived by Daniel Burnham and Frank Swales in the United States, it was built under the supervision of British architects R. F. Atkinson and John Burnet. The store brought American sales methods to London, using eye-catching window displays to attract customers inside and showing stock to its best advantage. When it was separated from the American-owned Sears group in 1998, it was valued at just over £360 million on the London **Stock Exchange**.

SERPENTINE. The 28-acre lake in **Hyde Park** was built at the suggestion of Caroline of Ansbach, wife of King George II. From the windows of **Kensington Palace**, she could see a string of small ponds, separated by marshland, which she believed could be linked to form a single, curving stretch of water by damming the Westbourne River. The work was carried out in 1730–31 and the lake used by the royal family for yachting. A bridge (designed by George Rennie), which provides fine views of **Westminster Abbey**, was built in 1826 and an Italian water garden added at the northern end in 1861. On the west side, in **Kensington Gardens**, George Frampton's bronze statue of Peter Pan (the little boy who never grew up) was erected in 1912, paid for by an anonymous admirer of author J. M. Barrie, who created the character. The lake is still used for boating, as well as fishing and swimming (one group of masochists insists on taking a dip every New Year's Day). The Serpentine Gallery, a showcase for contemporary art and sculpture, was opened in 1972, not far from Rennie's bridge, in a building opened as a tea house in 1907.

SEWAGE DISPOSAL. Until the second half of the 19th century, little provision was made for the disposal of London's sewage, which was allowed to flow freely into the **River Thames** and its tributaries. In 1858, however, Parliament passed legislation designed to reduce **water pollution** in the river and, the following year, work began on plans, prepared by **Joseph William Bazalgette**, to provide a drainage system for the city. A 1,300-mile network of brick tunnels was built in three layers leading to outfalls 11 miles downstream from **London Bridge**. Initially, the sewage was disgorged straight into the Thames, with the result that much reappeared in central London at high tide, but, even so, as construction neared completion in 1875, it was clear that the incidence of diseases such as **cholera**, contracted through contaminated drinking water, was declining rapidly. In 1879, the system was augmented by some 12 miles of storm sewer and, after 1887, waste was treated chemically, with much taken by boat for disposal in the North Sea. Further improvements were made by the **London County Council** between 1900 and 1935. From 1936, small treatment plants were increasingly replaced by larger and more efficient units, culminating in the opening of the **Beckton** works (the largest in Europe) in 1975. The previous year, responsibility for sewage disposal had been transferred from **local government** to the Thames Water Authority, which was privatized by the Conservative government in 1989 and concentrates its purification processing at Beckton and at Crossness (where plants that use bacteria to purify sewage have operated since 1964). (*See also* GREAT STINK; HUNGERFORD BRIDGE.)

SEX PISTOLS. During the late 1970s, the Sex Pistols rock band was the musical focus of the **punk** movement. Its members, all Londoners, were Paul Cook, Steve Jones, John Lydon (who adopted the stage name of Johnny Rotten), Glen Matlock, and John Ritchie (better known as Sid Vicious). Brought together in 1976 by Malcolm McLaren to promote Sex, a store that sold clothing favored by extremist political movements, they adopted a musical style that mixed the rhythms of such nonconformist stars as Iggy and the Stooges with the influences of groups such as The Who and the Small Faces, who had dominated British popular music a decade earlier. *Anarchy in the UK*, their first single, released in 1976, shocked orthodox society with its violent, aggressive imagery but appealed to many rebellious, urban, working-class youngsters, particularly in London. Confrontational stage performances, persistent profanities in television interviews, and nihilistic lyrics led to bans by the media and local authorities, but despite official disapproval their records sold well, *God Save the Queen*, *Pretty Vacant*, *Holidays in the Sun*, and *Never Mind the Bollocks, Here's the Sex Pistols* all reaching the top ten in the charts during 1977 through sophisticated manipulation of the press and television. By late that year, however, the group's momentum had slowed. An unsuccessful tour of the United States led to a split in 1978, then, in February 1979, Vicious died of a heroin overdose in New York while on bail awaiting trial on a charge of murdering his girlfriend, Nancy Spungen. The remaining members of the band reformed for a reunion tour in 1996 but, by that time, punk had been replaced by other fashions and the Pistols were a fond memory in the minds of middle-aged parents rather than contemporary musical hell-raisers who seemed to be threatening the fabric of British society.

SHADWELL. Shadwell lies northeast of **Wapping** on the marshy north bank of the **River Thames**, in the heart of London's **Docklands**. It developed from the mid-17th century, when Thomas Neale erected St. Paul's Church, opened a water works, established a **market**, and built houses to accommodate workers in tanneries, rope-making works, **breweries**, and other small industries. Within two centuries, the community had grown to nearly 12,000 people, although that number declined during the 1850s, when many buildings were demolished to make way for improved harbor facilities at Shadwell Basin. Construction of the King Edward VII Memorial Park in 1922 resulted in further slum removal. The area, still characterized by industry and by a largely working-class population, was incorporated within the **London Borough of Tower Hamlets** when the city's **local government** was reorganized in 1965. (*See also* ROTHERHITHE.)

SHAFTESBURY AVENUE. During the last quarter of the 19th century, **Joseph William Bazalgette** (the **Metropolitan Board of Works**' Engineer) planned a series of new roads in order to reduce traffic congestion in central London. A critical element of that strategy, Shaftesbury Avenue was built during the 1880s to facilitate movement between **Piccadilly Circus** and **Bloomsbury**. In addition, its construction allowed the authorities to demolish some of the city's most notorious slums (the street was named after the seventh Earl of Shaftesbury, a social reformer who had done much to ease the plight of poor families living in the area). Much of the new property was taken over by **theater**s; the Lyric was the first, opening in 1888, but it was soon followed by the Palace (established as the Royal English Opera house in 1891), the Apollo (1901), the Globe (1906), the Queen's (1907), the Shaftesbury (1911), and later by the Saville (1931). The Shaftesbury was damaged by bombs in 1941, during the **Blitz**, and later demolished, but cinemas and other forms of entertainment continued to move in after the Second World War, turning the street into the heart of the **West End**.

SHAKESPEARE, WILLIAM (1564–1616). Shakespeare, acknowledged by most literary scholars as the world's greatest playwright, was born in Stratford-Upon-Avon to merchant John Shakespeare and his wife, Mary. The child was baptized in Holy Trinity Church on 26 April 1564; his birth date is unknown but traditionally recognized as April 23. John Shakespeare was a significant figure in Stratford—a burgess who was appointed bailiff (a post similar to that of mayor) in 1568—so his son almost certainly attended the local grammar school.

Late in 1582, he married Anne Hathaway, who bore him a daughter (Susanna) in May of the following year and twins (Hamnet and Judith) in 1585. His activities over the next seven years or so are less certain. There are stories that he ran away from Stratford when he got into trouble for poaching deer, that he served as a soldier, and that he worked as a schoolmaster, but there are no records to authenticate any of these claims. By 1594, however, he was certainly in London and attached to the Lord Chamberlain's Company, which presented entertainments at **Bankside** and **Shoreditch**. He also, apparently, attracted the attention of the nobility because his first published poems (*Venus and Adonis* [1593]) and *The Rape of Lucrece* [1594]) were dedicated to Henry, Earl of Southampton. In 1596, he was living in Bishopsgate (*see* **Bishop's Gate**) close to the two **theater** districts, and in 1599 at **Southwark**, near the newly built **Globe Theatre**. By 1604, he was lodging in **Cripplegate** with the Mountjoys, a **Huguenot** family, and in 1613 he bought his first London home, the gatehouse at **Blackfriars**, where the former monastery hall had been converted into a playhouse.

Although it is not possible to produce an accurate chronology of Shakespeare's texts, the comments of contemporaries indicate that his reputation grew and that he was highly regarded by his peers (**Ben Jonson**, for example, wrote that he was "not of an age but for all time"). Although he made little effort to devise plots (for example, *The Comedy of Errors* is based on the plays *Menaechmi* and *Amphitruo* by Plautus, a Roman author), he was adept at reworking tales in order to heighten characterization and increase the dramatic effect of a story's climax. Early dramas, such as *The Taming of the Shrew* (1593–94) and *Romeo and Juliet* (1594–95) (both of which were performed when he was still in his twenties), were simply the precursors of a great range of historical plays, tragedies, and comedies that drew audiences from all social classes and earned him enduring fame. He also collaborated with other writers, as when he worked with John Fletcher on *The Two Noble Kinsmen*, but these contributions were often unattributed, leaving later scholars to debate the true extent of his influence on Elizabethan and Jacobean drama in London. After 1613, he produced no new work, though he may have continued to act. He returned to Stratford in 1614 and died there on 23 April 1616, allegedly from an illness that developed after a drinking session with Jonson and other cronies. (*See also* GEORGE INN; OLD VIC; PUBLIC RECORD OFFICE [PRO]; REGENT'S PARK; ROYAL NATIONAL THEATRE; SOUTHWARK CATHEDRAL; WESTMINSTER ABBEY.)

SHENE PALACE. *See* RICHMOND PALACE.

SHEPHERD'S BUSH. Best known as the site of the **British Broadcasting Corporation**'s Television Centre, Shepherd's Bush is located between **Notting Hill** (which lies to the east) and **Acton** (to the west). It developed during the 19th century, as the expansion of the **railway** network encouraged suburban **housing** growth, but retained some open space because eight acres of common land (once known as Gabblegoose Green) were protected by parliamentary legislation in 1872 and 30 acres of **park** land owned by the Manor of Ravenscourt were acquired by the **Metropolitan Board of Works** in 1887 and converted into playing fields. In 1914, an outdoor **market** opened near Goldhawk Road; surviving serious damage during the **Blitz** and threats of closure after the Second World War, it expanded from the 1950s, drawing custom from nearby **immigrant** communities by offering fruit, vegetables, and household goods with a strong West Indian emphasis. (*See also* STREET MARKETS.)

SHERIFF. The Sheriff is one of the principal officers of the **Corporation of London**, second only to the **Lord Mayor** in status. The post dates from 1132, when King Henry I awarded the **City of London** a charter empowering it to appoint a Sheriff (or Shire Reeve) for the County of Middlesex as well as for its own area. Until 1189, when the Mayor was first appointed, they ran the City as the monarch's representatives, collecting taxes and administering justice. The **Local Government** Act of 1888 removed their jurisdiction over Middlesex but allowed the City of London to retain two Sheriffs, who are now appointed annually by the members of the City **livery companies** on Midsummer Day (24 June) and take their oath of office on Michaelmas Eve (28 September). Usually, one Aldermanic Sheriff is appointed from the ranks of the **Aldermen** (only those who follow this route can become Lord Mayor). A second official (known as the Lay Sheriff) may be an Alderman or a member of the **Court of Common Council** or neither (though if he does not hold one of these positions, he must retire from the Corporation at the end of his year of office). The Sheriffs accompany the Lord Mayor on official occasions, attend sessions at the **Central Criminal Court**, and may present petitions from the City of London to Parliament.

SHOREDITCH. By the early 12th century, a settlement had formed at Scoredich (or Sceorf's Ditch), where two Roman routeways met outside the northeast walls of the **City of London**. For much of the Medieval period, the land was owned by the Roman Catholic Church, but following the dissolution of the English **monasteries** from 1532 it fell into secular hands and in 1576 became the site of The Theatre, the first playhouse built in England (several Elizabethan entertainers are buried nearby in St. Leonard's Church, including Gabriel Spencer, who was killed in a duel with writer **Ben Jonson** in 1598). From the late 17th century, the area was increasingly developed, evolving into a densely populated inner-city suburb. During the 20th century, many of the older properties were removed to make way for **housing** that would meet modern standards, but some older buildings remain, notably the former Georgian almshouses in Kingsland Road that house the **Geffrye Museum**. In 1965, when **local government** in the metropolitan area was reorganized, Shoreditch was included within the **London Borough of Hackney**.

SIR HENRY WOOD PROMENADE CONCERTS. *See* PROMS, THE.

SIR JOHN SOANE'S MUSEUM. A thoroughly personal collection of *objets d'art*, the **museum** holds the lifetime acquisitions of John Soane (1753–1837). The son of a bricklayer, Soane established himself as an architect in 1781 and was responsible for designing many important London buildings during the late 18th and early 19th centuries, including the **Bank of England**, the Law Courts in **Westminster**, the library at the House of Lords (*see* **Palace of Westminster**), and some of the **Waterloo churches**. Many of these have been demolished or radically altered, but his home (erected in 1658 and extensively renovated under his direction in 1792) still stands in **Lincoln's Inn Fields**, housing his eclectic purchases. Soane's wealth was supplemented by that of his wife, the heiress of a rich builder, so he was able to indulge an interest in painting, manuscripts, sculpture, precious stones, and other artefacts. He took over neighboring houses in order to provide space for his acquisitions, then, in 1833, made arrangements for everything to be preserved as a public museum. The exhibits include the eight canvases of William Hogarth's *Rake's Progress* (1735), paintings by Antonio Canaletto, books from architect **Robert Adam**'s library and 55 volumes of drawings from his office, **Christopher Wren**'s watch, Napoleon Bonaparte's pistols, the sarcophagus of the Egyptian pharaoh Seti I (who died in 1290 B.C.), a 13th-century Bible, and many other treasures. (*See also* CHELSEA HOSPITAL.)

SLOANE, HANS (1660–1753). The plants, rocks, animals, and other objects collected by Hans Sloane provided the foundation for the **British Museum**'s collections. The seventh son of tax collector Alexander Sloane and his wife, Sarah, Hans was probably born in Killyleagh, Ireland, on 16 April 1660. He studied medicine in London, Paris, Montpellier, and Orange, graduating in 1683. Through an association with Thomas Sydenham, one of the most renowned physicians of the late 17th century, he built up a large practice, supported by wealthy clients, and earned a scientific reputation that won him Fellowships of the **Royal Society** (1685) and the **Royal College of Physicians of London** (1687). In 1687, he traveled to Jamaica as doctor to the island's Governor, the Duke of Albermarle, but returned when his employer died the following year, was appointed Physician to Queen Anne in 1712, created a baronet in 1718, was made Physician General to the Army in 1722, accepted the post of Physician in Ordinary to King George II in 1727, and served as President of the Royal Society from 1727 to 1741. In 1712, he bought the Manor of **Chelsea** and settled there when he retired from practice in 1741. He died on 11 January 1753.

Sloane's interest in natural history dated from his childhood and was pursued at university alongside his medical studies. When he returned from Jamaica, he carried over 800 plant species with him (he also tried, but failed, to transport a live crocodile, an iguana, and a seven-foot snake). In his herbarium, he included a sample of *Theobroma cacao*, which Jamaicans used to make a drink Sloane found unpalatable. However, in the spirit of experiment, he mixed the liquid with milk and thus became the father of the chocolate industry.

As affluent patients flocked to his surgery in **Bloomsbury** Square, Sloane used the fees he collected to add books, medals, coins, mathematical instruments, and other artefacts to his collection. In 1749, he made a will bequeathing the acquisitions to the nation in return for a sum of £20,000 paid to his family. Six months after his death, the gift was accepted by Act of Parliament and trustees were appointed to manage it. In 1754, they purchased Montague House, not far from his Bloomsbury practice, and merged his collections with the libraries of Sir Robert Bruce Cotton (1571–1631) and Edward Harley, Earl of Oxford (1689–1741), to form the British **Museum**. Sloane is commemorated in several London street names, including **Sloane Square** and Hans Road, which runs alongside **Harrods**. (*See also* CHELSEA PHYSIC GARDEN; NATURAL HISTORY MUSEUM.)

SLOANE RANGER. *See* SLOANE SQUARE.

SLOANE SQUARE. A busy traffic junction towards the eastern end of **King's Road**, the square is named after **Hans Sloane**, President of the **Royal Society** from 1727 to 1741 and Lord of the Manor of **Chelsea** from 1712 until his death in 1753. It was developed as a residential area from 1771 but was increasingly infiltrated by commercial interests during the 19th century and redesigned just before the Second World War to improve the circulation of traffic. Peter Jones, one of London's principal department stores, has stood on the west side of the square since 1877 and the Royal Court Theatre (which has developed a reputation for avant-garde productions) on the east since 1887. During the 1980s, the area became a fashionable shopping haunt for affluent, young professionals who became known as "Sloane Rangers" or "Sloanes," terms still used to describe the Barbour jacket wearing, Land Rover driving, polo playing upper middle class.

SMITH, W. H., LTD. In 1792, Henry Walton Smith opened a small newsagent's shop in Little Grosvenor Street. Although he died shortly afterwards, the business flourished under the management of his family and, in 1828, assumed its present name when his son, William Henry, took full control. By the middle of the century, the firm had developed a reputation for speedy distribution of newspapers (it chartered a special boat to carry reports of the death of King George IV to Irish readers in 1830) and had opened bookstalls to cater to travellers at railway stations. When contracts to trade on the platforms were terminated, W. H. Smith established shops nearby, building up a nationwide chain by the 1940s. It became a public company in 1948 and subsequently acquired interests abroad, opening over 500 stores in the United States alone, principally at airports and luxury hotels. In 1998, it bought the retail interests of John Menzies, its biggest British competitor, to became the largest retailer of books, stationery, and music in the United Kingdom.

SMITHFIELD MEAT MARKET. London's largest wholesale meat **market** grew up on the "smooth field" just outside the walls of the **City of London**. From at least the 12th century, sales of horses, sheep, pigs, and other animals were held alongside **Bartholomew Fair** (which initially specialized in cloth). These were formally recognized in 1638, when the **Corporation of London** established a cattle market on the site under the terms of a royal charter, but problems arose over the next 200 years as the urban area expanded; drovers took a perverse pleasure in the disruption caused by driving herds through confined streets, beasts were slaughtered in the open, blood flowed along drainage channels, and entrails were dumped on the ground to rot. In 1855, Bartholomew Fair was closed because it was accompanied by drunkenness and public disorder, sales of live animals were moved to the **Metropolitan Cattle Market** in **Islington**, and the field was converted for trade in slaughtered meat. A covered hall, designed by Horace Jones, was opened in 1868, with additions in 1875 and 1899 extending the area to over 10 acres. During the second half of the 20th century, there were continual rumors of Smithfield's demise as retailers changed buying practices and other major markets (notably **Billingsgate Fish Market** and **Covent Garden** fruit and vegetable market) moved to new sites away from the city center. However, major rebuilding in the 1960s (following a fire in the poultry section in 1958) and refurbishment during the 1990s have upgraded facilities, providing better refrigerated storage and improved hygiene. Nearby, there is a wide range of public houses, cafés, and restaurants that cater to the needs of early morning workers. Smithfield employs about 1,000 people and sells about 150,000 tons of meat each year.

SNOW, JOHN (1813–1858). For 40 years during the 19th century, cholera was one of London's killer diseases. Introduced from India as British ships expanded their trading contacts, it caused a series of epidemics in 1831–32, 1848–49, 1854, and 1856, with over half of the sufferers dying. Its decline during the second half of the century was a direct result of John Snow's willingness to follow up his belief that the disease was transmitted by water. Born into a farming family in York on 15 March 1813, Snow was educated at a private school in the city before taking up an apprenticeship with Newcastle surgeon William Hardcastle in 1827.

Nine years later, he moved to London in order to study medicine formally and, in 1838, became a member of the **Royal College of Surgeons of England** and a licentiate of the Society of Apothecaries. He graduated from the University of London (*see* **universities**) with the degree of Doctor of Medicine in 1844, then, in 1850, was made a licentiate of the **Royal College of Physicians of London**. In 1849, Snow published a monograph suggesting that cholera (then a little-understood illness) was waterborne, a view that was challenged by Dr. Robert Baker (who believed that it was associated with slum conditions) and Dr. Henry Acland (who felt that marshy conditions were the cause). During the late summer of 1854, an outbreak of the disease in **Soho** caused at least 500 deaths over a period of 10 days. Snow, who had a practice in the area at Golden Square, prepared a map showing the location of the house where each victim lived, adding the pumps that were the only source of drinking water at the time. The map depicted a distinct cluster of deaths close to a pump in Broad Street, so the authorities removed the handle. Within days, the epidemic was over but skeptics argued that it was on the wane anyway, so some years passed before Snow's thesis was fully accepted.

The use of anesthetics in London hospitals also owes much to Snow's advocacy. In 1846, he was one of the first doctors in the city to use ether while treating patients. Also, he did much to promote acceptance of chloroform by employing it when Queen Victoria gave birth to Prince Leopold in 1853 and Princess Beatrice in 1858. He died on 16 June 1858 and was buried at **Brompton** Cemetery. Although he was a lifelong teetotaller (as well as a vegetarian and nonsmoker), he is commemorated by a pub that bears his name at the corner of Broadwick Street (the Broad Street of Snow's day) and Lexington Street.

SOCCER. *See* FOOTBALL.

SOHO. The Soho area of the **City of Westminster** is one of London's principal entertainment foci, bounded by **Oxford Street** to the north, **Regent Street** to the west, **Shaftesbury Avenue** to the south, and **Charing Cross Road** to the east. The land was used by aristocrats for hunting during the Medieval period ("So-ho!" was a common cry when hares were roused) but was increasingly built over during the 17th century, particularly around Soho Square, which was laid out by builder Richard Frith during the 1680s and attracted such noble residents as the Duke of Monmouth and Viscount Preston. The area also proved attractive to foreign **immigrants**, including **Huguenots** fleeing persecution (in 1739,

William Maitland wrote that "Many parts of this parish so greatly abound with French that it is an easy Matter for a Stranger to imagine himself in France"). They were followed by writers and artists, giving this section of the city a distinctively cosmopolitan, bohemian character. Around the middle of the 19th century, **theater**s and **music halls** became increasingly common, attracting restaurants, drinking places, prostitutes, and other services in their wake. Waiters and other workers, many from abroad, crammed into small rooms, forcing population densities up and facilitating the spread of infectious disease (*see* **Snow, John**).

From the 1960s, the area's reputation as a red light district flourished, with strip clubs, sex shops, and sellers of pornographic books boosting a tourist trade seeking the risqué and salacious, but, in 1972, members of the Soho Society (which represented local residents) initiated a campaign designed to reverse the growth of the industry. Several **police** officers were found guilty of corruption and the ensuing publicity led Parliament to introduce licensing programs for firms selling sex; as a result, the number of premises involved fell sixfold during the 1980s. In the decade that followed, the social composition of Soho changed radically. A housing association was formed to erect homes for families to rent, the proportion of school-age residents rose, a new parish church and community hall were built, and a **museum** was opened to improve knowledge of the neighborhood's history. (*See also* CHINATOWN; WARDOUR STREET.)

SOMERSET HOUSE. During the Medieval period, the London residences of the Bishops of Chester and Worcester occupied the site in the **Strand** where Somerset House now stands. In 1547–50, these buildings were swept away and replaced by England's first Renaissance palace, erected for Edward Seymour, Duke of Somerset and Lord Protector of England. After Seymour's execution in 1552, the mansion passed to the Crown which, over the next 200 years, used it as a residence for members of the royal family and as government offices. It was demolished in 1775 and replaced, between 1776 and 1786, by a structure, designed on classical lines by **William Chambers**, which is set around a courtyard measuring 350 feet by 310 feet and faced with **Portland stone**. An 800-foot-long facade fronts the **River Thames**, which flowed past the south terrace until embankments were built during the late 19th century (*see* **Bazalgette, Joseph William**). Initially, the **Royal Academy of Arts**, the **Royal Society**, and the Society of Antiquaries were housed in the north wing, the Royal Navy in the west and part of the south wings, and government officials in the remaining areas. Since then, occupants have included the **Courtauld Institute of Art**, the Inland Revenue, and the General Register of Births, Marriages and Deaths. In 1997, a trust was formed to prepare plans for the conservation of the building, oversee refurbishment, and provide housing for a collection of European decorative art gifted to the nation by Mr. Arthur Gilbert. (*See also* ATHENAEUM, THE; KNIGHTS HOSPITALLER; ROYAL COLLEGE OF ART; ST. MARGARET'S CHURCH, WESTMINSTER; UNIVERSITIES.)

SOTHEBY'S. In 1744, Samuel Baker, a London bookseller, began a series of annual auctions. A decade later, he embarked on a more regular series of sales from premises near **Covent Garden**, expanding the firm and taking on additional employees, including (in 1776) his nephew, John Sotheby. Expansion also necessitated moves to more capacious accommodation near the **Strand** in 1818 and then, in 1917, to the present address at 34–35 New **Bond Street**. From the 1860s until 1913, the firm concentrated on books but, from the First World War, increasingly challenged **Christie's** as a major auctioneer of fine art, finally surpassing its rival in 1954 and remaining ahead for 43 years. In 1997, the firm's worldwide income from auctions exceeded £1.1 billion.

SOUTH BANK. From the late 1940s, the derelict properties that lined the south bank of the **River Thames** between **Hungerford Bridge** and **Waterloo Bridge** were swept away. In their place, one of the world's largest art complexes was built, beginning with the **Royal Festival Hall**, erected for the **Festival of Britain** in 1951. The **National Film Theatre** followed five years later, two concert venues—the Purcell Room and the **Queen Elizabeth Hall**—in 1967, and the **Hayward Gallery** (which houses art exhibitions) in 1968. The **Royal National Theatre** opened in 1976 and, most recently, the **Museum of the Moving Image** was added in 1988. Some commentators have complained that the concrete structures are unnecessarily bleak but others have praised the views across the water to the **City of London**. In 2000, plans were unveiled for a £150 million facelift for the area. The project would involve construction of a 1,400-seat amphitheater underneath a six-acre landscaped park but would retain much of the concrete and would be supervised by American architect Rick Mather.

SOUTHWARK. As the Romans established control of their new British colony during the first century A.D., they built a bridge across the **River Thames** to provide access to their settlement at **Londinium**. Southwark developed at the southern end of that bridge, evolving into a significant market town, with a fair held annually from 1462 until petty crime and prostitution forced the authorities to ban the event in 1763. Because of its importance as a route focus and commercial center, it housed many taverns (including the Tabard, where poet Geoffrey Chaucer describes the gathering of his pilgrims in *The Canterbury Tales*, published c. 1387–1400) and, at the end of the 16th century, became London's principal entertainment area, with playhouses (such as the **Globe Theatre**) attracting large audiences. Many of the buildings were destroyed by fire in 1676 but, even so, the land was heavily developed by the end of Queen Anne's reign in 1714. The completion of **Westminster Bridge** in 1750 and Blackfriars Bridge in 1769 hastened the development process, so by the mid-19th century Southwark had become part of central London, with a host of small industries, particularly brewing, food processing, and leather making. After the Second World War, it was made the focus of several urban renewal programs (as at **Elephant and Castle**) and in 1965, when **local government** in the metropolitan area was reorganized, gave its name to the **London Borough of Southwark**. (*See also* BANKSIDE; CLINK PRISON; GEORGE INN; HENSLOWE, PHILIP; MARSHALSEA PRISON; PUGIN, AUGUSTUS WELBY NORTHMORE; SOUTHWARK BRIDGE; SOUTHWARK CATHEDRAL; THEATER.)

SOUTHWARK, LONDON BOROUGH OF. Southwark was created, following the dissolution of the **London County Council** in 1965, by the merger of the formerly independent authorities of **Bermondsey**, **Camberwell**, and **Southwark**. Lying on the south bank of the **River Thames**, opposite the **City of London**, it covers 11 square miles and has a population of 232,000 (1998). The three-mile river frontage is a complex mixture of old and new, with the 13th-century **Southwark Cathedral** sitting close to modern office developments and the re-created **Globe Theatre**. Much of the remainder of the borough is covered by rows of 19th-century terraced **housing** and modern local authority estates occupied by clerical and manual workers, although **Dulwich**, at the southern tip, has a high proportion of professional and managerial families. The area is one of the poorest in the United Kingdom, with a considerable black population and unemployment rates generally above the city average. Moreover, the urban landscape is often bleak, with few open spaces for recreation and several places (such as **Elephant and Castle**) where road improvements have taken precedence over community development. However, the local authority has invested heavily in regeneration

The City of London from Southwark in 1616 (Museum of London)

programs, tearing down high-density skyscraper blocks built in the 1960s and replacing them with conventional streets. Also, improved access during the 1990s (notably through the extension of **London Underground**'s Jubilee Line and the opening of the international rail terminal at nearby **Waterloo**) has helped to attract such new business as the £1.4 billion office complex planned for a site between **London Bridge** and **Tower Bridge** by the CIT Group. (*See also* BANKSIDE; KENNINGTON; PECKHAM; ROTHERHITHE.)

SOUTHWARK BRIDGE. Erected despite protests that it would interfere with navigation on the **River Thames**, the first Southwark Bridge, designed by James Rennie, linked **Bankside** (on the south shore of the river) to the **City of London** (on the north). It was built in 1814–19, with three arches and a 240-foot central span, the largest ever made of cast iron. The structure was replaced by the present five-span steel **bridge**, constructed to Ernest George's plans, in 1912–21.

SOUTHWARK CATHEDRAL. The cathedral occupies a site, southwest of **London Bridge**, that has been a Christian place of worship for 1,400 years. According to tradition, the first chapel was built by a ferryman early in the seventh century but destroyed by fire and replaced in about 852 under the supervision of St. Swithun, Bishop of Winchester. That structure, too, burned down (in 1106) and was rebuilt by Augustinian monks but survived for only a century before succumbing to another blaze. Work on a new church, dedicated to St. Mary Overie, began in 1220 and continued until the tower was completed in 1520. London's first example of religious **architecture** in Gothic style, it is considered (with **Westminster Abbey**) to be one of the two most important medieval properties remaining in the city. The building was extensively refurbished during the 19th century (in particular, the nave was declared unsafe and, in 1890–97, replaced to plans prepared by Sir Arthur Blomfield) then elevated in status from parish church to cathedral, with a dedication to St. Saviour and St. Mary Overie, in 1897 (a decision that reflected the growing population south of the **River Thames**). The building is particularly noted for its monuments, the earliest of which, dating from about 1275, is an effigy of a knight. A memorial to playwright **William Shakespeare** (who lived in Southwark from 1599 until 1604) stands in the south aisle underneath a stained glass window, designed by Christopher Webb and erected in 1954, which shows characters from the plays. The Harvard Chapel, adjoining the north choir aisle, was built in 1907 as a memorial to John Harvard, who was baptized in the church in 1607, emigrated to North America, and, when he died, left his books and property to the Massachusetts college that became Harvard University. In 2000, the church celebrated the millennium by forming London's first cathedral girls' choir and embarking on a £10 million restoration program.

SPANIARDS, THE. A 16th-century weather-boarded building, The Spaniards, in Hampstead Lane, is one of the best-known **public houses** in London. The origin of its name is contested; some writers believe that it was the home of the Spanish ambassador to the court of King James VII and II during the 17th century, others that it was owned by two Spanish brothers who killed themselves in a duel over a woman. More certainly, it was used by highwayman Dick Turpin, who stabled Black Bess, his mare, on the other side of the road. And, in 1780, rioters on their way to destroy nearby **Kenwood House** were delayed by the landlord, who plied them with alcohol until soldiers arrived to arrest them. The pub's location on the edge of **Hampstead Heath**, made it a popular haunt of the literary men who frequented Hampstead village during the 19th century. Poets Lord Byron, John Keats (*see* **Keats's House**), and Percy Bysshe Shelley were regular visitors, and author **Charles Dickens** clearly knew the place because, in *The Pickwick Papers* (1836–37), he describes how Mrs. Bardell and her friends met there to plot against Mr. Pickwick. (*See also* JACK STRAW'S CASTLE.)

SPEAKERS' CORNER. At the northeastern edge of **Hyde Park**, Speakers' Corner stands close to **Tyburn**, where criminals were hanged in public from 1388 until 1783. Condemned men and women were allowed to make a statement from the gallows before they were executed, and over the years, that privilege was extended to more general acceptance of a right to free speech at the site. During the 1850s and 1860s, a series of mass meetings in the park sometimes led police to arrest inflammatory orators, but, since 1872, the authorities have accepted both that crowds have a right to assemble and that speakers have a right to address them on any subject they choose provided there is no blasphemy or obscenity and no incitement to breach the peace. Traditionally, the soap boxes are brought out on Sunday mornings and passersby listen to impassioned arguments on all matter of religious, political, and social themes. Heckling is common but most speakers have a quick wit, readily turning criticisms to their own advantage.

SPITALFIELDS. About 1197, Walter and Rose Bruno founded an Augustinian priory, known as St. Mary Spital, on land to the east of the **City of London**. The fields nearby remained open until the 17th century, when proximity to the main urban area encouraged building. From 1685, when King Louis XIV of France revoked legislation giving French Protestants freedom of worship, **Huguenot** refugees flooded into the area, attracted by its reputation as a nonconformist heartland. They brought with them a heritage of silk weaving, reestablishing their businesses in England and turning Spitalfields into a center of textile production (houses in Fournier Street still have the large attic windows that the **immigrants** built in order to provide sufficient light for them to work their looms). The industry's reputation attracted dyers, weavers, bobbin makers, and other workers, creating an interdependent complex of small companies that still characterizes the suburb, even though silk has long been superseded by artificial fibers. The growing population led to a rash of church building (*see*, for example, **Christ Church, Spitalfields**) but the economics of the trade meant that most workers were poor, so much of the religious bodies' effort was concentrated on charitable work. During the 18th and 19th centuries, employment opportunities diversified with the growth of Black Eagle **Brewery** (which was founded in 1660 and produced a popular black stout) and the Spitalfields **Market** (established in 1682 to sell vegetables). Also, the ethnic composition changed with an influx of Jewish migrants from about 1880. The most recent incomers are the Bengalis, who arrived in the early 1960s and have established themselves in the clothing industry and retail services. Spitalfields was incorporated within the **London Borough of Tower Hamlets** when the metropolitan area's **local government** system was reformed in 1965 and, since then, has benefited from slum clearance programs and conservation efforts that have retained much of the early Georgian **housing**. (*See also* PEABODY, GEORGE.)

SQUARE MILE. The **City of London**, with its complex of financial services, is sometimes referred to as "The Square Mile" because it covers an area of 677 acres, just over one square mile.

STAMFORD HILL. Stamford Hill, in the **London Borough of Hackney**, has one of the largest concentrations of ultraorthodox Jews (known as Hasidim) in London. The only Jewish community in Britain to use the Yiddish language extensively, it has its roots in 18th-century Poland, where Ba'al Shem Tov led a charismatic movement that emphasized a nonintellectual relationship with God and a strict code of personal conduct. The black frock coats and wide-brimmed fur hats worn by the Polish nobility were adopted as the distinctive form of dress, making the men easily identifiable in the north London community. The women wear wigs, believing that only their husbands should see their real hair, and mix only with males to whom they are related. Divorce is unusual and disputes are solved according to traditional rules rather than by the tenets of English law. Stamford Hill developed during the 18th century, when it was popular with **City** bankers and financiers, many of whom had a Jewish background. The pace of expansion increased with the arrival of the **railway** in 1872, and the social composition of the area altered with the construction of flats specifically for working-class families in the period between the two world wars but, since then, the suburb has altered little. Jewish worshippers meet at a synagogue in Egerton Road and buy bread, groceries, and other goods at shops catering to their needs in the commercial heart of the area at the crossroads of Stamford Hill and Amhurst Park.

STANMORE. Stanmore, on the northwest fringe of the metropolitan area in the **London Borough of Harrow**, was settled by Neolithic times and was the location of a battle between the Celtic Catuvellauni people and an invading Roman army in 54 B.C. Ranulf de Glanville, Chief Justiciary of England, founded a priory in the area in 1170, but development was limited until the 20th century, when the proximity of the **Chiltern Hills** and the restrictions on building imposed by **green belt** legislation attracted successful **City** bankers and stockbrokers. The church of St. John the Evangelist dates from Saxon times, but the present building, designed by Henry Clutton, was erected in 1850; Lord Aberdeen (Prime Minister from 1852 to 1855) is buried in the vaults of its brick predecessor, which stands nearby, and the remains of Sir W. S. Gilbert, poet and writer of comic operas, lie in the churchyard.

STANSTED AIRPORT. *See* AIRPORTS.

STATE OPENING OF PARLIAMENT. In a ceremony little changed since Elizabethan times, the monarch rides in procession from **Buckingham Palace** to **Westminster Palace**, usually in November each year, to declare each session of Parliament open. Since 1852, Kings and Queens have travelled to the event in the Irish State Coach (bought by Queen Victoria specifically for the occasion), flanked by heralds and pursuivants.

The Foot Guards and cavalry of the **Household Division** form a guard of honor for dignitaries, who include the Earl Marshal, a hereditary post (held by the Dukes of Norfolk) that involves responsibility for all state ceremonial events. When the royal party reaches the Houses of Parliament (*see* **Palace of Westminster**), it enters by the Victoria Tower then makes its way to the Robing Room before processing to the House of Lords. Members of Parliament (MPs) are summoned from the House of Commons by the Gentleman Usher of the Black Rod, who has the door slammed in his face three times as a reminder of the elected body's independence, then, when the whole group is assembled (with the MPs standing and the Lords seated), the sovereign reads a speech that is written by the government and outlines its intentions for the coming session.

STEELYARD. The London center of the Hanseatic League stood on the north bank of the **River Thames**, taking its name from the large scales used to weigh imports. The League was created from 1241 as the Hansas (groups of German merchants trading with foreign countries) formed alliances with the ports from which they operated in order to further their commercial interests and restrict piracy. It reached the height of its power during the 14th century but was much resented by Londoners, partly because members of the League did not mix with representatives of other business interests in the city and partly because they had privileges not accorded to local people (they did not have to pay rent on the Steelyard, for example). In 1551, King Edward VI confiscated their property and revoked the privileges, then, in 1598, Queen Elizabeth I expelled them. The Steelyard was converted into a storehouse for the Royal Navy and burned down in the **Great Fire** of 1666. In 1865, **Cannon Street Station** was built on the site.

STEPNEY. Stepney forms part of London's working-class **East End**, lying some 3.5 miles from **Charing Cross**. Although settled by the Romans, the area remained agricultural until the 16th century, when buildings spread along the north bank of the **River Thames** as the **City of London** expanded beyond its defensive walls. From 1802, when the West India Dock opened on the **Isle of Dogs**, the area experienced a rapid influx of **immigrants** from other parts of the British Isles as well as from abroad, many of them unskilled and poor. The clothing industry was also an important source of employment but wages were low, so workers crammed into small, overcrowded houses, where infectious disease spread easily and educational standards were low. German attempts to bomb riverside industries during the **Blitz** caused much damage to residential property (one in three homes was destroyed) but left many sites available for redevelopment when the Second World War ended. Stepney was incorporated within the **London Borough of Tower Hamlets** when the metropolitan area's **local government** was reorganized in 1965 and, since then, has been the focus of many urban renewal programs, which have reduced populations and replaced 19th-century slums with modern **housing**.

STOCK EXCHANGE (LSE). The origins of the London Stock Exchange—the most important in the world for international business—lie in the city's 17th- and 18th-century **coffee houses**, where brokers sold stocks and shares to private buyers. In 1773, a group of these brokers purchased a **Threadneedle Street** building, which they called the Stock Exchange, opened it to members (who paid a daily subscription), and organized regulatory committees. Disputes over the rules led, in 1801, to a breakaway movement, which involved some 500 traders, who established their own Exchange at Capel Court (off Old Broad Street, in the **City of London**), with its own governing bodies. The capital generated by the Industrial Revolution contributed to their success, so, by 1850, their numbers had grown to well over 800 and, by 1905, to more than 5,500. In addition, regional cities established their own exchanges around Britain.

The 20th century brought a series of alterations to operating procedures, including the admission of women as members (in 1973) and the amalgamation of London with the provincial United Kingdom exchanges and the Dublin exchange as the International Stock Exchange of the United Kingdom and the Republic of Ireland (also in 1973). In 1979, the abolition of foreign exchange controls enabled British savings institutions to invest money overseas in non-UK securities, initiating competition with foreign brokers, then, during the 1980s, following government pressure, major changes to the rules were made in order to increase trade (and alter the widely held public view that the institution was a **gentlemen's club** that had adopted a whole range of restrictive practices). In particular, the LSE was converted, in 1986, from an association of members into a nonprofit-making limited company, with individual firms becoming shareholders, each with a single vote. The separation between brokers (who bought or sold on behalf of clients) and jobbers (who acted as middlemen between brokers) was ended, promoting merger of financial services companies, and outside concerns were permitted to take over member businesses, enabling them to increase their capital base. Also in 1986, the traditional face-to-face dealing on the trading floor was replaced by a computerized technology (known as SEAQ—the Stock Exchange Automated Quotations service), which allowed quotes to be displayed on screens and deals to be confirmed by telephone.

In 1991, the governing Council was replaced by a Board of Directors, with a membership drawn from several sources, including the LSE's customers. Then, in 1995, in response to a European Union directive that each state must have its own statutory regulation, Dublin business was redirected to a new exchange in the Irish Republic. In combination, the reforms swept away much of the excitement and tradition (including the attendants, who had been known as waiters since the coffee house days), but they introduced up-to-date business practices. In 1998, it announced an alliance with the Deutsche Borse in Frankfurt, but plans for a full merger proved controversial and were abandoned two years later. A major shake-up of the board, the appointment of Clara Furse (formerly of Crédit Lyonnais Rouse) as chief executive, and a decision to list the Exchange on its own market followed in 2001. (*See also* BIG BANG.)

STOKE NEWINGTON. Archaeological studies suggest that Stoke Newington, located four miles northeast of **Charing Cross**, was populated as early as Palaeolithic times. The site of a Saxon settlement, it was (according to legend) given by King Aethelstan to the monks of **St. Paul's Cathedral** in 939. By the 18th century, it had evolved into a sizable agricultural village, providing a particular attraction for nonconformists, who were not allowed to take up residence in the **City of London** because they refused to worship in the Church of England. One of them—author Daniel Defoe—went to school in Stoke Newington and gave the surname of Thomas Cruso, his classmate, to the hero of the novel, *Robinson Crusoe*, published in 1719. Isaac Watts (who wrote *When I Survey the Wondrous Cross* and other hymns), essayist William Hazlitt, and short story writer Edgar Allan Poe were also educated in the area, which still retains its dissenting tradition. During the 18th century, London began a process of encroachment that would ultimately engulf the community. In the early phase, a series of substantial mansions were built to house affluent families, then, from 1830, **Thomas Cubitt** erected large villas in the Greek Revival style popular at the time, and, after 1860, developers designed more modest terraced homes, filling the remaining open spaces. In the second half of the 20th century, local authorities undertook a number of urban renewal programs and the area became the focus for small groups of **immigrants** from the Caribbean, India, and the Turkish sector of Cyprus. Stoke Newington was included within the **London Borough of Hackney** when **local government** in the metropolitan area was reformed in 1965. (*See also* KRAY TWINS.)

STOW, JOHN (c.1525–1605). Stow's *Survey of London*, published in 1598, provides scholars with a detailed account of the city's buildings and businesses in the late Elizabethan period of transition from medieval to modern. Stow lived his entire life in London. Born in the parish of St. Michael, **Cornhill**, he is known to have had an address in **Aldgate** in 1549 and then to have moved to Leadenhall Street, where he remained for the rest of his life. Nothing is known of his parents, though some writers conjecture that his father was a tailor because Stow followed that trade, establishing a prosperous business until, from about 1560, he turned increasingly to writing and to collecting documents dealing with English history. In 1561, he published an edition of the works of Geoffrey Chaucer, then, in 1565, completed a *Summarie of Englyshe Chronicles*, which included the names, and periods in office, of "all the Bylyffes, Maiors, and Sheriffes of the Citie of London Sens the Conquest" and was regularly updated over the next 40 years. The 1598 *Survey* (which was revised and enlarged in 1603) described the city's foundation and growth, listed details of monuments and buildings, outlined urban customs, and provided insights into the habits and occupations of the citizenry. Modern historians regard the painstaking work as accurate but, at the time, Stow's honesty and diligence were much impugned by rivals. In 1562, for example, Richard Grafton, with a pun designed to deceive nobody, scoffed (in his *Abridgement of the Chronicles of England*) at the "memories of superstitious foundations, fables, and lyes foolishly stowed together." Stow was well able to defend himself, however, responding in 1567 with a similarly obvious swipe at the "thundering noise of empty tonnes and unfruitful graftes of Momus' offspring."

As his passion for history and for recording the events of his day consumed more and more of his time, Stow wandered the country, collecting texts and talking to the great men of the period, including playwright **Ben Jonson** and Archbishop of Canterbury Matthew Parker (who employed him to edit some medieval papers). Inevitably, his business suffered and he became increasingly dependent on charity. Moreover, his Roman Catholic leanings led to accusations of disloyalty by government officials sworn to defend the reformed Church of England, so he was called, on several occasions, to face courts of inquiry. He appears, however, to have accepted the vicissitudes with good grace and survived to see the succession of King James VI and I when he was nearly 80. Stow died on 6 April 1605 and was buried in **St. Andrew Undershaft Church** near his Leadenhall Street home.

STRAND. Running for three-quarters of a mile westward from the **Royal Courts of Justice** to **Trafalgar Square**, the Strand links London's commercial core in **The City** to the political complex at **Whitehall**. Originally a path running alongside the **River Thames**, it attracted residential development as early as the 12th century and by the Elizabethan period was lined with the mansions of bishops and courtiers (*see*, for example, **Somerset House**). By the time King George I ascended the throne in 1714, it had become well known for its **coffee shops**, many of them frequented by the metropolitan literati, such as **James Boswell**, who picked up his prostitutes from the plentiful supply in neighboring alleys. Redevelopment began around **Charing Cross** in the 1830s and spread along the street to include construction of **hotels** such as the Savoy (1884), several restaurants (including Simpson's, opened in 1904), and numerous **theater**s, of which only the Vaudeville (which presented its first performance in 1870), the Savoy (which was originally built in 1881), and the Adelphi (now in a building dating from 1930) remain. During the second half of the 20th century, further reconstruction involved the erection of administrative accommodation for commercial, government, and educational interests, but the road is still lined with cafeterias and specialist shops (such as the stamp dealer Stanley Gibbons). (*See also* ST. CLEMENT DANES CHURCH, STRAND; WATERLOO.)

STRATFORD. A mixed residential and industrial area in the northwest of the **London Borough of Newham**, Stratford takes its name from Stratford Langthorne Abbey, which was founded by William de Montfichet in 1135 and became one of the richest Cistercian **monasteries** in the country. The processing and manufacturing activities were begun by the monks, who built mills along the banks of the **River Lea**, and continued after the abbey's dissolution in 1538 with the development of gunpowder works, distilleries, textile printing shops, and porcelain furnaces. Then, in the 19th century, the Eastern Counties **Railway** made Stratford its major center for locomotive and rolling stock maintenance (1847) and facilitated the growth of a fruit and vegetable **market** from 1879. These sources of employment attracted a large working-class population, who found accommodation in densely packed streets of terraced houses (many of which were erected by the railway company). Little evidence of the area's early history remains (the abbey site is now covered by factories, for example), though a plaque in St. John's Church commemorates 18 Protestant martyrs burned at the stake in 1555–56 for refusing to give up their beliefs.

STRAWBERRY HILL. In 1747, author Horace Walpole, Earl of Oxford, acquired a small property overlooking the **River Thames** at **Twickenham**. For over 40 years, he worked on the building, converting it into a Gothic castle with battlements, molded ceilings, and quatrefoil windows. To assist him, he appointed a Committee of Taste, which scoured pictures of other structures, identified architectural features that seemed attractive, and adapted them to suit his needs. Thus, one of the chimney pieces was modelled on details of Edward the Confessor's tomb in **Westminster Abbey** and another on that of Archbishop Wareham in Canterbury Cathedral. Friends were commissioned to find appropriate furnishings and detailed inventories kept of all acquisitions. In 1757, Walpole installed a printing press in the house and published many of his own works (notably the novel *Castle of Otranto* in 1765) as well as those of other writers, such as poet Thomas Gray's Pindaric *Odes* (1757). After his death, the estate passed through the hands of several owners before it was inherited by Frances, Countess Waldegrave, in 1846. She enlarged the building to make it more appropriate for grand receptions, then, for 30 years, held gatherings attended by the major political figures of the mid-Victorian era. In 1923, the house was bought by the Catholic Education Council and turned into a teacher training college, which was later integrated with the University of Surrey.

STREATHAM. Streatham lies towards the southern end of the **London Borough of Lambeth**. During late Saxon times, it was the property of the Abbey of Chertsey but, after the Norman Conquest in 1066, was given to Richard of Tonbridge (a cousin of King William I), who gifted it to the Benedictine order. Although Streatham gained the right to hold a fair in the 13th century, the small settlement experienced little development until 1659, when a ploughman discovered a spring with waters, which, doctors declared, had medicinal qualities. Crowds flocked to the village, which developed a considerable reputation as a spa, attracting **Huguenot** weavers fleeing persecution in France and London merchants seeking suitable locations for their country homes. The latter included the Thrales, who had made their wealth from **breweries** and, in 1740, built Streatham Place, which became a favorite haunt of actor **David Garrick**, writer **Samuel Johnson** (who conducted chemistry experiments in an oven in the garden), playwright and poet Oliver Goldsmith, artist Joshua Reynolds, and other representatives of the arts. During the Georgian and Victorian periods, **transport** links improved, encouraging further immigration, notably after the opening of the **railway** station in 1856. By 1881, the population had reached 20,000 and, by 1901, had soared to 70,000. Agricultural land was covered by houses, roads, and commercial properties, a process that continued into the second half of the 20th century as Streatham earned a reputation as an entertainment focus (with an ice rink as well as a dance hall, a theater, and cinemas) and became a suburb within the metropolitan area rather than an independent community.

STREET LIGHTING. Until the early 19th century, the darkness of the London night was relieved only by candles flickering in windows, oil lamps suspended over doorways, and the glimmer of the moon. In 1804, however, Frederick Winsor (a German immigrant) formed the New Light and Heat Company and, three years later, provided a demonstration of **gas** lighting on the north side of **Pall Mall** in celebration of the birthday of the Prince of Wales (later King George IV). The Prince gave his enthusiastic support to advocates of the new fuel, a patronage that helped lead to the formation of the Gas Light and Coke Company, which, in 1812, received the rights to light streets in the **City of London**, **Southwark**, and **Westminster**. Lamps were placed on **Westminster Bridge** in 1814 and the rest of the central city soon followed. By 1840, a dozen firms employed an army of 380 lamplighters to light the burners at dusk and shut them off at dawn, though some communities (such as the aristocratic residents of **Grosvenor Square**) resisted the newfangled technology. Initially, the lamps were simply open flames that were frequently blown out by winds, but, from 1885, changes in design greatly improved the efficiency of the system. By that time, however, gas was giving way to **electricity**. Westminster Bridge was lit by electricity as early as 1858, but its use was limited until vacuum bulbs with incandescent carbon filaments were introduced in 1878–82. During the 20th century, gas lighting was gradually superseded by the more reliable, and increasingly sophisticated, electric systems, though some lamps in the area near **Temple Church** were hand lit as late as 1986.

STREET MARKETS. Until the second half of the 19th century, most Londoners did their shopping at street **markets** or with street traders. As late as 1851, the census showed that more than 30,000 people in the city earned a living as costermongers, selling fish, vegetables, meat, and other products from barrows. Usually, they announced their presence with shouted cries or some other noise (such as the handbell of the muffin man). The markets, where traders congregated, developed from the tradition of fairs (such as **Bartholomew Fair**), which were sanctioned by the authorities from as early as the 12th century but suppressed from the Georgian period, often because of **crime** and other antisocial behavior with which they became associated. The Industrial Revolution dealt a further blow, introducing mass-produced products more easily sold in department stores than at roadside stalls. And, more recently, a welter of legislation governing food hygiene has forced many of the barrow boys out of business. However, the hot chestnut man still sells his wares during the winter months, office workers buy their lunch from street traders in **Oxford Street** throughout the year, and Tubby Isaac's whelk bar offers jellied eels in Goulston Street. Also, the open air market tradition has survived, supported by increasing numbers of bargain-seeking tourists. **Petticoat Lane**, with its **Cockney** traders, offers a wide range of fruit, vegetables, clothing, and domestic goods, as does East Street (near **Elephant and Castle**). **Brixton** and **Shepherd's Bush** have become well known for their West Indian products, **Portobello Road Market** and the New Caledonian Market in **Bermondsey** Square for antiques, Leather Lane for crockery, Columbia Road for house plants, and Camden Lock (*see* **Camden Town**) on the **Regent's Canal** for bric-a-brac, including books and records. (*See also* LAMBETH WALK; RAG FAIR.)

SURBITON. Surbiton, located some 12 miles southwest of **Charing Cross**, owes its existence to the **railway**. When local authorities in **Kingston Upon Thames** refused to allow railway developments, the transport companies swung their routes south, opening a station at rural Surbiton in 1838. The improved access to the **City of London** attracted wealthy businessmen and -women, who built substantial villas in the area, earning it a reputation for affluence that it still retains. The suburb expanded rapidly, gaining borough status in 1938 and becoming part of the **London Borough of Kingston Upon Thames** in 1965. During the second half of the 20th century, many of the larger houses were converted into offices, but in the churches of St. Andrew, St. Mark, St. Matthew, and St. Raphael it retains some of the best small-scale

Victorian church **architecture** in the city. Also, a number of residential neighborhoods are protected from development by conservation legislation. (*See also* BARNARDO, THOMAS JOHN.)

SUTTON. Sutton, some 10 miles southwest of **Charing Cross**, was probably settled by Saxon immigrants during the sixth or seventh century (its name is derived from the Old English *sudtuna* or "southern settlement") but remained an agricultural village until the **railway** spurred urban development from 1847. During the second half of the 19th century, developers built **housing** for all classes of society, and private benefactors contributed to the establishment of institutions such as Thomas Wall's adult and nursery schools, opened in 1895 and 1909 respectively. Residential growth continued into the 20th century, so, in 1965, when the town became the administrative heart of the new **London Borough of Sutton**, a major program of urban reconstruction was initiated, with a new civic center, offices, and retail units opening in 1965 and an additional shopping mall added in 1991. As a result, little evidence of the old village remains, but St. Nicholas Church, founded in the seventh century, has survived, although it was substantially rebuilt to Edwin Nash's designs in 1862–44.

SUTTON, LONDON BOROUGH OF. The London Borough of Sutton lies on the southern rim of the London conurbation. Created in 1965, when **local government** in the metropolitan area was reformed, it consists of a series of small towns and villages covering some 17 square miles of what was previously part of the County of Surrey. Although there are several big employers (such as Reed Business Publishing, Canon, and Securicor), the borough is largely residential, with a high proportion of white-collar workers, particularly in **Sutton** and in **Cheam**. For many of the 177,100 residents (1998), the principal attraction is the quality of life, with regular rail services to central London, easy access to the M25 motorway and Gatwick **Airport**, and large areas of open space (including the **North Downs**) within easy reach.

SWEENEY TODD. Sweeney Todd is probably a mythical figure who set up a barber's shop at 186 **Fleet Street** then killed his customers, passing their bodies to his neighbor, Mrs. Lovett, who used them as the principal ingredient for meat pies, which earned a reputation as the best in London. The character first appears in the story "A String of Pearls," which was printed in *The People's Periodical and Family Library* in 1846. A dramatized version of the tale was staged at the Britannia Theatre the following year and caught the public imagination, so, in succeeding decades, the details of the enterprising business were fashioned and refashioned in various forms. For over a century, Sweeney was presented as an unlovely individual but, in 1973, Christopher Bond recast him in a more sympathetic light, suggesting that he was the victim of society because his wife and daughter were taken from him by a lecherous judge and that he was cast into jail unjustly. That version of the story was turned into a musical by Stephen Sondheim, Harold Prince, and Hugh Wheeler in 1979, winning eight Tony awards but, by Broadway standards, failing at the box office. It is not known whether the original character was solely a figment of a penny dreadful writer's imagination but, in 1880, when houses at the western end of Fleet Street were demolished during an urban renewal program, piles of human bones were discovered in a pit beneath No. 186.

SWISS COTTAGE. The area northwest of **Primrose Hill**, on the fringe of central London, developed from 1826, when a turnpike road was opened to link **Regent's Park** to **Hampstead**. An alpine style inn, erected beside the toll gate, gave the area its name. As transport links improved, the largely agricultural landscape was increasingly urbanized, particularly after a **bus** terminus was established in 1859 and a station for the **London Underground**'s Metropolitan Line was built in 1868. Expansion continued during the 20th century, enmeshing the suburb in the metropolitan area, so in 1965, it was absorbed by the **London Borough of Camden**. Still essentially residential, it houses the Hampstead Public Library, designed by Basil Spence and constructed in 1964. Sigmund Freud, who developed the science of psychoanalysis, lived nearby at 20 Maresfield Gardens (*see* **Freud's House.**)

SYDENHAM. Sydenham lies some six miles southeast of **Charing Cross**. Throughout the Middle Ages, it had low populations, serving largely as grazing land and a source of firewood. From the mid-17th century, however, the allegedly medicinal properties of local springs attracted crowds of visitors, many of whom built country homes in the area. In 1810, as agricultural practices changed, the open common was enclosed by hedges, then increasingly sold to builders. Lower Sydenham developed as a working-class area, with Upper Sydenham, higher on the hill slopes, attracting more wealthy families, particularly after 1854, when the erection of the **Crystal Palace** to the south enhanced its fashionable status.

Explorer Ernest Shackleton lived at 12 Westwood Hill and John Logie Baird (the first man to transmit television pictures) at 3 Crescent Wood Road, but, as the 20th century progressed and the metropolitan area expanded, many of the more affluent families moved further into the countryside, and Sydenham evolved into a residential suburb with a high proportion of residents commuting to work in central London. Office accommodation and retail developments increasingly infiltrated after the Second World War and local authorities used some of the remaining open space for public **housing**, but the site of the wells that originally promoted urban growth remains, converted into a municipal **park**. Sydenham was incorporated within the **London Borough of Lewisham** in 1965.

SYON HOUSE. Syon House overlooks the west bank of the **River Thames** near **Brentford**, in west London. It stands on the site of a Bridgettine **monastery,** which was founded by King Henry V in 1415 but appropriated in 1534 by King Henry VIII, who confined his fifth wife, Catherine Howard, in the building before her execution in 1542. Five years later, while Henry's body was lying in state overnight at Syon, his coffin burst open and, some hours later, dogs were discovered consuming his remains. When Edward VI succeeded to the throne in 1547, the estate passed to Edward, Duke of Somerset (who erected a house), then, following his execution in 1552, it was acquired by John Dudley. It was there, the following year, that Lady Jane Grey, Dudley's daughter-in-law, was offered the Crown of England, beginning a reign that lasted for only nine days. In 1594, Syon was leased to the Percy family, heirs to the Dukedom of Northumberland, who have made it their home ever since.

Under successive Dukes, the house has taken the form of a block, some 140 feet square, built round an open courtyard and with a turret at each corner. **Inigo Jones** designed an arcade for the east side in 1632, then, from 1761, **Robert Adam** transformed the interior by creating a suite of rooms, which included a great hall, a dining room, a drawing room (with crimson silk wall hangings), and a gallery that runs for the full length of the east front. Further alterations were made during the 19th century, when a conservatory was added and the north front rebuilt then faced with Bath stone. Many of the furnishings, which include 17th-century portraits of members of the royal family, were brought from a Percy property, which was demolished to make way for the construction of Northumberland Avenue. The gardens, laid out between 1767–73 by Capability Brown, were opened to the public in 1834 and now house a large motor

museum (which contains British vehicles dating from 1895) and a butterfly exhibition. (*See also* LONDON TRANSPORT MUSEUM.)

– T –

TATE GALLERY. The Tate was opened in 1897, when sugar refiner Sir Henry Tate gifted his collection of 65 paintings to the nation and financed the construction of exhibition rooms at Millbank (on the north shore of the **River Thames** near **Vauxhall** Bridge amidst the middle-class homes erected by **Thomas Cubitt** during the 1840s). An additional wing was provided by art dealer Sir Joseph Duveen for J. M. W. Turner's works, which had previously hung at the **National Gallery**. Extensions to the property were added in 1926 and 1937 (both funded by Duveen's son, who was later made Lord Duveen of Millbank), in 1979 (when the Gulbenkian Foundation paid a large part of the building costs), and in 1987 (when donations from the family and charitable foundation of property developer Charles Clore provided cash for new halls in which the Turners could be displayed). The gallery housed a British Collection (which included paintings, drawings, engravings, and sculptures from c.1550 to c.1900) and a Modern Collection (which concentrated on British artists working from about 1880 and foreign artists from the time of the French impressionists in the late 19th century). Initially, the two foci were considered distinct, but in 1989, the exhibits were rearranged into a single chronological sequence tracing the development of British art and its associations with foreign schools during the 20th century. In 2000, however, they were separated again when the representatives of modern art from 1900 (including Matisse, Picasso, Salvador Dalí, and the Cubists) were rehoused in the former **Bankside** Power Station, which was renamed Tate Modern. The British painters (including William Hogarth, Joshua Reynolds, Thomas Gainsborough, William Blake, John Constable, Edwin Landseer, and the pre-Raphaelites) remained at the Millbank site, which was rechristened Tate Britain. In its last full year on a single London site, the Tate attracted 1.8 million visitors.

TAXIS. In 1897, mechanically driven taxicabs began to compete with the horse-drawn carriages that had transported city dwellers for hundreds of years. Powered by electricity, they could travel for about 30 miles before their batteries needed recharging, but were extremely unreliable. Tires quickly wore out and vibration caused both an uncomfortable ride and mechanical problems, so, within three years, they had vanished. However, the disappearance provided only a temporary stay of execution for the horses. From 1904, petrol-driven vehicles became increasingly popular (there were 8,397 registered in 1914), gradually replacing the slower, more uncomfortable hansom cabs, which finally disappeared in 1947. In 1906, the Metropolitan **Police** drew up a set of regulations for the new form of transport. One of these rules stipulated that taxis must have a turning circle of no more than 25 feet; that regulation is still in force and accounts for the legendary maneuverability of the vehicles. Before they are allowed to pick up passengers, drivers must undergo exacting tests on "the knowledge"—a corpus of information that involves map-like understanding of street patterns and destinations within six miles of **Charing Cross**. They are also required to be physically fit and to meet high character standards. Over 20,000 of those who have qualified are active, using about 17,000 taxis, most of them diesel powered. In recent years, to the annoyance of traditionalists, many of the vehicles have replaced the traditional black coloring with advertisements. (*See also* TRANSPORT.)

TEA AUCTIONS. *See* LONDON TEA AUCTIONS.

TELEVISION CENTRE. *See* BRITISH BROADCASTING CORPORATION (BBC).

TEMPLE BAR. Temple Bar marks the western limit of the **City of London**, taking its name from nearby land formerly owned by the **Knights Templar**. Records from the later 13th century indicated that it was originally a simple chain attached to wooden posts, but by 1351 a larger gateway had been constructed. It was repaired on several occasions, then rebuilt in the 1670s to designs prepared by **Christopher Wren** and, from 1684 until 1746, used to mount the heads of traitors. By 1878, complaints about traffic congestion led to the dismantling of the obstruction and its transfer to the Hertfordshire estate of Sir Henry Bruce Meux. A memorial marking the original site of Temple Bar was erected in 1880. In 1588, when Queen Elizabeth I was on her way to a service in **St. Paul's Cathedral**, where she gave thanks for the defeat of the Spanish Armada, her entourage passed through the gate. Ever since, when a monarch has had to enter The City on state occasions, a ceremony has been held at the site; the sovereign asks for permission to pass through, the **Lord Mayor** presents his sword as a token of loyalty, and the weapon is returned to indicate that the head of the realm is under his protection.

TEMPLE CHURCH. In 1185, the **Knights Templar** erected a circular church on the north shore of the **River Thames**, just under a mile east of **Charing Cross**. According to some scholars, the design reflects that of the church of the Holy Sepulcher in Jerusalem; others claim that the Dome of the Rock was a more likely model. Dedicated to the Blessed Mary, the building was consecrated by Heraclius (Roman Catholic Patriarch of Jerusalem) at a service attended by King Henry II. It made much use of Purbeck marble (the first time the stone had been used extensively in London) and was extended in 1220–40 by the addition of a rectangular choir and a small chapel with a crypt where initiation rights were performed. When the Knights were disbanded in 1312, the land was given to the **Knights Hospitaller**, who leased it to lawyers. It was acquired by the Crown during the reign of King Henry VIII but, in 1608, King James VI and I gave the freehold jointly to the Inner Temple and the Middle Temple (*see* **Inns of Court**) on condition that they maintained the fabric, and the religious services, for all time. The church, a mixture of Norman and Gothic styles, was badly damaged on 10 May 1941, the last night of the **Blitz**, but restored under the direction of Walter Godfrey after the Second World War. Technically, it is a Royal Peculiar, a status that makes its clergy answerable to the monarch and the Archbishop of Canterbury rather than to the Bishop of London.

TEMPLE OF MITHRAS. In 1889, suspicions that a temple might lie under the streets of the **City of London** were aroused when a relief of Mithras, the Persian god of light, was discovered in the **Walbrook**. Those suspicions were confirmed in 1954, during redevelopment of a section of Queen Victoria Street, when excavations by Professor W. F. Grimes revealed a temple, known as the Mithraeum and built by the Romans during the second century. Mithras was an important rival to Jesus Christ in the Roman world but, even so, his place of worship bears a distinct resemblance to a Christian church, with an entrance to the east, a nave, and a raised sanctuary. Its discovery so caught the public's imagination that the building was reconstructed in front of Bucklesbury House, the office block built on the site. It is on permanent view to visitors but an unreliable guide to the original (the floor is modern paving rather than earth, for example, and the open location is the antithesis of the original, underground sanctum). Sculptures and other artefacts (including a silver incense box) found during the excavation are on display in the **Museum of London**.

THAMES, RIVER. The Thames, which flows through the center of London, rises in the Cotswold Hills (in the west of England) and flows eastward for 210 miles to the North Sea. Only the final 65 miles are tidal. The river was named Tamesis by Julius Caesar but is variously spelled in documents, with Tamis, Tamisa, and Tamensim common. The banks consist largely of clays and unconsolidated sediments, leaving only one point—on the south bank at **Southwark** and on the north bank immediately opposite—where the technology available to the Romans allowed bridge construction along the tidal stretch. Roads converged at the wooden crossing point, a small port developed, and the settlement eventually evolved into **Londinium**. In 1197, the **Corporation of London** paid King Richard I a sum of 1,500 marks for the right to control the river, then, for centuries, entrepreneurs siphoned off the flow, filled containers, and sold water from door to door along the city streets. Boats carried goods of all kinds from sellers to buyers, with barges able to travel as far upriver as Oxford by 1624.

Navigation improved with the construction of locks between Staines and Teddington in 1810–15, but disputes were common, particularly over fishing rights. The friction came to a head during the 1830s, when the Crown claimed ownership of the river banks and bed between the ebb and flow of the tides. The City initially disputed the claim but eventually conceded defeat, enabling Parliament to enact legislation forming a Board of Conservancy in 1857. Nine years later, that body was reformed as the Thames Conservancy Board and given authority over the entire navigable area of the river. Further change in 1908 awarded the **Port of London Authority** control from Teddington to the river mouth and the Conservancy Board responsibility for the remainder of the waterway. Both, however, lost some of their power following the passage of the Water Act (1973) which created the Thames Water Authority (TWA), giving it supremacy over other organizations in the river's 5,000-square mile catchment and requiring it to manage the entire water cycle, making provision for supply, **sewage disposal**, prevention of **water pollution**, and recreational facilities. The same legislation established a National Rivers Authority, whose Thames Region deals with drainage, navigation, fisheries, and **flood control**.

Until the 20th century, the river was a major routeway, developing extensive **docks**, particularly downriver from **London Bridge**. However, most of the ferries have vanished (the exceptions are those which ply between Woolwich and North Woolwich and between Gravesend and Tilbury), as has the bulk of the local industrial traffic. A water bus service takes passengers from **Greenwich** to **Putney**, stopping at piers en route, but an increasing number of the boats are recreational. Yachts crowd into St. Katharine's Marina in the redeveloped **Docklands**, and particularly during the summer months, larger vessels take tourists on outings to centers such as **Kew**. (*See also* BRIDGES; DOGGETT'S COAT AND BADGE RACE; FROST FAIRS; GREAT STINK; ROYAL NAVAL DOCKYARDS; WATER SUPPLY.)

THAMES BARRIER. *See* FLOOD CONTROL.

THAMESMEAD. Shortly after its formation in 1965, the **Greater London Council (GLC)** prepared plans to drain 1,600 acres of marshland on the south bank of the **River Thames** near **Abbey Wood** and create a new suburb that could house 100,000 people, with transport links to the central city and extensive provision for community activities. The first homes, however, were built of precast concrete blocks in skyscraper developments, which proved hard to maintain and were prone to dampness. Although advertised as "the city of the 21st century," they seemed soulless to many critics (and certainly to movie producer Stanley Kubrick, who used Thamesmead as the location for *A Clockwork Orange*, the violent futuristic movie filmed in 1971). By 1974, only 12,000 residents had moved in, so planners abandoned high-rise construction and made greater use of brick in an attempt to produce a more welcoming environment. At the dismemberment of the GLC in 1986, administrative responsibilities passed to a private company, but new management failed to cure the malaise as complaints about high rents and poor provision of services mounted, so, in 1999, the town was split into three units, each run by an Estate Management Board. At the end of the century, the population numbered only 30,000 and the yachting marina, commuter boat service, and other facilities envisaged in the early plans had still not materialized. (*See also* BEXLEY, LONDON BOROUGH OF.)

THEATER. London's first playhouse (known as The Theatre) was built at **Shoreditch** in 1576 (prior to that, dramatic performances had been presented at alehouses or churches). A second (The Curtain) opened nearby the following year, but the regulations imposed by the **Corporation of London** encouraged managers to move across the **River Thames** to the more liberal environment of **Southwark**. By 1600, a sizable entertainment complex had evolved in **Bankside**, with the **Globe Theatre**, the Rose, and the Swan attracting large audiences to performances of works by **William Shakespeare** and his contemporaries. All of the buildings were made of wood and operated as theaters in the round, with tiered rows of seats facing inward to a central stage. Mid-century Puritan authorities, led by Oliver Cromwell, enforced their closure, but from about 1660 they began to reappear north of the river, particularly around **Covent Garden** (*see*, for example, **Theatre Royal**). Revivals of Shakespeare's plays and dramatizations of works by popular authors such as Walter Scott created a large Victorian demand for popular entertainment, resulting in the construction of new playhouses and refurbishment of the old. As a result, many of London's largest commercial theaters date from the late 19th or early 20th century, including the Criterion (which has an 1870s interior), the Albery (which opened in 1903 and has a distinctive Edwardian design), and the Palladium (which presented its first performance in 1910). More recently, the **Royal National Theatre** (completed in 1976) and the **Barbican** Centre (opened in 1982) have added modern venues. About 40 companies present plays regularly in the **West End**, with countless other repertory groups, amateur dramatic societies, and pub players adding to the variety in other parts of the city. Many suburban locations, such as **Richmond** and **Wimbledon**, have their own theaters, which are usually subsidized by local authorities and present plays before they appear in the big cities. (*See also* BLACKFRIARS; GOLDERS GREEN; HAYMARKET; HENSLOWE, PHILIP; HOXTON; LEICESTER SQUARE; LLOYD WEBBER, ANDREW; *MOUSETRAP, THE*; MUSIC HALLS; OLD VIC; REGENT'S PARK; ROYAL ACADEMY OF DRAMATIC ART [RADA]; SADLER'S WELLS; SHAFTESBURY AVENUE; STRAND; SWEENEY TODD; THEATRE MUSEUM.)

THEATRE MUSEUM. Proposals for a **museum** displaying the story of British **theater** were first advanced by Laurence Irving (grandson of actor Henry Irving) in 1955. Following a series of donations, displays were mounted at a site in **Kensington** in 1963. The exhibits were taken over by the **Victoria and Albert Museum** eight years later, then, in 1987, transferred to the basement of the former **Covent Garden** flower **market** in Tavistock Street. The core of the collection is the Irving Archives, the Gabrielle Enthoven collection of playbills and programs (which include items from the 1920s), and material from the Richard Buckle Museum of Performing Arts. Paintings, scripts, costumes, stage designs, prompt copies, and other material are used to illustrate the development of London's entertainment complex and the contributions of individual actors, producers, and impresarios.

THEATRE ROYAL, DRURY LANE. In 1663, a **theater** was built in **Drury Lane** (near **Covent Garden**), but it survived for only nine years before being burned down. Its replacement, designed by **Christopher Wren**, provided the stage where, in 1742, **David Garrick** made his debut, then, over the next 30 years, built a reputation for Shakespearean drama (Sarah Siddons made a less successful first appearance as Portia in *The Merchant of Venice* in 1775). In 1776, Garrick retired and dramatist Richard Brinsley Sheridan took over, commissioning Henry Holland to redesign the building in 1794. On 24 February 1809, that structure, too, was destroyed by fire. (Sheridan sat in a nearby **coffee house** philosophically drinking port; "Surely," he said, "a man may take a glass of wine by his own fireside.") The fourth building, which still stands, was modelled on the theater in Bordeaux (France), designed by Benjamin Wyatt, and completed in 1812. James Spiller added a porch in 1820 and Samuel Beazley gave the eastern front a colonnade of pillars in 1831. During the 20th century, it has become best known for its musicals (*My Fair Lady* ran for 2,281 performances from 30 April 1958). The maximum audience is 2,188 people and one ghost, which appears in the Circle at matinees (it is believed that the apparition dates from 1840, when the skeleton of a man with a knife in his ribs was discovered behind a wall). In 2000, the venue was acquired by **Andrew Lloyd Webber** through the purchase of the Stoll Moss company. (*See also* PUGIN, AUGUSTUS WELBY NORTHMORE.)

THREADNEEDLE STREET. This 500-yard-long street in the heart of the **City of London** is best known as the home of the **Bank of England**. The road may get its name from the needle and thread used by the Merchant Taylors and the Needlemakers (two of the **livery companies**). In 1243, a community of French Protestants, known as the Hospital of St. Anthony, was established on the north side of the street to give aid to travellers and collect alms. Two hundred years later, a school was attached to the site (Sir Thomas More, Lord Chancellor of England from 1529 to 1532 and King Henry VIII's man for all seasons, was educated there), but the buildings (apart from the chapel) were destroyed in the **Great Fire** of 1666. The southwestern end of the street was occupied by the **Royal Exchange** (whose first two premises were also burned down) in 1565, the **Stock Exchange** moved into offices farther to the east in 1733, and the Bank of England built its headquarters near the junction of Threadneedle and Princes Streets in 1734, expanding its location in 1765. Financial concerns, such as the Bank of Scotland, NatWest Bank, and the Midland Bank, now line most of the remainder of the pavement. (*See also* BALTIC EXCHANGE.)

TIMES, THE. England's oldest national daily newspaper was founded on 1 January 1785 by John Walter, a coal dealer and insurance underwriter who acquired the rights to use logotypes (fonts of words rather than letters). In an attempt to popularize the system, he bought a disused printing shop in **Blackfriars** and established the *Daily Universal Register*. The failure of the printing process encouraged him to concentrate on the broadsheet newspaper, which he renamed *The Times* in 1788. Under Thomas Barnes, editor from 1817 to 1841, the paper flourished, adopting an avowedly liberal political stance and earning a reputation as *The Thunderer* because of its impassioned advocacy of parliamentary reform. In 1853, it employed the world's first war correspondent (William Howard Russell), but by the end of the century was in considerable financial trouble, surviving only through the intervention of Alfred Harmsworth, Viscount Northcliffe, in 1908. Journalistic standards also left much to be desired until William Haley (then Director General of the **British Broadcasting Corporation**) was appointed editor in 1952 and adopted a more lively reporting style (which included replacing front page advertisements with news in 1966).

The acquisition of new production technologies provoked a lengthy dispute with the print unions, which resulted in suspension of publication in 1978–79. The bitterness continued after the business was acquired, in 1981, by Rupert Murdoch, who attempted to replace hot metal with computers in the publishing process. At the time, the newspaper industry was heavily overmanned and printers were able to command wages well beyond those of other employees in skilled trades. However, employers allowed the situation to continue because the high costs of production kept potential competitors from entering the industry. Murdoch changed the situation one weekend in January 1985, when he moved *The Times* from its headquarters near **Fleet Street** to a new plant at **Wapping**, where journalists could compose their stories on computer screens. The action provoked a violent response from the printers, who besieged the new site in a yearlong dispute marked by bitter clashes with the police, but were eventually forced to concede defeat (*see* **Wapping Dispute**). Since then, the newspaper has aggressively challenged its rivals in a price war. In addition to its conventional paper editions, it also publishes on an Internet site.

TOOTING. Throughout the Middle Ages, Tooting (which lies six miles south of **Charing Cross**) was owned by aristocratic and monastic interests. The economy was primarily agricultural until well into the 19th century, though wealthy Londoners built country mansions in the area from about 1715. Villa developments were common by 1850, encouraged by improving **transport** links with the central city, but urban expansion was limited until the **London County Council** erected a housing estate at Totterdown in the 1890s. Private construction companies followed, throwing up rows of small houses for working-class families. As the urban area expanded, Tooting was enmeshed in the metropolis, becoming part of the **London Borough of Wandsworth** in 1965, but some of the open space has survived, notably the 150 acres of Tooting Bec Common, where villagers once dug gravel and cut firewood.

TOTTENHAM. A suburb of densely packed, largely working-class **housing** located amidst pockets of light industrial activity, Tottenham lies some six miles north of **Charing Cross**. It was probably settled during Saxon times; the *Domesday Book*, King William I's record of property, indicates a population of about 60 farmers in 1086, and some scholars suggest that All Hallows Church was founded before the Norman Conquest 20 years earlier. The village developed during the Middle Ages and, by the early 17th century, had evolved into a relatively prosperous agricultural community, but that rural economy was swept away by the Industrial Revolution. In 1840, the Great Eastern **Railway** laid a line through the area, then, in 1872, publicized its services by offering workmen cheap transport to **Liverpool Street Station**. That promotion resulted in a vast increase in demand for houses, which builders satisfied by erecting rows of small terraced homes. These were followed by manufacturing premises, institutional developments (such as the Prince of Wales Hospital, opened in 1868), and recreational services (notably Tottenham Hotspur **Football** Club, formed in 1880 and now one of the great powers of English soccer), so, by 1920, the area was totally urbanized, leaving very limited open space. Tottenham was incorporated within the **London Borough of Haringey** when **local government** in the metropolitan area was reorganized in 1965. Since then, the local authority has undertaken several urban renewal projects, including the construction of public housing. Bruce Castle, a 13th-century structure originally owned by King Robert the Bruce of Scotland but confiscated by Edward I of England in 1306, was bought in 1827 by Rowland Hill (who invented adhesive stamps and founded the penny post system in 1840); it now functions as a **museum** of local and postal history and as the regimental museum of the Middlesex Regiment, which was raised in 1755, saw service in the Peninsular War (1808–14), the Zulu War (1879), and the Boer Wars (1880–81 and 1899–1902) but was absorbed in the Queen's Regiment in 1967.

TOURISM. Because of its role as a capital city, London has long catered to tourists. Initially, most of those who came to gaze were affluent representatives of foreign courts or dignitaries from other parts of the country, but improved mass **transport** systems (beginning with the development of the **railway** network in the 19th century), greater leisure time, and more widespread wealth have combined to widen the range of visitors and increase their numbers. By the mid-1990s, over 250 million people spent one night or more in the city each year, contributing £7.5 billion to the economy. About half were from overseas, with 17 percent of the foreign cohort from the United States and 10 percent from each of France and Germany. The most popular foci were the traditional attractions at the **British Museum** (which received over six million visitors a year), the **National Gallery** (5 million), **Madame Tussaud's Waxworks** (2.7 million), the **Tower of London** (2.6 million), and **Westminster Abbey** (2.5 million), but newer ventures, such as the World of Adventures theme park at **Chessington** (1.7 million), were experiencing increases in revenue as they became more widely known.

TOWER BRIDGE. The first and, until the Queen Elizabeth II Bridge was completed at Dartford in 1991, the only **bridge** to be built downstream of **London Bridge**, Tower Bridge is one of London's best-known landmarks. Designed by architect Horace Jones (who died before the work was completed) and engineer John Wolfe-Barry, it was opened in 1894, linking the commercial and industrial area around the **Tower of London** to the **Bermondsey** docks. Constructed of stone, with a steel skeleton, the bridge has two 200-foot-high Gothic towers, one at each end. Two walkways connect them 142 feet above high tide level. Underneath, bascules (in effect, a double drawbridge) can be raised to allow ships into the upper area of the **Pool of London** (this operation was electrified in 1976 but the original steam-powered machinery has been preserved). Suspension spans at the sides connect the towers to the river banks. In 1982, a **museum** was opened inside the bridge, allowing visitors to inspect the Victorian engines and view the river from the walkways, which have been enclosed in glass. (*See also* TRANSPORT.)

TOWER HAMLETS. During the Medieval period, the garrison in the **Tower of London** was responsible for the safety of surrounding communities. In 1564, a militia from the villages was formed in order to secure the settlements' defense, then, in 1605, the area north of the **River Thames** and east of the **City of London** was formally named Tower Hamlets for military purposes. A parliamentary borough with the same title was created in 1832, but secessions brought boundary changes and the unit was dissolved in 1918. However, when **local government** within the metropolitan area was reorganized in 1965, the traditional nomenclature was resurrected for the **London Borough of Tower Hamlets**.

TOWER HAMLETS, LONDON BOROUGH OF. The borough lies immediately east of the **City of London**, covering eight square miles of the **East End**. It was created in 1965 through the merger of **Bethnal Green**, **Poplar**, and **Stepney**, all of which were independent authorities during the **London County Council**'s jurisdiction. The great majority of the 170,500 residents (1998) are semi-skilled or unskilled and many have immigrant backgrounds because this is a traditional home for newcomers to Britain; the Bangladeshi community, 37,000 strong, is the largest in Europe and there are sizeable groups of Bengalis, Chinese, Jews, Somalis, and West Indians. Since the 1960s, the local economy has undergone radical change, with the closure of the **docks** leaving large acreages of vacant land and many derelict buildings, which were transformed by the injection of £6 billion of public and private capital. **Canary Wharf** on the **Isle of Dogs** has derived much of the benefit, but the lower valley of the **River Lea** (traditionally an industrial area) and the western fringe of the borough adjoining **The City** have also undergone considerable transformation. However, most of the investment has concentrated on office building and the provision of a transport infrastructure, which has attracted a skilled workforce who leave for suburban homes every evening. The residents are among the most deprived in Europe, with unemployment rates often twice the London average, only 37 percent of homes owner-occupied, and levels of educational attainment significantly below those of the more affluent suburbs. (*See also* BETHNAL GREEN; BLACKWALL; BOW; CUBITT TOWN; DOCKLANDS; LIMEHOUSE; MILE END; MILLWALL; SHADWELL; SPITALFIELDS; TOWER HAMLETS; VICTORIA PARK; WAPPING; WHITECHAPEL).

TOWER HILL. Most prisoners in the **Tower of London** who were condemned to death met their fate outside the fortress on Tower Hill. A total of 75 men and women were executed, including Sir Thomas More (Lord Chancellor of England) in 1535, Thomas Cromwell (one of the architects of the English Reformation) in 1540, and William Laud (Archbishop of Canterbury) in 1645. In 1747, so many spectators gathered to see the death of Lord Lovat, a Jacobite supporter, that a wooden grandstand collapsed, killing several from the crowd. A plaque at the western end of the Trinity Square gardens marks the site of the executions, the last of which took place in 1780.

TOWER OF LONDON. Work on the Tower of London was begun by King William I in 1078, following the Norman invasion, and finished during the reign of Edward I, more than 200 years later (by which time it covered more than 18 acres and consisted of a series of concentric defenses). Originally erected as a fortress designed to provide security for the invaders, dominate access along the **River Thames**, and impress the conquered people, it has also served as a royal palace, prison, mint, astronomical observatory and record office. The oldest structure is the White Tower (which gets its name from the whitewash applied during the 13th century). Probably completed about 1100, it has walls 90 feet high and 15 feet thick and is now used as a **museum** of arms and armor. Other principal buildings include the Bell Tower (where Thomas More was kept prisoner before his execution in 1535), the Bloody Tower (by tradition, the place where Edward V and his brother, Richard, were murdered on the orders of Richard III in 1483), Traitor's Gate (the principal entrance to the castle from the river during the Middle Ages), and the Chapel of St. Peter ad Vincula (under the floor of which lay the bodies of Anne Boleyn and Catherine Howard, the second and fifth wives of King Henry VIII). King Stephen, in 1140, was the first monarch to use the place as a royal residence; from then, it was popular with England's kings and queens until James VI and I became more interested in **Whitehall Palace**.

Involuntarily, many prisoners spent time there, though dungeons and cells were never an integral part of the building. Captives were simply placed in whatever rooms were available (one in the White Tower was only four feet square). The first person incarcerated was Ranulf, Bishop of Durham, who was confined in 1101 for selling benefices, but many others followed, including, during the 20th century, traitor Roger Casement and Nazi fugitive Rudolf Hess. Frequently, supervision of captives was lax so many escaped, including the Welsh baron Roger Mortimer, who was helped to freedom in 1324 by his mistress, Isabella (wife of

The Tower of London (Museum of London)

Edward II), and Jacobite Lord Nithsdale, who disguised himself as a maid and walked out with his wife the day before his scheduled execution in 1716.

For over 600 years, the Tower also housed a menagerie, which provided both amazement and amusement for the royal court. It originated in 1235 with a gift of three leopards from the Holy Roman Emperor to King Henry III (leopards adorned the coat of arms of England's Plantagenet rulers). A polar bear (presented by the King of Norway) arrived in 1252 (the **Corporation of London** was ordered to provide it with a long chain so that it could catch fish in the Thames), and an elephant house was added in 1255. James VI and I enjoyed watching dogs fight lions, but later monarchs took less interest in the collection, so, by 1822, all that remained was a bear, an elephant, and a few birds. In that year, however, Alfred Copps was appointed Royal Keeper and set about rebuilding the menagerie, which numbered 59 species by the time it was transferred to **London Zoo** in 1839 after lions had attacked some passersby. The only remaining nonhuman residents are ravens; there is a legend that when these birds leave, the country will fall, so the authorities keep their wings clipped rather than tempt fate.

Although the Tower is located within the area of the **City of London**, it is considered outside the jurisdiction of the **Lord Mayor**. A permanent garrison is maintained, headed by a Constable (who always holds the rank of field marshal) and a resident Governor. Queen Victoria restored many parts of the fortress and opened it to the public. During the 1990s, further restoration work was carried out, particularly in the 13th-century Wakefield Tower, built by King Henry III as a private lodging. (*See also* BEEFEATER; CEREMONY OF THE KEYS; CROWN JEWELS; TOWER HILL.)

TOYNBEE HALL. In 1884, Samuel Barnett (vicar at St. Jude's Church in **Whitechapel**) established Toynbee Hall, in Commercial Street, as a center where he could "educate citizens in the knowledge of one another" as well as "provide teaching for those willing to learn and recreation to those who are weary." These were ambitious goals, for the Hall (named after social philosopher Arnold Toynbee) was located in one of London's poorest districts, but, aided by **university** students who shared his ideals, he provided a program of educational and cultural activities that spawned nationwide organizations such as the Workers' Educational Association and the Workers' Travel Association. Locally, the art exhibitions he organized led to the establishment of Whitechapel Art Gallery in

1901. During the 20th century, Barnett's work was continued by resident workers who included Clement Attlee (Prime Minister from 1945 to 1951), social reformer William Beveridge (architect of Britain's welfare state), and philosopher R. H. Tawney. (*See also* HAMPSTEAD GARDEN SUBURB.)

TRAFALGAR SQUARE. Trafalgar Square is central London's only large public square, so it has become a place where people congregate for political rallies and national celebrations. Located on a site used to stable royal horses during the 16th century and as an army barracks during the 17th, it was originally proposed, in 1812, as part of **John Nash**'s urban renewal scheme for **Charing Cross** but not completed (to **Charles Barry**'s plans) until 1840. Nelson's Column, 172 feet 2 inches high, dominates the space. One of London's best-known landmarks, it was designed by William Railton, shaped from Devonshire granite, and erected in 1839–42. The 17-foot-high statue of Admiral Horatio Nelson that stands atop the column is the work of Edward Hodges Baily. At the base, four bronze reliefs (cast from captured French cannon and finished in 1849) depict scenes from Nelson's victories at Cape St. Vincent (1797) and the Nile (1798), his bombardment of Copenhagen (1801), and his death at Trafalgar (1805). The four bronze lions that guard the column were designed by Edwin Landseer, cast by Baron Carlo Marochetti, and completed in 1867.

The fountains that form the other main features of the square were originally erected in 1845 but remodelled by Edward Lutyens in 1939 as memorials to two First World War naval commanders—Admiral Earl David Beatty and Admiral Earl John Jellicoe. The oldest of the statues is the bronze of King Charles I, which was cast in 1633. In 1649, parliamentarian authorities ordered brazier John Rivett to destroy it so the metal could be used for armaments, but he buried it in his garden instead. It was later acquired by King Charles II and placed in its present position in 1675: the Royal Stuart Society places a wreath beside it on January 30, the anniversary of Charles I's death. At the southeast corner of Trafalgar square, the smallest **police** station in Britain is located in a lamp post. Each December, the people of Norway provide a Christmas tree for the Square and on New Year's Eve there is a lively party atmosphere. During the year, visitors derive much pleasure from feeding the pigeons that flock on the open ground. On occasion, the authorities have tried to limit the practice because of the nuisance caused by the birds, but it has survived all efforts to eliminate it, although, early in 2001 Bernard Rayner (whose family had sold pigeon seed at a site on the square for half a century) was persuaded to close his booth and accept compensation for loss of livelihood from the **Greater London Authority**. Plans to close the area in front of the **National Gallery** to traffic and create a pedestrian piazza were announced in 2000. (*See also* ST. MARTIN-IN-THE-FIELDS CHURCH, TRAFALGAR SQUARE.)

TRAMS. The first tramcars appeared on London's streets in 1861, when George Francis Train introduced a service between Victoria Street and Bayswater Road. The vehicles were supposed to capitalize on the more limited friction between wheels and metal rails than between wheels and the normal road surface used by horse **buses** but actually created friction because pedestrians, and other traffic, found the tracks (which projected above the street level) a considerable hazard. In 1869, however, three tramways were built on the outskirts of the city and, with rails sunk into macadamized roads, proved a popular form of travel that was speedily replicated elsewhere. In 1899, most of the network was taken over by the **London County Council**, which, four years later, began an extensive development program. The local authority found the venture highly profitable, despite a low fare policy, but failed to invest either in track or in vehicles, so, when all public transport was handed over to the London Passenger Transport Board (*see* **London Transport**) in 1933, it seemed more economical to replace the 2,500 trams with trolleybuses, which used overhead power lines. Also, from 1945, diesel engine buses became increasingly popular so, by the end of 1952, the trams had been phased out. Nevertheless, they may make a comeback. In modern cities, buses are considered unreliable because of traffic congestion, so civic authorities in Amsterdam, Berlin, Los Angeles, Zurich, and elsewhere are placing increasing emphasis on tramcars as a form of mass **transport**. They were reintroduced to **Croydon** in 2000 and London Transport was also considering their potential.

TRANSPORT. The earliest forms of transport in the London area were probably by water along the **River Thames** and by horse along the marshy shores. Until comparatively recently, the river was an important thoroughfare. Archaeological evidence shows that the Romans and Saxons used it extensively (the remains of a Roman ship were discovered during excavation for the site of **County Hall**, for example), then, during the Medieval period, **docks** developed for sailing ships as trading contacts expanded and ferries conveyed travellers (and even wagons) across the water. The horse dominated land travel, though the poor had little option but to walk. Public transport along city streets was introduced during the late 16th century with the arrival of the hackney cab, named from the French *haquenée* (meaning "a slow moving old nag"). The hackney was an exclusive way of getting around—two horses drew a carriage, which contained two seats, one of which was occupied by the driver—but it quickly became popular, threatening the incomes of those who made their living moving people by boat.

In 1711, the sedan chair provided a further alternative, favored by those who did not want to be exposed to the elements as they made their way from a cab to their home. Sedans survived for over a century (there are reports of their use in **Hampstead** and **Mayfair** during the 1830s and 1840s), but their sedate rate of progress made them less attractive as the city spread. Wealthy Londoners preferred coaches, some maintaining their own, others hiring from local stables (the hire business survived until the 1920s). Additionally, public stage coaches offered a means of getting around the city during the late 18th and early 19th centuries. Carriages normally carried six people in relative comfort inside, with an additional three on top, but, from 1829, were challenged by the horse-drawn omnibus (which could carry up to 18 passengers).

The foundations of the modern mass transit system were laid from 1836, with the development of the **railway** network. The **London Underground** extended its route system from 1863, then, in 1897, the first motorized **buses** appeared, making commuting a way of life by the turn of the century. The private car revolutionized movement during the 20th century, with over 1.1 million arriving in central London each day by the 1990s, causing congestion in a road system designed for the horse and cart age. Also, the growth of air travel following the opening of **Hounslow** aerodrome in 1919 (and particularly after the end of the Second World War) attracted increasing numbers of tourists from throughout the world. In the modern city, public transit systems remain extremely important, primarily because of the lack of parking facilities for motorists and the rush hour traffic jams that slow drivers' journeys. Every weekday, **London Transport**'s Underground network carries 2.5 million passengers in 470 trains along 254 miles of track and the buses move a further 1.2 million. (*See also* AIRPORTS; ARCHWAY; BLACKFRIARS; BRIDGES; CANNON STREET STATION; DRAIN; GRAND UNION CANAL; LONDON REGIONAL PASSENGERS' COMMITTEE [LRPC]; POOL OF LONDON; PORT OF LONDON AUTHORITY [PLA]; REGENT'S CANAL; TAXIS; TRAMS; TUBE; TURNPIKES; VICTORIA; WANDSWORTH; WATERLOO.)

TRANSPORT FOR LONDON. *See* LONDON TRANSPORT (LT).

TREASURY BUILDINGS. The British government's principal finance officers work in the Treasury Buildings on the western side of **Whitehall**. Originally erected in 1845 (to designs by **Charles Barry**) on a site previously occupied by **Whitehall Palace**'s cock fighting pit, the offices were redesigned in 1960–64 (when construction work revealed the walls of the Tudor palace's tennis courts). An underground passage (known as Cockpit Alley) runs beneath the property, linking **Downing Street** with **Horse Guards Parade**, but is closed for security reasons.

TRINITY HOUSE. From Trinity Square, near the **Tower of London**, Trinity House manages the lighthouses along the coastlines of England, Wales, and the Channel Islands. The organization has its origins in the **Deptford** Guild of Mariners, which, in 1514, was granted a royal charter authorizing it to provide pilotage on the **River Thames**. The charter was renewed in 1547, when the guild was renamed The Corporation of Trinity House on Deptford Strand, and again in 1553, 1558, 1604, and 1685 (the last of these documents, drafted by **Samuel Pepys**, is the basis of Trinity House's modern responsibilities). The first lighthouse was built at Lowestoft (the easternmost point in England) in 1609 and the first light vessel anchored in The Nore (an area of the Thames estuary some four miles southeast of Shoeburyness) in 1732. Control of all English and Welsh lighthouses was assumed in 1836. In addition, the corporation has responsibility for providing navigation aids such as buoys and beacons as well as for making assistance available to sailors suffering financial hardship. Its policies are determined by a board consisting of Elder Brethren (that is, senior members of the corporation) and representatives of commercial interests. The lighthouse service has a separate committee.

TROOPING THE COLOUR. One of the most popular of London's annual ceremonies, the Trooping of the Colour takes place at **Horse Guards Parade** to honor the monarch on his or her official birthday in early June. It has its roots in the practice of medieval military commanders, who paraded banners in front of their armies before battle so that soldiers would be familiar with the colors that would be their rallying point, and was first held as a formal event in 1755. One of the five regiments of Foot Guards in the **Household Division** is the focus of the parade, with the monarch (who wears the uniform of that regiment) taking the salute. The other regiments and the Household Cavalry, with their massed bands, add bustle and music. Over 1,400 infantrymen and 200 mounted horsemen participate, demonstrating intricate and precise marching maneuvers. Demand for seats vastly exceeds supply, so tickets for the event are allocated by ballot; unsuccessful applicants line **The Mall** to watch the procession to and from Horse Guards.

TUBE. Although the term "Tube" is sometimes used loosely as a synonym for the whole of the **London Underground** system, it is most properly applied to the 85 miles of deep track on the central city sections of the **Waterloo** and **City**, Bakerloo, Central, Jubilee, Northern, **Picadilly**, and **Victoria** lines. The name was first applied to the City and South London **Railway**, which opened in 1890 with services from King William Street (near the **Bank of England**) to **Stockwell** (south of the **River Thames**). Designed by James Greathead, it incorporated tubular tunnels built 40 feet under the ground (earlier track had been constructed using a "cut and cover" method, which simply involved digging up a road, laying track, providing roofing, and then replacing the street). Modern tube trains travel at an average depth of 80 feet but reach over 221 feet on the Northern Line at Holly Bush hill and **Hampstead**. Hampstead, 192 feet at its lowest point, is the deepest station.

TUFNELL PARK. Tufnell Park lies east of **Kentish Town** some three miles north of **Charing Cross**, taking its name from the Tufnells, a brewing family who owned large estates in the area. In the years prior to the Industrial Revolution, the land supplied milk and other dairy products to London's growing population, but from the second quarter of the 19th century much of the pasture was used for villa developments. Initially, these were sold to well-to-do families. By 1900, however, many of the wealthy had left, leaving homes that were subdivided for poorer occupiers. In 1965, the suburb was incorporated within the **London Borough of Islington**, which introduced several local authority **housing** projects but retained the essentially Victorian character of the area.

TULSE HILL. A residential suburb located south of **Brixton**, Tulse Hill takes its name from the Tulse family, which owned estates in the area during the 17th century (Sir Henry was **Lord Mayor** of London in 1683). By 1800, much of the land was controlled by Dr. Thomas Edwards, who saw potential for urban development as city residents sought homes with access to the countryside. Plots were leased to wealthy business and professional people, who built large residences that could house an entourage of servants as well as members of the family, and in 1856 Holy Trinity Church, designed by T. D. Barry, was completed. However, such an exclusive estate inevitably attracted growth on its fringes (a growth hastened by the construction of a **railway** station in 1869), so, by the end of the 19th century, many of the richer occupants were moving farther out to sites that retained some semblance of rural life and provided greater privacy. Since then, apartment blocks have replaced several of the older properties, particularly in the north of the area. Tulse Hill was incorporated within the **London Borough of Lambeth** in 1965.

TURNPIKES. By the late 18th century, many roads in and around London (as elsewhere in England) were in a state of disrepair. Legally, parishes were responsible for their upkeep, but few authorities considered the task important, so Parliament eventually passed a series of acts creating Turnpike Trusts, which were empowered to charge tolls to travellers using the routeways under their control, with the funds invested in highway maintenance. These bodies undoubtedly wrought considerable improvement (building bridges and raising the standard of drainage, for example), but, over the years, much of the income was siphoned into the pockets of members rather than used for upkeep. Profits were high and the potential for fraud was considerable, so trusts, which could be bought and sold, were attractive commodities even though some forms of traffic (such as soldiers in uniform and ministers carrying out parish duties) were exempt from payment. Those at **Elephant and Castle**, **Mile End** Road, Tottenham Court Road, **Hyde Park Corner**, **Islington**, and **Tyburn** proved particularly lucrative, but users complained bitterly about the prices charged and, from 1864, they were phased out. The gates at Mile End, London's last major turnpike, were removed in 1866, although some smaller trusts survived into the 20th century.

TWICKENHAM. Modern Twickenham is a predominantly residential suburb 10 miles southwest of **Charing Cross**. Until the mid-19th century, it was a village located well outside London with an economy based largely on agriculture, fishing, and ferry services for travellers requiring transport across the **River Thames**. Wealthy courtiers built grand mansions on their estates (*see*, for example, **Marble Hill House**), and there was something of a tourist trade because steamers from the city carried parties upriver for picnics on Eel Pie Island (author **Charles Dickens** describes a typical outing in *Nicholas Nickleby*, published in 1839). In 1848, however, the Windsor, Staines, and South Western **Railway** laid track through Twickenham to **Richmond** and Windsor. The London and South Western Company added lines to **Kingston** in 1863 and the District Railway to **Hounslow** in 1883, making the area's open spaces attractive to builders providing homes for commuters keen to work in central London but raise families near the countryside. In addition, some 17 acres were acquired by the Rugby **Football** Union for its headquarters in 1907 (England plays its home international matches at the stadium, which now has a capacity of 57,400 spectators). Also, in 1933, a **bridge** (the first in Britain to use three-hinged reinforced concrete arches) was built to carry the Great Chertsey Road across the Thames to Richmond. In spite of the surge of development during the late 19th and early 20th centuries, much of the older property survived, particularly towards the south of the area. The church of St. Mary the Virgin was built in 1714–15 but incorporates elements of previous places of worship on the site, including the west tower, which dates from the 14th century. Poet Alexander Pope, who lived in Twickenham from 1719 to 1744, was buried in the church, and the graveyard contains a memorial to Thomas Twining, founder of the firm of tea merchants. Writers Alfred Lord Tennyson and Walter de la Mare had homes in Montpelier Row, a brick terrace erected as a speculative development in 1720, and, in 1747–91, **Strawberry Hill** (now occupied by St. Mary's College) was converted from a cottage to a Gothic castle by novelist Horace Walpole. (*See also* RICHMOND UPON THAMES, LONDON BOROUGH OF.)

TYBURN. From 1388 until 1783, public executions were carried out at Tyburn (the name is taken from a small stream that ran nearby). These events were public holidays (the authorities believed that watching men be hanged would deter members of the audience from committing **crimes**), so crowds of up to 200,000 people congregated around the gallows. Condemned prisoners dressed for the occasion, travelling from **Newgate Prison** in an open cart but stopping at **St. Giles-in-the-Fields Church** for a last mug of ale and at St. Sepulchre Church, **Holborn**, (where the bellman asked citizens to pray for the soul of the felons). After the death, the hangman claimed the victim's clothes and onlookers pressed forward to touch the corpse in the belief that it had the power to cure illnesses. The site of the gallows (which was sometimes known as Tyburn Tree) is marked by a stone in the traffic island at the junction of Bayswater Road and Edgware Road. Those dispatched included Perkin

Warbeck (who claimed he was heir to the English throne and mounted two invasions to prove his case but was put to death in 1499), Oliver Plunket (who died in 1681, the last Englishman to be martyred for his religious convictions), and highwayman Jack Sheppard (1714). After King Charles II was restored in 1660, the bodies of Oliver Cromwell and two of his supporters were exhumed from their graves, hanged at Tyburn, then beheaded and buried beneath the gallows. (*See also* CHARTERHOUSE; KETCH, JACK.)

– U –

UNDERGROUND. *See* LONDON UNDERGROUND.

UNITED STATES' EMBASSY. The United States established its London embassy on the east side of Grosvenor Square in 1938 but, after the Second World War, attempted to acquire the west side from the **Grosvenor Estate** so that its representatives could move into more commodious quarters. The estate agreed to sell but only if the United States would return 12,000 acres of Florida that were confiscated from the Grosvenor family at the time of the American War of Independence. The U.S. government felt that price was a little too high but leased the site, making it the only location where the country has an embassy but does not own the freehold. The building, faced with **Portland stone**, was designed by Saarinen and Associates and erected in 1956–59. It is surmounted by a gilded golden eagle, made of aluminum and with a wingspan of 35 feet. Most architectural critics are unimpressed by the structure, claiming that it is fussy, muddled, and too short to command the square.

UNIVERSITIES. The first center of higher **education** in London was University College, founded in 1826 by poet Thomas Campbell and other religious noncomformists who wanted to provide classes for students barred from Oxford and Cambridge, which only admitted members of the Church of England. The Anglicans responded in 1828 by creating King's College, then, in 1836, the Whig government established a University of London, with a charter in which King William IV declared that it was a duty of his royal office "to hold forth to all classes and denominations of his faithful subjects an encouragement for pursuing a regular and liberal course of education." University College, King's College, and other institutions presented male students for examination by the new body from 1838, but women were unable to graduate for a further 40 years. Under the terms of the University of London Act (1898), the institution, originally based in **Somerset House** but now in Malet Street, is governed by a Senate consisting of 55 members.

A second university was founded in 1962, when Brunel College of Advanced Technology (which took its name from engineer Isambard Kingdom Brunel) was renamed Brunel University and allowed to award its own degrees. Four years later, City University (with particular strengths in the arts, business studies, and the social sciences) was formed around Northampton Polytechnic. At the same time, the Labour government amalgamated groups of technical colleges to create nine polytechnics, designed to specialize in vocational subjects and award degrees through a Council for National Academic Awards. Under the terms of the Further and Higher Education Act of 1992, these institutions were allowed to call themselves universities and confer their own degrees, so, by the end of the decade, London had 14 independent universities (including the London Business School and the **Royal College of Art**). Together, they taught some 265,000 students. The largest was the University of London, where 93,600 undergraduates and postgraduates attended 47 colleges as disparate as the **London School of Economics and Political Science**, the **Courtauld Institute of Art**, and the School of Slavonic Studies. (*See also* AVERY HILL; BARNET, LONDON BOROUGH OF; BLOOMSBURY; CUSTOM HOUSE; DEPTFORD; GREAT ORMOND STREET HOSPITAL FOR SICK CHILDREN; KINGSTON UPON THAMES, ROYAL BOROUGH OF; LORD MAYOR; ROTHERHITHE; ROYAL ARSENAL; ROYAL COLLEGE OF SURGEONS OF ENGLAND; ROYAL NAVAL COLLEGE; RUSSELL SQUARE; UXBRIDGE.)

UNIVERSITY BOAT RACE. In 1829, crews from Oxford and Cambridge Universities held a race along the **River Thames** from Hambledon Lock to Henley (Oxford won). Sixteen years later, the event was held over a 4.5-mile course from **Putney** to **Mortlake**, a route used ever since. The race became an annual competition in 1856, attracting crowds of onlookers, but in recent years the number of spectators lining the banks has declined (although live television coverage ensures a national audience). In 1998, Cambridge broke the course record (with the heaviest crew on record) in a time of 16 minutes 19 seconds. By 2001, that university had 77 wins, eight more than Oxford. The 1912 race was the most sensational because both eights sank.

UXBRIDGE. Uxbridge is the commercial heart of the **London Borough of Hillingdon**. Probably settled in Saxon times (the name is said to derive from a tribe known as the Wixan), it was an established market center by the 12th century, building up a considerable trade in arable crops during the Middle Ages. Flour mills were built to the west of the settlement, using streams and rivers as a source of water power and beginning a process of industrialization enhanced by the opening of the Grand Junction Canal, which linked the community to **Paddington** in 1801 and to the English midlands in 1805. The arrival of the Great Western **Railway** in 1838 promoted further development, encouraging the establishment of market gardens supplying fresh fruit, vegetables, and flowers to London's rapidly growing urban population. During the 20th century, the creation of additional **transport** links (including the opening of Heathrow **Airport** in 1946) attracted international as well as British businesses, including light manufacturing interests (such as makers of precision instruments) and offices. Brunel **University** (named after Isambard Kingdom Brunel, the Great Western's engineer) was built on a site south of the town in 1966–67, building on local skills by concentrating on engineering disciplines and developing strong research links with the incoming firms. As the town expanded, much open space made way for buildings (the university is located on 150 acres of former horticultural land, for example) and many of the older properties were demolished to facilitate the construction of a new civic center, designed by Robert Matthew, Johnson-Marshall, and Partners, which opened in 1979. However, part of High Street, with structures dating from the late 15th century, is protected by conservation area legislation and the Treaty House, where Parliamentary and Royalist factions unsuccessfully attempted to resolve their differences in 1645, still stands (paneling taken from the House in 1929 to line walls in New York's Empire State Building was returned in 1955, as a gift to Queen Elizabeth II, and reinstalled).

– V –

VAUXHALL. Although it is now an urban area in the north of the **London Borough of Lambeth**, Vauxhall retained all the characteristics of a village until the beginning of the 19th century. The area derives its name from an early 13th-century mansion built by Falkes de Breauté and variously known as Fulke's Hall, Faukeshall, or Foxhall. Although it was a popular location for the country homes of the rich (Sir Noel Caron, English Ambassador to Holland, built a mansion there in the early 16th century, for example), its main attraction from about 1660 until 1859 was the New Spring Garden (renamed Vauxhall Gardens in 1785), which was a major recreational resource for city residents. Diarist **Samuel Pepys** admired the facilities, writing on 18 May 1667 of the pleasure of listening to "the nightingales and other birds, and here fiddles and there a harp, and here a jews trump, and here laughing." At night, the walkways were lit by hundreds of lights. Although they were accessible only by river until 1750, the gardens became very fashionable; Frederick, Prince of Wales, attended a ball on the site in 1732, writers **Samuel Johnson** and **James Boswell** were frequent visitors, and a grand fete was held to celebrate the Duke of Wellington's victory over the French at Vitoria (Spain) in 1813.

In 1816, the opening of a **bridge** to **Pimlico** (the first iron structure across the **River Thames** in London) added to the traffic entering the little settlement and encouraged development, as did the construction of the terminus of the London and Southampton Railway in 1838 and the building of **The Oval** as the headquarters of the Surrey County Cricket Club during the 1840s. Then, in 1859, Vauxhall Gardens was closed, despite various attempts to resuscitate them after the owners went bankrupt in 1840, and the site was built over. With the demise of the gardens, the area lost its social prestige and, during the second half of the 19th century, became one of the less affluent parts of the city as the working-class poor crowded in, attempting to find jobs at the rail depot and with the host of small industries—such as glove making, chemical production, and laundering—that sprang up nearby (St. Peter's Church, designed by John Loughborough Pearson, one of the most distinguished church architects of the time, was built at Kennington Lane in 1863–64, specifically to cater to these largely illiterate and lowly paid immigrants).

From 1895 to 1906, the Thames bridge was replaced by a structure with five steel arches and granite piers, designed by Alexander Binnie, in order to improve transport but, during the 20th century, the area retained its reputation as one of the more rundown parts of London, with a mixture of **housing** and commercial concerns. However, the transfer of **Covent Garden** market to **Nine Elms**, at the western edge of Vauxhall, has led to some regeneration of industrial activity.

VICTORIA. The Victoria area, 1.25 miles southwest of **Charing Cross** in the **City of Westminster**, is one of London's major route foci. Until the early 19th century, it was an extensive marsh forming the north bank of the **River Thames** but, in 1816, when Vauxhall Bridge was opened to provide a connection between **Westminster** and **Lambeth**, builders grasped the opportunity to provide homes along the approach road. The Grosvenor Canal, originally built in 1725, was upgraded in the 1820s, encouraging industrial concerns (such as engineering works) to locate alongside, then, two decades later, **Thomas Cubitt** developed land to the south. By 1851, slums were being cleared to make way for Victoria Street (named after Queen Victoria), which linked the area to the Houses of Parliament (*see* **Palace of Westminster**), encouraging the appropriately named American businessman, George Train, to lay **tram** lines along it.

In 1860, the London, Brighton, and South Coast **Railway** built the Grosvenor Bridge (the first rail **bridge** over the Thames in London) to bring the line from **Pimlico** to the rapidly expanding **West End** and constructed a new station at the western end of Victoria Street. At the same time, the London, Chatham, and Dover Company opened an adjacent terminus (which, within weeks, became the point at which most travellers from Europe entered the city). Shortly afterwards, the **London Underground** arrived, and inevitably **hotels**, **public houses**, cafeterias, restaurants, and shops were established to serve the transient clientele as the area flourished. Development during the 20th century further improved transport, with the two railway termini functioning as a single unit from 1921 and a coach station built only 400 yards away. Also, the Victoria Line, central London's first **Tube** route since 1907, was tunnelled from **Brixton** to **Walthamstow** in 1962–71, intersecting the Circle and District Lines at Victoria, which is now one of the busiest stations in the system with over 86 million passengers every year.

In the process of change, many of the 19th-century buildings were swept away. Few remain along the route to Vauxhall Bridge, most of the original Victoria Street is gone (including the Stag Brewery, which was demolished in 1959, after 318 years in the same location, to make way for a 27-story office block), and the shops in front of **Westminster Cathedral** have been knocked down to create the open space of a piazza. (*See also* BAZALGETTE, JOSEPH WILLIAM; BUSES.)

VICTORIA AND ALBERT MUSEUM (V&A). Part of a complex of **museums**, learned societies, and educational institutions in the **Brompton** area of south **Kensington** (*see*, for example, **Natural History Museum**, **Royal College of Art**, **Royal Geographical Society**, **Science Museum**), the V&A concentrates on the fine and applied arts of all periods and societies. It was founded in 1857, when the collections of the School of Design (created in 1837) and the Museum of Manufactures (established in 1852) were merged. Initially, exhibits were housed in wooden sheds and an enormous cast iron and glass structure, built by William Cubitt, which was quickly christened "the Brompton Boilers" (*see* **Bethnal Green Museum of Childhood**). As acquisitions accumulated, through purchase and donation, the V&A became, in the words of former director Roy Strong, "an extremely capacious handbag" exhibiting an eclectic range of artefacts with no obvious thematic link. Paintings (including a fine collection of works by British artists, donated by textile manufacturer John Sheepshanks in 1857) competed for space with the National Art Library (opened in 1884), the contents of the India Museum (transferred from the India Office), and individual items such as Raphael's Tapestry Cartoons (lent by Queen Victoria).

As space ran out, a competition, held to choose plans for new exhibition galleries, was won by Aston Webb (who was responsible for the Natural History Museum, erected in 1881). The foundation stone of the present 12-acre building, constructed to his designs, was laid in 1899 by Queen Victoria (performing the last major public engagement of her reign), but the flamboyant terracotta brick edifice, with its central tower shaped to resemble an imperial crown, was not completed until 1909. During the 20th century, the collection continued to grow (the Nehru Gallery of Indian Art was opened in 1990, for example), so the V&A authorities have attempted to solve display problems by dispersing material to other sites, such as the Museum of Childhood at Bethnal Green, the Wellington Museum (*see* **Hyde Park Corner**), and the **Theatre Museum** in **Covent Garden**. However, the Kensington site still houses an enormous variety of artwork, with particular strengths in the early Medieval, Gothic, and Renaissance periods, regional emphases on India and the Far East, and thematic concentrations on continental and decorative arts prior to 1825, English furniture and decorative arts from 1500 to 1860, portrait miniatures, and costumes.

In 1988, the museum's new Director, Elizabeth Esteve-Coll, incurred the wrath of traditionalists when she announced plans to make the institution more accessible to the public. Sir John Pope-Hennessey, one of her predecessors, claimed that proposals to mount more exhibitions focusing on popular culture and employ advertising agents who marketed the place as "An ace café with quite a nice museum attached" were vulgar. A restructuring of senior staff responsibilities caused further problems, leading to job losses and serious internal tensions. However, visitor numbers increased markedly, particularly among young people, who numbered only 10,000 in 1990 but totalled 100,000 in 1994. Alan Borg, appointed to succeed Esteve-Coll in 1995, introduced further changes to operating practices (including imposition of admission charges and a reduction in the number of volunteer helpers) and, in 1998, announced plans for a major refurbishment of the British Galleries. Some 950,000 people now tour the exhibits every year. (*See also* HAM HOUSE.)

VICTORIA PARK. During the middle years of the 19th century, central and local authorities were placed under increasing pressure to alleviate social conditions in the working-class areas of London by providing public **parks**. In 1842, Robert Peel's Conservative government used the funds acquired through the lease of **Lancaster House** to buy 290 acres of land in the **East End**, including the former site of **Stepney** Manor House. James Pennethorne (who also designed **Battersea Park**) was employed to landscape the area, which opened in 1845 as Victoria Park. Lakes were added the following year and an open-air swimming pool built in 1936. The park, which lies on the boundary of the **London Borough of Hackney** and the **London Borough of Tower Hamlets**, has frequently been used for mass demonstrations designed to attract support from the manual workers who dominate the eastern side of the city (as early as 1848, for example, a crowd of over 1,000 gathered to support the Chartist claims for universal adult male suffrage).

– W –

WALBROOK. The Walbrook rose in **Finsbury** and flowed south to the **River Thames**, providing a **water supply** for the Roman occupants of **Londinium**, who built the **Temple of Mithras** nearby. Following the Norman conquest of England in 1066, several Christian churches were erected close to the stream, notably **St. Stephen's** (founded before 1096), St. Mildred's (first mentioned in documents dating from 1175), and St. Margaret's (built by 1197), all of which were destroyed during the **Great Fire** of 1666 and reerected to designs prepared by **Christopher Wren**. However, the watercourse was only about 14 feet wide, too narrow for navigation and too easily polluted by refuse as the **City of London** expanded. As a result, it was covered over in 1440. A street of the same name, running from **Mansion House** to **Cannon Street Station**, follows the former east bank.

WALLACE COLLECTION. During the late 18th and the 19th centuries, the Seymour-Conway family (Marquesses of Hertford) amassed a fine private collection of European art. The initial works were acquired by the first Marquess, patron of Joshua Reynolds (1723–1792) and Allan Ramsay (1713–1834). His son added several family portraits and his grandson (a flamboyant socialite on whom William Thackeray modelled the sinister Marquis de Steyne in *Vanity Fair*, published in 1848) contributed a series of Dutch cabinet paintings as well as *Perseus and Andromeda* by Titian (c.1488–1576), and portraits by Anthony Van Dyck (1599–1641) and Thomas Gainsborough (1727–1788). The fourth Marquess was a recluse, who lived at the Château Bagatelle in the Bois de Boulogne, outside Paris, and devoted himself entirely to his collection, concentrating on French art at a time when it was very unfashionable. With the help of Richard, his illegitimate son (the product of a relationship with Mrs. Agnes Jackson), he purchased canvases by François Boucher (1703–1770), Jean-Honoré Fragonard (1732–1806), and Antoine Watteau (1684–1721), along with several 17th-century Dutch masterpieces (including Frans Hals's *Laughing Cavalier*, painted in 1624) and select pieces of Sèvres china. Richard (who, in 1842, adopted Wallace, his mother's maiden name, as his own surname) inherited the entire collection, adding Renaissance gold, armor, and Italian majolica. When he died in 1890 (having been knighted in recognition of his services to British nationals living in Paris during the Franco-Prussian War in 1870–71), the works passed to his wife, Julie, who (in accordance with her husband's wishes) bequeathed them to the nation in 1897. The collection was opened to the public three years later at Hertford House, the Wallaces' 18th-century home in Manchester Square. In 2000, the rooms were remodelled by American architect Rick Mather.

WALTHAM FOREST, LONDON BOROUGH OF. Waltham Forest, like the other **London borough**s, was created in 1965, when the **London County Council** was dissolved and replaced by a new structure of **local government**. In the process, **Chingford**, **Leyton**, and **Walthamstow**—all previously part of the County of Essex—were grouped together to form Waltham Forest, which took its name from the woodlands that once covered the area. Its 15 square miles are dominated by **housing**, though there is considerable open space in the north of the authority's territory. Chingford is the most affluent community, with relatively high proportions of clerical and skilled manual workers who own their own homes. However, some two-thirds of the 221,400 population (1998) live in

Leyton and Walthamstow, which occupy the southern half of the borough. There, the workforce is less highly trained, more likely to live in rented properties, and composed, to a considerable extent, of people from ethnic minorities (Waltham Forest has a large Pakistani community, which accounts for about 8 percent of the population, and a black Caribbean component only slightly smaller). Unemployment is higher than the **Outer London** average and concentrated among the young and nonwhite groups.

WALTHAMSTOW. The hamlet of Walthamstow developed as a farming community about seven miles northeast of **Charing Cross** on the road from the **City of London** to Waltham Abbey. Settlement dates from the Bronze Age but, although wealthy incomers were attracted from about 1500 (George Monoux, **Lord Mayor** of London in 1514, endowed a school, for example), there was little growth until the Industrial Revolution transformed the local and national economies during the 19th century. The marshes to the west were flooded to create reservoirs sufficient to supply water to expanding commercial interests as well as to meet domestic demands (*see* **water supply**). The arrival of the **railways** led to speculative **housing** developments, and entrepreneurs took advantage of the new technologies to establish manufacturing plants (the Brewer Car—the first British automobile to use the internal combustion engine—was built in Walthamstow in 1892–95). Population increased as workers moved to jobs and commuters took advantage of houses less expensive than those in the increasingly congested city center. Improved road access in 1930 fuelled construction (particularly in the north of the area) and local authority building added to the provision of homes. In the process, many of the older properties were destroyed but, following Walthamstow's incorporation within the **London Borough of Waltham Forest** in 1965, conservation orders were placed on several of those that remained (including the chapel at Forest Road School, which has stained glass windows designed by local craftsman and socialist William Morris in 1875–80). About 990 acres of the neighboring marshland were purchased by the Lea Valley Regional Park Authority (*see* **Lea, River**) in 1972; most is maintained in its natural state but provisions have also been made for sporting and recreational pursuits. (*See also* PARKS; WILLIAM MORRIS GALLERY.)

WANDSWORTH. Wandsworth lies on the south bank of the **River Thames** about 4.5 miles southwest of **Charing Cross**. It takes its name from the River Wandle, which rises near **Croydon** and flows into the Thames just west of the bridge that links the settlement to **Fulham** (*see* **Wandsworth Bridge**). The water in the Wandle provided the power for a series of small mills, and these, in turn, acted as a focus for the development, as early as the 13th century, of an industrial community that concentrated on flour making, bleaching and dyeing, brewing, metal working, and sewing hats (officials of the Roman Catholic Church at the Vatican bought their headgear from Wandsworth companies, earning the area a European reputation for craftsmanship). The factory owners used their firms' profits to build substantial homes, but their attempts to acquire land were not always successful; during the 18th century they tried to appropriate Wandsworth Common but were effectively resisted by other residents, so the area is still a public open space, incorporating a cricket ground.

The 19th century brought considerable expansion, much of it a result of the development of the **railways**. In 1803, the Surrey Iron Railway—a horse-drawn system—began to carry goods along the Wandle Valley, connecting factories along the route. Later, the London and Southampton Company brought its lines through Wandsworth as it introduced services to **Nine Elms** in 1838 and then to **Waterloo** a decade later. In addition to attracting commuters who wanted to live outside the city center but relatively close to their work, the accessibility provided by the railway, coupled with the availability of land for building, led to the establishment of a series of institutions, such as the prison (opened in 1851) and an asylum (which admitted its first inmates in 1857). A five-span lattice girder bridge connected the settlement to Fulham in 1870–73 (*see* **Wandsworth Bridge**), enhancing the **transport** infrastructure, but, even so, the area avoided becoming a wholly working-class community of the kind that evolved at **Battersea** (David Lloyd George, who became Prime Minister in 1916, lived at 3 Routh Road while he was President of the Board of Trade, for example). Most of the pre–Industrial Revolution buildings were, nevertheless, swept away during the building boom of the late 19th and early 20th centuries, with the exception of All Saints' Church (largely built in 1779–80, but incorporating the tower erected for an earlier place of worship in 1630) and a terrace of six early 18th-century houses nearby in Wandsworth Plain. The community is now part of the **London Borough of Wandsworth**. (*See also* HUGUENOTS.)

WANDSWORTH, LONDON BOROUGH OF. The authority was created, in 1965, as part of a restructuring of **local government** within the city. One-third of the administrative area of **Wandsworth**, as it had existed under the **London County Council**, was incorporated within a new **London Borough of Lambeth**; the remainder joined with **Battersea** to form the **London Borough of Wandsworth**. Although considered part of the inner city, it has a considerable amount of open space, incorporating **Battersea Park**, along with extensive areas of **Clapham Common**, Putney Heath, and other recreational land within its 13 square miles. Some traditional manufacturing industry survives along the **River Thames** frontage, but local employment is now based primarily on service industries (including the fruit and vegetable **market** at **Nine Elms**) and over 60 percent of the resident workforce commutes to jobs elsewhere, notably in central London. During the 1980s, Wandsworth aggressively supported the Conservative government's policy of reducing local council expenditure and, partly as a result, attracted growing numbers of well-paid, young professionals to its rows of terraced **housing** (Battersea, in particular, experienced a process of gentrification that increasingly confined manual workers to the local authority estates). However, lack of investment in infrastructure during that period left many areas somewhat shabby, encouraging the development of urban regeneration projects in more recent years, notably in Wandsworth town center. In 1998, the borough (which includes **Roehampton** and parts of **Balham** and **Clapham**) had a population of 220,800. (*See also* BATTERSEA POWER STATION; TOOTING.)

WANDSWORTH BRIDGE. The first **bridge** connecting **Wandsworth** (on the south bank of the **River Thames**) to **Fulham** (on the north) was a lattice girder structure, with five spans, built in 1870–73. It was replaced in 1936–40 by the present cantilever bridge, which has three spans and was designed by T. Pierson Frank.

WANSTEAD. A relatively prosperous suburb on the fringe of London, Wanstead lies some eight miles northeast of **Charing Cross**. It was settled at least by Roman times and was owned by religious interests from the Saxon period until the late Middle Ages but is best known for the 16th-century mansion built by the aptly named Sir Richard Rich, who, in 1544 (following the dissolution of the English monasteries by King Henry VIII), acquired the buildings attached to the church of **St. Bartholomew-the-Great**. The house, which was visited frequently by members of the royal family and courtiers such as poet Sir Philip Sidney, was extended by the Earl of Leicester (a favorite of Queen Elizabeth I) then purchased, in 1667, by Sir Joseph Child, Chairman of the **East India Company**. In 1715, his son, Richard, demolished the building and erected a new home, designed by Colen Campbell in Palladian style, which would influence a whole generation of architects, including John Wood the Elder, who was responsible for much of the layout of Georgian Bath. The luxurious interior is evident in William Hogarth's picture of Sir Richard and his family with their guests in the main salon, painted in 1729 and now owned by the Philadelphia Museum of Art. Unfortunately, within a few generations, the Childs' wealth was dissipated and the building knocked down so that the fabric could be sold as building stone. Only the stables survive, converted for use as a clubhouse for golfers and lawn bowlers. During the 18th and 19th centuries, several other large villas were erected in the area, but these, too, have vanished. Wanstead has developed, since the arrival of the **railway** in 1856, as a largely residential community surrounded by **Epping Forest** and areas of open space laid out for **football** and other sports. It was incorporated within the **London Borough of Redbridge** when the metropolitan area's **local government** system was reorganized in 1965.

WAPPING. A riverside suburb on the north bank of the **River Thames** some three miles east of **Charing Cross**, Wapping has seen its social and economic structures transformed since the end of the Second World War. The settlement grew from the 16th century as London's maritime importance increased and ship repairers, mast makers, suppliers of goods to seagoing vessels, sailors, and prostitutes vied for employment in a rough, working-class community where, along High Street alone, there were 36 drinking establishments in 1750. During the 19th century, many of these small businesses were pushed out as large companies erected warehouses close to the **docks**, then, in the 20th century, bomb damage and the decline of the harbor industries led to further out-migration and an increasingly derelict fabric. However, following the reorganization of **local government**, which placed Wapping in the **London Borough of Tower Hamlets** from 1965, and the establishment of the London **Docklands** Development Corporation in 1981, major urban regeneration projects were initiated. Buildings were demolished or renovated as **housing** estates were built, leisure facilities were laid out, and commercial concerns (such as News International, publishers of ***The Times***) were attracted to the area. In the process, many of the remaining working-class groups moved away, to be replaced by more affluent office workers seeking homes close to the facilities of the central city. (*See also* ROTHERHITHE; WAPPING DISPUTE.)

WAPPING DISPUTE. In the early 1980s, restrictive practices by labor unions led to heavy overemployment in the newspaper industry's production units and allowed printers to command wages many times higher than those of other craft workers. Most newspaper proprietors acquiesced, knowing that the resultant high costs deterred rival publishing firms from entering the market. However, when Rupert Murdoch acquired ***The Times*** in 1981 he faced the unions head on in an attempt to replace traditional printing methods (such as typesetting by compositors and the use of hot metal) with computerized technologies and built a plant at **Wapping** to replace the paper's cramped central London site off **Fleet Street**. The printers were incensed by the contracts offered to members who were offered jobs at the new site, resisting clauses that insisted on total flexibility of labor in the workplace, no strikes, and management power to hire and fire at will. Undaunted by threats of disrupted production, Murdoch, under the guise of recruiting for a new paper (the *London Post*), which he had no intention of publishing, hired journalists, executives, and printers sympathetic to his cause. Then, over a weekend in January 1985, he moved the entire production process to Wapping, where writers could compose their copy on computer screens. Furious, the print workers besieged the plant for a full year, clashing violently with the police and accusing them of supporting Prime Minister Margaret Thatcher's plans to crush union powers. In 1986, they were forced to concede, a defeat that led to considerable job losses and lower wages in the industry.

WARD. London's **local government** areas (*see* **City of London** and **London borough**s) are subdivided into wards, each of which elects representatives to the Borough Council. In the City of London, these units date from the period following the Norman Conquest in 1066, when William the Conqueror made London his capital. By 1206, there were 24 wards. In 1394, Farringdon was divided in order to simplify its administration but, since then, the pattern has remained unchanged (with the exception of Bridge Ward, which was created in 1550 to provide a sinecure post for former **Lord Mayor**s but abolished in 1978). Formerly, beadles were appointed in each ward to ensure that the law was observed, trading practices maintained, and sanitation rules kept, but these posts are now entirely ceremonial. Annual meetings (known as **wardmote**s) are held on the first Friday of September, providing an opportunity for voters (who include residents qualified to vote at parliamentary elections and all other people who own or rent property in the area) to choose representatives for the **Court of Common Council**. (*See also* CORPORATION OF LONDON.)

WARDMOTE. On the first Friday of September each year, electors in the **ward**s of the **City of London** meet to select their representatives to the **Court of Common Council**, the **Corporation of London**'s principal **local government** committee. The number of individuals chosen varies from one to four, according to the population of the ward. All adults entitled to vote at parliamentary elections may attend, along with those who rent or own property in the area. Wardmotes (which can be held at other times if a vacancy for an **Alderman** arises) also provide an opportunity for citizens to petition their Common Council members.

WARDOUR STREET. Wardour Street, which runs from north to south through **Soho**, is considered by cinema enthusiasts to be the center of the British film industry. It was originally built in the 1680s and named after Edward Wardour, a local landowner. During the 18th century, it became a focus for London's cabinetmaking industry (Thomas Sheraton was a resident during the 1790s) and for antique dealers, but the trade declined during the Victorian period and was replaced, in the early 1900s, by entertainment interests. In 1906, architect Frank Loughborough Pearson designed Nos. 152–60 as a headquarters for music publisher Novello and Company, modelling the building on the Renaissance Rathaus in Bremen (Germany). At the same time, theater costumier Willy Clarkson moved into Nos. 41 and 43, and firms making musical instruments occupied other premises. The movie companies established themselves from the 1930s, taking over many of the buildings and lining the street with stills from their latest productions.

WATERLOO. The northeast corner of the **London Borough of Lambeth** gets its name from the bridge that first linked the area to the **Strand**, on the northern bank of the **River Thames**. Built of granite to John Rennie's designs, the structure had nine elliptical arches and a pair of Doric columns at each end. It was opened on 18 June 1817 and was named by Parliament to commemorate the Duke of Wellington's victory over Napoleon Bonaparte's troops at Waterloo (near Brussels, Belgium) exactly two years earlier. In 1848, the London and South Western **Railway** built a station at the southern end, then, in 1864, the South Eastern Railway added a second, bringing commuters pouring in from the growing suburbs. By the early 1890s, more than 10,000 of the 50,000 passengers who arrived at the platforms every weekday morning were heading for work in the **City of London**, so a **London Underground** track, known as the **Drain**, was built to link the **Bank of England** to Waterloo, emphasizing the area's growing importance as a **transport** focus. The opening of the Bakerloo Line on the Underground in 1906 and the **Charing Cross** to **Kennington** section of the Northern Line in 1937 added to the traffic, attracting office developers (in 1922, for example, the **London County Council** moved into purpose-built headquarters at nearby **County Hall**) and encouraging the establishment of shops, **public houses**, and other services for travellers. In 1923, however, two of the piers supporting Rennie's bridge proved unsound, so it was demolished and replaced by a five-span concrete structure designed by **Giles Gilbert Scott** (Scott's bridge, opened in 1945, was built largely by women because of the lack of male laborers during the Second World War). The railway station itself was much damaged during the **Blitz** and significantly redeveloped afterwards (including a major extension designed by Nicholas Grimshaw and opened in 1993 to accommodate the trains serving the continent of Europe through the Channel Tunnel); as a result, little of the original fabric remains. Also, the neighboring areas of **Lambeth** were greatly altered in the process of reconstruction after the war, with semi-derelict Victorian property along the riverside removed and replaced by the **South Bank** arts complex and the 25-story office accommodation in the Shell Centre. (*See also* CARDBOARD CITY.)

WATERLOO CHURCHES. In 1818, Parliament passed a Church Building Act that authorized expenditure of over £1 million for building places of worship as a thanksgiving for Britain's victory over Napoleon Bonaparte's French armies at the Battle of Waterloo. In London, the 38 that were erected became popularly known as the Waterloo churches. They include St. John on **Bethnal Green** and St. Peter Walworth, both of which were designed by Sir John Soane (*see* **Sir John Soane's Museum**).

WATERMEN. While the **River Thames** was an important routeway, watermen had a monopoly over the carriage of passengers. The business was regulated by various Acts of Parliament and by the **Corporation of London**, which, from 1555, introduced a system of licensing and an apprenticeship training program. In the second half of the 16th century, the 40,000 watermen formed a **livery company** to represent their interests and, in particular, to protect members from abduction for service in the

Royal Navy. They united with the **lightermen** in 1700 but lost power as the river was spanned by **bridges** (reducing the demand for ferries), as land journeys became increasingly safe and comfortable (encouraging people to travel by coach), and as steam ships replaced sail (carrying more passengers and reducing demand for the watermen's services). By the beginning of the 20th century, they had almost vanished, although a few survive to represent the ancient trade and the Watermen's Company still accepts apprentices. (*See also* WESTMINSTER BRIDGE.)

WATER POLLUTION. Although, during Roman times, the **River Thames** contained salmon, trout, and other fish, population growth and the lack of sewers combined, by the early 19th century, to turn the waterway and its tributaries into a polluted sewer in which little life could survive. By 1290, the monks of the Carmelite priory in **Fleet Street** were complaining that the stench from the **Fleet River** had caused the death of several of their number, and, during the 17th century, Paul Hentzner (a German visitor to the city) claimed that his clothes never lost the smell of slime after they had been washed in water from the Thames. Even by the 1850s, the **City of London** had only 15 miles of sewer. Most houses had their own cesspits, which contaminated water percolating through the ground towards the wells from which people drew their supplies for drinking and washing. As a result, outbreaks of such infectious diseases as cholera were frequent and devastating (*see* **Snow, John**). In 1858, Parliament was forced into action, passing legislation, designed to clean up the Thames, which allowed **Joseph William Bazalgette** to prepare plans for the construction of a **sewage disposal** system ultimately completed in 1875. The improvements were considerable but, until the 1960s, discharges from vessels using the **docks** and from the industrial premises that lined the banks proved difficult to control, causing continuing deoxygenation. From 1965, however, the closure of most of the harbor facilities and their associated factories, coupled with stricter environmental standards, resulted in major improvements in water quality. Salmon and trout returned to the Thames, along with flounder, prawns, and eels, bringing birds such as heron, cormorant, and grebe, which depend on them for food. Under the terms of the Water Act of 1973, the Thames Water Authority was made responsible for pollution control throughout the river basin. (*See also* AIR POLLUTION; GREAT STINK; HUNGERFORD BRIDGE.)

WATER SUPPLY. During the early stages of its development, London drew most of its water from the **River Thames** or from wells. However, as the city grew, these became increasingly tainted by industry (such as tanneries) and by human refuse (*see* **water pollution**), so, from 1245, conduits were constructed in an attempt to transport purer supplies from further afield (for example, between 1439 and 1471, the **Corporation of London** built a pipeline in order to divert the flow from springs at **Paddington** to consumers in **Fleet Street**). The new channels helped to meet demand as the medieval city expanded but were limited by technology, relying solely on the force of gravity and therefore needing a source that was at a higher elevation than the user.

Seasonal variations in the flow caused problems as well, so from 1581, pumps were developed in order to widen the sources of supply, then, following the **Great Fire** in 1666, private companies began to provide water to wealthy householders and commercial concerns. These firms undoubtedly enhanced provision (although consumers had access to water for only a few hours each day) but also posed problems because they made little attempt to consult with one another over plans to install their wood and lead pipes. As a result, roads were sometimes dug up by one supplier, relaid, then dug up by another shortly afterwards. Also, as more and more water companies were established, particularly during the first decade of the 19th century, competition became intense, prices dropped, and profits fell. Desperate to avoid bankruptcy, the companies reached agreements that created monopoly suppliers in specific areas of the city. A committee of the House of Commons registered concern in 1821, fearing that users would face escalating costs, and claimed that water supply should not be determined by market forces but, in the absence of legislation, the providers took little notice. Nine years later, another parliamentary committee, unhappy that most of London's water was being taken from the heavily polluted Thames, considered the possibility of using other sources of supply but, again, failed to have any legislative impact (partly because many Members of Parliament were shareholders in the water companies).

By mid-century, however, the tide of educated opinion was forcing change. In 1849, a pamphlet published by **John Snow** convinced many Londoners that **cholera** was caused by contaminated drinking water, and, the following year, Edwin Chadwick (of the General Board of Health) argued that the city should find new sources of water, with public authorities taking responsibility for supply. Parliament was nudged into action and, in 1852, passed a Metropolitan Water Act, which stopped companies from taking supplies from the heavily polluted tidal area of the Thames below Teddington. Also, they were prevented from turning down requests for provision and made to cover all reservoirs within a five-mile radius of **St. Paul's Cathedral**. The **sewage disposal** system designed by **Joseph William Bazalgette** (and completed in 1875) contributed greatly to an improvement in the quality of drinking water—so much so that a Parliamentary Commission was able to report, in 1893, that "the water supplied to the consumer in London is of a very high standard of excellence and of purity"—but, even so, the suppliers remained unpopular, much criticized for their unwillingness to make provisions available in the poorer parts of the city and for the speed with which they cut off water if payments were late.

Ultimately, in 1897, Parliament appointed the Llandaff Commission to investigate the complaints and, as a result of its recommendations, passed the Metropolis Water Act, which created a Metropolitan Water Board in 1902. The board (consisting of 66 members appointed by the **Corporation of London**, the **London County Council**, and other local authorities) took over responsibility for water supply in London and initiated an extensive program of reservoir construction in order to meet the needs of a growing population with increasing living standards. In 1974, its duties were assumed by the Thames Water Authority, which was required to manage the full water cycle within the Thames's 5,000-square-mile catchment area. The Authority, privatized by the Conservative government in 1989, uses a mixture of natural sources and reservoirs to meet the metropolis's industrial and domestic needs. (*See also* CHINGFORD; WALTHAMSTOW.)

WEBBER, ANDREW LLOYD. *See* LLOYD WEBBER, ANDREW.

WELLINGTON ARCH. *See* HYDE PARK CORNER.

WELLINGTON MUSEUM. *See* HYDE PARK CORNER.

WEMBLEY. Despite evidence of settlement before the Norman Conquest of 1066, Wembley (some eight miles northwest of **Charing Cross**) remained largely agricultural until after the First World War. Moreover, the **railway**, which led to rapid growth in other suburbs, did little to encourage development when it arrived in 1844. Towards the end of the century, however, the **transport** companies began to promote recreational travel by advertising the attractions of the Wembley Park Leisure Gardens, with their cricket and **football** pitches, running track, flower beds, fountains, and waterfalls. Interest in its residential possibilities increased when the **trams** improved access in 1908 and expanded further as a result of the publicity surrounding the **British Empire Exhibition** of 1924–25, so by the beginning of the Second World War in 1939, terraced houses, small detached villas, and light industry had replaced the fields. In 1965, when metropolitan **local government** was reorganized, Wembley became the administrative heart of the new **London Borough of Brent**.

The major building in the area is Wembley Stadium, designed in concrete by Sir John Simpson and Maxwell Ayerton, with Owen Williams as consultant engineer. The stadium, built as the centerpiece of the Empire Exhibition, opened on 28 April 1923 in time to stage the Football Association (FA) Cup Final between Bolton Wanderers and West Ham United, an event that proved memorable for reasons other than soccer as an estimated 200,000 people crammed over the terraces and spilled onto the pitch. With cancellation of the game a real possibility, Police Constable George Storey on Billie, his white horse, gently pressed the crowd back from the playing area so that the match could begin, earning national celebrity as the public read of his actions in the press and watched news film in cinemas. Since then, the 80,000-seat arena has become the home of England's national football team and has housed other major sports competitions (such as the 1948 Olympic Games) and pop concerts. An indoor arena was added in 1933–34 (when it was known as the Empire Pool) and a conference center in 1973–76. In 1999, the building was sold to the FA-owned English National Stadium Development Company. The new owners immediately announced a £300 million refurbishment program. (*See also* WHITE CITY.)

WESLEY'S CHAPEL. The chapel, which is built on a site in City Road where more than 50,000 tons of rubble were dumped before **Christopher Wren** could begin work on **St. Paul's Cathedral**, was opened by John Wesley (cofounder of the Methodist faith with his brother, Charles) in 1778. Between 1972 and 1978, it was substantially renovated following an international appeal for funds that raised nearly £1 million. Wesley is buried behind the chapel. The house next door, where he lived in 1779–91, has been converted into a **museum** that displays his furniture, books, and other personal items. The church crypt is devoted to a display depicting the history of Methodism.

WEST END. In the northern hemisphere, the prevailing winds blow from west to east. As a result, the growth of coal-fired industry and the expansion of population from the late 18th century intensified concentrations of smoke and other forms of **air pollution** towards the east of cities and wealthy citizens in the more environmentally attractive west. London's distinctive West End emerged in just such conditions, coalescing around residential districts such as **Mayfair** and exclusive shopping areas such as **Bond Street**. Since then, the term has evolved to refer also to the **theater** and restaurant district, focusing on **Leicester Square**, which flourished as a result of its proximity to affluent families with money to spend on entertainment. In 2000, the **City of Westminster** issued a series of regulations designed to stem the proliferation of clubs and bars in the area and to restrict skyscraper developments. (*See also* HAYMARKET; LLOYD WEBBER, ANDREW; SHAFTESBURY AVENUE.)

WEST HAM. West Ham, lying six miles east of **Charing Cross** in the **London Borough of Newham**, was an early center of industry in the London area, with flour, oil, and timber milling, gunpowder production, distilling, leather making, textile printing, and porcelain production all evident by the 18th century. From 1802, the expansion of the **docks** alongside the **River Thames** brought further employment, then the **railway**, which arrived in 1839, improved accessibility and attracted additional business. In 1844, the Metropolitan Buildings Act enhanced the growing manufacturing complex by confining "offensive trades" such as sulfuric acid, paint, and soap production to a limited number of sites (notably places where dirty, odorous, or noisy firms already operated) but also emphasized West Ham's working-class character by attracting relatively unskilled labor to the area. Small, terraced houses mixed with coal-burning factories in an environment that bred socialist sentiment; the London Co-operative Society was established in 1862 by railway workers in West Ham, one of the earliest of the modern labor unions (now the large General, Municipal, Boilermakers and Allied Trades Union), was founded in 1889, and **James Keir Hardie** was elected to represent the southern part of the community in the **House of Commons** in 1892, becoming one of the first two representatives of the Labour Party to win a parliamentary constituency in London. Strongly paternalistic local authorities embarked on major house building programs between the two world wars in an attempt to alleviate some of the effects of poverty resulting from the world trade recession, and the decline in harbor industries from the 1950s provided space for urban renewal projects, but the population is still heavily dominated by manual groups with strong left-wing sympathies.

WEST LONDON EXTENSION BRIDGE. *See* BATTERSEA BRIDGE.

WESTMINSTER. Scholars suggest that Sebert (King of the East Saxons) founded a **monastery** on a marshy island in the **River Thames** west of the former Roman settlement of **Londinium** during the first half of the eighth century. In 1060, Edward the Confessor (King of England from 1042 to 1066) moved his palace to the site and ordered the building of a new **abbey** dedicated to St. Peter (*see* **Westminster Abbey**), thereby establishing a politico-ecclesiastical focus that would eventually rival the commercial center of the **City of London** in power. Because of their importance, church and court promoted urban expansion as lodging houses and services were established to meet the needs of visiting dignitaries. However, the wealthy residents attracted the poor, who hoped for charity and were particularly in evidence when monarchs moved their entourage (and, therefore, the affluent citizens) to other parts of England, so by the 19th century much of the area was a pestilential slum, with homeless beggars, overcrowded rooms, and a high incidence of infectious disease. However, the construction of new roads from 1850 and the building of Parliament Square as an approach to the **Palace of Westminster** in 1868 cleared away many of the worst properties. During the 20th century, government offices increasingly infiltrated **Whitehall** and a growing tourist industry brought souvenir shops in its wake. Westminster was given city status in 1900 and became a **London borough** in 1965 (*see* **Westminster, City of**). (*See also* WESTMINSTER BRIDGE; WESTMINSTER CATHEDRAL; WESTMINSTER HALL.)

WESTMINSTER, CITY OF. Westminster was designated a **London Borough** (when London's **local government** was reformed in 1965) by merging the formerly independent authorities of **Paddington**, **St. Marylebone**, and **Westminster**. Its eight square miles include many of the attractions that draw tourists to the capital, including **Buckingham Palace**, **Harrods**, **Madame Tussaud's Waxworks**, the **National Gallery**, the **National Portrait Gallery**, the **Palace of Westminster**, the **Royal Opera House**, **Trafalgar Square**, the **West End**, and over one-fifth of all the historic buildings in London considered sufficiently important to be given legal protection against insensitive development. Some 90 percent of the adults in the 220,800 population (1998) are employed in service industries, particularly banking and other financial activities, the **hotel** trade, retailing, and public administration. Most of those residents are professional and managerial workers, nearly two-thirds of them living in rented accommodations. About one-fifth are members of ethnic minorities, though (as a result of the long history of immigration by French **Huguenots**, Italians, Cypriots, Chinese, south Asians, Arabs, and Afro-Caribbeans) no single group dominates. The borough includes the districts of **Bayswater**, **Belgravia**, **Charing Cross**, **Covent Garden**, **Mayfair**, **Piccadilly**, **Pimlico**, **Regent Street**, **Soho**, the **Strand**, **Victoria**, and **Whitehall**.

WESTMINSTER ABBEY. Westminster **Abbey** stands close to the **Palace of Westminster** on the north bank of the **River Thames**. The first church on the site (probably founded by Sebert, King of the East Saxons, in about 750) was replaced in 1065, when Edward the Confessor (England's sovereign) authorized the construction of an abbey dedicated to St. Peter. These early structures have vanished under the present buildings, begun by command of King Henry III in 1245 and completed nearly three centuries later in 1532. The basic design is French Gothic (the apse is modelled on the church at Amiens, for example), but it incorporates typically English features (such as a double aisle) and makes use of local building materials (notably Reigate stone and Purbeck marble). The nave, 103 feet high, is taller than any other in the country. Over the past three centuries, the fashion for erecting funerary and memorial monuments has detracted somewhat from the simple architectural line of the interior but, even so, these structures have their own interest.

A shrine dedicated to Edward the Confessor (who died on 5 January 1066, just eight days after his church was consecrated) stands behind the high altar, close to the marble tomb of Henry III, and Henry VII's chapel (built in 1503–12) contains the remains of Henry himself, King Edward VI, Queen Mary I, Queen Elizabeth I, Mary Queen of Scots, King James VI and I, King Charles II, King William III, Queen Mary II, Queen Anne, and King George II. Commoners, buried in the building from the reign of King Richard II in the last quarter of the 14th century, include such notable politicians as Prime Ministers William Pitt the Elder, William Pitt the Younger, and William Gladstone. The south transept is widely known as Poet's Corner because, following Geoffrey Chaucer's interment in 1400, other prominent writers requested that they be laid close to the same spot. In fact, few poets found their last resting place there, though **Ben Jonson**, John Dryden, **Samuel Johnson**, and Alfred Lord Tennyson were accorded that honor. Others (such as Robert Burns and **William Shakespeare**) are commemorated only by tablets, often erected long after the writers died because their lifestyles did not appeal to conservative clergy. Elsewhere in the abbey, tombs and inscriptions laud British citizens who made significant contributions to their country's history, including explorer David Livingstone, scientists Michael Faraday and Isaac Newton, and architect **Robert Adam**.

Since the 14th century, English monarchs have been crowned in the abbey on the oak Coronation Chair fashioned by Master Walter of Durham. The Stone of Scone, the coronation stone of Scottish sovereigns, which was seized by King Edward I in 1297, lay underneath it until 1996, when it was returned to Edinburgh. In recent years, the rising number of tourists has led to access restrictions in certain areas (such as the garden) and, more controversially, to the introduction of admission charges. Eyebrows were also raised in 1999, when James O'Donnell was appointed Organist and Master of the Choristers, the most senior musical post in the Church of England. O'Donnell is the first Roman Catholic to win the job since the Reformation. Technically, the abbey is a Royal Peculiar and thereby under the jurisdiction of the monarch rather than the Church of England, but several Members of Parliament have argued that the ecclesiastical authorities should have more influence on management. (*See also* ARCHITECTURE; BARRY, CHARLES; CHAMBERS, WILLIAM; COVENT GARDEN; GARRICK, DAVID; GIBBONS, GRINLING; GIBBS, JAMES; HENDON; HOLBORN; HYDE PARK; MONASTERIES; PUBLIC RECORD OFFICE [PRO]; ST. PAUL'S CATHEDRAL; STRAWBERRY HILL; TOURISM; WESTMINSTER.)

WESTMINSTER BRIDGE. By the early 18th century, **London Bridge** was still the only road crossing between the north and south banks of the **River Thames** in the vicinity of the city. Proposals for a second structure further upstream had been consistently sabotaged by the protests of **watermen** who made a living by ferrying travellers over the river, shopkeepers who sold their wares on London Bridge, and the **Corporation of London**, which controlled access to the settlement. However, as a result of increased traffic caused by the growth of **Westminster**, and the promise of financial compensation for ferry operators, the arguments of the Earl of Pembroke and other advocates of improved **transport** eventually prevailed. Construction began in 1738, when Swiss engineer Charles Labelye was appointed engineer to the project, and was completed in 1750. Built of stone, the new edifice incorporated 15 arches and had its piers founded in chambers knows as caissons (the first time the technique had been employed in Britain). Londoners were proud of their new bridge—so much so that dogs were not allowed on it (in case they fouled it) and anyone caught decorating the sides with graffiti could be sentenced to death without a priest in attendance. **James Boswell**, the Scottish commentator on social life in the capital, called it a "noble edifice" and, in 1768, was sufficiently impressed to pick up "a strong, jolly young damsel" in **Haymarket** and make love to the lady above the arches while the Thames rolled, uncaring, beneath them. In 1802, poet William Wordsworth, less vigorously but more romantically, observed that "Earth hath not anything to show more fair" than the view of London, wearing "the beauty of the morning," from Westminster Bridge. However, there were continual technical problems with the foundations and Parliament decided that a replacement was needed. Thomas Page was appointed to design the crossing, with **Charles Barry** as a consultant, and, in 1862, the present bridge, with seven arches resting on granite piers, was opened to traffic. It is 84 feet wide, extremely large by mid-19th-century standards. (*See also* ALBERT, PRINCE; BOADICEA; BRIDGES; GAS; STREET LIGHTING.)

WESTMINSTER CATHEDRAL. Westminster Cathedral, dedicated to the Precious Blood of Our Lord Jesus Christ, is the mother church of the Roman Catholic faith in Great Britain. Construction work began in 1896 at a site, near **Victoria** Station, which was previously occupied by a women's **prison**, and was completed in 1903. Designed by John Francis Bentley, it is constructed of brick in Byzantine style (the more traditional Gothic was rejected so that the building would not look like a poor relation of nearby **Westminster Abbey**), and parts are deliberately left unfinished so that the financial burden of decoration can be assumed by worshippers of the future. The interior, described by architectural historian Nikolaus Pevsner as "one of the most moving of any church in London" is 342 feet long, 156 feet wide, and 117 feet high. Marble brought from over a hundred sites around the world adorns the walls, and the aisles are lined with chapels. The Fourteen Stations of the Cross were carved on the piers of the nave by Eric Gill, and the Metropolitan throne (gifted by the English Bishops in memory of Cardinal Herbert Vaughan, who initiated the building program) placed in the Sanctuary, close to an altar fashioned from Cornish granite. The body of John Southworth, hanged for his faith at **Tyburn** in 1654, was brought from France in 1930 and now lies in the Chapel of St. George. Visitors to the cathedral can take the elevator to the top of the 273-foot-high campanile, which provides a magnificent view over central London.

WESTMINSTER HALL. Westminster Hall, built in 1097–99 by William Rufus (son of William the Conqueror), is the only substantial surviving fabric of the original **Palace of Westminster**. In 1394–1401, a hammer beam roof, covering the 68-foot width of the room in a single span, was installed by Henry Yevele (Master Mason to King Richard II) and Hugh Herland (the Master Carpenter). Initially, the building provided space for banquets, but, from the 13th century, it was used for administrative purposes, housing law courts, meetings of Parliament, and other formal gatherings. William Wallace (leader of Scotland's struggle for freedom from English rule during the 13th century), Thomas More (who defied the edicts of King Henry VIII), Guy Fawkes (implicated in the **Gunpowder Plot**), and King Charles I (considered a tyrant by Oliver Cromwell's Puritan supporters) were all tried and condemned to death in the hall, which was also the site of coronation festivities until 1882. Today, it is used primarily for ceremonial events.

WHITECHAPEL. The Whitechapel area of London's **East End** lies close to the **City of London**, taking its name from the white stone walls of the 13th-century church of St. Mary Matfelon and developing as a center for trades that were considered a nuisance in **The City** because of their noise or other pollution (the Whitechapel Bell Foundry moved from Houndsditch in 1583, for example; its products include **Big Ben** and the United States's original Liberty Bell). Because of the suburb's location on the main road to Essex, residents also earned an income from coaching inns and **markets**, but wages in these trades were low, so the area was characterized by poverty, attracting **immigrants** because of the cheap **housing** and becoming widely known for its high **crime** rates (*see* **Jack the Ripper**). In an attempt to improve conditions, Samuel Barnett (vicar at St. Jude's Church) founded **Toynbee Hall** in 1884 and the Whitechapel Art Gallery in 1901, but the area retained its reputation throughout the 20th century. Since the 1970s, finance houses have expanded into the western fringe of the area from The City, replacing derelict property with office blocks, and services, such as **public houses**, have responded by upgrading facilities for the middle-class lunchtime trade. Also, young, single people have purchased some of the cheap housing and carried out improvements. However, Whitechapel remains predominantly working class, with a large Bangladeshi community. In 1965, it was incorporated within the **London Borough of Tower Hamlets**. (*See also* BOOTH, CHARLES; KRAY TWINS; PETTICOAT LANE.)

WHITE CITY. In 1908, impresario Imre Kiralfy staged an exhibition at **Shepherd's Bush** in an effort to cement a political *entente* between Britain and France. Because the displays were housed in light-colored buildings, the site became known as "White City," a name still used to refer to the area. The athletics events at the fourth modern Olympic Games were held in a specially constructed stadium erected in the same year as the exhibition. The climax was the marathon, held over a 26-mile route from Windsor Castle and establishing the length of the event until a further 385 yards were added at the **Wembley** games in 1948 so that the finishing line would be in front of the royal box. White City forms part of the **London Borough of Hammersmith and Fulham**.

WHITEFRIARS. The Whitefriars area of the **City of London** takes its name from the mantle of the Carmelite monks, who established a priory in the area during the second half of the 13th century. When Richard, Duke of Cornwall and brother of King Henry II, returned from a visit to the Holy Land in 1241, he was accompanied by a group of hermits whom the Saracens had expelled from a monastery on Mount Carmel. It proved impossible for them to observe strict rules of silence and exclusion in England, so, in 1247, Pope Innocent IV decreed that they could live in urban areas provided they were dependent on charity for their survival. A church was erected at the City site, close to **St. Paul's Cathedral**, in 1253, and, over the next 300 years, numerous wealthy patrons (including John of Gaunt, Regent of England while King Richard II was too young to rule) contributed to their welfare. When King Henry VIII broke up Roman Catholic religious houses from 1536, much of the property (which extended from **Fleet Street** to the **River Thames** and included a cemetery and garden) was taken over by the Royal Armourer and the Royal Physician. The Great Hall, for a period during late Elizabethan and early Jacobean times, served as a playhouse. Most of the fabric of the priory has now vanished, but excavations in 1927 revealed a 14th-century crypt and the paving of the cloister walk.

WHITEHALL. Whitehall runs for some 600 yards from **Trafalgar Square** towards the Houses of Parliament (*see* **Palace of Westminster**), getting its name from **Whitehall Palace**, which stood on its western side from 1529 until 1698. It took its present form in the 18th century, when neighboring buildings were demolished in order to widen the roadway and improve traffic flow. Over the past 200 years, as the duties of Parliament have multiplied, work places for ministers and civil servants have replaced the homes that formerly stood on the site (so much so that "Whitehall" is now a synonym for "government administration"). **The Admiralty**, the Foreign and Commonwealth Office, the Ministry of Agriculture, the Ministry of Defence, the Scottish Office, the **Treasury Buildings**, the Welsh Office, and other departments all have entries from the street or nearby. Also, the official homes of the Prime Minister and the Chancellor of the Exchequer are in **Downing Street**, an alley leading off Whitehall. The area lies within the **City of Westminster**. (*See also* BANQUETING HOUSE; CENOTAPH; PORTLAND STONE.)

WHITEHALL PALACE. In 1529, King Henry VIII acquired property (previously owned by Thomas Wolsey, his former Lord Chancellor), which stood on the bank of the **River Thames** just south of the present **Trafalgar Square**. Dissatisfied with his aging palace at **Westminster**, he set about converting the premises into a new residence named Whitehall (probably because it was fashionable at the time to accord that title to any place given over to feasting and celebration but possibly also because of the light color of the stonework). A 2,000-room warren of corridors and staircases, with gardens, orchards, a real tennis court, a tiltyard for jousting, and a cockpit, it became the fulcrum of social life for the Tudor and Stuart monarchs. Henry celebrated his marriages to Anne Boleyn and Jane Seymour there in 1533 and 1536 respectively, Elizabeth I used the Great Hall as a theater, James VI and I commissioned **Inigo Jones** to build the **Banqueting House**, Charles I acquired an extensive collection of paintings during the second quarter of the 17th century, Oliver Cromwell ruled from Whitehall as Lord Protector of England from 1653 until his death five years later, Charles II installed his mistresses as soon as he regained the Crown in 1660, and in 1688 the Roman Catholic James VII and II sneaked out of the palace to seek safety in France from his Protestant persecutors. In 1689, however, William III, believing that the **air pollution** in London was affecting his asthma, moved the royal court to **Kensington Palace**. Nine years later, the building burned to the ground, apparently because a servant woman left clothes drying too close to a fire. (*See also* DOWNING STREET; HORSE GUARDS PARADE; NATIONAL GALLERY; TREASURY BUILDINGS.)

WHITTINGTON, RICHARD "DICK" (c. 1358–1423). One of the most enduring children's tales in the English language tells how Dick Whittington, a poor orphan, went to seek his fortune in London. He found a job as a kitchen boy in the home of a rich merchant, who allowed his servants to include articles for sale with his own goods in the ships he dispatched abroad. Dick's only possession was his beloved cat, so he sent that—a decision that made his fortune because the animal devoured the mice and rats at a foreign potentate's court, persuading the ruler to purchase it for an enormous sum. Unaware of his unexpected income, Dick had forsaken the merchant's house, driven out by the constant criticism of a nagging cook. He headed north but, as he rested at **Highgate**, heard **Bow Bells** ring out, telling him to return because he would be **Lord Mayor** of London one day. He retraced his steps, learned of his new wealth, married Alice, the merchant's daughter, and lived happily ever after, serving as Lord Mayor three times.

The story, which evolved during the early 17th century, is completely unsubstantiated by evidence though Whittington was real enough. He was the son of wealthy parents—Sir William Whittington and his wife, Joan—but knowledge of his childhood and youth are scanty, though records show that he was living in London by 1379 and earning a living as a mercer. He played a part in the government of the city, serving as an **Alderman** for Broad Street in 1393 and as a **Sheriff** in 1393–94, before being appointed Lord Mayor in 1397, when the previous incumbent died. He held the post again in 1406–7 and 1419–20 but was distinguished more by the size of the loans he made to King Richard II and King Henry IV than by his impact on urban affairs. Whittington died, childless, in March 1423, predeceased by his wife (who really was called Alice). His estate was used to rebuild **Newgate Prison** and support other civic developments.

WILLESDEN. A working-class residential suburb within the **London Borough of Brent**, some six miles northwest of **Charing Cross**, Willesden became urbanized during the second half of the 19th century as a result of the expansion of the **railway** system. Stations opened near the village of Harlesden (1842), at Willesden Junction (1866), and at Willesden Green (1880), with the result that the population grew from less than 800 in 1811 to over 100,000 in 1901. The first houses were occupied by well-to-do **City** businesspeople (in Nicol Road, for example), but these were quickly outnumbered by rows of semidetached and terraced homes built for families with lower incomes. Churches (mainly nonconformist) were erected to minister to spiritual needs and shops established to meet secular wants. Such open space as remains has been developed by local authorities for recreational use (as at Roundwood **Park**) or is used as

burial grounds (notably at the Jews' Cemetery, consecrated in Pound Lane in 1873).

WILLIAM MORRIS GALLERY. An artist, designer, poet, and socialist, Morris (1834–96) believed that human potential could be realized through development of good craftsmanship. His wallpaper, textiles, tapestry, and typefaces revolutionized design during the second half of the 19th century and are still widely used. In 1950, Water House, his home in **Walthamstow** from 1848 to 1856, opened as a **museum**, with rooms displaying examples of his own work and that of his associates, notably Edward Burne-Jones and Frank Brangwyn. There is also an extensive collection of pre-Raphaelite paintings gifted by Brangwyn as a memorial to Morris. (*See also* KELMSCOTT PRESS.)

WIMBLEDON. The remains of an Iron Age fort indicate that Wimbledon, some seven miles southwest of **Charing Cross**, was settled in Prehistoric times. In the Medieval period, it was owned by the Archbishops of Canterbury, developing as a small hilltop village close to St. Mary's Church. During the 19th century, it spread downhill towards the **railway** station, which opened in 1838, then expanded in the 1870s and 1880s as it attracted office workers willing to commute to jobs in central London. However, despite the urban encroachment, over 1,000 acres of common remains as rough grassland, providing an important open space for recreation. The area is well provided with sporting facilities, with a professional **football** club founded in 1889 and an extensive golf course, but is best known for the tennis championships held each June at the All England Club in Church Road. The club was founded by croquet enthusiasts in 1869, adding lawn tennis eight years later. There are 19 grass courts and 10 clay, with the former used only during the championship tournament. A **museum**, opened in 1977 (the centenary of the championships), contains exhibits illustrating the history of the sport and an extensive library. Wimbledon was incorporated within the **London Borough of Merton** in 1965, when the metropolitan area's **local government** was reorganized. (*See also* BAZALGETTE, JOSEPH WILLIAM.)

WOODFORD. The suburb of Woodford occupies the northwestern section of the **London Borough of Redbridge**. It developed as an agricultural village during the Middle Ages, when it was controlled by the monks of Waltham **Abbey**, then became a popular site for the country homes of rich gentry after the estate was broken up in 1540 as part of King Henry

VIII's campaign to dissolve the English **monasteries**. The arrival of the **railway** in 1856 presaged the sale of the farms and parks to urban developers who paid large sums for the right to build homes suitable for workers willing to commute to office jobs in the **City of London**. As a result, by the early 20th century, Woodford was absorbed within the metropolitan area. Sir Winston Churchill, Prime Minister during the Second World War, represented the constituency in the House of Commons (*see* **Palace of Westminster**) from 1924 to 1964.

WOOLWICH. Woolwich developed as a fishing village on the south bank of the **River Thames** about eight miles east of **Charing Cross**. It was settled at least by Roman times but grew significantly from 1512, when King Henry VIII converted the small harbor into a **Royal Naval Dockyard** specifically to build *Great Harry* as the flagship for his fleet. In subsequent years, the port was a focus for much maritime activity—from Woolwich, Walter Raleigh set off for the Americas and Martin Frobisher for the Arctic—so ancillary industries such as rope making flourished nearby, along with glass production, brass manufacture, and other activities that benefited from a location where raw materials could easily be imported by sea. In 1715, the **Royal Arsenal** (where armaments were made and tested) was transferred from the **City of London**, in 1716 two regiments of artillery were formed at the base, then, in 1719, a school for officers was opened. A flourishing reputation for turning cadets into commanders led, in 1741, to the school's designation as a Royal Military Academy, which, over the next two centuries, trained many of Britain's military leaders, including General Charles Gordon and Earl Kitchener.

By the mid-19th century, Woolwich was a prosperous working-class town, its wealth indicated by the establishment of the Woolwich Building Society, founded in 1847 and now one of the United Kingdom's largest financial institutions. Since then, however, the local economy has changed significantly. The dockyard closed in 1869 (most of the site is now covered by local authority **housing** built during the 1970s). Much of the Royal Arsenal depot has also been cleared and the land used for homes. The Military Academy merged with its sister institution at Sandhurst in 1947, and part of the barracks was turned into a **museum** for the Royal Regiment of Artillery, with an extensive research library. Nearby, the Rotunda—a tent-like structure designed by **John Nash**—houses Britain's most comprehensive collection of guns in a display that traces the development of ordnance since the 13th century. Modern Woolwich is predominantly an administrative and educational center, serving as the focus of **local government** for the **London Borough of Greenwich**. The administrative headquarters of the building society (which surrendered its mutual status and became a public limited company in 1997) dominate the small town square, the **University** of Greenwich has a local campus, and technical skills are taught at Woolwich College. A free ferry (which first opened in 1889) provides vehicles and pedestrians with a link to communities on the north shore of the Thames.

WOOLWICH ARSENAL. *See* ROYAL ARSENAL.

WOOLWICH DOCKYARD. *See* ROYAL NAVAL DOCKYARDS.

WORCESTER PARK. The residential suburb of Worcester Park, on the borders of the **Royal Borough of Kingston Upon Thames** and the County of Surrey, lies on land that was once part of the **Nonsuch Palace** estate. It takes its name from Worcester House, built by the Earl of Worcester when he was keeper of the palace park in the 17th century and later the farmhouse base for pre-Raphaelite artists John Everett Millais and William Holman Hunt (Hunt painted *The Light of the World*, which brought his work to public attention in 1854, in the orchard). Residential development began with the arrival of the **railway** in 1865 and continued until after the Second World War.

WORLD HERITAGE SITES. Governments may nominate locations within their boundaries for listing as World Heritage Sites by the United Nations Educational, Scientific, and Cultural Organization (UNESCO). Before formal recognition is granted, states must have demonstrated their adherence to Article 4 of the 1972 World Heritage Convention, which requires them to conserve their natural and cultural environments. In London, three areas of the city have been designated—the neighborhood of the **Palace of Westminster**, **Westminster Abbey**, and **St. Margaret's Church** (which was recognized in 1987); the **Tower of London** (also listed in 1987); and maritime **Greenwich** (1997).

WORMWOOD SCRUBS. One of Britain's largest jails, the "Scrubs" was designed by Edmund Du Cane (an advocate of **prison** reform) and built by convict labor in 1874–80. Originally, it housed criminals of both sexes but, since 1902, has accommodated men only, normally taking about 1,000 inmates, many of whom are serving the initial stages of life sentences. After spy George Blake escaped from the premises in 1966 and made his way to the Soviet Union, security was tightened, but the strict regime, coupled with the inevitable lack of privacy and other problems in a building erected during the Victorian era, led to riots by the prisoners in 1979. There was further controversy in 1999 when Sir David Ramsbotham, the Chief Inspector of Prisons, claimed that the Scrubs was a hotbed of racism in which prison officers were destructive and self-seeking, over-influencing management decisions.

WREN, CHRISTOPHER (1632–1723). Following the **Great Fire**, which destroyed much of the **City of London** in 1666, Wren greatly influenced the way in which the urban area was rebuilt through his plans for **St. Paul's Cathedral** and other places of worship. Born in East Knowle (Wiltshire), he was the son of the local rector, also called Christopher, and his wife, Mary. He showed considerable aptitude for the sciences while he was at Westminster School and continued to pursue these interests at Oxford University, where he graduated in 1653. After a further four years of research, he was appointed lecturer at Gresham College (*see* **Thomas Gresham**), but in 1661 he returned to Oxford as Savilian Professor of Astronomy. Initially, he investigated the planet Saturn, carried out experiments designed to evaluate the moon's influence on barometric observations (the use of the barometer as a means of predicting weather is often attributed to Wren), and worked out a graphical method of explaining solar and lunar eclipses. He also played a large part in the discussions that led to the formation of the **Royal Society**, which he later served as President in 1681–83, but, from the early 1660s, became increasingly involved in architectural work (possibly because he had a reputation for preparing very precise drawings).

In 1663–65, Wren designed a new chapel for Pembroke College, Cambridge, and, in 1664–69, he was involved in preparing plans for the Sheldonian Theatre at Oxford. On 12 September 1666, less than a week after the Great Fire had burned itself out, he presented King Charles II with proposals for the rebuilding of the City. That grand scheme was never fully put into effect, but even so, he was made a member of the commission responsible for planning the new London and is usually credited with designs for the replacement for St. Paul's as well as those for 51 parish churches, 36 **livery company** halls, the **custom house**, and many private homes.

The reconstruction of the new cathedral was the most complex of these undertakings in terms both of **architecture** and of politics. The Church of England clergy clearly wanted a church built in traditional medieval style. Wren, however, had visited Paris in 1665 and preferred the domed structures he had seen there. As a result, drawings were constantly changed and refined in an attempt to satisfy both tastes, so it was not until 1675 that a satisfactory compromise was reached. At other sites, he was able to impose more of his own preferences, relying, for his interiors, on simple shapes adapted and molded to suit the needs of site and congregation, as at **St. Mary Abchurch Church**. By contrast, the exteriors were often more flamboyant, with elaborately crafted spires that heightened individuality and made the churches conspicuous from a great distance (the steeple at **St. Bride's Church, Fleet Street**, was the inspiration for the design of the traditional tiered wedding cake). Major secular commissions included the open courtyards of **Chelsea Hospital** (1681–91), the reconstruction of Cardinal Wolsey's Tudor palace at **Hampton Court** (1689–94), the conversion of **Kensington Palace** into a residence for King William III and Queen Mary II (1689–1702), the erection of a Royal Naval Hospital at **Greenwich** (from 1696), and additions to **Westminster Abbey** (where he was appointed Surveyor in 1698). Outside London, he was responsible for repair work to Salisbury Cathedral (1668), the design of Trinity College library at Cambridge University (1676–84), the building of a new chapel at Queen's College, Oxford, and other works.

In 1669, Wren was appointed Surveyor General for London. Four years later, he was knighted by King Charles II. He retained the patronage of the Stuarts through the reigns of William and Mary, and of Queen Anne, but the accession of the first Hanoverian monarch, King George I, in 1714 allowed his enemies to plot his downfall. He was replaced as Surveyor General in 1718 and spent most of his remaining years at Hampton Court. On a visit to his London house at St. James's Street, **Piccadilly**, early in 1723 he caught a cold and on 23 February he died. He was buried in St. Paul's, where an inscription in his honor, at the entrance to the choir, finishes with the words *Lector si monumentum requiris, circumspice* ("Reader, if you seek a monument, look around you").

In recent years, some scholars have questioned traditional attributions of church and other designs to Wren, claiming that he could not have achieved everything credited to his name. For example, the more baroque parts of St. Paul's, according to some critics, were the work of **Nicholas Hawksmoor** and **St. Benet's Church, Paul's Wharf** that of Robert Hooke. (*See also* ADMIRALTY, THE; BANQUETING HOUSE; BLACKFRIARS; BOW BELLS; BUSHY PARK; COLE ABBEY CHURCH, DISTAFF LANE; CORNHILL; GUILDHALL; JONES,

INIGO; LOMBARD STREET; MARLBOROUGH HOUSE; MONUMENT; PORTLAND STONE; QUEEN'S HOUSE; ROYAL OBSERVATORY; ST. ANDREW'S CHURCH, HOLBORN; ST. CLEMENT DANES CHURCH, STRAND; ST. JAMES'S CHURCH, PICCADILLY; ST. JAMES'S PALACE; ST. STEPHEN WALBROOK CHURCH, WALBROOK; SIR JOHN SOANE'S MUSEUM; TEMPLE BAR; THEATRE ROYAL, DRURY LANE; WALBROOK.)

– Y –

YEOMAN WARDER OF THE TOWER. *See* BEEFEATER.

YEOMEN OF THE GUARD. The Yeomen of the Guard are reputed to be the world's oldest surviving company of royal bodyguards. Formed by King Henry VII in 1485, their tasks are now largely ceremonial. Members, who wear a scarlet uniform of Tudor design, with royal emblems embroidered in gold, all formerly served with the armed forces. (*See also* HONOURABLE CORPS OF GENTLEMEN AT ARMS.)

– Z –

ZOOLOGICAL GARDENS. See CHESSINGTON; LONDON ZOO; TOWER OF LONDON.

Appendix 1

London Local Government Authorities: Addresses and Telephone Numbers

Corporation of London
Guildhall, London, EC2P 2EJ (Telephone: 020 7606 3030)

Barking and Dagenham
Civic Centre, Rainham Road North, Dagenham, RM10 7BN (Telephone: 020 8592 4500)

Barnet
Town Hall, The Burroughs, Hendon, NW4 4BG (Telephone: 020 8202 8282)

Bexley
Civic Offices, Broadway, Bexleyheath, DA6 7LB (Telephone: 020 8303 7777)

Brent
Town Hall, Forty Lane, Wembley, HA9 9HZ (Telephone: 020 8908 7127)

Bromley
Civic Centre, Stockwell Close, Bromley, BR1 3UH (Telephone: 020 8464 3333)

Camden
Town Hall, Euston Road, Camden, NW1 2RU (Telephone: 020 7278 4444)

Croydon
Taberner House, Park Lane, Croydon, CR9 3JS (Telephone: 020 8686 4433)

Ealing
Town Hall, New Broadway, Ealing, W5 2BY (Telephone: 020 8579 2424)

Enfield
Civic Centre, Silver Street, Enfield, EN1 3XY (Telephone: 020 8366 6565)

Greenwich
Town Hall, Wellington Street, Greenwich, SE18 6PW (Telephone: 020 8854 8888)

Hackney
Town Hall, Mare Street, Hackney, E8 1EA (Telephone: 020 8986 3123)

Hammersmith and Fulham
Town Hall, King Street, London, W6 9JU (Telephone: 020 8748 3020)

Haringey
Civic Centre, High Road, Wood Green, London, N22 4LE (Telephone: 020 8975 9700)

Harrow
Civic Centre, Station Road, Harrow, HA1 2UH (Telephone: 020 8863 5611)

Havering
Town Hall, Romford, RM1 3BD (Telephone: 01708 772222)

Hillingdon
Civic Centre, High Street, Uxbridge, UB8 1UW (Telephone: 01895 250111)

Hounslow
Civic Centre, Lampton Road, Hounslow, TW3 4DN (Telephone: 020 8570 7728)

Islington
Town Hall, Upper Street, Islington, N1 2UD (Telephone: 020 7226 1234)

Kensington and Chelsea
Town Hall, Hornton Street, London, W8 7NX (Telephone: 020 7937 5464)

Kingston Upon Thames
Guildhall, Kingston Upon Thames, KT1 1EU (Telephone: 020 8546 2121)

Lambeth
Town Hall, Brixton Hill, London, SW2 1RW (Telephone: 020 7926 1000)

Lewisham
Town Hall, Catford, SE6 4RU (Telephone: 020 8695 6000)

Merton
Civic Centre, London Road, Morden, SM4 5DX (Telephone: 020 8543 2222)

Newham
Town Hall, East Ham, E6 2RP (Telephone: 020 8472 1430)

Redbridge
Town Hall, High Road, Ilford, IG1 1DD (Telephone: 020 8478 3020)

Richmond Upon Thames
Civic Centre, York Street, Twickenham, TW1 3AA (Telephone: 020 8891 1411)

Southwark
Town Hall, Peckham Road, London, SE5 8UB (Telephone: 020 7525 7175)

Sutton
Civic Offices, St. Nicholas Way, Sutton, SM1 1EA (Telephone: 020 8770 5000)

Tower Hamlets
Mulberry Place, 5 Clove Crescent, London, E14 2BG (Telephone: 020 7512 4200)

Waltham Forest
Town Hall, Forest Road, Walthamstow, E17 4JF (Telephone: 020 8527 5544)

Wandsworth
Town Hall, Wandsworth High Street, London, SW18 2PU (Telephone: 020 8871 6000)

Westminster
City Hall, Victoria Street, London, SW1E 6QP (Telephone: 020 7828 8070)

Appendix 2
World Wide Web Addresses

The following list of Web addresses is not exhaustive but provides many links to related sites. Compendium sites (such as those for the London Tourist Board and the National Trust) are particularly helpful, as are those of local government bodies.

Readers are reminded, however, that Web addresses can change. Those listed below were current at the time of going to press but may have been altered since then. Judicious use of search engines could help to uncover the new locations.

Cathedrals and Churches

St. Paul's Cathedral. http://www.stpauls.co.uk/index.htm

Southwark Cathedral. http://www.max.roehampton.ac.uk/link/dswart/cath/index.htm

Westminster Abbey. http://www.westminster-abbey.org

Westminster Cathedral. http://www.westminstercathedral.org.uk

Commerce and Industry

Baltic Exchange. http://www.balticexchange.co.uk

Harrods. http://www.harrods.com

Lloyd's of London. http://www.lloydsoflondon.co.uk

London Chamber of Commerce and Industry. http://www.londonchamber.co.uk

London Clearing House. http://www.lch.co.uk

London First. http://www.london-first.co.uk

London International Finance and Futures Options Exchange (LIFFE). http://www.liffe.com

London Metal Exchange. http://www.lme.co.uk

London Stock Exchange. http://www.londonstockexchange.com

Port of London Authority. http://www.portoflondon.co.uk

Selfridge's. http://www.selfridges.com

Sotheby's. http://www.sothebys.com

Education

Association of Colleges, London Region. http://www.londoncolleges.com

Birkbeck College, University of London. http://www.goldsmiths.ac.uk

Brunel University. http://www.brunel.ac.uk

City University. http://www.city.ac.uk

East London, University of. http://www.uel.ac.uk

Greenwich, University of. http://www.gre.ac.uk

Imperial College, University of London. http://www.ic.ac.uk

Institute of Education, University of London. http://www.ioe.ac.uk

King's College, University of London. http://www.kcl.ac.uk

Kingston University. http://www.kingston.ac.uk

London Business School. http://www.lbs.ac.uk

London Guildhall University. http://www.lgu.ac.uk

London School of Economics, University of London. http://www.lse.ac.uk

Middlesex University. http://www.mdx.ac.uk

Queen Mary and Westfield College, University of London. http://www.qmw.ac.uk

Royal College of Art. http://www.rca.ac.uk

South Bank University. http://www.sbu.ac.uk

Thames Valley University. http://www.tvu.ac.uk

Westminster, University of. http://www.wmin.ac.uk

Emergency Services

City of London Police. http://www.cityoflondon.gov.uk/citypolice/index.htm

London Fire Brigade. http://london-fire.gov.uk/index.htm

Metropolitan Police. http://www.met.police.uk

Entertainment

London Theatre Guide. http://www.londontheatre.co.uk

Royal Festival Hall. http://www.rfh.org.uk

Society of London Theatre. http://www.officiallondontheatre.co.uk

TheatreNet. http://www.theatrenet.com

What's On Stage. http://www.whatsonstage.com

Government

Association of London Government. http://www.alg.gov.uk

Barking and Dagenham, London Borough of. http://www.barking-dagenham.gov.uk

Barnet, London Borough of. http://www.barnet.co.uk
Bexley, London Borough of. http://www.bexley.gov.uk
Brent, London Borough of. http://www2.brent.gov.uk
Bromley, London Borough of. http://www.bromley.gov.uk
Camden, London Borough of. http://www.camden.gov.uk
City of London. http://www.cityoflondon.gov.uk
Corporation of London. http://www.cityoflondon.gov.uk
Croydon, London Borough of. http://www.croydon.gov.uk
Ealing, London Borough of. http://www.ealing.gov.uk
Enfield, London Borough of. http://www.enfield.gov.uk
Greenwich, London Borough of. http://www.greenwich.gov.uk
Hackney, London Borough of. http://www.hackney.gov.uk
Hammersmith and Fulham, London Borough of. http://www.lbhf.gov.uk
Haringey, London Borough of. http://www.haringey.gov.uk
Harrow, London Borough of. http://www.harrow.gov.uk
Havering, London Borough of. http://www.havering.gov.uk
Hillingdon, London Borough of. http://www.hillingdon.gov.uk
Hounslow, London Borough of. http://www.hounslow.gov.uk
Houses of Parliament. http://www.parliament.uk
Islington, London Borough of. http://www.islington.gov.uk
Kensington and Chelsea, Royal Borough of. http://www.rbkc.gov.uk
Kingston Upon Thames, Royal Borough of. http://www.kingston.gov.uk
Lambeth, London Borough of. http://www.lambeth.gov.uk
Lewisham, London Borough of. http://www.lewisham.gov.uk
London Assembly. http://www.london.gov.uk
Merton, London Borough of. http://www.merton.gov.uk
Newham, London Borough of. http://www.newham.gov.uk
No. 10 Downing Street. http://www.number-10.gov.uk
Redbridge, London Borough of. http://www.redbridge.gov.uk
Richmond Upon Thames, London Borough of. http://www.richmond.gov.uk
Southwark, London Borough of. http://www.southwark.gov.uk
Sutton, London Borough of. http://www.sutton.gov.uk
Tower Hamlets, London Borough of. http://www.towerhamlets.gov.uk
Waltham Forest, London Borough of. http://www.lbwf.gov.uk
Wandsworth, London Borough of. http://www.wandsworth.gov.uk
Westminster, City of. http://www.westminster.gov.uk

Libraries

British Library. http://www.bl.uk
Family Records Centre. http://www.pro.gov.uk
M25 Consortium of Higher Education Libraries. http://www.M25lib.ac.uk/M25/welcome.html
Public Libraries. http://www.harden.dial.pipex.com/weblibs.html
Public Record Office. http://www.pro.gov.uk

Media

British Broadcasting Corporation. http://www.bbc.co.uk
BBC London Live. http://www.bbc.co.uk/londonlive
Daily Express. http://www.express.co.uk
Daily Mirror. http://www.mirror.co.uk
Daily Telegraph. http://www.dailytelegraph.co.uk
Evening Standard. http://thisislondon.co.uk:80/dynamic/index.htm
Financial Times. http://www.ft.com
Guardian. http://www.guardian.co.uk
Independent. http://www.independent.co.uk
LBC Radio. http://www.lbc.co.uk
Morning Star. http://www.poptel.org.uk/morning-star
Observer. http://www.observer.co.uk
Times. http://www.the-times.co.uk

Museums and Galleries

British Museum. http://www.thebritishmuseum.ac.uk
Cabinet War Rooms. http://www.iwm.org.uk/cabinet/cabinet.htm
Design Museum. http://www.designmuseum.org
Dickens House Museum. http://www.rmplc.co.uk/orgs/dickens/DHM/DHM2/index.html
Geffrye Museum. http://www.geffrye-museum.org.uk
Hayward Gallery. http://www.hayward-gallery.org.uk
HMS *Belfast*. http://www.iwm.org.uk/belfast.belfast.htm
Horniman Museum. http://www.horniman.demon.co.uk
Imperial War Museum. http://www/iwm.org.uk
London Dungeon. http://www.thedungeons.com
London Transport Museum. http://www.ltmuseum.co.uk
Museum of Childhood. http://www.vam.ac.uk
Museum of London. http://www.museum-london.org.uk
National Army Museum. http://www.national-army-museum.ac.uk
National Gallery. http://www.nationalgallery.org.uk

National Maritime Museum. http://www.nmm.ac.uk
National Portrait Gallery. http://www.npg.org.uk
Natural History Museum. http://www.nhm.ac.uk
Royal Academy of Arts. http://www.royalacademy.org.uk
Science Museum. http://www.nmsi.ac.uk/science_museum_fr.htm
Serpentine Gallery. http://www.serpentinegallery.org
Sir John Soane's Museum. http://www.soane.org
Tate Gallery. http://www.tate.org.uk
Tower of London. http://www.tower-of-london.com
Victoria & Albert Museum. http://www.vam.ac.uk
Wallace Collection. http://www.the-wallace-collection.org.uk
Whitechapel Art Gallery. http://www.whitechapel.org
William Morris Gallery. http://www.lbwf.gov.uk/wmg/home.htm

Palaces and Stately Homes

Buckingham Palace. http://www.royal.gov.uk/palaces/bp.htm
English Heritage. http://www.english-heritage.co.uk
Hampton Court Palace. http://www.the-eye.com/hcintro.htm
Kensington Palace. http://www.royal.gov.uk/palaces/kensington.htm
National Trust. http://www.nationaltrust.org.uk
Palace of Westminster. http://www.parliament.uk/parliament/guide/palace.htm
St. James's Palace. http://www.royal.gov.uk/palaces/stjamess.htm

Parks and Gardens

English Heritage. http://www.english-heritage.co.uk
London Zoo. http://www.londonzoo.co.uk/londonzoo/index.html
National Trust. http://www.nationaltrust.org.uk
Royal Botanic Gardens. http://www.rbgkew.org.uk
Royal Parks. http://www.open.gov.uk/rp/rphome.htm

Sports

Cricket Clubs. http://www-uk.cricket.org
Crystal Palace National Sports Centre. http://www.crystalpalace.co.uk
Football Association. http://www.the-fa.org
Rugby Football Union. http://www.rfu.com
Wembley National Stadium. http://www.wembleynationalstadium.com

Tourist Information

London Tourist Board. http://londontouristboard.co.uk

Transport

Gatwick Airport. htttp://www.gatwick.co.uk

Heathrow Airport. http://www.heathrow.co.uk

London City Airport. http://www.airwise.com/airports/europe/LCY/LCY_01.html

London Transport. http://www.londontransport.co.uk

Railtrack. http://www.railtrack.co.uk

Stansted Airport. http://www.stansted.co.uk

Bibliography

Bibliographies of settlements as large and diverse as London can include only a small portion of the literature about the city, so compilers must be selective. In this Historical Dictionary, citations are restricted to English-language publications registered by the British Library, which receives reference copies of all books and periodicals distributed in the United Kingdom. Most are readily obtainable by readers in the United States, either at local university and public libraries or through interlibrary loan services, and further details of those texts that are difficult to trace can be obtained through the search facility of the British Library's Internet site (http://www.bl.uk).

In addition, for reasons of space, references are confined to books and monographs, thus excluding articles in professional journals, newspaper reports, and information available only on microfiche or other nonprint sources. Also, all of the items listed have appeared since 1980. Students interested in older material may find suitable sources in Heather J. Creaton, ed., *Bibliography of Printed Works on London History to 1939* (London: Library Association Publishing, 1994), and Patricia L. Garside, ed., *Capital Histories: A Bibliographical Study of London* (Aldershot, UK: Ashgate, 1998). In addition, Kenneth J. Panton and Keith A. Cowlard, *Historical Dictionary of the United Kingdom*, 2 vols. (Lanham, Md.: Scarecrow Press, 1997, 1998) includes extensive reference to texts that place London in the wider context of British history and provides details of monarchs, prime ministers, and others who lived in the city as well as national events for which London was a focus. The *London Journal* regularly prints bibliographical studies, as does *Urban History* (and its predecessor, the *Urban History Yearbook*). The books cited in the bibliography below also incorporate extensive lists of references.

Many other sources of information are available to researchers pursuing specific enquiries. Scholarly journals, such as the *Transactions of the Royal Historical Society*, frequently contain papers dealing with the city, and the *London Evening Standard* (the city's evening newspaper) carries daily reports on crime, government, theater, transport, and other topics. These are supplemented by articles in the quality daily press (notably the *Daily Telegraph*, *The Financial Times, The Guardian*, *The Independent*, and *The Times*), allowing workers to trace historical developments as far back as the 18th century. Also, national and local government organizations regularly publish statistics summarizing quantifiable aspects of economic and social conditions, and special interest groups prepare documents outlining aspects of political or environmental concern. The Office of Population Censuses and Surveys has produced decennial returns describing the demographic characteristics of Londoners, and their living standards, since 1801, and the Ordnance Survey has charted the expansion of the city for nearly 200 years (parts of London were mapped at a scale of 60 inches to the mile by the middle of the 19th century). Specialist collections (such as the Museum of London's extensive archive of photographs and the government documents held at the Public Record Office) provide sources of ancillary information.

For ease of use, and to eliminate unnecessary repetition of citations, the bibliography is subdivided thematically rather than chronologically. However, no division of knowledge is precise, so readers are encouraged to refer to several categories rather than limit themselves to a single topic. For example, scholars seeking material on London's social history will find a lengthy list of books under that heading but will find further material in the sections dealing with biography, education, health, and ethnic groups, which together provide several hundred texts for reference.

By using the material provided here as a basis of study, scholars can readily widen the scope of their enquiries to provide additional depth and detail. However, authors differ in their approach to urban studies, so it is usually helpful to rely on several sources in order to obtain a balanced view. For example, Michael Hebbert's overview of the city's growth in *London: More by Fortune than Design* (Chichester,

UK: John Wiley, 1998) concentrates heavily on the 20th century and reveals a metropolitan area full of vitality because it has resisted attempts by planners to slow the pace of change. On the other hand, in *London: A History* (Oxford: Oxford University Press, 1998) Francis Sheppard places greater emphasis on earlier time periods, though noting concern about London's ability to retain its commercial dominance as technology facilitates movement of business to less central sites, and Stephen Inwood in *A History of London* (London: Macmillan, 1998) focuses on "the sick, the disgruntled, the hungry and the disreputable" in a work that suggests the time has come for greater control of development.

Ann Saunders's *The Art and Architecture of London* (Oxford: Phaidon, 1988) is a valuable single-volume survey of the city's most important buildings but is best used in conjunction with the more lavishly illustrated and comprehensive *Guide to the Architecture of London* by Edward Jones and Christopher Woodward (London: Weidenfeld and Nicolson, 1992). Additionally, access to a good street map, such as those published by Nicholson and A to Z, is essential to any researcher who wants to understand the relationship between neighborhoods, business zones, and transport nodes, or simply to acquire a sense of place.

The reasons for London's role as an international center of commerce are outlined by S. D. Chapman in *The Rise of Merchant Banking* (London: Unwin Hyman, 1988), and by L. D. Schwarz in *London in the Age of Industrialisation: Entrepreneurs, Labour Force and Living Conditions* (Cambridge: Cambridge University Press, 1992). Education receives special treatment from Stuart Maclure in *A History of Education in London, 1879–1990* (London: Allen Lane, 1990), and health in the edited volume by W. F. Bynum and Roy Porter on *Living and Dying in London* (London: Wellcome Institute for the History of Medicine, 1991). John Davis analyzes the strengths and weaknesses of the metropolitan area's local government during the second half of the 19th century in *Reforming London: The London Government Problem, 1855–1900* (Oxford: Clarendon, 1998), and Andrew Saint, ed., covers the first half of the 20th century in *Politics and the People of London: The London County Council, 1889–1965* (London: Hambledon, 1989). Roy Porter's *London: A Social History* (London: Hamish Hamilton, 1994) synthesizes a vast range of material on disease, housing conditions, and other factors conditioning quality of life.

Scholars fortunate to have access to the city will find all of the works listed above in the collections of the Guildhall Library, the first port of call for Londoners seeking documents dealing with aspects of the metropolitan area's development.

ARCHITECTURE

Allibone, Finch, and Lynn Quiney. *The Law Society's Hall: An Architectural History, 1823–1995*. London: Law Society, 1995.

Allinson, Kenneth, and Victoria Thornton. *Guide to London's Contemporary Architecture*. Oxford: Butterworth Architecture, 1993.

Amery, Colin. *Wren's London*. Luton, UK: Lennard, 1988.

———. *A Celebration of Art and Architecture: The National Gallery Sainsbury Wing*. London: National Gallery, 1991.

Atkinson, Frank. *St Paul's: The Cathedral Guide*. London: Pitkin, 1983.

Barker, Felix, and Ralph Hyde. *London as It Might Have Been*. London: John Murray, 1982.

Bayley, Stephen. *The Albert Memorial: The Monument in Its Social and Architectural Context*. London: Scolar, 1981.

Beattie, Susan. *A Revolution in London Housing: LCC Housing Architects and Their Work*. London: Architectural Press, 1980.

Binney, Marcus. *Palace on the River: Tony Farrell's Redevelopment of Charing Cross*. London: Wordsearch, 1991.

Binski, Paul. *Westminster Abbey and the Plantagenets: Kingship and the Representation of Power, 1200–1400*. New Haven, Conn.: Yale University Press, 1995.

Blatch, Mervyn. *A Guide to London's Churches*. London: Constable, 1995.

Blundell, Joe Whitlock. *Westminster Abbey: The Monuments*. London: Murray, 1989.

Boyne, Sir Harry. *The Houses of Parliament*. London: Batsford, 1981.

Bradley, Simon, and Nikolaus Pevsner. *The London Churches*. London: Penguin, 1998.

Brooks, Chris. *The Albert Memorial*. London: English Heritage/The Victorian Society. Westminster City Council, 1995.

Browne, John, and Timothy Dean. *Building of Faith: Westminster Cathedral*. London: Booth-Clibborn, 1995.

Brownless, David B. *The Law Courts: The Architecture of George Edmund Street*. New York: Architectural History Foundation, 1984.

Burman, Peter. *St. Paul's Cathedral*. London: Bell and Hyman, 1987.

Byrne, Andrew. *London's Georgian Houses*. London: Georgian Press, 1986.

———. *Bedford Square: An Architectural Study*. London: Athlone, 1990.

Cassidy, G. E. *The Architectural History of St. Anne's Church, Kew Green*. London: Richmond Local History Society, 1986.

Casson, Sir Hugh. *Hugh Casson's London*. Boston: Little, Brown, 1993.

Cherry, Bridget, and Nikolaus Pevsner. *London: South*. Harmondsworth, UK: Penguin, 1983.

———. *London: North West*. London: Penguin, 1991.

———. *London: North*. London: Penguin, 1998.

Cobb, Gerald. *London City Churches*. London: Batsford, 1989.

Cocke, Thomas. *900 Years: The Restorations of Westminster Abbey*. London: Harvey Miller, 1995.

Cox, Alan. *Docklands in the Making: The Redevelopment of the Isle of Dogs, 1981–1995*. London: Athlone/Royal Commission on the Historical Monuments of England, 1995.

Crowe, A. J. *Inns, Taverns and Pubs of the London Borough of Sutton: Their History and Architecture, With 61 Original Drawings*. London: London Borough of Sutton, 1980.

Cruickshank, Dan, and Peter Wyld. *Georgian Town Houses and Their Details*. London: Butterworth Architecture, 1990.

Darley, Gillian, ed. *The Living Heritage of Westminster: Celebrating 400 Years of Architectural Development in the City of Westminster*. London: Westminster City Council, 1984.

Darwin, John. *The Triumphs of Big Ben*. London: Hale, 1986.

Davies, Philip, and Delcia Keate. *In the Public Interest: London's Civic Architecture at Risk*. London: English Heritage, 1995.

Dow, Helen Jeanette. *The Sculptural Decoration of the Henry VII Chapel, Westminster Abbey*. Edinburgh: Pentland, 1992.

Downes, Kerry. *Sir Christopher Wren: The Design of St. Paul's Cathedral*. London: Trefoil, 1988.

Edwards, Brian. *London Docklands: Urban Design in an Age of Deregulation*. Oxford: Butterworth Architecture, 1992.

Farrell, Terry. *Terry Farrell: Urban Design*. London: Academy Editions, 1993.

Fletcher, Geoffrey. *The London Nobody Knows*. London: Cassell, 1996.

Foreman, Susan. *From Palace to Power: An Illustrated History of Whitehall*. Brighton, UK: Alpha, 1995.

Girouard, Mark. *Alfred Waterhouse and the Natural History Museum*. London: British Museum (Natural History), 1981.

Gough, Piers. *Albert Gate, Embankment Place, Vauxhall Cross: Architect Terry Farrell*. London: Wordsearch, 1993.

Guillery, Peter. *The Buildings of London Zoo*. London: Royal Commission on the Historical Monuments of England, 1993.

Gurr, Andrew. *Rebuilding Shakespeare's Globe*. London: Weidenfeld and Nicolson, 1989.

Hancox, Joy. *The Byrom Collection and the Globe Theatre Mystery*. London: Jonathan Cape, 1997.

Hardingham, Samantha. *London: A Guide to Recent Architecture*. London: Artemis, 1993.

Hare, Susan M. *Goldsmith's Hall in the City of London*. Norwich, UK: Jarrold, 1996.

Harris, John. *The Palladian Revival: Lord Burlington, His Villa and Garden at Chiswick*. New Haven, Conn.: Yale University Press, 1994.

Harvey, Anthony, and Richard Mortimer. *The Funeral Effigies of Westminster Abbey*. Woodbridge, UK: Boydell, 1994.

Harwood, Elain, and Andrew Saint. *London*. London: Her Majesty's Stationery Office/English Heritage, 1991.

Hawkes, Jason. *London Landmarks from the Air*. London: Ebury, 1996.

Heritage of London Trust. *Historic Buildings in Covent Garden*. London: Heritage of London Trust, 1984.

Hessenberg, Ian, ed. *London in Detail*. London: Murray, 1986.

Hibbert, Christopher. *London's Churches*. London: Macdonald/Queen Anne Press, 1988.

Hitchmough, Wendy. *Hoover Factory: Wallis, Gilbert and Partners*. London: Phaidon, 1992.

Hobhouse, Hermione. *London Survey'd: The Work of the Survey of London, 1894–1994*. Swindon, UK: Royal Commission on the Historical Monuments of England, 1994.

Hunter, Michael. *The Victorian Villas of Hackney*. London: Hackney Society, 1981.

Hunting, Penelope. *Cutlers Gardens*. London: Standard Life Assurance Company, 1984.

Jeffrey, Paul. *The City Churches of Sir Christopher Wren*. London: Hambledon Press, 1996.

Jeffrey, Sally. *The Mansion House*. Chichester, UK: Phillimore/Corporation of London, 1993.

Jenner, Michael. *London Heritage: The Changing Style of a City*. London: Mermaid, 1990.

Jodard, Paul. *Lightweight Classic: Terry Farrell's Covent Garden Nursery Building*. London: Cheerman, 1993.

Jones, Christopher. *No. 10 Downing Street: The Story of a House*. London: British Broadcasting Corporation, 1985.

Jones, Edward, and Christopher Woodward. *A Guide to the Architecture of London*. London: Weidenfeld and Nicolson, 1992.

Kirkman, Ken. *A History of Pinner Hill House and Estate*. London: Albury Enterprises, 1993.

Klatt, Bebbe, ed. *GLC/ILEA Architecture, 1976–1986: An Illustrated Record of the Work of the GLC/ILEA Department of Architecture and Civic Design in the Decade 1976 to 1986*. London: Architectural Press, 1986.

Leonard, John. *London's Parish Churches*. Derby, UK: Breedon, 1997.

Lindsay, Paul. *The Synagogues of London*. London: Vallentine Mitchell, 1993.

Mason, Martin, and Malcolm Sanders. *The City Companion*. London: Hale, 1994.

McKellar, Elizabeth. *The German Hospital, Hackney: A Social and Architectural History*. London: Hackney Society, 1991.

Menear, Laurence. *London's Underground Stations: A Social and Architectural Study*. Tunbridge Wells, UK: Midas, 1983.

Milward, R. J. *The Rectory: Wimbledon's Oldest House*. London: Artscan, 1992.

Montgomery-Massingberd, Hugh, and David Watkin. *The London Ritz: A Social and Architectural History*. London: Aurum, 1980.

Morrison, Kathryn. *One Hundred Years of Suburbia: The Aldershot Estate in Wanstead, 1899–1999*. London: Royal Commission on the Historical Monuments of England, 1999.

Mulryne, Ronnie, and Margaret Shewring. *Shakespeare's Globe Rebuilt*. Cambridge: Cambridge University Press, 1997.

Munsell, F. Darell. *The Victorian Controversy Surrounding the Wellington War Memorial: The Archduke of Hyde Park Corner*. Lewiston, N.Y.: Edwin Mellen, 1991.

Murray, Michael G. *Middle Temple Hall: An Architectural Appreciation*. London: Middle Temple, 1991.

Newton, Miranda H. *Architects' London Houses: Homes of Thirty Architects Since the 1930s*. Oxford: Butterworth Architecture, 1992.

Olsen, Donald J. *The City as a Work of Art: London, Paris, Vienna*. New Haven, Conn.: Yale University Press, 1986.

Orrell, John. *The Quest for Shakespeare's Globe*. Cambridge: Cambridge University Press, 1983.

Papadakis, Andreas C. *Post-Modern Triumphs in London*. London: Architectural Design, 1991.

Pearce, David. *London—Capital City*. London: Batsford, 1988.

Pearman, Hugh. *The Ark, London: Architect, Ralph Erskine*. London: Wordsearch, 1993.

Pevsner, Nikolaus, and Simon Bradley. *London: The City*. London: Penguin, 1997.

Physick, John. *The Victoria and Albert Museum: The History of Its Building*. Oxford: Phaidon, 1982.

Port, M. H. *Imperial London: Civil Government Building in London, 1850–1915*. New Haven, Conn.: Yale University Press, 1995.

Porter, Stephen, ed. *Poplar, Blackwell and the Isle of Dogs: The Parish of All Saints*. London: Athlone, 1994.

Powell, Kenneth. *London*. London: Academy Editions, 1993.

———. *Lloyd's Building: Richard Rogers Partnership*. London: Phaidon, 1994.

Richardson, Margaret. *66 Portland Place: The London Headquarters of the Royal Institute of British Architects*. London: Royal Institute of British Architects, 1984.

Ringshall, Ron, Dame Margaret Miles, and Frank Kelsall. *The Urban School: Buildings for Education in London, 1870–1980*. London: Greater London Council, 1983.

Ruffinière du Prey, Pierre de la. *Hawksmoor's London Churches*. Chicago: University of Chicago Press, 2000.

St. Aubyn, Fiona. *A Portrait of Georgian London, Based on Ackermann's "The Microcosm of London," Published 1808–1810*. Churt, UK: D. Leader, 1985.

St. John Wilson. *The Design and Construction of the British Library*. London: British Library, 1998.

Salvadori, Renzo. *Architect's Guide To London*. London: Butterworth Architecture, 1990.

Saunders, Ann. *The Art and Architecture of London: An Illustrated Guide*. Oxford: Phaidon, 1988.

Schofield, John. *Medieval London Houses*. New Haven, Conn.: Yale University Press, 1995.

Schumann-Bacia, Eva. *John Soane and the Bank of England*. New York: Princeton Architectural Press, 1991.

Stamp, Gavin, and Colin Amery. *Victorian Buildings of London, 1837–1887: An Illustrated Guide*. London: Architectural Press, 1980.

Thackrah, J. R. *The Royal Albert Hall*. Lavenham, UK: Terence Dalton, 1983.

Thorne, Robert. *Covent Garden Market: Its History and Restoration*. London: Architectural Press, 1980.

Toplis, Ian. *The Foreign Office: An Architectural History*. London: Mansell, 1987.

Trench, Richard. *Philip's London: Architecture, History, Art*. London: George Philip, 1991.

Walker, Annabel. *Kensington and Chelsea: A Social and Architectural History*. London: Murray, 1987.

Wedgwood, Alexandra. *Rebuilding the Houses of Parliament: Drawings from the Kennedy Albums and the Thomas Greene Papers*. London: House of Lords Record Office, 1984.

Weiner, Deborah E. B. *Architecture and Social Reform in Late-Victorian London*. Manchester, UK: Manchester University Press, 1994.

Weinreb, Matthew. *London Architecture: Features and Façades*. London: Phaidon, 1993.

Wickham, D. E. *Clothworkers' Hall*. Norwich, UK: Jarrold, 1989.

Williams, Andy. *Historic London*. London: Weidenfeld and Nicolson, 1994.

Williamson, Elizabeth, and Nikolaus Pevsner. *London Docklands*. London: Penguin, 1998.

Young, Elizabeth, and Wayland Young. *London's Churches*. London: Grafton, 1986.

ARTS AND ENTERTAINMENT

Adams, Elizabeth. *Chelsea Porcelain*. London: Barrie and Jenkins, 1987.

Allan, D. G. C. *Some Noble Men—And Women!: RSA Members and Prize Winners of the Twickenham Area*. London: Borough of Twickenham Local History Society, 1994.

Antor, Heinz. *The Bloomsbury Group: Its Philosophy, Aesthetics and Literary Achievement*. Heidelberg: C. Winter, 1986.

Ashwin, Clive. *A Century of Art Education*. London: Middlesex Polytechnic, 1982.

Baer, Marc. *Theatre and Disorder in Late Georgian London*. Oxford: Clarendon, 1992.

Bailey, Martin. *Van Gogh and Sir Richard Wallace's Pictures*. London: Trustees of the Wallace Collection, 1998.

Baird, David. *Shakespeare at the Globe*. London: MQ, 1998.

Balakier, Ann Stewart, and James J. Balakier. *The Spatial Infinite at Greenwich in Works by Christopher Wren, James Thornhill, and James Thomson: The Newton Connection*. Lewiston, N.Y.: Edwin Mellen, 1995.

Ball, Alan W. *The Countryside Lies Sleeping, 1685–1950: Paintings, Prints and Drawings of Pinner, Stanmore and Other Former Villages Now in the London Borough of Harrow*. London: Riverhill, 1981.

Baron, Xavier, ed. *London, 1066–1914: Literary Sources and Documents*. Robertsbridge, UK: Helm Information, 1997.

Barr, Charles. *Ealing Studios*. Berkeley: University of California Press, 1998.

Beard, Geoffrey. *The Work of Christopher Wren*. Edinburgh: Bartholomew, 1982.

———. *The Work of Grinling Gibbons*. London: Murray, 1989.

Beasley, Maureen. *Five Centuries of Artists in Sutton: A Biographical Dictionary of Artists Associated With Sutton, London*. London: London Borough of Sutton, 1989.

Berry, Herbert. *Shakespeare's Playhouses*. New York: AMS, 1987.

Berry, Patricia. *Theatrical London*. Stroud, UK: Alan Sutton, 1995.

Bond, Henry. *The Cult of the Street: Photographs of London*. London: Emily Tsingou Gallery, 1998.

Bond, Maurice, ed. *Works of Art in the House of Lords*. London: Her Majesty's Stationery Office, 1980.

Boursnell, Clive. *The Royal Opera House, Covent Garden*. London: Hamilton, 1982.

Bowsher, Julian. *The Rose Theatre: An Archaeological Discovery*. London: Museum of London, 1998.

Brandt, Bill. *London in the Thirties*. London: Gordon Fraser, 1983.

Brown, John Russell. *Shakespeare and His Theatre*. London: Viking, 1993.

Bryant, Julius. *Finest Prospects: Three Historic Houses—A Study in London Topography*. London: English Heritage, 1986.

———. *The Iveagh Bequest, Kenwood*. London: London Historic House Museums Trust, 1990.

———. *London's Country House Collections*. London: Scala Books/English Heritage, 1993.

Burling, William J. *A Checklist of New Plays and Entertainments on the London Stage, 1700–1737*. Rutherford, N.J.: Fairleigh Dickinson University Press, 1993.

Burrows, Donald. *Handel and the English Chapel Royal*. London: Royal Hospital, Chelsea, 1985.

Casteras, Susan P., and Colleen Denney. *The Grosvenor Gallery: A Palace of Art in Victorian England*. New Haven, Conn.: Yale University Press, 1996.

Cheshire, D. F., Sean McCarthy, and Hilary Norris. *The Old Vic Refurbished*. London: Old Vic, 1983.

Clarke, Mary. *London Contemporary Dance Theatre: The First 21 Years*. London: Dance Books, 1988.

Coke, Thomas. *Vice-Chamberlain Coke's Theatrical Papers, 1706–1715*. Carbondale: Southern Illinois University Press, 1982.

Collin, Francesca. *The Arts & Entertainment in London*. London: Ward Lock, 1997.

Cook, Ann Jennalie. *The Privileged Playgoers of Shakespeare's London, 1576–1642*. Princeton, N.J.: Princeton University Press, 1981.

Coren, Michael. *Theatre Royal: 100 Years of Stratford East*. London: Quartet, 1984.

Cosh, Mary, ed. *Angus McBean in Islington*. London: Isledon Publications Trust, 1982.

Cowgill, J., M. de Neergard, and N. Griffiths. *Medieval Finds from Excavations in London: Knives and Scabbards*. London: Her Majesty's Stationery Office, 1987.

Cox, Jeffrey N. *Poetry and Politics in the Cockney School: Keats, Shelley, Hunt and Their Circle*. Cambridge: Cambridge University Press, 1998.

Cross, Tom. *Artists and Bohemians: 100 Years with the Chelsea Arts Club*. London: Quiller, 1992.

Crowfoot, Elisabeth, Frances Pritchard, and Kay Staniland. *Textiles and Clothing, c. 1150–c. 1450*. London: Her Majesty's Stationery Office, 1992.

Cruickshank, Graeme, ed. *The Palace Theatre, 1891–1991*. London: Palace Theatre, 1991.

Dakers, Caroline. *The Holland Park Circle: Artists and Victorian Society*. New Haven, Conn.: Yale University Press, 1999.

Day, Barry. *This Wooden "O": Shakespeare's Globe Reborn*. London: Oberon, 1996.

Donaldson, Frances. *The Royal Opera House in the Twentieth Century*. London: Weidenfeld and Nicolson, 1988.

Donkin, Ellen. *Getting into the Act: Women Playwrights in London, 1776–1829*. London: Routledge, 1995.

Doty, Gresdna A., and Billy J. Harbin. *Inside the Royal Court Theatre, 1956–1981: Artists Talk*. Baton Rouge: Louisiana State University Press, 1990.

Down, Michael, and Derek West. *Sketches at Lord's: The Cricket Lithographs of John Corbet Anderson*. London: Willow, 1990.

Drogheda, Lord, Ken Davison, and Andrew Wheatcroft. *The Covent Garden Album: 250 Years of Theatre, Opera and Ballet*. London: Routledge and Kegan Paul, 1981.

Duff, Charles. *The Lost Summer: The Heyday of the West End Theatre*. London: Nick Hern, 1995.

Dunn, Sheila. *The Theatres of Bromley: A Century of Theatre in Bromley*. London: Lanthorn, 1984.

Ehrlich, Cyril. *First Philharmonic: A History of the Royal Philharmonic Society*. Oxford: Clarendon, 1995.

Evans, Graeme. *An Urban Renaissance?: The Role of the Arts in Urban Regeneration—A Survey of Local Authorities in Greater London*. London: University of North London Press, 1993.

Eyles, Allen, and Keith Skone. *London's West End Cinemas*. London: Premier Bioscope, 1984.

———. *The Cinemas of Croydon*. London: Keytone, 1989.

Farr, Dennis, and John Newman. *Guide to the Courtauld Institute Galleries at Somerset House*. London: Courtauld Institute of Art, 1990.

Findlater, Richard, ed. *At the Royal Court: 25 Years of the English Stage Company*. Ambergate, UK: Amber Lane, 1981.

Fox, Celina. *Londoners*. London: Thames and Hudson, 1987.

Frayling, Christopher. *The Royal College of Art: 150 Years of Art and Design*. London: Barrie and Jenkins, 1987.

Freeman, Terence M. *Dramatic Representations of British Soldiers and Sailors on the London Stage, 1660–1880: Britons Strike Home*. Lewiston, N.Y.: Edwin Mellen, 1995.

Gair, Reavley. *The Children of St. Paul's: The Story of a Theatre Company, 1553–1608.* Cambridge: Cambridge University Press, 1982.

Gale, Maggie B. *West End Women: Women and the London Stage, 1918–1962.* London: Routledge, 1996.

Galinou, Mireille, and John Hayes. *London in Paint: Oil Paintings in the Collection at the Museum of London*. London: Museum of London, 1996.

Gascoigne, Bamber. *Images of Twickenham, with Hampton and Teddington*. London: Saint Helena, 1981.

George, Ken. *Two Sixpennies Please: Lewisham's Early Cinemas*. London: Lewisham Local History Society, 1987.

Gielgud, Kate Terry. *A Victorian Playgoer*. London: Heinemann, 1980.

Gillam, Geoffrey. *Theatres, Music Halls and Cinemas in the London Borough of Enfield*. London: Enfield Archaeological Society, 1986.

Girdham, Jane. *English Opera in Late Eighteenth-Century London: Stephen Storace at Drury Lane*. Oxford: Clarendon, 1997.

Goodman, Andrew. *Gilbert and Sullivan's London*. London: Faber, 2000.

Gray, Marcus. *London's Rock Landmarks: The A-Z Guide to London's Rock Geography.* London: Omnibus, 1985.

Green, Oliver. *Underground Art: London Transport Posters, 1908 to the Present.* London: Studio Vista, 1990.

Grew, Francis, and Margarethe de Neergard. *Medieval Finds from Excavations in London: Shoes and Pattens*. London: Her Majesty's Stationery Office, 1988.

Griswold, Wendy. *Renaissance Revivals: City Comedy and Revenge Tragedy in the London Theatre, 1576–1980*. Chicago: University of Chicago Press, 1986.

Guest, Ivor. *Ballet in Leicester Square: The Alhambra and the Empire, 1860–1915.* London: Dance Books, 1992.

Gurr, Andrew. *Rebuilding Shakespeare's Globe*. London: Weidenfeld and Nicolson, 1989.

———. *Playgoing in Shakespeare's London*. Cambridge: Cambridge University Press, 1996.

———. *The Shakespearian Playing Companies*. Oxford: Clarendon, 1996.

Hamlyn, Robert. *Robert Vernon's Gift: British Art for the Nation*. London: Tate Gallery, 1993.

Hancox, Joy. *The Byrom Collection and the Globe Theatre Mystery*. London: Jonathan Cape, 1997.

Harvey, A. D. *The Public Record Office as a Source for English Literary Studies.* Paris: Didier Érudition, 1990.

Harvey, Anthony, and Richard Mortimer, eds. *The Funeral Effigies of Westminster Abbey*. Woodbridge, UK: Boydell, 1994.

Hawkins, Frank V. *A Hundred Years of Chamber Music*. London: South Place Ethical Society, 1987.

Hay, Malcolm, and Jacqueline Riding. *Art in Parliament: The Permanent Collection of the House of Commons—A Descriptive Catalogue*. London: Palace of Westminster/Jarrold, 1996.

Haynes, John. *Taking the Stage: Twenty-One Years of the London Theatre*. London: Thames and Hudson, 1986.

Hayter, Alethea. *A Sultry Month: Scenes of London Literary Life in 1846*. London: Robin Clark, 1992.

Hewison, Robert. *Under Siege: Literary Life in London, 1939–45*. London: Methuen, 1988.

Hicks, Alistair. *The School of London: The Resurgence of Contemporary Painting*. Oxford: Phaidon, 1989.

Hill, David. *Turner on the Thames: River Journeys in the Year 1805*. New Haven, Conn.: Yale University Press, 1993.

Honigman, Ernst, and Susan Brock, eds. *Playhouse Wills, 1558–1642: An Edition of Wills by Shakespeare and His Contemporaries in the London Theatre*. Manchester, UK: Manchester University Press, 1993.

Honri, Peter. *John Wilton's Music Hall: The Handsomest Room in Town*. Hornchurch, UK: Henry, 1985.

Hornsey, Brian. *Ninety Years of Cinema in Harrow*. Stamford, UK: Fuchsiaprint, 1997.

Hume, Robert D., ed. *The London Theatre World, 1660–1800*. Carbondale: Southern Illinois University Press, 1980.

Hunkin, James F. *Changing Faces: A Decade at the National Theatre*. London: Oberon, 1997.

Huth, Andrew. *The Proms in Pictures: A Pictorial History Celebrating the Centenary of the Proms*. London: BBC, 1995.

Huxley, Paul. *Exhibition Road: Painters at the Royal College of Art*. Oxford: Phaidon, 1988.

Hyde, Ralph. *The Streets of London, 1880–1928: Evocative Watercolours by H. E. Tidmarsh*. Colchester, UK: Red Scorpion/Corporation of London, 1993.

Ingamells, John. *The Wallace Collection*. London: Scala, 1990.

Ingram, William. *The Business of Playing: The Beginnings of the Adult Professional Theater in Elizabethan London*. Ithaca, N.Y.: Cornell University Press, 1992.

Isherwood, Andrew. *An Introduction to the Kelmscott Press*. London: Victoria and Albert Museum, 1986.

Jackson, Allan Stuart. *The Standard Theatre of Victorian England*. Rutherford, N.J.: Fairleigh Dickinson University Press, 1993.

Jacobs, Michael, and Malcolm Warner. *Art in London*. Norwich, UK: Jarrold, 1980.

Jenkins, Simon. *Images of Hampstead*. London: Ackermann, 1982.

Johnson, Roger, and Jean Upton, eds. *Back to Baker Street: An Appreciation of Sherlock Holmes and London*. London: Sherlock Holmes Society of London, 1994.

Keen, Michael E. A *Bibliography of the Microfilms in the National Art Library, Victoria and Albert Museum*. London: Victoria and Albert Museum, 1980.

Kimmey, John L. *Henry James and London: The City in His Fiction*. New York: P. Lang, 1991.

King, T. J. *Casting Shakespeare's Plays: London Actors and Their Roles, 1590–1642*. Cambridge: Cambridge University Press, 1992.

Knif, Henrik. *Gentlemen and Spectators: Studies in Journals, Opera and the Social Scene in Late Stuart London*. Helsinki: Finnish Historical Society, 1995.

Knight, Vivien. *The Works of Art of the Corporation of London: A Catalogue of Paintings, Watercolours, Drawings, Prints and Sculpture*. Cambridge: Woodhead-Faulkner, 1986.

Knutson, Roslyn Lander. *The Repertory of Shakespeare's Company, 1594–1613*. Fayetteville: University of Arkansas Press, 1991.

LaRue, C. Steven. *Handel and His Singers: The Creation of the Royal Academy Operas, 1720–1728*. Oxford: Clarendon, 1995.

Lebrecht, Norman. *Music in London: A History and Handbook*. London: Aurum, 1992.

Lee, Edward. *Musical London*. London: Omnibus, 1995.

Leggatt, Alexander. *Jacobean Public Theatre*. London: Routledge, 1992.

Levey, Michael. *The National Gallery Collections*. London: National Gallery Publications, 1987.

Longford, Elizabeth. *Images of Chelsea*. London: Saint Helena Press, 1980.

Low, Crail, and Lucy Minto. *Rock and Pop London from Bedsit to Stadium: Places Where the Stars Made It Happen*. London: Handbook Publishing, 1997.

Lowe, T. W., ed. *A Century of Comic Operas: A Tribute to Sir W. S. Gilbert and the D'Oyly Carte Opera Company*. London: Grayson and Lowe, 1988.

Lukins, Jocelyn. *The Fantasy Factory: Lime Grove Studios, London, 1915–1991: A History*. London: Venta Books, 1996.

Macweeney, Alen, and Susan Allison. *Bloomsbury Reflections*. Peterborough, UK: Ryan, 1989.

Manley, Lawrence. *Literature and Culture in Early Modern London*. Cambridge: Cambridge University Press, 1995.

Marcus, Jane, ed. *Virginia Woolf and Bloomsbury: A Centenary Celebration*. Basingstoke, UK: Macmillan, 1987.

Marler, Regina. *Bloomsbury Pie: The Making of the Bloomsbury Boom*. London: Virago, 1997.

Mazower, David. *Yiddish Theatre in London*. London: Jewish Museum, 1996.

McCarthy, Steve. *The Crystal Palace Dinosaurs: The Story of the World's First Prehistoric Sculptures*. London: Crystal Palace Foundation, 1994.

McDowell, Paula. *The Women of Grub Street: Press, Politics and Gender in the London Literary Marketplace, 1678–1730*. Oxford: Clarendon, 1998.

McVeigh, Simon. *Concert Life in London from Mozart to Haydn*. Cambridge: Cambridge University Press, 1993.

Mellor, David. *The Sixties Art Scene in London*. Phaidon/Barbican Art Gallery, 1993.

Milhous, Judith, and Robert D. Hume, eds. *Vice-Chamberlain Coke's Theatrical Papers, 1706–1715*. Carbondale: Southern Illinois University Press, 1982.

Milligan, Thomas B. *The Concerto and London's Musical Culture in the Late Eighteenth Century*. London: Bowker, 1983.

Mosse, Kate. *The House: Inside the Royal Opera House, Covent Garden*. London: BBC Books, 1995.

Mullin, Donald. *Victorian Plays: A Record of Significant Productions on the London Stage, 1837–1901*. New York: Greenwood, 1987.

Mulryne, Ronnie, and Margaret Shewring. *Shakespeare's Globe Rebuilt*. Cambridge: Cambridge University Press, 1997.

Musgrave, Michael. *The Musical Life of the Crystal Palace*. Cambridge: Cambridge University Press, 1995.

Nadel, Ira Bruce, and F. S. Schwarzbach. *Victorian Artists and the City: A Collection of Critical Essays*. New York: Pergamon, 1980.

Nagler, A. M. *Shakespeare's Stage*. New Haven, Conn.: Yale University Press, 1981.

Naylor, Gillian, ed. *Bloomsbury: The Artists, Authors and Designers by Themselves*. London: Pyramid, 1990.

Neighbarger, Randy L. *An Outward Show: Music for Shakespeare on the London Stage, 1660–1830*. Westport, Conn.: Greenwood, 1992.

Newall, Christopher. *The Grosvenor Gallery Exhibitions: Change and Continuity in the Victorian Art World*. Cambridge: Cambridge University Press, 1995.

Norrie, Ian, ed. *Writers and Hampstead: Observations on the Place and the People—101 Commentators from Domesday to Drabble*. London: High Hill, 1987.

Olsen, Donald J. *The City as a Work of Art: London, Paris, Vienna*. New Haven, Conn.: Yale University Press, 1986.

Orrell, John. *The Quest For Shakespeare's Globe*. Cambridge: Cambridge University Press, 1983.

Parry, Linda, ed. *William Morris: Art and Kelmscott*. Woodbridge, UK: Boydell and Brewer, 1996.

Pearce, J. E., A. G. Vince, and M. A. Jenner. *London-Type Ware*. London: London and Middlesex Archaeological Society, 1985.

Pearce, Jacqueline. *Post-Medieval Pottery in London, 1500–1700: Border Wares*. London: Her Majesty's Stationery Office, 1992.

Pearce, Jacqueline, and Alan Vince. *Surrey Whitewares*. London: London and Middlesex Archaeological Society, 1988.

Pedicord, Harry William. "*By Their Majesties' Command*": *The House of Hanover at the London Theatres, 1714–1800*. London: Society for Theatre Research, 1991.

Perry, George. *George Perry Presents Forever Ealing: A Celebration of the Great British Film Studio*. London: Pavilion, 1981.

Peterson, William S. *The Kelmscott Press: A History of William Morris's Typographical Adventure*. Oxford: Clarendon, 1989.

Petty, Frederick C. *Italian Opera in London, 1760–1800*. Ann Arbor, Mich.: UMI Research Press, 1980.

Philip, Neil, and Victor Neuberg. *A December Vision: His Social Journalism—Charles Dickens*. London: Collins, 1986.

Pick, John. *The West End: Mismanagement and Snobbery*. Eastbourne, UK: Offord, 1983.

Piper, David. *Artists' London*. London: Weidenfeld and Nicolson, 1982.

Platt, John. *London's Rock Routes*. London: Fourth Estate, 1985.

Prentice, Rina. *A Celebration of the Sea: The Decorative Art Collections of the National Maritime Museum*. London: Her Majesty's Stationery Office, 1994.

Price, Curtis, Judith Milhous, and Robert D. Hume. *The Impresario's Ten Commandments: Continental Recruitment for Italian Opera in London, 1763–64*. London: Royal Musical Association, 1992.

———. *Italian Opera in Late Eighteenth-Century London: The King's Theatre, Haymarket, 1778–1791*. Oxford: Clarendon, 1995.

Ranger, Paul. *"Terror and Pity Reign in Every Breast": Gothic Drama in the London Patent Theatres, 1750–1820*. London: Society for Theatre Research, 1991.

Ravenhill, William, and David J. Johnson. *Joel Gascoyne's Engraved Maps of Stepney, 1702–04*. London: London Topographical Society/Guildhall Library, 1995.

Reed, Nicholas. *Sisley and the Thames: A Pilgrimage in the Steps of Alfred Sisley, Impressionist Painter, Who Came to London in 1874*. London: Lilburne, 1992.

Rice, Charles. *Tavern Singing in Early Victorian London: The Diaries of Charles Rice for 1840 and 1850*. London: Society for Theatre Research, 1997.

Richards, Nick. *Picture This: An Overview of Visual Arts Activity in Four East London Boroughs*. London: University of East London, 1996.

Riddell, Jonathan. *By Underground to Kew: London Transport Posters—1908 to the Present*. London: Studio Vista, 1994.

Roberts, Philip. *The Royal Court Theatre, 1965–1972*. London: Routledge and Kegan Paul, 1986.

Rogers, Jean Scott. *Stage by Stage: The Making of the Theatre Museum*. London: Her Majesty's Stationery Office, 1985.

Rogers, Pat. *Hacks and Dunces: Pope, Swift and Grub Street*. London: Methuen, 1980.

Rosenbaum, S. P. *Victorian Bloomsbury*. Basingstoke, UK: Macmillan, 1987.

———. *Edwardian Bloomsbury*. Basingstoke, UK: Macmillan, 1994.

Rosenbaum, S. P., ed. *The Bloomsbury Group: A Collection of Memoirs and Commentary*. Toronto: University of Toronto Press, 1995.

Rowell, George. *The Old Vic Theatre: A History*. Cambridge: Cambridge University Press, 1993.

Rutter, Carol Chillington, ed. *Documents of the Rose Playhouse*. Manchester, UK: Manchester University Press, 1984.

Scanlon, Ann. *Those Tourists Are Money: The Rock 'n' Roll Guide to Camden*. London: Tristia, 1997.

Scharf, George. *George Scharf's London: Sketches and Watercolours of a Changing City, 1820–50*. London: Murray, 1987.

———. *Drawings of Westminster*. London: London Topographical Society, 1994.

Schreuders, Piet, Mark Lewisohn, and Adam Smith. *The Beatles' London*. London: Hamlyn, 1994.

Seaborne, Mike. *Photographers' London, 1839–1994*. London: Museum of London, 1995.

Shanes, Eric. *The Genius of the Royal Academy*. London: Royal Academy, 1981.

Sharland, Elizabeth. *From Shakespeare to Coward, From the Globe to the Phoenix Theatre: A Guide to Historic Theatrical London and the World Beyond*. Watchet, UK: Barbican, 1997.

Sheridan, Paul. *Penny Theatres of Victorian London*. London: Dobson, 1981.

Sidnell, Michael J. *Dances of Death: The Group Theatre of London and the Thirties*. London: Faber, 1984.

Sizemore, Christine Wick. *A Female Vision of the City: London in the Novels of Five British Women*. Knoxville: University of Tennessee Press, 1989.

Smith, David L., Richard Strier, and David Bevington. *The Theatrical City: Culture, Theatre, and Politics in London, 1576–1649*. Cambridge: Cambridge University Press, 1995.

Smith, Irwin. *Shakespeare's First Playhouse*. Dublin: Liffey, 1981.

Southall, Brian. *Abbey Road: The Story of the World's Most Famous Recording Studios*. Cambridge: Stephens, 1982.

Stone, George Winchester. *The Stage and the Page: London's "Whole-Show" in the Eighteenth-Century Theatre*. Berkeley: University of California Press, 1981.

Thesing, William B. *The London Muse: Victorian Poetic Responses to the City*. Athens, Ga.: University of Georgia Press, 1982.

Thomson, Peter. *Shakespeare's Theatre*. London: Routledge, 1992.

Tooley, John. *In House: Covent Garden—Fifty Years of Opera and Ballet*. London: Faber, 1999.

Toynbee, J. M. C. *The Roman Art Treasures from the Temple of Mithras*. London: London and Middlesex Archaeological Society, 1986.

Trench, Richard. *Philip's London: Architecture, History, Art*. London: George Philip, 1991.

Trewin, Wendy. *The Arts Theatre, London, 1927–1981*. London: Society for Theatre Research, 1986.

Twyning, John. *London Dispossessed: Literature and Social Space in the Early Modern City*. Basingstoke, UK: Macmillan, 1998.

Upstone, Robert. *Treasures of British Art: The Tate Gallery*. New York: Abbeville, 1996.

Waddell, Heather. *London Art and Artists Guide*. London: London Art and Artists Guide, 1997.

Wade, Allan. *Memories of the London Theatre, 1900–1914*. London: Society for Theatre Research, 1983.

Walker, Kathrine Sorley, and Sarah C. Woodcock. *The Royal Ballet: A Picture History*. London: Threshold, 1986.

Waterfield, Giles, ed. *Art for the People: Culture in the Slums of Late Victorian Britain*. London: Dulwich Picture Gallery, 1994.

Wearing, J. P. *The London Stage, 1900–1909: A Calendar of Plays and Players*. Metuchen, N.J.: Scarecrow, 1981.

———. *The London Stage, 1910–1919: A Calendar of Plays and Players*. Metuchen, N.J.: Scarecrow, 1982.

———. *The London Stage, 1920–1929: A Calendar of Plays and Players*. Metuchen, N.J.: Scarecrow, 1984.

———. *The London Stage, 1930–1939: A Calendar of Plays and Players*, 3 vols. Metuchen, N.J.: Scarecrow, 1990 (vols. 2 and 3), 1991 (vol. 1).

———. *The London Stage, 1940–1949: A Calendar of Plays and Players*, 2 vols. Metuchen, N.J.: Scarecrow, 1991.

———. *The London Stage, 1950–1959: A Calendar of Plays and Players*. Metuchen, N.J.: Scarecrow, 1993.

Wegner, Nicholas. *Depart from Zero: The Development of the Gallery London, 1973–1978*. London: Gallery Trust, 1987.

Weightman, Gavin. *Bright Lights, Big City: London Entertained, 1830–1950*. London: Collins and Brown, 1992.

Whitcombe, Vincent. *London's Art and Artists*. Spelhurst, UK: Spellmount, 1991.

Wilcox, Denys J. *The London Group, 1913–1939—The Artists and Their Works*. Aldershot, UK: Scolar, 1995.

Williamson, Paul, ed. *The Medieval Treasury: The Art of the Middle Ages in the Victoria and Albert Museum*. London: Victoria and Albert Museum, 1986.

Wilson, Jean. *The Archaeology of Shakespeare: The Material Legacy of Shakespeare's Theatre*. Stroud, UK: Alan Sutton, 1995.

Wilson, Robin J., and Frederic Lloyd. *Gilbert and Sullivan: The D'Oyly Carte Years*. London: Weidenfeld and Nicolson, 1984.

Wilson, Simon. *Tate Gallery: An Illustrated Companion*. London: Tate Gallery, 1991.

Woodcock, Sarah C. *The Sadler's Wells Royal Ballet, Now the Birmingham Royal Ballet*. London: Sinclair-Stevenson, 1991.

AUTOBIOGRAPHY AND BIOGRAPHY

Ackroyd, Peter. *Dickens*. London: Sinclair-Stevenson, 1990.

Ackroyd, Peter, ed. *Dickens' London: An Imaginative Vision*. London: Headline, 1987.

Aldrich, Megan, Paul Atterbury, Barry Bergdoll, and Margaret H. Floyd, eds. *A. W. N. Pugin: Master of Gothic Revival*. New Haven, Conn.: Yale University Press, 1995.

Ames-Lewis, Frances, ed. *Sir Thomas Gresham and Gresham College: Studies in the Intellectual History of London in the 16th–17th Centuries*. Aldershot, UK: Ashgate, 1999.

Aronson, Theo. *Prince Eddy and the Homosexual Underworld*. London: Murray, 1994.

Atterbury, Paul, and Clive Wainwright, eds. *Pugin: A Gothic Passion*. New Haven, Conn.: Yale University Press, 1994.

Attwood, John. *Dick Whittington: Fact and Fable*. London: Regency, 1988.

Bagshaw, H. A. E. *Coasting Sailorman: A First-Hand Account of Life and Trade Aboard Thames Sailing Barges Between the Years 1915 and 1945*. Ware, UK: Chaffcutter, 1998.

Bailey, Doris M. *Children of the Green: A True Story of Childhood in Bethnal Green, 1922–1937*. London: Stepney Books, 1981.

Baker, Frank. *John Wesley: London Publisher, 1733–1791*. London: Friends of Wesley's Chapel, 1984.

Barker, Sybil. *Sybil Barker's War: The Wartime Diary of a Director of Music and Organist at the Royal Holloway College (University of London)*. Worthing, UK: Churchman, 1989.

Barnes, Annie. *Tough Annie: From Suffragette to Stepney Councillor*. London: Stepney Books, 1980.

Barrett, Daniel. *T. W. Robertson and the Prince of Wales's Theatre*. New York: P. Lang, 1995.

Batchelor, Mary. *Catherine Bramwell-Booth*. Tring, UK: Lion, 1986.

Beasley, Maureen. *Five Centuries of Artists in Sutton: A Biographical Dictionary of Artists Associated with Sutton, London*. London: Sutton Libraries, 1989.

Benn, Caroline. *Keir Hardie*. London: Richard Cohen, 1997.

Bennett, J. A. *William Booth and the Salvation Army: Up and Down the City Road*. Basingstoke, UK: Marshall Pickering, 1987.

———. *The Mathematical Science of Christopher Wren*. Cambridge: Cambridge University Press, 1982.

Bloch, Sidney. *No Time for Tears: Childhood in a Rabbi's Family*. London: Kimber, 1980.

Bond, W. H. *Thomas Hollis of Lincoln's Inn: A Whig and His Books*. Cambridge: Cambridge University Press, 1990.

Boswell, James. *Boswell's London Journal*. London: Futura, 1982.

———. *The Journals of James Boswell, 1762–1795*. London: Mandarin, 1990.

———. *The Life of Samuel Johnson*. London: David Campbell, 1992.

Brady, Frank. *James Boswell: The Later Years, 1769–1795*. London: Heinemann, 1984.

Briggs, Asa, and John Mair. *Marx in London: An Illustrated Guide*. London: British Broadcasting Corporation, 1982.

Brown, Antony. *Cuthbert Heath, Maker of the Modern Lloyd's of London*. Newton Abbot, UK: David and Charles, 1980.

Brown, Irene. *One Woman's War: Reflections of a Cockney Kid*. London: Excalibur, 1991.

Bryant, Arthur. *Samuel Pepys*, 3 vols. London: Panther, 1984 (vol. 1) and 1985 (vols. 2 and 3).

Bryant, Julius. *Robert Adam, 1728–1792: Architect of Genius.* London: English Heritage, 1992.

Carvel, John. *Citizen Ken.* London: Hogarth, 1987.

Cashmore, T. H. R. *The Orleans Family in Twickenham, 1800–1932.* London: London Borough of Twickenham Local History Society, 1982.

Cave, Richard Allen. *Ben Jonson.* Basingstoke, UK: Macmillan Education, 1991.

Cave, Richard, Elizabeth Schafer, and Brian Woolland, eds. *Ben Jonson and Theatre: Performance, Practice and Theory.* London: Routledge, 1999.

Chambers, James. *Christopher Wren.* Stroud, UK: Alan Sutton, 1998.

Chesshyre, Hubert, and Adrian Ailes. *Heralds of Today: A Biographical List of the Officers of the College of Arms, London, 1963–86.* Gerrards Cross, UK: Van Duren, 1986.

Clingham, Greg. *James Boswell: The Life of Johnson.* Cambridge: Cambridge University Press, 1992.

Corfield, John. *Thomas Smith, 1798–1875—Architect and Surveyor, Hertford and London.* Hertford, UK: Hertford and Ware Local History Society, 1998.

Cox, Don Richard. *Arthur Conan Doyle.* New York: F. Ungar, 1985.

Cullen, Tom. *Crippen: The Mild Murderer.* Harmondsworth, UK: Penguin, 1988.

Cutler, Horace. *The Cutler Files.* London: Weidenfeld and Nicolson, 1982.

Cutpurse, Moll. *The Life and Death of Mrs. Mary Frith, Commonly Called Moll Cutpurse.* New York: Garland, 1993.

Darley, Gillian. *John Soane: An Accidental Romantic.* New Haven, Conn.: Yale University Press, 1999.

Dickson, John. *Murder Without Conviction: Inside the World of the Krays.* London: Sidgwick and Jackson, 1986.

Donoghue, Albert, and Martin Short. *The Krays' Lieutenant.* London: Smith Gryphon, 1995.

Downes, Kerry. *Hawksmoor.* London: Thames and Hudson, 1987.

Dutton, Richard. *William Shakespeare: A Literary Life.* New York: St. Martin's Press, 1989.

Eddowes, John. *The Two Killers of Rillington Place.* London: Warner, 1995.

Edwards, Owen Dudley. *The Quest for Sherlock Holmes: A Biographical Study of Arthur Conan Doyle.* Harmondsworth, UK: Penguin, 1984.

Evans, Robert C. *Ben Jonson and the Poetics of Patronage.* Lewisburg, Pa.: Bucknell University Press, 1989.

———. *Jonson and the Contexts of His Time.* Lewisburg, Pa.: Bucknell University Press, 1994.

Falconer, David. *The Bengal Merchant: The Story of Thomas Falconer, Servant of the Honourable East India Company.* Trowbridge, UK: Angel Publications, 1982.

Fawcett, Patrick. *Memories of a Wimbledon Childhood, 1906–1918.* London: John Evelyn Society, 1981.

Fay, Stephen. *Power Play: The Life and Times of Peter Hall.* London: Coronet, 1996.

Finer, S. E. *The Life and Times of Sir Edwin Chadwick*. London: Methuen, 1980.
Finlayson, Iain. *The Moth and the Candle: A Life of James Boswell*. London: Constable, 1984.
Finn, Ralph L. *Grief Forgotten: The Tale of an East End Jewish Boyhood*. London: Futura, 1985.
———. *Time Remembered: The Tale of an East End Jewish Boyhood*. London: MacDonald, 1985.
Foot, John. *The Illustrated Diary of a Thames Pilot*. Ringwood, UK: Navigator, 1995.
Fraser, Frankie. *Mad Frank: Memoirs of a Life of Crime*. London: Warner, 1994.
Fraser, Russell A. *Young Shakespeare*. New York: Columbia University Press, 1988.
———. *Shakespeare: The Later Years*. New York: Columbia University Press, 1992.
Friedman, Terry. *James Gibbs*. New Haven, Conn.: Yale University Press, 1984.
Fryer, Jonathan. *Soho in the Fifties and Sixties*. London: National Portrait Gallery, 1998.
Gamble, Rose. *Chelsea Child*. London: Ariel, 1982.
Garnett, Angelica. *Deceived with Kindness: A Bloomsbury Childhood*. London: Pimlico, 1995.
Giddings, Robert, ed. *The Changing World of Charles Dickens*. London: Vision, 1983.
Girouard, Mark. *Alfred Waterhouse and the Natural History Museum*. London: British Museum (Natural History), 1981.
Glazebrook, George. *Where No Flowers Grow: A Child's Eye View of Deptford*. Rainham, UK: Glazebrook, 1989.
Goodman, Jonathan. *The Crippen File*. London: Allison and Busby, 1985.
Guilmartin, G. Harry. *Bare, Empty Sheds: A London Tramwayman's Autobiography*. Brightlingsea, UK: Tramway and Light Railway Society, 1986.
Hamilton, Charles. *In Search of Shakespeare: A Study of the Poet's Life and Handwriting*. London: Hale, 1986.
Hancox, Joy. *The Byrom Collection and the Globe Theatre Mystery*. London: Jonathan Cape, 1997.
Harding, Arthur. *East End Underworld: Chapters in the Life of Arthur Harding*. London: Routledge and Kegan Paul, 1981.
Hardy, Barbara. *Charles Dickens: The Writer and His Work*. Windsor, UK: Profile, 1983.
Harris, John, and Michael Snodin, eds. *Sir William Chambers: Architect to George III*. New Haven, Conn.: Yale University Press, 1996.
Hartwell, William Michael Berry. *William Camrose: Giant of Fleet Street*. London: Weidenfeld and Nicolson, 1992.
Harvey, Charles, and Jon Press. *Art, Enterprise and Ethics: The Life and Work of William Morris*. London: Frank Cass, 1996.
Hattersley, Roy. *Blood and Fire: William and Catherine Booth and Their Salvation Army*. London: Abacus, 2000.
Hauer, Christian E., ed. *Christopher Wren and the Many Sides of Genius: Proceedings of a Christopher Wren Symposium*. Lewiston, N.Y.: Edwin Mellen, 1997.

Heren, Louis. *Growing Up Poor in London*. London: Indigo, 1996.
Hibbert, Christopher. *The Making of Charles Dickens*. Harmondsworth, UK: Penguin, 1983.
———. *The Personal History of Samuel Johnson*. London: Pimlico, 1998.
Hilton, Della. *Christopher Marlowe and the New London Theatre*. Edinburgh: Pentland, 1993.
Hobhouse, Hermione. *Thomas Cubitt, Master Builder*. Didcot, UK: Management Books, 1995.
Hollis, Henry. *Farewell Leicester Square*. Glasgow: MacLellan, 1983.
Holman, Bob. *Good Old George: The Life of George Lansbury*. Oxford: Lion, 1990.
Honan, Park. *Shakespeare: A Life*. Oxford: Oxford University Press, 1998.
Honigman, E. A. J. *Shakespeare: The Lost Years*. Manchester, UK: Manchester University Press, 1985.
Howat, Gerald. *Plum Warner*. London: Unwin Hyman, 1987.
Hughes, Peter. *The Founders of the Wallace Collection*. London: Trustees of the Wallace Collection, 1981.
Hume, Robert D. *Henry Fielding and the London Theatre*. Oxford: Clarendon, 1988.
Humphreys, Anne. *Travels into the Poor Man's Country: The Work of Henry Mayhew*. Firle, UK: Caliban, 1982.
Hutchinson, Roger. *All the Sweets of Being: A Life of James Boswell*. Edinburgh: Mainstream, 1995.
Isaacs, Jeremy. *Never Mind the Moon: My Time at the Royal Opera House*. London: Bantam, 1999.
Jacob, Jack. *A Londoner's Diary, 1926–1980*. Montreux, Switzerland: Minerva, 1995.
Jameson, Derek. *Send in the Angels: From Fleet Street to Showbiz*. London: Ebury, 1990.
———. *Last of the Metal Men: From Fleet Street to Showbiz*. London: Penguin, 1991.
Kay, Dennis. *Shakespeare: His Life, Work and Era*. London: Sidgwick and Jackson, 1992.
Kay, W. David. *Ben Jonson: A Literary Life*. Basingstoke, UK: Macmillan, 1995.
Kosky, Jules. *Mutual Friends: Charles Dickens and the Great Ormond Street Hospital*. London: Weidenfeld and Nicolson, 1989.
Kray, Reg. *Born Fighter*. London: Century, 1990.
———. *Villains We Have Known*. London: Arrow, 1996.
Kray, Reg, and Ron Kray. *Our Story*. London: Sidgwick and Jackson, 1988.
Lambrianou, Chris. *Escape from the Kray Madness*. London: Sidgwick and Jackson, 1995.
Lamerton, Richard. *East End Doc*. Cambridge: Lutterworth, 1986.
Legh, Sarah. *Sarah: The Letters and Diaries of a Courtier's Wife, 1906–1936*. London: Owen, 1989.
Lellenberg, Jon L., ed. *The Quest for Sir Arthur Conan Doyle: Thirteen Biographers in Search of a Life*. Carbondale: Southern Illinois University Press, 1987.

Le Rougetel, Hazel. *The Chelsea Gardener: Philip Miller, 1691–1770*. London: Natural History Museum, 1990.

Levi, Peter. *The Life and Times of William Shakespeare*. London: Macmillan, 1988.

Lewis, Jeremy. *Kindred Spirits: Adrift in Literary London*. London: Flamingo, 1996.

Lippincott, Louise. *Selling Art in Georgian London: The Rise of Arthur Pond*. New Haven, Conn.: Yale University Press, 1983.

Livingstone, Ken. *If Voting Changed Anything, They'd Abolish It*. London: Fontana, 1988.

MacGregor, Arthur, ed. *Sir Hans Sloane: Collector, Scientist, Antiquary, Founding Father of the British Museum*. London: British Museum Press, 1994.

Mackail, J. W. *The Life of William Morris*. New York: Dover, 1995.

Maria, Robert de. *Life of Samuel Johnson: A Critical Biography*. Oxford: Blackwell, 1994.

Marsh, Jan. *Bloomsbury Women: Distinct Figures in Life and Art*. London: Pavilion, 1995.

Martin, Peter. *A Life of James Boswell*. London: Weidenfeld and Nicolson, 1999.

Masters, Anthony. *Inside Marbled Halls: Life Above and Below Stairs in the Hyde Park Hotel*. London: Futura, 1980.

McIntyre, Ian. *Garrick*. London: Allen Lane, 1999.

McLaren, Angus. *A Prescription for Murder: The Victorian Serial Killings of Dr. Thomas Neill Cream*. Chicago: University of Chicago Press, 1993.

McLeod, Herbert. *Chemistry and Theology in Mid-Victorian London: The Diary of Herbert McLeod, 1860–1870*. London: Mansell, 1987.

Mercer, Vaudrey. *The Frodshams: The Story of a Family of Chronometer Makers*. Ticehurst, UK: Antiquarian Horological Society, 1981.

Miles, Rosalind. *Ben Jonson: His Life and Work*. London: Routledge and Kegan Paul, 1986.

Mitchell, L. G. *Holland House*. London: Duckworth, 1980.

Moore, Lucy. *The Thieves' Opera: The Remarkable Lives of Jonathan Wild, Thief-Taker, and Jack Sheppard, House-Breaker*. London: Viking, 1997.

Neary, E. A. *The Memoirs of a Victorian London Gutter-Snipe*. Lewes, UK: Book Guild, 1990.

Nicholson, Shirley. *A Victorian Household, Based on the Diaries of Marion Sambourne*. London: Barrie and Jenkins, 1988.

Orel, Harold, ed. *Sir Arthur Conan Doyle: Interviews and Recollections*. London: Macmillan, 1991.

Palmer, Alan, and Veronica Palmer. *Who's Who in Bloomsbury*. Brighton, UK: Harvester, 1987.

Palmer, Francis C. *Just a Cockney: A Cockney's Story*. Isleworth, UK: Jestico, 1992.

Parker, Robert. *Rough Justice*. London: Fontana, 1981.

Payne, John. *William Morris and London: A Personal View*. London: London Borough of Merton, 1996.

Pearson, Hesketh. *A Life of Shakespeare*. London: Hamilton, 1987.

Pearson, John. *The Profession of Violence: The Rise and Fall of the Kray Twins*. London: Granada, 1984.

Perrett, Bryan. *The Real Hornblower: The Life of Admiral of the Fleet Sir James Alexander Gordon, Last Governor of the Royal Naval Hospital, Greenwich*. London: Arms and Armour, 1998.

Powell, Kerry. *Oscar Wilde and the Theatre of the 1890s*. Cambridge: Cambridge University Press, 1990.

Read, Leonard. *Nipper: The Story of Leonard 'Nipper' Read*. London: Warner, 1992.

Richardson, Charles. *My Manor*. London: Sidgwick and Jackson, 1991.

Richardson, Margaret, and Mary Anne Stevens, eds. *John Soane, Architect: Master of Space and Light*. London: Royal Academy of Arts, 1999.

Riggs, David. *Ben Jonson: A Life*. Cambridge, Mass.: Harvard University Press, 1989.

Roach, Arthur W. *I Am a Victorian: Just an Edwardian Childhood in Streatham*. London: Streatham Society, 1992.

Rockett, Dorothy, and Brenda Hargreaves. *Two Streatham Childhoods*. London: Streatham Society, 1980.

Rodaway, Angela. *A London Childhood*. London: Virago, 1985.

Rowse, A. L. *Shakespeare the Man*. New York: St. Martin's Press, 1988.

Ruffinière du Prey, Pierre de la. *John Soane: The Making of an Architect*. Chicago: University of Chicago Press, 1982.

Sanders, Peter. *The Simple Annals: The History of an Essex and East End Family*. Gloucester, UK: Alan Sutton, 1989.

Sawyer, Paul. *Christopher Rich of Drury Lane: The Biography of a Theatre Manager*. Lanham, Md.: University Press of America, 1986.

Saxby, David. *William Morris at Merton*. London: Museum of London, 1995.

Schneer, Jonathan. *George Lansbury*. Manchester, UK: Manchester University Press, 1990.

Schumann-Bacia, Eva. *Sir John Soane and the Bank of England*. New York: Princeton Architectural Press, 1991.

Seaver, Paul S. *Wallington's World: A Puritan Artisan in Seventeenth-Century London*. London: Methuen, 1985.

Shears, Elsie. *The Cockney Lady*. London: New Millenium, 1995.

Shone, Richard. *Bloomsbury Portraits: Vanessa Bell, Duncan Grant and Their Circle*. London: Phaidon, 1993.

Sisman, Adam. *Boswell's Presumptuous Task*. London: Hamish Hamilton, 2000.

Slipper, Jack. *Slipper of the Yard*. London: Sidgwick and Jackson, 1981.

Smith, Grahame. *Charles Dickens: A Literary Life*. Basingstoke, UK: Macmillan, 1996.

Southgate, Walter. *That's the Way It Was: A Working Class Autobiography, 1890–1950*. Oxted, UK: New Clarion, 1982.

Spencer-Silver, Patricia. *Pugin's Builder: The Life and Work of George Myers*. Hull, UK: University of Hull Press, 1993.

Stansky, Peter. *On or About December 1910: Early Bloomsbury and Its Intimate World*. Cambridge, Mass.: Harvard University Press, 1996.

Stevens, R. J. S. *Recollections of R. J. S. Stevens: An Organist in Georgian London*. London: Macmillan, 1992.

Stroud, Dorothy. *Sir John Soane, Architect*. London: De la Mare, 1996.

Summerson, John. *The Life and Work of John Nash, Architect*. Cambridge, Mass.: MIT Press, 1980.

Swift, Catherine M. *Catherine Bramwell Booth*. Basingstoke, UK: Marshall Pickering, 1989.

Tait, A. A. *Robert Adam: Drawings and Imagination*. Cambridge: Cambridge University Press, 1993.

Taylor, S. J. *The Great Outsiders: Northcliffe, Rothermere and the* Daily Mail. London: Weidenfeld and Nicolson, 1996.

Thomas, John Birch. *Shop Boy: An Autobiography*. London: Century, 1985.

Thompson, J. Lee. *Northcliffe: Press Baron in Politics, 1865–1922*. London: Murray, 2000.

Tyack, Geoffrey. *Sir James Pennethorne and the Making of Victorian London*. Cambridge: Cambridge University Press, 1992.

Wain, John. *Samuel Johnson*. London: Papermac, 1988.

Watkin, David. *Sir John Soane: Enlightenment Thought and the Royal Academy Lectures*. Cambridge: Cambridge University Press, 1996.

Watts, Alan S. *The Life and Times of Charles Dickens*. London: Studio Editions, 1991.

Webb, Billy. *Running with the Krays: My Life in London's Gangland*. Edinburgh: Mainstream, 1995.

Wedgwood, Alexandra. *A. W. N. Pugin and the Pugin Family*. London: Victoria and Albert Museum, 1985.

Wenham, L. P. *James Tate, Master of Richmond School, Yorkshire, and Canon of St. Paul's Cathedral, London*. Northallerton, UK: North Yorkshire County Record Office, 1991.

White, Derek. *The No-Nonsense Vicar: Twenty Years of Working with the Homeless*. London: Janus, 1995.

Wilcox, Denys J. *The London Group, 1913–1939: The Artists and Their Works*. Aldershot, UK: Scolar, 1995.

Williams, Guy. *Augustus Pugin versus Decimus Burton: A Victorian Architectural Duel*. London: Cassell, 1990.

Wilson, Angus. *The World of Charles Dickens*. London: Panther, 1983.

Wilson, David M. *The Forgotten Collector: Augustus Wollaston Franks of the British Museum*. London: Thames and Hudson, 1984.

Wilton, Frederick C. *The Britannia Diaries, 1863–1875: Selections from the Diaries of Frederick C. Wilton*. London: Society for Theatre Research, 1992.

Yarde, Doris M. *Sarah Trimmer of Brentford and Her Children, With Some of Her Early Writings*. London: Hounslow and District History Society, 1990.

COMMERCE AND INDUSTRY

Alcok, N. W. *Warwickshire Grazier and London Skinner, 1552–1555: The Account Book of Peter Temple and Thomas Heritage*. London: Oxford University Press, 1981.

Alexander, Sally. *Women's Work in Nineteenth-Century London: A Study of the Years 1820–1850*. London: Journeyman, 1983.

Alley, Hugh. *Hugh Alley's Caveat: The Markets of London in 1598*. London: London Topographical Society, 1988.

Arnold, Wendy. *The Historic Hotels of London*. London: Thames and Hudson, 1989.

Augar, Philip. *The Death of Gentlemanly Capitalism: The Rise and Fall of London's Investment Banks*. London: Penguin, 2000.

Avis, F. C. *The 16th Century Long Shop Printing Office in the Poultry*. London: Glenview, 1982.

Back, D. H. L. *Forsyth and Co.: Patent Gunmakers, 1806–1852*. Norwich, UK: Historical Firearms, 1995.

Baladouni, Vahé. *Armenian Trade with the English East India Company: An Aperçu*. Roma: Banco di Roma, 1986.

Barty-King, Hugh. *The Baltic Story: Baltick Coffee House to Baltic Exchange, 1744–1994*. London: Quiller, 1994.

Beaumont, Richard. *Purdey's: The Guns and the Family*. Newton Abbot, UK: David and Charles, 1984.

Beaver, Patrick. *The Match Makers*. London: Melland, 1985.

Beer, Reg. *The Match Girls' Strike*. London: Museum of Labour, 1983.

Belanger, Terry. *Booksellers' Sales of Copyright: Aspects of the London Book Trade, 1718–1768*. Ann Arbor: University of Michigan Press, 1993.

Bennett, Eric. *The Worshipful Company of Carmen of London*. Buckingham, UK: Barracuda, 1982.

Bird, Peter J. W. N. *The Weak Form Efficiency of the London Metal Exchange*. Stirling, UK: University of Stirling, 1983.

Blakey, George G. *The Post-War History of the London Stock Market: 50 Years of Business, Politics and People*. Chalford, UK: Management Books 2000, 1997.

Blayney, Peter W. M. *The Bookshops in Paul's Cross Churchyard*. London: Bibliographical Society, 1990.

Braithwaite, David. *Building in the Blood: The Story of the Dove Brothers of Islington, 1781–1981*. London: Godfrey Cave, 1981.

Broomhead, Frank. *The Zaehnsdorfs (1842–1947): Craft Bookbinders*. London: Private Libraries Association, 1986.

Brown, Anthony. *Edward Lloyd: 300 Years of Lloyd's*. London: Lloyd's List, 1988.

Brown, Maisie. *The Market Gardens of Barnes and Mortlake: The Rise and Fall of a Local Industry*. London: Barnes and Mortlake History Society, 1985.

Brown, Philip A. H. *London Publishers and Printers, c. 1800–1870*. London: British Library, 1982.

Brown, Robert H. and John Wormell. *An Introduction to Working in the Lloyd's Market*. London: Witherby, 1987.

Bruce, George. *A Wine Day's Work: The London House of Deinhard, 1835–1985*. London: Deinhard, 1985.

Burk, Kathleen. *Morgan Grenfell, 1838–1988: The Biography of a Merchant Bank*. Oxford: Clarendon, 1989.

Byatt, Derrick. *Promises to Pay: The First Three Hundred Years of the Bank of England Notes*. London: Spink, 1994.

Callery, Sean. *Harrods, Knightsbridge: The Story of Society's Favourite Store*. London: Ebury, 1991.

Campbell, John, and William Bonner. *Media, Mania and the Markets*. London: Fleet Street, 1994.

Carter, Robert L., and Peter Falush. *The London Insurance Market*. London: Association of British Insurers, 1996.

Cassis, Youssef. *City Bankers, 1890–1914*. Cambridge: Cambridge University Press, 1994.

Chakrabarty, Phanindranath. *Rise and Growth of English East India Company: A Study of British Mercantile Activities in Mughal India*. Calcutta: Punthi Pustak, 1994.

Chapman, Colin. *How the Stock Exchange Works*. London: Hutchinson Business, 1988.

Chapman, S. D. *The Rise of Merchant Banking*. London: Unwin Hyman, 1988.

Christianson, C. Paul. *Memorials of the Book Trade in Medieval London: The Archives at Old London Bridge*. Cambridge: Brewer, 1987.

Clarke, Michael. *Regulating the City: Competition, Scandal and Reform*. Milton Keynes, UK: Open University Press, 1986.

Clarke, William M. *How the City of London Works: An Introduction to Its Financial Markets*. London: Sweet and Maxwell, 1995.

Clay, C. J. J., and B. S. Wheble, eds. *Clay and Wheble's Modern Merchant Banking: A Guide to the Workings of the Accepting Houses of the City of London and Their Services to Industry and Commerce*. Cambridge: Woodhead-Faulkner, 1983.

Coakley, Jerry, and Laurence Harris. *The City of Capital: London's Role as a Financial Centre*. Oxford: Blackwell, 1993.

Cobb, H. S., ed. *The Overseas Trade of London Exchequer Customs Accounts, 1480–1*. London: London Record Society, 1990.

Cobbett, Donald. *Before the Big Bang: Tales of the Old Stock Exchange*. Horndean, UK: Milestone, 1986.

Cockerell, H. A. L. *Lloyd's of London: A Portrait*. Cambridge: Woodhead-Faulkner, 1984.

Coggan, Philip. *The Money Machine: How the City Works*. Harmondsworth, UK: Penguin, 1986.

Cooper, Jeremy. *Dealings with Dealers: The Ins and Outs of the London Antiques Trade*. London: Thames and Hudson, 1985.

Coover, James. *Music at Auction: Puttick and Simpson (of London), 1794–1971*. Warren, Mich.: Harmonie Park, 1988.

Courtney, Cathy, and Paul Thompson. *City Lives: The Changing Voice of British Finance*. London: Methuen, 1996.

Dale, Tim. *Harrods: The Store and the Legend*. London: Pan, 1981.

———. *Harrods: A Palace in Knightsbridge*. London: Harrods, 1995.

Daniels, P. W. *The Location of Foreign Banks and Metropolitan Development: London and New York*. Liverpool: University of Liverpool, 1986.

Davies, Brinley. *Business Finance and the City of London*. London: Heinemann Educational, 1982.

Dawson, Frank G. *The First Latin American Debt Crisis: The City of London and the 1822–1825 Loan Bubble*. New Haven, Conn.: Yale University Press, 1990.

Davis, C. T. *Industries of Wandsworth*. London: London Borough of Wandsworth, 1983.

Desai, Tripta. *The East India Company: A Brief Survey from 1599 to 1857*. New Delhi: Kanak, 1984.

Doolittle, I. G. *The City of London and Its Livery Companies*. Dorchester, UK: Gavin, 1982.

Edwards, Marjorie. *Up the Cally: The History and Recollections of London's Old Caledonian Market*. London: Marketprompt, 1989.

Ellinger, A. G., and T. H. Stewart. *A Post-War History of the Stock Market*. Cambridge: Woodhead Faulkner/Investment Research, 1980.

Ellmers, Chris, and Alex Werner. *Dockland Life: A Pictorial History of London's Docks*. Edinburgh: Museum of London/Mainstream, 1991.

Fainstein, Susan S. *The City Builders: Property, Politics and Planning in London and New York*. Oxford: Blackwell, 1994.

Falkus, Malcolm. *Always Under Pressure: The Story of North Thames Gas Since 1949*. Basingstoke, UK: Macmillan, 1988.

Faulder, J. S., ed. *The Worshipful Company of Builders' Merchants, 1961–1986*. London: The Worshipful Company of Builders' Merchants, 1986.

Fay, Stephen. *Portrait of an Old Lady: Turmoil at the Bank of England*. London: Penguin, 1988.

———. *The Collapse of Barings*. London: Arrow, 1996.

Feldman, Hugh. *Letter Receivers of London, 1652–1857: A History of Their Offices and Handstamps within the General, Penny and Twopenny Posts*. Bristol, UK: Stuart Rossiter Trust Fund, 1998.

Flower, Raymond, and Michael Wynn Jones. *Lloyd's of London: An Illustrated History*. Colchester, UK: Lloyd's of London Press, 1987.

Forshaw, Alec, and Theo Bergström. *The Markets of London*. Harmondsworth, UK: Penguin, 1983.

Fox, Celina, ed. *London—World City, 1800–1840*. New Haven, Conn.: Yale University Press/Museum of London, 1992.

Frostick, Michael. *Bentley: Cricklewood to Crewe*. London: Osprey, 1980.
Galletly, Guy. *The Big Bang: The Financial Revolution in the City of London and What It Means for You After the Crash*. Plymouth, UK: Northcote House, 1988.
Gapper, John, and Nicholas Denton. *All that Glitters: The Fall of Barings*. London: Penguin, 1997.
Gaskell, Martin. *Harry Neal Ltd.: A Family of Builders*. Cambridge: Granta, 1989.
Geddes, Philip. *Inside the Bank of England*. London: Boxtree, 1987.
Gibson-Jarvie, Robert. *The London Metal Exchange: A Commodity Market*. Cambridge: Woodhead-Faulkner, 1988.
Gower, Graham. *The Tile and Brickmakers of Streatham*. London: Local History Publications, 1998.
Grafton Green, Brigid. *Milk for the Millions*. London: London Borough of Barnet, 1983.
Greenwood, John. *The Industrial Archaeology and Industrial History of London: A Bibliography*. Cranfield, UK: Kewdale, 1988.
Grimwade, Mary. *Shopping in Barnes Between the Two World Wars*. London: Barnes and Mortlake History Society, 1989.
Gumbel, H. Edward. *Insurance and Reinsurance as Financial Services in the London Market*. London: Witherby, 1988.
Gunn, Cathy. *Nightmare on Lime Street: Whatever Happened to Lloyd's of London?* London: Smith Gryphon, 1992.
Hall, Maximilian. *The City Revolution: Causes and Consequences*. Basingstoke, UK: Macmillan/Loughborough University, 1987.
Hamilton, J. E. *The Industries of Crayford: A Brief History*. London: London Borough of Bexley, 1980.
Hancock, David. *Citizens of the World: London Merchants and the Integration of the British Atlantic Community, 1735–1785*. Cambridge: Cambridge University Press, 1995.
Harding, Vanessa, and Laura Wright, eds. *London Bridge: Selected Accounts and Rentals, 1381–1538*. London: London Record Society, 1995.
Hartley, Peter. *The Story of Royal Enfield Motor Cycles*. Cambridge: Stephens, 1981.
Hawkes, H. G. *Tottenham Shops: A Personal Memory*. London: Edmonton Hundred Historical Society, 1983.
Hennessy, Elizabeth. *A Domestic History of the Bank of England*. Cambridge: Cambridge University Press, 1992.
Hewer, Chris. *A Problem Shared: A History of the Institute of London Underwriters, 1884–1984*. London: Witherby, 1984.
Hewlett, Nick, and Jan Toporowski. *All Change in the City: A Report on Recent Changes and Future Prospects in London's Financial Markets*. London: Economist Publications, 1985.
Higlett, Susan. *Business and Trade in High Street, Hounslow, 1803–1982: A Study of Twelve Families*. London: Hounslow and District History Society, 1982.
Hinde, K. S. G. *The City of London Solicitors' Company, 1908–1994*. London: City of London Solicitors' Company, 1994.

Hobson, Dominic. *The Pride of Lucifer: Morgan Grenfell, 1838–1990—The Unauthorised Biography of a Merchant Bank*. London: Mandarin, 1991.

Hope, Valerie, Clive Birch, and Gilbert Torry. *The Freedom: The Past and Present of the Livery, Guilds and City of London*. Buckingham, UK: Barracuda, 1982.

———. *The Worshipful Company of Weavers of the City of London*. London: Worshipful Company of Weavers, 1994.

Houston, J. F. *Featherbedds and Flock Bedds: Notes on the History of the Worshipful Company of Upholders of the City of London*. Sandy, UK: Three Tents, 1993.

Howcroft, J. B., and J. Lavis. *A Strategic Profile of the Payment Systems of London Clearing Banks*. Bangor, UK: University College of North Wales, 1996.

Huffman, Joseph P. *Family, Commerce and Religion in London and Cologne: Anglo-German Emigrants, c. 1000–1300*. Cambridge: Cambridge University Press, 1998.

Ingham, Geoffrey K. *Capitalism Divided?: The City and Industry in British Social Development*. Basingstoke, UK: Macmillan, 1984.

Irving, Joe. *The City at Work: A Guide to the Institutions That Make Up the City of London and Their Roles*. London: Deutsch, 1981.

Jenkin, Roger. *The Wig-Making Clarksons: In Search of Their Life and Times*. Ilfracombe, UK: Stockwell, 1982.

Jenkins, Peter R., ed. *The London Bankers Clearing House: Rules and Regulations, 1910*. Pulborough, UK: Dragonwheel, 1994.

Jones, P. E. *The Worshipful Company of Poulters of the City of London: A Short History*. London: Poulters' Company, 1981.

Joseph, Vivian. *A History of the British East India Company, 1615–1858*. Cheddar, UK: Tallis, 1987.

Kay, William. *The Big Bang: An Investor's Guide to the Changing City*. London: Weidenfeld and Nicolson, 1986.

Kay, William, ed. *The Stock Exchange: A Marketplace for Tomorrow*. London: Stock Exchange Press, 1986.

Keay, John. *The Honourable Company: A History of the English East India Company*. London: HarperCollins, 1991.

Kershen, Anne J. *Uniting the Tailors: Trade Unionism Among the Tailoring Workers of London and Leeds, 1870–1939*. London: Frank Cass, 1995.

Kirkham, Pat, Rodney Mace, and Julia Porter. *Furnishing the World: The East London Furniture Trade, 1830–1980*. London: Journeyman, 1987.

Kynaston, David. *The City of London*, 4 vols. London: Chatto and Windus, 1994 (vol. 1), 1995 (vol. 2), 1999 (vol. 3), and 2001 (vol. 4).

Lacey, Robert. *Sotheby's: Bidding for Class*. London: Little, Brown, 1998.

Landau, Nick. *London from the 1979 Labour Force Survey*. London: Greater London Council, 1983.

Lang, R. G., ed. *Two Tudor Subsidy Assessment Rolls for the City of London*. London: London Record Society, 1993.

Lawson, Philip. *The East India Company: A History*. London: Longman, 1993.

Lazar, David. *Markets and Ideology in the City of London*. London: Macmillan, 1990.

Leedale, Mark. *Intervention and the East London Clothing Industry*. Oxford: Oxford Polytechnic, 1988.

Leeson, Nick. *Rogue Trader*. London: Warner, 1997.

Lovett, Vivien. *Surrey Street, Croydon: A Stall Story—100 Years of Market Trading*. Coulsdon, UK: Frosted Earth, 1995.

Lyth, Torolf. *J. John Masters and Company Ltd.: The Inside Story*. Kidlington, UK: Gwyn-Smith, 1986.

MacLennan, Emma. *Child Labour in London*. London: Low Pay Unit, 1982.

Maitland, Robert. *London's Printing and Publishing Industry*. London: Greater London Council, 1980.

Manser, W. A. P. *Regulation in the City*. London: FT Financial Publishing, 1997.

Mantle, Jonathan. *For Whom the Bell Tolls: The Lessons of Lloyd's of London*. London: Mandarin, 1993.

Marshall, James. *The History of the Great West Road: Its Social and Economic Influence on the Surrounding Area*. London: Heritage Publications, 1995.

Massey, Doreen. *Docklands: A Microcosm of Broader Social and Economic Trends*. London: Docklands Forum, 1991.

Massil, William I. *Immigrant Furniture Workers in London, 1881–1939, and the Jewish Contribution to the Furniture Trade*. London: Jewish Museum/Geffrye Museum, 1997.

Masters, Roy. *The Royal Arsenal, Woolwich*. Stroud, UK: Alan Sutton, 1995.

McCartney, Wilf. *Dare to Be a Daniel! A History of One of Britain's Earliest Syndicalist Unions: 38 Strikes Fought, 38 Won!—The Life and Struggles of an Agitator and the Fight to Free the Catering Slaves of the West End of London (1910–1914)*. London: Kate Sharpley Library, 1992.

McDowell, Paula. *The Women of Grub Street: Press, Politics and Gender in the London Literary Marketplace, 1678–1730*. Oxford: Clarendon Press, 1998.

McRae, Hamish, and Frances Cairncross. *Capital City: London as a Financial Centre*. London: Methuen, 1991.

Meadows, Pamela, Hilary Cooper, and Richard Bartholomew. *The London Labour Market*. London: Her Majesty's Stationery Office, 1988.

Melling, John Kennedy. *Discovering London's Guilds and Liveries*. Aylesbury, UK: Shire, 1981.

Michie, Ranald. *The London and New York Stock Exchanges, 1850–1914*. London: Allen and Unwin, 1987.

———. *The London Stock Exchange*. Oxford: Oxford University Press, 2000.

Montgomery-Massingberd, Hugh, and David Watkin. *The London Ritz: A Social and Architectural History*. London: Aurum, 1980.

Myers, Robin, and Michael Harris, eds. *The Stationers' Company and the Book Trade, 1550–1990*. Winchester, UK: St. Paul's Bibliographies, 1997.

Newall, Sir Paul. *Japan and the City of London*. London: Athlone, 1996.

Nightingale, Pamela. *A Medieval Mercantile Community: The Grocers' Company and the Politics and Trade of London, 1000–1485*. New Haven, Conn.: Yale University Press, 1995.

Oliver, Kingsley M. *Hold Fast, Sit Sure: The History of the Worshipful Company of Saddlers of the City of London, 1160–1960*. Chichester, UK: Phillimore, 1995.

Osborn, Helen. *Inn and Around London: A History of Young's Pubs*. London: Young and Company, 1991.

Packer, Maurice. *Bookbinders of Victorian London*. London: British Library, 1991.

Paige, John. *The Letters of John Paige, London Merchant, 1648–1658*. London: London Record Society, 1984.

Paris, Michael. *Silvertown, 1917*. Hornchurch, UK: Henry, 1986.

Perlmutter, Kevin. *London Street Markets*. London: Wildwood, 1983.

Peterson, William S. *The Kelmscott Press: A History of William Morris's Typographical Adventure*. Oxford: Clarendon, 1989.

Philips, C. H. *The East India Company*, 6 vols. London: Routledge, 1998.

Plender, John, and Paul Wallace. *The Square Mile: A Guide to the City Revolution*. London: Hutchinson Business, 1986.

Pohl, Manfred, and Kathleen Burk. *Die Deutsche Bank in London, 1873–1998*. Munich: Piper, 1998.

Price, Jacob M. *Perry of London: A Family and a Firm on the Seaborne Frontier, 1615–1753*. Cambridge, Mass.: Harvard University Press, 1992.

Prince, Leslie B. *The Farrier and His Craft: The History of the Worshipful Company of Farriers*. London: J. A. Allen, 1980.

Pullen, Bob. *London Street People: Past and Present*. Oxford: Lennard, 1989.

Rappaport, Erika Diane. *Shopping for Pleasure: Women in the Making of London's West End*. Princeton, N.J.: Princeton University Press, 2000.

Rawnsley, Judith. *Going for Broke: Nick Leeson and the Collapse of Barings Bank*. London: HarperCollins, 1996.

Rees, Jane, and Mark Rees. *Christopher Gabriel and the Tool Trade in 18th-Century London: A Commentary in the Business Records of Christopher Gabriel, Planemaker and Tool Seller in London, 1770–1809, and His Connection with the London Tool Making and Selling Trade*. Ipswich, UK: Roy Arnold, 1997.

Reid, Margaret. *All Change in the City: The Revolution in Britain's Financial Sector*. Basingstoke, UK: Macmillan, 1988.

Roberts, Richard, and David Kynaston, eds. *The Bank of England: Money, Power and Influence, 1694–1994*. Oxford: Clarendon, 1995.

Robinson, Jeffrey. *The Hotel: Upstairs, Downstairs in a Secret World*. London: Simon and Schuster, 1996.

Rudden, Bernard. *The New River: A Legal History*. Oxford: Clarendon, 1985.

Saunders, Ann, ed. *The Royal Exchange*. London: London Topographical Society, 1997.

Sayers, R. S. *The Bank of England, 1891–1944*. Cambridge: Cambridge University Press, 1986.

Schmiechen, James A. *Sweated Industries and Sweated Labour: The London Clothing Trades, 1860–1914*. London: Croom Helm, 1984.

Schwarz, L. D. *London in the Age of Industrialisation: Entrepreneurs, Labour Force and Living Conditions*. Cambridge: Cambridge University Press, 1992.

Shaw, E. R. *The London Money Market*. London: Heinemann, 1981.

Shenker, Israel. *The Savoy of London: Reflections on the First Hundred Years*. London: Chesler, 1988.

Sheppardson, Chris. *The Luxury Hotels of London*. Lewes, UK: Book Guild, 1991.

Shipley, Debra, and Mary Peplow. *London Street Markets*. Aylesbury, UK: Shire, 1987.

Solman, David. *Loddiges of Hackney: The Largest Hothouse in the World*. London: Hackney Society, 1995.

Sutton, Jean. *Lords of the East: The East India Company and Its Ships*. London: Conway Maritime, 1981.

Thomas, W. A. *The Big Bang*. Oxford: Philip Allan, 1986.

Urwin, A. C. B. *Commercial Nurseries and Market Gardens*. London: Twickenham Local History Society, 1982.

Wainwright, David. *Stone's Ginger Wine: Fortunes of a Family Firm, 1740–1990*. London: Quiller, 1990.

Ward, Michael. *Red Flag over the Workhouse: The Unemployed in South West London, 1918–1923*. London: Wandsworth History Workshop, 1992.

Webb, G. H. *The Bigger Bang: Growth of a Financial Revolution*. London: Waterlow, 1987.

Welsh, Frank. *Uneasy City: An Insider's View of the City of London*. London: Weidenfeld and Nicolson, 1986.

Whetnall, Norman. *How the Stock Exchange Works*. Reading, UK: Flame, 1987.

White, Patrick. *Lloyd's: Post Reconstruction and Renewal*. London: FT Financial Publishing, 1997.

Whone, Adam. *Edward Withers Ltd.: 230 Years of Violin Craft in Soho*. London: Mill Hill, 1996.

Willson, E. J. *West London Nursery Gardens: The Nursery Gardens of Chelsea, Fulham, Hammersmith, Kensington and a Part of Westminster, Founded Before 1900*. London: Fulham and Hammersmith Historical Society, 1982.

Ziegler, Dieter. *Central Bank, Peripheral Industry: The Bank of England in the Provinces, 1826–1913*. Leicester, UK: Leicester University Press, 1990.

Ziegler, Philip. *The Sixth Great Power: Barings 1762–1929*. London: Collins, 1988.

EDUCATION AND LEARNING

Allan, D. G. C. *Some Noble Patriotic Men—And Women*. London: Twickenham Local History Society, 1994.

Allan, D. G. C., and John L. Abbott, eds. *The Virtuoso Tribe of Arts and Science: Studies in the Eighteenth-Century Work and Membership of the London Society of Arts*. Athens, Ga.: University of Georgia Press, 1992.

Ames-Lewis, Frances, ed. *Sir Thomas Gresham and Gresham College: Studies in the Intellectual History of London in the 16th–17th Centuries*. Aldershot, UK: Ashgate, 1999.

Ashwin, Clive. *A Century of Art Education*. London: Middlesex Polytechnic, 1982.

Attfield, John. *With Light of Knowledge: A Hundred Years of Education in the Royal Arsenal Co-operative Society, 1877–1977*. London: Royal Arsenal Co-operative Society, 1981.

Barber, Michael, ed. *Education in the Capital*. London: Cassell, 1992.

Barker, Nicholas. *Treasures of the British Library*. London: British Library, 1988.

Barnes, William. *Managerial Catalyst: The Story of London Business School, 1964–1989*. London: Paul Chapman, 1989.

Barrett, Anne, and Kevin Brown, eds. *St. Mary's Hospital Medical School: An Historical Anthology*. London: Imperial College/St. Mary's Hospital and Medical School Archives, 1990.

Batchelor, Meston. *Cradle of Empire: A Preparatory School Through Nine Reigns*. London: Phillimore, 1981.

Bentley, Linna. *Educating Women: A Pictorial History of Bedford College, University of London, 1849–1985*. St. Albans, UK: Alma, 1991.

Bingham, Caroline. *The History of the Royal Holloway College, 1886–1986*. London: Constable, 1987.

Black, Gerry. *JFS: The History of the Jews' Free School, London, Since 1732*. London: Tymsder, 1998.

Bryant, Margaret E. *The London Experience of Secondary Education*. London: Athlone, 1986.

Burgess, Tyrrell, Michael Locke, John Pratt, and Nick Richards. *Learning for Living: Higher Education in East London, 1890–1992*. London: Athlone, 1994.

Calnan, James. *The Hammersmith: The First 50 Years of the Royal Postgraduate Medical School at Hammersmith Hospital*. Lancaster, UK: MTP, 1985.

Cannon, Rupert. *The Bolt Court Connection: A History of the LCC School of Photo Engraving and Lithography, 1893–1949*. London: London College of Printing, 1985.

Carle, B. *Libraries for All: An Illustrated History of Kensington and Chelsea Libraries Service, 1887–1987*. London: Royal Borough of Kensington and Chelsea, 1987.

Copelman, Dina M. *London's Women Teachers: Gender, Class and Feminism, 1870–1930*. London: Routledge, 1996.

Cotchin, Ernest. *The Royal Veterinary College, London: A Bicentenary History*. Buckingham, UK: Barracuda Books, 1990.

Crombie, A. E. O. *A View of Christ's College, Blackheath*. Gillingham, UK: Meresborough, 1980.

Dahrendorf, Ralf. *LSE: a History of the London School of Economics and Political Science, 1895–1995*. Oxford: Oxford University Press, 1995.

Desmond, Adrian. *Archetypes and Ancestors: Palaeontology in Victorian London, 1850–1875*. London: Blond and Briggs, 1982.

———. *The Politics of Evolution: Morphology, Medicine and Reform in Radical London*. Chicago: University of Chicago Press, 1989.

Devereux, W. A. *Adult Education in Inner London, 1870–1980*. London: Shepheard-Walwyn/Inner London Education Authority, 1982.

Dixon, C. Willis. *The Institute: A Personal Account of the History of the University of London Institute of Education, 1932–1972*. London: Institute of Education, 1986.

Eagling, Geoffrey J. *A History of a London School for the Deaf: Ackmar Road, 1898–1983*. Feltham, UK: British Deaf History Society, 1998.

Field, John. *The King's Nurseries: The Story of Westminster School*. London: James and James, 1987.

Firth, A. E. *Goldsmiths' College: A Centenary Account*. London: Athlone, 1991.

Floud, Roderick, and Sean Glynn. *London Higher: The Establishment of Higher Education in London*. London: Athlone, 1998.

Frayling, Christopher. *The Royal College of Art: 150 Years of Art and Design*. London: Barrie and Jenkins, 1987.

Gage, Andrew Thomas, and William Thomas Stearn. *A Bicentenary History of the Linnean Society of London*. London: Academic, 1988.

Gleason, Mary Louise. *The Royal Society of London: Years of Reform, 1827–1847*. New York: Garland, 1991.

Grunfeld, Judith. *Shefford: The Story of a Jewish School Community in Evacuation, 1939–1945*. London: Soncino Press, 1980.

Hall, Marie Boas. *All Scientists Now: The Royal Society in the Nineteenth Century*. Cambridge: Cambridge University Press, 1984.

Hammond, Carolyn. *Chiswick Library: One Hundred Years of Service to the Community*. London: London Borough of Hounslow, 1991.

Harte, Negley. *The University of London, 1836–1996*. London: Athlone, 1986.

Hemming, T. D., E. Freeman, and D. Meakin, eds. *The Secular City: Studies in the Enlightenment Presented to Haydn Mason*. Exeter, UK: University of Exeter Press, 1994.

Hepper, F. Nigel. *Plant Hunting for Kew*. London: Her Majesty's Stationery Office, 1989.

Hill, Alan. *One Hundred Years of Libraries in Barking: A Centenary Report*. London: London Borough of Barking, 1989.

Hodges, Sheila. *God's Gift: A Living History of Dulwich College*. London: Heinemann, 1981.

Hunter, Michael. *The Royal Society and Its Fellows, 1660–1700: The Morphology of an Early Scientific Institution*. London: British Society for the History of Science, 1994.

Huxley, Paul. *Exhibition Road: Painters at the Royal College of Art*. Oxford: Phaidon, 1988.

Jackson, Winefride. *The Royal School of Needlework Yesterday and Today*. Blaby, UK: Anderson/Royal School of Needlework, 1981.

Jessel, Camilla. *Life at the Royal Ballet School*. London: Methuen, 1985.

Jones, Valentino. *We Are Our Own Educators!: Josina Machel from Supplementary to Black Complementary School*. London: Karia, 1986.

Keeling, C. H. *They All Came into the Ark: A Record of the Zoological Society of London in Two World Wars*. Shalford, UK: Clam, 1988.

Keeling, Denis F. *Orphans of Commerce: The Commercial Travellers' Schools at Wanstead*. London: Tylney, 1992.

Kenny, Anthony. *The British Library and the St. Pancras Building*. London: British Library, 1994.

Knapp, John M., ed. *The Universities and the Social Problem*. New York: Garland, 1985.

Lawrence, Susan C. *Charitable Knowledge: Hospital Pupils and Practitioners in Eighteenth-Century London*. Cambridge: Cambridge University Press, 1996.

Leaf, John. *Harrow School*. Andover, UK: Pitkin, 1991.

Lee, Raymond, and John A. Hay. *Bermondsey 1792*. Feltham, UK: National Union of the Deaf, 1993.

Lichfield, Patrick, and Richard Shymansky. *An Illustrated History of Harrow School*. London: Michael Joseph, 1988.

Maclure, Stuart. *A History of Education in London, 1879–1990*. London: Allen Lane, 1990.

Marsden, W. E. *Educating the Respectable: A Study of Fleet Road Board School, Hampstead, 1879–1903*. London: Woburn, 1991.

Marsh, Neville. *The History of Queen Elizabeth College, One Hundred Years of University in Kensington*. London: King's College, 1986.

McIntosh, John, Fred Naylor, and Laurence Norcross. *The Inner London Education Authority After the Abolition of the Greater London Council*. London: Centre for Policy Studies, 1983.

Nelson, Helen McCutcheon, and Brian Louis Pearce. *The Happiest Days: A History of Education in Twickenham*, 2 vols. London: Twickenham Local History Society, 1994 (vol. 1) and 1996 (vol. 2).

Nicholls, Michael. *Some Trends in Theological Education in London, 1830–1890*. Leicester, UK: UCCEF.

Pearce, B. L. *Free for All: The Public Library Movement in Twickenham*. London: Twickenham Local History Society, 1985.

Pyatt, Edward C. *The National Physical Laboratory: A History*. Bristol, UK: Hilger, 1983.

Quader, Dil Afroze. *Learning in Deprivation*. Dacca, Bangladesh: University Press, 1993.

Quick, Anthony. *Charterhouse: A History of the School*. London: James and James, 1990.

Ranger, Sir Douglas. *The Middlesex Hospital Medical School: Centenary to Sesquicentenary, 1935–1985*. London: Hutchinson Benham, 1985.

Ringshall, Ron, Dame Margaret Miles, and Frank Kelsall. *The Urban School: Buildings for Education in London, 1870–1980*. London: Greater London Council, 1983.

Rosen, Harold, and Tony Burgess. *Language and Dialects of London School Children: An Investigation*. London: Ward Lock, 1980.

Shorney, David. *Teachers in Training, 1906–1985: A History of Avery Hill College*. London: Thames Polytechnic, 1989.

Smith, Eric E. F. *Macaulay School: The Story of a Church School, 1648–1987*. London: Clapham Press, 1987.

Smith, Ernest G., and Beryl D. Cottell. *The Royal Dental Hospital of London and School of Dental Surgery, 1858–1985*. London: Athlone, 1997.

Teague, S. John. *The City University: A History*. London: City University, 1980.

Topping, James. *The Beginnings of Brunel University: From Technical College to University*. Oxford: Oxford University Press, 1981.

Towle, Angela. *Undergraduate Medical Education: London and the Future*. London: King's Fund Initiative, 1992.

Turner, H. D. T. *The Cradle of the Navy: The Story of the Royal Hospital School at Greenwich and at Holbrook, 1694–1988*. York, UK: William Sessions, 1990.

Wake, Roy. *The Nightingale Training School, 1860–1996*. London: Haggerston, 1998.

Willson, F. M. G. *Our Minerva: The Men and Politics of the University of London, 1836–1858*. London: Athlone, 1995.

Wright, Nigel. *Free School: The White Lion Experience*. Bristol, UK: Libertarian Education, 1989.

Wright, Simon. *Waterfield's School: A Preparatory School in Its Victorian Heyday*. Heron's Ghyll, UK: Heron's Ghyll Press, 1994.

ETHNIC GROUPS

Alderman, Geoffrey. *London Jewry and London Politics, 1889–1986*. London: Routledge, 1989.

Al-Rasheed, Madawi. *Iraqi Assyrian Christians in London: The Construction of Ethnicity*. Lewiston, N.Y.: Edwin Mellen, 1998.

Anim-Addo, Joan. *Longest Journey: A History of Black Lewisham*. London: Deptford Forum, 1995.

———. *Sugar, Spices and Human Cargo: An Early Black History of Greenwich*. London: London Borough of Greenwich, 1996.

Ashgar, Mohammad Ali. *Bangladeshi Community Organisations in East London*. London: Bangla Heritage, 1996.

Baumann, Gerd. *Contesting Culture: Ethnicity and Community in West London*. Cambridge: Cambridge University Press, 1996.

Beckman, Morris. *The Hackney Crucible*. London: Vallentine Mitchell, 1996.

Bennett, Christopher. *The Housing of the Irish in London: A Literature Review*. London: Polytechnic of North London, 1991.

Benson, Susan. *Ambiguous Ethnicity: Interracial Families in London*. Cambridge: Cambridge University Press, 1981.

Benyon, John, ed. *Scarman and After: Essays Reflecting on Lord Scarman's Report, the Riots and Their Aftermath*. Oxford: Pergamon, 1984.

Berrol, Selma C. *East Side/East End: Eastern European Jews in London and New York, 1870–1920*. Westport, Conn.: Praeger, 1994.

Black, Gerry. *Living Up West: Jewish Life in London's West End*. London: London Museum of Jewish Life, 1994.

———. *JFS: The History of the Jews' Free School Since 1732*. London: Tymsder, 1998.

Brinson, Charmian. *The Strange Case of Dora Fabian and Mathilde Wurm: A Study of German Political Exiles in London During the 1930s*. Berne, Switzerland: Peter Lang, 1997.

Brooks, Alan. *1991 Census: Ethnic Groups in Hammersmith and Fulham*. London: London Borough of Hammersmith and Fulham, 1994.

Campbell, Alistair. *Two Hundred Years: The Highland Society of London*. London: Highland Society of London, 1983.

Catholic Family History Society. *The Registers of the Venetian Chapel in London: Baptisms 1744–1796, Marriages 1744–1754, 1772–1788*. London: Catholic Family History Society, 1996.

Chippendale, Neil, ed. *Reminiscences from the Asian Community in Hounslow*. London: Heritage Publications, 1993.

———, ed. *Reminiscences from the Afro-Caribbean Community in Hounslow*. London: Heritage Publications, 1994.

Donovan, Jenny. *We Don't Buy Sickness; It Just Comes: Health, Illness and Health Care in the Lives of Black People in London*. Aldershot, UK: Gower, 1986.

Eade, John. *The Politics of Community: The Bangladeshi Community in East London*. Aldershot, UK: Avebury, 1989.

Ethnic Communities Oral History Project. *Passport to Exile: The Polish Way to London*. London: Ethnic Communities Oral History Project, London Borough of Hammersmith and Fulham, 1988.

———. *In Exile: Iranian Recollections*. London: Ethnic Communities Oral History Project, London Borough of Hammersmith and Fulham, 1989.

———. *Xeni: Greek-Cypriots in London*. London: Ethnic Communities Oral History Project, London Borough of Hammersmith and Fulham, 1990.

———. *Such a Long Story!: Chinese Voices in Britain*. London: Ethnic Communities Oral History Project, London Borough of Hammersmith and Fulham, 1994.

Fleming, Scott. *Home and Away: Sport and South Asian Male Youth*. Aldershot, UK: Avebury, 1995.

Flood, Aidan. *The Irish in Camden*. London: London Borough of Camden, 1990.

Gillespie, Marie. *Television, Ethnicity and Cultural Change*. London: Routledge, 1995.

Green, J. *A Social History of the Jewish East End in London, 1914–1939: A Study of Life, Labour and Liturgy*. Lewiston, N.Y.: Edwin Mellen, 1991.

Grunfeld, Judith. *Shefford: The Story of a Jewish School Community in Evacuation, 1939–1945*. London: Soncino, 1980.

Huffman, Joseph P. *Family, Commerce and Religion in London and Cologne: Anglo-German Emigrants, c. 1000–c. 1300*. Cambridge: Cambridge University Press, 1998.

Jaulmes, Yves. *The French Protestant Church of London and the Huguenots*. London: Église Protestante Française de Londres, 1993.

Kershen, Anne J. *London, the Promised Land?: The Migrant Experience in a Capital City*. Aldershot, UK: Avebury, 1997.

Leech, Kenneth. *Brick Lane 1978: The Events and Their Significance*. Birmingham, UK: AFFOR, 1980.

Lingayah, Sam. *A Comparative Study of Mauritian Immigrants in Two European Cities: London and Paris*. London: Mauritians' Welfare Association, 1991.

London Research Centre. *A Survey of the Armenian Community in London*. London: London Research Centre, 1990

Luthra, Manmohan. *Black Minorities and Housing in Ealing: A Comparative Study of Asian, West Indian and Native White Communities in Ealing and Southall*. London: Shakti, 1982.

Mannick, A. R. *Mauritians in London*. Mayfield, UK: Dodo, 1987.

Marks, Lara V. *Model Mothers: Jewish Mothers and Maternity Provision in East London, 1870–1939*. Oxford: Clarendon, 1994.

Marmoy, Charles F. A., ed. *The Case Book of "La Maison de Charité de Spittlefields," 1739–41*. London: Huguenot Society of London, 1981.

Massil, William I. *Immigrant Furniture Workers in London, 1881–1939, and the Jewish Contribution to the Furniture Trade*. London: Jewish Museum/Geffrye Museum, 1997.

Mazower, David. *Yiddish Theatre in London*. London: Jewish Museum, 1996.

McAuley, Ian. *Ethnic London: A Complete Guide to the Many Faces and Cultures of London*. Chicago: Passport, 1993.

McKellar, Elizabeth. *The German Hospital, Hackney: A Social and Architectural History*. London: Hackney Society, 1991.

O'Grady, Anne. *Irish Immigration to London in the 1940s and 1950s*. London: Polytechnic of North London, 1988.

Okokon, Susan. *Black Londoners, 1880–1990*. Stroud, UK: Alan Sutton, 1998.

Pollins, Harold. *Hopeful Travellers: Jewish Immigrants and Settlers in Nineteenth-Century Britain*. London: London Museum of Jewish Life, 1989.

Quader, Dil Afroze. *Learning in Deprivation*. Dacca, Bangladesh: University Press, 1993.

Rozin, Mordechai. *The Rich and the Poor: Jewish Philanthropy and Social Control in Nineteenth-Century London*. Brighton, UK: Sussex Academic, 1999.

Sanders, Moshe. *Jewish Books in Whitechapel: A Bibliography of Narodiczky's Press*. London: Duckworth, 1991.

Sebba, Mark. *London Jamaican: A Case Study in Language Contact*. London: Longman, 1993.

Shaw, R. A., R. D. Gwynn, and P. Thomas. *Huguenots in Wandsworth*. London: London Borough of Wandsworth, 1985.

Sinha, Rachana. *The Cultural Adjustment of Asian Lone Mothers Living in London*. Aldershot, UK: Ashgate, 1998.

Srebrnik, Henry Felix. *London Jews and British Communism, 1935–1945*. London: Vallentine Mitchell, 1995.

Tambs-Lyche, Harald. *London Patidars: A Case Study in Urban Ethnicity*. London: Routledge and Kegan Paul, 1980.

Taylor, Seamus. *Smalltown Boys and Girls: Emigrant Irish Youth in London*. London: Polytechnic of North London, 1988.

Wann, Mai. *Chiot Shipowners in London: An Immigrant Elite*. Coventry, UK: Centre for Research in Ethnic Relations, 1987.

Whooley, Finbarr. *Irish Londoners: Photographs from the Paddy Fahey Collection*. Stroud, UK: Alan Sutton, 1997.

Wraight, John. *The Swiss in London: A History of the City Swiss Club, 1856–1991*. London: City Swiss Club, 1991.

Wulff, Helena. *Twenty Girls: Growing Up, Ethnicity and Excitement in a South London Microculture*. Stockholm: University of Stockholm, 1988.

Zucchi, John E. *The Little Slaves of the Harp: Italian Child Street Musicians in Nineteenth-Century Paris, London and New York*. Montreal: McGill-Queen's University Press, 1992.

GOVERNMENT AND POLITICS

Alderman, Geoffrey. *London Jewry and London Politics, 1889–1986*. London: Routledge, 1989.

Anson, Brian. *I'll Fight You for It!: Behind the Struggle for Covent Garden*. London: Cape, 1981.

Atkinson, Diane. *Suffragettes in the Purple, White and Green: London, 1906–14*. London: Museum of London, 1992.

Barry, Jim. *The Women's Movement and Local Politics: The Influence on Councillors in London*. Aldershot, UK: Avebury, 1991.

Beattie, Susan. *A Revolution in London Housing: LCC Housing Architects and Their Work, 1893–1914*. London: Greater London Council/Architectural Press, 1980.

Billingham, David. *The Creation of the London Docklands Development Corporation: A Study of the Conflict Between Central and Local Government*. London: Polytechnic of Central London, 1981.

Binski, Paul. *Westminster Abbey and the Plantagenets: Kingship and the Representation of Power, 1200–1400*. New Haven, Conn.: Yale University Press, 1995.

Boyne, Sir Harry. *The Houses of Parliament*. London: Batsford, 1981.

Burke, Barry, and Ken Worpole. *Hackney Propaganda: Working Class Club Life and Politics in Hackney, 1870–1900*. London: Centerprise, 1980.

Bush, Julia. *Behind the Lines: East London Labour, 1914–1919*. London: Merlin, 1984.

Butler, Sir Thomas. *The Crown Jewels and the Coronation Ceremony*. London: Pitkin, 1989.

Carter, Peter. *Islington at Westminster: The Story of Members of Parliament for Islington and Finsbury, 1884–1983*. London: Islington Fabian Society, 1984.

Clifton, Gloria C. *Professionalism, Patronage, and Public Services in Victorian London: The Staff of the Metropolitan Board of Works, 1856–1889*. London: Athlone, 1992.

Cooke, Sir Robert. *The Palace of Westminster: Houses of Parliament*. London: Burton Skira, 1987.

Cormack, Patrick. *Westminster Palace and Parliament*. London: Warne, 1981.

Cox, Jeffrey N. *Poetry and Politics in the Cockney School: Keats, Shelley, Hunt and Their Circle*. Cambridge: Cambridge University Press, 1998.

Cutler, Horace. *The Cutler Files*. London: Weidenfeld and Nicolson, 1982.

Davis, John. *Reforming London: The London Government Problem, 1855–1900*. Oxford: Clarendon, 1988.

De Krey, Gary Stuart. *A Fractured Society: The Politics of London in the First Age of Party, 1688–1715*. Oxford: Clarendon, 1985.

Dove, Iris. *Yours in the Cause: A Brief Account of Suffragettes in Lewisham, Greenwich and Woolwich*. London: London Borough of Lewisham/London Borough of Greenwich, 1988.

Eade, John. *The Politics of Community: The Bangladeshi Community in East London*. Aldershot, UK: Avebury, 1989.

Evans, Graeme. *An Urban Renaissance?: The Role of the Arts in Urban Regeneration—A Survey of Local Authorities in Greater London*. London: University of North London Press, 1993.

Fainstein, Susan S. *The City Builders: Property, Politics and Planning in London and New York*. Oxford: Blackwell, 1994.

Fell, Bryan H., and K. R. MacKenzie. *The Houses of Parliament: A Guide to the Palace of Westminster*. London: Her Majesty's Stationery Office, 1988.

Forrester, Andrew, Stewart Lansley, and Robin Pauley. *Beyond Our Ken: A Guide to the Battle for London*. London: Fourth Estate, 1985.

Fraser, Antonia. *The Gunpowder Plot: Terror and Faith in 1605*. London: Weidenfeld and Nicolson, 1996.

Fuller, Ken. *Radical Associates: London Busworkers from the 1880s to the 1980s*. London: Lawrence and Wishart, 1985.

Garbutt, E. *London Transport and the Politicians*. London: Ian Allan, 1985.

Gelb, Joyce, and Michael Lyons. *A Tale of Two Cities: Housing Policy and Gentrification in London and New York*. London: South Bank Polytechnic, 1991.

Glassberg, Andrew D. *Representation and Urban Community*. London: Macmillan, 1991.

Goss, Sue. *Local Labour and Local Government: A Study of Changing Interests, Politics and Policy in Southwark from 1919 to 1982*. Edinburgh: Edinburgh University Press, 1988.

Harris, Tim. *London Crowds in the Reign of Charles II: Propaganda and Politics from the Restoration Until the Exclusion Crisis*. Cambridge: Cambridge University Press, 1987.

———. *A Patriot Press: National Politics and the London Press in the 1740s*. Oxford: Clarendon, 1993.

Hay, Malcolm. *Westminster Hall and the Medieval Kings*. London: British Museum, 1995.

Haynes, Alan. *The Gunpowder Plot: Faith in Rebellion*. Stroud, UK: Alan Sutton, 1994.

Hebbert, Michael, and Ann Dickins Edge. *Dismantlers: The London Residuary Body*. London: London School of Economics and Political Science, 1994.

Hennessy, Peter. *Whitehall*. London: Fontana, 1990.

Hone, J. Ann. *For the Cause of Truth: Radicalism in London, 1796–1821*. Oxford: Clarendon, 1982.

Hope, Valerie. *My Lord Mayor: Eight Hundred Years of London's Mayoralty*. London: Weidenfeld and Nicolson/Corporation of London, 1989.

Ikin, C. W. *Hampstead Heath: How the Heath Was Saved for the Public*. London: High Hill Press, 1985.

Jenkins, Hugh. *Rank and File*. London: Croom Helm, 1980.

Jones, Christopher. *The Great Palace: The Story of Parliament*. London: British Broadcasting Corporation, 1983.

———. *No. 10 Downing Street: The Story of a House*. London: British Broadcasting Corporation, 1985.

Jones, Leslie. *Hyde Park and Free Speech*. London: Museum of Labour History, 1981.

Lang, R. G., ed. *Two Tudor Subsidy Assessment Rolls for the City of London*. London: London Record Society, 1993.

Lawes, Aidan. *Chancery Lane: "The Strong Box of Empire."* London: Public Record Office, 1996.

Leech, Kenneth. *Brick Lane, 1978: The Events and Their Significance*. Birmingham, UK: AFFOR, 1980.

Lindley, Keith. *Popular Politics and Religion in Civil War London*. Aldershot, UK: Scolar, 1997.

Linehan, Thomas P. *East London for Mosley: The British Union of Fascists in East London and South-West Essex, 1933–40*. London: Cass, 1996.

Marriott, John. *The Culture of Labourism: The East End Between the Wars*. Edinburgh: Edinburgh University Press, 1991.

Marten, Henry. *Letters from the Tower of London, 1660–2*. Chepstow, UK: Moss Rose, 1983.

Masters, Betty R. *Chamber Accounts of the Sixteenth Century*. London: London Record Society, 1984.

McCalman, Iain. *Radical Underworld: Prophets, Revolutionaries and Pornographers in London, 1795–1840*. Cambridge: Cambridge University Press, 1988.

McDowell, Paula. *The Women of Grub Street: Press, Politics and Gender in the London Literary Marketplace, 1678–1730*. Oxford: Clarendon, 1998.

Milford, Anna. *Lord Mayors of London*. London: Comerford and Miller, 1989.

Nicholls, Mark. *Investigating the Gunpowder Plot*. Manchester, UK: Manchester University Press, 1991.

Nicol, Bill. *Regional Disincentive Policies and Inner Area Problems: A Comparison of London and Paris*. Newcastle Upon Tyne, UK: University of Newcastle Upon Tyne, 1980.

Nightingale, Pamela. *A Medieval Mercantile Community: The Grocers' Company and the Politics and Trade of London, 1000–1485*. New Haven, Conn.: Yale University Press, 1995.

Olechnowicz, Andrzej. *Working-Class Housing in England Between the Wars: The Becontree Estate*. Oxford: Clarendon, 1997.

Oliver, Hermia. *The International Anarchist Movement in Late Victorian London*. London: Croom Helm, 1983.

Owen, David. *The Government of Victorian London, 1855–1889: The Metropolitan Board of Works, the Vestries and the City Corporation*. Cambridge, Mass.: Belknap, 1982.

Panayiotopoulos, Prodromos Ioannou. *Local Government Economic Initiatives: Planning, Choice and Politics—The London Experience*. Swansea, UK: University College Swansea, 1992.

Parry, José. *Greening London: Environmental Policies and Practices of the London Boroughs*. London: London Research Centre, 1991.

Pennybacker, Susan D. *A Vision for London, 1889–1914: Labour, Everyday Life and the LCC Experiment*. London: Routledge, 1995.

Peters, Marie. *Pitt and Popularity: The Patriot Minister and London Opinion During the Seven Years War*. Oxford: Clarendon, 1980.

Phelps, Barry. *Power and the Party: A History of the Carlton Club, 1832–1982*. London: Carlton Club/Macmillan, 1983.

Roberts, Patricia. *Governmental Action and the Residential Environment: A Case Study of Battersea, London Borough of Wandsworth*. London: Polytechnic of the South Bank, 1985.

Rowlands, David. *The Impact of the Introduction of Corporate Management on the London Borough of Waltham Forest*. London: Polytechnic of the South Bank, 1981.

Saint, Andrew, ed. *Politics and the People of London: The London County Council, 1889–1965*. London: Hambledon, 1989.

Savitch, Harold V. *Post-Industrial Cities: Politics and Planning in New York, Paris, and London*. Princeton, N.J.: Princeton University Press, 1988.

Shoemaker, Robert B. *Prosecution and Punishment: Petty Crime and the Law in London and Rural Middlesex, c. 1660–1725*. Cambridge: Cambridge University Press, 1991.

Smith, David L., Richard Strier, and David Bevington. *The Theatrical City: Culture, Theatre and Politics in London, 1576–1649*. Cambridge: Cambridge University Press, 1995.

Sofer, Anne. *The London Left Takeover*. London: J. Caslake, 1987.

Squires, Mike. *The Aid to Spain Movement in Battersea, 1936–1939*. London: Elmfield, 1994.

Srebrnik, Henry Felix. *London Jews and British Communism, 1935–1945*. London: Vallentine Mitchell, 1995.

Stoker, Gerry, and Vivien Lowndes. *Tower Hamlets and Decentralisation: The Experience of Globe Town Neighbourhood*. Luton, UK: Local Government Management Board, 1991.

Tatchell, Peter. *The Battle for Bermondsey*. London: Heretic, 1983.

Taylor, Rosemary. *In Letters of Gold: The Story of Sylvia Pankhurst and the East London Federation of the Suffragettes in Bow*. London: Stepney Books, 1993.

Thale, Mary. *Selections from the Papers of the London Corresponding Society, 1792–1799*. Cambridge: Cambridge University Press, 1983.

Ward, Michael. *Red Flag Over the Workhouse: The Unemployed in South West London, 1918–1923*. London: Wandsworth History Workshop, 1992.

Westgate, Alison. *A Green and Pleasant London: A Review of Boroughs' Commitment to the Environment—An LBA Review*. London: London Boroughs Association, 1991.

Wilson, Robert. *The Houses of Parliament*. Norwich, UK: Jarrold, 1994.

Willson, F. M. G. *Our Minerva: The Men and Politics of the University of London, 1836–1858*. London: Athlone, 1995.

Young, Ken, and Patricia L. Garside. *Metropolitan London: Politics and Urban Change, 1837–1981*. London: Edward Arnold, 1982.

HEALTH AND HEALTH CARE

Allderidge, Patricia. *The Bethlem Royal Hospital: An Illustrated History*. London: Bethlem and Maudsley National Health Service Trust, 1995.

Amidon, Lynne. *An Illustrated History of the Royal Free Hospital*. London: Special Trustees for the Royal Free Hospital, 1996.

Barrett, Anne, and Kevin Brown, eds. *St. Mary's Hospital Medical School: An Historical Anthology*. London: Imperial College/St. Mary's Hospital and Medical School Archives, 1990.

Bell, Walter George. *The Great Plague of London*. London: Bracken, 1994.

Benzeval, Michaela, Ken Judge, and Michael Solomon. *The Health Status of Londoners: A Comparative Perspective*. London: King's Fund Initiative, 1992.

Boyle, Sean, and Chris Smaje. *Acute Health Services in London: An Analysis*. London: King's Fund Initiative, 1992.

Broadley, Margaret E. *Patients Come First: Nursing at 'The London' Between the Two World Wars*. Tunbridge Wells, UK: Pitman Medical, 1980.

Bruce, Nigel. *Reducing Unplanned Pregnancy: An Investigation of High Rates of Abortion in Camden and Islington*. London: Hampstead Health Authority, 1992.

Bynum, W. F., and Roy Porter, eds. *Living and Dying in London*. London: Wellcome Institute for the History of Medicine, 1991.

Calnan, James. *The Hammersmith: The First 50 Years of the Royal Postgraduate Medical School at Hammersmith Hospital*. Lancaster, UK: MTP, 1985.

Champion, J. A. I., ed. *Epidemic Disease in London*. London: Centre for Metropolitan History, 1993.

Clifton, Gloria C. *Professionalism, Patronage, and Public Services in Victorian London: The Staff of the Metropolitan Board of Works, 1856–1889*. London: Athlone, 1992.

Cook, Harold J. *The Decline of the Old Medical Regime in Stuart London*. Ithaca, N.Y.: Cornell University Press, 1986.

Cornwell, Jocelyn. *Hard Earned Lives: Accounts of Health and Illness from East London*. London: Tavistock, 1984.

Curle, B. *St. Charles Hospital, 1881–1981: A Century of Service*. London: St. Charles Hospital, 1981.

Daunton, Claire, ed. *The London Hospital Illustrated 250 Years*. London: Batsford, 1990.

Donaldson, J. A. *The National Dental Hospital, 1859–1914*. London: British Dental Association, 1992.

Donovan, Jenny. *We Don't Buy Sickness; It Just Comes: Health, Illness and Health Care in the Lives of Black People in London*. Aldershot, UK: Gower, 1986.

Gould, Terry, and David Uttley. *A Short History of St. George's Hospital and the Origins of Its Ward Names*. London: Athlone, 1997.

Granshaw, Lindsay. *St. Mark's Hospital, London: A Social History of a Specialist Hospital*. London: King Edward's Hospital Fund for London, 1985.

Halliday, Stephen. *The Great Stink of London: Sir Joseph Bazalgette and the Cleansing of the Victorian Capital*. Stroud, UK: Alan Sutton, 1999.

Hardy, Anne. *The Epidemic Streets: Infectious Disease and the Rise of Preventive Medicine, 1856–1900*. Oxford: Clarendon, 1993.

Hogg, Christine. *Centering Excellence?: National and Regional Health Services in London*. London: King's Fund Initiative, 1992.

Kosky, Jules. *Mutual Friends: Charles Dickens and the Great Ormond Street Hospital*. London: Weidenfeld and Nicolson, 1989.

Kosky, Jules, and Raymond J. Lunnon. *Great Ormond Street and the Story of Medicine*. London: Hospitals for Sick Children/Granta, 1991.

Laing, William. *Going Private: Independent Health Care in London*. London: King's Fund Initiative, 1992.

Lawrence, Susan C. *Charitable Knowledge: Hospital Pupils and Practitioners in Eighteenth-Century London*. Cambridge: Cambridge University Press, 1996.

Marks, Lara. *Model Mothers: Jewish Mothers and Maternity Provision in East London, 1870–1939*. Oxford: Clarendon, 1994.

———. *Metropolitan Maternity: Maternal and Infant Welfare Services in Early Twentieth-Century London*. Amsterdam: Rodopi, 1996.

McKellar, Elizabeth. *The German Hospital, Hackney: A Social and Architectural History*. London: Hackney Society, 1991.

Meara, Richard. *London's Legacy: Aspects of the NHS Estate in London*. London: King's Fund Initiative, 1992.

Mercer, Derrik, and Gillian Mercer. *Children First and Always: A Portrait of Great Ormond Street*. London: Futura, 1987.

Murphy, Elaine. *London Views: Three Essays on Health Care in the Capital*. London: King's Fund Initiative, 1992.

O'Keefe, Eileen. *Divided London: Towards A European Public Health Approach*. London: University of North London Press, 1993.

Ranger, Sir Douglas. *The Middlesex Hospital Medical School: Centenary to Sesquicentenary, 1935–1985*. London: Hutchinson Benham, 1985.

Russell, David. *Scenes from Bedlam: A History of Caring for the Mentally Disordered at Bethlem Royal Hospital and the Maudsley*. London: Baillière Tindall, 1997.

Samman, P. D., ed. *A History of St. John's Hospital for Diseases of the Skin, 1963–1988*. Oxford: Radcliffe Medical, 1990.

Sargent, Margaret. *Women, Drugs, and Policy in Sydney, London, and Amsterdam: A Feminist Interpretation*. Aldershot, UK: Avebury, 1992.

Seccombe, Ian J. *Health Care Labour Markets: Supply and Change in London*. London: King's Fund Initiative, 1992.

Sleator, Alan, and Denise Winn. *Great Ormond Street: Behind the Scenes at the World's Most Famous Children's Hospital*. London: Ebury, 1996.

Smith, Ernest G., and Beryl D. Cottell. *The Royal Dental Hospital of London and School of Dental Surgery, 1858–1985*. London: Athlone, 1997.

Smith, Jane, ed. *London After Tomlinson: Reorganising Big City Medicine*. London: BMJ Publishing, 1993.

Thompson, Phyllis. *No Bronze Statue: A Living Documentary of the Mildmay Mission Hospital*. Eastbourne, UK: Kingsway, 1982.

Towle, Angela. *Undergraduate Medical Education: London and the Future*. London: King's Fund Initiative, 1992.

Wake, Roy. *The Nightingale Training School, 1860–1996*. London: Haggerston, 1998.

Weedon, Brenda. *A History of Queen Mary's University Hospital, Roehampton*. London: Richmond, Twickenham and Roehampton Healthcare NHS Trust, 1996.

Yeo, Geoffrey. *Images of Bart's: An Illustrated History of St. Bartholomew's Hospital in the City of London*. London: Historical Publications, 1992.

THE LAW

Andrew, Donna T. *Philanthropy and Police: London Charity in the Eighteenth Century*. Princeton, N.J.: Princeton University Press, 1989.

Barker, Felix, and Silvester-Carr, Denise. *Crime and Scandal: The Black Plaque Guide to London*. London: Constable, 1995.

Beadle, William. *Jack the Ripper*. Dagenham, UK: Wat Tyler, 1995.

Begg, Paul, Martin Fido, and Keith Skinner. *The Jack the Ripper A–Z*. London: Headline, 1996.

Begg, Paul, and Keith Skinner. *The Scotland Yard Files*. London: Headline, 1992.

Belcher, Victor. *Boodle, Hatfield and Co.: The History of a London Law Firm in Three Centuries*. London: Boodle, Hatfield and Co., 1985.

Benn, Melissa, and Ken Worpole. *Death in the City: An Examination of Police Related Deaths in London*. London: Canary, 1986.

Benyon, John, ed. *Scarman and After: Essays Reflecting on Lord Scarman's Report, the Riots and Their Aftermath*. Oxford: Pergamon, 1984.

Binet, Helene. *The Inns of Court*. London: Black Dog, 1996.

Borowitz, Albert. *The Woman Who Murdered Black Satin*. Columbus: Ohio State University Press, 1981.

Brimson, Dougie, and Eddy Brimson. *Capital Punishment: London's Violent Football Following*. London: Headline, 1997.

Brown, John W. *The Streatham Grave Robbers: A Tale of Attempted Body Snatching in Streatham in 1814*. London: Local History Publications, 1998.

Brown, Roger Lee. *A History of the Fleet Prison, London: The Anatomy of the Fleet*. Lewiston, N.Y.: Edwin Mellen, 1996.

Buchanan, Charles. *Bow Street Runner*. Saffron Walden, UK: Anglia Young, 1992.

Budworth, Geoffrey. *The River Beat: The Story of London's River Police Since 1798*. London: Historical Publications, 1997.

Bunker, John. *From Rattle to Radio*. Studley, UK: K. A. F. Brewin, 1988.

Burford, E. J., and Joy Wotton. *Private Vices—Public Virtues: Bawdry in London from Elizabethan Times to the Regency*. London: Robert Hale, 1995.

Byrne, Richard. *Prisons and Punishments of London*. London: Harrap, 1989.

Casale, Silvia. *Women Inside: The Experience of Women Remand Prisoners in Holloway*. London: Civil Liberties Trust, 1989.

Chesshyre, Robert. *The Force: Inside the Police*. London: Pan, 1990.

Clarke, Kate. *The Pimlico Murder: The Strange Case of Adelaide Bartlett*. London: Souvenir, 1990.

Coldham, Peter Wilson. *Lord Mayor's Court of London: Depositions Relating to Americans, 1641–1736*. Washington, D.C.: National Genealogical Society, 1980.

Cole, Harry. *Policeman's Ball*. London: Fontana, 1992.

Cooper, Jeremy, and Tarek Qureshi. *Through Patterns Not Our Own: A Study of the Regulation of Violence on the Council Estates of East London*. London: Nereg, 1993.

Coquillette, Daniel R. *The Civilian Writers of Doctors' Commons, London: Three Centuries of Juristic Innovation in Comparative, Commercial and International Law*. Berlin: Duncker and Humblot, 1988.

Cowper, Francis. *A Prospect of Gray's Inn*. London: GRAYA, 1985.

Darbyshire, Neil. *The Flying Squad*. London: Headline, 1993.

Dickson, John. *Murder without Conviction: Inside the World of the Krays*. London: Sidgwick and Jackson, 1986.

Donoghue, Albert, and Martin Short. *The Krays' Lieutenant*. London: Smith Gryphon, 1995.

Elliott, Bryn. *A History of Loughton and Chigwell Police*. Loughton, UK: Chigwell and Loughton History Society, 1991.

Evans, Stewart P., and Paul Gainey. *The Lodger: The Arrest and Escape of Jack the Ripper*. London: Century, 1995.

Fairfax, Norman. *From Quills to Computers: The History of the Metropolitan Police Civil Staff, 1829–1979*. London: Metropolitan Police, 1980.

Feldman, Paul H. *Jack the Ripper: The Final Chapter*. London: Virgin, 1997.

Fido, Martin. *Murder Guide to London*. London: Grafton, 1987.

Fisher, Peter. *An Illustrated Guide to Jack the Ripper*. Runcorn, UK: P. and D. Riley, 1996.

Fleming, Robert. *Scotland Yard*. London: Signet, 1995.

Fuller, Jean Overton. *Sickert and the Ripper Crimes: An Investigation into the Relationship Between the Whitechapel Murders of 1888 and the English Tonal Painter Walter Richard Sickert*. Oxford: Mandrake, 1990.

Goodman, Andrew. *The Court Guide*. London: Sweet & Maxwell, 1980.

———. *The Royal Courts of Justice Guide*. London: Longman Professional, 1985.

Gould, Robert W., and Michael J. Waldren. *London's Armed Police: 1829 to the Present*. London: Arms & Armour, 1986.

Hardwicke, Glyn. *Keepers of the Door: The History of the Port of London Authority Police*. London: Peel Press, 1980.

Herber, Mark D. *Clandestine Marriages in the Chapel and Rules of the Fleet Prison, 1680–1754: Transcripts of Registers at the Public Record Office*. London: Francis Boutle, 1998.

Hobbs, Dick. *Doing the Business: The Working Class and Detectives in the East End of London*. Oxford: Oxford University Press, 1989.

———. *Bad Business: Professional Crime in Modern Britain*. Oxford: Oxford University Press, 1995.

Holmes, Thomas. *Known to the Police*. New York: Garland, 1984.

James, P. D., and T. A. Critchley. *The Maul and the Pear Tree: The Ratcliffe Highway Murders, 1811*. Bath, UK: Chivers, 1988.

Jennings, Andrew, Paul Lashmar, and Vyv Simson. *Scotland Yard's Cocaine Connection*. London: Cape, 1990.

Jones, Trevor. *The Islington Survey: Crime, Victimization and Policing in Inner-city London*. Aldershot, UK: Gower, 1986.

Kelland, Gilbert. *Crime in London*. London: Grafton, 1987.

Kennedy, Ludovic. *10 Rillington Place*. London: HarperCollins, 1995.

Lansdowne, Andrew. *A Life's Reminiscences of Scotland Yard*. New York: Garland, 1984.

Lefebure, Molly. *Murder on the Home Front*. London: Grafton, 1990.

Lemmings, David. *Gentlemen and Barristers: The Inns of Court and the English Bar, 1680–1730*. Oxford: Clarendon, 1990.

Linebaugh, Peter. *The London Hanged: Crime and Civil Society in the Eighteenth Century*. London: Penguin, 1993.

Lock, Joan. *Marlborough Street: The Story of a London Court*. London: Hale, 1980.

———. *Tales from Bow Street.* London: Hale, 1982.

Loftie, W. J. *The Inns of Court and Chancery*. Southampton, UK: Ashford, 1985.

Martin, Frank. *Rogue's River: Crime on the River Thames in the Eighteenth Century*. Hornchurch, UK: Henry, 1983.

Mayhew, Henry. *London Characters and Crooks*. London: Folio Society, 1996.

McLaren, Angus. *A Prescription for Murder: The Victorian Serial Killings of Dr. Thomas Neill Cream*. Chicago: University of Chicago Press, 1993.

Moore, Lucy. *Conmen and Cutpurses: Scenes from the Hogarthian Underworld*. London: Allen Lane/Penguin Press, 2000.

Morton, James. *Gangland: London's Underworld*. London: Warner, 1993.

Murphy, Robert. *Smash and Grab: Gangsters in the London Underworld, 1920–60*. London: Faber and Faber, 1993.

Murphy, Theresa. *The Old Bailey: Eight Centuries of Crime, Cruelty and Corruption*. Edinburgh: Mainstream, 1999.

Murray, Michael G. *Middle Temple Hall: An Architectural Appreciation*. London: Middle Temple, 1991.

Nicholson, John. *The Great Liberty Riot of 1780: Being an Account of How the People Destroyed the Prisons of London and Set Free the Prisoners, Together with a Thorough Examination of How This Event Has Been Portrayed in History and Literature*. London: Bozo, 1985.

Norris, Henry. *Justice in Eighteenth-Century Hackney: The Justicing Notebook of Henry Norris and the Hackney Petty Sessions Book*. London: London Record Society, 1991.

O'Donnell, Kevin. *The Jack the Ripper Whitechapel Murders*. St. Osyth, UK: Ten Bells, 1997.

Paley, Bruce. *Jack the Ripper: The Simple Truth*. London: Headline, 1995.

Palmer, Scott. *Jack the Ripper: A Reference Guide*. Lanham, Md.: Scarecrow Press, 1995.

Pearson, John. *The Profession of Violence: The Rise and Fall of the Kray Twins*. London: Granada, 1995.

Petrow, Stefan. *Policing Morals: The Metropolitan Police and the Home Office, 1870–1914*. Oxford: Clarendon Press, 1994.

Plimmer, John F. *In the Footsteps of the Whitechapel Murders: An Examination of the Jack the Ripper Murders Using Modern Police Techniques*. Lewes, UK: Book Guild, 1998.

Porter, Bernard. *The Origins of the Vigilante State: The London Metropolitan Police Special Branch Before the First World War*. Woodbridge: Boydell, 1991.

Rock, Paul. *The Social World of an English Crown Court: Witness and Professionals in the Crown Court Centre at Wood Green*. Oxford: Clarendon, 1993.

———. *Reconstructing a Women's Prison: The Holloway Redevelopment Project, 1968–88*. Oxford: Clarendon, 1996.

Rose, Andrew. *Scandal at the Savoy: The Infamous 1920s Murder Case*. London: Bloomsbury, 1991.

Rose, David. *Climate of Fear: Blakelock Murder and the Tottenham Three*. London: Bloomsbury, 1992.

Rumbelow, Donald. *The Triple Tree: Newgate, Tyburn and the Old Bailey*. London: Harrap, 1982.

———. *The Houndsditch Murders & the Siege of Sidney Street*. Harmondsworth, UK: Penguin, 1990.

Runnicles, Dorothy. *Co-operation and Conflict: A Study of Social Service Work with Juveniles in Trouble*. Hatfield, UK: Hatfield Polytechnic, 1983.

Salgado, Gamini. *The Elizabethan Underworld*. Gloucester, UK: Alan Sutton, 1984.

Sheptycki, J. W. E. *Innovations in Policing Domestic Violence: Evidence from Metropolitan London*. Aldershot, UK: Avebury, 1993.

Shoemaker, Robert B. *Prosecution and Punishment: Petty Crime and the Law in London and Rural Middlesex, c. 1660–1725*. Cambridge: Cambridge University Press, 1991.

Shore, Heather. *Artful Dodgers: Youth and Crime in Early Nineteenth-Century London*. London: Royal Historical Society, 1999.

Smith, Phillip Thurmond. *Policing Victorian London: Political Policing, Public Order, and the London Metropolitan Police*. Westport, Conn.: Greenwood, 1985.

Sugden, Keith, ed. *Criminal Islington: The Story of Crime and Punishment in a Victorian Suburb*. London: Islington Archaeology and History Society, 1989.

Sugden, Philip. *The Complete History of Jack the Ripper*. London: Robinson, 1995.

Taylor, Laurie. *In the Underworld*. Oxford: Blackwell, 1984.

Thomas, Donald. *The Victorian Underworld*. London: Murray, 1999.

Thorne, Samuel E., and J. H. Baker, eds. *Readings and Moots at the Inns of Court in the Fifteenth Century: Moots and Readers' Cases*. London: Selden Society, 1990.

Tullett, Tom. *Murder Squad: Famous Cases of Scotland Yard's Murder Squad*. London: Granada, 1981.

Tully, James. *Prisoner 1167: The Madman Who Was Jack the Ripper*. New York: Carroll and Graf, 1997.

Turnbull, Peter. *The Killer Who Never Was: A Re-appraisal of the Whitechapel Murders of 1888*. Hull, UK: Clark, Lawrence, 1996.

Waddell. Bill. *The Black Museum: New Scotland Yard*. London: Little, Brown, 1995.

Waddington, P. A. J. *Liberty and Order: Public Order Policing in a Capital City*. London: UCL Press, 1994.

Ward, Tony. *Death and Disorder: Three Case Studies of Public Order and Policing in London*. London: INQUEST, 1986.

Whittington-Egan, Richard. *The Riddle of Birdhurst Rise: The Croydon Poisoning Mystery*. Harmondsworth, UK: Penguin, 1988.

Wunderli, Richard M. *London Church Courts and Society on the Eve of the Reformation*. Cambridge, Mass.: Medieval Academy of America, 1981.

LOCAL STUDIES: AREAS NORTH OF THE RIVER THAMES

Abbott, Simon, ed. *Suburb 75: Hampstead Garden Suburb, 1907–1982—A Seventy-Fifth Anniversary Celebration*. London: Hampstead Garden Suburb Residents' Association, 1982.

Addison, Sir William. *Epping Forest: Figures in a Landscape*. London: Hale, 1991.

Allemandy, Victor H. *Enfield Past and Present*. London: Enfield Preservation Society, 1983.

Ashby, Margaret. *The Book of the River Lea*. Buckingham, UK: Barracuda, 1991.

Bartholomew, James. *The City of London: A Photographer's Portrait*. London: Herbert, 1989.

Bentley, James. *East of the City: The London Docklands Story*. London: Pavilion, 1997.

Bernard, Philippa. *Chelsea: A Visitor's Guide*. London: Chelsea Rare Books, 1983.

Binney, Marcus. *Palace on the River: Tony Farrell's Redevelopment of Charing Cross*. London: Wordsearch, 1991.

Bloch, Howard. *Newham Dockland*. Stroud, UK: Chalford, 1995.

Bloch, Howard, and Nick Harris. *Canning Town*. Stroud, UK: Chalford, 1995.

Borer, Mary Cathcart. *The Story of Covent Garden*. London: Hale, 1984.

Bowden, Richard. *Marylebone and Paddington*. Stroud, UK: Alan Sutton, 1995.

Brown, R. S. *The Book of Wealdstone: The History of a Victorian Suburb*. Buckingham, UK: Barracuda, 1989.

Cameron, Andrea. *Hounslow, Isleworth, Heston, and Cranford: A Pictorial History*. Chichester, UK: Phillimore, 1995.

Clark, Roger George. *Chelsea Today*. London: Hale, 1991.

———. *Richmond Today, Including Kew Gardens and Hampton Court*. London: Hale, 1994.

Clegg, Gillian. *Chiswick Past*. London: Historical Publications, 1995.

Connell, Jim. *Illustrated History of Upper Street, Islington*, 2 vols. London: Islington Local History Education Trust, 1989 (vol. 1) and 1991 (vol. 2).

Cosh, Mary. *The Squares of Islington*, 2 vols. London: Islington Archaeology and History Society, 1990 (vol. 1) and 1993 (vol. 2).

Cox, Jane. *London's East End: Life and Traditions*. London: Phoenix Illustrated, 1997.

Cull, Elizabeth. *Portrait of the Chilterns*. London: Hale, 1982.

Curtis, Peter. *In Times Past: Wood Green and Tottenham with West Green and Harringay: An Illustrated Journey into More Peaceful Life Styles*. London: Hornsey Historical Society, 1991.

Dalling, Graham. *A Guide to Enfield Street Names*. London: Enfield Preservation Society, 1983.

———. *Enfield Town*. London: Enfield Preservation Society, 1988.

———. *Southgate and Edmonton Past: A Study in Divergence*. London: Historical Publications, 1996.

Darby, Madge. *Waeppa's People: A History of Wapping*. Colchester, UK: Connor and Butler, 1988.

Davis, Fred. *Finchley Common: A Notorious Place*. London: London Borough of Barnet, 1981.

Davis, Leonard. *Chingford in 1891*. London: Chingford Historical Society, 1994.

Dearden, James S. *John Ruskin's Camberwell*. St. Albans, UK: Brentham, 1990.

Delvin, S. *A History of Winchmore Hill*. London: Regency, 1987.

Denny, Barbara. *Notting Hill and Holland Park Past: A Visual History*. London: Historical Publications, 1993.

———. *Hammersmith and Shepherds Bush Past*. London: Historical Publications, 1995.

———. *Chelsea Past*. London: Historical Publications, 1996.

Denny, Barbara, and Carolyn Starren. *Kensington and Chelsea*. London: Royal Borough of Kensington and Chelsea, 1995.

Dowling, Ian, and Nick Harris. *Wanstead and Woodford*. Bath, UK: Chalford, 1994.

Draper, Warwick H. *Hammersmith: A Study in Town History*. London: Anne Bingley, 1989.

Dumayne, Alan. *The London Borough of Enfield*. Stroud, UK: Alan Sutton, 1996.

Essen, Richard. *Ealing and Northfields*. Stroud, UK: Alan Sutton, 1996.

———. *Ealing, Hanwell, Perivale and Greenford*. Stroud, UK: Alan Sutton, 1997.

Evans, Brian. *Bygone Romford*. Chichester, UK: Phillimore, 1988.

———. *Bygone Barking*. Chichester, UK: Phillimore, 1991.

Farmer, Alan. *Hampstead Heath*. London: Historical Publications, 1984.

Farmer, Jack. *Epping Town Fire Brigade: A History*. London: Epping Forest District Museum, 1986.

Farrell, Jerome, and Christine Bayliss. *Hammersmith and Shepherds Bush*. Stroud, UK: Alan Sutton, 1995.

Farson, Daniel. *Soho in the Fifties*. London: Pimlico, 1993.

Fisher, J. L. *Epping*. Chelmsford, UK: Essex Libraries, 1984.

Fishman, William J. *East End and Docklands*. London: Duckworth, 1990.

Forshaw, Alec. *Smithfield Past and Present*. London: Hale, 1990.

Gay, Ken. *Forest to Suburb: The Story of Hornsey Retold*. London: Hornsey Historical Society, 1988.

———. *Palace on the Hill: A History of Alexandra Palace and Park*. London: Hornsey Historical Society, 1992.

———. *Hornsey and Crouch End*. Stroud, UK: Chalford, 1998.

Gillies, Stewart, and Pamela Taylor. *Finchley and Friern Barnet: A Pictorial History*. Chichester, UK: Phillimore, 1992.

Girling, Brian. *Harrow*. Stroud, UK: Chalford, 1996.

Grynberg, Warren. *The Square Mile: The City of London in Historic Postcards*. Moreton-in-Marsh, UK: Windrush, 1995.

Hammond, Carolyn, and Peter Hammond. *Chiswick*. Bath, UK: Alan Sutton, 1994.

———. *Brentford*. Stroud, UK: Chalford, 1996.

Hart, Valerie, Richard Knight, and Lesley Marshall. *Camden Town, 1791–1991: A Pictorial Record*. London: London Borough of Camden, 1991.

Hasker, Leslie. *The Place Which Is Called Fulanham: An Outline History of Fulham from Roman Times Until the Start of the Second World War*. London: Fulham and Hammersmith Historical Society, 1981.

———. *Hammersmith and Fulham Through 1500 Years: A Brief History*. London: Fulham and Hammersmith Historical Society, 1992.

Hearmon, Caroline. *Uxbridge: A Concise History*. London: London Borough of Hillingdon, 1982.

Hedley, Owen. *The City of London*. London: Pitkin, 1982.

Hepple, Leslie W., and Alison M. Doggett. *The Chilterns*. Chichester, UK: Phillimore, 1994.

Holmes, Malcolm J. *Hampstead to Primrose Hill*. Stroud, UK: Alan Sutton, 1995.

Home, Robert, and Sebastian Loew. *Covent Garden*. London: Surveyors, 1987.

Hounsell, Peter. *Ealing and Hanwell Past: A Visual History of Ealing and Hanwell*. London: Historical Publications, 1991.

Howson, James. *A Brief History of Barking and Dagenham*. London: London Borough of Barking and Dagenham, 1984.

Hunter, Michael. *The Victorian Villas of Hackney*. London: Hackney Society, 1981.

Hunter, Michael, and Robert Thorne, eds. *Change at King's Cross from 1800 to the Present*. London: Historical Publications, 1990.

Hunting, Penelope. *Royal Westminster: A History of Westminster Through Its Royal Connections*. London: Royal Institute of Chartered Surveyors, 1981.

———. *Cutler's Gardens*. London: Standard Life Assurance Company, 1984.

Keene, Derek. *Cheapside Before the Great Fire*. London: ESRC, 1985.

Kelter, Catherine. *Hayes Past*. London: Historical Publications, 1996.

Kentfield, Steve. *A Riverside Journey: Tower Bridge to Blackwell Pier in Picture Postcards c. 1900 to 1930s*. London: History of Wapping Trust, 1990.

Kimber, Jane. *Fulham*. Stroud, UK: Alan Sutton, 1996.

Kirwan, Paul. *Southall: A Brief History*. London: London Borough of Ealing, 1980.

Knott, Bettie. *The Hub of Hoxton: Hoxton Street, 1851–1871, Based on a Study of the Censuses*. London: London Borough of Hackney, 1981.

Law, A. D. *Walthamstow Village*. London: Walthamstow Antiquarian Society, 1984.

Lawrence, Peter. *Woodford: A Pictorial History*. Chichester, UK: Phillimore, 1995.

Loobey, Patrick. *Chiswick and Brentford*. Thrupp, UK: Alan Sutton, 1997.

Mander, David. *Hackney, Homerton and Dalston: Prints and Engravings, 1720–1948*. Stroud, UK: Alan Sutton, 1996.

———. *More Light, More Power: An Illustrated History of Shoreditch*. Stroud, UK: Alan Sutton, 1996.

———. *Look Back, Look Forwards!: An Illustrated History of Stoke Newington*. Stroud, UK: Alan Sutton, 1997.

———. *Strength in the Tower: An Illustrated History of Hackney*. Stroud, UK: Alan Sutton, 1998.

Manton, Colin. *Bygone Billingsgate*. Chichester, UK: Phillimore, 1989.

Marsh, Phyllis. *Chelsea Through the Ages*. Liss, UK: Triplegate, 1984.

Marshall, Lesley. *Kentish Town: Its Past in Pictures*. London: London Borough of Camden, 1993.

Mason, Martin, and Malcolm Sanders. *The City Companion*. London: Hale, 1994.

Massey, Doreen. *Docklands: A Microcosm of Broader Social and Economic Trends*. London: Docklands Forum, 1991.

McDonald, Erica, and David J. Smith. *Artisans and Avenues: A History of the Queen's Park Estate*. London: City of Westminster, 1990.

Meads, R. J. *Southall 830–1982*. Braunton, UK: Merlin, 1983.

Miller, Mervyn. *Hampstead Garden Suburb: Past and Present*. Stroud, UK: Chalford, 1995.

Miller, Mervyn, and A. Stuart Gray. *Hampstead Garden Suburb*. Chichester, UK: Phillimore, 1992.

Nelson, John. *The History, Topography and Antiquities of the Parish of St. Mary, Islington, in the County of Middlesex*. London: Philip Watson, 1980.

O'Leary, J. G. *Dagenham*. London: London Borough of Barking and Dagenham/London Borough of Redbridge, 1988.

Owusu, Kwesi, and Jacob Ross. *Behind the Masquerade: The Story of the Notting Hill Carnival*. London: Arts Media Group, 1988.

Oxley, J. E. *Barking and Ilford*. London: London Borough of Barking and Dagenham/London Borough of Redbridge, 1987.

Pam, D. O. *The Hungry Years: The Struggle for Survival in Edmonton and Enfield Before 1400*. London: Edmonton Hundred Historical Society, 1980.

———. *The Story of Enfield Chase*. London: Enfield Preservation Society, 1984.

———. *A Parish Near London: A History of Enfield*, 3 vols. London: Enfield Preservation Society, 1990 (vol. 1), 1992 (vol. 2), and 1994 (vol. 3).

Parkinson, Michael. *Visiting, Living and Working in Hammersmith and Fulham*. Gloucester, UK: British Publishing, 1992.

Pearce, K. R. *Uxbridge, 1950–1970: The Changing Town*. Stroud, UK: Alan Sutton, 1997.

Pewsey, Stephen. *Chingford*. Stroud, UK: Chalford, 1996.

———. *East Ham*. Stroud, UK: Alan Sutton, 1996.

———. *Stratford, West Ham and the Royal Docks*. Stroud, UK: Alan Sutton, 1996.

Reboul, Percy, and John Heathfield. *The London Borough of Barnet Past and Present*. Stroud, UK: Alan Sutton, 1997.

Richardson, John. *Islington Past: A Visual History of Islington*. London: Historical Publications, 1988.

———. *Highgate Past: A Visual History of Highgate*. London: Historical Publications, 1989.

———. *Camden Town and Primrose Hill Past: A Visual History of Camden Town and Primrose Hill*. London: Historical Publications, 1991.

———. *Covent Garden Past*. London: Historical Publications, 1995.

———. *Kentish Town Past*. London: Historical Publications, 1997.

Robinson, A. J., and D. H. B. Chesshyre. *The Green: A History of the Heart of Bethnal Green and the Legend of the Blind Beggar*. London: London Borough of Tower Hamlets, 1986.

Roe, William P. *Glimpses of Chiswick's Place in History*. London: Alwyn, 1990.

Scannell, Dorothy. *Mother Knew Best: An East End Childhood*. Bath, UK: Firecrest, 1987.

———. *Dolly's Mixture*. Bath, UK: Firecrest, 1988.

Schwitzer, Joan. *Highgate Village*. London: Hornsey Historical Society, 1989.

Schwitzer, Joan, ed. *People and Places: Lost Estates of Highgate, Hornsey and Wood Green*. London: Hornsey Historical Society, 1996.

Schwitzer, Joan, and Ken Gay. *Highgate and Muswell Hill: A Visual Portrait*. Stroud, UK: Chalford, 1995.

Sheaf, John. *Hampton in the 1890s Through the Eyes of Captain Christie of Beveree*. London: Twickenham Local History Society, 1995.

———. *Edwardian Hampton: The Story of Hampton and Hampton Hill from 1900–1914*. London: Twickenham Local History Society, 1997.

Smith, Hector. *A Perambulation at Ealing in 1776*. London: Ealing Museum Art and History Society, 1980.

Smith, Margery M. *Woodford: Village to Suburb*. London: Woodford and District Historical Society, 1982.

Snow, Len. *Brent: Wembley, Willesden and Kingsbury—A Pictorial History*. Chichester, UK: Phillimore, 1990.

Spencer, Adam. *Wembley and Kingsbury*. Stroud, UK: Alan Sutton, 1995.

———. *Willesden*. Stroud, UK: Alan Sutton, 1996.

Sugden, Keith. *History of Highbury*. London: Islington Archaeology and History Society, 1984.

Tames, Richard. *Soho Past*. London: Historical Publications, 1994.

Taylor, Pamela, and Joanna Corden. *Barnet, Edgware, Hadley and Totteridge: A Pictorial History*. Chichester, UK: Phillimore, 1994.

Taylor, Rosemary, and Christopher Lloyd. *Stepney, Bethnal Green and Poplar*. Stroud, UK: Alan Sutton, 1995.

———. *The Changing East End: Stepney, Bethnal Green and Poplar, 1860–1960*. Stroud, UK: Alan Sutton, 1997.

Thomas, Ben. *Ben's Limehouse Recollections*. London: Ragged School Books, 1987.

Thomson, David. *In Camden Town*. Harmondsworth, UK: Penguin, 1983.

Tindall, Gillian. *The Fields Beneath: The History of One London Village*. London: Paladin, 1980.

Turner, Christopher. *Hampton Court, Richmond and Kew Step by Step*. London: Faber, 1987.

Usborne, Ann. *A Portrait of Islington*. London: Damien Tunnacliffe, 1981.

———. *A Portrait of Hampstead*. London: Damien Tunnacliffe, 1984.

———. *A Portrait of Highgate*. London: Damien Tunnacliffe, 1986.

Wade, Christopher. *Hampstead Past: A Visual History of Hampstead*. London: Historical Publications, 1989.

Walker, Annabel. *Kensington and Chelsea: A Social and Architectural History*. London: Murray, 1987.

Walter, Don. *The Book of Harrow on the Hill*. Whittlebury, UK: Baron, 1996.

———. *Harrow and Pinner*. Stroud, UK: Alan Sutton, 1996.

Wesker, Arnold. *Say Goodbye—You May Never See Them Again: Scenes from Two East-End Backgrounds*. London: Cape, 1983.

West, Jack. *Personal Memories of Dagenham Village: 1920 Onward*. Ilfracombe, UK: Stockwell, 1993.

Willment, Diana. *Brentford: New Brentford and the Grand Union Canal*. London: Greater London Industrial Archaeology Society, 1993.

———. *Brentford: Old Brentford and the River Thames*. London: Greater London Industrial Archaeology Society, 1993.

Woodford, F. Peter, ed. *Streets of Bloomsbury and Fitzrovia: A Survey of Streets, Buildings and Former Residents in Part of Camden*. London: Camden History Society, 1997.

LOCAL STUDIES: AREAS SOUTH OF THE RIVER THAMES

Aslet, Clive. *The Story of Greenwich*. Cambridge, Mass.: Harvard University Press, 1999.

Aubrey, John. *Aubrey's History of Streatham*. London: Local History Reprints, 1989.

———. *Aubrey's History of Tooting*. London: Local History Reprints, 1989.

Barker, Felix. *Greenwich and Blackheath Past*. London: Historical Publications, 1993.

Battle, Arthur. *Edwardian Chislehurst: Memories of the Village Baker*. Rainham, UK: Meresborough, 1988.

Beasley, John D. *East Dulwich: An Illustrated Alphabetical Guide*. London: South Riding Press, 1998.

Blomfield, David. *The Story of Kew*. London: Leyborne, 1992.

———. *Kew Past*. Chichester, UK: Phillimore, 1994.

Bloom, J. Harvey. *Bygone Balham and Tooting Bec*. London: Local History Reprints, 1993.

Boast, Mary. *The Story of Bankside from the River Thames to St. George's Circus*. London: London Borough of Southwark, 1985.

———. *The Story of Camberwell.* London: London Borough of Southwark, 1996.

Brayley, Edward W. *Brayley's History of Streatham*. London: Local History Reprints, 1989.

———. *Brayley's History of Tooting*. London: Local History Reprints, 1989.

Brown, John W. *The Victoria History of Streatham*. London: Local History Reprints, 1989.

———. *The Victoria History of Tooting*. London: Local History Reprints, 1989.

———. *A Topographical Dictionary of Streatham in 1823*. London: Local History Reprints, 1991.

———. *Dulwich Past and Present*. London: Local History Reprints, 1995.

Brown, Maisie, ed. *Barnes and Mortlake Past, With East Sheen*. London: Historical Publications, 1997.

Burgess, Frank. *No Small Change: 100 Years of Sutton High Street*. London: London Borough of Sutton, 1983.

Bushell, T. A. *Imperial Chislehurst: The Story of a Kentish Village*. Buckingham, UK: Barracuda, 1980.

Cashmore, T. H. R. *Alexander Pope's Twickenham: 18th-Century Views of His "Classic Village*." London: Twickenham Local History Society, 1988.

Chamberlain, Mary. *Growing Up in Lambeth*. London: Virago, 1989.

Ching, Pamela A. *Teddington in 1800: The Year of the Enclosure*. London: Twickenham Local History Society, 1983.

Clark, Roger George. *Richmond Today, Including Kew Gardens and Hampton Court*. London: Hale, 1994.

Cloake, John. *Richmond's Links with North America*. London: Richmond Local History Society, 1989.

———. *Richmond Past: A Visual History of Richmond, Kew, Petersham and Ham*. London: Historical Publications, 1991.

———. *The Growth of Richmond*. London: Richmond Local History Society, 1993.

Coulter, John. *Lewisham: History and Guide*. Stroud, UK: Alan Sutton, 1994.

Cox, Dorothy. *The Book of Orpington*. Buckingham, UK: Barracuda, 1988.

Dixon, Ken. *Brixton: The Story of a Name*. London: Brixton Society, 1991.

Dudman, Jill. *Lambeth, Kennington and Clapham*. Stroud, UK: Alan Sutton, 1996.

Egan, Michael. *Kidbrooke, Eight Hundred Years of a Farming Community*. London: Greenwich and Lewisham Antiquarian Society, 1983.

Essen, Richard. *Richmond and Kew*. Stroud, UK: Chalford, 1995.

Everson, Tim. *Kingston, Surbiton and Malden*. Stroud, UK: Alan Sutton, 1995.

Gascoigne, Bamber. *Images of Twickenham, With Hampton and Teddington*. London: Saint Helena Press, 1981.

Gerhold, Dorian. *Putney and Roehampton Past*. London: Historical Publications, 1994.

Glazebrook, George. *Where No Flowers Grow: A Child's Eye View of Deptford, 1921–1931*. Rainham, UK: Meresborough, 1989.

Gower, Graham. *A Brief History of Streatham.* London: Streatham Society, 1990.
———. *Streatham Farms*. London: Local History Publications, 1991.
Green, Brian. *Victorian and Edwardian Dulwich*. Buckingham, UK: Barracuda, 1988.
Green, James, Judith Filson, and Margaret Watson. *The Streets of Richmond and Kew*. London: Richmond Local History Society, 1989.
Hailstone, Charles. *Alleyways of Mortlake and East Sheen.* London: Barnes and Mortlake Historical Society, 1983.
Harris, Christopher. *West Wickham, 1880–1980*. London: London Borough of Bromley, 1983.
Heffernan, Hilary. *South Thames: Tower Bridge to Thamesmead*. Stroud, UK: Chalford, 1996.
Henry, William. *Bromley Memories: Boyhood*. Bolton, UK: Stylus, 1992.
Hewson, Don. *Putney and Roehampton*. Stroud, UK: Alan Sutton, 1997.
Humphrey, Stephen. *Southwark, Bermondsey, and Rotherhithe in Old Photographs*. Stroud, UK: Alan Sutton, 1995.
———. *Camberwell, Dulwich and Peckham*. Stroud, UK: Alan Sutton, 1996.
———. *Southwark, Bermondsey and Rotherhithe: A Second Selection*. Stroud, UK: Alan Sutton, 1997.
Inman, Eric R., and Nancy Tonkin. *Beckenham*. Chichester, UK: Phillimore, 1993.
Kennett, John. *Eltham: A Pictorial History*. Chichester, UK: Phillimore, 1995.
Knowlden, Patricia. *West Wickham: Past into Present*. London: Hollies, 1986.
Knowlden, Patricia, ed. *Bromley: A Pictorial History*. Chichester, UK: Phillimore, 1990.
Loobey, Patrick. *Battersea and Clapham*. Stroud, UK: Chalford, 1994.
———. *Barnes, Mortlake and Sheen*. Stroud, UK: Alan Sutton, 1995.
Loobey, Patrick, and John W. Brown. *Balham and Tooting in Old Photographs*. Stroud, UK: Alan Sutton, 1994.
Lysons, Daniel. *Lysons's History of Streatham*. London: Local History Reprints, 1989.
———. *Lysons's History of Tooting*. London: Local History Reprints, 1989.
MacRobert, Scott. *Putney and Roehampton: A Brief History*. London: Putney Society, 1992.
McGormack, Anne. *Kingston Upon Thames: A Pictorial History*. Chichester, UK: Phillimore, 1989.
Mercer, John. *Sidcup: A Pictorial History*. Chichester, UK: Phillimore, 1994.
Milward, Richard. *Early and Medieval Wimbledon*. London: Wimbledon Society, 1983.
———. *Historic Wimbledon: Caesar's Camp to Centre Court*. Moreton-in-Marsh, UK: Windrush and Fielders of Wimbledon, 1989.
Overton, Eric. *A Guide to the Manorial History of Tooting Graveney and the King's Champion*. London: Local History Publications, 1995.

Peters, John. *Woolwich Remembered*. Edinburgh: Pentland, 1994.

Piper, Alan. *A History of Brixton*. London: Brixton Society, 1996.

Plastow, Norman, ed. *A History of Wimbledon and Putney Commons*. London: Conservators of Wimbledon and Putney Commons, 1986.

Platts, Beryl. *A History of Greenwich*. London: Proctor, 1986.

Prichard, John A. *Belvedere and Bostall: A Brief History*. London: London Borough of Bexley, 1994.

Ratcliffe, Eric. *Winstanley's Walton, 1649: Events in the Civil War at Walton-on-Thames—The "Lights" in Walton St. Mary, Gerrard Winstanley and the Digger*s. Stevenage, UK: Astrapost, 1994.

Reed, Nicholas. *Crystal Palace and the Norwoods*. Stroud, UK: Chalford, 1995.

Rhind, Neil. *Blackheath Village and Environs*, 2 vols. London: Bookshop Blackheath, 1983.

———. *The Heath*. London: Bookshop Blackheath, 1987.

Sampson, June. *Kingston Past*. London: Historical Publications, 1997.

Scott, Mick. *Bromley, Keston, and Hayes in Old Photographs*. Stroud, UK: Alan Sutton, 1993.

Scott, Pat, Alison Edwards, and Eileen Pulfer, eds. *The Perfect Playground: Childhood Memories of Crystal Palace*. London: Crystal Palace Foundation, 1990.

Sexby, J. J. *Sexby's History of Streatham Common*. London: Local History Reprints, 1989.

———. *Sexby's History of Tooting Common*. London: Local History Reprints, 1989.

Simmons, Roger, ed. *Eltham in the Making: From Roman Times Until 1939*. London: Eltham Society, 1990.

Smith, Eric. *Clapham*. London: Clapham Society, 1990.

Steele, Jess. *Turning the Tide: The History of Everyday Deptford*. London: Deptford Forum, 1993.

Thornhill, Lilian. *Conservation Areas of Croydon, Including Central Croydon and the Parish Church: An Illustrated History by the Croydon Society*. London: Croydon Society, 1987.

Turner, Christopher. *Hampton Court, Richmond and Kew Step by Step*. London: Faber, 1987.

Wagstaff, John, and Doris Pullen, ed. *Beckenham: An Anthology of Local History to Celebrate the Golden Jubilee of Beckenham's Charter of Incorporation, 1935*. London: Historical Association, 1984.

Walford, Edward. *Walford's History of Tooting*. London: Local History Reprints, 1989.

———. *Walford's History of Norwood and Streatham*. London: Local History Reprints, 1993.

Warhurst, R. J. *A View of Dulwich, Peckham and Camberwell Around 1300*. London: Grain, 1993.

THE MEDIA

Allen, Robert, and John Frost. *Daily Mirror*. Cambridge: Stephens, 1981.

———. *Voice of Britain: The Inside Story of* The Daily Express. Cambridge: Stephens, 1983.

Baistow, Tom. *Fourth Rate Estate: An Anatomy of Fleet Street*. London: Comedia, 1985.

Barson, Susie, and Andrew Saint. *A Farewell to Fleet Street*. London: Historic Buildings and Monuments Commission for England/Allison and Busby, 1988.

Bishop, Diana. *King Penguins: Their Place in 20th-Century Publishing*. Cambridge: Andrew Dalby, 1982.

Boston, Ray. *The Essential Fleet Street: Its History and Influence*. London: Blandford, 1990.

Bourne, Richard. *Lords of Fleet Street*. London: Unwin Hyman, 1990.

Briggs, Asa. *The BBC: The First Fifty Years*. Oxford: Oxford University Press, 1985.

Brown, Philip A. H. *London Publishers and Printers, c. 1800–1870*. London: British Library, 1982.

Cain, John. *The BBC: 70 Years of Broadcasting*. London: British Broadcasting Corporation, 1992.

Campbell, John, and William Bonner. *Media, Mania and the Markets*. London: Fleet Street, 1994.

Crozier, Michael. *The Making of* The Independent. Sevenoaks, UK: Coronet, 1988.

Draper, Alfred. *Scoops and Swindles: Memoirs of a Fleet Street Journalist*. London: Buchan and Enright, 1988.

Edwards, Robert. *Goodbye Fleet Street*. Sevenoaks, UK: Coronet, 1988.

Fountain, Nigel. *Underground: The London Alternative Press, 1966–74*. London: Routledge, 1988.

Garland, Nicholas. *Not Many Dead: Journal of a Year in Fleet Street*. London: Hutchinson, 1990.

Gillespie, Marie. *Television, Ethnicity and Cultural Change*. London: Routledge, 1995.

Goldsmith, Sam, ed. *Britain in the Eye of the World: The Foreign Press Association in London, 1888–1988*. London: Foreign Press Association in London, 1988.

Gray, Tony. *Fleet Street Remembered*. London: Heinemann, 1990.

Griffiths, Dennis. *Plant Here the Standard*. Basingstoke, UK: Macmillan, 1996.

Grose, Roslyn. *The Sun-sation: Behind the Scenes of Britain's Bestselling Daily Newspaper*. London: Angus and Robertson, 1989.

Hamilton, Sir Denis. *Editor-in-Chief: The Fleet Street Memoirs of Sir Denis Hamilton*. London: Hamilton, 1989.

Harris, Michael. *London Newspapers in the Age of Walpole: A Study of the Origins of the Modern English Press*. Rutherford, N.J.: Fairleigh Dickinson University Press, 1987.

Harris, Robert. *A Patriot Press: National Politics and the London Press in the 1740s*. Oxford: Clarendon, 1993.

Hart-Davis, Duff. *The House the Berrys Built*. London: Hodder and Stoughton, 1990.

Hatton, Joseph. *Journalistic London: Being a Series of Sketches of Famous Pens and Papers of the Day*. London: Routledge/Thoemmes, 1998.

Hennessey, Brian. *Savoy Hill: The Early Years of British Broadcasting*. Romford, UK: Ian Henry, 1996.

Hickman, Tom. *What Did You Do in the War, Auntie?: The BBC at War, 1939–45*. London: BBC Books, 1995.

Holden, Anthony. *Of Presidents, Prime Ministers and Princes: A Decade in Fleet Street*. London: Weidenfeld and Nicolson, 1984.

Howard, Philip. *We Thundered Out: 200 Years of* The Times, *1785–1985*. London: Times Books, 1985.

Howsam, Leslie. *Kegan Paul, a Victorian Imprint: Publishers, Books and Cultural History*. London: Kegan Paul International, 1998.

Hudson, Len. *Almost a Century: A History of London Town Magazine*. London: Alexius, 1995.

Jacobs, Eric. *Stop Press: The Inside Story of* The Times *Dispute*. London: Deutsch, 1980.

Jenkins, Simon. *The Market for Glory: Fleet Street Ownership in the Twentieth Century*. London: Faber, 1986.

Kersch, Cyril. *A Few Gross Words: The Street of Shame and My Part in It*. London: Simon and Schuster, 1990.

Lamb, Larry. *Sunrise: The Remarkable Rise and Rise of the Best-Selling Soaraway* Sun. London: Papermac, 1989.

Leapman, Michael. *The Treacherous Estate: The Press After Fleet Street*. London: Hodder and Stoughton, 1992.

Lind, Harold. *The Evening Newspapers Market: How Bad Is It and Can It Get Worse?* London: ADMAP, 1984.

Littleton, Suellen M. *The Wapping Dispute: An Examination of the Conflict and Its Impact on the National Newspaper Industry*. Aldershot, UK: Avebury, 1992.

MacArthur, Brian. *Deadline Sunday: A Life in the Week of* The Sunday Times. London: Hodder and Stoughton, 1991.

Macdonald, Ian. *The Times*. Paisley, UK: Gleniffer, 1984.

Maitland, Robert. *London's Printing and Publishing Industry*. London: Greater London Council, 1980.

Martin, Roderick. *New Technology and Industrial Relations in Fleet Street*. Oxford: Clarendon, 1981.

Nash, Paul W. *The Corvinus Press: A History and Bibliography*. Aldershot, UK: Scolar, 1994.

Peterson, William S. *The Kelmscott Press: A History of William Morris's Typographical Adventure*. Oxford: Clarendon, 1989.

Randall, Mike. *The Funny Side of the Street*. London: Bloomsbury, 1988.

Richards, Huw. *The Bloody Circus:* The Daily Herald *and the Left*. London: Pluto, 1997.

Robinson, Duncan. *William Morris, Edward Burne-Jones and the Kelmscott Chaucer*. London: Fraser, 1982.

Solomon, Harry M. *The Rise of Robert Dodsley: Creating the New Age of Print*. Carbondale: Southern Illinois University Press, 1996.

Waterhouse, Keith. *Daily Mirror Style*. London: Mirror, 1981.

Wilson, Keith M. *A Study in the History and Politics of the Morning Post, 1905–1926*. Lewiston, N.Y.: Edwin Mellen, 1990.

Winkworth, Stephen. *Room Two More Guns: The Intriguing History of the Personal Column of* The Times. London: Allen and Unwin, 1986.

Wintour, Charles. *The Rise and Fall of Fleet Street*. London: Hutchinson, 1989.

Woods, Oliver, and James Bishop. *The Story of* The Times: *Bicentenary Edition, 1785–1985*. London: Michael Joseph, 1985.

MUSEUMS, EXHIBITIONS, AND GALLERIES

Abbott, G. *The Beefeaters of the Tower of London*. Newton Abbot, UK: David and Charles, 1985.

Amery, Colin. *A Celebration of Art and Architecture: The National Gallery Sainsbury Wing*. London: National Gallery, 1991.

Beaver, Patrick. *The Crystal Palace: A Portrait of Victorian Enterprise*. Chichester, UK: Phillimore, 1986.

Bennett, J. A. *Science at the Great Exhibition*. Cambridge: Whipple Museum of the History of Science, 1983.

Burton, Anthony. *Bethnal Green Museum of Childhood*. London: Victoria and Albert Museum, 1986.

———. *Vision and Accident: The Story of the Victoria and Albert Museum*. London: V&A Publications, 1999.

Butler, Sir Thomas. *The Crown Jewels and Coronation Ritual*. London: Pitkin, 1982.

Casson, Sir Hugh. *The Tower of London: An Artist's Portrait*. London: Herbert/Her Majesty's Tower of London, 1993.

Casteras, Susan P., and Colleen Denney. *The Grosvenor Gallery: A Palace of Art in Victorian England*. New Haven, Conn.: Yale University Press, 1996.

Caygill, Marjorie L. *Treasures of the British Museum*. London: British Museum, 1985.

———. *The Story of the British Museum*. London: British Museum, 1992.

Chamberlin, E. R. *The Tower of London: An Illustrated History*. Exeter, UK: Webb and Bower, 1989.

Cocks, Anna Somers. *The Victoria and Albert Museum: The Making of the Collection*. Leicester, UK: Windward, 1980.

Cork, Richard, Balraj Khanna, and Shirley Read. *Art on the South Bank: An Independent Report*. London: Greater London Council, 1986.

Daniels, Jeffery. *Geffrye Museum*. Derby, UK: English Life, 1986.

Desmond, Ray. *The India Museum, 1801–1879*. London: Her Majesty's Stationery Office, 1982.

Edwards, Alison, and Keith Wyncoll. *"The Crystal Palace Is On Fire!": Memories of the 30th November 1936*. London: Crystal Palace Foundation, 1986.

Farr, Dennis, and John Newman. *Guide to the Courtauld Institute Galleries at Somerset House*. London: Courtauld Institute of Art, 1990.

Fisher, Jean. *Matt's Gallery*. London: Serpentine Gallery, 1984.

Galinou, Mireille, and John Hayes. *London in Paint: Oil Paintings in the Collection at the Museum of London*. London: Museum of London, 1996.

Gibbs-Smith, C. H. *The Great Exhibition of 1851*. London: Her Majesty's Stationery Office, 1981.

Girouard, Mark. *Alfred Waterhouse and the Natural History Museum*. London: British Museum (Natural History), 1981.

Goode, C. T. *Ally Pally: The Alexandra Palace, Its Transport and Its Troubles*. Bracknell, UK: Forge, 1983.

Goodman, Jonathan, and Bill Waddell. *The Black Museum: Scotland Yard's Chamber of Crime*. London: Harrap, 1987.

Gorman, John. *Images of Labour: Selected Memorabilia from the National Museum of Labour History, London*. London: Scorpion, 1985.

Greenhill, Basil. *Guide to the National Maritime Museum, Greenwich*. London: Her Majesty's Stationery Office, 1981.

Greenhill, Basil, ed. *The National Maritime Museum*. Paris: Scala, 1982.

Gunther, A. E. *The Founders of Science at the British Museum, 1753–1900: A Contribution to the Centenary of the Opening of the British Museum (Natural History) on 18th April 1981*. Halesworth, UK: Halesworth, 1980.

Hamlyn, Robin. *Robert Vernon's Gift: British Art for the Nation*. London: Tate Gallery, 1993.

Hammond, Peter. *Royal Armouries: Official Guide*. London: Trustees of the Royal Armouries/Philip Wilson, 1986.

———. *Her Majesty's Royal Palace and Fortress of the Tower of London*. London: Department of the Environment, 1987.

Hughes, Peter. *The Founders of the Wallace Collection*. London: Trustees of the Wallace Collection, 1981.

Ingamells, John. *The Wallace Collection*. London: Scala, 1990.

James, Elizabeth. *The Victoria and Albert Museum: A Bibliography and Exhibition Chronology, 1852–1996*. London: Fitzroy Dearborn/Victoria and Albert Museum, 1998.

Jervis, Simon, and Maurice Tomlin. *Wellington Museum*. London: Victoria and Albert Museum, 1984.

Johnson, Lewis. *Prospects, Thresholds, Interiors: Watercolours from the National Collection at the Victoria and Albert Museum*. Cambridge: Cambridge University Press, 1994.

Keen, Michael E. *A Bibliography of the Microfilms in the National Art Library, Victoria and Albert Museum, 1980*. London: Victoria and Albert Museum, 1980.

Levey, Michael. *The National Gallery Collections*. London: National Gallery, 1987.

McCrimmon, Barbara. *Power, Politics and Print: The Publication of the British Museum Catalogue, 1881–1900*. Hamden, Conn.: Bingley, 1981.

McIlwain, John. *Cutty Sark*. Andover, UK: Pitkin, 1994.

McKean, John. *Crystal Palace, Joseph Paxton and Charles Fox*. London: Phaidon, 1994.

Mears, Kenneth J. *The Crown Jewels, Tower of London*. London: Department of the Environment, 1986.

———. *The Tower of London: 900 Years of English History*. Oxford: Phaidon, 1988.

Murdoch, John. *The Courtauld Gallery at Somerset House*. London: Courtauld Institute of Art/Thames and Hudson, 1998.

Newall, Christopher. *The Grosvenor Gallery Exhibitions: Change and Continuity in the Victorian Art World*. Cambridge: Cambridge University Press, 1995.

Nicolson, Adam. *Regeneration: The Story of the Dome*. London: HarperCollins, 1999.

Parnell, Geoffrey. *The Tower of London Past and Present*. Stroud, UK: Alan Sutton, 1998.

Physick, John. *The Victoria and Albert Museum: The History of Its Building*. Oxford: Phaidon, 1982.

Prentice, Rina. *A Celebration of the Sea: The Decorative Art Collections of the National Maritime Museum*. London: Her Majesty's Stationery Office, 1994.

Prescott, Norman S. *Dual Heritage: The Bible and the British Museum*. Luton, UK: Cortney, 1986.

Rogers, Jean Scott. *Stage by Stage: The Making of the Theatre Museum*. London: Her Majesty's Stationery Office, 1985.

Rogers, Malcolm. *Museums and Galleries of London*. London: Black, 1991.

Rothstein, Natalie. *Silk Designs of the Eighteenth Century in the Collection of the Victoria and Albert Museum, London, with a Complete Catalogue*. London: Thames and Hudson, 1990.

Scimone, G. M. S., and M. F. Levey. *London Museums and Collections*. London: Canal, 1989.

Shanes, Eric. *The Genius of the Royal Academy*. London: Royal Academy, 1981.

Shepherd, John, ed. *Post-War Archaeology in the City of London, 1946–1972: A Guide to the Records of Excavations by Professor W. F. Grimes Held by the Museum of London*. London: Museum of London, 1998.

Sheppard, F. H. W. *The Treasury of London's Past: An Historical Account of the Museum of London and Its Predecessors, the Guildhall Museum and the London Museum*. London: Her Majesty's Stationery Office, 1991.

Somerset Fry, Plantagenet. *The Tower of London: Cauldron of Britain's Past*. London: Quiller, 1990.

Spalding, Frances. *The Tate: A History*. London: Tate Gallery, 1998.

St. Clair, William. *Lord Elgin and the Marbles*. Oxford: Oxford University Press, 1983.

Stearn, William T. *The Natural History Museum at South Kensington: A History of the Museum, 1753–1980*. London: Natural History Museum, 1998.

Stephens, Peter, John Freeborn, and Oliver Green. *London Transport Museum*. London: London Transport Museum, 1980.

Thackray, John C. *A Guide to the Official Archives of the Natural History Museum, London*. London: Society for the History of Natural History, 1998.

Thompson, Alan, Andrew Westman, and Tony Dyson, eds. *Archaeology in Greater London, 1965–1990: A Guide to Records of Excavations by the Museum of London*. London: Museum of London, 1998.

Thornton, Peter, and Helen Dorey. *A Miscellany of Objects from Sir John Soane's Museum, Consisting of Paintings, Architectural Drawings and Other Curiosities from the Collection of Sir John Soane*. London: Laurence King, 1992.

Upstone, Robert. *Treasures of British Art: The Tate Gallery*. New York: Abbeville, 1996.

Waddell, Bill. *The Black Museum, New Scotland Yard*. London: Little, Brown, 1995.

Walford, Edward. *Walford's History of the Crystal Palace*. London: Local History Reprints, 1993.

Warren, Valerie. *The Wimbledon Lawn Tennis Museum*. London: The Museum, 1982.

Wegner, Nicholas. *Depart from Zero: The Development of the Gallery London, 1973–1978*. London: Gallery Trust, 1987.

———. *Journal of the Gallery London: Notes and Observations, 1978–1990*. London: Cv Publications, 1991.

Whitehead, Peter. *The British Museum (Natural History)*. London: Philip Wilson/British Museum (Natural History), 1981.

Whitten, Faith, and Geoff Whitten. *The Chelsea Flower Show*. London: Elm Tree/Royal Horticultural Society, 1982.

Williamson, Paul, ed. *The Medieval Treasury: The Art of the Middle Ages in the Victoria and Albert Museum*. London: Victoria and Albert Museum, 1986.

Wilson, Anthony. *The Science Museum*. London: Science Museum, 1988.

Wilson, David M. *The British Museum: Purpose and Politics*. London: British Museum, 1989.

———. *The Collections of the British Museum*. London: British Museum, 1989.

Wilson, Derek. *The Tower of London: A Thousand Years*. London: Allison and Busby, 1998.

Wilson, Michael. *The National Gallery, London*. Paris: Scala, 1982.

Wilson, Simon. *Tate Gallery: An Illustrated Companion*. London: Tate Gallery, 1991.

Yanni, Carla. *Nature's Museums: Victorian Science and the Architecture of Display*. London: Athlone, 1999.

THE NATURAL ENVIRONMENT

Archer, John, and David Curson. *Nature Conservation in Richmond Upon Thames*. London: London Ecology Unit, 1993.

Archer, John, and Ian Yarham. *Nature Conservation in Newham*. London: London Ecology Unit, 1992.

Astbury, A. K. *Land and Water in the Lower Thames Basin*. London: Carnforth, 1980.

Attrill, Martin J. *A Rehabilitated Estuarine Ecosystem: The Environment and Ecology of the Thames Estuary*. Dordrecht, The Netherlands: Kluwer Academic, 1998.

Barton, N. J. *The Lost Rivers of London: A Study of Their Effects Upon London and Londoners, and the Effects of London and Londoners Upon Them*. London: Historical Publications, 1982.

Bellamy, David. *The Queen's Hidden Garden: Buckingham Palace's Treasury of Wild Plants*. Newton Abbot, UK: David and Charles, 1984.

Bridgeland, D. R. *Quaternary of the Thames*. London: Chapman and Hall, 1994.

Bridgeland, D. R., P. Allen, and B. A. Haggart, eds. *The Quaternary of the Lower Reaches of the Thames: Field Guide*. Durham, UK: Quaternary Research Association, 1995.

Brimblecombe, Peter. *The Big Smoke: A History of Air Pollution in London Since Medieval Times*. London: Routledge, 1988.

Burley, Robert, Meg Game, and Mathew Frith. *Nature Conservation in Waltham Forest*. London: London Ecology Unit, 1989.

Burton, Rodney M. *Flora of the London Area*. Eynsford, UK: London Natural History Society, 1983.

Clenet, Deirdre, Bob Britton, and Meg Game. *Nature Conservation in Croydon*. London: London Ecology Unit, 1988.

Corbet, Gordon B. *Jubilee Park: The Natural History of a Country Park*. London: London Borough of Bromley/Orpington Field Club, 1993.

Currie, Ian. *Frosts, Freezes and Fairs: Chronicles of the Frozen Thames and Harsh Winters in Britain Since 1000 A.D.* Coulsdon, UK: Frosted Earth, 1996.

Curson, David. *Nature Conservation in Barking and Dagenham*. London: London Ecology Unit, 1992.

Farino, Teresa, and Meg Game. *Nature Conservation in Hillingdon*. London: London Ecology Unit, 1988.

Friends of the Earth. *London's Air Pollution*. London: Friends of the Earth, 1987.

Gibbard, Philip L. *The Pleistocene History of the Middle Thames Valley*. Cambridge: Cambridge University Press, 1985.

———. *Pleistocene History of the Lower Thames Valley*. Cambridge: Cambridge University Press, 1994.

Goode, David. *Wild in London*. London: Michael Joseph, 1986.

Greater London Council. *Ecology and Nature Conservation in London*. London: Greater London Council, 1984.

Greater London Ecology Unit. *A Nature Conservation Strategy for London: The London Borough of Brent*. London: Greater London Ecology Unit, 1987.

Hanson, M. W. *Lords Bushes: The History and Ecology of an Epping Forest Woodland*. London: Essex Field Club, 1983.

Hare, Tony. *London's Meadows and Pastures*. London: London Ecology Unit, 1988.

Hawkins, Roy. *Green London: A Handbook*. London: Sidgwick and Jackson, 1987.

Hepple, Leslie W., and Alison M. Doggett. *The Chilterns*. Chichester, UK: Phillimore, 1994.

Jefferies, Richard. *Nature Near London*. London: John Clare Books, 1980.

Luckin, Bill. *Pollution and Control: A Social History of the Thames in the Nineteenth Century*. Bristol, UK: Hilger, 1986.

Marshall, Tim. *Environmental Sustainability: London's Unitary Development Plans and Strategic Planning*. London: South Bank University, 1992.

Pape, David. *Nature Conservation in Hounslow*. London: London Ecology Unit, 1990.

Parry, José. *Greening London: Environmental Policies and Practices of the London Boroughs*. London: London Research Centre, 1991.

Ramsey, Winston G. *Epping Forest Then and Now*. London: Battle of Britain Prints International, 1986.

Robinson, Eric. *London: Illustrated Geological Walks*, 2 vols. Edinburgh: Scottish Academic, 1984 (vol. 1) and 1985 (vol. 2).

Schwar, M. J. R., and D. J. Ball. *Thirty Years On: A Review of Air Pollution in London*. London: Greater London Council, 1983.

Sumbler, M. G. *British Regional Geology: London and the Thames Valley*. London: Her Majesty's Stationery Office, 1996.

Swales, Sue, Meg Game, and Ian Yarham. *Nature Conservation in Greenwich*. London: London Ecology Unit, 1989.

Swales, Sue, Ian Yarham, and Bob Britton. *Nature Conservation in Kingston Upon Thames*. London: London Ecology Unit, 1989.

Tyssen-Gee, Robert. *Hampstead Weather, 1860–1981*. London: Camden History Society, 1982.

Venis, Ernest. *The Natural History of Hatch End*. London: Hatch End Association, 1995.

Waite, Michael. *Nature Conservation in Islington*. London: London Ecology Unit, 1992.

Weightman, Gavin, and Mike Birkhead. *City Safari: Wildlife in London*. London: Sidgwick and Jackson, 1986.

Westgate, Alison. *A Green and Pleasant Land: A Review of Boroughs' Commitment to the Environment*. London: London Boroughs Association, 1991.

White, Jim. *Jim White's Diary: A Countryman's Year on the North Downs of Kent*. London: Blue Cat, 1985.

Wood, Leslie B. *The Restoration of the Tidal Thames*. Bristol, UK: Hilger, 1982.

PALACES, MANSIONS, AND COUNTRY HOUSES

Barber, Peter, Oliver Cox, and Michael Curwen. *Lauderdale Revealed—A History of Lauderdale House, Highgate: The Building, Its Owners and Occupiers, 1582–1993*. London: Lauderdale House Society, 1993.

Bellamy, David. *The Queen's Hidden Garden: Buckingham Palace's Treasury of Wild Plants*. Newton Abbot, UK: David and Charles, 1984.

Boulding, Anthony. *The History of Hampton Court Palace Gardens*. London: Hampton Court Palace, 1994.

Bryant, Julius. *Finest Prospects: Three Historic Houses—A Study in London Topography*. London: English Heritage, 1986.

———. *Marble Hill House, Twickenham*. London: English Heritage, 1988.

———. *The Iveagh Bequest, Kenwood*. London: London Historic House Museums Trust, 1990.

———. *The Landscape of Kenwood*. London: English Heritage, 1990.

———. *London's Country House Collections*. London: Scala, 1993.

Burrows, Donald. *Handel and the English Chapel Royal*. London: Royal Hospital, Chelsea, 1985.

Carswell, John. *The Saving of Kenwood and the Northern Heights*. Henley-on-Thames, UK: Aidan Ellis, 1992.

Charlton, John. *Kew Palace, Richmond Upon Thames*. London: Department of the Environment, 1983.

———. *A History and Description of Chiswick House and Gardens*. London: Her Majesty's Stationery Office, 1984.

Cloake, John. *Palaces and Parks of Richmond and Kew*, 2 vols. Chichester, UK: Phillimore, 1995 (vol. 1) and 1996 (vol. 2).

Collett-White, Ann, and James Collett-White. *Gunnersbury Park and the Rothschilds*. London: Heritage Publications, 1993.

Cryer, Mary. *A Short History of Lambeth Palace*. Worthing, UK: Churchman, 1988.

Davis, Fred. *Finchley Manor: Influential Families*. London: London Borough of Barnet, 1982.

Edgar, Donald. *Palace: A Fascinating Behind-the-Scenes Look at How Buckingham Palace Really Works*. London: W. H. Allen, 1983.

Fishlock, Michael. *The Great Fire at Hampton Court*. London: Herbert, 1992.

French, Anne. *Ranger's House, Blackheath*. London: English Heritage, 1992.

Harris, Eileen. *Osterley Park, Middlesex*. London: National Trust, 1994.

Harris, John. *The Palladian Revival: Lord Burlington, His Villa and Garden at Chiswick*. New Haven, Conn.: Yale University Press, 1994.

Hayes, John. *Kensington Palace*. London: Department of the Environment, 1985.

Hedley, Olwen. *Hampton Court Palace*. London: Pitkin, 1991.

Hoey, Brian. *Buckingham Palace*. Andover, UK: Pitkin, 1990.

Jones, Christopher. *No. 10 Downing Street: The Story of a House*. London: British Broadcasting Corporation, 1985.

Kirkman, Ken. *A History of Pinner Hill House and Estate*. London: Albury Enterprises, 1993.

Minter, Sue. *The Greatest Glasshouse: The Rainforests Recreated*. London: Her Majesty's Stationery Office, 1990.

Morris, Gillian M. *The History of Hounslow Manor and the Bulstrode Family*. London: Hounslow and District History Society, 1980.

Morton, Andrew. *Inside Kensington Palace*. Bath, UK: Chivers, 1988.

———. *Inside Buckingham Palace*. London: Michael O'Mara, 1991.

Nash, Roy. *Buckingham Palace: The Palace and the People*. London: Macdonald, 1980.

———. *Hampton Court: The Palace and the People*. London: Macdonald, 1983.

National Maritime Museum. *The Queen's House: A Royal Palace by the Thames*. London: National Maritime Museum, 1992.

National Trust. *Ham House, Surrey*. London: National Trust, 1995.

Osborne, June. *Hampton Court Palace*. London: Her Majesty's Stationery Office, 1990.

Robinson, John Martin. *Royal Palaces: Buckingham Palace: A Short History*. London: Royal Collection, 1995.

Stewart-Wilson, Mary. *The Royal Mews*. London: Bodley Head, 1991.

Thurley, Simon. *Henry VIII's Kitchens at Hampton Court*. London: Hampton Court Palace, 1994.

———. *The Whitehall Palace Plan of 1670*. London: London Topographical Society, 1998.

Urwin, A. C. B. *The Houses and Gardens of Twickenham Park, 1227–1805*. London: Twickenham Local History Society, 1984.

Wilson, Ken. *Camden Place, Chislehurst: The Story of a Country House in Words and Drawings*. Bromley: Bromley Library Services, 1981.

———. *"A Tied Cottage": The Story of Buckingham Palace*. London: Lanthorn, 1985.

Wright, Patricia. *The Strange History of Buckingham Palace*. Stroud, UK: Alan Sutton, 1996.

PARKS AND GARDENS

Bartholomew, James. *The Magic of Kew*. Herbert/Royal Botanic Gardens, 1988.

Batey, Mavis, and Jan Woudstra. *The Story of the Privy Garden at Hampton Court*. London: Barn Elms, 1995.

Beasley, John D. *Peckham Rye Park Centenary*. London: South Riding, 1995.

Bellamy, David. *The Queen's Hidden Garden: Buckingham Palace's Treasury of Wild Plants*. Newton Abbot, UK: David and Charles, 1984.

Boulding, Anthony. *The History of Hampton Court Palace Gardens*. London: Hampton Court Palace, 1994.

Brace, Marianne. *London's Parks and Gardens*. Cambridge: Pevensey, 1986.
Brown, Michael Baxter. *Richmond Park: The History of a Royal Deer Park*. London: Hale, 1985.
Bryant, Julius. *The Landscape of Kenwood*. London: English Heritage, 1990.
Charlton, John. *A History and Description of Chiswick House and Gardens*. London: Her Majesty's Stationery Office, 1984.
Church, Richard. *London's Royal Parks*. London: Her Majesty's Stationery Office, 1993.
Cloake, John. *Palaces and Parks of Richmond and Kew*, 2 vols. Chichester, UK: Phillimore, 1995 (vol. 1) and 1996 (vol. 2).
Crowe, Andrew. *The Parks and Woodlands of London*. London: Fourth Estate, 1987.
Desmond, Ray, and F. Nigel Hepper. *A Century of Kew Plantsmen: A Celebration of the Kew Guild*. London: Kew Guild, 1993.
Edgar, Donald. *The Royal Parks*. London: W. H. Allen, 1986.
Farmer, Alan. *Hampstead Heath*. London: Historical Publications, 1984.
Fletcher Jones, Pamela. *Richmond Park: Portrait of a Royal Playground*. Chichester, UK: Phillimore, 1983.
Galinou, Mireille, ed. *London's Pride: The Glorious History of the Capital's Gardens*. London: Anaya, 1990.
Gunn, Spence. *Kew Gardens: A Resource for the World*. London: Royal Botanic Gardens, 1996.
Harris, John. *The Palladian Revival: Lord Burlington, His Villa and Garden at Chiswick*. New Haven, Conn.: Yale University Press, 1994.
Hawkins, Roy. *Green London: A Handbook*. London: Sidgwick and Jackson, 1987.
Hepper, F. Nigel. *Plant Hunting for Kew*. London: Her Majesty's Stationery Office, 1989.
Ikin, C. W. *Hampstead Heath: How the Heath Was Saved for the Public*. High Hill Press/Heath and Old Hampstead Society, 1985.
King, Ronald. *Royal Kew*. London: Constable, 1985.
Lennox-Boyd, Arabella. *Private Gardens of London*. London: Weidenfeld and Nicolson, 1990.
Le Rougetel, Hazel. *The Chelsea Gardener: Philip Miller, 1691–1770*. London: Natural History Museum Publications, 1990.
Nichols, Beverley. *Green Grows the City: The Story of a London Garden*. Woodbridge, UK: Antique Collectors Club, 1997.
Pierce, Pat. *Bushy Park*. London: Royal Parks, 1993.
———. *Greenwich Park*. London: Royal Parks, 1993.
———. *Hyde Park and Kensington Gardens*. London: Royal Parks, 1993.
———. *The Regent's Park and Primrose Hill*. London: Royal Parks, 1993.
———. *Richmond Park*. London: Royal Parks, 1993.
———. *St. James's Park and the Green Park*. London: Royal Parks, 1993.
Plastow, Norman, ed. *A History of Wimbledon and Putney Commons*. London: Conservators of Wimbledon and Putney Commons, 1986.

Plummer, Brian, and Don Shewan. *City Gardens: An Open Spaces Survey in the City of London*. London: Belhaven, 1992.

Sands, Mollie. *The Eighteenth-Century Pleasure Gardens of Marylebone, 1737–1777*. London: Society for Theatre Research, 1987.

Solman, David. *Clissold Park*. London: Abney Park Cemetery Trust, 1992.

Urwin, A. C. B. *The Houses and Gardens of Twickenham Park, 1227–1805*. London: Twickenham Local History Society, 1984.

Varriale, Olga. *Leaves from My Diary: Kew Gardens, London*. Perugia, Italy: Studio d'Arte Tipografia, 1984.

Weekes, David. *The Origins of Lexham Gardens and Lee Abbey in London*. Leominster, UK: Gracewing, 1996.

Winterman, M. A. *Croydon's Parks: An Illustrated History*. London: London Borough of Croydon, 1988.

RELIGION, BURIAL GROUNDS, AND PLACES OF WORSHIP

Atkinson, Frank. *St. Paul's: The Cathedral Guide*. London: Pitkin, 1983.

———. *St. Paul's and the City*. London: Michael Joseph, 1985.

Bale, Malcolm. *Marching On!: The Salvation Army—Its Origin and Development*. London: Salvation Army, 1990.

Barker, Felix. *Highgate Cemetery: Victorian Valhalla*. London: Murray, 1984.

Beasley, John D. *Peckham and Nunhead Churches*. London: South Riding, 1995.

Bennett, David. *William Booth and the Salvation Army: Up and Down the City Road*. Basingstoke, UK: Marshall Pickering, 1987.

Binski, Paul. *Westminster Abbey and the Plantagenets: Kingship and the Representation of Power*. New Haven, Conn.: Yale University Press, 1995.

Black, Jerry. *JFS: The History of the Jews' Free School, London, Since 1732*. London: Tymsder, 1998.

Blakebrough, Eric. *Called to Be Giants: The Faith Which Inspired a City Mission*. Basingstoke, UK: Marshall Pickering, 1987.

Blakebrough, Eric, ed. *Church for the City*. London: Darton, Longman and Todd, 1995.

Blatch, Mervyn. *A Guide to London's Churches*. London: Constable, 1995.

Blundell, Joe Whitlock. *Westminster Abbey: The Monuments*. London: Murray, 1989.

Bogdanescu, Sylvia. *The Life and Times of St. Dunstan-in-the-West*. London: Guild Church Council, 1986.

Bradley, Simon, and Nikolaus Pevsner. *The London Churches*. London: Penguin, 1998.

Brigden, Susan. *London and the Reformation*. Oxford: Clarendon, 1989.

Browne, John, and Timothy Dean. *Building of Faith: Westminster Cathedral*. London: Booth-Clibborn, 1995.

Bruce, Penny. *Merton Priory*. London: Museum of London, 1993.

Burman, Peter. *St. Paul's Cathedral*. London: Bell and Hyman, 1987.

Burrows, Donald. *Handel and the English Chapel Royal*. London: Royal Hospital, Chelsea, 1985.

Carpenter, Edward, and David Gentleman. *Westminster Abbey*. London: Weidenfeld and Nicolson, 1987.

Cassidy, G. E. *The Architectural History of St. Anne's Church, Kew Green*. London: Richmond Local History Society, 1986.

Chandler, Arthur R. *The Church That Stood on the Hill: A Commemoration of St. Barnabas Church, Dulwich, 1894–1992*. London: Heritage Consultancy, 1993.

Cloake, John. *Richmond's Great Monastery: The Charterhouse of Jesus of Bethlehem of Shene*. London: Richmond Local History Society, 1990.

Cobb, Gerald. *London City Churches*. London: Batsford, 1989.

Cocke, Thomas. *900 Years: The Restorations of Westminster Abbey*. London: Harvey Miller, 1995.

Cox, Jane. *Hatred Pursued Beyond the Grave: Tales of Our Ancestors from the London Church Courts*. London: Her Majesty's Stationery Office, 1993.

Cryer, Mary. *A Short History of Lambeth Palace*. Worthing, UK: Churchman, 1988.

Cunningham, Kit. *St. Etheldreda's, Ely Place*. Andover, UK: Pitkin, 1992.

Denny, Barbara. *Kings Bishop: The Lords Spiritual of London*. London: Alderman, 1985.

Dow, Helen Jeanette. *The Sculptural Decoration of the Henry VII Chapel, Westminster Abbey*. Edinburgh: Pentland, 1992.

Downes, Kerry. *Sir Christopher Wren: The Design of St. Paul's Cathedral*. London: Trefoil, 1988.

Doyle, Peter. *Westminster Cathedral, 1895–1995*. London: Geoffrey Chapman, 1995.

Ellis, Roger. *Viderunt Eam Filie Syon: The Spirituality of the English House of a Medieval Order from Its Beginnings to the Present Day*. Salzburg, Austria: Universität Salzburg, 1984.

Evinson, Denis. *Pope's Corner: An Historical Survey of the Roman Catholic Institutions in the London Borough of Hammersmith and Fulham*. London: Fulham and Hammersmith Historical Society, 1980.

———. *Catholic Churches of London*. Sheffield, UK: Sheffield Academic, 1998.

Fairbank, Jenty. *Booth's Boots: The Beginnings of Salvation Army Social Work*. London: Salvation Army, 1983.

Field, John. *Kingdom, Power and Glory: A Historical Guide to Westminster Abbey*. London: James and James, 1997.

Gibbins, Ronald C. *Methodist East Enders*. Peterborough, UK: Foundery Press, 1995.

Glasman, Gina. *East End Synagogues*. London: Museum of the Jewish East End, 1987.

Hackman, Harvey. *Wates's Book of London Churchyards: A Guide to the Old Churchyards and Burial-Grounds of the City and Central London*. London: Collins, 1981.

Harvey, Anthony, and Richard Mortimer. *The Funeral Effigies of Westminster Abbey*. Woodbridge, UK: Boydell, 1994.

Harvey, Barbara F. *Living and Dying in England, 1100–1540: The Monastic Experience*. Oxford: Clarendon, 1993.

Hattersley, Roy. *Blood and Fire: William and Catherine Booth and Their Salvation Army*. London: Little, Brown, 1999.

Hauer, Christian E. *A Comprehensive History of the London Church and Parish of St. Mary the Virgin, Aldermanbury, the Phoenix of Aldermanbury*. Lewiston, N.Y.: Edwin Mellen, 1994.

Huelin, Gordon. *Vanished Churches of the City of London*. London: Guildhall Library, 1996.

Hibbert, Christopher. *London's Churches*. London: Macdonald/Queen Anne Press, 1988.

Huffman, Joseph P. *Family, Commerce and Religion in London and Cologne: Anglo-German Emigrants. c. 1000–c. 1300*. Cambridge: Cambridge University Press, 1998.

Jaulmes, Yves. *The French Protestant Church of London and the Huguenots*. London: Église Protestante Française de Londres, 1993.

Jeffree, Richard. *The Story of Mortlake Churchyard*. London: Barnes and Mortlake History Society, 1983.

Jeffrey, Paul. *The City Churches of Sir Christopher Wren*. London: Hambledon Press, 1996.

Johnson, Malcolm. *Outside the Gate: St. Botolph's and Aldgate, 950–1994*. London: Stepney Books, 1994.

Knighton, C. S. *Acts of the Dean and Chapter of Westminster, 1543–1609: The First Collegiate Church (1543–1556*). Woodbridge, UK: Boydell, 1997.

Kollar, Rene. *Westminster Cathedral: From Dream to Reality*. Edinburgh: Faith and Life Publications, 1987.

———. *The Return of the Benedictines to London: A History of Ealing Abbey from 1896 to Independence*. London: Burns and Oates, 1989.

Leonard, John. *London's Parish Churches*. Derby, UK: Breedon, 1997.

Lindley, Keith. *Popular Politics and Religion in Civil War London*. Aldershot, UK: Scolar, 1997.

Lindsay, Paul. *The Synagogues of London*. London: Vallentine Mitchell, 1993.

Manchester, Sean. *The Highgate Vampire: The Infernal World of the Undead Unearthed at London's Highgate Cemetery and Environs*. London: Gothic, 1991.

Mason. Emma. *Westminster Abbey and Its People, c. 1050–c. 1216*. Woodbridge, UK: Boydell and Brewer, 1996.

Mason, Emma, ed. *Westminster Abbey Charters, 1066–c. 1214*. London: London Record Society, 1988.

McIlhiney, David B. *A Gentleman in Every Slum: Church of England Missions in East London, 1837–1914*. Allison Park, Penn.: Pickwick, 1988.

McIlwain, John. *Westminster Cathedral: The Roman Catholic Metropolitan Cathedral of Westminster*. Andover, UK: Pitkin, 1994.

Milne, Gustav. *St. Bride's Church, London: Archaeological Research, 1952–60 and 1992–5*. London: English Heritage, 1997.

Milward, R. J. *A Parish Church Since Domesday: St. Mary's, Wimbledon*. London: Parish of Wimbledon, 1993.

Morris, J. N. *Religion and Urban Change: Croydon, 1840–1914*. Woodbridge, UK: Royal Historical Society/Boydell, 1992.

Murdoch, Norman H. *Origins of the Salvation Army*. Knoxville: University of Tennessee Press, 1994.

Napier, Michael, and Alistair Laing. *The London Oratory Centenary, 1884–1984*. London: Trefoil, 1984.

Pannett, James P. *St. George's Cathedral, Southwark*. Andover, UK: Pitkin, 1996.

Perkins, Richard. *St. Anne's Church, Kew Green*. Much Wenlock, UK: R. J. L. Smith, 1993.

Pierce, Pat. *Brompton Cemetery*. London: Royal Parks, 1993.

Rice, Hilary Stainer. *Country Churches of the Chilterns*. Burnham, UK: Corinthian, 1983.

Rowles, Rosemary. *St. Mary Abbots: The Parish Church of Kensington*. Andover, UK: Pitkin, 1992.

Smith, Eric E. F. *Macaulay School: The Story of a Church School, 1648–1987*. London: Clapham Press, 1987.

Sullivan, David. *The Westminster Corridor: An Exploration of the Anglo-Saxon History of Westminster Abbey and Its Nearby Lands and People*. London: Historical Publications, 1994.

Thomas, Christopher, Barnley Stone, and Christopher Phillpotts. *Excavations at the Priory and Hospital of St. Mary Spital, London*. London: Museum of London, 1997.

Thompson, Phyllis. *To the Heart of the City: The Story of the London City Mission*. London: Hodder and Stoughton, 1985.

Turner, Christopher. *London Churches Step by Step*. London: Faber, 1987.

Walker, Henry. *East London: Sketches of Christian Work and Workers*. High Wycombe, UK: Marcan, 1984.

Wittich, John. *Catholic London*. Leominster, UK: Fowler Wright, 1988.

Woodward, Max W. *One at London: Some Account of Mr. Wesley's Chapel and London House*. London: Friends of Wesley's Chapel, 1983.

Wunderli, Richard M. *London Church Courts and Society on the Eve of the Reformation*. Cambridge, Mass.: Medieval Academy of America, 1981.

Young, Elizabeth, and Wayland Young. *London's Churches*. London: Grafton, 1986.

THE RIVER THAMES

Astbury, A. K. *Land and Water in the Lower Thames Basin*. London: Carnforth, 1980.

Attrill, Martin J. *A Rehabilitated Estuarine Ecosystem: The Environment and Ecology of the Thames Estuary*. Dordrecht, The Netherlands: Kluwer Academic, 1998.

Bagshaw, H. A. E. *Coasting Sailorman: A First-Hand Account of Life and Trade Aboard Thames Sailing Barges Between the Years 1915 and 1945*. Ware, UK: Chaffcutter, 1998.

Banks, Leslie, and Christopher Stanley. *The Thames: A History from the Air*. Oxford: Oxford University Press, 1990.

Bates, L. M. *The Spirit of London's River: Memoirs of the Thames Waterfront*. Woking, UK: Gresham, 1980.

Belloc, Hilaire. *The Historic Thames*. Exeter, UK: Bower and Webb, 1988.

Bridgeland, D. R. *Quaternary of the Thames*. London: Chapman and Hall, 1994.

Bridgeland, D. R., P. Allen, and B. A. Haggart, eds. *The Quaternary of the Lower Reaches of the Thames: Field Guide*. Durham, UK: Quaternary Research Association, 1995.

Budworth, Geoffrey. *The River Beat: The Story of London's River Police Since 1798*. London: Historical Publications, 1997.

Burstall, Patricia. *The Golden Age of the Thames*. Newton Abbot, UK: David and Charles, 1981.

Cracknell, Basil E. *Portrait of London River: The Thames from Teddington to the Sea*. London: Hale, 1980.

Currie, Ian. *Frosts, Freezes and Fairs: Chronicles of the Frozen Thames and Harsh Winters in Britain Since 1000 A.D.* Coulsdon, UK: Frosted Earth, 1996.

Dix, Frank L. *Royal River Highway: A History of the Passenger Boats and Services on the River Thames*. Newton Abbot, UK: David and Charles, 1985.

Ebel, Suzanne, and Doreen Impey. *A Guide to London's Riverside: Hampton Court to Greenwich*. London: Constable, 1985.

Ellmers, Chris. *London's Lost Riverscape: A Photographic Panorama*. London: Viking, 1988.

Foot, John. *The Illustrated Diary of a Thames Pilot*. Ringwood, UK: Navigator, 1995.

Gibbard, Philip L. *The Pleistocene History of the Middle Thames Valley*. Cambridge: Cambridge University Press, 1985.

———. *Pleistocene History of the Lower Thames Valley*. Cambridge: Cambridge University Press, 1994.

Gilbert, Stuart, and Ray Horner. *The Thames Barrier*. London: Telford, 1984.

Hawthorne, Edward. *Electric Boats on the Thames, 1889–1914*. Stroud, UK: Alan Sutton, 1995.

Heffernan, Henry. *South Thames: Tower Bridge to Thamesmead*. Stroud, UK: Chalford, 1996.

Hill, David. *Turner on the Thames: River Journeys in the Year 1805*. New Haven, Conn.: Yale University Press, 1993.

Leapman, Michael. *London's River: A History of the Thames*. London: Pavilion, 1991.

Luckin, Bill. *Pollution and Control: A Social History of the Thames in the Nineteenth Century*. Bristol, UK: Hilger, 1986.

Martin, Frank. *Rogues' River: Crime on the River Thames in the Eighteenth Century*. Hornchurch, UK: Henry, 1983.

Milne, Antony. *London's Drowning*. London: Thames Methuen, 1982.

Mindell, Ruth, and Jonathan Mindell. *Bridges Over the Thames*. Poole, UK: Blandford, 1985.

Murray, Ernest G. *Tales of a Thames Lighterman*. Whittlebury, UK: Baron Birch, 1992.

Palmer, Kenneth Nicholls. *Ceremonial Barges on the River Thames: A History of the Barges of the City of London Livery Companies and of the Crown*. London: Unicorn, 1997.

Phillips, Geoffrey. *Thames Crossings: Bridges, Tunnels and Ferries*. Newton Abbot, UK: David and Charles, 1981.

Reed, Nicholas. *Sisley and the Thames: A Pilgrimage in the Steps of Alfred Sisley, Impressionist Painter, Who Came to London in 1874*. London: Lilburne, 1992.

Reynolds, John E. *Thames Ship Towage, 1933–1992*. Edinburgh: Pentland, 1993.

Sumbler, M. G. *British Regional Geology: London and the Thames Valley*. London: Her Majesty's Stationery Office, 1996.

Waters, Tony. *Bridge by Bridge Through London: The Thames from Tower Bridge to Teddington*. Whitstable, UK: Pryor, 1989.

Weightman, Gavin. *London River: The Thames Story*. London: Collins and Brown, 1990.

Wilson, Sheila, and Ken Wilson. *Thames Barrier*. London: New Century, 1991.

Wood, Leslie B. *The Restoration of the Tidal Thames*. Bristol, UK: Hilger, 1982.

SOCIAL HISTORY

Ackroyd, Peter. *London: The Biography*. London: Chatto and Windos, 2000.

Adlard, John. *In Sweet St. James's Clerkenwell: The Musical Coal-Man and His Friends and Neighbours in the Golden Age of a London Suburb*. London: London Borough of Islington, 1984.

Aldous, Tony. *The "Illustrated London News" Book of London's Villages*. London: Secker and Warburg, 1990.

Alexander, Sally. *Women's Work in Nineteenth-Century London: A Study of the Years 1820–1850*. London: Journeyman, 1983.

Archer, Ian W. *The Pursuit of Stability: Social Relations in Elizabethan London*. Cambridge: Cambridge University Press, 1991.

Arnold, Dana, ed. *The Metropolis and Its Image: Constructing Identities for London*. Oxford: Blackwell, 2000.

Barker, Felix. *Edwardian London*. London: Laurence King, 1995.

Barret-Ducrocq, Françoise. *Love in the Time of Victoria: Sexuality, Class and Gender in Nineteenth-Century London*. London: Verso, 1991.

Barron, Caroline M., and Anne F. Sutton, eds. *Medieval London Widows, 1300–1500*. London: Hambledon, 1994.

Beauchamp, Michelle. *On the Streets: A Journey Through London with the Young Homeless*. London: Harrap, 1989.

Beckson, Karl. *London in the 1890s: A Cultural History*. New York: Norton, 1992.

Belcher, Victor. *The City Parochial Foundation, 1891–1991: A Trust for the Poor of London*. Aldershot, UK: Scolar, 1991.

Bond, Henry. *The Cult of the Street: Photographs of London*. London: Emily Tsingou Gallery, 1998.

Bosanquet, Charles B. P. *London: Some Account of Its Growth, Charitable Agencies and Wants*. New York: Garland, 1984.

Boulton, J. P. *Neighbourhood and Society: A London Suburb in the Seventeenth Century*. Cambridge: Cambridge University Press, 1987.

Boyle, Thomas. *Black Swine in the Sewers of Hampstead: Beneath the Surface of Victorian Sensationalism*. London: Hodder and Stoughton, 1989.

Brandt, Bill. *London in the Thirties*. London: Gordon Fraser, 1983.

Burford, E. J. *Wits, Wenchers and Wantons: London's Low Life—Covent Garden in the Eighteenth Century*. London: Hale, 1986.

———. *Royal St. James's, Being a Story of Kings, Clubmen and Courtesans*. London: Hale, 1988.

Burford, E. J., and Joy Wotton. *Private Vices—Public Virtues: Bawdry in London from Elizabethan Times to the Regency*. London: Robert Hale, 1995.

Burke, Barry, and Ken Worpole. *Hackney Propaganda: Working Class Club Life and Politics in Hackney, 1870–1900*. London: Centerprise, 1980.

Bynum, W. F., and Roy Porter, eds. *Living and Dying in London*. London: Wellcome Institute for the History of Medicine, 1991.

Carr, Gregg. *Residence and Social Status: The Development of Seventeenth-Century London*. New York: Garland, 1990.

Clarke, Sam. *Sam, an East End Cabinet-Maker: The Pocket Book Memoir of Sam Clarke, 1907–1979*. London: Geffrye Museum, 1983.

Connor, J. E., and Critchley, B. J. *Palaces for the Poor*. Colchester, UK: Connor and Butler, 1984.

———. *The Red Cliffs of Stepney: The Buildings of the East End Dwellings Co., the 4% Industrial Dwellings Co. and Related Groups*. Colchester, UK: Connor and Butler, 1987.

Cooper, Christine. *The Changing Social Structure of Greater London*. London: Greater London Council, 1982.

Cooper, Jilly. *The Common Years*. London: Mandarin, 1989.

Courtney, Carol-Ann. *A Shilling for the Axe-Man*. London: Signet, 1993.

Cox, Jane. *London's East End Life and Traditions*. London: Weidenfeld and Nicolson, 1994.

Crowe, A. J. *Inns, Taverns and Pubs of the London Borough of Sutton: Their History and Architecture, With 61 Original Drawings*. London: London Borough of Sutton, 1980.

Curl, James Stevens. *The Londonderry Plantation, 1609–1914: The History, Architecture, and Planning of the Estates of the City of London and Its Livery Companies in Ulster.* Chichester, UK: Phillimore, 1986.

Davin, Anna. *Growing Up Poor: Home, School and Street in London, 1870–1914.* London: Rivers Oram Press, 1996.

Delarue, Jean. *No. 1 Clapham Road: The Diary of a Squat*. Pontefract, UK: Peaceprint, 1990.

Denny, Barbara. *Ladybirds on the Wall: Growing Up in West Kensington, 1920–1940*. London: Fulham and Hammersmith Historical Society, 1993.

Dobson, Anita. *My East End*. London: Pavilion, 1987.

Down, Catherine. *A Child From "The Borough."* Ilfracombe, UK: Stockwell, 1992.

Earle, Peter. *A City Full of People: Men and Women of London, 1650–1750*. London: Methuen, 1994.

Egan, Geoff, and Frances Pritchard. *Dress Accessories c. 1150–c. 1450*. London: Her Majesty's Stationery Office, 1991.

Emsley, Ian. *The Development of Housing Associations, With Special Reference to London and Including a Case Study of the London Borough of Hammersmith.* New York: Garland, 1986.

Everett, Michael D. *Victorian London Street Life*. Sheffield, UK: MDE, 1986.

Farson, Daniel. *Limehouse Days: A Personal Experience of the East End.* London: Michael Joseph, 1991.

Finn, Ralph L. *Grief Forgotten: The Tale of an East End Jewish Boyhood.* London: Macdonald, 1985.

———. *Time Remembered: The Tale of an East End Jewish Boyhood.* London: Macdonald, 1985.

Fishman, W. J. *East End 1888: A Year in a London Borough Among the Labouring Poor*. London: Duckworth, 1988.

Forrest, Denys. *St. James's Square: People, Houses, Happenings.* London: Quiller, 1986.

Fox, Celina, ed. *London—World City, 1800–1840*. New Haven, Conn.: Yale University Press/Museum of London.

Friedman, Danny, and Hal Pawson. *One in Every Hundred: A Study of Households Accepted as Homeless in London*. London: London Research Centre, 1989.

Fryer, Jonathan. *Soho in the Fifties and Sixties*. London: National Portrait Gallery, 1998.

Gale, Maggie B. *West End Women: Women and the London Stage, 1918–1962*. London: Routledge, 1996.

Gamble, Rose. *Chelsea Child*. London: Ariel, 1982.

Gelb, Joyce, and Michael Lyons. *A Tale of Two Cities: Housing Policy and Gentrification in London and New York*. London: South Bank Polytechnic, 1991.

George, M. Dorothy. *London Life in the Eighteenth Century*. London: Routledge/Thoemmes, 1996.

Glasheen, Joan. *St. James's, London*. Chichester, UK: Phillimore, 1987.

Goldman, Willy. *East End, My Cradle: Portrait of an Environment*. London: Robson, 1988.
Gowing, Laura. *Domestic Dangers: Women, Words and Sex in Early Modern London*. Oxford: Clarendon, 1996.
Grana, Joanna. *Nobody Nicked 'Em: How We Started a Toy Library in the East End of London*. London: Calouste Gulbenkian Foundation, 1983.
Green, David R. *People of the Rookery: A Pauper Community in Victorian London*. London: King's College, 1986.
Green, Mike. *The 1950s and Swinging Sixties and London Memories*. Wymondham, UK: Stylus, 1994.
———. *Christmas 1950 in Hammersmith*. Wymondham, UK: Stylus, 1996.
Halsey, A. H., Roger Jowell, and Bridget Taylor, eds. *The Quality of Life in London*. Aldershot, UK: Dartmouth, 1995.
Hanawalt, Barbara A. *Growing Up in Medieval London: The Experience of Childhood in History*. Oxford: Oxford University Press, 1993.
Harley, Ed. *An Eastender*. Braunton, UK: Merlin, 1989.
Harrison, Paul. *Inside the Inner City: Life Under the Cutting Edge*. Harmondsworth, UK: Penguin, 1983.
Harvey, Barbara. *Living and Dying in England, 1100–1540: The Monastic Experience*. Oxford: Clarendon, 1993.
Hawkes, Herbert Granville. *Reynardson's Almshouses, Tottenham, Middlesex, Mainly Based on the Accounts and Minute Books of that Charity in Bruce Castle Museum*. London: Enfield Hundred Historical Society, 1980.
Hermann, Bernard. *London: City of Contrasts*. London: W. H. Allen, 1989.
Holloway, Sally. *Courage High!: A History of Firefighting in London*. London: Her Majesty's Stationery Office, 1992.
Holme, Anthea. *Housing and Young Families in East London*. London: Routledge and Kegan Paul, 1985.
Huffman, Joseph P. *Family, Commerce and Religion in London and Cologne: Anglo-German Emigrants c. 1000–c. 1300*. Cambridge: Cambridge University Press, 1998.
Hutton, Richard. *Richard Hutton's Complaints Book: The Notebook of the Steward of the Quaker Workhouse at Clerkenwell, 1711–1737*. London: London Record Society, 1987.
Jackson, Alan A. *Semi-Detached London: Suburban Development, Life and Transport, 1900–39*. Didcot, UK: Wild Swan, 1991.
Johnson, Nichola. *Eighteenth Century London*. London: Her Majesty's Stationery Office, 1991.
Jowett, Evelyn M. *Raynes Park, With West Barnes and Cannon Hill: A Social History*. London: Merton Historical Society, 1987.
Joyce, Patrick. *The History of Morden College, Blackheath: 1695 to the Present*. Henley-on-Thames, UK: Gresham/Trustees of Morden College, 1982.
King, John. *Grove Park: The History of a Community*. London: Grove Park Community Group, 1982.

Knif, Henrik. *Gentlemen and Spectators: Studies in Journals, Opera and the Social Scene in Late Stuart London*. Helsinki: Finnish Historical Society, 1995.

Lees, Lynn Hollen. *Poverty and Pauperism in Nineteenth-Century London*. Leicester, UK: University of Leicester, 1988.

MacDonald, Michael, ed. *Witchcraft and Hysteria in Elizabethan London: Edward Jorden and the Mary Glover Case*. London: Tavistock/Routledge, 1991.

MacLennan, Emma. *Child Labour in London*. London: Low Pay Unit, 1982.

Madge, Charles, and Peter Willmott. *Inner City Poverty in Paris and London*. London: Routledge and Kegan Paul, 1981.

Marcus, Sharon. *Apartment Stories: City and Home in Nineteenth-Century Paris and London*. Berkeley: University of California Press, 1999.

Marshall, James. *The History of the Great West Road: Its Social and Economic Influence on the Surrounding Area*. London: Heritage Publications, 1995.

Massey, Doreen. *Docklands: A Microcosm of Broader Social and Economic Trends*. London: Docklands Forum, 1991.

Matthews, Rupert. *London: Moments in Time*. Derby, UK: Breedon, 1997.

Mayhew, Henry. *The "Morning Chronicle" Survey of Labour and the Poor: The Metropolitan Districts*. Firle, UK: Caliban Brooks, 1980.

———. *London's Underworld*. London: Bracken, 1983.

———. *The Unknown Mayhew: Selections from the* Morning Chronicle, *1849–50*. Harmondsworth, UK: Penguin, 1984.

———. *London Labour and the London Poor*. Harmondsworth, UK: Penguin, 1985.

———. *The Illustrated Mayhew's London: The Classic Account of London Street Life and Characters in the Time of Charles Dickens and Queen Victoria*. London: Weidenfeld and Nicolson, 1986.

———. *London Characters and Crooks*. London: Folio Society, 1996.

McCalman, Iain. *Radical Underworld: Prophets, Revolutionaries and Pornographers in London, 1795–1840*. Cambridge: Cambridge University Press, 1988.

McDonald, Erica. *Artisans and Avenues: A History of the Queen's Park Estate*. London: City of Westminster, 1990.

McDowell, Linda. *Capital Culture: Gender at Work in the City*. Oxford: Blackwell, 1997.

McDowell, Paula. *The Women of Grub Street: Press, Politics and Gender in the London Literary Marketplace, 1678–1730*. Oxford: Clarendon, 1998.

Montgomery-Massingberd, Hugh, and David Watkin. *The London Ritz: A Social and Architectural History*. London: Aurum, 1980.

Morris, J. N. *Religion and Urban Change: Croydon, 1840–1914*. Woodbridge, UK: Royal Historical Society, 1992.

Murie, Alan, and Syd Jeffers. *Living in Bed and Breakfast: The Experience of Homelessness in London*. Bristol, UK: University of Bristol, 1988.

Murray, Venetia, ed. *Echoes of the East End*. London: Viking, 1989.

Neary, E. A. *The Memoirs of a Victorian London Gutter-Snipe*. Lewes, UK: Book Guild, 1990.

O'Day, Rosemary, and David Englander. *Mr. Charles Booth's Inquiry: Life and Labour of the People in London Reconsidered*. London: Hambledon, 1993.

Olechnowicz, Andrzej. *Working-Class Housing in England Between the Wars: The Becontree Estate*. Oxford: Clarendon, 1997.

O'Mahony, Brendan. *A Capital Offence: The Plight of the Young Single Homeless in London*. London: Routledge, 1988.

O'Neill, Gilda. *My East End: A History of Cockney*. London: Viking, 2000.

Palmer, Alan. *The East End: Four Centuries of London Life*. London: Murray, 1989.

Palmer, Kenneth Nicholls. *Ceremonial Barges on the River Thames: A History of the Barges of the City of London Livery Companies and of the Crown*. London: Unicorn, 1997.

Pam, D. O. *The Hungry Years: The Struggle for Survival in Edmonton and Enfield Before 1400*. London: Edmonton Hundred Historical Society, 1980.

Panteli, Stavros. *London: The Royal City*. London: Interworld, 1989.

Parker, Tony. *The People of Providence: A Housing Estate and Some of Its Inhabitants*. London: Picador, 1992.

Paterson, Sir Alexander. *Across the Bridges: Life by the South London River-Side*. New York: Garland, 1980.

Paterson, John. *Edwardians: London Life and Letters, 1901–1914*. Chicago: I. R. Dee, 1996.

Pepys, Samuel. *The Diary of Samuel Pepys*. London: Bell and Hyman, 1985.

———. *The Great Fire of London*. London: Phoenix, 1996.

Picard, Liza. *Restoration London*. London: Weidenfeld and Nicolson, 1997.

———. *Dr. Johnson's London: Life in London, 1740–1770*. London: Weidenfeld and Nicolson, 2000.

Playfair, Guy Lyon. *This House Is Haunted: The Investigation of the Enfield Poltergeist*. London: Sphere, 1981.

Pointer, Frank Erik. *Cockney Glotalling: A Study on the Phonetics of Contemporary London Speech*. Essen, Germany: Verlag die Blaue Eule, 1996.

Porter, Roy. *London: A Social History*. London: Hamish Hamilton, 1994.

Puxley, Ray. *Cockney Rabbit: A Dick 'n' Arry of Rhyming Slang*. London: Robson, 1992.

Rappaport, Erika Diane. *Shopping for Pleasure: Women in the Making of London's West End*. Princeton, N.J.: Princeton University Press, 2000.

Richardson, John. *London and Its People: A Social History from Medieval Times to the Present Day*. London: Barrie and Jenkins, 1995.

Rose, June. *For the Sake of the Children: Inside Barnardo's—120 Years of Caring for Children*. London: Futura, 1987.

Rosen, Harold, and Tony Burgess. *Language and Dialects of London School Children: An Investigation*. London: Ward Lock, 1980.

Rosenbaum, S. P. *Victorian Bloomsbury*. Basingstoke, UK: Macmillan, 1987.

Rothstein, Andrew. *A House on Clerkenwell Green*. London: Marx Memorial Library, 1983.

Rubenstein, Antonia, ed. *Just Like the Country: Memories of London Families Who Settled the New Cottage Estates, 1919–1939*. London: Age Exchange, 1991.

Schneer, Jonathan. *The Imperial Metropolis*. New Haven, Conn.: Yale University Press, 2000.

Schwarz, L. D. *London in the Age of Industrialisation: Entrepreneurs, Labour Force and Living Conditions*. Cambridge: Cambridge University Press, 1992.

Shipley, Stan. *Club Life and Socialism in Mid-Victorian London*. London: Journeyman, 1983.

Shonfield, Zuzanna. *The Precariously Privileged: A Professional Family in Victorian London*. Oxford: Oxford University Press, 1987.

Smedley, Bunny. *Lord North Street, 1725–1996: A Westminster Portrait*. London: Hyde Park Antiquarian, 1996.

Smuts, R. Malcolm. *Court Culture and the Origins of a Royalist Tradition in Early Stuart England*. Philadelphia: University of Pennsylvania Press, 1987.

Springle, W. B. *The Vanishing Cockney: In and About London*. London: Langdale, 1990.

Sullivan, David. *The Westminster Corridor: An Exploration of the Anglo-Saxon History of Westminster Abbey and Its Nearby Lands and People*. London: Historical Publications, 1994.

Sutherland, Douglas. *Portrait of a Decade: London Life, 1945–1955*. London: Harrap, 1988.

Sykes, Christopher Simon. *Private Palaces: Life in the Great London House*. London: Chatto and Windus, 1985.

Thomas, Christopher, Barnley Stone, and Christopher Philpotts. *Excavations at the Priory and Hospital of St. Mary Spital, London*. London: Museum of London, 1997.

Thompson, Liz. *Just a Cotchell: Tales from a Docklands Childhood and Beyond*. London: Basement Writers, 1987.

Thomson, Arline K. *Discovering Elizabethan London: Diary and Sketches*. Orono: University of Maine Press, 1994.

Thomson, John. *Victorian Street Life in Historic Photographs*. New York: Dover, 1994.

Thornley, Andy, ed. *The Crisis of London*. London: Routledge, 1992.

Townsend, Peter, with Paul Corrigan and Ute Kowarzik. *Poverty and Labour in London: Interim Report of a Centenary Survey*. London: Low Pay Unit/Poverty Research (London) Trust, 1987.

Trench, Richard. *London Under London*. London: Murray, 1993.

Tuffin, Rachel. *"There Ain't Much to Play—Most Things Are for Adults": Children in an Urban Environment*. London: University of East London, 1996.

Wade, Christopher. *For the Poor of Hampstead, for Ever: Three Hundred Years of the Hampstead Wells Trust*. London: Camden History Society, 1998.

Walker, Annabel. *Kensington and Chelsea: A Social and Architectural History*. London: Murray, 1987.

Walkowitz, Judith R. *City of Dreadful Delight: Narratives of Sexual Danger in Late-Victorian London*. London: Virago, 1992.
Waller, Maureen. *1700: Scenes from London Life*. London: Hodder and Stoughton, 2000.
Ward, Michael. *Red Flag Over the Workhouse: The Unemployed in South West London, 1918–1923*. London: Wandsworth History Workshop, 1992.
Warne, Joan. *My Other Family: A Woodford Children's Home in the Thirties*. Harlow, UK: Virtual Valley, 1996.
Weiner, Deborah E. B. *Architecture and Social Reform in Late-Victorian London*. Manchester, UK: Manchester University Press, 1994.
Weinstein, Rosemary. *Tudor London*. London: Her Majesty's Stationery Office, 1994.
Wells, Keith. *The History of Avery Hill Housing Estate*. Nottingham, UK: Local History Press, 1995.
White, Jerry. *Rothschild Buildings: Life in an East End Tenement Block, 1887–1920*. London: Routledge and Kegan Paul, 1980.
———. *The Worst Street in North London: Campbell Bunk, Islington, Between the Wars*. London: Routledge and Kegan Paul, 1986.
Whiteford-Engholm, Sylvia. *Roll-ups and Teacups*. London: Macmillan, 1990.
Whitehouse, Roger. *A London Album: Early Photographs Recording the History of the City and Its People from 1840 to 1915*. London: Secker and Warburg, 1980.
Williams, Norman Lloyd. *Tudor London Visited*. London: Cassell, 1991.
Willmott, Phyllis. *A Green Girl*. London: Peter Owen, 1983.
Wilson, Robert McLiam, and Donovan Wylie. *The Dispossessed*. London: Picador, 1992.
Wright, Laura. *Sources of London English: Medieval Thames Vocabulary*. Oxford: Clarendon, 1996.
Wulff, Helena. *Twenty Girls: Growing Up, Ethnicity and Excitement in a South London Monoculture*. Stockholm: University of Stockholm, 1988.
Wyndham, Joan. *Love Lessons: A Wartime Diary*. London: Heinemann, 1985.
Yelling, J. A. *Slums and Slum Clearance in Victorian London*. London: Allen and Unwin, 1986.
Young, Michael. *The Symmetrical Family: A Study of Work and Leisure in the London Region*. Harmondsworth, UK: Penguin, 1980.
Young, Michael, and Peter Willmott. *Family and Kinship in East London*. London: Routledge and Kegan Paul, 1986.

SPORTS AND RECREATION

Bass, Howard. *Glorious Wembley: The Official History of Britain's Foremost Entertainment Centre*. London: Guinness Superlatives, 1982.
Berry, Herbert. *The Noble Science: A Study and Transcription of Sloane Ms. 2530, Papers of the Masters of Defence of London, Temp. Henry VIII to 1590*. Newark, N.J.: University of Delaware, 1991.

Brimson, Dougie, and Eddie Brimson. *Capital Punishment: London's Violent Football Following*. London: Headline, 1997.

Brown, John W. *Streatham Races*. London: Local History Publications, 1990.

Campbell, Denis, and Andrew Shields. *Soccer City: The Future of Football in London*. London: Mandarin, 1993.

Cheshire, Scott. *Chelsea: A Complete Record, 1905–1991*. Derby, UK: Breedon, 1991.

———. *Chelsea: An Illustrated History*. Derby, UK: Breedon, 1997.

Coton, Ken. *Fulham's Golden Years: A Pictorial Memoir of Fulham Football Club, 1958–1983*. London: Ashwater, 1992.

Crossley, Lionel. *Crystal Palace Speedway: The Thrills and Spills of the 20s and 30s*. London: Crystal Palace Foundation, 1986.

Dodd, Christopher. *The Oxford and Cambridge Boat Race*. London: Stanley Paul, 1983.

Doggart, Hubert, and John Woodcock. *Lord Be Praised*. Derby, UK: English Life, 1988.

Down, Michael, and Derek West. *Sketches at Lord's: The Cricket Lithographs of John Corbet Anderson*. London: Willow, 1990.

Farrar, Dave, and Peter Lush. *Touch and Go: A History of Professional Rugby League in London*. London: London League Publications, 1995.

Fleming, Scott. *Home and Away: Sport and South Asian Male Youth*. Aldershot, UK: Avebury, 1995.

Goodwin, Bob. *An Illustrated History of Tottenham Hotspur*. Derby, UK: Breedon, 1997.

Heald, Tim, ed. *My Lord's: A Celebration of the World's Greatest Cricket Ground*. London: Willow, 1990.

Hayes, Dean. *The White Hart Lane Encyclopedia: An A–Z of Tottenham Hotspur FC*. Edinburgh: Mainstream, 1996.

Hyde, Ralph. *The Regent's Park Colosseum, Or, "Without Hyperbole, the Wonder of the World," Being an Account of a Forgotten Pleasure Dome and Its Creators*. London: Ackermann, 1982.

Kaufman, Neil, and Alan Ravenhill. *Leyton Orient: A Complete Record, 1881–1990*. Derby: Breedon, 1990.

Kerr, Charles. *West Ham United: The Making of a Football Club*. London: Duckworth, 1986.

Kerr, Diana Rait, and Ian Peebles. *Lord's, 1946–1970*. London: Pavilion, 1987.

Leatherdale, Clive. *Wimbledon: From Southern League to Premiership—A Complete Record*. Westcliff-on-Sea, UK: Desert Island, 1995.

Lemmon, David. *The Official History of Middlesex County Cricket Club*. London: Christopher Helm, 1988.

Lewis, Tony. *Double Century: The Story of MCC and Cricket*. London: Hodder and Stoughton, 1987.

Lidbury, Michael. *Wimbledon Football Club: The First 100 Years*. London: Wimbledon Football Club, 1991.

Lindsay, Richard. *Millwall: A Complete Record, 1885–1991*. Derby, UK: Breedon, 1991.

Little, Alan. *The Changing Face of Wimbledon*. London: Wimbledon Lawn Tennis Museum, 1989.

Little, Alan, and Lance Tingay. *Wimbledon Men: A Hundred Championships, 1877–1986*. London: Wimbledon Lawn Tennis Museum, 1986.

Moorhouse, Geoffrey. *Lord's*. London: Hodder and Stoughton, 1983.

Northcutt, John, and Roy Shoesmith. *West Ham United: An Illustrated History*. Derby, UK: Breedon, 1994.

Ollier, Fred. *Arsenal: A Complete Record, 1886–1992*. Derby, UK: Breedon, 1992.

Peters, H. W. de B. *The London Playing Fields Society: Centenary History, 1890–1990*. Brentford, UK: London Playing Fields Society, 1990.

Redden, Richard. *The Story of Charlton Athletic, 1905–1990*. Derby, UK: Breedon, 1990.

Rippon, Anton. *The Story of Middlesex County Cricket Club*. Ashbourne, UK: Moorland, 1982.

Sands, Mollie. *The Eighteenth-Century Pleasure Gardens of Marylebone, 1737–1777*. London: Society for Theatre Research, 1987.

Sands, Nigel. *Crystal Palace Football Club, 1905–1997: The History of the Club*. Whittlebury, UK: Sporting and Leisure, 1997.

Soar, Phil. *Tottenham Hotspur: The Official Illustrated History, 1882–1996*. London: Hamlyn, 1996.

Soar, Phil, and Martin Tyler. *Arsenal: The Official History, 1886–1996*. London: Hamlyn, 1996.

Thrave, Andrew. *The History of the Wembley FA Cup Final*. London: Weidenfeld and Nicolson, 1994.

Wade, Virginia. *Ladies of the Court: A Century of Women at Wimbledon*. London: Pavilion, 1984.

Warner, Pelhars. *Lord's, 1787–1945*. London: Pavilion, 1987.

Watson, J. N. P. *Horse and Carriage: The Pageant of Hyde Park*. London: Sportsman's Press, 1990.

Watt, Tom. *The End: 80 Years of Life on Arsenal's North Bank*. Edinburgh: Mainstream, 1993.

Watt, Tom, and Kevin Palmer. *Wembley, the Greatest Stage: The Official History of 75 Years at Wembley Stadium*. London: Simon and Schuster, 1998.

Yapp, Nick. *A History of the Foster's Oval*. London: Pelham, 1990.

Young, Michael, and Peter Willmott. *The Symmetrical Family: A Study of Work and Leisure in the London Region*. Harmondsworth, UK: Penguin, 1980.

TRANSPORT

Abbott, James. *Docklands Light Railway*. London: Ian Allen, 1991.

Appleyard, Donald. *Livable Streets*. Berkeley: University of California Press, 1981.

Atkinson, J. B. *The West London Joint Railways*. London: Ian Allen, 1984.

Bain, Gordon. *Gatwick Airport*. Shrewsbury, UK: Airlife, 1994.

Baker, Michael H. C. *Farewell to London's Trolleybuses*. Shepperton, UK: Ian Allen, 1994.

———. *London Transport, 1933–1962*. Shepperton, UK: Ian Allen, 1996.

———. *London Transport Since 1963*. Shepperton, UK: Ian Allen, 1997.

———. *The London Country Buses in Colour*. Shepperton, UK: Ian Allen, 1998.

Bancroft, Peter. *London Transport Records at the Public Record Office*. Alton, UK: Nebulous, 1995.

Barker, T. C. *Moving Millions: A Pictorial History of London Transport*. London: London Transport Museum, 1990.

Baxter, Nicola. *The London Bus and Tube Network: Sixty Years of Public Transport in London*. London: Hodder, 1994.

Bayliss, Derek A. *Retracing the First Public Railway*. London: Living History Publications, 1981.

Beer, Brian. *Diesels in the Capital*. Sparkford, UK: Haynes, 1990.

Blake, James. *Odd Men Out: An Illustrated Listing of Type Substitutions and Scheduled Operation of Mixed Types of London Transport Central Buses, 1959–1981*. London: Capital Transport, 1981.

Blake, Jim, and Barry Turner. *At London's Service: 50 Years of London Transport Road Services*. London: Regent, 1983.

Boag, Andrew. *Metrobus: The Company's First Ten Years*. London: Capital Transport, 1994.

Body, Geoffrey. *The Blackwall and Millwall Extension Railways*. Weston-Super-Mare, UK: Avon-Anglia, 1982.

Borley, H. V. *Chronology of London Railways*. Oakham, UK: Railway and Canal Historical Society, 1982.

Bosher, David J. *The District Line and Associated Routes: A Brief History*. London: Erix, 1997.

Bruce, J. Graeme. *Steam to Silver: A History of London Transport Surface Rolling Stock*. London: Capital Transport, 1983.

———. *Workhorses of the London Underground*. London: Capital Transport, 1987.

———. *The London Underground Tube Stock*. Shepperton, UK: Ian Allen, 1988.

Bruce, J. Graeme, and Piers Connor. *Underground Train Overhaul: The Story of Acton Works*. London: Capital Transport, 1991.

Bruce, J. Graeme, and Desmond F. Croome. *The Twopenny Tube*. London: Capital Transport, 1996.

Cluett, Douglas, Joanna Nash, and Bob Learmonth. *Croydon Airport: The Great Days, 1928–1939*. London: London Borough of Sutton, 1980.

Coles, C. R. L. *Railways Through the Chilterns*. London: Ian Allen, 1980.

———. *Railway Through London*. London: Ian Allan, 1983.

Connor, J. E. *All Stations to Poplar*. Colchester, UK: Connor and Butler, 1985.

———. *Stepney's Own Railway: A History of the London and Blackwall System*. Colchester, UK: Connor and Butler, 1987.

——. *Finsbury Park to Alexandra Palace*. Midhurst, UK: Middleton Press, 1997.

Connor, J. E., and B. L. Halford. *The Forgotten Stations of Greater London: A Gazetteer of Disused and Renamed Passenger Stations within the Area Covered by the Greater London Boroughs*. Colchester, UK: Connor and Butler, 1991.

Connor, Piers. *Going Green*. London: Capital Transport, 1994.

Course, Edwin. *London's Railways Then and Now*. London: Batsford, 1987.

Croome, Desmond F., and Alan A. Jackson. *Rails Through the Clay: A History of London's Tube Railways*. London: Capital Transport, 1993.

Curtis, Colin H. *The Routemaster Bus: A Comprehensive History of a Highly Successful London Bus Type from Its Design, Development and Introduction into the Fleet*. Tunbridge Wells, UK: Midas, 1981.

Davies, Reg. *Rails to the People's Palace*. London: Hornsey Historical Society, 1980.

Davies, R., and M. D. Grant. *London and Its Railways*. Newton Abbot, UK: David and Charles, 1983.

Day, John R. *A Source Book of London Transport*. London: Ward Lock, 1982.

Dewe, George, and Michael Dewe. *Fulham Bridge, 1729–1886: The Predecessor of Putney Bridge*. London: Fulham and Hammersmith Historical Society, 1986.

Dix, Frank L. *Royal River Highway: A History of the Passenger Boats and Services on the River Thames*. Newton Abbot: David and Charles, 1985.

Edwards, Dennis. *The Golden Years of the Metropolitan Railway and the Metro-Land Dream.* Tunbridge Wells, UK: Midas, 1983.

Elliot, Alan. *Wimbledon's Railways*. London: Wimbledon, 1982.

Elwin, Geoff, and Cathleen King. *The Grand Union Canal from the Chilterns to the Thames*. Northolt, UK: Blackthorn, 1981.

Falconer, Jonathan. *Heathrow*. London: Ian Allen, 1990.

Faulkner, J. N. *Clapham Junction*. London: Ian Allen, 1991.

——. *Railways of Waterloo*. Shepperton, UK: Ian Allen, 1994.

Fuller, Ken. *Radical Associates: London Busworkers from the 1880s to the 1980s*. London: Lawrence and Wishart, 1985.

Garbutt, E. *London Transport and the Politicians*. London: Ian Allen, 1985.

Garland, Ken. *Mr. Beck's Underground Map*. London: Capital Transport, 1994.

Gent, John B., and John H. Meredith. *Croydon's Tramways, Including Crystal Palace, Mitcham and Sutton*. Midhurst, UK: Middleton Press, 1994.

Georgano, G. N. *The London Taxi*. Princes Risborough, UK: Shire, 1985.

Glover, John. *London Transport: Buses and Trains Since 1933*. London: Ian Allen, 1988.

——. *London Transport Railways*. Shepperton, UK: Ian Allen, 1991.

——. *London Underground*. Shepperton, UK: Ian Allen, 1997.

Glover, John, and Colin J. Marsden. *London Transport Railways and PTE Systems*. London: Ian Allen, 1985.

Goode, C. T. *Ally Pally: The Alexandra Palace, Its Transport and Its Troubles*. Bracknell, UK: Forge, 1983.

Goudie, F. W. *Metropolitan to Jubilee: Wembley Park to Stanmore*. Bracknell, UK: Forge, 1986.

Goudie, F. W., Robert Barker, and Douglas Stuckley. *Railways of Wembley*. Wokingham, UK: Forge, 1996.

Gray, Adrian. *The London, Chatham and Dover Railway*. Rainham, UK: Meresborough, 1984.

Green, Oliver. *The London Underground: An Illustrated History*. London: Ian Allen, 1987.

Green, Oliver, and Jeremy Rewse-Davies. *Designed for London: 150 Years of Transport Design*. London: Laurence King, 1995.

Hailstone, Charles. *Hammersmith Bridge*. London: Barnes and Mortlake Historical Society, 1987.

Hands, Peter. *British Railways Steaming Through London*. Solihull, UK: Defiant, 1996.

Hardy, Brian. *L.P.T.B. Rolling Stock, 1933–1948*. Truro, UK: Barton, 1981.

———. *London Underground Rolling Stock*. London: Capital Transport, 1990.

Harley, Robert J. *Camberwell and West Norwood Tramways*. Midhurst, UK: Middleton, 1993.

———. *Embankment and Waterloo Tramways*. Midhurst, UK: Middleton, 1994.

———. *Greenwich and Dartford Railways, Including Eltham and Bexley*. Midhurst, UK: Middleton, 1993.

———. *Lewisham and Catford Tramways*. Midhurst, UK: Middleton, 1994.

———. *Southwark and Deptford Tramways*. Midhurst, UK: Middleton, 1994.

———. *East Ham and West Ham Tramways*. Midhurst, UK: Middleton, 1995.

———. *Ilford and Barking Tramways*. Midhurst, UK: Middleton, 1995.

———. *Kingston and Wimbledon Tramways*. Midhurst, UK: Middleton, 1995.

———. *Victoria and Lambeth Tramways*. Midhurst, UK: Middleton, 1995.

———. *Walthamstow and Leyton Tramways*. Midhurst, UK: Middleton, 1995.

———. *Woolwich and Dartford Trolleybuses*. Midhurst, UK: Middleton, 1995.

———. *Aldgate and Stepney Tramways*. Midhurst, UK: Middleton, 1996.

———. *Eltham and Woolwich Tramways*. Midhurst, UK: Middleton, 1996.

———. *Holborn and Finsbury Tramways*. Midhurst, UK: Middleton, 1996.

———. *Barnet and Finchley Tramways*. Midhurst, UK: Middleton, 1997.

———. *Edgware and Willesden Tramways*. Midhurst, UK: Middleton, 1998.

Hawthorne, Edward. *Electric Boats on the Thames*. Stroud, UK: Alan Sutton, 1995.

Higginson, Martin, ed. *Tramway London: Background to the Abandonment of London's Trams, 1931–1952*. London: Light Rail Transit Association/Birkbeck College, 1993.

Holloway, Sally. *Moorgate: Anatomy of a Railway Disaster*. Newton Abbot, UK: David and Charles, 1988.

Holman, Printz P. *The Amazing Electric Tube: A History of the City and South London Railway*. London: London Transport Museum, 1990.

Hornby, Frank. *London Suburban: An Illustrated History of the Capital's Commuter Lines Since 1948*. Peterborough, UK: Silver Link, 1995.

Horne, M. A. C. *The Central Line: A Short History*. London: Douglas Rose, 1987.

———. *The Northern Line: A Short History*. London: Douglas Rose, 1987.

———. *The Victoria Line: A Short History*. London: Douglas Rose, 1988.
———. *The Bakerloo Line: A Short History*. London: Douglas Rose, 1990.
Horne, Mike, and Bob Bayman. *The First Tube*. London: Capital Transport, 1990.
Huntley, Ian. *The London Underground: Surface Stock Planbook, 1863–1959*. London: Ian Allen/London Transport, 1988.
Jackson, Alan A. *London's Termini*. Newton Abbot, UK: David and Charles, 1985.
———. *London's Metropolitan Railway*. Newton Abbot, UK: David and Charles, 1986.
———. *Semi-Detached London: Suburban Development, Life and Transport, 1900–39*. Didcot, UK: Wild Swan, 1991.
Jackson, Alan A., ed. *The Memories and Writings of a London Railwayman: A Tribute to Harold Vernon Borley (1895–1989)*. Mold, UK: Railway and Canal Historical Society, 1993.
Jones, Dave. *Enfield and Wood Green Tramways*. Midhurst, UK: Middleton, 1997.
Joyce, J. *"Operation Tramway": The End of London's Trams, 1950–1952*. London: Ian Allan, 1987.
———. *London's Trams*. Shepperton: Ian Allan, 1990.
Kidner, R. W. *The London Tramcar, 1861–1952*. Headington, UK: Oakwood, 1992.
King, John, and Geoffrey Tait. *Golden Gatwick: 50 Years of Aviation*. Gatwick, UK: Royal Aeronautical Society, 1980.
Lambert, Anthony J. *Nineteenth-Century Railway History Through the Illustrated London News*. Newton Abbot, UK: David and Charles, 1984.
Lane, Kevin. *London's Buses*. London: Ian Allan, 1991.
Lascelles, T. S. *The City and South London Railway*. Oxford: Oakwood, 1987.
Leboff, David. *London Underground Stations*. Shepperton, UK: Ian Allan, 1994.
Marsden, Colin J. *This Is Waterloo*. London: Ian Allan, 1981.
Marsden, Peter. *Ships of the Port of London: Twelfth to Seventeenth Centuries A.D*. London: English Heritage, 1996.
Marshall, James. *The History of the Great West Road: Its Social and Economic Influence on the Surrounding Area*. London: Heritage Publications, 1995.
McCall, Albert William. *Green Line: The History of London's Country Bus Services*. London: New Cavendish Books, 1980.
McCormack, Kevin. *The Heyday of the London Bus*, 3 vols. Shepperton, UK: Ian Allen, 1992 (vol. 1), 1995 (vol. 2), and 1996 (vol. 3).
McLachlan, Tom. *London Buses, 1985–1995: Managing the Change*. Glossop, UK: Venture, 1996.
Menear, Laurence. *London's Underground Stations: A Social and Architectural Study*. Tunbridge Wells, UK: Midas, 1983.
Millichip, Malcolm. *The Era of Gas Light and Steam: Steam Transport of the North Thames Gas Board and Constituent Companies*. London: London and Southern Gas Association, 1995.
Mitchell, Vic. *Charing Cross to Dartford*. Midhurst, UK: Middleton, 1990.
Mitchell, Vic, and Keith Smith. *London Bridge to East Croydon*. Midhurst, UK: Middleton, 1988.

———. *Charing Cross to Dartford*. Midhurst, UK: Middleton, 1990.

———. *Holborn Viaduct to Lewisham, Including the Greenwich Park Branch*. Midhurst, UK: Middleton, 1990.

———. *Lewisham to Dartford via Bexleyheath and Sidcup*. Midhurst, UK: Middleton, 1991.

———. *Mitcham Junction Lines*. Midhurst, UK: Middleton, 1992.

———. *Victoria to Bromley South*. Midhurst, UK: Middleton, 1992.

———. *South London Line*. Midhurst, UK: Middleton, 1995.

———. *Wimbledon to Epsom*. Midhurst, UK: Middleton, 1995.

———. *Lines Around Wimbledon*. Midhurst, UK: Middleton, 1996.

———. *Willesden Junction to Richmond*. Midhurst, UK: Middleton, 1996.

———. *North London Line: Broad Street to Willesden Junction via Hampstead Heath*. Midhurst, UK: Middleton, 1997.

Montague, Keith. *Paddington Steam*. Norwich, UK: Becknell, 1982.

Oakley, E. R. *The London County Council Tramways*, 2 vols. London: London Tramways History Group, 1989 (vol. 1) and 1991 (vol. 2).

Oakley, E. R., and C. L. Withey. *Improving London's Trams (1932–7)*. London: London Regional Transport Association, 1988.

Pennick, Nigel. *Waterloo and City Railway*. Cambridge: Electric Traction, 1984.

———. *Bunkers Under London*. Cambridge: Valknut, 1988.

———. *London's Early Tube Railways*. Cambridge: Valknut, 1988.

Phillips, Geoffrey. *Thames Crossings: Bridges, Tunnels and Ferries*. Newton Abbot, UK: David and Charles, 1981.

Platt, Edward. *Leadville: A Biography of the A40*. London: Picador, 2000.

Pond, C. C., ed. *The Walthamstow and Chingford Railway*. London: Walthamstow Antiquarian Society, 1982.

Reed, John. *London Tramways*. London: Capital Transport, 1997.

Reynolds, John E. *Thames Ship Towage, 1933–1992*. Edinburgh: Pentland, 1993.

Robertson, Reg. *Steaming Through the War Years: Reminiscences on the Ex-GER Lines in London*. Oxford: Oakwood, 1996.

Rolt, L. T. C. *The Making of a Railway*. Stroud, UK: Alan Sutton, 1990.

Russell, Terry. *Croydon's Trolleybuses*. Midhurst, UK: Middleton, 1996.

Scott, Peter G. *The Harrow and Stanmore Railway*. London: Hartest, 1981.

———. *The London and Birmingham Railway Through Harrow, 1837–1987: A Celebration of 150 Years of the Euston Main Line Through the London Borough of Harrow*. London: London Borough of Harrow, 1987.

Sherwood, Tim. *The Railways of Richmond-Upon-Thames*. Wokingham, UK: Forge, 1991.

Smeeton, C. S. *The Metropolitan Electric Tramways*, 2 vols. London: Light Rail Transit Association/Light Railway Society, 1984 (vol. 1) and 1986 (vol. 2).

———. *Modernisation of the London Company Tramways*. Ambergate, UK: Tramway and Light Railway Society, 1989.

———. *The London United Tramways*, 2 vols. London: Light Rail Transit Association/Tramway and Light Railway Society, 1994.

Smith, Martin. *Steam on the Underground*. Shepperton, UK: Ian Allen, 1994.
Taylor, Hugh. *London Trolleybus Routes*. London: Capital Transport, 1994.
Taylor, Sheila. *A Journey Through Time: London Transport Photographs, 1880 to 1965*. London: Laurence King, 1992.
Thompson, Julian. *London's Trams Then and Now*. Shepperton, UK: Ian Allen, 1992.
Turner, Barry. *All Change!: Through the Years at Some Busy London Bus Terminals*. London: Regent, 1984.
Vaughan, J. A. M. *This Is Paddington*. Shepperton, UK: Ian Allen, 1982.
Waller, Wally. *The Busman's Story*. Bognor Regis, UK: New Horizon, 1982.
Warren, Kenneth. *Fifty Years of the Green Line*. London: Ian Allen, 1980.
———. *The Motorbus in Central London*. London: Ian Allen, 1986.
Webber, Mick. *London Trolleybus Chronology, 1931–1962*. Shepperton, UK: Ian Allen, 1997.
White, H. P. *Greater London*. Vol. 3 of *A Regional History of the Railways of Great Britain*. Newton Abbot, UK: David St. John Thomas, 1987.
Williams, Stephanie. *Docklands*. London: Phaidon, 1993.
Winter, James. *London's Teeming Streets, 1830–1914*. London: Routledge, 1993.
Woodman, Trevor. *The Railway to Hayes: An Historical Review of the Development of the Railway and Locality of Hayes, Kent*. London: Hayes Village Association, 1982.

URBAN DEVELOPMENT

Abbott, Simon. *Suburb 75: Hampstead Garden Suburb, 1907–1982—A Seventy-Fifth Anniversary Celebration*. London: Hampstead Garden Suburb Residents Association, 1982.
Appleyard, Donald. *Livable Streets*. Berkeley: University of California Press, 1981.
Bacon, George W. *The A to Z of Victorian London*. Lympne Castle, UK: Harry Margary, 1987.
Barker, Felix, and Ralph Hyde. *London As It Might Have Been*. London: Murray, 1982.
Barker, Felix, and Peter Jackson. *The History of London in Maps*. New York: Cross River, 1992.
Beier, A. L., and Roger Finlay, eds. *London 1500–1700: The Making of the Metropolis*. London: Longman, 1986.
Bell, Walter George. *The Great Fire of London*. London: Bracken, 1994.
Bentley, James. *East of the City: The London Docklands Story*. London: Pavilion, 1997.
Besant, Walter. *London in the Nineteenth Century*. New York: Garland, 1985.
Binney, Marcus. *Palace on the River: Terry Farrell's Redevelopment of Charing Cross*. London: Wordsearch, 1981.
Bird, Joanna, Mark Hassall, and Harvey Sheldon, eds. *Interpreting Roman London: Papers in Memory of Hugh Chapman*. Oxford: Oxbow, 1996.

Bosanquet, Charles B. P. *London: Some Account of Its Growth, Charitable Agencies and Wants*. New York: Garland, 1984.

Branigan, Keith, ed. *The Archaeology of the Chilterns from the Ice Age to the Norman Conquest*. Chesham, UK: Chess Valley Archaeological and Historical Society, 1994.

Butler, Tim, and Michael Rustin, eds. *Rising in the East?: The Regeneration of East London*. London: Lawrence and Wishart, 1996.

Calvocoressi, Paul. *Conservation in Dockland: Old Buildings in a Changing Environment*. London: Docklands Forum, 1990.

Cammen, Hans van der, ed. *Four Metropolises in Western Europe: Development and Urban Planning of London, Paris, Randstad Holland and the Ruhr Region*. Assen, The Netherlands: Van Gorcum, 1988.

Carr, Gregg. *Residence and Social Status: The Development of Seventeenth-Century London*. New York: Garland, 1990.

Carter, Valerie. *Fighting for the Future: The Story of Enfield Preservation Society, 1936–1996*. London: Enfield Preservation Society, 1997.

Clark, John. *Saxon and Norman London*. London: Her Majesty's Stationery Office, 1989.

Clegg, Gillian. *The Archaeology of Hounslow*. London: West London Archaeological Field Group, 1991.

Clout, Hugh, and Peter Wood, eds. *London: Problems of Change*. Harlow, UK: Longman, 1986.

Connor, J. E., and Critchley, B. J. *Palaces for the Poor*. Colchester, UK: Connor and Butler, 1984.

Cotton, Jonathan, John Mills, and Gillian Clegg. *Archaeology in West Middlesex: The London Borough of Hillingdon from the Earliest Hunters to the Late Medieval Period*. London: London Borough of Hillingdon, 1986.

Cox, Alan. *Docklands in the Making: The Redevelopment of the Isle of Dogs, 1981–1995*. London: Athlone/Royal Commission on the Historical Monuments of England, 1995.

Daniels, P. W. *The Location of Foreign Banks and Metropolitan Development: London and New York*. Liverpool: University of Liverpool, 1986.

Davies, B. J., B. Richardson, and R. S. Tomber. *A Dated Corpus of Early Roman Pottery from the City of London*. London: Museum of London/Council for British Archaeology, 1994.

Davis, K. Rutherford. *Britons and Saxons: The Chiltern Region, 400–700*. Chichester, UK: Phillimore, 1982.

Edgar, Donald. *The Royal Parks*. London: W. H. Allen, 1986.

Edwards, Brian. *London Docklands: Urban Design in an Age of Deregulation*. Oxford: Butterworth Architecture, 1992.

Emsley, Ian. *The Development of Housing Associations, With Special Reference to London and Including a Case Study of the London Borough of Hammersmith*. New York: Garland, 1986.

Evans, Graeme. *An Urban Renaissance?: The Role of the Arts in Urban Regeneration—A Survey of Local Authorities in Greater London*. London: University of North London Press, 1993.

Fainstein, Susan S. *The City Builders: Property, Politics and Planning in London and New York*. Oxford: Blackwell, 1994.

Farrell, Terry. *Urban Design*. London: Academy Editions, 1993.

Fisher, John. *A Collection of Early Maps of London, 1553–1667*. Lympne Castle, UK: Harry Margary/Guildhall Library, London.

Fox, Celina, ed. *London—World City, 1800–1840*. New Haven, Conn.: Yale University Press/Museum of London, 1992.

Gayler, Hugh J. *Geographical Excursions in London*. Lanham, Md.: University Press of America, 1996.

Gelb, Joyce, and Michael Lyons. *A Tale of Two Cities: Housing Policy and Gentrification in London and New York*. London: South Bank Polytechnic, 1991.

Hall, Jenny, and Ralph Merrifield. *Roman London*. London: Her Majesty's Stationery Office, 1986.

Hall, John. *Metropolis Now: London and Its Region*. Cambridge: Cambridge University Press, 1990.

Hamnett, Chris, and Bill Randolph. *Cities, Housing and Profits: Flat Break-Up and the Decline of Private Renting*. London: Hutchinson, 1988.

Hawkes, Jason. *London Landmarks from the Air*. London: Ebury, 1996.

Hebbert, Michael. *London: More by Fortune than Design*. Chichester, UK: John Wiley, 1998.

Hibbert, Christopher. *London: The Biography of a City*. Harmondsworth, UK: Penguin, 1980.

Hill, Charles, Martin Millett, and Thomas Blagg. *The Roman Riverside Wall and Monumental Arch in London: Excavations at Baynard's Castle, Upper Thames Street, London, 1974–76*. London: London and Middlesex Archaeological Society, 1980.

Hobley, Brian. *Roman and Saxon London: A Reappraisal*. London: Museum of London, 1985.

Hoggart, Keith, and David R. Green. *London: A New Metropolitan Geography*. London: Edward Arnold, 1991.

Holgate, Robin. *Neolithic Settlement of the Thames Basin*. Oxford: British Archaeological Reports, 1988.

Holgate, Robin, ed. *Chiltern Archaeology—Recent Work: A Handbook for the Next Decade*. Dunstable, UK: Book Castle, 1995.

Hollamby, Ted. *Docklands: London's Backyard into Front Yard*. London: Docklands Forum, 1990.

Home, Gordon. *Medieval London*. London: Bracken, 1994.

Horsman, Valerie, Christine Milne, and Gustav Milne. *Building and Street Development Near Billingsgate and Cheapside*. London: London and Middlesex Archaeological Society, 1988.

Horwood, Richard. *The A to Z of Regency London*. Lympne Castle, UK: Harry Margary/Guildhall Library, London/London Topographical Society, 1985.

Ikin, C. W. *Hampstead Garden Suburb: Dreams and Realities*. London: New Hampstead Garden Suburb Trust, 1990.

Inwood, Stephen. *A History of London*. London: Macmillan, 1998.

Jackson, Alan A. *Semi-Detached London: Suburban Development, Life and Transport, 1900–39*. Didcot, UK: Wild Swan, 1991.

Jenner, Michael. *London Heritage: The Changing Style of a City*. London: Mermaid, 1990.

Keene, Derek, and Vanessa Harding. *A Survey of Documentary Sources for Property Holding in London Before the Great Fire*. London: London Record Society, 1985.

———. *Historical Gazetteer of London Before the Great Fire—Cheapside: Parishes of All Hallows Honey Lane, St. Martin Pomary, St. Mary le Bow, St. Mary Colechurch, and St. Pancras Soper Lane*. Cambridge: Chadwyck-Healey, 1987.

Leapman, Michael. *The Book of London: The Evolution of a Great City*. London: Weidenfeld and Nicolson, 1989.

Ledgerwood, Grant. *Urban Innovation: The Transformation of London's Docklands, 1968–84*. Aldershot, UK: Gower, 1985.

Lenon, Barnaby J. *London*. London: Unwin Hyman, 1988.

Lobel, Mary D. *The City of London from Prehistoric Times to c. 1520*. Oxford: Oxford University Press/Historic Towns Trust, 1989.

Lyons, Charles Barker. *London—Isle of Dogs*. London: London Docklands Development Corporation, 1981.

Maloney, Catharine. *The Upper Walbrook Valley in the Roman Period*. York, UK: Museum of London/Council for British Archaeology, 1990.

Marsden, Peter. *Roman London*. London: Thames and Hudson, 1980.

———. *The Roman Forum Site in London: Discoveries Before 1985*. London: Her Majesty's Stationery Office, 1987.

Marshall, Tim. *Environmental Sustainability: London's Unitary Development Plans and Strategic Planning*. London: South Bank University, 1992.

McDonald, Erica. *Artisans and Avenues: A History of the Queen's Park Estate*. London: City of Westminster, 1990.

Merrifield, Ralph. *London: City of the Romans*. London: Batsford, 1983.

Merriman, Nick. *Prehistoric London*. London: Her Majesty's Stationery Office, 1990.

Miller, Mervyn, and A. Stuart Gray. *Hampstead Garden Suburb*. Chichester, UK: Phillimore, 1992.

Milne, Gustav. *The Port of Roman London*. London: Batsford, 1985.

———. *The Great Fire of London*. London: Historical Publications, 1986.

———. *Book of Roman London: Urban Archaeology in the Nation's Capital*. London: Batsford/English Heritage, 1995.

Milne, Gustav, ed. *From Roman Basilica to Medieval Market: Archaeology in Action in the City of London*. London: Her Majesty's Stationery Office, 1992.

Morris, J. N. *Religion and Urban Change: Croydon, 1840–1914*. Woodbridge, UK: Royal Historical Society/Boydell, 1992.

Morris, John. *Londinivm: London in the Roman Empire*. London: Weidenfeld and Nicolson, 1982.

Munton, Richard. *London's Green Belt: Containment in Practice*. London: Allen and Unwin, 1983.

Ogborn, Miles. *Spaces of Modernity: London's Geographies, 1680–1780*. New York: Guilford Press, 1998.

Ogden, Philip, ed. *London Docklands: The Challenge of Development*. Cambridge: Cambridge University Press, 1992.

Ogilby, John. *The A to Z of Restoration London* (*The City of London, 1676*). Lympne Castle, UK: Harry Margary/Guildhall Library, London.

Olechnowicz, Andrzej. *Working-Class Housing in England Between the Wars: The Becontree Estate*. Oxford: Clarendon, 1997.

Olsen, Donald J. *Town Planning in London: The Eighteenth and Nineteenth Centuries*. New Haven, Conn.: Yale University Press, 1982.

Page-Roberts, James. *Guide to a Dockland of Change: A Present Day, Historical, Anecdotal and (1949–1969) Photographic Guide to the Riverside Docks and Wharves Between the Tower of London and Limehouse*. London: Mudlark, 1997.

Parry, José. *Greening London: Environmental Policies and Practices of the London Boroughs*. London: London Research Centre, 1991.

Pearce, Graham, Les Hems, and Brian Hennessy. *The Conservation Areas in London and the South East*. London: Historic Buildings and Monuments Commission for England, 1990.

Perring, Dominic. *Roman London*. London: Seaby, 1991.

Perring, Dominic, and Steve Roskams. *Early Development of Roman London West of the Walbrook*. London: British Council for Archaeology, 1991.

Philp, Brian. *The Forum of Roman London: Excavations of 1968–9*. Dover, UK: Kent Archaeological Rescue Unit, 1982.

———. *The Crofton Roman Villa at Orpington*. Dover, UK: Kent Archaeological Rescue Unit, 1992.

———. *The Roman Villa Site at Orpington, Kent*. Dover, UK: Kent Archaeological Rescue Unit, 1996.

Philp, Brian, and Peter Keller. *The Roman Site at Fordcroft, Orpington* (*The Detailed Excavation of a Site at Poverest Road and a Consideration of the Roman Settlement in the Fordcroft–Kent Road Area*). London: Kent Archaeological Trust, 1995.

Porter, Stephen. *The Great Fire of London*. Stroud, UK: Alan Sutton, 1996.

Rasmussen, Steen Eiler. *London: The Unique City*. Cambridge, Mass.: Massachusetts Institute of Technology Press, 1982.

Rawcliffe, Michael. *Victorian London*. London: Batsford, 1985.

Roberts, Patricia. *Governmental Action and the Residential Environment: A Case Study of Battersea, London Borough of Wandsworth*. London: Polytechnic of the South Bank, 1985.

Rocque, John. *The A to Z of Georgian London*. Lympne Castle, UK: Harry Margary/London Topographical Society, 1982.

Rogers, Richard, and Mark Fisher. *A New London*. London: Penguin, 1992.

Savitch, Harold V. *Post-Industrial Cities: Politics and Planning in New York, Paris, and London*. Princeton, N.J.: Princeton University Press, 1988.

Schofield, John. *The Building of London from the Conquest to the Great Fire*. London: British Museum/Museum of London, 1993.

———. *Medieval London Houses*. New Haven, Conn.: Yale University Press, 1995.

Schofield, John, and Tony Dyson. *Archaeology of the City of London*. London: Museum of London, 1980.

Sheppard, Francis. *London: A History*. Oxford: Oxford University Press, 1998.

Simmie, J. M. *Planning London*. London: UCL Press, 1994.

Simo, Melanie Louise. *London and the Landscape: From Country Seat to Metropolis, 1783–1843*. New Haven, Conn.: Yale University Press, 1988.

St. Aubyn, Fiona. *A Portrait of Georgian London Based on Ackermann's "The Microcosm of London," Published 1808–1810*. Churt, UK: D. Leader, 1985.

Stoker, Gerry, and Vivien Lowndes. *Tower Hamlets and Decentralisation: The Experience of Globe Town Neighbourhood*. Luton, UK: Local Government Management Board, 1991.

Stow, John. *A Survey of London Written in the Year 1598*. Stroud, UK: Alan Sutton, 1994.

Summerson, John. *Georgian London*. London: Pimlico, 1991.

Tames, Richard. *Bloomsbury Past*. London: Historical Publications, 1993.

———. *City of London Past*. London: Historical Publications, 1995.

Thomas, Christopher, Barnley Stone, and Christopher Phillpotts. *Excavations at the Priory and Hospital of St. Mary Spital, London*. London: Museum of London, 1997.

Thomson, Arline K. *Discovering Elizabethan London: Diary and Sketches*. Orono: University of Maine Press, 1994.

Underwood, Jacky. *Town Planners in Search of a Role: A Participant Observation Study of Local Planners in a London Borough*. Bristol, UK: University of Bristol, 1980.

Urwin, A. C. B. *Twickenham Before 704 A.D.* London: Twickenham Local History Society, 1980.

———. *Saxon Twickenham: The Evidence of the Charters, 704–948 A.D.* London: Twickenham Local History Society, 1981.

Vince, Alan G. *Saxon London: An Archaeological Investigation*. London: Seaby, 1990.

Watson, Isobel. *Gentlemen in the Building Line: The Development of South Hackney*. London: Padfield, 1989.

Weinstein, Rosemary. *Tudor London*. London: Her Majesty's Stationery Office, 1994.

Wells, Keith. *The History of Avery Hill Housing Estate*. Nottingham, UK: Local History Press, 1995.

Williams, Norman Lloyd. *Tudor London Visited*. London: Cassell, 1991.
Williams, Tim. *Public Buildings in the South-West Quarter of Roman London*. London: Museum of London/Council for British Archaeology, 1993.
Wyngaerde, Anton van den. *The Panorama of London circa 1544*. London: London Topographical Society, 1996.
Yelling, J. A. *Slums and Slum Clearance in Victorian London*. London: Allen and Unwin, 1986.
Young, Ken, and Patricia L. Garside. *Metropolitan London: Politics and Urban Change, 1837–1981*. London: Edward Arnold, 1982.

WARFARE AND THE ARMED FORCES

Allen, W. D., and R. F. H. Cawston. *Carpiquet Bound: A Pictorial Tribute to the 4th County of London Yeomanry (Sharpshooters), 1939–1944*. Ewell, UK: Chiavari, 1997.
Barfoot, John. *Over Here and Over There: Ilford Aerodromes and Airmen in the Great War*. Romford, UK: Ian Henry, 1998.
Barker, Sybil. *Sybil Barker's War: The Wartime Diary of a Director of Music and Organist at the Royal Holloway College (University of London)*. Worthing, UK: Churchman, 1989.
Barlow, L., and R. J. Smith. *3rd County of London (Sharpshooters)*. Aldershot, UK: Robert Ogilby Trust, 1983.
Bates, L. M. *The Thames on Fire: The Battle of London River, 1939–1945*. Lavenham, UK: Terence Dalton, 1985.
Beardmore, George. *Civilians at War: Journals, 1938–1946*. Oxford: Oxford University Press, 1984.
Bloch, Howard, ed. *Black Saturday: The First Day of the Blitz—East London Memories of September 7th, 1940*. London: THAP Books, 1984.
Brown, Irene. *One Woman's War: Recollections of a Cockney Kid*. London: Excalibur, 1991.
Bryant, Kenneth. *Streatham's 41: An Account of the German V-1 Offensive Against England As It Affected Streatham*. London: Streatham Society, 1998.
Chappell, Mike. *The Guards Divisions, 1914–45*. London: Osprey, 1995.
Chippendale, Neil. *The Battle of Brentford: The Hounslow Area in the Civil War*. Leigh-on-Sea, UK: Partizan, 1991.
Clifford, Tony, Kathryn Abnett, and Peter Grisby. *On the Home Front: Barking and Dagenham in World War II*. London: London Borough of Barking and Dagenham, 1990.
Cluett, Douglas, Joanna Bogle, and Bob Learmonth. *Croydon Airport and the Battle for Britain, 1939–1940*. London: London Borough of Sutton, 1984.
Creaton, Heather J., ed. *Sources for the History of London, 1939–45: A Guide and Bibliography*. London: British Records Association, 1998.

Cross, Arthur, and Fred Tibbs. *The London Blitz*. London: Nishen, 1987.

Davis, Leonard. *Chingfliers, Chingboys and Chingford Aerodrome: The Story of the Royal Naval Air Station Chingford and, to a Limited Extent, of Chingford During the Great War of 1914–1918*. London: Chingford Historical Society, 1997.

Demarne, Cyril. *The London Blitz: A Fireman's Tale*. London: Battle of Britain Prints International, 1991.

Dunstan, Simon. *The Guards: Britain's Household Division*. London: Windrow and Green, 1996.

Emberton, Wilfred. *Skippon's Brave Boys: The Origins, Development and Civil War Service of London's Trained Bands*. Buckingham, UK: Barracuda, 1984.

Golden, Jenny. *Hackney at War*. Stroud, UK: Alan Sutton, 1995.

Green, Brian. *Dulwich: The Home Front, 1939–1945*. London: Dulwich Society, 1995.

Green, Mike, ed. *Shelling of London*. Wymondham, UK: Stylus, 1993.

Greer, Day, ed. *London's Burning: Memories*. Bolton, UK: Stylus, 1991.

Hardy, Clive, and Nigel Arthur. *London at War*. London: Quoin, 1989.

Harrison, Roy. *Blitz Over Westminster: City of Westminster Civil Defence Bomb Incident Photographs, 1940–1944*. London: City of Westminster, 1990.

Hasker, Leslie. *Fulham in the Second World War*. London: Fulham and Hammersmith Historical Society, 1984.

Hatton, D. M. "*The Devil's Own*": *A History of the Inns of Court Regiment*. London: J. A. Allen, 1992.

Her Majesty's Stationery Office. *The Royal Hospital, Chelsea*. London: Her Majesty's Stationery Office, 1985.

Hewison, Robert. *Under Siege: Literary Life in London, 1939–45*. London: Methuen, 1988.

Hickman, Tom. *What Did You Do in the War, Auntie?: The BBC at War, 1939–45*. London: BBC Books, 1995.

Hill, Maureen. *The London Blitz, September 1940–May 1941*. London: Chapman, 1990.

Hostettler, Eve, ed. *The Island at War: Memories of War-Time Life on the Isle of Dogs, East London*. London: Island History Trust, 1990.

Hovey, John. *A Tale of Two Ports: London and Southampton*. London: Industrial Society, 1990.

Johnson, David. *The City Ablaze: The Second Great Fire of London, 29th December 1940*. London: Kimber, 1980.

King, John. *Grove Park in the Great War*. London: Grove Park Community Group, 1983.

Mack, Joanna, and Steve Humphries. *London at War: The Making of Modern London, 1939–1945*. London: Sidgwick and Jackson, 1985.

Malin, M. A., ed. *The Villager at War: A Diary of Home Front Pinner, 1939–1945*. London: Pinner Association, 1995.

Mansel, Philip. *Pillars of Monarchy: An Outline of the Political and Social History of the Royal Guards*. London: Quartet, 1984.

Mitchinson, K. W. *Gentlemen and Officers: The Impact and Experience of War on a Territorial Regiment, 1914–1918*. London: Imperial War Museum, 1995.

Neville, John. *The Blitz: London Then and Now*. London: Hodder and Stoughton, 1990.

Nixon, Barbara. *Raiders Overhead: A Diary of the London Blitz*. London: Scolar/Gulliver, 1980.

O'Leary, John. *Danger Over Dagenham, 1939–1945*. London: London Borough of Barking and Dagenham, 1995.

Oliver, David. *Hendon Aerodrome: A History*. Shrewbury, UK: Airlife, 1994.

Paget, Julian. *The Yeomen of the Guard: Five Hundred Years of Service, 1485–1985*. Poole, UK: Blandford, 1984.

Porter, Stephen, ed. *London and the Civil War*. London: Macmillan, 1996.

Rason, Paul. *Memories of the Many 50 Years On: A Collection of Memories of People from the London Borough of Bromley Reflecting on Their War*. London: Environment Bromley, 1995.

Roberts, Keith. *London and Liberty: Ensigns of the London Trained Bands*. Leigh-on-Sea, UK: Partizan, 1987.

Roebuck, Margaret Thelwell. *From Me to You: Wartime Memories, 1939–1946*. Pittsburgh, Pa.: Dorrance, 1995.

Scott, Mick. *Home Fires: A Borough at War*. London: London Borough of Bexley, 1986.

Sellers, Leonard. *Shot in the Tower: The Story of the Spies Executed in the Tower of London During the First World War*. London: Leo Cooper, 1997.

Skilton, W. *The Household Division*. Leicester, UK: Midland, 1992.

Stewart, James D. *Bermondsey in War, 1939–1945*. London: London Borough of Southwark, 1981.

Taylor, Gordon. *London's Navy: A Story of the Royal Navy Volunteer Reserve*. London: Quiller, 1983.

Trench, Richard. *London Before the Blitz*. London: Weidenfeld and Nicolson, 1989.

Tuner, H. D. *The Cradle of the Navy: The Story of the Royal Hospital School at Greenwich and at Holbrook, 1694–1988*. York, UK: William Sessions, 1990.

Wallington, Neil. *Firemen at War: The Work of London's Fire-Fighters in the Second World War*. Newton Abbot, UK: David and Charles, 1981.

Watson, Elizabeth. *Don't Wait for It, Or, Impressions of War, 1939–1941*. London: Imperial War Museum, 1994.

Watson, J. N. P. *The Story of the Blues and Royals: Royal Horse Guards and 1st Dragoons*. London: Leo Cooper, 1993.

———. *Through Fifteen Reigns: A Complete History of the Household Cavalry*. Staplehurst, UK: Spellmount, 1997.

Weller, Ken. *"Don't Be a Soldier!": The Radical Anti-War Movement in North London, 1914–1918*. London: Journeyman, 1985.

Williams, Alan, and Anthony de Reuck. *The Royal Armoury at Greenwich, 1515–1649: A History of Its Technology*. London: Trustees of the Royal Armouries, 1995.

Williams, David. *The Black Cats at War: The Story of the 56th (London) Division T.A., 1939–1945*. London: Imperial War Museum, 1995.
Winter, Jay, and Jean-Louis Robert. *Capital Cities at War: Paris, London, Berlin, 1914–1919*. Cambridge: Cambridge University Press, 1997.
Ziegler, Philip. *London at War, 1939–1945*. London: Sinclair-Stevenson, 1995.

REFERENCE WORKS

Allinson, Kenneth, and Victoria Thornton. *Guide to London's Contemporary Architecture*. Oxford: Butterworth Architecture, 1993.
Armstrong, Bill. *1981 Census: Ward and Borough Indices for Greater London*. London: Greater London Council, 1984.
Armstrong, William. *A Ward Level Atlas of London from the 1991 Census*. London: London Research Centre, 1996.
Ashton, Geoffrey. *Catalogue of Paintings at the Theatre Museum, London*. London: Victoria and Albert Museum/Society for Theatre Research, 1992.
Atkins, P. J. *The Directories of London, 1677--1977*. London: Mansell, 1990.
Atkinson, Frank. *St. Paul's: The Cathedral Guide*. London: Pitkin, 1983.
Bacon, George W. *The A to Z of Victorian London*. Lympne Castle, UK: Harry Margary/Guildhall Library, London, 1987.
Baker, Christopher, and Tom Henry. *The National Gallery Complete Illustrated Catalogue*. London: National Gallery, 1995.
Bancroft, Peter. *London Transport Records at the Public Record Office*. Alton, UK: Nebulous, 1995.
Barker, Felix, and Denise Silvester-Carr. *Crime and Scandal: The Black Plaque Guide to London*. London: Constable, 1995.
Baron, Xavier, ed. *London, 1066–1914: Literary Sources and Documents*. Robertsbridge, UK: Helm Information, 1997.
Beasley, John D. *East Dulwich: An Illustrated Alphabetical Guide*. London: South Riding Press, 1998.
Beasley, Maureen. *Five Centuries of Artists in Sutton: A Biographical Dictionary of Artists Associated with Sutton, London*. London: London Borough of Sutton, 1989.
Blackmore, Howard L. *A Dictionary of London Gunmakers, 1350–1850*. Oxford: Phaidon Christie's, 1986.
Blatch, Mervyn. *A Guide to London's Churches*. London: Constable, 1995.
Brace, Marianne. *London's Parks and Gardens*. Cambridge: Pevensey, 1986.
Buckingham Palace. *List of Pictures and Works of Art*. London: Buckingham Palace, 1993.
Burman, Peter. *St. Paul's Cathedral*. London: Bell and Hyman, 1987.
Carpenter, Edward, and David Gentleman. *Westminster Abbey*. London: Weidenfeld and Nicolson, 1987.

Carr, R. J. M. *Docklands History Survey: A Guide to Research*. London: Greater London Council, 1984.

Cherry, Bridget, and Nikolaus Pevsner. *London: South*. Harmondsworth, UK: Penguin, 1983.

———. *London: North West*. London: Penguin, 1991.

Clout, Hugh, ed. *The Times History of London*. London: Times Books, 1999.

Collin, Francesca. *The Arts and Entertainment in London*. London: Ward Lock, 1997.

Creaton, Heather J., ed. *Bibliography of Printed Works on London History to 1939*. London: Library Association Publishing, 1994.

———. *London*. Oxford: Clio, 1996.

———. *Sources for the History of London, 1939–45: A Guide and Bibliography*. London: British Records Association, 1998.

Crowe, Andrew. *The Parks and Woodlands of London*. London: Fourth Estate, 1987.

Department of Transport. *Transport Statistics for London*. London: Her Majesty's Stationery Office, published with periodic revision since 1989.

Dolphin, Philippa, Eric Grant, and Edward Lewis. *The London Region: An Annotated Geographical Bibliography*. London: Mansell, 1981.

Edmonds, Mark. *Inside Soho*. London: Nicholson, 1988.

Essex Record Office. *Essex in London: A Guide to the Records of the London Boroughs Formerly in Essex Deposited in the Essex Record Office—Barking and Dagenham, Havering, Newham, Redbridge, Waltham Forest*. Chelmsford, UK: Essex Record Office, 1992.

Fairbairn, Lynda. *Italian Renaissance Drawings from the Collection of Sir John Soane's Museum*. London: Azimuth Editions, 1998.

Fairfield, Sheila. *The Streets of London: A Dictionary of Their Names and Origins*. London: Macmillan, 1983.

Fell, Sir Brian H., and K. R. MacKenzie. *The Houses of Parliament: A Guide to the Palace of Westminster*. London: Her Majesty's Stationery Office, 1988.

Fitch, Marc. *Index to Testamentary Records in the Archdeaconry Court of London Now Preserved in Guildhall Library, London: 1661–1700*. London: British Record Society, 1985.

Galinou, Mireille, and John Hayes. *London in Paint: Oil Paintings in the Collection at the Museum of London*. London: Museum of London, 1996.

Gardner, Douglas. *The Covent Garden Guide*. London: Benn, 1980.

Garside, Patricia L., ed. *Capital Histories: A Bibliographical Study of London*. Aldershot, UK: Ashgate, 1998.

Gibson, J. S. W., and Heather Creaton. *Lists of Londoners*. Birmingham, UK: Federation of Family History Societies, 1997.

Gibson, Peter. *The Capital Companion: A Street-by-Street Guide to London and Its Inhabitants*. Exeter, UK: Webb and Bower, 1985.

Glinert, Ed. *A Literary Guide to London*. London: Penguin, 2000.

Government Office for London. *London Research: A Directory of Academic Expertise*. London: Government Office for London, 1998.

Government Office for London/London Research Centre/Office for National Statistics. *Focus on London '98*. London: Her Majesty's Stationery Office, 1998.

Gray, Marcus. *London's Rock Landmarks: The A–Z Guide to London's Rock Geography.* London: Omnibus, 1985.

Greater London Council. *Statistical Series*. London: Greater London Council, 1980–86.

Greenwood, John. *The Industrial Archaeology and Industrial History of London: A Bibliography*. Cranfield, UK: Kewdale, 1988.

Guildhall Library. *Registers of Church of England Parishes and Other Source Material Relating to Anglican Baptising, Marriages and Burials within the City of London*. London: Guildhall Library, 1984.

———. *City Livery Companies and Related Organisations: A Guide to Their Archives in Guildhall Library*. London: Guildhall Library, 1989.

Hackman, Harvey. *Wates's Book of London Churchyards: A Guide to the Old Churchyards and Burial-Grounds of the City and Central London*. London: Collins, 1981.

Hall, Christopher A. *A Guide to the Lloyd's Marine Collection at Guildhall Library*. London: Guildhall Library, 1985.

Hammond, Peter. *Royal Armouries: Official Guide*. London: Trustees of the Royal Armouries/Philip Wilson, 1986.

Harris, T. C. *Guide to the Parish Registers Deposited in the Greater London Record Office*. London: Greater London Record Office, 1991.

Harvey, A. D. *The Public Record Office as a Source for English Literary Studies*. Paris: Didier Érudition, 1990.

Harvey, Richard. *A Guide to Genealogical Sources in Guildhall Library*. London: Guildhall Library, 1997.

Hawkins, Roy. *Green London: A Handbook*. London: Sidgwick and Jackson, 1987.

Hay, Malcolm, and Jacqueline Riding. *Art in Parliament: The Permanent Collection of the House of Commons—A Descriptive Catalogue*. London: Palace of Westminster/Jarrold, 1996.

Heritage of London Trust. *Historic Buildings in Covent Garden*. London: Heritage of London Trust, 1984.

Her Majesty's Stationery Office. *The Royal Botanic Gardens, Kew*. London: Her Majesty's Stationery Office, 1987.

Horwood, Richard. *The A to Z of Regency London*. Lympne Castle, UK: Harry Margary/Guildhall Library, London/London Topographical Society, 1985.

James, Elizabeth. *The Victoria and Albert Museum: A Bibliography and Exhibition Chronology, 1852–1996*. London: Fitzroy Dearborn/Victoria and Albert Museum, 1998.

Jones, Edward, and Christopher Woodward. *A Guide to the Architecture of London*. London: Weidenfeld and Nicolson, 1992.

Keen, Michael E. *A Bibliography of the Microfilms in the National Art Library, Victoria and Albert Museum*. London: Victoria and Albert Museum, 1980.

Keene, Derek, and Vanessa Harding. *A Survey of Documentary Sources for Property Holding in London Before the Great Fire*. London: London Record Society, 1985.

———. *Historical Gazetteer of London Before the Great Fire: Cheapside—Parishes of All Hallows Honey Lane, St. Martin Pomary, St. Mary le Bow, St. Mary Colechurch, and St. Pancras Soper Lane*. Cambridge: Chadwyck-Healey, 1987.

Kelly's Directories. *Kelly's Post Office London Business Directory*. East Grinstead, UK: Kelly's Directories, published with periodic revision since 1985.

Kirby, John. *The Festival of Britain—A List of Information Sources*. Sheffield, UK: PAVIC, 1993.

Knight, Vivien. *The Works of Art of the Corporation of London: A Catalogue of Paintings, Watercolours, Drawings, Prints and Sculpture*. Cambridge: Woodhead-Faulkner, 1986.

Lee, Edward. *Musical London*. London: Omnibus, 1995.

Levey, Michael. *The National Gallery Collections*. London: National Gallery, 1987.

London Research Centre. *London Housing Statistics*. London: London Research Centre, published with periodic revision since 1990.

———. *Education in London: Key Facts*. London: London Research Centre, published with periodic revision since 1994.

Low, Crail, and Lucy Minto. *Rock and Pop London from Bedsit to Stadium: Places Where the Stars Made It Happen*. London: Handbook Publishing, 1997.

Markert, Lawrence W. *The Bloomsbury Group: A Reference Guide*. Boston: G. K. Hall, 1990.

McBurney, Valerie. *Guide to Libraries in London*. London: British Library, 1995.

Morton, Brian N. *Americans in London: An Anecdotal Street Guide to the Homes and Haunts of Americans from John Adams to Fred Astaire*. London: Macdonald, 1986.

Mullin, Donald. *Victorian Plays: A Record of Significant Productions on the London Stage, 1837–1901*. New York: Greenwood, 1987.

Newson, Gerald. *American London: People and Places of Popular and Historic Interest*. London: Q Books, 1982.

Ogilby, John. *The A to Z of Restoration London* (*The City of London, 1676*). Lympne Castle, UK: Harry Margary/Guildhall Library, London, 1992.

Office for National Statistics. *Regional Trends*. Her Majesty's Stationery Office (published annually).

Pevsner, Nikolaus, and Simon Bradley. *London: The City*. London: Penguin, 1997.

Pond, C. C., and K. N. H. Parry. *Access to Parliamentary Resources and Information in London Libraries*. London: Public Information Office, 1997.

Post Office. *Postcode Areas within the Greater London Area*. London: Post Office, published with periodic revision since 1980.

———. *Post Office London Directory, 1846*. King's Lynn, UK: Michael Winton, 1994.

Prentice, Rina. *A Celebration of the Sea: The Decorative Art Collections of the National Maritime Museum*. London: Her Majesty's Stationery Office, 1994.

Raymond, Stuart. *London and Middlesex: A Genealogical Bibliography*. Birmingham, UK: Federation of Family History Societies, 1994.

———. *Londoners' Occupations: A Genealogical Guide*. Birmingham, UK: Federation of Family History Societies, 1994.

Reed Information Services. *Kelly's Post Office London Professional Services Directory: A Unique Guide to the Financial, Legal and Property Sectors of London*. East Grinstead, UK: Reed Information Services, published with periodic revision since 1992.

Richardson, Elizabeth P. *A Bloomsbury Iconography*. Winchester, UK: St. Paul's Bibliographies, 1989.

Rogers, Malcolm. *Museums and Galleries of London*. London: Black, 1991.

Rosen, Barbara, and Wolfgang Zuckermann. *The Mews of London: A Guide to the Hidden Byways of London's Past*. Exeter, UK: Webb and Bower, 1982.

Ross, Thomas W. *Good Old Index: The Sherlock Holmes Handbook—A Guide to the Sherlock Holmes Stories by Sir Arthur Conan Doyle: Persons, Places, Themes, Summaries of All the Tales, with Commentary on the Style of the Author*. Columbia, S.C.: Camden House, 1997.

Rothstein, Natalie. *Silk Designs of the Eighteenth Century in the Collection of the Victoria and Albert Museum, London, with a Complete Catalogue*. London: Thames and Hudson, 1990.

Sanders, Moshe. *Jewish Books in Whitechapel: A Bibliography of Narodiczky's Press*. London: Duckworth, 1991.

Scimone, G. M. S., and M. F. Levey. *London Museums and Collections*. London: Canal, 1989.

Seaborne, Mike. *Photographers' London, 1839–1994*. London: Museum of London, 1995.

Shepherd, John, ed. *Post-War Archaeology in the City of London, 1946–1972: A Guide to the Records of Excavations by Professor W. F. Grimes Held by the Museum of London*. London: Museum of London, 1998.

Silverthorne, Elizabeth, ed. *London Local Archives: A Directory of Local Authority Record Offices and Libraries*. London: Guildhall Library/Greater London Archives Network, 1994.

Stamp, Gavin, and Colin Amery. *Victorian Buildings of London, 1837–1887: An Illustrated Guide*. London: Architectural Press, 1980.

Thompson, Alan, Andrew Westman, and Tony Dyson, eds. *Archaeology in Greater London, 1965–1990: A Guide to Records of Excavations by the Museum of London*. London: Museum of London, 1998.

Thompson, Arline K. *Discovering Elizabethan London: Diary and Sketches*. Orono: University of Maine Press, 1994.

Trench, Richard. *Philip's London: Architecture, History, Art*. London: George Philip, 1991.

Turner, Christopher. *London Churches Step by Step*. London: Faber, 1987.

Turner, Tom, and Simon Rendel. *London Landscape Guide*. London: Landscape Institute, 1983.

Upstone, Robert. *Treasures of British Art: The Tate Gallery*. New York: Abbeville, 1996.

Waddell, Heather. *London Art and Artists Guide*. London: London Art and Artists Guide, 1997.

Webb, Cliff. *London Livery Company Apprenticeship Registers: Tinplateworkers' Company, 1666, 1668, 1676, 1681, 1683–1800*. London: Society of Genealogists, 1998.

Weinreb, Ben, and Christopher Hibbert. *The London Encyclopaedia*. London: Macmillan, 1993.

Williamson, Elizabeth, and Nikolaus Pevsner. *London Docklands*. London: Penguin, 1998.

Wittich, John. *Discovering London Street Names*. Princes Risborough, UK: Shire, 1996.

Wolfston, Patricia S. *Greater London Cemeteries and Crematoria*. London: Society of Genealogists, 1994.

Woodford, F. Peter, ed. *Streets of Bloomsbury and Fitzrovia: A Survey of Streets, Buildings and Former Residents in Part of Camden*. London: Camden History Society, 1997.

About the Author

Kenneth J. Panton is a professor of geography and director of British Studies Programs at the University of Southern Mississippi. A Scot by birth, he received his first degree at the University of Edinburgh and his doctorate at King's College in the University of London. For 25 years, before moving to the United States, he lectured in the department of geography at London Guildhall University. Dr. Panton coauthored Scarecrow's two-volume *Historical Dictionary of the United Kingdom* and has published professionally both in the United States and Europe.

About the Author

[illegible]